A GRAMMAR OF NEW TESTAMENT GREEK.

"MELANCTHONIS HOC DICTUM EST: SCRIPTURAM NON POSSE INTELLIGI THEOLOGICE, NISI ANTEA SIT INTELLECTUM GRAMMATICE."

A

GRAMMAR

OF THE

NEW TESTAMENT GREEK.

BY

ALEXANDER BUTTMANN.

AUTHORIZED TRANSLATION,

WITH NUMEROUS ADDITIONS AND CORRECTIONS BY THE AUTHOR.

Andover:

WARREN F. DRAPER, PUBLISHER.

MAIN STREET.

1895.

ANDOVER: PRINTED BY WARREN F. DRAPER.

TRANSLATOR'S PREFACE.

It is to be hoped that the reproduction of the following work in English will not be regarded as a superfluous labor. The day has gone by, indeed, when the extravagant maxim could find acceptance, "The better grammarian, the worse logician and theologian;" but the some- what indiscriminate depreciation of the study of the dead languages at the present day is not without injurious influence upon those who are preparing themselves to be expounders of the Divine Word. Even in that land which is reputed to be the home of philological studies, the prince of New Testament expositors has recently said: "We theo- logians are still far too deficient in a comprehensive and positive knowledge of Greek Grammar."[1] The sense of such a deficiency which the general progress of linguistic science must sooner or later awaken, and especially the recognition (which the growing tendency to break away from traditional opinions will force upon theologians) of the need of taking a new inventory of the biblical data, as preliminary to a revision of the scientific statements of the Christian faith, will eventually secure a welcome for works like the present.

Its author is the youngest son of the late Philip Buttmann, whose Grammars, which have been in use now for more than eighty years, have rendered the name familiar wherever Greek is studied. After completing his training at the universities of Berlin and Bonn, he became, in 1837, a teacher in the gymnasium at Potsdam, where, by successive promotions, he attained, in 1854, to the rank of Professor. But in the same year he resigned his office, in order to secure the leisure needed for his literary labors; and he has lived since in retire- ment, except that he has held the position of "Schulrath," to which the city appointed him in 1864.

Intrusted by the other members of the family with the care of his father's grammatical works, he has edited at least eight editions of the so-called Intermediate Grammar (which in its eighteenth edition was translated into English by the late Dr. Edward Robinson), and seven

[1] Meyer's Commentary on the Ep. to the Romans (5th ed.). Pref. p. vii note.

v

editions of the School Grammar. Under his hand these works have
undergone essential changes, especially in the syntax, and have been so
judiciously adapted to the steady progress in grammatical science, as
still (forty-four years after the death of their author) to be able to
maintain themselves in many German schools and universities against
the competition of recent Grammars, like those of Curtius and
Krüger.

Besides many essays upon grammatical, critical, and exegetical topics,
which Professor Buttmann has prepared from time to time for the
Studien und Kritiken, and other periodicals, he published, in 1856, a
book on " German Names of Places." But his chief work, and that
especially for the preparation of which he withdrew from the labor of
teaching, is his N. T. Grammar. This is confessedly the most important
treatise on the subject which has appeared since Winer's. The author
makes generous acknowledgments of indebtedness to Winer ; but a
slight examination of the book will convince the reader that it has a
valid claim to be regarded as an original work. In fact, the general
attitude and drift of the two writers differ perceptibly. While Winer
— owing, doubtless, to the lax views respecting the N. T. language
which prevailed when he began to write — seems loath to recognize
incipient departures from classic usage, Prof. Buttmann, on the other
hand, is quick to concede and to trace out the general tendency of the
language to degenerate from the classic standard, is inclined to give
greater prominence than Winer to the influence of the Septuagint, and
even to detect traces of the Latin in the syntax of the N. T. Hence
it comes to pass that respecting several details, such as the unemphatic
use of αὐτός in the Nom. (p. 107), the use of periphrases for the Genitive (p. 156), of the Indic. Pres. for the Subjunc. in deliberative
questions (p. 208 sq.), etc., his views vary materially from those of his
predecessor. On other and broader topics, too, such as the use of the
Art. (cf. pp. 90, 93), the apparently indiscriminate employment of Aor.
and Perf. (p. 197), the so-called Gnomic Aor. (pp. 201 sqq.), the use
and force of the particle ἵνα (pp. 235 sqq.) and of the Infin. with τοῦ
(pp. 266 sqq.), his clear and thorough discussions will be read with
interest; while his full exhibition of grammatical forms,[1] especially those
of the verb, will prove to be specially helpful. And as his discussion of
the principles of the N. T. language, both supplementing and qualifying,
as it does, the views of Winer, will interest the student of grammar ;
so his extended application of these principles in elucidating obscure

---

[1] Cf. Tischendorf's commendatory remark in his N. T. ed. Sept. Crit. Maj.
Prolegg. p. lx.

passages will be welcomed by those who care for little more than the results of exegesis.

The form which the author thought best to give his treatise, viz. that of an Appendix to Ph. Buttmann's Griechische Grammatik (the work which Dr. Robinson translated), has doubtless retarded its circulation.[1] By adopting that form, he was enabled, while devoting, at the most, but a passing remark to those points which the language of the N. T. has in common with classic Greek, to exhibit what is peculiar to the N. T. in a more sharp and consecutive treatment than would have been possible otherwise. But the scientific precision of the plan is counterbalanced, in the result, by the practical inconveniences to which those students are subjected who are not familiar with the grammatical method of Buttmann. It seemed desirable to the translator, therefore, while, on the one hand, retaining as far as possible the author's exclusive treatment of his department, on the other hand, to adapt the work to the easy use of students drilled in other grammatical text-books. In order to accomplish this twofold object, I have introduced into the translation so much only from Buttmann's classical Grammar as was necessary, in every case, to render the matter under discussion intelligible to the student without recourse to that work; and, on the other hand, I have added to the references to that Grammar (which is designated by the letter B.) running references to the other classical Grammars most in use in this country and in Great Britain, viz. to those of Hadley, Crosby, Donaldson, Jelf. These Grammars, as well as Buttmann's, are referred to by sections,[2] and designated respectively by the initials H., C., D., J.

Owing to diversity in the arrangement and treatment of topics, these references will not be found to be all equally pertinent. But in making them I have been governed by the conviction that a reference to a familiar work, and one at hand, is more serviceable, especially to a beginner, than a reference, though better in itself, to a work less accessible or less easily understood.

In addition to the Grammars already named, references have been given to Prof. Goodwin's Syntax of Moods and Tenses, to Winer's

[1] Since the arrangements for this translation were completed with Prof. Buttmann and his publisher, large use of the original has been made in the notes of Prof. Moulton's excellent translation of the *Sixth* edition of Winer's N. T. Grammar. But it is believed that those who obtain their knowledge of it through that medium can hardly fail to desire to possess the entire work in English.

[2] Occasionally it has been convenient to refer to Buttmann's Classical Grammar by *pages*. In that case the page given is that of Dr. Robinson's translation of the eighteenth German edition, published in 1851, by Harper and Brothers, N. Y.

N. T. Grammar, and occasionally to Prof. Short's Essay on the Order of Words in Attic Greek Prose.[1] These works are represented by G., W., and S. respectively. The references to Winer are to the pages of the authorized translation of the *Seventh* German edition, and are followed in each case by the number of the corresponding page in the original, inclosed within a parenthesis. The references to the "Lehrgebäude" of Gesenius have been supplemented, so far as possible, by references to the corresponding matter in his Hebrew Grammar. The general references to Pape and to Wahl have, for the most part, been retained. But the sixth edition of Liddell and Scott will ordinarily serve the student quite as well as the former; and the revised edition of Dr. Robinson's N. T. Lexicon, or, still better, Prof. Grimm's edition of Wilke's Clavis[2] may be substituted for the latter.

The matter incorporated from Buttmann's classical Grammar, and the references to the other grammatical works above mentioned, are generally introduced without any distinctive mark; but all other additions made by me are carefully distinguished from the original by square brackets.

With the exception of the slight modification of the plan of the work which has been already described, and the omission of a paragraph from the author's Preface which this modification rendered irrelevant, the translation reproduces the original in full and without change. But Prof. Buttmann has very kindly furnished me with two hundred and sixty-one manuscript additions and corrections for this edition — many of them of considerable length and much importance. In weaving them into the text, I have taken pains not to obscure the author's change of opinion, when any has occurred.

The Greek text of the N. T. generally adopted by the author is that of Lachmann's larger edition; see the remarks on this subject at the close of the Introduction, p. 4. In the same place, the reader will discover that the printing of this book was begun nearly two years ago. But the delay is the less regretted, because in the interim the eighth edition of Tischendorf's text and the Greek Testament of Tregelles have both been completed, so that in passages where allusion is made

---

[1] Prefixed to Dr. Drisler's edition of Yonge's English-Greek Lexicon. N. Y. Harper and Brothers. 1870.

[2] The translation of Prof. Grimm's Lexicon which was promised in the Bibliotheca Sacra for October, 1864, has been lying in manuscript now for many months. The protracted work of verifying the references is drawing towards a close, and the book will be published as soon as leisure can be found for the editorial labor requisite to adapt it to the needs of English-speaking students.

to variation in the text, the reading adopted by both these editors has been indicated. To accomplish this at the least expense of alteration in the plates, the ordinary abbreviations Tdf. and Treg. have occasionally been superseded by the simple T. and Tr. respectively. For the same reason the codex Sinaiticus has been referred to by cod. Sin., Sin., and א indifferently.

The Biblical references have all been carefully verified. The N. T. Index has been enlarged so as to include all the passages from the N. T. referred to in the Grammar; and a separate index has been added, comprising the passages cited from the Septuagint. For the labor which these improvements involved, as well as for valuable assistance in correcting the press, my grateful acknowledgments are due to my friend Rev. Geo. B. Jewett, D.D.

The other indexes have been materially augmented; the cross-references have been multiplied; chapter and verse added to many of the fragmentary quotations from the N. T.; the pagination of the German original has been given in the margin; and at the end of the book a Glossary of technical terms encountered more or less frequently in commentaries and grammatical works has been added for the convenience of students.

Finally, I would reiterate the closing words of the author's Preface, in reliance upon the promise made to those who shall agree as touching what they ask.

J. H. THAYER.

THEOLOGICAL SEMINARY, ANDOVER, MASS.
August, 1873.

PREFACE.

As long ago as the appearance of the nineteenth edition of my father's Greek Grammar, I designed to give, as an Appendix for the practical purposes of schools, a summary of the grammatical usage of the N. T. in so far as it differs from ordinary usage, in order subsequently to follow it with a copious and scientific exposition of the entire department. To this twofold undertaking I was led by the persuasion that Winer's Grammar is, on the one hand, too comprehensive and learned for school use; and that on the other hand, for those who have been taught according to the plan of Buttmann's Grammar, it prepares manifold difficulties by its arrangement and whole method of treatment, and requires for its correct understanding almost an independent training of its own. But my work also grew under my hands. The further I entered upon my theme, the more I perceived that such a summary as I had originally designed could only get a sure foundation and make claim to scientific worth in case the entire department had previously been explored as far as possible in all directions, and received a sustained exposition; and that, at any rate, it is a more correct and safe procedure to let a practical outline follow a larger work, executed on scientific principles, than the reverse. Thus arose this Grammar. That I venture to present it to the learned public in face of the many and undisputed excellences of Winer's, does not arise from the mistaken and self-complacent opinion that the work of my respected predecessor ought to be supplanted by a new one. On the contrary, it is my firm persuasion that Winer's work will long continue to maintain its honorable position in philological as well as theological science; and it is my highest wish that my work may only succeed in winning for itself a modest place in this department of literature behind, or by the side of, its predecessor and master.

Winer's Grammar originated at a time when modern philological criticism, especially as applied by Lachmann and Tischendorf, had not yet given to the text of the N. T. that form which it now has in most of the editions used in schools and universities. It is true, the recent revisions of the text remained by no means unnoticed by Winer. On the contrary, the indefatigable labors of the man in this particular are shown by the circumstance that almost every new edition of his Grammar underwent the most important and radical alterations, in order to conform it to the stage of criticism at the time. But the work as a whole acquired by these frequent changes a somewhat ragged look, and a form often extremely inconvenient for practical use, especially for citation. Since, too, hardly any performance within his department escaped the notice of this thorough investigator, inasmuch as he took notice of all publications in any way relating to it, — as well those of specifically theological science as of philological, both oriental and classical, — and wrought the acquired results into his work, he imparted to it by degrees such a character that it may be regarded almost as a grammatically arranged Commentary on the N. T.; a commentary which, by its copious wealth and its searching treatment of many particular passages, is, and will remain, indispensable to every member of the theological profession. But on the other hand it is not to be denied, that by the accumulation (often unlimited) of learned material the clear grammatical outlook was frequently cut off. Furthermore, as the work did not adopt any given system of classical Greek grammar, but traversed anew, in the syntax at least, the entire realm of grammatical phenomena, much was of necessity given which strictly belonged to the general grammar, or at least might have been assumed as sufficiently well-known already. The inevitable consequence of this was, that for an unpractised eye what is distinctive and peculiar in N. T. usage is not discriminated sharply enough from what, as being common property to all who spoke and wrote Greek, pertains to Greek grammar in general.

Taking, then, the critical investigations of the recent editors as my basis, and adopting the philological views which underlie Buttmann's Greek Grammar, particularly the nineteenth and following editions edited by me, I have given my N. T. Grammar the form of an Appendix to that work. In this way the first part of my book, which relates to Forms and Inflection, has acquired, it must be confessed, a somewhat fragmentary aspect, as the honored reviewer in Zarncke's literary "Centralblatt" correctly remarks. Since, however, the deviations, in the matter of Forms, of the language of the N. T. writers, (with the exception, perhaps, of the text of the Apocalypse as established by modern criticism) from the current literary language, especially the then prevalent κοινή, so-called, are by no means very important, a work undertaking to bring out only what is distinctive in the N. T. language cannot assume any other shape; — just as the same description holds true of that portion of Winer's Grammar also which treats of Forms.

As respects Syntax the case is different. Here what is characteristic and peculiar is incomparably more marked, in consequence of the nature of the contents of the N. T. books on the one hand, and of many foreign influences on the other. That the mental impulse given by the new doctrine must produce a noticeable effect upon language, does not need to be shown at length. Of the foreign influences which impart to the Greek of the N. T. that complexion which distinguishes it so noticeably from the classic tongue, there are in particular four: First, the influence of the linguistic spirit of the Orient, especially of the O. T. Hebrew and of the Aramaic of the Palestinian Jews of that day (Hebraisms); Secondly (and closely connected with this), the influence of the Greek translation of the Bible by the Seventy interpreters, generally diffused as it was among the Jews of that region and so much in use (the Septuagint); Thirdly, the influence coming from the popular language prevalent in all portions of the Greek world of that day, as distinguished from the literary diction of the repositories of classic Greek literature and culture (the Common or Colloquial language); Fourthly, the influence of the Latin language upon the later Greek or so-called κοινή (Latinisms).

*   *   *   *   *   *

A complete exhibition of the linguistic peculiarities of the N. T. would comprise a discrimination between the styles peculiar to the different N. T. authors. For it is not to be overlooked, that (leaving the Apocalypse aside) there exists a difference not only between the historic writings and the epistolary, but also within these main divisions, between the synoptists and John; between the Pauline and the Catholic epistles; between individual Evangelists; in fact, between the several writings of one and the same author; — an assertion which is true, for example, of the Gospel of Luke and the Book of Acts. A detailed exposition of these differences, however, would carry us quite too far, and lies beyond the limits of this Grammar, which is primarily concerned only with grouping as far as possible all characteristics together, and so taking a combined view of the N. T. diction and style. The compass of the several writings, also, is too small to afford a basis for separate expositions of the various peculiarities in language; and an author must be satisfied to treat this subject in a fragmentary way as opportunity offers. Moreover, a minute elaboration of this topic falls rather to the department of N. T. stylistics, or of exegesis, whose business it is to examine and elucidate the individual writings on all sides. The reader, therefore, may be the more readily referred to these exegetical works, as more thorough treatment and careful investigation have already been bestowed upon the subject by the recent commentators;[1] and in consequence of the critical renovation of the text will continue to be given it in the future. Whatever grammatical results, however, could already be mentioned, I have carefully endeavored to note: by speaking of them in their place as special peculiarities, and by giving as complete a list of them as possible in the Index under the head of the respective N. T. authors. The same has been done in reference to the four aspects of the language previously mentioned, with regard to which the Index may be consulted under the topics, Hebraisms, Septuagint, Language (popular and later Greek), Latinisms.

On two other points it seems to me necessary to say a word in this place, viz. the proper attitude and relations of New Testament Grammar to Exegesis and to Lexicography. The contents of the N. T., especially of the Epistles, are so exceptional both as respects difficulty and importance, and the compass of the several books is so small, that in the domain of interpretation the most diverse results could not fail to be brought to light. Evidence of this is afforded by the extremely numerous and voluminous exegetical writings, the like of which in amount can probably be shown by no literary productions of ancient or modern times. Owing to the variety of religious parties and theological sects, which from the first centuries down have been so numerous and changeful, as well as in consequence of the restricted views or one-sided partizanship of individuals, the diversity of exegetical principles is very considerable; — in fact there are for many passages almost as many different interpretations as interpreters (see ex. gr. Winer on Gal. iii. 20). And to what assaults from the same quarter and for the same reasons the sacred text itself has been exposed from the very earliest times, the collection of various readings affords many a striking proof; (see ex. gr. 1 Tim. iii. 16 ; 1 John v. 7 ; 1 Cor. xv. 51, etc.). Nowhere, however, do the opinions of interpreters diverge more widely than where a knowledge of grammatical principles was wanting, and consequently the caprice of the private understanding had free course, so that often N. T. Grammar was made responsible for the strangest hypotheses and chimeras. Although the knowledge of grammar is not the only, still

---

[1] Among many others I may mention the commentaries of Bleek on the Epistle to the Hebrews, of Lücke and Tholuck on John, of Fritzsche on the first two Gospels, of the same author and of Rückert and Reiche on the Epistles to the Romans and the Corinthians, of de Wette and Meyer on all the books of the N. T the numerous N. T. Introductions, etc.

it is the primary and the main, foundation of interpretation; at any
rate, it is a check to subjective caprice and inordinate excesses. Without this foundation there can be no talk about certainty in explaining
the Scriptures; for we possess no inspired interpretation. Linguistic
products, even the most sacred, are like all others, subject to the restraint
of linguistic laws, which, be they ever so special, are nevertheless *Laws*,
which every author spontaneously and unconsciously obeys. To establish
such definite linguistic laws, together with the just as definitely-limited
exceptions (so far forth as the latter either rest upon analogies in ordinary usage, or at least group themselves together under a distinctly
traceable special analogy), and to combine all these phenomena into
one systematic whole, is the business of a special grammar.

Many passages of Scripture, however, are of such a kind that, owing
to the limited extent of the several books, they are destitute of any
other analogy. These, to be sure, must then be explained from themselves, from the context and the tenor of Scripture, or by the aid of
ancient tradition (which must have for us the greater authority the
nearer it stands to the time of composition of the Scriptures), in a word,
historically rather than grammatically. Such cases must be left principally to Exegesis. If Grammar notices them, it does so rather incidentally, and for the sake of completeness; their value to Grammar
can only be determined by their relation to analogies already established. For she can adopt, and work up as solid portions of the system
she would found, only those results of Hermeneutics which rest upon
analogies, if she will not run the risk of being compelled to pull to
pieces to-morrow what she to-day perhaps has laboriously built up, and
to cast away as useless material what she has over-hastily made the
corner pillar of her structure. On the other hand, it would be just as
erroneous, if she in haughty self-sufficiency should wish utterly to
seclude herself from the results of Hermeneutics. Both sciences must
continually go hand in hand. As Hermeneutics has in Grammar her
constant monitor and the touchstone of her results, so Grammar receives
from the discreet critico-historical inquiry of Exegesis perpetually new
enrichment. It is an unscientific, irrational demand, — and one which
misjudges man's powers, — that the one science should not begin to act
till after the other has finished its work; since, on the contrary, they
are *both at the same time* called and commissioned for the understanding
of the Scriptures. By progressive discernment, with the help of Grammar and under the guidance of critico-historical research, continually to
diminish the number of passages which refuse to submit to any linguistic analogy (and consequently as to whose meaning commentators

generally diverge in all directions) is one of the leading and abiding aims of Hermeneutics.

Further: it is difficult to draw a sharp boundary line between Lexicography and the explanation of words (Semasiology) on the one hand, and Grammar on the other; since both departments often encroach upon each other, and stand in relations of reciprocity. Indeed, from a scientific point of view every syntactic phenomenon connected with a word ought to be included in syntax, of whatever nature that phenomenon may be: for example, the different significations of a word so far forth as they proceed from a difference of construction, or on the other hand occasion a different construction. But a particular grammar, like that of the N. T., always subserves, in the main, practical necessities; and it would be obliged to extend its limits far too wide, if in the respect under consideration it would attain to merely relative completeness even. Here also, therefore, a separation must take place between what can be traced back to definite laws and perceptible analogies, and what as an isolated peculiarity can be conveniently left to the dictionaries. It is true, the general lexicons in common use in the schools, as they are all based on classical usage, are not sufficient in many cases for the understanding of the N. T. (compare ex. gr. the words πιστεύειν, ἐλπί-ζειν, ὁμολογεῖν; the prepositions ἐν, εἰς, ἀπό, etc.); and accordingly, a great number of special dictionaries have been prepared by scholars, among which may be named those of Schöttgen, Schleusner, Wahl, Bretschneider, Wilke, Schirlitz, etc. Grammar, however, obliged as it is continually to impose upon itself firm restrictions, cannot possibly include all that is lexically important — unless the fulness of details is to destroy the evident perspicuity of the whole, but must regard its task as completely performed when all the combinations and constructions occurring in the N. T., especially those relating to cases and verbs, are linguistically accounted for. The possession of a special dictionary, therefore, will always be requisite to theologians and every one who desires to investigate the N. T. writings minutely.

These are the principles and the most important aims which have guided me in the composition of this work. Whether I have a right to appear before the literary public with a book which originated in this way and has been wrought out according to these principles, those must judge who join to linguistic knowledge an unprejudiced view of the great difficulties to be overcome. Whether I hereafter venture to make an abridgment of this work for the use of schools, will depend upon the invitation especially of those gentlemen who have charge of religious instruction in the Gymnasia.

In conclusion, let me be permitted, with allusion to the closing words of Winer's Preface to the last [i.e. the 6th] edition of his Grammar, to utter the deep-felt desire, that under God's assistance it may be reserved for this book also (in fellowship with the work of my honored predecessor, to which it owes very much, indeed the greatest part, of its value) to further the knowledge of Biblical truth so far as any such work can.

POTSDAM, Nov. 1858.

CONTENTS

PART FIRST: FORMS.

PART SECOND: SYNTAX.

B. § 1, N. 8; C. § 88; H. § 4 f.; D. § 13.

1. THE basis of the Hellenistic language of the N. T. is the so-called Macedo-Alexandrian dialect, which, as is well known, became current in the time of the Ptolemies, especially at Alexandria, then the seat of culture; and this again was founded upon the κοινὴ διάλεκτος which sprang from the Attic dialect. From Alexandria Greek speech and culture spread over the Asiatic kingdoms which arose from the Macedonian conquest, and accordingly over Syria. Here, of course, much that was local and foreign was mixed with it, not only in the mouth of the people, but also of the educated who wrote for the people. Consequently, in the language of the N. T. when compared with the Attic dialect, — the general basis of the (prose) literary language, — we may distinguish, first, the peculiarities belonging to the Alexandrian (Macedonian) dialect; and secondly, especially in the Syntax, the so-called Hebraisms (Aramaisms).

REMARK. Since the N. T. writings, however, are (perhaps with the exception of Matthew) the free products of authors who thought and spoke in Greek, they do not exhibit nearly as many Hebraisms as the language of the Seventy, who translated immediately from the Hebrew; they consequently constitute an independent idiom. But as the translated Scriptures of the O. T. exercised a manifold influence upon the composition of the N. T. books — being referred to very often by the N. T. writers, who inwove into their language quotations from them, now literal, now free, — a N. T. Grammar must often take notice of the language of the Septuagint.

2. The language of the several books of the N. T. again 2 varies according as every individual writer 1) has his peculiar modes of expression, 2) and even certain dialectic peculiarities, 3) and approximates more or less to the Hebrew style. In particular the historic books differ from the epistolary in consequence of their differing aim and contents; inasmuch

as the historic, especially the Gospels of Matthew, Mark, and John, approximate more to the (Aramaizing) language of the people; the Epistles, on the other hand, particularly those written by Paul to Greek-speaking churches and persons in Europe and Asia, are connected as respects language with the literary Greek then in use, yet not without noticeable deviations in construction and in the formation and meaning of words, since the common Greek habits of thought and speech were not adequate to the expression of the new ideas. The strictly Greek style of writing is approximated most closely by the writings of Luke, especially by the Acts, of which the diction and entire mode of expression is often suggestive of Attic elegance and is full of genuine Greek turns and constructions, although instances of the opposite are not wanting in them. Lastly, the language of the Apocalypse is distinguished from all the rest by great and sometimes very anomalous peculiarities in word and structure.

3. Since the Alexandrian dialect arose from the κοινή, it is not surprising that writers speak even of so-called Ionisms, Dorisms, etc. (though very limited in number) in the N.T. also. But neither the language of the N. T., nor that of the κοινοί in general, can be regarded as a mixture, as is sometimes assumed, of the various Greek dialects; since all the dialectic phenomena in question are in part quite isolated and in part of doubtful origin.

4. Although we possess a large number of MSS.[1] of the N. T. Scriptures, some of which are very old, and the writings 3 of the oldest church fathers bear witness largely to the text current in their times, yet very divergent forms of the text have come down to us. This makes it often very difficult — indeed, owing to the equal authority for the readings, almost impossible — to distinguish between what originally belonged

---

[1] The most important among the so-called uncial Codices (i.e. MSS. written in uncial letters) are the Cod. Alexandrinus (A) now in the British Museum, London, Cod. Vaticanus (B) in Rome, Cod. rescriptus Ephræmi (C) in Paris, Cod. Cantabrigiensis (D), etc. To these must now be added the Cod. Sinaiticus (א) in St. Petersburg (recently discovered by Tischendorf in the Convent of Mt. Sinai). The oldest MSS. are Codd. Vat. and Sin., both of the 4th century. See, for details concerning the MSS., the Prolegomena of Tischendorf and Scholz, the Introductions of Hug, [Tregelles, Scrivener], Griesbach's Symb. Crit., [Smith's Bible Dict. Art. *New Testament*, especial y in the Am. ed.], etc.

to the author, and what to the transcribers and the time in which and for which they wrote. The earlier editions of the N. T. — as the editio princeps which appeared (at Alcala) in Spain, (the so-called Complutensian); then the various editions by Erasmus which appeared in the sixteenth century (and which Luther used in his translation), and particularly that by Robert Stephens (1550), Theodore Beza (1565), and the Elzevirs (1624, — which last gradually acquired general currency in the Western Church, and hence its text is called the Textus Receptus) — all rest more or less upon a very imperfect, in fact, arbitrary, collation of a number of MSS. apparently for the most part the more modern. In the 17th century, accordingly, and particularly in the 18th, a great multitude of various readings was collected through the more careful collation of the most important of the older MSS., and by the labors of many scholars, as Bengel, Wetstein, Bentley, Birch, Griesbach, etc. ; but the text of most of the subsequent editions [1] differed in the main but little from the textus receptus, since the editors (generally theologians) did not venture to depart too far from that to which usage had given a kind of ecclesiastical sanction. Hence the need of a text founded upon a purely philological process became more and more pressing. The merit of having prepared the way for su h a thorough revision of the text upon critical and philolo al principles, belongs unquestionably to Carl Lachmann (Lch .), who first in 1831 prepared a smaller edition of the N. T. nd subsequently in 1842 a larger edition [2] furnished with a cri cal apparatus and Jerome's Latin version, the so-called Vul ate Almost at the same time and in pursuance of essentiall the 4 same method, — yet often reaching different results, p rtly because starting with other critical views,[3] partly in c nse-quence of using a much greater number of MSS., collat ons, and critical helps of every kind — L. F. C. Tischendorf (1 df.)

[1] The greatest reputation among those of more recent date was won by the editions of Griesbach which were prepared with judicious criticism and great care: smaller ed. Leips. 1825 ; larger ed. Vol. I. Halle, 1796 (3d ed. care of David Schulz, Berlin, 1827), Vol. II. Hal. 1806.

[2] Novum Testamentum gr. et lat. Car. Lachmannus rec., Ph. Buttmannus Græcæ lect. auctoritates apposuit. Berol. 1842, 1850.

[3] On the critical principles of the two editors see the Prefaces to their respective editions, and the discussions and expositions in the theol. Stud. u. Krit. there referred to.

undertook to restore the text in a series of editions of the N.T., the first of which appeared in 1841. After making several journeys expressly for this purpose, collating for himself nearly all the most important Codices, and publishing several ancient and newly-discovered manuscript documents,[1] he prepared a second larger edition [1849],[2] provided with a copious critical apparatus, which was followed (in 1854) by the Triglot edition, comprising the Greek text, the Vulgate and the oldest Lutheran translation [cf. note [3] below]. Respecting other modern editions, as that of Scholz, Ed. von Muralt, the Acts by Bornemann, see Tisch. pref. [Tregelles, on the Printed Text of the Gr. N. T. 1854; cf. the Introductions, etc., referred to p. 2, note [1]]. The present work will in the main take as its basis the text of Lachmann's large edition, yet constant regard is paid to the readings of Tischendorf;[3] and, where it seemed necessary, to those of Griesbach (Grsb.) also, as well as of the textus receptus (Rec.). [In disputed passages the reading adopted by Tregelles (Treg.), in his Greek New Testament (exclusive of the Revelation, which is not yet published[4]), 1857–70, will also be indicated.]

[1] See the list of them given in the Preface to the editions of 1849 and 1854 [more fully in his 7th ed. 1859], and at the end of his second edition of the Sept. (Lips. 1856), [4th ed. 1869].

[2] Novum Testamentum Graece. Ad. antiq. testes rec., appar. crit. apposuit, etc. C. Tischendorf. ed. II. Lips. 1849.

[3] There is just appearing [1855 sqq.] in separate numbers, a new (7th) edition of Tischendorf's text of 1849, considerably modified in the text, but more especially furnished with the critical Commentary of the edition of 1849 greatly enlarged and perfected, so that the reader is now enabled in every single case to see the entire stock of variants, and the kind of support given to every reading (even to those not received) by MSS., versions, fathers, etc.; the compendious nature of the former Commentary rendered this often quite impossible, at least very troublesome and uncertain. Regard will be paid to this edition also as far as it has already appeared. [Of his most recent (8th) critical edition (1864 sqq.), eight parts (extending to 1 Cor. v. 7) have already (Sept. 1871) been published. Unless some indication to the contrary be given, this is the text of Tischendorf uniformly referred to. He has edited besides, *N. T. Gr. ex cod. Sin.* Lips. 1865, and *N. T. Vaticanum,* Lips. 1867; to both of these reference will be occasionally made when the text of a passage is in question.] [The *text* of Tdf.'s 8th ed. is now complete.]

[4] It has appeared since the printing of this book was begun, and its readings will be referred to so far as practicable.]

ETYMOLOGY.

PRONUNCIATION, ORTHOGRAPHY.
B. § 8, 2; C. § 79; W. p. 48 (47); Tdf. ed. 7 Prol. xxxvii. sq. 1. sqq.

The letter ι is often represented in the MSS. of the N. T. by ει; yet no inference can be drawn from this respecting its quantity, for the change occurs in the case of long vowels (θλειψις, γεινωσκω) and of short (ηγγεικεν, καθεισας) alike. Under the influence of Itacism also it is often reproduced by η (as Κηλικια, πρωτοκλησια, βραχηονι), and on the other hand ει is represented by ι (απεστιλεν, αιτισθαι D). In foreign words the use of ει for ι has been in part adopted into the text (see p. 6 note [1]). In genuine Greek words the usual spelling is followed in the printed editions. But in Matt. xxviii. 3 all the (older) MSS. give ειδέα for ιδέα (Lchm.); and it has consequently been received into the text by Tischendorf [and Tregelles]. This was the general mode of writing the word. Hence even Suidas so spelt it, adding expressly οἱ νῦν διὰ τοῦ ῑ γράφουσι; cf. Bhdy. praef. ad Suid. p. 39; Fischer on Plat. Euthyphr. p. 125.

A similar vacillation is found in the M. between ε and αι (several instances of which are given on p. 0, note [1]) and other vowels, especially between οι and υ (thus almost always ἠνύγην for ἠνοίγην). On the various Itacistic in changes in the MSS. see Tdf. praef. ad Vet. Test. pp. 72, 80 [ed. , and N.T. as above]; Sturz, Dial. Alex. p. 117 sq. Before μ ζ is often written instead of σ, as Ζμύρνης (adopted by Tdf. [ed. 8, Rev. i. 11 and ii. 8]), which spelling, according to Lucian (ud. voc. 9), must have been pretty general.

TERMINAL LETTERS.
B § 4, 5; H. § 74 sq.; C. § 160; D. § 83 sq.

Hebrew proper nouns in the Greek text, either, 1) appear unaltered (and are then indeclinable), so that the eye must

6 accustom itself to a multitude of unusual terminal letters, as
in Δανείδ, 'Ραχάβ, Βοόζ, Ναζαράθ, etc.[1]; or, 2) they receive a
Greek termination (and are then inflected according to analogy), as Μωυσῆς, 'Ησαίας, 'Ιερεμίας, 'Ιωνᾶς, 'Ιησοῦς ; or, 3)
they appear in both forms, the foreign form then always being
indeclinable ; e.g. ἡ 'Ιερουσαλήμ and τὰ 'Ιεροσόλυμα, Μαριάμ
and Μαρία, 'Ιακώβ (so always of Jews, Matt. i. 15, etc.) and
'Ιάκωβος (so of the various Christians), Σαούλ (so of the son
of Kish, Acts xiii. 21) and Σαῦλος (so always, in narration,
of the apostle before he took the name of Παῦλος ; but even
then, whenever he is addressed, the national form Σαούλ is
uniformly used, Acts ix. 4, etc.).   Latin names are always
Grecized, as Πιλᾶτος,[2] 'Ιοῦστος, Φῆλιξ, etc.   Concerning the
inflection of Grecized proper names see p. 15 sq. below.

ENCLITICS.

B. 14, 4. and N. 1; H. § 106 sq.; C. § 787 sq.; J. § 64 obs. 1; D. § 55.

The general laws of *Inclination* hold to their full extent in
the N. T. writings ; — that is to say, this method of accentuation has been carried out consistently in the N. T. because
there was no reason for following there different rules in
reference to the accents from those followed in all other Greek

---

[1] As respects the spelling of foreign names there is naturally enough considerable diversity, not only in the mss., but also in the several editions.   Thus Lachmann, for instance, gives the name Nazareth not only in the form Ναζαράθ Matt.
iv. 13, but also Ναζαρέθ ii. 23 and Ναζαρέτ Mark i. 9 ; [Tdf. and Treg. use the
forms in -εθ and -ετ, and also (Matt. iv. 13) the form Ναζαρά.   Tdf. in his 7th ed.
(see Prol. p. lv. note) had decided that -εθ was the form everywhere to be used in
Matt. and -ετ in John.   In the note on Luke i. 26 in his 8th ed. he thinks this evangelist used the form in -εθ, with the exception of -ρά in iv. 16].   The name David
(in the mss. commonly written Δαδ) appears now in Lachmann in the form
Δανείδ throughout (not Δαυίδ or Δαβίδ), and Tdf. [and Treg.] have followed him
in this respect.   In reference to other names there is no such harmony between the
editions, e.g. Κίς and Κείς [Lchm. with whom Tdf. now and Treg. agree], Χοραζίν
[Lchm.] and -ζείν [Tdf. Treg.], ῥαββί [Lchm. Treg.] and ῥαββεί [Tdf., cf. Prol.
ed. 7, p. li.], Χερουβίμ and χερουβείν Lchm. [Tdf. ed. 8 ; Treg.] Heb. ix. 5.   The
Greek mode of writing the name Beelzebub (as Luther [so A. V.] has it after the
Vulgate) is Βεελζεβούλ, that of Belial is more probably Βελίαρ 2 Cor. vi. 15 Tdf.
[ed. 8 ; Treg.].   See on this subject Tdf. ed. 2. p. 34 [Alf. N. T. Vol. I. prol. p.
94 sq.].

[2] As respects the accentuation Πιλᾶτος see Fritzsche on Mark p. 671 ; Winer p.
52 (51).   Bekker in his edition of Josephus always marks this and similar proper
names with the circumflex ; and the recent editors of the N. T. have decided in
favor of this mode of writing.   See Tisch. pref. p. 36 [ed. 7, p. lxi.   In ed. 8 he
writes Πειλᾶτος ; see his note on Matt. xxvii. 2].   Elsewhere the long α in words
of Latin origin appears marked simply with the acute (not circumflex) ; as, σενάτο.
(Plut. Romul. 13), λιγάρε, ἀλλιγάρε (26), κωμεσσάτοι (Moral. p. 726).

writings.[1] Dissyllables after perispomena are not marked as
enclitic ; hence παῖς ἐστίν, γυναικῶν τινῶν, etc.   Cf. Herm. de
emend. rat. I. 71, 73.

MUTATIONS OF THE CONSONANTS.
B. § 16, N. 3; H. §§ 41 sq. 60; C. § 151 sqq.; J. §§ 34. 33;

The use of σσ for ττ, described as mainly Ionic, is in the
N. T. the only traditional spelling with most words, as περισσός,
θάλασσα, γλῶσσα, τάσσω, etc.   In the Comparative, the forms
κρείσσων, ἐλάσσων are interchanged with κρείττων, ἐλάττων ;
and in certain words derived from them the ττ has become
established, as ἐλαττόω, ἐλαττονέω, ἥττημα, ἡττᾶσθαι.

The combination ρρ is exchanged with ρσ, e.g. θαρρέω and
θαρσέω (see Wahl, clav. min.).   But instead of ἄρρην Lchm.
has everywhere (even in Rev. xii. 5, 13) restored the form
with ρσ [so Treg. ; and Tdf. also except in Rom. i. 27].

ASPIRATES.
B. § 17, N. 1; H. § 72; C. § 167; J. § 23.

The use of an aspirate before a smooth breathing conflicts,
indeed, with the general rules of orthography, which are observed also in the N. T., yet in several instances is pretty well
established.   Thus we have, e.g. ἔφιδε Acts iv. 29 [ἔπιδε Tdf.],
ἀφίδω Phil. ii. 23, ἐφεῖδεν Luke i. 25 Tdf. [ed. 7], ἀφελπίζοντες
vi. 35 Lchm., οὐχ Ἰουδαϊκῶς Gal. ii. 14 (Tdf. οὐχ', as cod. A has,
e.g. in οὐχ' ὄψεσθε Luke xvii. 22) — to write it thus with the
apostrophe was the almost universal usage, see Schneider on Plat.
Rep. p. 455 ; Anecd. Bekk. p. 683 sq.   On the other hand, in
the MSS. we also find often οὐκ εὗρον (Exod. xvi. 27), οὐκ ἕνεκα
in Hermas, etc. ; but see below p. 10.   On the omission of aspiration (οὐκ ἕστηκεν) see Tdf.'s note on John viii. 44.   [He
writes ἐπίσταται for ἐφίσταται in 1 Thess. v. 3.]   Further
ἐφ' ἐλπίδι Acts ii. 26 [(Tdf. ἐλπ.); Rom. viii. 20 Tdf. ; iv. 18
Lchm.], οὐχ ἠγάπησαν Rev. xii. 11, οὐχ ἰδού Acts ii. 7, οὐχ
ὀλίγος xix. 23 Lchm., cf. xii. 18 ; see Lachmann's pref. p. 42.
The aspiration ἐλπις occurs also in inscriptions ; see Franz,
Epigr. 111.   It is possible that the retention of the digamma in
single words (cf. the Lat. video) occasioned these irregularities,
which occur elsewhere also, see Winer p. 45 (44).

B. § 18, N. 2; H. § 65, c.; C. § 159, d.; J. § 31, a.; W. p. 44.

The form ἐθύθη, which formerly stood in the text (1 Cor
v. 7) has now given place again to the regular form ἐτύθη.

[1] The oldest manuscripts have in general few or no accents ; s e Hug, Einl. § 50.

DOUBLING OF CONSONANTS.
B. § 21, 3; H. § 40 b.; C. § 159; D. § 95; J. § 22, 3.

Lachmann, following manuscripts, has often introduced again in spelling proper names θθ instead of τθ, and Tischendorf [and Tregelles also] has in part followed him in this. Thus in Lchm. [Tdf. Treg.] we always find Ματθαῖος (even in Acts i. 13) Ματθάν, but in Lchm. [Treg.] Ματθάτ Luke iii. 24 [Tdf. Ματθάθ; Treg. Ματθάτ in Luke iii. 29]; and in Lchm. Ματθίας Acts i. 23 [Treg. Tdf. Ματθ.]. Since in matters of orthography no uniformity can be attained either by following 8 MSS. or inscriptions, it seems advisable here, where the two modes of writing cannot have been governed by any difference in sound (cf. Lchm. pref. p. 40), to follow out consistently either the spelling with θθ (which occurs here and there in inscriptions also), or that with τθ as the grammarians prescribe.

The name Zacchaeus is written Ζακχαῖος by all; on the other hand, the spelling of Ἀπφία Philem. 2, Σάπφειρα Acts v. i, is doubtful.

On the neglect to double ρ see p. 32.

CHANGES OF ν.

B. § 25, N. 3; H. § 52; C. § 166; D. § 101; J. 28; W. p. 48; Tdf. ed. 7, Prol. p. xlvii sq.

The rule that σύν in composition, before σ followed by another consonant, and before ζ, drops its ν, is often disregarded in the N. T.; thus we always find συνσταυροῦν, συνστρατιώτης, συνζῆν, συνζητεῖν, σύνζυγος. In other words, however, the omission is made, e.g. συστατικός, συστενάζω, συστοιχεῖν, συστρέφω, συστροφή, συσχηματίζειν. See Wahl's clavis, and Lachmann's pref. p. 40. Further, the oldest (uncial) MSS. often omit the assimilation of the ν in the two prepositions σύν and ἐν before labials and palatals, sometimes also before λ and σ, thus συνπαραλαβεῖν, συνμαθητής, συνκαθισάντων, ἐνκακεῖν, ἐνγεγραμμένος, συνλυπούμενος, σύνσωμα, etc., and likewise in separated words ἐν μέσῳ (only in the Apocalypse does Tdf. [ed. 7; cf. Prol. to Sept. ed. 4, p. lxxii] write them always as one word: ἐμμέσῳ), ἐν Κανᾶ. In particular it may be noticed that in compounds with ἐν and σύν cod. Vat. (and Sin.) almost always neglects assimilation when these prepositions preserve their proper signification; see Bttm.'s Rev. of Kuenen and Cobet's ed. of cod. Vat. in the theol. Stud. u. Krit. for 1862 p. 180. On the

other hand, the mode of writing as one word is often found, as ἐμμέσῳ, ἐγκανᾶ, συμπᾶσι, etc. [Tdf. writes ἔνπροσθεν in Rev. iv. 6.]

MOVABLE FINAL LETTERS.
B. § 26, 2 and 4; H. § 78 sq.; C. § 162 sq.; D. § 85; J. § 20. 2; W. p. 41 sq.

In the earlier editions the rules of the grammarians in reference to ν ἐφελκυστικόν were followed. These, however, were
found to be so seldom sustained by the manuscripts, that at
present Tischendorf has retained ν ἐφελκυστικόν before every
consonant without exception, and has carried out this rule
consistently, with very few exceptions, throughout the N. T.
[i.e. in ed. 7, cf. Prol. p. liii; in ed. 8 he has dropped it in
several cases, following the best MSS.; see the note below.]
Lachmann (in his large edition) also writes it before all the
consonants; yet in particular cases, following the MSS., he has
not admitted it; these, however, almost disappear in the multitude that remain: e.g. Matt. vi. 24; John ix. 30, 32; Acts ii.
6, 22, 40; vii. 25; ix. 22; x. 40; xii. 6; xxi. 33; Rom. ii. 8;
Rev. xix. 17; Luke xvii. 29, etc.[1]

The numeral εἴκοσι appears everywhere, even at the end of 9
a sentence and before a vowel (Acts i. 15 [yet Treg. -σιν]),
without ν ἐφελκυστικόν. So too in the O. T., see Tdf's. ed.
praef. p. xxxiv. [ed. 4; cf. N. T. ed. 7, p. liv.].

Precisely the same procedure occurs in connection with
οὕτως, so that the other form οὕτω is at present almost completely banished from the text [cf. Tdf. ed. 7, p. liii]. There
are rare exceptions again in Lchm.; as, Phil. iii. 17; Acts xxiii.
11; Rom. i. 15; vi. 19, etc.

---

[1] Perhaps we can hardly hope ever to succeed in clearing up this point, since, as
the liberty of later times in the use of ν was manifestly unrestrained, and the thing
itself is so trivial, the transcribers (learned and unlearned) of the N. T. books felt
little hesitation in employing or omitting it at option. Consequently the consistent introduction of the ν ἐφελκυστικόν throughout may be justified as a silent confession of the impossibility of tracing out the original mode of spelling of the
authors themselves; and so much the more, as the cases in which *all* the MSS. employ ν contrary to the grammatical rule appear to be very frequent, while cases of
the other class (in which *all* MSS. omit it), are extremely rare. It would only be
necessary, then, to bring one's self to use the ν in these rare cases contrary to the
MSS., as in Luke xvi. 13; Matt. vi. 24 (δυσί Tdf. [so too Treg.] even in ed. 7, with
the remark: sic codd. unc. omnes, *ut videtur* [cf. note on Luke l. c. ed. 8]). If we are
unwilling to do this, then Lachmann's [and Tdf.'s?] method of allowing here as
elsewhere the authority of the oldest MSS. to decide, deserves unqualifiedly the
preference, as affording the only stable anchorage in the matter. To be sure, we
should need in that case a more careful collation of the manuscripts in reference
to this particular than we now possess.

The case is quite different with respect to μέχρις and ἄχρις. Both these forms never occur before consonants, but always μέχρι and ἄχρι. On the other hand, μέχρις is regularly used before vowels, e.g. μέχρις οὗ, μέχρις αἵματος Heb. xii. 4. Only ἄχρι stands several times even before vowels; but not always without reason. For while in the common phrase ἄχρις οὗ the word remains everywhere unaltered, ἄχρι is everywhere used, manifestly to avoid cacophony, in the phrase ἄχρι ἧς ἡμέρας: Matt. xxiv. 38; Luke i. 20; xvii. 27; Acts i. 2, cf. xxiii. 1. Elsewhere the two forms are interchanged before vowels, as ἄχρις [-ρι Treg. Tdf.] αὐγῆς Acts xx. 11, ἄχρις [-ρι Treg. Tdf.] Ἀππίου φόρου xxviii. 15, ἄχρι (ἄχρις Rec.) ἡμερῶν πέντε xx. 6.

B. § 27, N. 1; H. § 24 D. c.; C. § 130 c.; J. § 10, obs. 2; W. p. 43.

Instead of ἕνεκα, ἕνεκεν (p. 72), the Ionic form εἵνεκεν sometimes occurs (which is not unknown to the Attics also, see Buttmann's ausf. Sprachl.), as οὗ εἵνεκεν Luke iv. 18, εἵνεκεν τῆς δόξης 2 Cor. iii. 10. As respects termination, the forms ἕνεκεν and εἵνεκεν stand before vowels and consonants, but ἕνεκα only before consonants (Matt. xix. 5; Acts xxvi. 21, cf. the variant in Mark xiii. 9).

CRASIS AND ELISION.
B. §§ 29. 30; H. §§ 68. 70; C. §§ 124. 127; D. §§ 130. 133; J. §§ 13. 17; W. p. 46.

Since the writers of the New Testament were far from feeling such a dislike to *hiatus*, as, for example, the Attic orators felt, the two means of preventing it, viz. Crasis and Elision, are no longer employed in all the cases mentioned in the Grammars.

As respects Crasis, although it is by no means wanting in the N.T., yet it is restricted to a number of customary instances, very common in other writings also; and even in these it is far from being uniform. Thus we find, for example, κἀμοί and καὶ ἐμοί, κἀγώ and καὶ ἐγώ, κἀκεῖ and καὶ ἐκεῖ, ταὐτά and τὰ αὐτά; further, τοὐναντίον, τοὔνομα, κἄν for καὶ ἐάν (for so it is to be taken even in Mark vi. 56, — for details respecting κἄν see the Syntax, p. 360), etc. In the recent printed editions, however, there is little agreement in this particular, because the manuscripts very often exhibit both modes of writing.

Elision continues to be most frequently observed with ἀλλά and the prepositions, as ἀπό, διά, etc. Yet the elided and the full mode of writing are constantly interchanged; and indeed, th.s is more or less the case in profane authors also. As respects other words, frequently written elsewhere with the apostrophe, as δέ, τέ, γέ, οὐδέ, ὥςτε, ἄρα, ἵνα, thus much at least may be positively affirmed : that elision has passed almost completely out of use; hence these words are regularly written in full, even where ordinary prose certainly would not have neglected elision. However, in such a matter as elision (and crasis) it is not advisable to proceed with rigorous consistency, as Winer maintains [p. 40], since every writer must be allowed the liberty of occasionally employing elision at his option, even in cases where he ordinarily neglects it (Matt. xxiii. 16; 1 John ii. 5; Acts xix. 2; Heb. viii. 4; ix. 25; Rom. ix. 7, etc.).

REMARK. The quotation from Menander in 1 Cor. xv. 33 is written by Tdf. [so אּ] in full (χρηστά [Treg. χρῆστα]), according to the mss., by Lchm. with the apostrophe χρήσθ' (as a quotation), but not as the earlier editions have it χρῆσθ', contrary to the rule (B. § 30, 3; H. § 100; C. § 774; D. § 138; J. § 63, 2).

The current formula τοῦτ' ἔστιν is always written with the apostrophe, and by many (Lchm. also [Treg. in the majority of instances]) as a single word, because it had become a complete adverb (like δηλονότι, etc.).

DECLENSION : THE DUAL.

B. § 33, 3; H. § 115; C. § 178; D. § 149; J. § 72.

The Dual, in the language of the N. T. as in Latin, has wholly passed out of use, in nouns as well as in verbs.

FIRST DECLENSION.

B. § 34, 2; H. § 134; C. § 194 sq.; D. § 161; J. § 78.

The rule that after ρ the Gen. ends in ας is sometimes disregarded ; as, σπείρης, πρώρης (Acts xxvii. 30 Lchm. [Tdf.]), πλημμύρης Luke vi. 48 [Treg.] Tdf. (cod. Sin.), μαχαίρης, -ρη, but not throughout (Acts xii. 2 etc. [Lchm.]), Σαπφείρῃ Acts **11** v. 1 Tdf. [אּ*]. This is not to be looked upon as an Ionism otherwise the Nom. also would be σπείρη, πρώρη. But ρ in these words has only the influence of any other consonant before α; that is to say, it allows the flexion in η to follow in the Gen. and Dat. Now as these words according to the rule for quantity (B. § 34, N. II, 1.) have a short in the Nom., the accentuation must be σπεῖρα and also by consequence πρῶρα (Lchm. [Tdf.] πρῷρα Acts xxvii. 41, — on this spelling, which is common in mss., see Dindorf in Steph. Thesaur. sub voce ; Etym. Magn. 692; Cobet, Praef. ad N. T. Vat. p. 12; Nov. Lect. 204.); see besides, Lchm. pref. I. p. 43.

Quite isolated, yet sufficiently attested by mss. [Sin. also], is the Gen. in ης also from a pure in συνειδυίης Acts v. 2 ; cf. Tdf. pref. (1849) p. xxiv, note 1, [ed. 7, p. liv], Exod. viii. 21. 24 ; 1 Sam. xxv. 20 (Vat.).

To the examples of abstract substantives in εία with a long may be added from the N. T. the following: ἐριθεία *working for hire* — commonly accented falsely, and ἀρεσκεία *desire to please*, from ἐριθεύομαι and ἀρεσκεύομαι (ἀρέσκεια Col. i. 10 Lchm. Tdf. [eds. 2, 7 ; Treg. ; Tdf. ed. 8 -κία]).

Concerning the Doric Genitive in α of proper names in ας see below, p. 20.

Second Declension.
B. § 35; H. § 138 sq.; C. § 199; D. § 166 sq.; J. § 85 sq.

Several substantives in ος, which ordinarily have but one gender, occur in the N. T. now as M a s c u l i n e, now as F e m i n i n e. Thus :

1) ἡ λιμός *famine*, — a use noted as Doric by old grammarians, and common also in the Sept., see Is. viii. 21. As Fem. it appears in Luke xv. 14 ; Acts xi. 28 (where formerly the Masc. stood, and some mss. give even λιμὸν μέγαν ... ἥτις, respecting which see in the Syntax, p. 81); as Masc. in Luke iv. 25.

2) ἡ βάτος *bramble*, elsewhere also the current form (see Pape) Luke xx. 37 ; Acts vii. 35. On the other hand τοῦ βάτου (τῆς βάτου Rec.) Mark xii. 26.

3) Respecting ὁ and ἡ ληνός see § 123, 7, p. 81.

To the feminines which are properly Adjectives add from the N. T. ἡ ἄβυσσος *bottomless deep*, in the earlier writers only an adjective ; see Pape.

The Voc. in ε of words in ος is very common in the N. T., as κύριε, διδάσκαλε, φαρισαῖε, τυφλέ, etc. Yet the other form also (like the Nom.) is not rare, as υἱὸς Δαυείδ Matt. i. 20, etc.; and it is the less so, since, as will be shown in § 129 a. 5, p. 140, even the full form of the Nom. with the Article takes the place of the Voc., as ὁ θεός, etc. As a rare exception must be noted θεέ μου Matt. xxvii. 46, found also in the Sept., e.g. 2 Esdr. ix. 6 ; Judd. xvi. 28 ; xxi. 3 ; Sap. ix. 1.

Contracts.
B. § 36; H. § 144; C. § 200; D. § 169; J. § 85, 2.

The regular forms of the Gen. and Dat. of νοῦς (νοῦ, νῷ) are quite unknown to the writers of the N. T., and the heteroclite forms of the 3d Declension, in general more current in the later language (Ausf. Sprachl. I. p. 154), are the only ones in use: τοῦ νοός, τῷ νοΐ, see Wahl. The Gen. of πλοῦς also is πλοός in Acts xxvii. 9.

Of ὀστοῦν (John xix. 36) in the Plural only the uncontracted forms ὀστέα, ὀστέων occur: Matt. xxiii. 27; Luke xxiv. 39; Heb. xi. 22.

ATTIC DECLENSION.
B. § 37; H. § 146; C. § 200; D. § 170; J. § 86.

The forms λεώς, νεώς (from which comes νεωκόρος Acts xix. 35) of the Attic Declension are wholly unused in the N. T. : λαός, ναός are always used instead. Concerning proper names in -ως see p. 20 below. The N. T. form for ἀνώγεων (derived from ἄνω and γῆ) is ἀνάγαιον Lchm. Tdf. [Treg.], or ἀνώγαιον Tdf. [only in ed. 2 in Mark], Mark xiv. 15; Luke xxii. 12, — a Dorism (see An. Cram. II. p. 131, 14, and cf. Mullach, Gr. Vulgarspr. p. 21; Ahrens, Dial. Dor. p. 187). Cf. κτείνω p. 61.

THIRD DECLENSION.
B. § 41, N. 2; H. § 164.

Respecting the (later) accentuation φοῖνιξ, κῆρυξ (1 Tim. ii. 7) see Winer p. 50 (49) and the works there referred to [also Lipsius, Gram. Untersuch. p. 36 sq. ; Tdf. (eds. 7, 8) and Treg. write κήρυξ]. Like κῆρυξ we must then, with Tdf. [Treg.], accent Φῆλιξ also (Acts xxiv. 3, etc.).

ACCUSATIVE SINGULAR.
B. § 44; H. § 157; C. § 204; D. p. 102; J. § 92, 3 sq.

From χάρις the (rare and later) Accusative χάριτα twice occurs: Jude 4; Acts xxiv. 27 Lchm. [now Tdf. also, and Treg.], cf. xxv. 9.

As a peculiarity of the Alexandrian dialect in general is to be noticed the appending of the Acc. ν to the regularly formed Acc. in α, of which a great number of examples from the Sept. may be seen in Sturz, Dial. Alex. p. 127; on ν ἐφελκ. with the Acc. cf. Lob. Parall. p. 142 sq.; Tdf. 7 [cf. 8] on Heb. vi. 19 [and ed. 7 prol. p. lv]. Recent editors have with reason hesitated to adopt this form of the Case in the N. T. where it has been transmitted in a few instances, particularly by cod. Alex. (e.g. Rom. xvi. 11 συγγενῆν [Treg.]), because it is not sufficiently guaranteed by other MSS. Lchm. [Tdf. ed. 7, not 8] has admitted it only in the Apocalypse, e.g. ἄρσεναν xii. 13, εἰκόναν xiii. 14, μῆναν xxii. 2, ποδήρην i. 13 [Lchm. in ed. min. only]. In Heb. vi. 19 also, some [Tdf. ed. 7;

Treg.] would read ἀσφαλῆν; this form, however, Lchm. has not adopted (as Winer asserts p. 69 (67) — [yet correctly, as respects Lachmann's stereotype ed.]) as [in his larger ed.] he there accents ἀσφαλήν, and consequently takes it as a metaplasm after the 1st

13 declension. Tdf. [2, 8] has ἀσφαλῆ with cod. Vat. [and Sin.], which is perhaps to be preferred (cf. ἀκλινῆ x. 23, μονογενῆ xi. 17). The Acc. Δίαν (from Ζεύς) Acts xiv. 12 Tdf. ed. 7, is not sustained by codd. Vat. and Sin.

CONTRACTS.
B. § 49, N. 3; H. § 176 sq.; C. § 207; D. § 181; J. § 111, 1 b.

The Genitive Plural of neuters in ος, whenever it occurs in the N. T., retains the uncontracted form ὀρέων Rev. vi. 15, χειλέων Heb. xiii. 15. But that of ἔτος, *year*, is always ἐτῶν; see the Lexx.

PARTIAL CONTRACTION.
B. § 50; H. § 185 sq.; C. § 219; D. § 186 sq.; J. § 100.

The contraction of this class of words (which was often neglected by Attic writers, B. § 50, N. 3) is wholly omitted in the N. T., — and that not only in the Nominative (ἰχθύες Luke ix. 13), but also in the Accusative Plural ἰχθύας Matt. xiv. 17, στάχυας xii. 1, βόας Jno. ii. 14, 15, βότρυας Rev. xiv. 18, etc.; see Wahl.

CONTRACTS IN ις ETC. GEN. εως.
B. § 51; H. § 185 sq.; C. § 220; D. § 186 sq.; J. § 101.

Words of this class are uniformly contracted in the N. T.; indeed, contractions like πηχῶν and Gen. ἡμίσους Plur. τὰ ἡμίση (B. § 51, N. 5) from the later and less pure Attic seem to have been the only forms in use in the language of the N. T., thus τῶν πηχῶν John xxi. 8; Rev. xxi. 17, ἡμίσους Mark vi. 23, probably also τὰ ἡμίση Luke xix. 8 (ἡμίσεα Lchm. ἡμίσεια Tdf. [Treg.]). On the origin of the spelling τὰ ἡμίσεια (for which codd. Vat. and Sin. itacistically give ἡμίσια) see Bttm.'s Rev. of Kuenen and Cobet in the theol. Stud. u. Krit. 1862, p. 194.

The Genitive in -εως of neuter nouns of this class is used also in the N. T.; as, σινάπεως Matt. xiii. 31 and often.

CONTRACTS IN εύς.
B. § 52; H. § 189; C. § 220; D. § 190; J. § 97.

The Acc. Plural in έᾱς, as it is not found at all in later Greek, so too it does not occur in the language of the N. T., and the form in εῖς is the only one current; accordingly, ἀρχιερεῖς γραμματεῖς γονεῖς, ἱππεῖς, etc.; see Wahl.

VARYING CONTRACTION.
B. § 53; H. § 178; C. § 213 c.; J. § 129, 2.

The Acc. of ὑγιής which occurs four times (see Wahl) is never ὑγιᾶ, but always ὑγιῆ, as sometimes also even in the earlier writers.

NEUTERS IN ας.
B. § 54; H. § 168, 182 D.; C. § 222 e.; D. § 181; J. § 103, 2 sq.

The contracted forms of κέρας and τέρας are wholly unknown to the language of the N. T., as in general to the Alexandrian dialect; hence always κέρατα, τέρατα, κεράτων, etc. see Wahl. The Plural of κρέας, on the other hand, is τὰ κρέα, Rom. xiv. 21 etc.

The Ionic change of α into ε occurs once (Luke i. 36) in the Dative γήρει, which the Text. Recept. against all the MSS. has altered into γήρᾳ.

14

CONTRACTS IN ων.
B. § 55; H. § 175; C. § 211; D. § 184; J. § 129, Obs. 2.

The uncontracted forms of Comparatives in ων are, even in the Nom. Plur. (e.g. Acts xxvii. 12), used indiscriminately with the contracted forms (xix. 32 etc.).

ANOMALOUS DECLENSION.
B. § 56, N. 1; H. § 197 sq. ; C. § 223 sq.

It seems to be expedient for convenience of reference to bring together here under a single head what is to be said respecting the declension of

Foreign Proper Names,

as well as of certain other names of persons and forei ˙ (i.e. not Greek) words.

1. As was remarked above, p. 5 sq., proper names which re-main unaltered dispense with all inflection, even when the r ending seems to render them capable of it, as Ἱεριχώ, Φαραώ (Acts vii. 10), Ἐμμαούς, Ἐνώς, Γεθσημανῆ (Lchm. [Treg.] -νεῖ [Tdf. -νεί, cf. ed. 7 Prol. p. lxi]), Βηθφαγῆ [Lchm., Treg. (except Luke xix. 29) ; Tdf. -γή, cf. also ed. 7, Prol. p. lv, lxi] ; many in -ών, as Ἀαρών, Ἐσρών, Ζαβουλών, Σαμψών, Σιών, Γεδεών[1], and in -α, as Σάρα, Σινᾶ, μάννα, Βηθεσδά, Σάρεπτα, Γολγοθᾶ, Κανᾶ, etc.

2. As soon, however, as the word undergoes a change,

---

[1] That the inflection of the Lexicons Γεδεών, -ῶνος, is incorrect see Heb. xi. 32, and cf. in the O. T. Judges vii, 14, 18 etc.

especially such a change as gives it a declinable ending, inflection takes place according to analogy. It is not to be overlooked that names well-known and of frequent occurrence, such as Jesus, Moses, Solomon, Jerusalem, etc., have accommodated themselves in popular usage to the Greek vocal laws much more frequently than names less familiar. Cf. the Genealogies.

3. The transformation into Greek took place most simply with nouns which already had an ending resembling Greek, or whose ending allowed itself easily to be made such. So in particular with proper names in ων. These have ordinarily Gen. -ωνος, etc., as Σαρών Acc. Σαρῶνα Acts ix. 35 (Tdf. Σάρωνα [Treg. -νᾶ]), Σιδών -ῶνος, Σίμων -ωνος, (on the other hand the less altered name Συμεών is indeclinable, Rev. vii. 7). But the name Solomon has a twofold inflection: As it took in Greek the form Σολομων, there resulted according to the analogy of similar well-known names, like Ξενοφῶν, the inflection Σολομῶν (for so the Nom. must then be accented) Σολομῶντος, etc.; or, according to the analogy of Βαβυλών, the inflection Σολομών, -ῶνος, etc. Both modes of inflection have been received into the text in Lachmann's edition, even in the same writer (e.g. Matt. i. 6 and xii. 42),— a phenomenon which occurs several times in the case of such familiar names; see Moses, Jerusalem, etc. below. Tdf., however, has given the preference everywhere [except Acts iii. 11 and v. 12; in vii. 47 he writes Σαλωμών; cf. his note on Matt. vi. 29, and ed. 7, p. liv] to the inflection -ῶνος, etc. [so Treg., yet Acts vii. 47 -μῶν]. With the twofold inflection of Σολομῶν cf. that of the old Greek name Σαρπηδών Gen. Σαρπηδόνος and Σαρπήδοντες.

4. Latin words and proper names, likewise, are shaped according to analogy and inflected agreeably to Latin declension, as λεγεών (legio) λεγεῶνος, Matt. xxvi. 53 [Treg. also]; Luke viii. 30, on the other hand λεγιών Mark v. 9, 15 (the spelling λεγιών has on the whole the greatest MS. authority in its favor [cod. Sin. also]; so Tdf. everywhere, see ed. 7, Prol. p. 1 [and note on Mark v. 9 in ed. 8]); εὐρακύλων (Vulg. euroaquilo, it is wanting in the lexicons) Acts xxvii. 14 Lchm. [Treg. Tdf.] *Northeast wind*, formed like *euroauster,* εὐρόνοτος; Φῆλιξ -κος, Καῖσαρ -ος, etc. Nouns in *ens* receive in the Nom., in accordance with Greek vocal laws (B. § 25), the form in -ης,

as Κλήμης, Κρήσκης, Πούδης, and are declined Κλήμεντος, etc. Phil. iv. 3.

5. Further, the following nouns are Grecized by appending to them (or coining for them) Greek final syllables : [1]

Feminines in a Gen. -ης, etc. ; for example, Γάζα (Gen. -ης, Dat. -η in the O. T., as, Zech. ix. 5 ; Josh. xi. 22) Acc. -αν. Further, γέεννα, γεέννης, etc. ; from Latin, μεμβράνα Acc. plural -νας, αἱ ταβέρναι, etc.

6. Feminines in a Gen. -ας, as Μαρία, -ας, -ᾳ, -αν. In this noun, however, the inflected form is constantly interchanged with the indeclinable form Μαριάμ [yet according to Tdf. ed. 7, p. xxxv, the best MSS. favor the former] : Nom. Matt. xiii. 55 ; Luke i. 27 ; ii. 19 (John xi. 32 ; xx. 18, Tdf. [Treg.]), Dat. Luke ii. 5 (Acts i. 14 Tdf. [Treg.]), Acc. Matt. i. 20 ; Luke ii. 16 ; John xi. 19 (Rom. xvi. 6 Tdf.), Voc. Luke i. 30 (John xx. 16 Tdf. [Treg.]). Further, Σαμάρεια (not -εία, Acts viii. 14) [Tdf. now everywhere Σαμαρία] -είας, -είᾳ, Βηθανία, -ίας, -ίᾳ. Μάρθα John xi. 1 (to which Wahl incorrectly gives the Gen. -ης) and probably ᾿Άννα also (to judge from the Dative ᾿Άννᾳ in the O. T. 1 Sam. i. 2, 5, etc.) and Εὔα (not Εὖα) Εὔαν have the Genitive in -ας, contrary to the main rule, but in accordance with the inflection of other Greek proper names as Λήδα, etc. (B. § 34, 2 ; H. § 126 ; C. § 195). Of Σουσάννα, and ᾿Ιωάννα none of the inflected forms occur in the N. T.[2] Βηθσαϊδά forms its Accusative in -άν Mark vi. 45, etc., but is otherwise indeclinable : John i. 45 ; xii. 21. From the Latin κουστωδία, -ας, etc. 16

Feminines in η Gen. -ης : ἡ ᾿Ιόππη, Σαλώμη, etc.

7. Masculines in ης, -ου, -η, -ην, e.g. ᾿Ιωάννης, ᾿Ιορδάνης, and, from the Latin, κοδράντης (quadrans), φαιλόνης (paenula φαινόλης Poll.). ᾿Ιωάννης (in cod. Vat. almost always, in Sin. often written with one ν : ᾿Ιωάνης) forms its Dat. according to the same MSS. also ᾿Ιωάννει (᾿Ιωάνει), — heteroclitically therefore ; cf. Μωυσῆς No. 11, p. 19.

8. Masculines in ας, -ου, -ᾳ, -αν. This inflection appears in many words, but always with a preceding vowel, ι or ε, as Ιερεμίας, ᾿Ησαΐας, Βαραχίας, ᾿Εζεκίας (Lchm. -είας ; Gen. -ου

---

[1] In other writers, as Josephus, etc., this is done with a far larger number of names than in the Old and New Test.

[2] On the other hand, in the O. T. the Gen. of Σωσάννα (Σωσάννης) occurs in Sus. 27.

3

2 Kings xviii. 13, etc.), Ζαχαρίας, Ἠλίας, Ἰεχονίας (Gen. -ου
1 Chron iii. 17, -α Bar. i. 3), Ἰωσίας (-ου 2 Kings xxiii. 34, -α
Jer. xxv. 1), Ματταθίας, Οὐρίας, Ἀνδρέας; and probably also
Μεσσίας, Ματθίας, Ὀζίας, Ἰουνίας, of none of which has the
Gen. been preserved. Respecting Ἀνανίας see below, 13, c) p. 20.

9. Masculines and Feminines in ος, -ου, etc.; as, Ἰάκωβος,
Σαῦλος see p. 6, Ζακχαῖος, Ματθαῖος, Ἰάειρος, ἡ Δαμασκός, etc.,
and those formed by change of the Latin ending us : Πόντιος
Πιλᾶτος, Κουάρτος, Πόπλιος, Ποτίολοι (Puteoli), Χῶρος i.e.
Caurus or Corus Northwest wind (wanting in Pape) Acts
xxvii. 12.

Neuters in ον from the Latin : φραγέλλιον flagellum John ii.
15, σουδάριον, μίλιον a mile, etc.

10. Neuters in α, -ων, -οις, -α. This inflection is followed
by several names of cities, formed after the analogy of τὰ
Ἄβδηρα, Θυάτειρα, etc., — especially by Jerusalem : τὰ Ἱεροσόλυμα, -ων, -οις; this inflected form, however, is constantly interchanged (often in close proximity) with the O. T. indeclinable
form ἡ Ἱερουσαλήμ, e.g. Luke ii. 22 and 25, 42 and 43.   In
address the Jewish form is always used (Matt. xxiii. 37, etc.).
John uses only the first form τὰ Ἱ. (see Heydler, über die
Namen Hierosolyma, etc., Progr., Frankf. 1856).   The third
form given in the lexicons is found in only a single passage in
the whole Bible : Matt. ii. 3 πᾶσα Ἱεροσόλυμα. Yet we cannot
infer from this an inflection in -ης, -η, etc. as given in the lexicons, since in this passage Ἱεροσόλυμα seems to be used more
like the indeclinable Ἱερουσαλήμ (moreover πᾶσα is wanting
in cod. D), and consequently, as the name of a city, has been
construed as feminine. Such a combination certainly would
have been impossible to a native Greek author.

On the other hand Γόμορρα has both inflections : Gen. -ας,
and -ων Dat. -οις.   In the O. T. the forms in -ων and -οις do not
occur (but Nom. and Acc. -α Gen. -ας) so that these forms seem
to have been first developed in the N. T. by the word's being
17 frequently connected with τὰ Σόδομα (-ων, -οις) which is always
neuter.

Λύδδα has -ης in the Gen. (Acts ix. 38 [Tdf. Treg. give -ας]),
but just before it twice occurs inflected like a Neuter in α: Acc.
Λύδδα vs. 32, 35 ; Josephus (B. J. 1, 15, 6 ad fin.) uses it as a
Neut. Plur. ; cf. Γόμορρα in the O. T.   Θυάτειρα on the other

hand (of which the Gen. in -ων occurs Acts xvi. 14, the Dat. in -οις Rev. ii. 18) has once the Acc. in -αν, Rev. i. 11 ; and Λύστρα in Lycaonia has its Dat. in -οις, but for its Acc. τὴν Λύστραν Acts xiv. 6, 8, 21, etc.

11. Masculines in ης of the third declension. Here belongs especially the name Μωυσῆς. Its first syllable is in recent editions almost uniformly written ωυ, and probably therefore in the solitary passage where Lchm. has left the simple ω (Rom. ix. 15), the other spelling ωυ is with Tdf. [Treg., so א also] to be restored [Tdf. puts a diaeresis over the υ, see ed. 7, p. lxii ; and cf. Grimm's Lexicon]. The common inflection is Gen.(uniformly) -έως, Dat. -εῖ, Acc. -έα (Luke xvi. 29),— thus quite after the analogy of the Greek word ῎Αρης ; hence it is idle to assume an unused Nominative form in εύς, as is generally done in the lexicons. In addition to these forms there have been preserved (according to the Declension which follows) a Dative in -ῇ twice, Rom. ix. 15 (Tdf. Μωϋσεῖ [Treg. -εῖ] Acts vii. 44, and an Accusative -ῆν four times, Acts vi. 11 ; vii. 35 ; 1 Cor. x. 2 ; Heb. iii. 3. On the derivation and spelling of the word see also Fr. on Rom. ix. 15, and cf. Joseph. adv. Ap. 1. 31.

Further Μανασσῆς, — the Acc. of which ends in -ῆ Matt. i. 10 (Gen. -ῆ Sept.), and ᾿Ιωσῆς with a twofold inflection ᾿Ιωσῆτος (Mark vi. 3 ; xv. 40) and ᾿Ιωσῆ in accordance with the Declension which follows.

12. There still remain a large number of foreign names and words, which follow none of the modes of inflection described above, yet among which there exists a great and obvious analogy. Mehlhorn (Gr. Gram. p. 182) appropriately proposes for all these words a special declension, which on account of the simplicity of its endings he calls the *weak inflection*. The following is the Table :

ας	α	ᾳ	αν	α
ης	η	ῃ	ην	η
ως	ω	ῳ	ων	ω
ους	ου	ου	ουν	ου

The first two series, it will be noticed, are founded on the first declension, the remaining two upon the second. This inflection is ordinarily, but not invariably, distinguished by the circumflex on the last syllable.

13 A. *Words in* αϛ. The inflection of these, especially
when they are not perispomena, agrees closely with that of
words which have the Doric Genitive (p. 12 ; cf. H. § 136
Rem. d.), as 'Αννίβας etc., and has manifestly been formed after
18 the analogy of this declension.   In later times this was the
most usual inflection of foreign proper names, and of such as had
undergone a violent abbreviation (as 'Αλεξᾶς from 'Αλέξανδρος);
and many newly-formed words followed it.   Here belong

a) All circumflexed proper names, as 'Ιωνᾶς, Θωμᾶς, Βαρραβᾶς, Βαρσαβᾶς, Κηφᾶς, Κλωπᾶς (John xix. 25), Χουζᾶς ;
further 'Αρτεμᾶς, Δημᾶς, 'Επαφρᾶς, 'Ερμᾶς, Ζηνᾶς, Θευδᾶς,
Λουκᾶς, Μελεᾶς, 'Ολυμπᾶς, Παρμενᾶς, Σκευᾶς, Στεφανᾶς, supposed to be mere abbreviations of current Greek names, as
'Αρτεμίδωρος, Δημήτριος, 'Επαφρόδιτος, Ζηνόδωρος (Anec. Bek.
p. 857), Λουκιανός, Μελέαγρος, Παρμενίδης, etc.

b) Circumflexed appellatives of foreign origin, e.g. κορβανᾶς,
σατανᾶς, μαμωνᾶς Gen. -ᾶ, etc.

c) Barytone proper names whose last syllable is preceded
by a consonant, as "Αννας, 'Αρέτας, Βαρνάβας, 'Ιούδας Luke i.
39 ; Mark vi. 3, etc.), Καϊάφας (or Καΐφας Luke iii. 2 Lchm.) ;
from the Latin, 'Αγρίππας *Agrippa*.   The same analogy,
doubtless, was followed also by 'Αντίπας ('Αντίπατρος ?),
Κλεόπας (Κλεόπατρος ? Luke xxiv. 18), 'Ελύμας ; and from
the Latin, 'Ακύλας *Aquila*, Σίλας (Acts xv. 22, etc., always
called by Paul Σιλουανός *Silvanus*, 2 Cor. i. 19, etc.), — of
which no Genitive is found. 'Ανανίας is generally given in
the lexicons with Gen. -ᾶ, contrary to analogy (see No. 8, above),
but in the N. T. no Gen. is found ; in the O. T., indeed, occurs
the Gen. 'Ανανία (Neh. iii. 23), but also the regular 'Ανανίου
Tob. v. 12 (13).   Cf. 'Ιωσίας, etc. in No. 8, p. 18, above.

14 B. *Words in* ης. The proper name Φιλῆς, -ῆ, etc. serves
as the paradigm.   From the N. T. are to be referred to this
class only a few isolated forms, as the collateral forms of
Μωυσῆς given above, p. 19, and the Gen. 'Ιωσῆ from 'Ιωσῆς
(Matt. xxvii. 56 [Tdf. reads 'Ιωσήφ, after ‫א‬ etc.]).   The proper
names 'Ιαννῆς and 'Ιαμβρῆς have no oblique cases extant ;
yet according to Suidas (sub voce) the Gen. of 'Ιαμβρῆς was
'Ιαμβροῦ.   The Acc. 'Ιαμβρῆν occurs in Apocryphal writings.

15 C. *Words in* ωϛ. These, according to Mehlhorn, ought
properly all to be accented as perispomena, as is still done, for

example, in ταώς, ταῶ (B. § 58), according to the direction of the ancient grammarians. Commonly, however, this rule is not observed in the editions (and MSS.), but the words are accented as oxytones, and thus made to agree perfectly with the so-called Attic second Declension (B. § 37). And in general, amid the variety of views concerning this declension, even among the ancients, harmony can hardly be attained.

Accordingly, the proper name Ἀπολλώς is inflected in the N. T. after the Attic 2d Declension, thus Nom. Ἀπολλώς Acts xviii. 24, Gen. -ώ 1 Cor. i. 12, but likewise Acc. -ώ Acts xix. 1, yet in 1 Cor. iv. 6 Acc. Ἀπολλών (after A, B, ℵ) ; so too Κῶς the name of an island, Acc. Κῶ Acts xxi. 1.

19

16 D. *Words in οῦς.* In the N. T. only Ἰησοῦς, -οῦ, -οῦ, -οῦν, -οῦ. Lastly, the analogy of all these words is closely followed by the inflection of

E) Λευΐς [-είς, etc. Tdf. (except in Rev. vii. 7, ed. 7), Treg.] Luke v. 29, Gen. Λευΐ iii. 24, Acc. Λευΐν v. 27.

17. The *Gender of Proper Names* in the case of persons follows the sex. As a specialty it is to be noticed, that the name of the heathen god Βάαλ has the feminine article in a quotation by Paul from the O. T. (Rom. xi. 4). In the O. T. ὁ and ἡ Βάαλ occur ; see Winer 1.. (168).

Χερουβίμ (Lchm. [Tdf. 7, 8 ; Treg.] -βείν) is construed as a neuter plural in Heb. ix. 5.

18. *Names of cities,* even when indeclinable, follow the general rule, that is to say, are feminine ; as, ἡ Ἰερουσαλήμ, ἡ Βηθλεέμ, ἡ Κανᾶ, etc. (John iv. 46, etc.). But if they are declinable the general rules hold ; as, τὰ Σόδομα, Φίλιπποι, etc. On ἡ Ἰεροσόλυμα see No. 10 above, p. 18.

In like manner the *names of rivers* are Masculine, according to the general rule, as ὁ Ἰορδάνης ; so, too, when indeclinable : ὁ Κεδρών (John xviii. 1 Lchm.), ὁ Σιλωάμ John, Luke, (in Josephus also ἡ Σιλ. sc. πηγή, B. J. 5, 4, 2 ; 12, 2).

19. The names of the *mountains* Σινᾶ and Σιών are given in the lexicons as masculine. Their gender is not evident from the N. T., since they occur either without the article or in connection with τὸ ὄρος, and τὸ Σινᾶ (Gal. iv. 25 Lchm.) may be explained by the rule that a word regarded as an independent object is made neuter. When we consider, however, that proper names frequently take the gender of the most

current appellative belonging to them (here, therefore, τὸ ὄρος),
it is much more probable that these indeclinable names of
mountains are also neuter.   With this agrees the current O. T.
phrase τὸ ὄρος τὸ Σινᾶ (Exod. xix. 11, 18, etc.), and there is
no reason for giving a different explanation of this combination
from that of τὸν ποταμὸν τὸν Εὐφράτην (Rev. xvi. 12).   Further,
Σιών when, as is so often the case, it stands for all Jerusalem,
is always *feminine* in the prophetic writings of the O. T., as
Ps. cxxxii. 13 ; Lam. i. 17 ; Zech. viii. 2, etc.[1]

20   The Mt. of Olives, commonly called τὸ ὄρος τῶν ἐλαιῶν (Matt.
xxi. 1 etc.) also has the single name Ἐλαιών, Gen. -ῶνος (Acts
i. 12 ἀπὸ ὄρους τοῦ καλουμένου Ἐλαιῶνος), and must accordingly,
like Greek names of mountains of the same form (Κιθαιρών,
Ἑλικών, etc.), be masculine.   Nevertheless, in Luke xix. 29 ;
xxi. 37 it is treated as indeclinable, consequently as neuter :
πρὸς τὸ ὄρος τὸ καλούμενον Ἐλαιών ; so, too, in Josephus (e.g.
Antiq. 20, 8, 6 ; B. J. 5, 2, 3).   Recent editors have, accordingly, rejected the former accentuation -ῶν and write Ἐλαιών,
to distinguish it from the other designation τῶν ἐλαιῶν, which
Luke also uses just afterwards : xix. 37 ; xxii. 39.   Cf. Fritzsche
ad Marc. Exc. III.

ANOMALOUS DECLENSION.
B. § 56, N. 2; H. § 197; C. § 223 sq.; J. § 116 sq.

The word σκότος, which so frequently occurs, is of the *neuter*
gender throughout the N. T.   The statement in Wahl that it
is also masc. is supported only by the reading — long ago discarded — of the Rec. in Heb. xii. 18 (τῷ σκότῳ).

Ἔλεος, of the masculine gender in Attic authors (see Pape),
is in the N. T. only neuter, — in the four or five passages
where the Rec. had the masculine the neuter having now been
restored ; see the passages in Wahl.

Πλοῦτος, elsewhere only masculine, is often used by Paul as
neuter, but only in the Nom. and Acc., e.g. 2 Cor. viii. 2 ; Eph.

---

[1] Names of mountains, to judge from the Sept., have no established gender.
The neuter, however, is the most common.   Thus we have τὸ Ἰταβύριον (*Tabor*),
and, in the same combination as that given above with Sinai, τὸ ὄρος τὸ Ἐφραΐμ,
τὸ ὄρος τὸ Σηείρ, τὸ ὄρος τὸ Ἀβαρίμ, τὸ ὄρος τὸ Ἀερμών, etc.   Lebanon is masculine,
ὁ Λίβανος, likewise Carmel, ὁ Κάρμηλος or ὁ Χέρμελ Isa. xxxii. 15 sq.; Jer. xlvi.
(xxvi.), 18 ; but τὸ ὄρος τὸ Καρμήλιον also occurs (2 Kings ii. 25), and once even ἡ
Κάρμηλος (1 Kings xviii. 42), as also ἡ Ἀερμών Josh. xi. 3 etc.   But ἡ Θαβώο ὶν
1 Chron. vi. 77 is the city or region of Tabor.

i. 7, etc.; in the Gen. always of the 2d Declension, Rom. xi. 33, etc.; (the Dative does not occur).

Ζῆλος is masculine as it is everywhere in Greek authors; but in 2 Cor. ix. 2 (codd. Vat. and Sin.), perhaps also in Acts v. 17 (Vat.), the preference might be given to the neuter form (as in the Clem. Epp.). Only once, in the *adverbial* expression κατὰ ζῆλος (Phil. iii. 6), has the neuter been adopted by all the MSS. [Sin. also].

Ἦχος, altogether a later word (see Thom. Mag.), is masculine; but in Luke xxi. 25 the Genitive is ἤχους (if the reading [so Sin. also] is correct).

Instead of ἡ νίκη, which appears only once (1 John v. 4), the collateral form τὸ νῖκος, common elsewhere also in later writers, is usual; as, Matt. xii. 20; 1 Cor. xv. 57, etc.; so, too, in the Sept.

B. § 56, 6; H. § 200; C. § 226; D. § 284; J. § 85, Obs. 2.

Of δεσμός both plurals (-μά and -μοί) appear in the N. T. — 21 the first in Luke. That Paul takes the word as masculine follows from Phil. i. 13 (in the other passages the gender is not evident) and the usage of the Sept. (Jer. ii. 20; Job xxxix. 5, etc.).

A metaplasm of the N. T. language, which however is in plain analogy with other metaplasms (cf. πρόσωπον, ὄνειρον, B. § 58; H. § 199 and D; C. § 225 f.; D. § 284; J. § 117), is found in τὸ σάββατον which regularly has σαββάτου, -ῳ, Plur. τὰ σάββατα (Acts xvii. 2; see the following paragraph) σαββάτων. The Dative plural is almost uniformly σάββασιν — from the Hebr. שַׁבָּת, as if from a theme not in use. The regular form, τοῖς σαββάτοις, Lchm. has adopted from the single codex B in only two passages: Matt. xii. 1, 12; but between them (vs. 5), he gives σάββασιν as everywhere else.

DEFECTIVE, PLURAL, AND INDECLINABLE NOUNS.

B. § 57, 1; H. § 201; C. § 227 sq.; D. § 284; J. §§ 114. 118.

Jewish Names of Festivals have the plural form, according to Greek usage, as τὰ ἐγκαίνια, τὰ ἄζυμα; in like manner τὰ γενέσια *birth-day festival*, and sometimes οἱ γάμοι when it is synonymous with *convivium*, *epulae*, Matt. xxii. 2; Luke xii. 36; xiv. 8. Also the plural τὰ σάββατα, both when it signifies a festival and a week, frequently alternates with τὸ σάββατον; see Wahl, and cf. e.g. Luke xviii. 12 with xxiv. 1, etc.

The Plural τὰ σάββατα appears even in the Sept., e.g. Lev. xxiii. 32, etc. Respecting Names of Cities see above, p. 18.

Further, the following are sometimes used as Plurals in the N. T.: οἱ κόλποι in the phrase ἐν τοῖς κόλποις τοῦ Ἀβραὰμ εἶναι Luke xvi. 23 ; τὰ ἀργύρια in the sense of *money* Matt. xxviii. 12 (Vulg. *pecuniam*), cf. the common reading in Mark xiv. 11, where, as in most other passages, the Sing. has been adopted ; τὰ ὀψώνια *wages*, synonymous with τὸ ὀψώνιον (Luke iii. 14, etc., cf. the Lat. *stipendium*) ; and, agreeably to a Jewish mode of thought, οἱ αἰῶνες *the world* (עוֹלָמִים Ps. cxlv. 13) Heb. i. 2, and οἱ οὐρανοί (הַשָּׁמַיִם) Matt. iii. 16, etc. Also ' the holy place' in the temple and ' the holiest of all' are called in Heb. ix. 2, 3 τὰ ἅγια and ἅγια ἁγίων after Ezek. xli., xlii. etc. Also the newly-formed word μεγιστᾶνες (equivalent to μέγα δυνάμενοι, see Phryn. and Thom. Mag. sub voce) seems (like *proceres*) to have been ordinarily used only in the Plural.

In the case of αἱ θύραι (*fores*) and τὰ ἱμάτια (*clothing*) the Plural form is sufficiently accounted for by the meaning.

The foreign word τὸ σίκερα *intoxicating drink*, like τὸ πάσχα, is indeclinable ; in the N. T. it occurs only in the Acc. (Luke i. 15), but in the Sept. also in the oblique cases (Num. vi. 3 ; Deut. xiv. 26).

List of Anomalous Nouns.

B. § 58; H. § 202; C. § 223 sq.; D. § 284; J. § 112.

Instead of ὁ ἅλς *salt* (Mark ix. 49, 50) in the N. T. the later neuter form is more common : τὸ ἅλας (Gen. ἅλατος), Dat. ἅλατι Col. iv. 6, [in Mark ix. 50 Tdf. twice reads Nom. τὸ ἅλα, with א*, etc.].

The Acc. of ἀρτέμων (Gen. -ονος) is according to MSS. [Sin. also] ἀρτέμωνα in Acts xxvii. 40 ; so the Scholiast on Eurip. Med. 273.

In the N. T. ἔρις, after the analogy of ὄρνις, has the two Plur. forms ἔριδες, 1 Cor. i. 11, and ἔρεις — at present only in Tit. iii. 9. In the other passages the editors have given the preference to the Sing. ἔρις (2 Cor. xii. 20 ; Gal. v. 20 ; 1 Tim. vi. 4); yet in Cor. and Tim. Tdf. ed. 7 restores ἔρεις again, [so Treg. in Cor. ; א only ἔρις, which Tdf. now adopts uniformly.]

Of κλεῖς, likewise, both forms are found in Sing. and Plur. : κλεῖν Rev. iii. 7, κλεῖδα Luke xi. 52, τὰς κλεῖς Rev. i. 18, κλεῖδας Matt. xvi. 19.

Συγγενής, properly an Adjective, like all words in ης of the 3d Declension, regularly follows the analogy of τριήρης. Only once is the Dat. Plur. συγγενεῦσι found as an important variant Mark vi. 4 (also 1 Macc. x. 89). Whether this erroneous form, which arose probably from the resemblance between the inflection and that of nouns in εύς (cf. Μωυσῆς), is to be attributed in the above passage to the scribes or to the author, may be doubtful; and on this account the reading has not been adopted [yet so in Mark, Tdf. eds. 7 and 8, and Treg.]. But it makes in favor of the latter supposition that in another passage (Luke ii. 44) [many of] the *very same* MSS. (with the exception of cod. Vat. which here also exhibits συγγενεῦσι) do not repeat the termination -εῦσι but give the regular form συγγενέσι, which also harmonizes perfectly with the general accuracy of form characteristic of Luke, as on the other hand the form συγγενεῦσι is congruous with Mark. Further, that the form acknowledged to be erroneous should be early altered by other scribes into the regular one, is quite natural; and finally, it appears from the grammarian Herodian, in Cram. An. III. p. 246, that this corrupt form must have actually been in frequent use (πολλῶν σφαλλομένων κατὰ κλίσιν δοτικῆς πτώσεως καὶ λεγόντων συγγενεῦσι κτλ.). Otherwise he would have hardly found it necessary to demonstrate in detail, as he does, its erroneousness.

Κατήγωρ, a solecistic by-form of κατήγορος, occurs only in Rev. xii. 10; (it is wanting in the lexicons).

ADJECTIVES.
B. § 60; H. § 209 sq.; C. § 229 sq.; D. § 196; J. § 127.

In the distinction of Genders of Adjectives in ος certain irregularities and departures from the common usage occur in the N. T. The following deserve especial notice:

βέβαιος, in Attic authors generally of the common gender, always in the N. T. takes the form βεβαία in the Fem.; see Wahl. ἔρημος, on the other hand, which in Attic writers has three endings, has invariably the Fem. ἔρημος Gal. iv. 27, etc., and Wahl is to be corrected accordingly.

ἕτοιμος fluctuates between three terminations and two, cf. Matt. xxv. 10; 2 Cor. ix. 5; 1 Pet. i. 5.

ἀργή Fem. of ἀργός (1 Tim. v. 13; Jas. ii. 20) is altogether 23 a later form; see Pape, and cf. Tit. i. 12.

Not only ἐπουράνιος, which as a composite adj. must be of the common gender (Heb. iii. 1, etc.), but also the simple οὐράνιος, which is regularly of three endings (see Pape), has two terminations in the N. T.: στρατιὰ οὐράνιος Luke ii 13; ὀπτασία οὐράνιος Acts xxvi. 19.

ὅμοιος is always of three endings, only in Rev. iv. 3 we find ἶρις ὅμοιος (according to cod. A).

ὁσίους, too, in 1 Tim. ii. 8, as its very position indicates, is to be joined to χεῖρας, as is done by most of the commentators and the ancients. The Fem. does not occur elsewhere.

αἰώνιος, ordinarily even in the N. T. of the common gender, has the Fem. αἰωνία only in two passages : 2 Thess. ii. 16 ; Heb. ix. 12, (cf. the common reading in 1 John ii. 25 ; Acts xiii. 48).

B. § 60, 6; H. § 208; C. § 23; J. § 121, 2.

χρύσεος contracts its feminine χρυσῆ Heb. ix. 4 ; on the other hand, the Acc. χρυσᾶν is given by Lchm. [Tdf. Treg.; so cod. Sin.] in Rev. i. 13 (analogous to the Plural χρυσᾶς neut. χρυσᾶ). Contraction is neglected in the Gen. Plur. χρυσέων in Rev. ii. 1 Lchm.[Trg.,Tdf. 7]. In Rev. also occur according to cod. Sin. χρύσεα, χάλκεα, — forms which (according to Phryn. p. 207) must have been generally in use among writers of the κοινή.

B. § 62; H. § 212; C. § 23; J. § 122, 1.

The Genitive βαθέως, which now on MS. authority [Sin. also] is substituted in Luke xxiv. 1 for the regular βαθέος, rests on later usage ; see B. § 51 N. 2 ; H. § 186 ; D. § 101 ; J. l.c. ; Tdf. ed. 7, p. liv. Perhaps, too, in 1 Pet. iii. 4 πραέως [Tdf. Treg.] should be read instead of πραέος.

Respecting ἡμίσους, etc., see p. 14.

B. § 63, 1; H. § 217; J. § 130, 1.

The plural νῆστεις from νῆστις, Matt. xv. 32 ; Mark viii. 3 [here Tdf. now reads νῆστις ; so too in Matt. l.c. edd. manual. et stereot.], is a collateral form of the Plur., instead of νήστιες or νήστιδες, which occurs also elsewhere, but is censured by the Atticists ; see Lob. ad Phryn. p. 326 ; Fritzsche ad Marc. Exc. III. p. 796.

ANOMALOUS ADJECTIVES.
B. § 64, 2; H. § 219 a.; C. § 236 c.; D. § 216; J. § 125, Obs. 2.

The form πρᾶος seems to be wholly unknown to the language of the N. T. ; for not only in Matt. xi. 29 — the single passage where it still stood — has it been made by the editors to give way to the other form πραΰς, agreeably to all the other passages (see Wahl), but the abstract substantive πραότης also has been, at least by Tdf., everywhere altered into πραΰτης. And this procedure is the more defensible because in the two passages still remaining (Gal. vi. 1; Eph. iv. 2) in which Lchm. has left the form πραότης (which he writes without iota subscript), important ms. authorities [Sin. also] offer the other form; see the other passages in Wahl, to which Col. iii. 12 is to be added.

An example of the use of the indeclinable word ἐπάναγκες as an adjective by means of the article, after the manner of adverbs (see § 125, 10 p. 95), is Acts xv. 28 πλὴν τούτων τῶν ἐπάναγκες. Elsewhere the word does not occur in the N. T.

Comparison of Adjectives in -os.

B. § 65, N. 5; H. § 221; C. § 257; J. § 135.

The comparative of διπλοῦς, — which in its ethical sense antithetic to ἀπλοῦς (see Pape) is capable of comparison, — is in Matt. xxiii. 15 διπλότερος, a form which can be shown elsewhere also in later authors (Appian, Praef. 10) and is constructed as if from διπλός, of which the Neut. plural διπλᾶ can be authenticated, at least in later poets; see Steph. Thesaur. and Lob. ad Phryn. p. 234.

Other Forms of Comparison.

B. § 67; H. § 222; C. § 261; D. § 277; J. § 186.

The form of the comparative of ταχύς peculiar to later Greek: ταχίων, τάχιον, is the only form in use in the N. T. as well as in the Old. In the New Testament, however, it occurs only as an adverb in the neuter: John xx. 4, etc. The common form θᾶσσον has so completely passed out of use that it has not been preserved even as a variant.

Anomalous Comparison.

B. § 68; H. § 223; C. § 262; D. § 280; J. § 137.

The common comparison of ἀγαθός is κρείσσων, κράτιστος — the latter employed in addressing persons of rank and authority: Acts xxiii. 26; xxiv. 3; xxvi. 25 (cf. Luke i. 3; the Vulg. always uses optimus). Of the other forms of comparison only βέλτιον occurs once (as an adverb), 2 Tim. i. 18.

The ordinary comparative of κακός is χείρων — as well in the signification deterior as pejor, Matt. xxvii. 64, etc. The superlative does not occur.

DEFECTIVE COMPARISON.

B. § 69, 2; H. § 224; C. § 262; D. § 282; J. § 140.

The positive ἤρεμος (formed from ἠρέμα), which is very rare and not yet satisfactorily established from other writers, occurs in 1 Tim. ii. 2. Cf. Lobeck, Path. Proll. p. 158.

The adjectival forms of the comparative ἀνώτερος, etc., (questioned in B. § 69, 2 note) cannot be denied, at least in
25 later writers. Accordingly in the N. T. we have them not only used adverbially in the Neuter, ἀνώτερον Luke xiv. 10 etc., but even as adjectives : τὴν ἐσωτέραν φυλακήν (Acts xvi. 24, cf. Heb. vi. 19), τὰ κατώτερα μέρη Eph. iv. 9.

B. § 69, N. 3; C. § 262 (c); D. § 283; J. § 140.

Two examples of double comparison occur in the N. T. : 3 John 4 μειζότερος, and Eph. iii. 8 ἐλαχιστότερος. In general it is to be noticed, that in all such formations, which are not altogether rare either in poets or in prose writers, the two different kinds of comparison (by -τερος, etc. and -ίων, etc.) are always found united. The Latin language also presents analogous phenomena, which in general belonged probably more to the popular language and to the class of arbitrary formations.

NUMERALS.

B. § 70. 1; H. § 255; C. § 24 sq.; D. § 249 sq.; J. § 166.

Respecting εἷς καθ᾽ εἷς and similar expressions, see p. 30. The later spelling οὐθείς, μηθείς is found in the N. T. (see Tdf. 7, 8 on 1 Cor. xiii. 2) alternating with the common one ; indeed the two are found close beside each other, as in 1 Cor. xiii. 2, 3 (cf. Ἱεροσόλυμα, Μαρία above, pp. 17, 18). The same holds true of the derivative ἐξουθενέω, only that here the other form with δ is incomparably more rare ; Lchm. gives it only in Mark ix. 12 and 2 Cor. x. 10 ; [so Treg. in Mark].

REMARK. The Form ἐξουδενόω, which is given in the lexicons on account of Mark ix. 12, has been altered into the common form in -έω after preponderant MS. authority. On the other hand, the form in -όω is very common in the Sept., and has now been adopted again by Tdf. in Mark ix. 12 (after Sin.) The MSS. fluctuate between ἐξουδενέω, -όω, ἐξουθενέω, -όω ; cf. Steph. Thesaur. sub voce.

The form δυοῖν from δύο no longer occurs, but instead of it in the Genitive the indeclinable form δύο, e.g. Matt. xviii. 16, and in the Dative δυσί, Matt. vi. 24, etc.

The spelling τέσσερες, τεσσεράκοντα is probably hardly

to be called an Ionism, but rests merely on an erroneous usage
of the Alexandrian period. For we never find the inflections
τεσσέρων, -ερσι, as these cases run in Ionic, but invariably
(even in cod. Alex.) τεσσάρων, τέσσαρσι, e.g. Acts x. 11; Rev.
xxi. 17 (τεσσεράκοντα τεσσάρων). Since, however, the forms
with ε have been transmitted principally by the above codex,
whence they have often found their way into the O. T. (see
Sturz, Dial. Alex. p. 118), Lachmann, following the authority of cod. Vat., has adopted them but sparingly, e.g. Acts
i. 3; 2 Cor. xi. 24, and almost always in the Apocalypse.
Tischendorf [cf. ed. 7, p. il] has them more frequently, —
in particular τεσσεράκοντα throughout [so Treg.] and the neuter
τέσσερα, — but otherwise τέσσαρες, -ας, τεσσαρεσκαιδέκατος.
To maintain consistency throughout is not advisable, since it
is certain that both modes of spelling were in use, but it is 26
best everywhere to follow the MSS. Compare besides the form
(received by Lchm.) κεκαθερισμένος for κεκαθαρ. in Heb.
x. 2, and ἐκαθερίσθη in Tdf's. last ed. Matt. viii. 3; Mark i. 42,
ἐκαθέρισεν Acts x. 15 Tdf. [ed. 7; Treg.], μιερός for μιαρός Barn.
Act.19, p.71 ed.Tdf. [In Rev. xxi.17 Treg. prints τεσσαρά:οντα].

The rule of certain ancient grammarians relative to the
accent of the compounds of ἔτος (Etym. Magn. τριέ ης μὲν
χρόνος, τριετὴς δὲ παῖς, cf. Winer p. 50 (49)) has been o served
in the N. T. by Lchm.; hence τεσσερακονταέτης χρόι ς Acts
vii. 23; xiii. 18, but ἑκατονταετής sc. ἀνήρ Rom. iv. 1 (-έτης
Tdf.). In the Rec. the rule was reversed; [Treg. accents
the last syllable in every instance]. On the disag eement
among the old grammarians see Schol. ad Il. ψ. 266 and cf.
Lehrs, quaest. epp. pp. 136, 147.

ORDINAL, AND OTHER DERIVATIVE NUMBERS.
B. § 71, 1; H. § 256; C. § 240; D. § 253, Obs. 1 d.; J. § 165, 3.

As a later form for τεσσαρακαιδέκατος, and one p :culiar to
the N. T., τεσσαρες καιδέκατος is to be noticed: A :ts xxvii.
27, 33. Cf. the Ionic cardinal number B. § 70.

The *cardinal* εἷς takes the place in one case of t e *ordinal*
πρῶτος (cf. B. p. 92 note †), namely, in the commn phrase
ἡ μία τῶν σαββάτων i.e. *the first day of the week* (s ɛ p. 23);
as, Mark xvi. 2 (on the other hand, in vs. 9 πρώτ ɔ σ.) Acts
xx. 7, etc. Matt. xxviii. 1 also, where the article is wanting,
is nevertheless to be understood like the other passages; cf.

Rev. ix. 11 ἡ οὐαὶ ἡ μία with xi. 14. This use is borrowed from the Hebrew (see Wahl under εἷς, or Gesen. under אֶחָד), hence it is to be found frequently in the Sept. also, e.g. ἐν ἡμέρᾳ μιᾷ τοῦ μηνός Exod. xl. 2 ; Ezra x. 16, etc.   Corresponding to τίς for πότερος (B. § 78, 2) is the use of εἷς or ὁ εἷς in the sense of *alter*, ὁ ἕτερος ; see Wahl.

In 2 Pet. ii. 5 the ordinal number is used peculiarly, (having the force of the German *selb-*) ; thus ὄγδοον Νῶε *Noah with seven others.* Cf. αὐτὸς πέμπτος (B. § 127, N. 2 ; H. § 669 ; C. § 541 g. ; D. p. 462 ; J § 656 f.).

In compound numeral adverbs it is sufficient if the adverbial form occurs but once ; as, Matt. xviii. 22 ἑβδομηκοντάκις ἑπτά.

Distributive numerals are destitute of a special adjective-form in Greek. In the N. T. accordingly they are sometimes, as in other Greek authors, expressed by adverbial constructions, as ἀνὰ δύο Luke ix. 3 (see § 147 under ἀνά, p. 331), οἱ καθ᾿ ἕνα, κατὰ δύο, *singuli, bini* Eph. v. 33 ; 1 Cor. xiv. 27 (see § 147 under κατά, p. 335). In this case the combination (unknown to classic Greek) deserves notice, by virtue of which εἷς is treated like an indeclinable numeral, or 27 the preposition as a species of adverb, particularly in the formula εἷς καθ᾿ εἷς Mark xiv. 19 [Tdf. κατά]; John viii. 9 (Rev. iv. 8 ἓν καθ᾿ ἕν), and cf. Rom. xii. 5 τὸ δὲ καθ᾿ εἷς for εἷς ἕκαστος, Rev. xxi. 21 ἀνὰ εἷς ἕκαστος. Sometimes distributives are expressed by repeating the cardinal numeral, as is done in Hebrew (see Gesen. Lehrg. p. 703 ; Gr. § 118, 5), e.g. δύο δύο Mark vi. 7 with which the analogous expressions in 39, 40 συμπόσια συμπόσια, πρασιαί πρασιαί may be compared (Gesen. Lehrg. p. 669 ; Gr. § 106, 4).

B. § 71, 3; H. § 258; C. § 240, 5; D. § 256; J. § 161, 5.

The Multiplicative numerals are formed: in the parable of the Sower (Luke viii. 8) by means of -πλασίων, — a termination which in later writers came into frequent use (see Lob. Phryn. p. 411 note), καρπὸν ἑκατονταπλασίονα (like πολλαπλασίων Luke xviii. 30 ; see Pape, and cf. Xen. Oec. ii. 3 ἑκατονταπλασίονα) ; in Mark iv. 8 by circumlocution with a preposition, after the manner of distributives, as εἰς τριάκοντα, εἰς ἑκατόν[1] ; finally in Matt. xiii. 8, 23 by the simple cardinal.

[1] This, at least, is that one of the ancient readings which Tischendorf [so Treg.] has followed. As respects the other (Lchm. Grsb. etc.) see Syntax § 126, 3 p. 1)3.

PRONOUNS.
B. § 72; H. § 230; C. § 243 sq.; D. § 232; J. § 149, 1.

The reflexive forms of the 3d Pers. Sing. and Plur. (οὗ, etc.) have passed quite out of use in the language of the N. T. On ἑαυτοῦ, (αὑτοῦ), αὐτοῦ, etc. see below, Syntax § 127, 14 p. 111.

B. § 72, N. 3; H. § 232; C. § 788 e.; D. § 55 (c); J. § 64, 3 a.

The inclination of the accent in πρός με has been adhered to by the editors of the N. T., as in Matt. iii. 14, etc. And Lchm. accents also the 2d Pers. in the same way when no especial emphasis rests on the Pronoun, as πρός σε Matt. xiv. 28; xxv. 39; Mark ix. 17, etc. On the other hand, in John xxi. 22 τί πρὸς σέ; Matt. xxvi. 18 πρὸς σὲ ποιῶ τὸ πάσχα. With other prepositions the pronoun is always orthotone ; as, ἐν ἐμοί, ἐν σοί, ἐπὶ σέ, etc. ; see the rule of the old grammarians in Herm. de emend. rat. p. 75. The accentuation πρὸς μέ often employed by Tdf. is uniformly to be rejected.

αὐτός ; THE REFLEXIVE PRONOUN ; THE RECIPROCAL.
B. § 74; H. § 234 sq.; C. § 244; D. § 234 sq.; J. § 150 sq.

Respecting the N. T. use of αὐτός as well as of the reflexive pronoun ἐμαυτοῦ, etc., see the Syntax § 127, p. 107 sqq.

Though the use of the reciprocal pronoun ἀλλήλων is quite current in the N. T., yet the circumlocution by means of the numeral εἷς is also found, but only in isolated cases : 1 Thess. v. 11 οἰκοδομεῖτε εἷς τὸν ἕνα (interchanged with ἀλλήλους) ; cf. 1 Cor. iv. 6 ἵνα μὴ εἷς ὑπὲρ τοῦ ἑνὸς φυσιοῦσθε κατὰ τοῦ ἑτέρου. This use is not a Hebraism, see Winer, p. 173 (163), and cf. § 126, 3 p. 102.

τίς, τὶς.
B. § 77; H. § 244; C. § 253; D. § 240; J. § 156.

The secondary forms of τίς and τὶς are quite unknown to the N. T. ; the Gen ὅτου of the compound ὅστις occurs, indeed, but only in the conjunctional phrase ἕως ὅτου Matt. v. 25, etc. The un-Attic (and poetic) μήτις for μηδείς occurs 1 Cor. xvi. 11.

CORRELATIVES.
B. § 78, 2; H. § 247; C. § 53; J. § 874, Obs. 4.

The distinction between τίς and πότερος, which was sometimes neglected even by the Greeks (like the use of *quis* and *uter* by the Romans), seems to be wholly disregarded by the writers of the N. T. ; for the form πότερος occurs but once and

in the double conjunction πότερον . . . ἤ (John vii. 17), while
everywhere else τίς is used, even where there is the plainest
reference to two, as Matt. xxi. 31 τίς ἐκ τῶν δύο ἐποίησεν.
See Wahl under τίς, and cf. B. § 71, 1. An analogy to this is
offered by the obliteration of the difference between πρότερος
and πρῶτος, -ον (although the Latins in translating still observe
it in numerous instances), and likewise between ἄλλος and
ἕτερος. For example, Heb. viii. 7 εἰ γὰρ ἡ πρώτη ἐκείνη (Vulg.
illud *prius* sc. testamentum) ἦν ἄμεμπτος, οὐκ ἂν δευτέρας ἐζη-
τεῖτο τόπος, John xx. 4 ἔτρεχον οἱ δύο ὁμοῦ· ὁ δὲ ἄλλος μαθητὴς
ἦλθεν πρῶτος (*prior* a, b, c, d,) εἰς τὸ μνημεῖον. Hence πρῶτος
is even connected with the Gen. compar. (John i. 15, 30),
respecting which see Syntax § 123, 14 p. 84.

THE VERB.

SYLLABIC AUGMENT.

B. § 83, 2; H. § 43; C. § 277 sq.; D. § 305; J. § 171, and Obs. 6.

The doubling of ρ after the augment, which, as is well known,
was omitted only by the poets on account of the verse (B. §
21, N. 2) has sometimes been neglected also in the N. T.
Although double letters are often written singly in the MSS.
yet the doubling of ρ in most verbs is never, or only in extremely rare instances, omitted ; accordingly we find ἔρριψα,
ἔρρηξα, etc. Hesitation, therefore, has justly been felt at
making arbitrary alterations in those verbs in which the best
codices sustain almost unanimously the single ρ. They are
29 Matt. xxvi. 67 ἐράπισαν, Acts xvi. 22 περιρήξαντες (codd. Vat.
and Sin.), 2 Cor. xi. 25 ἐραβδίσθην, Heb. ix. 19 ἐράντισε (cf.
below, p. 33), 2 Tim. iii. 11 ; iv. 17 ἐρύσατο, ἐρύσθη, — (on the
other hand, ἐρρύσατο 2 Cor. i. 10 ; Col. i. 13 ; 2 Pet. ii. 7).
According to the analogy of these examples the cod. Alex.
[Sin. also] (and Tdf. [so Treg.]) writes in John xix. 23 ἄραφος
instead of ἄρραφος ; and so frequently in composition after
prepositions, as διαρήσσων Luke viii. 29, ἐπιρίψαντες xix. 35 ;
1 Pet. v. 7 ; cf. Mark ii. 21 ; Luke v. 6 ; Acts xvi. 22, etc.

B. § 83, N. 1; H. § 319 b.; C. § 280 b.; D. p. 195; J. § 175, Obs. 1.

The former reading μεμνηστευμένη Luke i. 27 ; ii. 5 is now set
aside on the authority of MSS.; yet it is often found in the N. T.
Apocrypha, and elsewhere also, e.g. in Diodor. (18. 23); see Lob.
Parall. p. 10 sq.

B. § 83, N. 4; H. § 319; C. § 159 e.; D. § 305 b) Obs.; J. § 176, 1.

The Homeric ῥερυπωμένα finds now two parallels in the text of the N.T., viz. ρ ε ρ ι μ μ έ ν ο ν Matt. ix. 36 (Lchm. after cod. D, ἐριμμ. Tdf. [Treg.]) and ρ ε ρ α ν τ ι σ μ έ ν ο ι Heb. x. 22 (according to codd. [‎א] A C). Similar instances in later authors are adduced by Lobeck, Parall. p. 13. As respects the aspiration of the first ρ, Lchm. has in both cases [so Treg. in Heb.] given the smooth breathing, see Ausf. Sprachl. § 6 Anm. 3 Note, and Lobeck as above, who besides puts a breathing over the second ρ, as ῥέριμμαι. But as the opinions of the old grammarians do not quite favor the adoption of this, Göttling (on Theodos. p. 213 and Acc. p. 205) advocates the retention of the rough breathing on the first ρ, except in words of Aeolic origin; and this is done by most editors. Cf. Steph. Byz. p. 543 Mein.

B. § 83, N. 5; H. § 308 a.; C. § 279; D. § 305 (1); J. § 171, Obs. 1.; Tdf. ed. 7, p. lvi.

With μ έ λ λ ω and δ ύ ν α μ α ι in the N. T. both kinds of augment are used promiscuously; as, ἤμελλεν John iv. 47, ἔμελλεν vi. 71, ἠδύνατο Matt. xxvi. 9, ἐδύναντο Mark iv. 33. But with βούλομαι the text of Lchm. [Treg. Tdf. apparently] always gives the simple augment: Impf. ἐβουλόμην Acts xv. 37; xxviii. 18; Philem. 13; Aor. ἐβουλήθην 2 John 12; on the other hand, the Aorist of δύναμαι is always ἠδ νήθην [-άσθην Tdf. in Mark vii. 24 after א B], as in Matt. xvii. 1 ?, 19; 1 Cor. iii. 1, etc. Cf. besides, the anomalous ἐθέλω.

B. § 83, N. 7; H. § 311; C. 284 c.; D. § 311; J. § 171, Obs. 4; Tdf. c.

The omission of the syllabic augment of the Pluperfect takes place, though not invariably (e.g. Luke xvi. 20; John x. 22), yet in the majority of cases; hence πεποιήκεισαν, ἐκβεβλήκει, γεγόνει Mark xv. 7, 10; Luke vi. 48, etc. See other examples in Winer § 12, 9 p. 72 (70).

TEMPORAL AUGMENT.

B. § 84, 2; H. § 312; C. § 278; D. § 305, Obs. 2; J. § 173, 7; Tdf. l.c.

With ἐργάζομαι the augment ει is the common one in the N. T. also; yet the other augment (η) has been received into the text on preponderant authority in Acts xviii. 3; Luke xix. 16 [Treg. ει-]. In the other passages it is commonly found as a noteworthy variant (particularly in codd. Cant. and Clarom.) 3C [and adopted by Tdf.], as in Matt. xxv. 16 [Sin. also]; xxvi. 10 [Sin. also]; Rom. vii. 8; 2 Cor. xii. 12.

The reading of the Rec. in Rev. vi. 14 εἰλισσόμενος is now set aside.

On the other hand, the number of the verbs that take the augment ει is increased in the N. T. by one, viz. ἑλκόω, Perf. Pass. Part. εἱλκωμένος Luke xvi. 20.

B. § 84, 5; H. § 310; C. § 278 d.; D. § 305 (2); J. § 173, 2; Tdf. 1. c.

Verbs beginning with εὐ have now εὐ, now ηὐ; and in fact, both kinds of augment alternately: εὐκαιρέω Mark vi. 31; Acts xvii. 21, εὐλογέω Luke ii. 34; Heb. xi. 20, 21, εὐφραίνω Acts ii. 26; vii. 41, εὐχαριστέω Acts xxvii. 35; Rom. i. 21, εὑρίσκω in the Imperf. Acts vii. 11; Luke xix. 48; Heb. xi. 5.

On the other hand, εὐ alone is used in the other tenses of εὑρίσκω, as εὗρον, εὕρηκα, εὑρέθην, also in εὐδοκέω (yet not without variants, see Col. i. 19), and in the following verbs, which occur but once in augmented forms: εὐθυδρομέω Acts xvi. 11, εὐνουχίζω Matt. xix. 12; εὐπορέω Acts xi. 29.

But εὔχομαι has everywhere only ηὐ-, as ηὐχόμην Rom. ix. 3; ηὔχοντο Acts xxvii. 29 [εὐ- Tdf. Treg.]; προσηύχετο, προσηύξαντο viii. 15; Luke xviii. 11; Jas. v. 17, 18, and in the case of εὐφορέω, Luke xii. 16, the MSS. are divided (Lchm. ηὐφόρησεν, [εὐ- א Tdf. Treg.]). Cf. further below, p. 35.

B. § 84, N. 3; H. § 309 D.; C. § 284 b.; D. p. 201; J. § 174, 3.

Neglect of the temporal augment, after the manner of the Ionians, occurs in the N. T. but very rarely. Thus the MSS. sustain ἐπαισχύνθη [ἐπη- א] 2 Tim. i. 16 (on the other hand, it is regular in 2 Cor. vii. 14), διερμήνευεν Luke xxiv. 27; there is preponderant authority also for ἀνορθώθη [א ἀνωρ-] Luke xiii. 13; further, for προορώμην Acts ii. 25, and ὁμοιώθημεν [ὠ- א Tdf. Treg.] Rom. ix. 29, — both in quotations from the O. T. (the latter, indeed, not taken into the text by Lchm., but placed on an equality with the reading adopted); also for οἰκοδόμησεν Acts vii. 47 Tdf. [ed. 2; Treg.] cf. Luke vii. 5 var. [in John ii. 20 Tdf. now reads οἰκοδομήθη], ἐποικοδόμησεν 1 Cor. iii. 14 Tdf. [Treg.] (on the forms of the Aug. of this verb see Tdf.'s crit. com. on Acts vii. 47), ὁμολόγησεν Acts vii. 17 (Sin.), διεγείρετο John vi. 18 (Vat. [Treg.]). See more examples of the kind from the Sept. in Sturz, Dial. Alex. p. 124.

The reading περιέστραψεν Acts ix. 3 Lchm., as if formed from περιστράπτω, may be noticed as an anomaly quite isolated. It is an instance of carelessness, which in such a writer as Luke is probably to be charged only to the transcribers, since in another passage (xxii. 6) of the same author the Inf. Aor. runs περιαστράψαι. Tdf. accordingly has not adopted it; see the various readings, and Steph. Thes. sub voce στράπτω.

The Augment in Composition.
B. § 86, 3; H. § 316; C. § 282; D. § 310; J. § 180, 2.

Of the verbs belonging under this head εὐαγγελίζω (also προευαγγ. Gal. iii. 8) always has the augment in the middle, also in 1 Cor. xv. 2, see Wahl. On the other hand, the Perf. Inf. of εὐαρεστέω is now read after cod. A without augment, εὐαρεστηκέναι, in Heb. xi. 5 [ℵ εὐη-].

B. § 86, N. 3; H. § 315; D. § 308, Obs. 2; J. § 181, 6.

Agreeably to the general rule, προφητεύω in the N. T. has its augment at the beginning: ἐπροφήτευον, -σαν, etc. (see Wahl); yet everywhere with the variant προεφήτευον, etc. 31 (especially in the Vat. cod., which the Rec. followed). Only once, Jude 14, has the text of Lchm. (not Tdf. [Treg.]) the augment in the middle. [Cf. Grimm's Lex. sub voce.]

B. § 86, N. 4; H. § 314; C. § 279 b.; D. p. 200; J. § 181.

The number of examples of a twofold augment can be increased from the N. T. Thus throughout we find ἀπεκατεστάθη Matt. xii. 13 etc. [so ἀπεκατέστη Mark viii. 25 Tdf. Treg.], and ἠνεῴχθησαν, see the anom. οἴγω p. 63. On the other hand, ἀνέχομαι and διακονέω have the simple augment: ἀνείχεσθε 2 Cor. xi. 1 (and 4 Tdf. [Treg.]) ἀνεσχόμην Acts xviii. 14 Lchm. [Tdf. Treg.], διηκόνουν -ησα frequently. On the double augment see Poppo on Thuc. 4, 130; and on this (common) διηκόνουν cf. An. Bekk. p. 1285; Moeris sub voce. Respecting ἀνορθόω see p. 34. (Cf. besides Ps. xlviii. 13, 21 cod. Alex.)

Future Subjunctive.
B. § 88, 1; H. § 262; C. § 269 b.

From the N. T. a number of examples of the Subjunctive form of the Future are adduced. In very late Greek, like that of the Byzantine writers and Scholiasts and N. T. Apocrypha (which swarm with similar anomalies), forms of this sort (ἔσωνται, ἐλεύσωνται) are not to be denied; but, according to Lobeck's judgment (Phryn. p. 721), in the earlier authors down to the κοινοί they are to be charged wholly to the copyists, whose ear had already become accustomed to such half-barbarous forms (ib. 720). How far back, however, the beginnings of this usage are to be carried, would be hard to decide. A basis for it is offered by μεμισθώσωνται in the Tabul. Heracl. (cf. Ahrens, Dial. Dor. p. 334). Respecting the usage of the N. T. authors, Lobeck, indeed, does not generally express himself; yet on the whole he seems to be opposed to the admission of such subjunctives even in the N.T. (p. 722). In point of fact, too, recent criticism has done away with most of the instances (cited by Winer p. 75 (72)) : e.g. 1 Pet. iii. 1 κερδηθήσονται, Rev. xviii. 14 εὑρήσουσιν (εὕρῃς Tdf. [eds. 2, 7], εὑρήσῃς Rec.). Also the first of the examples adduced there (1 Cor. xiii. 3 καυθήσωμαι) has been set aside by Tdf. yet is still admitted by Lchm. [Treg.] ; but the reading is altogether uncertain (the three leading MSS. have καυχήσωμαι). Cf. Lob. p. 722. The reading of the received text in Luke xiii. 35 ἥξῃ for ἥξει Lchm. Tdf. can likewise be referred to this head. Δώσῃ, which in John xvii. 2, owing to its strong support, can hardly be got rid of (although even in the Rev. it has yielded to the forms δώσει and δῶσιν, viii. 3; xiii. 16), may, if established, still be looked upon as an (erroneous) Aorist Subjunctive form, which in later times became more and more prevalent in the mouth of the people ; (some of the modern Greeks still say ἔδωσ). See the numerous forms of the kind from δίδωμι and τίθημι in Lobeck as above, also in Cobet's Nov. Lect. 266 : Var. Lect. 96. The same holds good of the clearly transposed Subj. ὄψησθε in Luke xiii. 28 [Tdf. Treg. read ὄψεσθ , with codd. B D etc.], formed from the elsewhere unused theme ὄπτω and the Aorist ὠψάμην which actually occurs here and there. See in particular Plat. legg. p. 947 ., and cf. Ausf. Sprachl. under ὁράω.

CHARACTERISTIC.

B. § 92, N. 3; H. § 328 b.; C. § 349.

Στηρίζω has commonly, in accordance with the rule, στηρίξω, ἐστήρικται, στηριχθῆναι ; but the Aor. Imperat. is always στήρισον Luke xxii. 32 ; Rev. iii. 2 (likewise Ezek. vi. 2), and besides, in cod. Vat. the same inflection is found also in Luke ix. 51 ἐστήρισε [so Tdf. Treg.], 2 Thess. iii. 3 στηρίσει (not in Lchm. [Treg.]). Hence the Perf. ἐστήρικα (not ἐστήριχα Jer. xxi. 10) and Fut. στηριῶ in the Sept.

Moreover σαλπίζω, though σάλπιγξ (var. σάλπιξ) -γγος Rev.
i. 10 etc. comes from it, invariably has the forms σαλπίσει,
ἐσάλπισεν Matt. vi. 2; 1 Cor. xv. 52 (and often in Rev., see
Wahl), and likewise the subst. σαλπιστής instead of σαλπιγκτής
Rev. xviii. 22.

THE FUTURE.
B. § 95, H. § 372 sqq.; C. § 305; D. § 302; J. § 203.

In the N. T. (as generally in later Greek, see Ausf. Sprachl.
II. 315) φορέω (φορέσω) ἐφόρεσα 1 Cor. xv. 49 (Sir. xi. 5)
belongs also to those verbs in έω which in inflection do not
lengthen the ε.

Respecting ἐπαινέσω see p. 53.

Contrary to rule, πεινάω has uniformly Fut. πεινάσω, Aor.
ἐπείνασα: Matt. xii. 1, 3, etc. See Lob. Phryn. p. 204.

The so-called Attic Future of verbs in ίζω is quite usual in
the N. T. Yet not from all these verbs; but, so far as can be
gathered from existing evidence, a portion of them have exclusively the Attic Future, others the ordinary Future, still
others both. By far the greater number, however, do not
occur in the Future, and it is not always safe to draw an
inference from the usage of the Sept. or of later authors respecting that of the N. T. The Attic Future forms in the N. T.
(in part quotations from the O. T.) are the following: ἀφοριεῖ,
-ιοῦσιν Matt. xiii. 49; xxv. 32, ἐλπιοῦσιν Matt. xii. 21; Rom.
xv. 12, παροργιῶ Rom. x. 19, καθαριεῖ Matt. iii. 12; Heb. ix.
14 etc., ἐδαφιοῦσιν Luke xix. 44, μακαριοῦσιν i. 48, μετοικιῶ
Acts vii. 43, ἐγγιεῖ Jas. iv. 8, χρονιεῖ Heb. x. 37, and in the
O. T. there are many more of them. The following, on the
other hand, have the Future in σω: γνωρίζω, invariably, John
xvii. 26, etc., also Col. iv. 9 (where Tdf. [Treg.] and the Rec.
read γνωριοῦσιν after [א] A C), θερίζω 1 Cor. ix. 11; Gal. vi.
7 etc., ἐμφανίζω John xiv. 21, ἐρίζω Matt. xii. 19, καθίζω Matt.
xix. 28; xxv. 31, καταρτίζω 1 Pet. v. 10, μετασχηματίζω Phil.
iii. 21, σχίζω Luke v. 36, χαρίζομαι Rom. viii. 32, χρηματίζω 33
vii. 3, χωρίζω viii. 35, and ῥαπίζω Matt. v. 39 Tdf. [eds. 2, 7].
But ἐξυπνίσω John xi. 11, σκανδαλίσω 1 Cor. viii. 13, are Aor.
Subjunctives. Κομίζομαι has both forms: 1 Pet. v. 4; 2 Pet.
ii. 13 (-ιοῦμαι), Eph. vi. 8; Col. iii. 25 (-ίσομαι); this may
have occurred often, as well as in the O. T., e.g. ποτιῶ Num.
v. 24, 26; Sir. xxiv. 31, ποτίσω Sir. xv. 3.

Respecting στηρίζω and σαλπίζω see above, p. 36 sq.

B. § 95, N. 13.

As proof of the statement that the N. T. writers give the Attic form
of the Future even to such verbs as lengthen the vowel, several
passages are cited with more or less reason (see Fisch. ad Well. II.
p. 359). After the rejection of those passages in which formerly a
Future was erroneously supposed to be discovered (τί ποιῶ, etc.), the
following have perhaps the greatest probability of such a use in their
favor: Matt. xxvi. 18 ποιῶ, Luke xiii. 32 τελειοῦμαι, Luke xii. 20
ἀπαιτοῦσιν; in particular, Matt. xii. 25 ἐρημοῦται and John xiv. 19; xvi.
16, 17 θεωρεῖ, θεωρεῖτε, since indubitable Futures (σταθήσεται, ὄψεσθε,
etc.) correspond to them both before and afterwards. The supposition
is opposed by (1) Its complete irregularity; (2) The entire silence of
the ancient grammarians, since, had the usage actually found place in
the language, it is hardly credible that they should not on any occasion
have taken notice of it; (3) The extraordinary circumstance that, if
this form of the Future was possible, the examples of it are so uncommonly rare, although the opportunity of employing it was so frequent,
while yet the use of the Attic Future of those verbs that can form it
regularly occurred so very extensively; finally (4) The fact that the
Vulgate in translating the form employs almost always the Present;
which, on the other supposition, would hardly have been done where
the temptation to use the Future lay so close at hand as e.g. in Matt.
xxvi. 18. Only ἐρημοῦται does it translate by *desolabitur* and θεωρεῖτε
by *videbitis*, probably on account of the other Future forms which
follow.[1] Hence the admission of this anomalous Attic Future is un-
warranted even in the language of the N. T., and such Futures are to
be explained syntactically as Presents in which the future signification
is included (§ 137, 10 p. 203). By this, however, it is not meant at
all to deny, that the N. T. writers, affected by their frequent use of
the Attic Future, were the more easily led to employ in pure verbs
the Present instead of the Future, inasmuch as the feeling which
demands the Future was in some measure satisfied by the circumflexed
34 form. Cf. τί ποιοῦμεν (*quid faciemus*) John xi. 47.

On γεννᾶται Matt. ii. 4 see Fritzsche on the passage, and below
§ 137, 9 p. 203.

---

[1] The other (Ital.) versions have some of them the Future in the other passages
also. But that this warrants an inference respecting the sense only, in no wise
respecting the form, is satisfactorily shown by the circumstance that they translate
other indubitable Presents also (leaving out of sight ἔρχομαι, ἐρχόμενος, see p. 58),
such as γινώσκεται, ἀναβαίνω, δύναται (Luke vi. 44; John vii. 8; Matt. xix. 25)
by the Future Cf. Lachmann's preface (Ph. Bttm.'s coroll.) p. 50.

ALEXANDRIAN AORIST.

B. § 96, N. 1; C. § 327; J. § 192, 8; Tdf. ed. 7, p. lvi; Scrivener's N. T. Crit. p. 416

Numerous examples from the O. T. of the Alexandrian Aorist in *a* with the characteristic of the 2d Aor. are given in Sturz, Dial. Alex. p. 60 sq., and from the N. T. in Winer § 13, 1, a. p. 73 (71). Moreover, it is to be particularly noticed that both Aorist forms are constantly found in use by the same writer, often in close proximity (e.g. Matt. xxii. 22 sq. ἀπῆλθαν . . . προςῆλθον, Acts xxviii. 13 sqq. ἤλθομεν . . . ἤλθαμεν . . . ἤλθον, xii. 10, etc.). This phenomenon is no more surprising than the simultaneous use by the Attics of the two Aorists εἶπον and εἶπα, ἤνεγκον and ἤνεγκα, formed after the same analogy. Accordingly, it is a very uncritical procedure (of which the Rec. has sometimes been guilty) to undertake by correction to carry through consistently the one form or the other in any writer; but here if anywhere the authority of the greater number of good MSS. alone should decide in every particular case. To be sure, the editors often arrive in this matter at different results, according as they give this class of MSS. or that the preference, (the cod. Alex., particularly, has the Alexandrian form in such cases). Yet in general it will be found that in the instances belonging here the Alexandrian forms occur most frequently in the 1st Pers. Sing., the Plural throughout, and the inflected forms of the Imperative but never in the Infin. and Partic. Active (seldom in the Middle). Cf. with this the somewhat variable use of the two Aorists in the anomalous φέρω and εἰπεῖν. For an example from the Sept. of the 2d Pers. Sing. see 2 Sam. iii. 34 ἔπεσας.

Thus in the N. T. we find used promiscuously the forms ἤλθον -ομεν -ετε, ἐλθέτω, and ἤλθαν etc. (the 1st Pers. ἤλθα is found only in Rev. x. 9), εἶδον and εἶδαν (John i. 4; Acts xii. 16 etc., εἴδαμεν in Acts iv. 20), but εἶδον always in the 1st Pers. almost without a single variant;[1] ἔπεσον [-αν Tdf.

---

[1] It is surprising that in the Apocalypse, amid the uncommonly numerous instances of the 1st Pers. Sing. εἶδον, nevertheless in one passage εἶδα is twice given (xvii. 3, 6); so that we are probably justified in attributing the form rather to the scribe of cod. A, which here is almost the sole authority [so T., Tr., א in s. 6]. It may be further noticed that Tdf. [ed. 7; cf. Prol. p. lii] in the Apocalypse has everywhere ['plerumque'] adopted the forms ἴδον, and ἴδα, which often occur in the Sept. [cf. Tdf.'s ed Prol. § 28, p. lxxii. ed. 4]. In other books they seldom occur in the MSS., see e.g. Mark xvi. 5 var.; Luke ii. 20 [Tdf.].

Treg.] Mark vi. 40 etc., and ἔπεσαν[1] Acts xii. 7 etc., also 1st
85 Pers. ἔπεσα Acts xxii. 7; Rev. i. 17, etc. and in the Sept.;
πέσετε Luke xxiii. 30 [-ατε Tdf. Treg.] and πέσατε Rev. vi. 16,
ἐξεπέσατε Gal. v. 4; εὗρον -ομεν and εὗραν Luke ii. 16 Tdf.
[Treg.], εὑράμενος Heb. ix. 12. In the Middle αἱρεῖσθαι the
Aor. εἱλάμην, εἵλατο has (except in the Partic. and Infin. Heb.
xi. 25; Acts vii. 34) wholly supplanted the other: Acts vii.
10, 21; xii. 11; xxiii. 27; 2 Thess. ii. 13, (in the Active
ἀνεῖλατε Acts ii. 23, ἀνεῖλαν x. 39).

Other forms, like ἔφυγαν, ἔλαβαν, ἐλάβαμεν, ἔβαλαν, ἐφάγα-
μεν, ἔφαναν, belong for the most part only to the O. T., yet are
found also in the MSS. of the N. T. and here and there in
modern texts, e.g. Luke v. 5 (A); Acts xxi. 27 (A [א, Tdf.
Treg.]); Mark xii. 8 (B); Acts xvi. 37; Rev. xviii. 19 Lchm.
Tdf. [ed. 7]. But the Imperfect form εἶχαν Mark viii. 7 (Rev.
ix. 8), παρεῖχαν Acts xxviii. 2, is wholly without analogy,
although the editors have adopted it into the text because sustained by the testimony of the leading codices A and B (and א
also). In the N. T. Apocrypha forms of the sort become more
and more numerous.

B. § 96, N. 2.

In the Active voice κρύπτω has commonly the 1st Aor., in
the Passive the 2d; yet once it has also the 2d Aor. Active
ἔκρυβον Luke i. 24 — [according to Sophocles, Gram. an Imperfect; cf. 2 Kings xi. 3; Soph. Lex. sub κρύβω; Lob. Phryn.
p. 317]. See B. § 92, Note 2, foot-note p. 122.

THIRD FUTURE.

B. § 99; H. § 394; C. § 319.

The Third Fut. (Passive), seldom used even by the Greeks
in its peculiar force as a Paulopost Future and Future Perfect,
belongs to the more delicate and artificial products of the
Greek tongue. In the N. T., therefore, it no longer appears.
On κεκράξομαι see the anomalous κράζω p. 61.

---

[1] In Matt. vii. 25 also the MSS. [א also] give προσέπεσαν, out of which Lchm.,
on account of the Latin translation and taking into consideration the frequent
interchange of ε and αι (see e.g. αναπεσαι for αναπεσε Luke xiv. 10; xvii. 7 [Tdf.
ed. 7, p. lvi], φαγεσε ib. 8, γυνεκαις 1 Cor. xiv. 34, and the still more uncouth
αισθειεται for ἐσθίετε 1 Cor. x. 25 cod. G), thought he must make προσέπαισαν.
Yet considering the rarity of the word προσπαίω (it occurs nowhere else in the
N. T., and in the O.T. also, as well as in other authors, its existence is almost
doubtful, see Stephanus sub voce; the usual word is προσπταίω) Tdf. [so Treg.]
has with reason given the preference to the MS. reading. Cf. besides the anomalous πίπτω, p. 67.

VERBS IN λ μ ν ρ.
B. § 101; H. § 345; C. § 152; J. § 222.

Examples from the N. T. of the later formation in *a* from verbs in *-αίνω, -αίρω* are, *σημᾶναι* Acts xi. 28 ; xxv. 27 ; Rev. i. 1, *ποιμάνατε* 1 Pet. v. 2, *ἐκκαθάρῃ* 2 Tim. ii. 21, *ἐβάσκανεν* Gal. iii. 1 and even *ἐπιφᾶναι* Luke i. 79 ; thence the Subjunc. *φάνῃ* (Rec. *φαίνῃ* or *φανῇ* [Tr.]) Rev. viii. 12 ; xviii. 23. Cf. the extended discussion in Lob. ad Phryn. p. 25. The spelling *σημᾶναι, καθᾶραι* in earlier authors (e.g. Xen. Hell. 1, 1, 2 ; Oec. 18, 8, etc.) probably arose only through later copyists. See Poppo and Dind. on Cyr. 4, 5, 36.

Ἀποκτείνω uniformly retains the *ν* in the 1st Aor. Passive ; thus, *ἀπεκτάνθην* Mark viii. 31, etc., see Winer § 15, p. 83 (79). With *κρίνω* and *κλίνω*, however, this is never the case. This **36** usage holds good in the N. T. Of *τείνω* and *πλύνω* no Aor. Pass. forms occur.

B. § 101, N. 7 and 8; C. § 50.

The Perfect Passive of *μιαίνω*, which in earlier authors (Plato, Thucyd.) is formed according to common analogy *μεμίασμαι*, is *μεμίαμμαι* in later writers (e.g. Dio C. p. 655, and cf. An. Cram. IV. p. 197) ; and this is the form given by all the manuscripts in Titus i. 15. The form *μεμίανται* which occurs in the same passage may be taken (according to B. § 101, N. 7) as 3d Pers. Plural ; commonly it is explained as 3d Pers. Singular, like *ἐξήρανται* Mark xi. 21.[1] This last-mentioned verb also has in the N. T. *ἐξήραμμαι* in the 1st Pers. Sing., cf. Mark iii. 1 ; xi. 20.

VERBALS IN τός.
B. § 102; H. § 398; C. § 269 d.; D. p. 190; J. § 318.

Verbals in *τος* take the accent on the last syllable, as *γραπτός*, *γνωστός, ὁρατός, ἀγαπητός, φθαρτός*, etc. When compounded,

---

[1] The Vulgate translates it inquina*tae sunt*. When we add to this the express testimony of the scholiast on Arist. Plut. 635 (*ἔχει δὲ τὸ λελάμπρυνται τρίτον πρόσωπον τῶν ἐνικῶν ὁμόφωνον τῷ τρίτῳ τῶν πληθυντικῶν, ὡς τὸ ἐξήρανται καὶ κατήσχυνται καὶ ὅσα τοιαῦτα*) and the other passages cited in the Ausf. Sprachl. I. 442, we can hardly regard the existence of the 3d Pers. Plural as so improbable as Schäfer on Dion. H. de comp. verb. p. 355 asserts it to be ; especially as to a Greek the ending *-νται* would naturally produce the impression of a plural. As further evidence towards establishing that form *μεμίανται* as plural, the quotation from an unknown poet in Suidas under *ψαφαρῇ* may serve : *Ἕστασαν, οὐδὲ κόμας ψαφαρῇ μεμίαντο κονίῃ*, where *μεμ.* is manifestly plural, whether we read *κόμας* or with Valckenaer *κόμαι.* Hermann also (on Aesch. Pers. 569) takes the form *ἔρρανται* as 3d Pers. Plur. of the Perfect.

6

however, they always draw back the accent if the composition first takes place in the Verbal; as, θεόπνευστος, δυσβάστακτος, εὔθετος, εὐπρόςδεκτος, εὔχρηστος, and all those compounded with a privative, the number of which is very great in the N. T., as ἄνιπτος, ἄφθαρτος, ἀπρόςιτος, ἀδιάκριτος, etc. On the other hand, if derived indubitably from verbs already compounded, they retain the accent on the last, as ἀνεκτός from ἀνέχομαι, εὐλογητός from εὐλογέω, ἐκλεκτός from ἐκλέγομαι, also συνεκλεκτός, συνετός from συνίημι, etc. Those that do not do this must be regarded as first compounded in the Verbal, as ἀπόδεκτος (simple δεκτός Luke iv. 19, etc.), σύμφυτος, ἔμφυτος, ἔκθετος, etc.

Verbals in τος derived from intransitive verbs have also an Active (intransitive) sense, as θνητός, παθητός (Acts xxvi. 23), ἄπταιστος (Jude 24), ἀρεστός, etc.   See further respecting Verbals below, § 134, 8, p. 190.   On προςήλυτος see p. 74.

37

REMARKS ON THE REGULAR VERB.
B. p. 162; H. § 349; C. § 293; D. p. 179; J. § 194.

Respecting the double form of the 1st Aor. Opt. Act. given in the paradigm, it may be remarked that in the 3d Pers. Sing. the form in αι is the only one in use (hence probably in the 3d Pers. Plur. more correctly ποιήσαιεν Luke vi. 11 Lchm. [Treg. Tdf.], ψηλαφήσαιεν Acts xvii. 27 var.), and in the 3d Pers. Plur. of the Imperative of all tenses the forms in -τωσαν and -σθωσαν. Examples of both verbal forms abound in all parts of the N. T., e.g. 1 Thess. iii. 11, 12 ; Heb. xiii. 21 ; Jas. v. 14 ; Rom. xv. 11 ; Luke xxi. 21, etc.

B. p. 162; H. § 363; C. § 331; J. § 196.

Instances of the form in σαι in the 2d Pers. Sing. of contract verbs — a form which indubitably occurs in the N. T., and is elsewhere also in use here a   there, and is accordingly censured by the Atticists   even the anti-Atticists (An. Bekk. II. 77, 98)—are t   ollowing : ὀδυνᾶσαι Luke xvi. 25, καυχᾶσαι, κατακαυχᾶσ   om. ii. 17, 23 ; xi. 18 ; 1 Cor. iv. 7.   Elsewhere it appe   only in the two Future forms πίεσαι and φάγεσαι ; se   ne anomalous πίνω p. 66, and ἐσθίω p. 58.

B. p. 162; H. § 363 a.; C. § 297 f.; J. § 196, Obs. 4.

The 2d Pers. βούλει has been retained in the N. T. (Luke xxii. 42), but the reading of the Rec. ὄψει is not found to be established by the codd.; hence recent editions have -η, as generally in the 2d Pers., also of the Future, thus ὄψῃ, μαίνῃ, παρέξῃ, ἀπαρνήσῃ, etc.; see Win. § 13. 2, p. 75 sq. (73). The 2d Pers. of οἴομαι does not occur. In the N. T. Apocrypha always βούλῃ, ὄψῃ (Nicod. B. 6, 9; Ep. Clem. 1, 39, etc.).

B. p. 163; H. § 355 sq.; C. § 330; D. p. 253; J. § 192.

The (Alexandrian, see An. Bekk. p. 91) termination, common in the Sept., of -οσαν for -ον especially in the 2d Aor. (see examples in Sturz, Dial. Alex. p. 59; Mullach, Vulg. Spr. p. 16), does not occur very often in the N. T. The reading of cod. A [ℵ also] in 2 Thess. iii. 6, παρελάβοσαν, has not been adopted by Lchm. [yet so Tdf. eds. 7, 8]; ἐδολιοῦσαν in Rom. iii. 13 is in a quotation from the O. T. (Ps. v. 9); and ἐδίδοσαν, which Winer p. 77 (74) adds to these, cannot be taken into account. In the 3d Pers. of 2d Aorists the ending -αν was more common (ἦλθαν, εἶδαν), as observed above, p. 39. Accordingly we have only εἴχοσαν (John xv. 22, 24) left, — an Imperfect form, therefore, which is as isolated here as εἶχαν was above; see respecting it my article in the Stud. u. Krit. for 1858, Heft 3, p. 485 sqq. It is remarkable that this very form has the authority of cod. Alex. against it.

B. p. 164; C. § 330; D. p. 253; J. § 191.

The ending -αν for -ασι in the Perfect is now established in many passages of the N. T., as John xvii. 7; Rev. xviii. 3 38 Lchm. [Tdf. Treg.]; Jas. v. 4; Acts xvi. 36 etc., see Winer § 13, p. 76 (73); yet not in all, see e.g. Luke ix. 36 [-αν Tdf. Treg.]; Rev. viii. 2; 1 John ii. 18 (γεγόνασιν, but in Rom. xvi. 7; Rev. xxi. 6 etc. γέγοναν), etc.

Quite without parallel is the 2d Pers. Sing. of the same tense with the ending -ες for -ας: Rev. ii. 3 κεκοπίακες. See Lchm. pref. p. 42 note, and cf. Exod. v. 22 Alex. This form of the Perf., however, was by no means uncommon in the Alexandrian dialect, as is apparent from Apollon. Synt. p. 37, 9; 71, 12, and is found both in cod. Vat. and cod. Sin. in many other passages also.

The 3d Pers. Plur. of the Pluperf. Act. is uniformly -εισαν, as πεποιήκεισαν Mark xv. 7, etc., even when in Attic the form in -εσαν is the only one in use see οἶδα, p. 51. (But ἀπ-, ἐξῇεσαν Acts xvii. 15, etc.)

CONTRACT VERBS.
B. § 105; H. § 370 sq.; C. § 309 sq.; D. § 332 sq.; J. § 238 sq.

The uncontracted Imperative ἀπόχεε (B. p. 174, note) has a parallel in the form (Rev. xvi. 1) ἐκχέετε (Rec. ἐκχέατε). Cf. Lchm. pref. p. 42 note.

B. p. 167, note; H. § 371; C. § 309 c.; D. p. 256; J. § 239.

In the more recent editions the ι subscript is omitted in the Infin. termination -ᾶν. Yet in consideration of the Infin. termination -οῖν for -οῦν in verbs in όω, which is here and there given and even accepted (Matt. xiii. 32, cf. Mark iv. 32; Heb. vii. 5 where Tdf. [so too Treg.] after cod. B reads ἀποδεκατοῖν), the other mode of writing is perhaps to be preferred in the N. T.

B. § 105, N. 5; H. § 371; C. § 120; D. p. 262; J. § 239.

Of the four verbs here mentioned, διψάω and πεινάω do not follow the rule, as they everywhere revert to the main rule and contract into a, e.g. Rom. xii. 20. That πεινάω (not διψάω) retains the a in the other tenses also see p. 37.

B. § 105, N. 8; C. § 322; H. § 370 D.; D. p. 263 sq.; J. § 240.

As in the case of the forms τέσσερα etc., see above p. 29, so when contractions of verbs in άω which have η in the Future occur occasionally as if from -έω (but only into -ου), we are hardly warranted in regarding them as Ionisms, but only as irregularities (perhaps of the scribes) occasioned by analogous forms. Thus we find ἠρώτουν Matt. **xv. 23** [Mark iv. 10 Tdf.], νικοῦντι Rev. ii. 7, 17 Lchm. [so T. Tr. **vs.** 17]; but νικῶντας again in xv. 2 (-οῦντας C.); [ἐμβριμούμενος John xi. 38 Tdf.; ἐνεβριμοῦντο Mark xiv. 5 Tdf.]. Numerous examples of the contraction in ου may be quoted, moreover, from the Apocrypha of the N. T., the Apost. Fathers, etc.; cf. also Cram. Anecd. IV. p. 412.

Respecting the opposite change of έω into άω see ἐλεέω and ξυρέω in the list of anomalous verbs, pp. 57, 63.

VERBS IN μι.
B. § 107; H. § 400; C. § 45; D. § 319; J. § 274.

The remark that the contracted forms of the 3d Pers. Plur. were those used in common Greek, does not hold at least in the N. T., for there only the ordinary Attic forms are in use, as τιθέασι, διδόασι Matt. v. 15; Rev. xvii. 13, etc.

Side by side with the common forms of the Pres. ἵστημι, the later Present form ἱστάνω occurs, especially in the Indic. 39 and Partic., as συνιστάνω Gal. ii. 18, συνιστάνομεν 2 Cor. v. 12, ἐξ- συν- καθιστάνων Acts i. 6; viii. 9; xvii. 15; 2 Cor. x.

12, 18, etc. Besides this, the Rec. often had by-forms of the Pres. from the theme in άω, see Winer 78 (75). These, however, in the Indic. and Partic. have all now been changed: some into the common form (as in 2 Cor. iv. 2 ; vi. 4), and some into that in νω (see above). The Infinitive in Lachmann's edition [and Treg.'s] is given, as commonly, ἱστάναι (1 Cor. xiii. 2), and once as from the collateral form in άω, viz. ἱστᾶν (2 Cor. iii. 1). But as important MSS. give in both passages [א Tdf. 8 in 2 Cor. l.c.] the form in -άνειν, Tdf. [eds. 2, 7] in consideration of the above examples has given it the preference.

The contracted forms of the Imperfect (B. p. 183), ἐτίθουν, ἐτίθει, ἐδίδουν, -ου are by far the most common forms in the N. T. as also in common prose, e.g. Matt. xxvi. 26 ; Mark iv. 8 ; vi. 7, 56 ; Luke xxiv. 30 ; Acts ii. 47 ; iii. 2 ; iv. 35 ; 2 Cor. iii. 13, etc. Instances like ἐδίδοσαν John xix. 3 ; Acts xvi. 4, ἐπετίθεσαν Acts viii. 17, are exceptional, (and have for the most part important variants against them). In the Present of both verbs only the common forms (τίθημι, -σι, etc.) are in use, and the neuter Partic. ἀποδιδοῦν Rev. xxii. 2 is quite isolated. In Rev. iii. 9 we find διδῶ, which Lchm. [Tdf. eds. 7, 8] following the two leading MSS. [but not Sin.] has adopted, manifestly for the Indic. (not Subjunc.), which here agreeably to the style of the Rev. stands for the Future (Vulg. dabo), the common form of which, δώσω, occurs ii. 17, etc.

The fourth formation in νμι occurs, indeed, in the N.T., yet perpetually alternating with the inflection in ύω (which is more common in later authors). For example, from δεικνύναι we have δείκνυμι 1 Cor. xii. 31, δεικνύεις John ii. 18, δείκνυσιν Matt. iv. 8 ; John v. 20, δεικνύειν Matt. xvi. 21, ἐπιδεικνύς, ἀποδεικνύντα Acts xviii. 28 ; 2 Thess. ii. 4, δεικνύοντος Rev. xxii. 8, ἐπιδεικνύμεναι Acts ix. 39 ; from ὀλλύναι: ἀπόλλυε Rom. xiv. 15, Ἀπολλύων Rev. ix. 11 (cf. Sir. xx. 22), ἀπόλλυται 1 Cor. viii. 11, -ύμεθα Matt. viii. 25, -ύμενοι 2 Cor. iv. 9, etc. In other verbs the form in νω has almost completely superseded the other ; for instance, from ὄμνυμι we have ὀμνύει, ὀμνύετε, ὀμνύουσι ; ὀμνύειν in Matt. xxvi. 74 (but in the parallel passage Mark xiv. 71 ὀμνύναι ; where, however, cod. A [so Sin.] also has -ύειν) ; further, ἐστρώννυον, ἐζώννυες, etc.

In the Subjunctive of the Pres. and 2d Aor. Act. the ordinary contracted forms (τιθῶ, θῶ, etc.) are everywhere found.

40 Yet of δίδωμι three forms of the 3d Pers. Sing. have been preserved, viz.

1) The regular (διδῷ) δῷ Matt. v. 25 ; John xv. 16 Lchm. [Treg. Tdf.], and often.

2) διδοῖ, δοῖ. These forms are not Optative [cf. e.g. Tdf. ed. 7, p. lvii] but Subjunctive, and have arisen by regular contraction from a theme in όω (cf. μισθόῃ, μισθοῖ): 1 Cor. xv. 24 ; Mark iv. 29 ; [viii. 37 T. Tr.] ; xiv. 10, 11 ; John xiii. 2, (and as important variants in John xiii. 29 ; Eph. iv. 29 ; 1 Thess. v. 15 ; Luke xxii. 4). And in like manner from the syncopated Aor. ἔγνων comes the 3d Pers. Subjunc. γνοῖ Mark v. 43 ; ix. 30 ; Luke xix. 15 (John xi. 57 var.). In 1 Macc. xi. 40 we find παραδοῖ ; in Hermas, Mand. iv., γνοῖ (Sin.). On the Subjunctive cf. § 139, 37, p. 233.

3) δώῃ (not δῴη or δῴῃ) as if from a lengthened form δώω. This form is the rarest and is quite without analogies in later Greek in its favor. It occurs in Eph. i. 17 Lchm. [δῴη Tdf. eds. 2, 7, 8 ; Treg.] (B δῷ), 2 Tim. ii. 25 Lchm. [δῴη Tdf. eds. 2, 7, 8 ; Treg.] and John xv. 16 Tdf. [eds. 2, 7 ; ed. 8, Lchm. Treg. δῷ].

The 2d Pers. Sing. appears always in the form δῷς, γνῷς : Mark vi. 25 ; Luke i. 4 ; Rev. iii. 3 [Tdf. Treg. γνώσῃ], etc.

The (Pres. and) Aor. Optative of δίδωμι, which in accordance with the syntax of the N. T. occurs but rarely, has the later form (διδῴην) δῴην ; see Lob. Phryn. p. 346. Of the passages cited by Winer p. 78 sq. (75) only Rom. xv. 5 ; 2 Tim. i. 16, 18 (according to Tdf. [eds. 2, 7] also Eph. i. 17 [ed. 8 ; so Tr.] ; iii. 16 ; 2 Tim. ii. 25 [ed. 8 ; so Tr.] ; iv. 14) belong under this head, as the others have been changed in modern editions, some into the Subjunctive (δῷ, δώῃ) some into the Future (δώσει).

B. § 107, N. I. 8;   H. § 402;   C. § 306 c.;   D. p. 183;   J. § 277.

The Aorist in κα of the three verbs τίθημι, δίδωμι, ἵημι is uniformly in use in the N. T., not only in the Sing. and 3d Pers. Plur. but also in the 1st and 2d Pers. Plur., so that in the Indicative it has almost completely supplanted the 2d Aorist ; as, ἐδώκαμεν, -τε, Matt. xxv. 35 ; Mark vii. 13 ; Gal. iv. 15 ; 1 Thess. iv. 2 ; ἀφήκαμεν, συνήκατε, etc. Matt. xiii. 51 ; xix. 27 ; xxiii. 23 ; Mark x. 28, etc. ; (only once παρέδοσαν Luke i. 2).

The Moods, on the other hand, are formed from the 2d Aor. throughout.

Respecting the very anomalous Subjunctive δώσῃ, see p. 36 above.

B. § 107, N. I. 14; H. § 401; C. § 297; J. § 274.

The 2d Aor. Imperative of ἵστημι occurs in both forms: ἀνάστα Acts xii. 7 etc., and ἀνάστηθι, ἐπίστηθι Acts ix. 6, 34; 2 Tim. iv. 2. Cf. the anomalous βαίνω, p. 54.

The Present Imperative Pass. of ἵστημι has only the full form ἵστασο: 2 Tim. ii. 16; Tit. iii. 9.

The 3d Pers. Sing. of the Imperf. and 2d Aor. Middle of δίδωμι ought, according to common usage, to run ἐδίδοτο, ἔδοτο, as Lchm. [so Treg.] reads in Matt. xxi. 33; Mark xii. 1; Luke xx. 9. But in other passages according to pretty trustworthy authority (and in the [last two of the] above three also according to cod. A [and in all three according to codd. א B]) it is preserved for us with the ending -ετο, as if from the theme δίδω. Thus διεδίδετο Acts iv. 35, ἀπέδετο Heb. xii. 16, παρεδίδετο 1 Cor. xi. 23, and often in the Sept. e.g. Ex. ii. 21; v. 13 Alex. That this erroneous inflection is not unexampled in later Greek may be seen from Stephanus, Thes. under δίδωμι; cf., too, the theme ἵω under ἵημι, p. 48. The more recent collations have shown that both cod. Vat. and cod. Sin. rather favor than oppose this form. Both codd. exhibit *prima manu* almost always -ετο. Hence it is not to be discarded from the N.T.; on the contrary, the form in -οτο is rather a later (Grecizing) correction.

The Future form ἐκδόσεται (Matt. xxi. 41) has been set aside.

B. § 107, m. 21; H. § 416; C. § 50; J. § 319.

The Aorist and Future Pass. ἐστάθην, σταθήσομαι occur very frequently in a purely neuter force, interchangeably with ἔστην, στήσομαι. Examples abound in all parts of the N. T., as Matt. xii. 25; Luke xviii. 10; xxi. 36; Rev. vi. 17; Rom. xiv. 4, etc. Both forms σταθῆναι and — ᷒ in Mark iii. 24 sq. Tdf. [Treg.]. Winer's statement p. 252 (237) that the 1st Aor. Act. ἔστησα also occurs in an intransitive sense is without foundation; for in the isolated instance, Acts xxvii. 28, an object (as ναῦν or ἑαυτούς) is to be supplied, according to the well-known rule (§ 130, 4 p. 144), which is to be applied also to the N. T.

Of the syncopated forms of the Perfect, we find most frequently in use — but always alternating with the full forms —

the Infin. ἑστάναι (Acts xii. 14 ; 1 Cor. x. 12) and the very common Partic. ἑστώς, ἑστῶσα. The Neuter in the abbreviated form is ἑστός Matt. xxiv. 15 ; Rev. xiv. 1 (Tdf. [ed. 2] ἑστώς [7, 8, Tr. ἑστός]). On the other hand, the full form ἑστηκός is found Mark xiii. 14 [-κότα T. Tr.]; Rev. v. 6 [-κώς T. Tr.].

Of the collateral form of the Present we find στήκει John i. 26 etc., στήκετε (Indic. and Imperat.), and the Subjunc. στήκητε 1 Thess. iii. 8, (see B. p. 187, Note *) ; and one example of the Perfect ἕστακα in a transitive sense, Acts viii. 11 (cf. 9 and 13).

ἵημι.

B. § 108, 109; H. § 403; C. p. 78; D. p. 295; J. § 283 sq.

It is by far the most difficult task to lay down the N. T. use of the verb ἵημι ; for nowhere do the MSS. (and consequently the editions also) vary so noticeably as in the case of this verb. Since its use is frequent, we will distribute the forms which occur under the various themes.

1) Present ἵημι : Under this head we comprise the common use, which is in the main that of the N. T. also, as is attested by the forms ἀφίησι, ἀφίετε, συνιᾶσι (2 Cor. x. 12 Lchm. [T. Tr.]), ἀφιέτω, συνιῶσιν (Mark, Luke), συνιείς ; Aorist συνῆκα (see p. 46), παρεῖναι (Luke xi. 42), συνῶ, ἀνῶ (Heb. xiii. 5), ἄφες, σύνετε (Mark vii. 14), ἀνείς ; Passive ἀφίεται, ἀφίενται, καθιέμενος, παρειμένος. The Aor. Pass. is only found unaugmented : ἀνέθη Acts xvi. 26, ἀφέθησαν Rom. iv. 7.

2) Theme ῾ΙΕΩ. Here belongs (besides the regular Pres. Subjunc. given above) the Indic. 3d Pers. Plur. if accented as perispome (συνιοῦσιν, ἀφιοῦσιν), as is done by Tdf. [eds. 2, 7] Matt. xiii. 13 [ed. 8 also] ; Rev. xi. 9 ; 2 Cor. x. 12. But the form has few analogies. Still, they are now offered us by Hermas ; who, indeed, in the Infin. uniformly has συνιέναι, but elsewhere always συνιῶ, συνιείς. Yet since (according to cod. Simon.) Hermas gives the Imperat. σύνιε, perhaps we ought also to read everywhere συνίω, συνίεις ; but in Mand. 6, 2 συνιεῖς is a Future. Lchm. [so Treg.] has accordingly sometimes (with cod. B) changed it into the regular form, and sometimes accented it as proparoxytone [cf. T. on Rev. l. c.]— in this way bringing it under the

3) Theme ῾ΙΩ. Here belong, besides this 3d Pers. Plur. ἵουσιν, the 1st Pers. ἀφίομεν Luke xi. 4 (and moreover, as an important variant in Matt. vi. 12, etc.), the Partic. συνίων Rom.

iii. 11 (Tdf. again from ʿΙΕΩ: συνιῶν, see above; but quite erroneously in the Rec. συνιών Matt. xiii. 23), Eph. v. 17 var., ἀφίονται in cod. D (Matt. ix. 2, 5 [cod. Sin. also], etc.), and especially, the thoroughly established Imperfect form ἤφιεν Mark i. 34; xi. 16, (on which cf. B. p. 194, 5; J. § 284, and Lchm. praef. p. 43). Finally

4) Theme ʿΕΩ — to which belongs the isolated ἀφεῖς Rev. ii. 20.

5) Besides, there is still the Perf. Pass. 3d Pers. Plur. ἀφέωνται, already mentioned in B. p. 191, Note *. This seems to be a Dorism not peculiar to the N. T. but, on the contrary, rather widely extended, and even received by Attic writers; see Ahrens, Dial. Dor. p. 344; Bredow, Dial. Herod. p. 395. Tdf. [eds. 2, 7] adopted it throughout, Lchm. [Tdf. ed. 8, Treg.] only in Luke and John (also in 1 John ii. 12), but in Matt. and Mark ἀφίενται instead. See the passages in Wahl, and Winer § 14, p. 80 (77).

ἧμαι.

The 2d Pers. Sing. κάθη and Imperat. κάθου, noticed (in B. p. 192) as later forms, are both found in the N. T. — the former in Acts xxiii. 3, the latter in a quotation from the O. T. (Ps. cx.) in several passages (Matt. xxii. 44, Acts, Heb., etc.), and elsewhere also: Jas. ii. 3.

ἔννυμι.

Instead of ἀμφιέννυμι (Matt. vi. 30, etc.) the N. T. has a by-form ἀμφιέζω Luke xii. 28 Tdf. [Treg.] which has been formed, it is supposed, from the ordinary Fut. ἀμφιέσω. Lchm. 43 (after cod. B) substitutes for it the still more anomalous form ἀμφιάζει, not found elsewhere in the N. T., with which we have to compare only the (unreceived) reading of cod. D ἠμφιασμένος in Matt. xi. 8. The form ἀμφιάζειν, however, is found in the O. T. (e.g. Job xxix. 14; xl. 5) and sometimes elsewhere also in later writers; see Steph. sub voce. On the derivation of this form (held by the ancient grammarians to be a Dorism) cf. Lobeck, Rhemat. p. 223.

εἰμί.

The later by-form of the Imperat. 3d Pers. Sing. (B. p. 193, Note †; C. p. 74 c.; D. p. 229; J. § 286, 2), ἤτω, is found in 1 Cor. xvi. 22; Jas. v. 12, (on the other hand, ἴσθι in Matt.

ii. 13; 1 Tim. iv. 15; ἔστω in 1 Pet. iii. 3; ἔστωσαν, etc.).
Further, the Imperf. 2d Pers. Sing. ἦς (questioned by Winer
80 (76)) is found without variant, and has accordingly been
received, in Matt. xxv. 21, 23; John xi. 21, 32; xxi. 18; Rev.
iii. 15. On the other hand ἦσθα as usual in Matt. xxvi. 69;
Mark xiv. 67.

The 2d Pers. Plur. of the Imperf. is only ἦτε, Rom. vi. 20,
etc. As to Luke ii. 33 (ἦν ... θαυμάζοντες) see § 129, 3 p. 127.

In the 1st Pers. Sing. the Imperf. has uniformly the Mid.
form ἤμην (so that ἦν in the N. T. is only 3d Pers. Sing.), as
Matt. xxv. 35, etc. (see Wahl); rarely in the 1st Pers. Plur.
ἤμεθα, Matt. xxiii. 30; Acts xxvii. 37. On the other hand,
ἦμεν as usual in Rom. vii. 5; Eph. ii. 3[Tdf. Treg. ἤμεθα], etc

With regard to the inclination of εἰμί the remarks made,
p. 6 above, hold true.

As an example of the peculiar style of the Apocalypse, often
setting at defiance the laws of Grammar, may be here set down
the frequently recurring formula ὁ ὤν καὶ ὁ ἦν; for here
the Imperf. 3d Pers. Sing. ἦν, in the want of a Partic. Pret. of
εἶναι, is not only used as such a Partic., but also the entire
expression itself (by the use of the Art.) is treated like an
indeclinable noun: i. 4, 8; iv. 8; xi. 17.

εἰμι.

This verb, so common with the Greeks, does not occur as a
simple verb in the whole N. T. (also not in the O. T., with
the exception, perhaps, of ἴθι Prov. vi. 6); but instead of it
other and more expressive verbs are everywhere used, as
ἔρχομαι, βαίνω, ὑπάγω, etc. Even in John vii. 34, 36, where
some would read εἶμι, the only correct reading is εἰμί.

In composition it appears, but almost exclusively in the
Acts (which approximates most closely to the Greek diction),
as ἐξ-, ἀπῄεσαν, εἰςιέναι, (εἴςιθι in cod. B Acts ix. 6), εἰςῄει,
44 ἐξιόντων, ἡ ἐπιοῦσα sc. ἡμέρα; see the passages in Wahl. Elsewhere isolated compound forms occur; but still only in Luke
(viii. 4) συνιόντος, and the Ep. to the Heb. (ix. 6) εἰςίασιν.

κεῖμαι.

This verb is plainly used as Perf. Pass. of τίθημι (B. p. 198, 4)
in Acts xxviii. 20 ταύτην τὴν ἄλυσιν περίκειμαι. Cf. § 134,
7 p. 189.

οἶδα.

Of οἶδα the regular (unsyncopated) forms of the Indicative are the only forms in use; thus 2d Pers. οἶδας (Matt. xv. 12, etc.), Plur. οἴδαμεν, οἴδατε (xxii. 16; xx. 25, etc.), also 3d Pers. οἴδασιν (Jude 10; Luke xi. 44, etc.). Only in the Acts again do we find once (xxvi. 4) the Attic 3d Pers. Plur. ἴσασιν, and in James i. 19 the best MSS. give ἴστε (Vulg. also *scitis*) instead of the reading of the Rec. ὥστε, although the author elsewhere (iv. 4) writes οἴδατε.

The forms of the Moods correspond to the Attic, even in the Imperat. of which the syncopated form ἴστε occurs Eph. v. 5; Heb. xii. 17.[1]

The Imperfect has only ᾔδεις in the 2d Pers. Sing., Luke xix. 22 etc., and in the 3d Pers. Plur. always ᾔδεισαν, according to what was said on p. 43; as, Mark xiv. 40; Luke iv. 41; John ii. 9; Acts xvi. 3, etc.

DEPONENTS PASSIVE.
B. § 113, 4; H. § 413; C. § 266; D. §§ 337. 433; J. § 320.

The custom of Deponent Verbs — or of such as in the Middle form receive a peculiar meaning, whether transitive or intransitive — to form their Aorist out of the Passive steadily increased in later times, as may be gathered, for example, from the list of those verbs which may have both Aorists, since then the Passive Aor. belongs for the most part to the later period. Thus ἀπεκρίθη, is far more common in the N. T. than ἀπεκρίνατο (this occurs e.g. Matt. xxvii. 12; Acts iii. 12, etc.); ἀνάγομαι, αὐλίζομαι, have only ἀνήχθην, etc. Yet there are also cases of the opposite kind, as ἀρνέομαι, ὁπλίζομαι, and others still are used quite promiscuously, as ἀγαλλιάομαι[2] (John v. 35; viii. 46

---

[1] At any rate the Vulg. has *scitote* in both passages. Still, in both passages it suits the contents better to take this form as 2d Pers. Plur. Indicative, — especially in the Ep. to the Heb., which, moreover, in many respects approximates to the classic Greek more nearly than do the other Epp.

[2] This verb (peculiar to the N. T. and Sept. and also to the ecclesiastical authors, but to profane writers almost unknown) is in all probability not a Greek word but of oriental origin, coined out of the Hebr. גִּיל (אָגִיל, רָגִיל, abstr. גִּילָה) *to rejoice*, which is often, especially in the prophetic writings, rendered by ἀγαλλιᾶσθαι. Accordingly, with the word ἀγάλλομαι it has originally nothing to do. Probably, however, it may have found support in this well-known word (as is the case with all languages in the adption of foreign words, Grimm, deutsch. Wörterb. Vorr. p. xxvi) to which in signification also it has a distant resemblance. The Hebr. consonant ר on the reception of the word took its place after the liquids, — a position better suited to the Greek utterance.

56, etc.), ἐμβριμάομαι (Matt. ix. 30 ; Mark i. 43). However, a complete exhibition of the use of all deponent and middle verbs would carry us too far, and the subject must consequently be left (as being of a lexical rather than a grammatical nature) to the special dictionaries, or to a more extended discussion.

But that in the language of the N. T. the Passive formation was employed in general, far more than was the case earlier, to denote the r e f l e x i v e or i n t r a n s i t i v e sense answering to the Active, may for example's sake be illustrated in a few instances. Thus we have already seen (on p. 47) that the Aor. Pass. ἐστάθην often stands precisely in the sense of ἔστην, and is interchanged with it. So e.g. in Matthew κριθῆναι means in v. 40 merely *litigate* (but vii. 1 μὴ κριθῆτε purely Pass. *be judged*), διακριθῆναι xxi. 21 *doubt*, ξηρανθῆναι xxi. 19 etc. *dry up*, φιμωθῆναι xxii. 12 *grow dumb*, σκανδαλισθῆναι, -θήσεσθαι xi. 6 etc. *take offence*, σπλαγχνισθῆναι ix. 36 etc. *feel compassion*, ἄρθητι καὶ βλήθητι xxi. 21 *raise yourself and cast yourself* (cf. Luke xvii. 6), ἠγέρθη xxvii. 64 *surrexit* (Vulg.), ἐγέρθητε xvii. 7, ἐνεβριμήθη ix. 30 *comminatus est*, συνήχθησαν xxii. 34 ; xxv. 32 *convenerunt*; and connected with a new object (according to § 135, 3 p. 191) : ἐντραπήσονται τὸν υἱόν μου xxi. 37 *vere-buntur filium meum*. Ἐγενήθην, γενηθήτω (vi. 10 ; ix. 29) alternates with the ordinary Aor. Mid. γενέσθαι ; and ὤφθη, so common (xvii. 3, etc.), means not *was seen* but *appeared*, and

46 hence is connected with the Dative αὐτοῖς (not ὑπ᾽ αὐτῶν ; with which cf. the familiar use § 134, 2 p. 187). Or to take examples from James : μαρανθήσεται i. 11 *will wither away*, ὑποτάγητε iv. 7 a pure reflexive *submit yourselves*, so too μεταστραφήτω iv. 9, ταπεινώθητε iv. 10, etc.

B. § 113, N. 6; H. § 415; C. § 588; J. § 368.

That certain tenses of deponent verbs, especially the Perf. Aor. and Fut. Pass., are used in a p a s s i v e s e n s e, abundant examples may be brought from the N. T. to show ; for in fact the usage was somewhat current among the Greeks. Thus are used θεαθῆναι Matt. vi. 1 ; xxiii. 5, ἀσφαλισθῆναι from ἀσφα-λίσασθαι xxvii. 64, 65, ἴαται Mark v. 29, ἰαθήσεται Matt. viii. 8, χαρισθῆναι, λογισθῆναι, μνησθῆναι (Acts x. 31), ἐπιλελησμένον ἐστίν (Luke xii. 6), etc. Very rarely (as also among Greek authors) does this take place in the Present, e.g. λογίζεται Rom. iv. 4, 5, and probably also βιάζεται Matt. xi. 12, see the commentaries and cf. Luke xvi. 16, and relative to the similar use of βιάζεσθαι by the Greeks see Pape.

B. § 113, N. 7; H. § 412; C. § 584; D. § 344; J. § 321.

Exactness in the employment of the Fut. Mid. of many verbs as an ordinary Fut. has undergone a marked diminution in the N. T. and among the κοινοί in general. To be sure, ἀκούσομαι still occurs often enough, especially in the Acts (the Mid. form almost exclusively in the 1st and 3d Pers. Plur., John v. 25, 28 ; Acts xxi. 22 ; xxviii. 28 ; xvii. 32 ; Rom. x. 14 var. ; Active, John x. 16. Cf. κλαίω p. 60 sq.), but likewise often ἀκούσω, -σετε Matt. xiii. 14 etc. ; further ἀπαντήσω Mark xiv. 13, γελάσω Luke vi. 21, διώξω John xv. 20 etc., ἐπαινέσω 1 Cor. xi. 22 Tdf. [eds. 2, 7, 8 ; Tr.], ἐπιορκήσω Matt. v. 33, κλέψω Rom. xiii. 9 etc., σπουδάσω 2 Pet. i. 15. The Future form in Luke xii. 9 cod. Sin. ἀπαρνήσεται (although in itself considered genuine Greek, see B. § 113, 6) rests probably on a mistake of the copyist (for -νηθήσεται).

B. § 113, N. 9; C. § 576.

The remark that the alleged Passive sense of the Aor. Mid. is extremely rare, holds good also in reference to the N. T., inasmuch as the examples referred by some to this head (G.¹ v. 12 ; 1 Cor. x. 2 Tdf. [eds. 2, 7 ; Treg.] ; 2 Cor. v. 4) are all to be taken in a Middle or Neuter (not Passive) sense. Acts xv. 22 even the Vulgate translates correctly, *eligere viros ex eis et mittere.*

ANOMALOUS VERBS.

B. § 114; H. § 451; C. § 50; D. § 353; J. § 250 sqq.

ἄγνυμι. The retention of the augment in tenses otherwise without it occurs Matt. xii. 20 (κατεάξει), John xix. 31 (κατεαγῶσιν). Cf. ἀνοίγω under οἴγω, p. 62.

ἄγω. For an example of the 1st Aor. in composition see 47 2 Pet. ii. 5 ἐπάξας. On the other hand, κατ-, ἐπαγαγεῖν Acts v. 28, etc.

αἱρέω. Respecting the Alexandrian Aor. 3d Pers. Plur. εἶλαν (Acts x. 39), Mid. εἱλάμην, etc., see p. 39. Examples of the Fut. ἑλῶ in composition see in Luke xii. 18 (καθελῶ), Rev. xxii. 19 (ἀφελεῖ) ; cf. Josh. ii. 13 ἐξελεῖσθε.

ἅλλομαι. The Aorist has the form ἥλατο Acts xiv. 10, but Partic. ἐφαλόμενος Acts xix. 16 Lchm. [Tdf. Treg.] (al. ἐφαλλ.).

ἁμαρτάνω. Future ἁμαρτήσω Matt. xviii. 21. The Aorist always has in the Indic. the form ἥμαρτον; in the Subjunc. alternate the 2d Aor. ἁμάρτῃ, ἁμάρτητε (1 John ii. 1, etc.) and the 1st Aor. ἁμαρτήσῃ Matt. xviii. 15, ἁμαρτήσωμεν Rom. vi. 15 (Rec. -σομεν), even in close proximity, as Luke xvii. 3, 4. The Partic. is always ἁμαρτήσας: Rom. v. 14, 16; 2 Pet. ii. 4; Heb. iii. 17. Hermas invariably uses ἡμάρτησα, ἁμαρτήσας, etc.

ἀπειλέω threaten, elsewhere only Active (1 Pet. ii. 23), is used by Luke as Mid. in the same sense, Acts iv. 17, 21.

ἁρπάζω has the first formation throughout: Fut. ἁρπάσω Matt. xii. 29; Mark iii. 27; John x. 28, Aor. ἥρπασα Acts viii. 39 etc., (Perf.) Pluperf. συνηρπάκει Luke viii. 29, 1st Aor. Pass. ἡρπάσθην Acts xxvii. 15; Rev. xii. 5. On the other hand, from the second formation it has only tenses with a pure characteristic: 2d Aor. Pass. ἡρπάγην 2 Cor. xii. 2, 4, Fut. ἁρπαγήσομαι 1 Thess. iv. 17.

αὐξάνω has not only the causative sense, make grow, 1 Cor. iii. 6, Fut. αὐξήσω 2 Cor. ix. 10 etc., but also the immediative, grow, (Matt. vi. 28, etc.), for which also the Mid. or Pass. form αὐξάνομαι is used, 2 Cor. x. 15; Col. i. 10. The Aorist in this sense is both ηὔξησα Acts vii. 17 and ηὐξήθην Matt. xiii. 32; 1 Pet. ii. 2. The simple Pres. form αὔξω only in the latter sense Eph. ii. 21, — also in Col. ii. 19 αὔξει τὴν αὔξησιν according to § 131, 5 p. 148.

βαίνω. The syncopated Imperat. Aor. has in composition both forms, as in the case of ἵστημι (see p. 47); thus κατά-, μετάβηθι John iv. 49; vii. 3 etc., μετάβα Matt. xvii. 20, ἀνάβα Rev. iv. 1 Tdf. [also Treg.]. The further inflection appears Matt. καταβάτω xxiv. 17 Lchm. [Tdf. Treg.], Mark xiii. 15; Luke xvii. 31, ἀνάβατε Rev. xi. 12.

βαρύνω. This theme does not occur at all in the N. T. (also no longer in Luke xxi. 34), but instead the un-Attic (except in the Perf., see Thom. Mag. sub voce) theme βαρέω: βαρείσθω, βεβαρημένος, βαρηθῶσιν, ἐπιβαρῆσαι, etc., [yet καταβαρυνόμενοι Mark xiv. 40 Lchm. Tdf. Treg.].

βιόω has been almost completely supplanted (in the Fut. 48 and Aor. also) by the verb ζῆν. as we find only βιῶσαι, 1 Pet. iv. 2. See ζῆν, p. 58.

βλαστάνω has in the Aorist only the later form of the 1st Aor. ἐβλάστησα Matt. xiii. 26 ; Heb. ix. 4 ; also in an Active sense Jas. v. 18, on which cf. § 131, 4 p. 147. The Subjunc. Pres. is βλαστᾷ in Mark iv. 27 (Rec. βλαστάνῃ) from a collateral form βλαστάω, hardly to be found elsewhere (see Schol. Pind. Pyth. 4. 113 θάλλει καὶ βλαστᾷ).

γαμέω. The Aor. runs indiscriminately now ἔγημα Luke xiv. 20 etc., now ἐγάμησα Mark vi. 17 etc., both side by side 1 Cor. vii. 28. As respects signification, it is used in the Active as well of the man as of the woman, as in the above passage from Cor., where the difference in form does not indicate a difference in sense, but is purely accidental ; for subsequently (vs. 34) γαμῆσαι is used also of the woman. In the Mid. (Pass.) it is always used of the woman, but in the Aor. it has only the Passive form γαμηθῆναι, instead of the Attic γήμασθαι, vs. 39 etc. On the collateral form γαμίζω, ἐκγαμίζω, see the lexicons.

γίνομαι. The Aorist has far more frequently the Attic form of the 2d Aor. Mid., especially in the Subjunc. and Optat. (μὴ γένοιτο), than the un-Attic 1st Aor. Pass. ἐγενήθην 1 Thess. ii. 5 etc., of which the Imperat. γενηθήτω often occurs in the Synoptics, the Partic. in Heb. iv. 3. Partic. γεγονώς in sense like natus, old, in 1 Tim. v. 9.

γινώσκω. Respecting γνοῖ (Aor. Subjunctive) see under δίδωμι, p. 46.

That the Pass. of γινώσκω should sometimes (1 Cor. viii. 3 ; xiii. 12 ; Gal. iv. 9) be taken as Pass. of the causative signification (cause to know, bring to the knowledge of) like the Heb. Hophal, so that ἐγνώσθην ὑπὸ θεοῦ would mean 'I was brought to knowledge by God,' is an error which modern interpretation has already left behind it. See the commentaries on the above passages, and Winer 263 247).

δέομαι. The uncontracted form ἐδέετο [Tdf., also cod. Sin.] in Luke viii. 38, Lchm. has altered after several MSS. into the still more anomalous form ἐδεεῖτο (cf. Job xix. 16 Alex.), thus formed as it were from the same theme from which comes the common Aor. ἐδεήθην Matt. ix. 38, etc. Cf. the form δεούμεθα in the anti-Atticist, Anecd. Bekk. I. p. 90.

δύναμαι. By the side of the common 2d Pers. Sing. δύνασαι is found sometimes the form (censured as Indic.) δύνῃ, Mark ix. 22 ; Rev. ii. 2. On the other hand, δυνήσῃ is now read [yct Treg. Tdf. ed. 8, δύνῃ; so א also] in Luke xvi. 2. Respecting the augment see p. 33.

49 δύω has in the Present, as often in later writers and the Sept., the intransitive sense: (of the sun) ἐπιδυέτω Eph. iv. 26. The neuter by-form δύνω, Luke iv. 40, ought to form the Aorist ἔδυν, as also was formerly read in Mark i. 32. But recent editors, after preponderant MS. authority [yet see below], give even here the 1st Aor. ἔδυσαν (in Luke iv. 40, also, cod. D has δύσαντος) used by Greeks only transitively; and the compound παρεισέδυσαν, Jude 4, also has this intransitive sense. Elsewhere the 1st Aor. Act. in composition (ἐκ-, ἐνδύω) regularly has the transitive signification; in the intransitive or reflexive (clothe one's self) the form of the 1st Aor. Mid. makes its appearance. The syncopated Aor. ἔδυν has consequently passed quite out of use in the N.T.; cf. φύω p. 68. Yet the reading ἔδυ (Mark i. 32 Tdf.) gains now a new support in cod. Sin. Instead of παρεισέδυσαν cod. Vat. gives -δύησαν, formed quite after the analogy of ἐφύην. Cf. Lobeck's note in Buttm.'s Ausf. Sprachl. II. p. 321, under φύω.

The Present by-form (διδύσκω) ἐνδιδύσκω, Mark xv. 17; Luke viii. 27; xvi. 19, analogously formed but unknown to earlier writers, has a transitive sense.

ἐγείρω. The Present Active has sometimes, but as it seems only in the Imperative (Matt. ix. 5, 6; Mark x. 49; Acts iii. 6; Eph. v. 14), the intransitive signification (similar to ἄγε). In the Rec. it was formerly, in opposition to settled authority, altered into the Mid. form ἔγειραι; this form was the less admissible as the Aorist in a neuter sense always in the N. T. has the Passive form ἠγέρθην; see p. 52 above. Cobet has everywhere restored ἔγειραι again. But Suidas (sub voce) censures expressly the erroneous (and hence actually occurring) use of ἔγειρε.

(ἕζομαι) καθέζομαι. The Imperf. ἐκαθεζόμην has everywhere plainly the Imperf. signification sat, was sitting, Matt. xxvi. 55; John iv. 6; xi. 20, synonymous therefore with the Imperf. ἐκαθήμην John vi. 3; Mark iii. 32, or with the very common periphrasis ἦν καθήμενος Acts ii. 2, etc. In the Present καθέζομαι is not in use except in the Participle (Luke ii. 46; Acts vi. 15). See the N.T. use of the forms which belong here under ἵζω, p. 60.

ἐθέλω. Although in the Present only the shorter form θέλω occurs, yet the augmented forms always take η: ἤθελον, ἠθέλησα. The Perf. does not occur. (On τεθέληκα Ps. xli. 12 see Phryn. sub voce and Sturz, Dial. Alex. p. 64.)

εἰπεῖν. Respecting εἶπον and εἶπα see p. 39. Besides the forms of εἶπα usual in Attic writers (εἶπας, εἴπατε, etc.) we find 1st Pers. εἶπα Heb. iii. 10 [Tdf. Tr. retain εἶπον] in quotation, Acts xxvi. 15, προείπαμεν 1 Thess. iv. 6, 3d Plur. εἶπαν frequently interchanged with εἶπον (e.g. Matt. xxvii. 4, 6), Partic. εἴπας Acts vii. 37 etc. and εἰπών vs. 60 etc. The Imperative with the ending 50 -ον is accented by the recent editors εἰπόν (Acts xxviii. 26; Mark xiii. 4, cf. Luke x. 40 var.). This accentuation, if the form is taken as 1st Aor. Imperat., conflicts with the rules of the old grammarians (Arcad. p. 169 δισύλλαβα παροξύνονται ἢ προπερισπῶνται· νεῖμον, εἶπον ἀντὶ τοῦ εἰπέ κ.τ.λ.), and εἶπον accordingly is the only correct Attic accentuation, see Ph. Buttm. Exc. I. ad Plat. Men. and Xen. Mem. 3, 6, 3. But as respects the Scriptures, the testimony of the old grammarian Jo. Charax (see Etym. Mag. sub voce; Varini Ecl. p. 172 Dind.) is too clear and definite to allow us to adhere to the same accentuation in the N. T. (λέγει ὁ Χάραξ, ὅτι τὸ παρὰ τῇ θείᾳ γραφῇ προστακτικὸν ὀξυτόνως λεγόμενον, οἷον εἰπόν ἀντὶ τοῦ εἰπέ, δευτέρου ἀορίστου ἐστὶ κατὰ τὴν Συρακουσίων γλῶσσαν λεγόμενον ... οἷον λάβε λάβον, καὶ τὸ ἄνελε ἄνελον. εἰ οὖν εἰπέ ὀξυτόνως, δῆλον ὅτι καὶ εἰπόν κ.τ.λ.); on the other hand, the same grammarian expressly lays down the accentuation εἶπον for Menander. Mid. ἀπειπάμην 2 Cor. iv. 2. The less Attic mode of writing the 1st Aor. Pass. ἐρρέθην instead of ἐρρήθην (Matt. v. 21, etc. [yet Tdf. reads -έθην even here]) is now everywhere established in Paul (Rom. ix. 12, 26; Gal. iii. 16) and in the Apocalypse (vi. 11; ix. 4), so also commonly in the Sept. (Gen. xv. 13; 2 Sam. v. 6, etc.). The Partic. is always ῥηθείς, even in the Sept. (Gen. xlv. 27).

ἐλεέω. The collateral Pres. form ἐλεάω is not only established by the mss., Rom. ix. 16 [so ℵ], (18 [not ℵ]); Jude 23 [so ℵ], but is also sufficiently attested by the testimony of the old grammarians (see Etym. Mag. and Steph. Thes. sub voce) as well as by other analogous examples (as ξυρέω, ξυράω). In such verbs, however, the forms that arise by flexion always take η: ἐλεήσω, ἐλέησον, ξυρήσωνται, ἐξυρημένος, etc. See

8

Etym. Mag. p. 129, 49 and cf. ἐλλογᾶτο Rom. v. 13 (A, [-αται א^a]), ἐλλόγα Philem. 18.

ἑλκόω. Respecting the augment see p. 34.

ἐραυνάω, the Alexandrian spelling (see Sturz, Dial. Alex. p. 117) for ἐρευνάω, hence often found in cod. Alex., as Rom. xi. 33; 1 Pet. i. 10; 1 Cor. ii. 10, has been received only once by Lchm., in Rev. ii. 23; on the other hand by [Treg. and] Tdf. everywhere (even in Rom. viii. 27 with cod. Sin.).

ἔρχομαι. Respecting the Alexandrian Aor. see p. 39. Since εἶμι is not used in the N. T. (except in composition, see p. 50), the Pres. in its mood-forms (ἔρχου καὶ ἴδε), the Imperf. ἠρχόμην, and the Fut. ἐλεύσομαι make their appearance again; in connection with which it is to be noticed, that (like the Pres. εἶμι in Attic authors) ἔρχομαι here, agreeably to its 51 signification, often has a future force, John ix. 4; xiv. 3 (πάλιν ἔρχομαι καὶ παραλήμψομαι) etc., (cf. the Germ. *ich komme*). See the passages in Winer 265 (249), and cf. p. 38 above; also § 137, 10 p. 203.

ἐσθίω. The by-form ἔσθω, otherwise only poetic (Zon. Lex. sub voce ἔσθειν σπανίως καὶ, εἴπερ ἄρα, οἱ ποιηταί), has sometimes, although not very strongly attested, been adopted into the text: Luke xxii. 30 ἔσθητε, Mark i. 6 Tdf. [Treg.] ἔσθων. Yet the form is found also in the O. T.: Lev. xvii. 10, 13; Sir. xx. 16, etc. [cf. Tdf. N. T. ed. 7 Proleg. p. il].

Instead of the Attic Fut. ἔδομαι the N. T. employs the analogous form φάγομαι, as Jas. v. 3 (ἔσται καὶ φάγεται), Rev. xvii. 16 (in the midst of Futures), Luke xiv. 15 (μακάριος ὃς φάγεται, Vulg. *manducabit*), and with a new anomaly in the 2d Pers. Sing. φάγεσαι, Luke xvii. 8 (Micah vi. 14, etc.). See p. 42.

εὑρίσκω. On the Alexandrian Aorist see p. 40, on the augment p. 34, and on the formerly received readings εὑρήσῃς, -σωμεν p. 36.

ἔχω. On εἶχαν see p. 40, εἴχοσαν p. 43. On the augment of ἀνέχομαι see p. 35.

ζάω. This verb, common in the N. T., has both forms of the Future: ζήσω John v. 25; 2 Cor. xiii. 4 etc. and ζήσομαι Matt. iv. 4 etc., see the lexicons. The Future and the Aorist ἔζησα have also the signification of ἀναζῆν come to *life (again)* in Matt. ix. 18; Rom. xiv. 9; Rev. xx. 4, 5; and in Luke xv.

24, 32 cod. B [and in vs. 32 א also, which Tdf. and Treg agree with] has ἔζησεν instead of the received ἀνέζησεν.

Instead of the Imperf. 1st Pers. Sing. ἔζων, Rom. vii. 9, cod. B exhibits ἔζην — a form analogous in structure to ἔζη, ζῆθι, ζῆναι; hence it early became current and has been often preserved in the manuscripts of Attic authors even. Respecting its doubtful Attic currency and the contradictory statements of the Atticists, see Ellendt, Lex. Soph. under ζάω, and Buttm. Ausf. Sprachl. § 114.

ἡγέομαι. The Perf. ἥγημαι in Phil. iii. 7, taken by some as a Pres., stands plainly in antithesis to the following ἡγοῦμαι. Cf. however Acts xxvi. 2 and Bhdy. Synt. p. 379.

ἥκω. The Perf. 3d Pers. Plur. ἥκασιν, very anomalous not only as respects form but signification also (for the Present has already the sense of the Perfect), Lchm. [so Tdf. Treg.] has adopted in Mark viii. 3, sustained by the codd. A D [א also] and the translation (venerunt). As the form does not occur again in the N. T., the readings ἥκουσιν (Rec.) and εἰσίν (Tdf. [eds. 2 and 7] after cod. B) seem plainly to be mere corrections. This Perfect is one of those isolated irregularities of the language, occasioned by the signification and perpetuated 52 by the thoroughly analogous appearance of the form (cf. διαπεφυλάκασι Xen. Cyr. 8, 6, 3), of which examples are to be met with not only in deteriorating Greek but in all ages, especially in dialects less cultivated than the Attic. Moreover, the form ἧκα as Perfect has Alexandrian precedent (ἥκαμεν, -τε, -σιν Gen. xlii. 7; xlv. 16; xlvii. 4; Job xvi. 22; Sus. 52, etc.), and is found elsewhere also in writers of the κοινή; see Steph. Thesaur.; Lob. ad Phryn.; Ep. Clem. 1, 12, etc.

Respecting the Subjunc. ἥξη see p. 36.

ἡττάομαι. The Ionic form of the 1st Aor. Pass. (but with the augment) ἡσσώθητε for ἡττήθητε (A) has been received by Lchm. [Treg.] after a few MSS. [א also] in 2 Cor. xii. 13.

θάλλω. The 2d Aor. ἀνεθάλετε, very rare elsewhere or even doubtful (Lob. Paral. p. 557), is used by Paul, Phil. iv. 10, as also sometimes in the O. T., Ps. xxviii. 7; Sap. iv. 4; Sir. xlvi. 12.

θαυμάζω. The Passive which elsewhere means only *to be wondered at* (2 Thess. i. 10) is used in the Apocalypse quite like a deponent Pass.: Aor. ἐθαυμάσθη *wondered*, Fut. θαυμασθήσονται, xiii. 3 [Tdf. reads ἐθαύμασεν ὅλη etc.] ; xvii. 8 [Tdf. Treg. read θαυμάσονται].

θνήσκω. The syncopated form τεθνάναι is given Acts xiv. 19 by Tdf. [ed. 2; but in eds. 7 and 8 τεθνηκέναι with Lchm. Treg.].

θύω. On ἐθύθην see p. 7.

(ἴζω) καθίζω. Respecting the Future see p. 37.

This verb is used by the N. T. writers in both senses (set, and seat one's self). The Middle occurs only twice in the Future, and that too in the 2d Pers. Plur. καθίσεσθε, Luke xxii. 30; Matt. xix. 28.

Further, since the ideas to sit and to seat one's self pass over into each other variously, the common N. T. uses of all these related verbs may be grouped as follows:

καθίζω set, καθίσω, καθιῶ, etc.

καθίζω seat one's self, Fut. καθίσω, -ιῶ (2d Pers. Plur. καθίσεσθε), Aor. ἐκάθισα. The Perf. κεκάθικα (Heb. xii. 2) synonymous with

κάθημαι sit (Imperat. κάθου see p. 49, Infin. καθῆσθαι, Partic. καθήμενος and καθεζόμενος), Imperf. ἐκαθήμην and ἐκαθεζόμην. The Future in this sense is supplied by the Fut. of καθίζω.

ἱκνέομαι appears only once, in the 3d Pers. Sing. of the 2d Aor. ἀφίκετο Rom. xvi. 19.

53 καίω. The 2d Aor. Pass. is κατεκάην, Rev. viii. 7; hence Fut. Pass. κατακαήσομαι 1 Cor. iii. 15; 2 Pet. iii. 10, but also καυθήσομαι Rev. xviii. 8. Respecting καυθήσωμαι (1 Cor. xiii. 3) see p. 36. The Fut. Act. is regularly καύσω, Rev. xvii. 16. But the Partic. καυσ ιιμενα, 2 Pet. iii. 10, 12, belongs to καυσόω, see the lexicons.

καμμύω see μύω p. 62.

κεράννυμι. The Perf. Pass. κεκέρασμαι occurs Rev. xiv. 10; Heb. iv. 2 Lchm. [Treg. Tdf., so ℵ] (where Tdf. [eds. 2, 7] reads κεκραμένος).

κερδαίνω. The formation (κερδήσομαι) Aor. ἐκέρδησα is almost the only one in use in the N. T.: Matt. xviii. 15, etc. Accordingly the Aor. Subjunc. κερδάνω 1 Cor. ix. 21, although the other form (κερδήσω) is used four times in the same connection either just before or afterwards, is surprising, but established by the MSS. [ℵ also].

κλαίω. Fut. 2d Pers. Plur. κλαύσετε Luke vi. 25; John

xvi. 20, 3d Pers. Plur. κλαύσονται Rev. xviii. 9, as in the case of ἀκούω, see p. 53 ; (cf. Origen on Luke vi. 25 πενθήσουσι καὶ κλαύσονται).

κράζω with long a (Herodian π. μον. p. 23), hence κρᾶζον Gal. iv. 6 (cf. Lob. Parall. p. 408), and 2d Perf. κέκραγα in sense of Pres. (John i. 15 μαρτυρεῖ καὶ κέκραγεν), never has [(except ἀν-έκραγον Luke xxiii. 18 Tdf.Treg.)] the 2d Aor., but always, as in later writers, the 1st ἔκραξα Matt. viii. 29 etc. The Future occurs only once : Luke xix. 40. But since the authorities there are divided between κεκράξονται A, κράξουσιν B [א], κράξονται D, and further, in favor of the first the usage of the Sept. (Ps. lxv. 14 etc.) [where κράξουσι is nowhere found ; see Tdf. crit. com. in Luc. l.c.] and the perhaps mutilated reading of cod. D may be adduced, while the authority of the [two] oldest MS[s.] and the usage of later authors (Lob.'s note in Buttm. Ausf. Sprachl. II. 223) weigh in favor of the second, a decision cannot be given with confidence in a case which stands so by itself. Among modern editors Lchm. has given the preference to the common form κεκράξονται, Tdf. [Treg.] to the reading κράξουσιν. With κρᾶζον may be compared προςπλᾶζον Il. μ, 285, — as according to the intimations of Lobeck (in the Ausf. Sprachl. II. 268) it is perhaps more correctly written.

κρεμάννυμι. From the Middle κρέμαμαι we have in Luke xix. 48 the regular ἐξεκρέματο. The oldest MS[s.], however, read instead ἐξεκρέμετο, probably not a clerical error, and certainly no more anomalous than ἐξέδετο, διεδίδετο (see δίδωμι p. 47). But on account of the little support which other codices give it, this rare form, which occurs besides only here and there in MSS., has not been adopted by the editors [except Tdf.].

κρύπτω. See p. 40. 54

κτείνω. Besides this form there exist two other by-forms of the Pres. : the most common ἀποκτέννω with a doubling of the liquid, after the Aeolic fashion (see Ahrens, Dial. Aeol. p. 52 sq.), Matt. x. 28 ; Luke xii. 4 ; Rev. vi. 11, and ἀποκταίνω, which is said to have been the Doric spelling (id. Dial. Dor. p. 186), 2 Cor. iii. 6 ; Rev. xiii. 10. Yet this last form, which is but weakly attested by the MSS., has with reason not been adopted by Tdf. [or Treg.], and seems, if it was really the original reading, to be less a (doubtful) Dorism, than to rest upon an erroneous spelling of the word, occasioned by the common Aorist ἀπεκτάνθην (see p. 41) and the familiar poetic forms ἔκταν, κτανέω, etc.

(κύω) ἀποκύω or ἀποκυέω (forms between which no difference can be found in Greek authors as respects signification, see Lob. ad Aj. p. 103) has, where it occurs, the transitive meaning, *bear, bring forth*, and forms the Aor. ἀπεκύησα Jas. i. 15, 18. Recent editors accentuate ἀποκύει.

λαμβάνω. In spelling this verb the recent editors have everywhere introduced the Alexandrian mode with μ (Sturz, p. 130) ; thus, Fut. λήμψομαι Acts i. 8 etc., Aor. Pass. ἐλήμφθην Mark xvi. 19 etc. In the same way in derivatives λῆμψις, ἀνα- ἀντι- μετα- πρόςλημψις, προςωπολημπτέω, etc.

The 2d Aor. Imperat. λάβε, according to the uniform direction of the old grammarians (e.g. Jo. Alex. p. 21 τὸ λαβέ καὶ ἰδέ ὀξυνόμενα ἀττικά ἐστι· τὰ γὰρ κοινὰ τούτων βαρύνεται), must, like ἴδε, be accented as paroxytone in the N. T.: Rev. x. 8, 9 ; John i. 47, etc.

λάσκω. The 1st Aor. ἐλάκησεν occurs once, Acts i. 18.

λείπω has as usual the 2d Aor., and only once the 1st Aor. καταλείψαντες Acts vi. 2. The collateral form λιμπάνω occurs 1 Pet. ii. 21.

μεθύω and μεθύσκομαι are both united without any important difference of meaning: 1 Thess. v. 7 οἱ μεθυσκόμενοι νυκτὸς μεθύουσιν. Aor. Pass. ἐμεθύσθην Rev. xvii. 2.

(μέλω) μεταμέλομαι, Fut. μεταμεληθήσομαι Heb. vii. 21 (in quotation), Aor. μετεμελήθην. On the other hand, from ἐπιμέλομαι we have the Fut. ἐπιμελήσομαι 1 Tim. iii. 5.

μιαίνω. Respecting the Perf. Pass. see p. 41.

55   (μύω). The abbreviated (after the Epic fashion, B. § 117 N. 2; H. § 73 D; C. § 136; D. § 140; J. § 19.) compound καμμύω for καταμύω, which is severely censured by Phrynichus (sub voce), appears, according to the words of the same grammarian, to have passed over into somewhat general use in prose from the time of the comic poet Alexis. At any rate the Alexandrians employ it frequently (Isa. xxix. 10 ; xxxiii. 15 ; vi. 10),[1] and from this last passage it passed over into the N. T. (Matt. xiii. 15 ; Acts xxviii. 27).

[1] Whether in Lam. iii. 43 we should accent καμμῦσαι after the poetic fashion, or καμμύσαι as commonly, may be doubtful. Yet in the case of a word manifestly

νίζω. Only the other Present *νίπτω* is in use in the N. T. (Matt. xv. 2 etc.) as in the Sept. (Ex. xxx. 18; 2 Chron. iv. 6).

(*νύσσω*) *κατανύσσω* forms, quite according to analogy, a 2d Aor. Pass. *κατενύγην* Acts ii. 37, which is not in use by the earlier writers, but frequent in the O. T.: Gen. xxxiv. 7, etc. This Aorist has everywhere the ethical sense; Hesych.: *κατενύγησαν, ἐλυπήθησαν*; Suidas sub voce.

ξυρέω. On the by-form *ξυράω* 1 Cor. xi. 6, see Etym. Magn. sub voce; Lob. on the Ajax p. 181; and under *ἐλεέω* p. 57.

(*οἴγω*) *ἀνοίγω*. The variations in the form of this very common verb are very great, both in the MSS. and in the different editions. In order to get a summary view of the forms we will bring them together as given in Lchm.'s text which here departs in many respects from the Rec.: FUTURE regularly *ἀνοίξω* Matt. xiii. 35; 1ST AORIST *ἤνοιξα*—John ix. 17, 21, 26, 30, 32; Acts v. 19; ix. 40; xii. 14; xiv. 27; Rev. throughout, (Subjunc. *ἀνοίξω* Luke xii. 36 etc., Imperat. *ἄνοιξον* xiii. 25, Infin. *ἀνοῖξαι* Acts xxvi. 18 etc., Partic. *ἀνοίξας* Matt. v. 2, etc.) —and *ἀνέῳξα* John ix. 14 (and frequently as a variant, as ix. 30 etc.); 2D PERFECT in an intransitive sense *ἀνέῳγα* 1 Cor. xvi. 9; 2 Cor. vi. 11 (Partic. *ἀνεῳγότα* John i. 52). PASSIVE: 1ST AOR. *ἠνοίχθην* Rev. xx. 12, *ἀνεῴχθην* Luke i. 64, and with double (threefold) augment *ἠνεῴχθην* Matt. iii. 16; ix. 30; John ix. 10; Acts xvi. 26 (Infin. *ἀνεῳχθῆναι* Luke iii. 21 with retention of the Augment, as in *ἄγνυμι*, which see); 1ST FUT. *ἀνοιχθήσομαι* Luke xi. 10; 2D AOR. *ἠνοίγην* (*was opened*, or *opened itself*) Acts xii. 10; Rev. xv. 5; xi. 19 (Subjunc. *ἀνοιγῶσιν* Matt. xx. 33); 2D FUT. *ἀνοιγήσομαι* Matt. vii. 7; Luke xi. 9; PERF. PARTIC. *ἀνεῳγμένος* Rev. iv. 1; Acts x. 11 etc.; 2 Cor. ii. 12, *ἠνεῳγμένος* Acts ix. 8; 56 Rev. x. 2, 8; xix. 11, and *διηνοιγμένος* Acts vii. 56 (also in ix. 8 *ἠνοιγμένος* according to A [א; adopted by Tdf.]). Moreover, we find several times in two of the oldest MSS. (A B) the 1st Aor. Act. with the double augment *ἠνέῳξε* John ix. 17, 21, 32 [but not so cod. Sin.], which has at least as much internal probability as *ἠνεῴχθην* etc. above. Of course, where the MSS. vary, different editors have decided in many passages now in

borrowed from the language of poetry the former accentuation is probably to be preferred.

favor of one reading and now in favor of another. As, however, the number of forms in use, which is all we are here concerned with, is the same (Tdf. agrees in the main with Lchm.), we will leave disagreements respecting particular instances to the reader's own observation.

οἰκτείρω: Fut. οἰκτειρήσω Rom. ix. 15 (as in the Sept. where we find also Aor. Imperat. οἰκτείρησον Ps. iv. 2).

(ὄλλυμι) ἀπόλλυμι. For the collateral form of the Pres. in ύω see p. 45. The Future Active is commonly ἀπολέσω Matt. xxi. 41 etc.; on the other hand, only once ἀπολῶ 1 Cor. i. 19, in a quotation from the O. T. In the Middle the Fut. is always ἀπολοῦμαι Matt. xxvi. 52; Rom. ii. 12; Matt. ix. 17 Tdf. [eds. 2, 7].

ὀμείρομαι is a by-form of ἱμείρομαι, given only in 1 Thess. ii. 8 (and a few times in the versions of the O. T.), but established by the MSS., and also attested by Hesychius and Photius sub voce. See Steph. Thesaurus, and Fritzsche on Mark, excurs. tert. p. 792.

ὄμνυμι. Respecting the form in ύω see p. 45.

ὁράω. The N. T. agrees in the main with the Attic use of this verb, excepting the forms of the Alexandrian Aor. (see p. 39) and the accentuation ἴδε (see under λαμβάνω p. 62). On isolated cases like προορώμην see p. 34; on the Subjunc. ὄψησθε see p. 36. The mode of spelling the Perf. (employed in Attic poetry, B. p. 251 Note †; H. § 450, 4; C. § 50) ἑόρακα is often exhibited by the MSS., but has not been received by the editors before Tdf., who in his 7th ed. introduced it several times, e.g. Luke ix. 36; John ix. 37, [but in ed. 8 appears to have returned to the usual form, — yet not in Col. ii. 18]. The Passive ὤφθην, ὀφθήσομαι commonly means to appear (apparere) cf. p. 52. Respecting ἰδού see p. 70.

παίζω. The Fut. Mid. παίξομαι is the common form in the Alexandrian dialect (Ezek. xxii. 5; Hab. i. 10), as with later writers in general (Luc. Dial. Deor. 4, 3; Apoll. Lex. Hom. under μωμήσονται); the Future occurs but once in the N.T., and then (according to B. § 113, N. 7) in the Active form ἐμπαίξουσιν Mark x. 34, which is not unknown to the Sept. also (Isa xxxiii. 4). The other tenses also occur in the guttural formation: ἔπαιξα, ἐπαίχθην, etc., Matt. xxvii. 31; ii. 16; Luke xviii. 32, etc.

παύω. The 2d Fut. Pass. of this verb is found once (Rev.

Infin. πῖναι existed, or at least can be proved. But that the Aorist ἔπιον had an inclination to form syncopated Aorists is shown by the Imperat. πῖθι ; and the abbreviation of the Infin., used as it must have been very frequently (δός μοι πῖν, πῖν βού-λομαι), would arise thus in the mouth of the people most naturally. Modern editors of the N. T. have accordingly retained this spelling, and Jacobs also in his Delectus Epigr. (6. 78) has returned to the form πῖν. [Tdf. ed. 8 everywhere reads πεῖν.]

πίπτω. Respecting the Alexandrian Aorist see p. 39 sq. But the former reading ἀνάπεσον (Rec.) or ἀνάπεσαι (Grsb.) is now changed into the common Imperative form ἀνάπεσε Luke xiv. 10 ; xvii. 7.

ῥέω has in the Future ῥεύσω John vii. 38 ; in the Aorist, as in Attic (ἐρρύην), Subjunc. παραρυῶμεν Heb. ii. 1. Cf. p. 32.

σαλπίζω, see p. 37.

(σκέπτομαι) ἐπισκέπτομαι the writers of the Old Test. and the New are fond of using in the Pres. and Imperf. ; see the lexicons.

στηρίζω, see p. 36.

(στορέννυμι) in the N. T. forms only from the other form, στρώννυμι, the Aor. ἔστρωσα, Perf. Pass. ἔστρωμαι, Aor. Pass. ἐστρώθην. On στρωννύω see p. 45.

τυγχάνω. The Perf. in later writers is commonly τέτευχα instead of τετύχηκα (Lob. ad Phryn. p. 395; Sturz, Dial. Alex. p. 198) and accordingly in the Sept. also : Job vii. 2, etc. This was formerly the reading also in Heb. viii. 6, but now instead a third form has been adopted from MSS. [Sin. also] into the text : τέτυχεν. As this form was apparently altogether unknown to the grammarians, Lobeck, as above, and Dind., in the Thesaurus of Steph., regard it as a mistake of the scribes, and it has been on this account expunged by the editors in classic authors, often it must be confessed against all MS. authority (e.g. Diod. 12, 17), and commonly changed into τέτευχα. In the language of the N. T. the unusual and even erroneous (B. § 97, 4 p. 134) form of the Perfect must always be allowed to stand.

φαίνω. Respecting ἔφανα see p. 41.

φαύσκω, a word formed from the stem φα (to shine) after the manner of iteratives, and used only in compounds (Job xxv. 5 etc.), to which, quite according to analogy, the form 60

(φαύσω) ἐπιφαύσει Eph. v. 14 is referred. In the O. T. we
find frequently the Aor. διέφανσε, διαφαύσῃ (e.g. ἕως διαφαύσῃ
ἡμέρα 1 Sam. xiv. 36 etc.). This rare word, which however
is found even in Herodotus (9, 45), was wholly unknown to
Attic authors.

In a few passages (Matt. xxviii. 1 ; Luke xxiii. 54) it has
the form ἐπιφώσκω, — in both instances of day-break. Cf. the
Lat. *illucesco*.

φέρω. On ἤνεγκον and ἤνεγκα see p. 39. Besides the forms
of the 1st Aor. usual also in Attic, we find most frequently
the Partic. ἐνέγκας (Luke xv. 23 etc.), which in the N. T. has
completely supplanted the other in ών, as on the other hand
the Infin. ἐνεγκεῖν (Jude 9 etc.) has superseded that in αι,
which is still read only in 1 Pet. ii. 5. The 1st Pers. ἤνεγκα
is found Acts xxvi. 10 etc., Imperat. προςένεγκον Matt. viii. 4
(-κε Rec.).

φθάνω. The Aorist ἔφθην is not in use, but only 1st Aor.
ἔφθασα: Matt. xii. 28 etc.

φύω. As the Aor. ἔφυν has been wholly superseded in the
language of the N. T. by the later 2d Aor. Pass. ἐφύην (hence
φυέν, συμφυεῖσαι Luke viii. 6, 7, 8), the Subjunc. must be
circumflexed ἐκφυῇ Matt. xxiv. 32 ; Mark xiii. 28 (ἐκφύῃ Rec.
[Tdf.]). Cf. δύω p. 56.

χαίρω. The Fut. is always χαρήσομαι Luke i. 14 etc., as
in the Sept., which, however, in composition always employs
the regularly formed yet elsewhere unheard of form in οῦμαι,
as κατα-, ἐπιχαροῦμαι.

χέω. Respecting the Imperative ἐκχέετε see p. 44. The
Future, after the manner of the so-called Attic Futures or of
the Fut. of liquid verbs (cf. Aor. ἔχεα), is circumflexed : ἐκχεῶ
Acts ii. 17, 18 in an O.T. citation (Joel iii. 1 sq.). We are prevented from accenting it ἐκχέω, as in Attic, on the one hand
by the testimony of the ancient grammarians (Choerob. in An.
Bekk. p. 1290 ; Cram. IV. p. 194 ; Etym. Magn. sub χέω) who
adduce it as an example of a second Future (τὸ ἐκχεῶ δευτέρου
μέλλοντος οἷον καὶ τὸ κατακλιεῖς παρ᾽ Εὐπόλιδι κ.τ.λ.) ; on the
other hand, especially by the further inflection of χεῶ: χεεῖς,
χεεῖ, χεεῖτε, χεοῦσιν, — forms which it so happens, indeed,
cannot be brought forward from the N. T., but are very frequent
in the Sept., as Ex. iv. 9 ; xxx. 19 ; Lev. iv. 12 ; Num. xix. 17 ;

Deut. xii. 16; 2 Kings xxiv. 4, etc. Ἐκχεῖται in Matt. ix. 17 is Pres.; probably also in Mark ii. 22 [yet dropped here by Tdf. Treg.].

The Aor. Pass. ἐχέθην, so common in later writers (Lob. Parerg. p. 732), has not yet been found either in the O. T. or the New, but always ἐχύθην, χυθήσομαι, as in the Perf. κέχυται. On account of this last form we often find χύω given 61 in the lexicons as a form of the Present; but it never occurs, at least in the N. T., but instead (χύνω) συνέχυνεν Acts ix. 22, or, after the Aeolic mode of writing sometimes, χύννω, (on this form used in codd. Vat. and Sin. see Tdf. N. T. Vat. pref. p. xxx Note [1]; [N. T. ed. 7, Prol. p. xlviii]) ἐκχυννόμενος Matt. xxiii. 35; xxvi. 28 and the parallel passages, συγχύννεται Acts xxi. 31 Lchm. [Tdf. Treg.]; xxii. 20. Cf. κτέννω under κτείνω, p. 61.

ψύχω. 2d Fut. Pass. ψυγήσομαι, Matt. xxiv. 12.

ὠθέω in the historic tenses loses again the syllabic augment, ἐξῶσεν, ἀπώσατο Acts vii. 27, 39, 45; Rom. xi. 1, 2, and so also in the Sept. ἀπώσθην Ps. lxxxvii. (lxxxviii.) 6, ἀπῶσμαι Jonah ii. 5 etc. This occurs sometimes also in earlier writers, see Poppo on Thuc. 2, 84.

ὠνέομαι does the same: ὠνήσατο Acts vii. 16.

ADVERBS.

B. § 115, N. 3; H. § 225 sq.; C. § 380 sq.; D. § 260 sq.; J. § 324.

Lachmann writes all adverbs, if they arose from the Dative of even an obsolete noun, — as λάθρα Matt. i. 19, εἰκῆ Col. ii. 18, πάντη Acts xxiv. 3, κρυφῆ Eph. v. 12, — again with the ι subscript, [so Treg. in the case of πάντη]; cf. B. § 116, Note 8 p. 272; C. § 109. In the mss. both modes were used. See Bast. ad Greg. Cor. p. 719, and Cobet, N. T. pref. p. 12, [Tdf. ed. 7, Prol. p. lxii].

B. § 115,5; H. § 228; C. § 263; D. § 282; J. § 141.

Adverbs in ως derived from the usual forms of comparison, accordingly in τέρως (τάτως) άτως (which, moreover, in earlier authors also are not uncommon, see the list in Matthiä's Greek Gram. § 262), occur also in the N. T. Thus always περισσοτέρως in Paul (Gal. i. 14 etc.), also in Heb. ii. 1, σπουδαιοτέρως Phil. ii. 28, the phrase ἐσχάτως ἔχειν Mark v. 23. Examples of the common adverbial form of the comparative in τερον are, περισσότερον Heb. vi. 17 ; vii. 15 ; Mark vii. 36, ἐκτενέστερον Luke xxii. 44, κι ιιψότερον John iv. 52, πορρώτεροι (-τέρω Rec. [Tdf.]) Luke xxiv. 28, ἀκριβέστερον Acts xxiv. 22, ἀνώτερον Heb. x. 8, etc. ; (but the present reading in Acts xxiv. 10 is εὐθύμως instead of εὐθυμότερον, and διπλότερον in Matt. xxiii. 15 is an adjective ; cf. p. 27).

The other form of comparison in ων, ιστος always forms its adverbs in the usual way : ἧττον, ἔλαττον, κάλλιον, βέλτιον, ἆσσον, τάχιον (see p. 27), τάχιστα, etc.

B. § 115, N. 7.

Instead of ἰδού ecce the N. T. writers, especially John, frequently use ἴδε ; both side by side in Mark xiii. 21 Lchm. Cf. also § 129 a. 2 p. 139. Examples of ἴδε with the Plural Matt. xxvi. 65 ; of ἄγε as an Interjection Jas. iv. 13 ; v. 1. Cf. with ἴδε attended by the Plur. the similar ἄφες ἴδωμεν (Matt. xxvii. 49), on which see § 139, 4 p. 139. The ordinary distinction between δεῦρο and δεῦτε, according to which the latter is used in addressing more than one (yet cf. Bttm. Lexil. II. No. 101), is observed in the N. T. ; see Wahl.

PARTICLES OF PLACE.
B. § 116; H. §§ 203. 879; C. §§ 192. 704; D. § 262; J. § 339.

The local ending -θεν has sometimes lost its origina. .ference to the question *whence*. Thus ἔσωθεν, ἔξωθεν, hardly u...or any longer from the adverbs ἔσω, ἔξω ; e.g. Matt. vii. 15 ; Rev. iv. 8 ; v. 1 ; and with the Article, τὸ ἔσωθεν ὑμῶν Luke xi. 39, 40 (cf. 2 Cor. iv. 16), κυκλόθεν *in circuitu* Rev. iv. 8. This, as is well known, often occurred in the earlier language and the poets with the termination -θεν, -θε ; as, ὄπισθεν, ἄνευθε, ἔμπροσθεν, προπάροιθε, etc. From the fact that the suffix -θεν came to take the place thus of a mere adverbial ending we can explain a pleonastic combination which is frequent in the N.T., viz. that to such an adverb, when the reference to the question *whence* is manifest, the prepositions ἀπό and ἐκ are still prefixed ; e.g. ἀπὸ μακρόθεν, ἀπ᾽ ἄνωθεν, ἐκ παιδιόθεν Matt. xxvi. 58 ; xxvii. 51 ; Mark ix. 21, etc., — combinations, however, which came into use very early, especially with poets (ἀπ᾽ οὐρανόθεν Hom.).

A strict observance of grammatica᾽ accuracy in the employment of the local particles is not to ᾽e expected of the N. T writers. A portion of these irregularities may be removed, to be sure, in some syntactical way, as e.g. the expression ἄξων τοὺς ἐκεῖσε ὄντας (Acts xxii. 5) by the attractive power of ἄξων (B. § 151, I. 8); but in general it does not accord with the language of the N. T. to explain all the passages of the sort in such artificial ways. On the contrary, the assumption of a certain inaccuracy in the employment of such particles seems to be the more admissible, as even the earlier prose writers by no means always adhered rigorously to the rule. And in particular, particles of rest as ἐκεῖ, ποῦ, οὗ, ὅπου, ἐνθάδε are constantly connected with verbs of motion in answer to the question *whither*, because the particles ποῖ, ὅποι, etc. seem to have passed wholly out of use, (a fact which explains the frequent corruption of these particles in the texts of Attic writers, and the instructions of Phrynichus ed. Lob. p. 43); as, ποῦ, ὅπου ὑπάγει, ἐκεῖ ἀπῆλθεν, ἐλθὲ ἐνθάδε,(with which the usage of earlier authors as given in B. § 116, 3 Note † and 7 Note may be compared). It is likewise undeniable that ὧδε, originally a particle having reference to manner, has in the N. T. already assumed completely a local signification : and that, too, not merely of rest, *here*, but, like all those previously mentioned, of direction also, *hither*,—a usage of which the beginnings can be traced very early (see B. § 149, 1 p. 429). It is indeed quite proper to be extremely abstemious in employing this method of explaining classic authors, but to insist on observing 63 the same restraint in reference to all passages of the N. T. would be to increase the difficulties of interpretation unnecessarily, and without any considerable gain either philological or logical. Examples of this local use of ὧδε (expressly censured by the old grammarians) occur, especially in the gospels, very frequently, as e.g. in Matt. xvi. 28 ; xvii. 4 ; viii. 29 ; xxii. 12 ; xiv. 8, 18, etc. ; and often in Hermas the expressions ὧδε κακεῖ, ὧδε κακεῖσε are met with (Simil. 6. 1 ; Mand. 5. 2, etc.).

Finally, compare with the general tenor of these remarks the N. T. use of the two prepositions which correspond most naturally to the two ideas of rest and motion (whither), viz. ἐν and εἰς, as given in the Syntax § 147, pp. 328, 332 sq.

CHANGES OF FORM IN PARTICLES. ANASTROPHE.

B. § 117, 2.

Of the three forms ἐάν, ἤν, ἄν, the first is used almost ex-clusively ; — ἄν is very rare indeed, or doubtful, John xiii. 20 ; xvi. 23 ; xx. 23 Tdf. [Treg.], ἤν not found at all.

Although only the un-Attic form of the adverb ἔσω (for εἴσω) is in use, yet the preposition is written only εἰς never ἐς. Instead of χθές modern editors have everywhere substituted the (Hellenistic) form ἐχθές, John iv. 52 etc.

Respecting ἕνεκεν before consonants see p. 10.

B. § 117, N. 1; H. § 872; C. § 619; J. § 423.

Instead of ἄν the form ἐάν is frequently found. Yet this interchange is not exactly arbitrary, since on comparing the passages it will be found that it occurs only in relative clauses with the Subjunctive : in clauses, therefore, of a general nature which (according to B. § 139, 3) include within themselves the supposition expressed by ἐάν, and allow themselves without violence to be transformed into such conditional clauses. This ἐάν, however, continually alternates with ἄν, and in printed editions there is no agreement in this particular. Since ex-amples of this manner of writing the word abound in all parts of the N. T., it may suffice here to illustrate what has been said by one or two cases : as Matt. xvi. 19 ὃ ἂν δήσῃς ἐπὶ τῆς γῆς, ἔσται δεδεμένον ἐν τοῖς οὐρανοῖς, καὶ ὃ ἐὰν λύσῃς ἐπὶ τῆς γῆς, ἔσται λελυμένον ἐν τ. ο. ; likewise vs. 25 ; John xv. 7 ὃ ἂν θέλητε Lchm. ἐὰν Tdf. [Treg.], etc. In the MSS. of other Greek writers, too, this ἐάν is found only in similar clauses, see Jacobs ad Achil. Tat. p. 130, 7 ; and the frequent occur-64 rence of this interchange warrants us in inferring the existence of this always erroneous (yet not altogether unfounded) mode of writing the word, at least in later authors.

B. § 117, 3, 2); H. § 615; C. § 785; J. § 63, Obs. 3.

This second case of anastrophe (i.e. when the primitive dissyllabic prepositions stand alone instead of a compound of εἶναι) also occurs in the N. T. in the use of ἔνι for ἔνεστι : 1 Cor. vi. 5 ; Gal. iii. 28 ; Col. iii. 11 ; Jas. i. 17.

The words οὐαί, οὐά, ἔα occur in the N. T. as Interjections.

FORMATION OF WORDS.

B. § 119; H. § 452 sqq.; C. § 359 sqq.; D. § 354 sqq.; J. § 329 sqq.

B. § 119, m. 19. Since in verbal Substantives in μα the
long vowel belongs to the earlier writers, the short vowel to
the later (cf. Cobet's N. T. pref. p. 50), we ought in the N. T.
to write uniformly κρίμα (not κρῖμα) ; so cod. Vat., though
very often writing κρεινω, constantly writes κριμα. The form
αἰτιώματα (Sin. also) for αἰτιάματα, Acts xxv. 7, is erroneously
formed, but unquestionable.

On φάγος and φαγός see Fritzsche on Mark, p. 790. On πειθός
in 1 Cor. ii. 4 (very likely a corrupted passage) cf. πηγός in
Homer. Yet probably ἐν πειθοῖ should be read, [ἐν πειθοῖς
σοφίας λόγοις is adhered to by Lchm. Tdf. Treg.] ; see the
interpreters.

B. § 119, m. 32. As respects substantives compounded with
ἀρχός ruler, or derived from ἄρχω, the ending ης, according
to the 1st Declension, is the most common, and passed over also
into the Latin language. Thus πατριάρχης, τετράρχης (pa-
triarcha, tetrarcha), ἐθνάρχης, πολιτάρχης, ἀσιάρχης, and many
others besides in the Sept. ; see the list in Winer 61 (60) and
the lexicons. Only in the case of χιλίαρχος is the form in ος the
exclusive form ; and ἑκατοντάρχης alternates with ἑκατόνταρχος,
even in close proximity, as in Acts xxii. 25, 26 ; Matt. viii. 8, 13.
Doubtful is στρατοπεδάρχης, Acts xxviii. 16, since it is wanting
in codd. [א] A B.

Examples from the N. T. (besides ἱερωσύνη given in B. §
119 m. 38) of words in σύνη with ω preceding are : ἀγαθωσύνη, ἁγιωσύνη, μεγαλωσύνη, all with a short vowel preceding
the antepenult. Instead of βασίλεια the N. T. has everywhere
the later form (see Sturz, Dial. Alex. p. 151) βασίλισσα.

B. § 119, m. 83. The adverbial ending ί occurs only
in the word πανοικί Acts xvi. 34, — for so the word should be
written, although several MSS. [Sin. also] give πανοικεί. See
Theodos. Gramm. p. 74 ed. Gttl., and among the moderns
especially Ellendt, Lex. Soph. under ἀνατεί and ἀνοιμωκτί.
According to his view, adverbs derived from words of the 2d
Declension have the ending ί, at least by preference.

To the new formations of later Greek belong also the two
adjectives ἐπιούσιος and περιούσιος, respecting whose doubtful

10

derivation and meaning ((Origen de Orat. 16 : ἐπιούσιος ἔοικε πεπλάσθαι ὑπὸ τῶν εὐαγγελιστῶν) see the lexicons.

B. § 121, 8; C. § 386 c.; D. p. 335; J. § 345, 2.

Among the words which in composition change the initial ε into η may be reckoned the new word προςήλυτος, so frequent in the later language, of which the Prep. πρός and the stem of ἦλθον, ἤλυθον Fut. ἐλεύσομαι, manifestly form the basis; hence the abstract προςήλυσις (Just. Mart.) for προςέλευσις (John Chrys.). See the lexicons, and compare the words ἔπηλυς, ἐπήλυτος, ἐπήλυσις, etc.

The practice of separating compound Names of Cities extends, as is evident from inscriptions, down to the latest times. Hence in Acts xvi. 11 we should read, with all the [most] ancient MSS., Νέαν πόλιν; and so, consistently, in Col. iv. 13 ἐν Ἱερᾷ πόλει (for Ἱεραπόλει). Thus it was the uniform practice to say Μεγάλη πόλις, Κωνσταντίνου πόλις, Ἀδριανοῦ πόλις, but in derivatives Μεγαλοπολίτης, Νεαπολίτης, Κωνσταντινοπολίτης; cf. on this Herodian de Adverb. p. 587; Cobet's N. T. pref. p. 12.

INTRODUCTION.

1. The language of the N. T. departs from the ordinary language in all that relates to the structure of clauses and style of expression far more than in the forms of words; — and that not merely from the Attic, but also from the later common Greek. The causes of this are: First, the want of classic-Greek training and erudition (Acts xxii. 3; 2 Cor. xi. 22; Gal. i. 14, etc.) which may be fairly assumed in the case of most of the N. T. writers; Secondly, their dependence upon the language of the O. T. (in particular that of the Septuagint), as well as upon Jewish modes of thought in general (the so-called Hebraisms pertain, strictly speaking, all of them to the syntactical part of grammar); Thirdly, their new Christian ideas. As was remarked, however, on p. 1 sq. respecting the Forms, so again in this particular the difference between the several writings composing the N. T. is not inconsiderable; and it is the Book of Acts again which distinguishes itself creditably from all the rest by its Greek mode of expression and combination of clauses. Among the Epistolary writings the Epistle to the Hebrews has most of the Greek complexion.[1] And the Apocalypse is farthest removed from the Greek diction, in consequence of its peculiar and free style of composition (of which we have already given an example p. 50), which often conflicts with all the laws of Greek syntax.

2. Strictly speaking, in a special Grammar only those phenomena should find place which are peculiar to the department treated of, — in the present case, to the N. T. And this principle has been in general adhered to in this Grammar. In this 66

---

[1] Cf. Origen in Euseb. H. E. 6, 25: ὅτι ἐστὶν ἡ ἐπιστολὴ συνθέσει τῆς λέξεως ἑλληνικωτέρα (i. e. than the Epp. of Paul) πᾶς ὁ ἐπιστάμενος κρίνειν φράσεων διαφορὰς ὁμολογήσαι ἄν.

instance, however, as in all things where practical requirements also come into consideration, rigid consistency in carrying out a principle would be injurious to the whole. Frequently it has been desirable to bring into prominence the agreement between the N. T. language and ordinary Greek usage, particularly in those cases where such agreement appears rather as exceptional, and a departure from the usage of the N. T. elsewhere. Moreover, the usage of the classic authors themselves varies so much, according to time, place, subject, etc., that it could not fail often to seem appropriate to indicate the coincidence between the N. T. usage and this or that department of classic Greek. And finally, it has been necessary occasionally, where the more thorough treatment of the peculiarities of a department relatively restricted required a more extended presentation of a topic, to give a more detailed delineation even of the ordinary usage than could be given in a general Greek Grammar for the use of schools. This has been particularly the case where the usage of later writers or of the Seventy, to which of course little or no regard is wont to be paid in school Grammars, has had unmistakable influence upon the language of the N. T.

SUBSTANTIVES AND ADJECTIVES.
The Substantive.
B. § 123.

When a substantive, whether concrete or abstract, in any Case, refers to another substantive (subject) in the Plural in such a way that it pertains equally to every individual of the plurality, accurate usage requires that it also should stand in the Plural.

67   The ancient languages, as is well known, are more consistent in this respect than, for instance, the German, which says unhesitatingly, and perhaps more frequently than not, *sie zogen sich das Kleid an, schlugen das Gesicht nieder, fielen auf das Knie*, etc. etc. But irregularities occur also in ancient authors, even (though seldom) in good Greek prose ;[1] hence no special N. T. usage can be established on such passages as Acts xviii. 6 τὸ αἷμα ὑμῶν ἐπὶ τὴν κεφαλὴν ὑμῶν, Luke xxiv. 4 ἐπέστησαν ἐν ἐσθῆτι ἀστραπτούσῃ, vs. 5 Lchm. (κλίνουσαι) τὸ πρόσωπον εἰς τὴν γῆν, 1 Thess. iii. 10 ὑμῶν τὸ πρόσωπον,

---

[1] The subject requires, according to Bhdy. Synt. p. 60 note [3], a more careful examination than has yet been given it. See the works there referred to.

1 Cor. vi. 19 τὸ σῶμα ὑμῶν, Rev. vi. 11 ἐδόθη αὐτοῖς στολὴ λευκή, xi. 8, 9 τὸ πτῶμα αὐτῶν.   On the other hand, the Plural occurs Acts i. 10 (ἐν ἐσθήσεσι λευκαῖς), Rev. xi. 9 (τὰ πτώματα αὐτῶν); and in several of the above passages important authorities (followed sometimes by Tdf. [Treg.]) have the Plural.   This fluctuation in the MSS. proves the currency of both modes of expression; and again, the frequent correction of the Sing. into the Plur. shows that offence was taken at the Sing. as the inferior form.

Respecting the Hebraistic circumlocutions διὰ χειρὸς, ἐκ χειρὸς, διὰ στόματος αὐτῶν, see § 133, 20 p. 182.

Most of the passages adduced by Winer 175 (165) where, on the   **1**
contrary, the Plural seems to stand instead of the Singular, rest upon no fixed usage, and accordingly the explanation of the Plural must be left to the interpretation of the individual passages; e.g. Matt. ii. 20 (οἱ ζητοῦντες), xxi. 7 (ἐπάνω αὐτῶν), xxvii. 44 (οἱ λῃσταί), 1 Cor. xvi. 3 (δι᾽ ἐπιστολῶν), Heb. ix. 23 (κρείττοσιν θυσίαις), etc.   The same holds true of passages in which the interpreters recognize a Hebraistic *pluralis excellentiae* (John ix. 3 τὰ ἔργα τοῦ θεοῦ, Heb. vii. 6 τὰς ἐπαγγελίας, etc.); in these the Plural, without any such assumption, has a natural foundation in the ordinary usage.   On the other hand, the following belong to an idiomatic usage:

1) Those substantives which are Plural only.   These, so far as they are peculiar to the N. T., have already found their place above on p. 23 sq.

2) The custom, belonging to ancient languages in general, of expressing abstract ideas by the Plural, inasmuch as in this way not the idea of the abstract, as such, is to be indicated, but rather its external manifestation, — its applicability to a certain plurality of persons or objects.   Thus in the N. T. occur frequently οἰκτιρμοί, προσωπολημψίαι, ὑποκρίσεις, ἐριθεῖαι, θυμοί, φθόνοι, μοιχεῖαι, κλοπαί, πλεονεξίαι, πονηρίαι, καταλαλιαί, πρωτοκλισίαι, etc.   In enumerations, the Plural and the Singular are wont to be interchanged; as, Mark vii. 22; Gal. v. 19 sq.

APPOSITION.   **68**

B. § 123, 2; H. § 500; C. § 393; D. § 407; J. § 467.

Appositive limitations which are separated from the sub-   **3**
stantive to which they belong by a relative clause referring to the same substantive, may also take the Case of the Relative, being attracted by it as the nearer word.

The clearest instance is Phil. iii. 18 πολλοὶ περιπατοῦσιν, οὓς πολλάκις

ἔλεγον ὑμῖν ..., τοὺς ἐχθροὺς τοῦ σταυροῦ τοῦ Χρ.　1 John ii. 25 ἡ
ἐπαγγελία, ἣν αὐτὸς ἐπηγγείλατο ἡμῖν, τὴν ζωὴν τὴν αἰώνιον, Philem. 10
τοῦ τέκνου, ὃν ἐγέννησα ἐν τοῖς δεσμοῖς, Ὀνήσιμον, τόν ποτε etc.　Cf.
Rev. xvii. 8 (ὧν ... βλεπόντων) ; and respecting 2 Cor. x. 13 (οὗ ...
μέτρου) see § 143, 9 p. 286.

4　The assertion that appositive limitations are also expressed by the
Genitive, rests upon an erroneous conception of such combinations
as πόλις τῆς Σαμαρείας Acts viii. 5, πόλεις Σοδόμων καὶ Γομόρρας 2 Pet.
ii. 6 (Lat. urbs Romæ, fluvius Euphratis), and it is only out of con-
descension to modern usage that an appositive relation is here assumed.
Just as erroneous is it to bring under apposition such phrases as τὸν
ἀρραβῶνα τοῦ πνεύματος, τὴν ἀπαρχὴν τοῦ πνεύματος, σημεῖον περιτομῆς,
etc., since such combinations are either to be taken literally, or at
most as circumlocutions of simple abstract ideas.　Such periphrases
are quite current in the ancient languages generally, and in the N. T.
preëminently with the apostle Paul.

5　In certain portions of the N. T., however, a noticeable departure from the grammatical usage of other writers is perceptible.　That is to say, appositives whether expressed by a
substantive, an adjective, or a participle, since they may be
regarded as an abbreviation of a relative clause (cf. § 125, 3
p. 92 sq.), frequently appear, not in the oblique case demanded
by the context, but in the Nominative, — still lingering, as
it were, after the rejection of the relative construction, in the
extraneous case, viz. the Nominative.

The most conspicuous examples of this incorrect grammatical usage
are found in the Apocalypse: i. 5 ἀπὸ Ἰησοῦ Χρ. ὁ μάρτυς ὁ πιστός, vii. 4
τὸν ἀριθμὸν τῶν ἐσφραγισμένων, ἑκατὸν ... χιλιάδες ἐσφραγισμένοι, xx. 2
ἐκράτησεν τὸν δράκοντα, ὁ ὄφις ὁ ἀρχαῖος ; particularly when the Partic.
with the Art. is used : ii. 20 τὴν Ἰεζάβελ, ἡ λέγουσα ἑαυτὴν προφῆτιν,
iii. 12 τῆς καινῆς Ἱερουσαλήμ, ἡ καταβαίνουσα, xiv. 12 τῶν ἁγίων, οἱ
τηροῦντες, viii. 9 τὸ τρίτον τῶν κτισμάτων, τὰ ἔχοντα ψυχάς, ix. 14 τῷ
ἕκτῳ ἀγγέλῳ, ὁ ἔχων τὴν σάλπιγγα ; and even many limiting participles
69　without the article [1] may be conveniently viewed as instances of
this construction, as xiv. 14 (εἶδον) ὅμοιον υἱῷ ἀνθρώπου, ἔχων etc.
whether we refer ἔχων to ὅμοιον (τινά) or to υἱῷ, cf. xix. 12 ; and with
especial harshness in vii. 9 Lchm. εἶδον ὄχλον πολὺν (Tdf. [so Treg.] καὶ
ἰδοὺ ὄχλος πολύς) ... ἑστῶτες ... περιβεβλημένους.　(See respecting

---

[1] That we are justified in assuming that the writer often, instead of the Participle,
had in mind a relative clause in very form, may be seen from such passages as
vi. 1 ἤκουσα ἑνὸς ... λέγοντος ὡς φωνὴ βροντῆς (Rec. by correction φωνῆς).　Cf.
on the other hand, Rom. i. 4 etc.

the very frequent loose annexation of participial clauses in the Nom.
and their use instead of other cases § 129 a. 6 p. 141, § 144, 3–7 and
especially 13 p. 298, and cf. the examples given in § 151, 12 p. 386
of loose connection of clauses in other constructions also). In the
other writers this use appears on the whole less frequently, although
there is reason for supposing that the number of passages of the sort
has been greatly diminished by later corrections (the Rec. in fact had
displaced it almost everywhere). A plain instance occurs in Mark xii.
39 sq. The recent editors, indeed, [Lchm. Tdf. Treg.] place one of
the larger punctuation marks before οἱ κατεσθίοντες [κατέσθοντες Treg.]
and let the Partic. be resumed by the following οὗτοι, according to
§ 144, 21 p. 306, so that vs. 40 forms an independent clause by itself.
But the asyndeton before οἱ κατεσθίοντες is not satisfactory, and still
less the assumption that the forcible close (οὗτοι λήμψονται etc.) is to
be referred merely to vs. 40, and not at the same time to vss. 38, 39.
On the contrary, by referring οἱ κατεσθίοντες immediately to τῶν γραμματέων not only does the passage gain in natural flow, but the construction assumed receives external confirmation also on comparing it
with the parallel passage in Luke (xx. 47 Tdf. [Treg.] οἳ κατεσθίουσιν).
An instance without the article is Mark vii. 19 (πᾶν εἰς τὸν ἀφεδρῶνα
ἐκπορεύεται, καθαρίζων πάντα τὰ βρώματα (Rec. καθαρίζον). Respecting
Luke xxiv. 47 Tdf. [Treg.] (ἀρξάμενοι) see § 150, 7 p. 374.

In Phil. iii. 19, therefore, it is not necessary to refer back the
loosely appended clause οἱ τὰ ἐπίγεια φρονοῦντες to the remote leading
subject of the sentence, and in Luke xx. 27 (τινὲς τῶν Σαδδ., οἱ ἀντιλέγοντες) the description οἱ ἀντιλέγοντες applies not merely to the part
(τινές), but to the whole. But Jas. iii. 8 (τὴν δὲ γλῶσσαν ... · ἀκατά-
στατον κακόν, μεστὴ ἰοῦ θανατηφόρου), 2 Cor. xi. 28 (ἡ ἐπίστασίς μοι ἡ
καθ᾽ ἡμέραν etc.) and similar passages are rather to be taken as independent clauses left incomplete and approximating to exclamation.[1]

---

[1] An extraordinary example of grammatical inaccuracy is given by the MSS.
[א also] in Acts vi. 5 Lchm. ἐξελέξαντο Στέφανον, ἄνδρα π λ ή ρ η ς πίστεως. In
such a writer as Luke (particularly in the Acts) such a combination may be held
to be impossible (ἀνὴρ πλήρης might have been tolerated) ; hence, in spite of the
emphatic testimony, Tdf. [so Treg.] has refused to accept the reading in this form.
Another example is Acts x. 37 οἴδατε τὸ γενόμενον ῥῆμα καθ᾽ ὅλης τῆς Ἰουδαίας,
ἀ ρ ξ ά μ ε ν ο ς ἀπὸ τῆς Γαλιλαίας μετὰ τὸ βάπτισμα (by the by : read κήρυγμα according to cod. Vat., Roman ed. 1868), sustained almost unanimously by the entire
collection of uncials (including Vat. and Sin.), and, what is strangest of all, not
called in question even by the correctors of the MSS., as may be gathered from the
collation of a yet larger number of MSS. The change into ἀρξάμενον is easily made,
and forces itself upon every one. But since not even the ancient correctors ven-
tured to make it, we are the less warranted in doing so, but must put up with the
grammatical anomaly, and assume that the formula ἀρξάμενος ἀπό to the mind of
the writer had become petrified almost into an indeclinable adverbial adjunct

Respecting the Accusative in appositional specifications see § 131, 13 p. 153.

70 REMARK. The question whether adjuncts in the correct gram-
6   matical case (as 1 Pet. iii. 21; Rom. viii. 23, etc.) are to be taken as appositive or not, pertains wholly to the exegesis of the several passages.

AGREEMENT OF ADJECTIVAL ADJUNCTS WITH THEIR SUBSTANTIVE.
CONSTRUCTIO AD SYNESIN.

B. § 123, 3 and N. 3; H. § 511, 23; C. §§ 492-98; D. p. 362; J. § 378.

7   The offences against grammatical accuracy in respect to Gender and Number in which the language of the N. T. allows itself, are far less frequent than as respects Case, (see the preceding chapter). Most instances of the sort, also, may be comprised under the grammatical categories of Attraction and Constructio ad Synesin; and accordingly reference may be made to the sections relative to these topics: §§ 127, 7 p. 105, 129, 8 p. 129, and 143, 4 p. 281. Hence only those passages will be spoken of here in which similar irregularities occur with attributive (i.e. adjectival) adjuncts of the substantive.

The strongest cases are furnished, again, by the Apocalypse. Yet they are hardly founded in the author's ignorance of the laws of the language, as there is reason enough for supposing that such roughnesses of expression were positively designed by him; cf. deWette on Rev. i. 4; Winer 534 sq. (497 sq.) : for instance, xii. 5 Lchm. [Tdf. Treg.] ἔτεκεν υἱὸν ἄρσεν (Tdf. [ed. 2] ἄρρενα), ὃς μέλλει etc., since the idea of τέκνον (which word actually follows just afterwards) is suggested by the verb ἔτεκεν (Germ. *sie gebar einen Sohn, ein Männliches, der* etc.). On the altogether analogous combinations θηρίον ὃς, ὀνόματα οἳ, and the like, see § 143, 4 p. 282. Still more surprising is the reading of Lchm. in xvii. 3 καθημένην ἐπὶ θηρίον κόκκινον, γέμοντα ὀνόματα βλασφημίας ἔχον κεφαλὰς, — a harshness which [Treg., not now Tdf.] avoids by separating the word into γέμον τὰ. But harsh expressions of this sort are quite common in the Rev., as witness immediately afterwards the

Still more surprising, and grammatically viewed almost inexplicable, are two ex-amples from the Apocalypse, yet whose genuineness we are not warranted on this account in questioning : xix. 20 Lchm. ἐβλήθησαν εἰς τὴν λίμνην τοῦ πυρὸς, τῆς καιομένης ἐν θείῳ (Tdf. [eds. 2, 7] τὴν κ.) and i. 15 Lchm. οἱ πόδες αὐτοῦ ὅμοιοι χαλκολιβάνῳ, ὡς ἐν καμίνῳ πεπυρωμένης (Tdf. [eds. 2, 7] -νοι). From the last passage it at least follows that the word is χαλκολίβανος, not -νον (it is wanting in the Sept.), and is of the Feminine gender, as the simple λίβανος is so often (Eurip. Nicand., see Steph. sub voce), and accordingly has pretty nearly the sense of *brazen incense* (amber ?). The gloss in Suidas under χαλοκλίβανον is not genuine; see Bernhardy in loc. [In i. 15 Tdf. ed. 8 reads -νῳ. Treg. in both agrees with Lchm.]

simultaneous dependence of the Acc. and the Gen. upon γέμον, see
§ 132, 12 p. 164. The language in the following passages is in complete antagonism to a sense of grammatical propriety, but sustained
by the MSS. [Sin. also]: xi. 4 οὗτοί εἰσιν ... αἱ δύο λυχνίαι αἱ ἐνώπιον
κυρίου τῆς γῆς ἑστῶτες, where no author would have written any
thing else than ἑστῶσαι (the correction of Rec.), and nevertheless
ἑστῶτες must be referred to the οὗτοι at the beginning, xxi. 9 Lchm.
εἷς ἐκ τῶν ἀγγέλων τῶν ἐχόντων τὰς ἑπτὰ φιάλας, τῶν γεμόντων (Tdf. 71
[eds. 2,7] γεμούσας) τῶν πληγῶν etc., where γεμόντων as respects sense
can have reference only to φιάλας, and yet has been attracted by τῶν
ἀγγέλων, so that the ἄγγελοι seem to be, as it were, identified with the
φιάλαι, xiv. 19 εἰς τὴν ληνὸν τοῦ θυμοῦ τοῦ θεοῦ τὸν μέγαν (Rec. [cod.
Sin. also] τὴν μεγάλην), which cannot be grammatically defended by
the fact that ληνός has two genders; see the lexicons, and cf. xiv. 20;
Deut. xvi. 13; Gen. xxx. 38, 41, etc. To the examples already given
may be added v. 12 Tdf. and xxi. 14 (Tdf. [Treg.; א* om., אᵉ εχον.]).

In the other writings of the N. T. such anomalies are seldom met
with, even in the MSS.; for such a combination as λιμὸν μέγαν ... ἥτις
in Acts (xi. 28), the reading given by several MSS., is very improbable;
see above p. 12. On the other hand, in Phil. ii. 1 εἴ τις σπλάγχνα καὶ
οἰκτιρμοὶ Lchm. [Tdf. eds. 7, 8, Treg.] is not only the reading almost
unanimously [Sin. also] attested, but, however offensive the combination may sound even to our ears, is to be preferred with Grsb. Lchm.
[Tdf. 7, 8, Treg.] to the manifest corrections τινα or τι, which also are
by no means satisfactory. We have nothing left us here except to connect τις, by virtue of the constr. ad syn. and in view of what precedes,
immediately with the abstract idea (compassion) which follows, although
such a connection is to be justified only by the license of epistolary
style. In Mark xiii. 14 Tdf. (even before the discovery of Sin.) had
adopted the reading ὅταν ἴδητε τὸ βδέλυγμα τῆς ἐρημώσεως ἑστηκότα [so
Treg.], the writer having had in mind a dimly conceived Masc. subst.,
either a heathen statue or a Roman army or something else of the
sort; cf. Fritzsche on Matt. xxiv. 15.

Acts iii. 11 πᾶς ὁ λαὸς ... ἔκθαμβοι is quite according to usage; the
passage falls under the head of Participles constructed ad synesin,
respecting which see especially § 129, 8 p. 129 sq.

OMISSION OF THE SUBSTANTIVE WITH ADJECTIVES.
B. § 123, 5 and N. 5; H. § 509; C. § 506; D. § 399; J. § 436.

Examples of the omission of easily supplied substantives 8
with adjectives are not uncommon in the N. T. Thus by the
omission of ἡμέρα we have τῇ ἐχομένῃ, ἐπιούσῃ, τρίτῃ, ἡ
ἑβδόμη (Heb. iv. 4), cf. the similar instances § 125, 10 p. 95;

11

of ὁδός Luke xix. 4 ἐκείνης ἤμελλεν διέρχεσθαι, v. 19 ποίας εἰςενέγκωσιν αὐτόν ; of χείρ : ἡ ἀριστερά, ἡ δεξιά, δεξιὰς διδόναι etc. ; of γῆ : ἡ ξηρά, ἡ περίχωρος, etc. ; of πύλη John v. 2 ἐπὶ τῇ προβατικῇ ; of ἄνδρες (more specifically διάκονοι) Acts xxi. 8 ἐκ τῶν ἑπτά (cf. vi. 5) ; of ἄγαλμα Acts xix. 35 τὸ διοπετές (cf. Eurip. I. T. 950 ; Herodian 1. 11).

What omitted word is to be supplied is not always so evident as in the above examples, and accordingly it has been proposed to regard the force of the subst. as inhering in the adjective, and (as in § 128, 1 p. 122) not to supply any definite word. With M a s c u l i n e s and F e m i n i n e s, however, this will hardly do, and accordingly we must, as in all languages, supply a more or less definite idea, although it may be but dimly conceived. Thus the idea of *Time*, conformably to ὁ χρόνος or ἡ ὥρα, ἡμέρα ; hence both ἀφ' ἧς 2 Pet. iii. 4 ; Luke vii. 45 etc. (cf. Col. i. 6, 9), and ἀφ' οὗ, ἐξ οὗ, ἄχρις οὗ, etc., further ἐξ αὐτῆς or ἐξαυτῆς Acts x. 33 ; xi. 11 etc., ἔτι τετράμηνός ἐστιν John iv. 35 ; *Space, Locality,* as it were after ἡ χώρα, as ἐξ ἐναντίας Mark xv. 39, 72 ἐκ τῆς ὑπὸ τὸν οὐρανὸν εἰς τὴν ὑπ' οὐρανὸν λάμπει Luke xvii. 24, further ἐν δεξιᾷ, plur. ἐκ δεξιῶν, ἐξ εὐωνύμων, and the like ; *Breeze,* after ἡ αὔρα : Acts xxvii. 40 τῇ πνεούσῃ ; *Water,* agreeably to τὸ ὕδωρ : Matt. x. 42 ποτήριον ψυχροῦ, Jas. iii. 11 ἡ πηγή ... βρύει τὸ γλυκὺ καὶ τὸ πικρόν ; more specifically *Rain* : Jas. v. 7 (γεωργὸς μακροθυμῶν) ἕως λάβῃ πρώϊμον καὶ ὄψιμον ; *Raiment* : John xx. 12 δύο ἀγγέλους ἐν λευκοῖς sc. ἱματίοις (a word which by subsequent correction was added Matt. xi. 8 Rec.), Rev. xviii. 12, 16 περιβεβλημένη βύσσινον, πορφυροῦν, etc. ; *Opinion,* in accordance with ἡ γνώμη, in the phrase ἀπὸ μιᾶς Luke xiv. 18.

An example also of the omission of a substantive i m p l i e d i n t h e i d e a o f t h e v e r b (τοῦτον ὀλίγας ἔπαισε sc. πληγάς B. § 123, N. 5) occurs in Luke xii. 47 δαρήσεται πολλάς ... ὀλίγας (with the Passive according to the usage treated of in § 134, 6 p. 189) ; and similarly 2 Cor. xi. 24 τεσσεράκοντα παρὰ μίαν ἔλαβον.

Respecting adverbial expressions, like κατ' ἰδίαν, δημοσίᾳ, etc., see B. § 115, 4 p. 266.

REMARK. The opposite case (B. § 123, N. 6), viz. the a d d i t i o n of ἀνήρ to substantives, as though it were an adjective, occurs only with Luke (xxiv. 19 ἀνὴρ προφήτης, Acts iii. 14 ἄνδρα φονέα, etc.) ; in respectful addresses (ἄνδρες ἀδελφοὶ, Γαλιλαῖοι, etc.) only in the Acts.

ADJECTIVES USED INSTEAD OF (ENGLISH) ADVERBS.

B. § 123, 6 ; H. § 488 ; C. § 509 ; D. p. 458 sq. ; J. § 714.

9   This use is quite current with the N. T. writers, so that it is not worth while to give the separate instances, since they

agree in the main with the specifications given in the Grammars; as, ἑκὼν πράσσω, δευτεραῖοι ἤλθομεν, πύλη αὐτομάτη ἠνοίχθη, ἑστῶτας ἀργούς (Matt. xx. 3), etc. In like manner these authors discriminate accurately between πρῶτος and πρῶτον, e.g. John xx. 4; i. 42 Tdf.; xviii. 13, etc.; μόνος and μόνον, e.g. Rom. xvi. 4; Matt. v. 47, etc.

COMPARATIVE AND SUPERLATIVE.
B. § 123, 7; H. § 662; C. § 514; D. § 415; J. § 784.

When the idea or the object with which the comparison is made is apparent at once from the connection, the Comparative not infrequently stands alone, and so gets the look of a Positive, as Acts xvii. 21 τὶ καινότερον. Especially is this the case with the Comparative of adverbs, as τάχιον, κάλλιον, μᾶλλον, ἆσσον, περισσοτέρως, etc.; cf. p. 69 sq. Moreover, this usage is by no means peculiar to the N. T.; see the literature in Winer 242 sq. (227 sq.).

B. § 123, N. 8; H. § 665; C. § 510; D. p. 392; J. § 784, 2.

Examples of the (pleonastic) strengthening of the Comparative by μᾶλλον are Mark vii. 36 μᾶλλον περισσότερον ἐκήρυσσον; still stronger Phil. i. 23 πολλῷ μᾶλλον κρεῖσσον. The strengthening by means of πολύ, ἔτι, etc. needs no explanation.

Respecting the Comparative force of the Positive see § 149 under ἤ p. 360.

B. § 123, N. 9; H. § 664 sq.; C. § 553; D. p. 396; J. § 870, Obs. 4.

The intensifications of the Superlative (by πολύ, μάλιστα, etc., the particles ὡς, ᾖ, etc., the pron. οἷος, etc.) usual in Greek authors do not occur in the N. T. On the other hand, certain constructions are brought forward by the interpreters as (in part intensive) circumlocutions for the Superlative. That sometimes the Positive may in a sense take the place of a Superlative is apparent in Matt. xxii. 36 ποία ἐντολὴ μεγάλη ἐν τῷ νόμῳ; cf. vs. 38. To this may be added Matt. v. 19 (μέγας κληθήσεται), Luke x. 42 (τὴν ἀγαθὴν μερίδα ἐξελέξατο) and the Hebraistic (Gesen. Lehrgeb. p. 692 [Gr. § 117]) phrase, Luke i. (28) 42 εὐλογημένη σὺ ἐν γυναιξίν. But in all these passages our Positive is fully adequate as a translation (and has been used for the most part), so that a peculiar (Hebraistic) *usus loquendi* cannot be founded upon them. Such a peculiarity might sooner be found in the circumlocution for the Superlative formed according to Hebrew precedent (קֹדֶשׁ הַקֳּדָשִׁים, see Gesen. as above), if it had been perpetuated in any other expression than τὰ ἅγια ἁγίων, already touched upon

p. 24; for, substantive phrases, such as βασ. λεὺς βασιλέων, κύριος κυρίων, can hardly be included under this head, as Winer 246 (231) correctly remarks.

Concerning μικρὸν ὅσον ὅσον see § 150 p. 373.

INTERCHANGE OF COMPARATIVE AND SUPERLATIVE.

13   Luther in his translation of the Bible [so A. V.] has availed himself, in a number of passages, of the (German) Superlative instead of the Greek Comparative, (an example, however, which de Wette has not followed); and consequently the opinion has been pretty general, that such an interchange of the degrees of comparison is a characteristic of the N. T. language. That this is not the case modern commentators have shown abundantly, and careful consideration of the sense will teach every attentive reader for himself.

Since, however, it is not to be denied that the modern languages in the majority of these cases would have employed the Superlative or other modes of expression, we will here designate the passages in question; but for the extended exposition of them, in particular of 1 Cor. xiii. 13, reference must be made to the commentaries. Besides this instance, we have Matt. xviii. 1 and the parallel passages (Mark ix. 34; Luke ix. 46), Matt. xi. 11; Luke vii. 28; xxii. 24. We must not number among them the passages in which the nature of the Comparative is preserved by the addition πάντων, and at the most we are to assume a very common circumlocution for the Superlative; hence Luther [so A. V. generally] translates such passages also (but with greater reason) by the Superlative: Matt. xiii. 32; Mark iv. 32; 1 Cor. xv. 19. Similar is John x. 29.

14   Lastly, it is said that on the other hand the Superlative can stand for the Comparative. This opinion rests upon the connection —
74   occurring here and there in native Greek writers — of the Superlative with the Genitive (e.g. Hom. Od. λ, 482) or with ἤ; respecting which see Herm. ad Vig. p. 718 and ad Eur. Med. p. 343 (V. 67). In the N. T. only John's connection of πρῶτος with the Genitive can here come into account; this, however, receives its natural explanation by the (later) usage spoken of p. 32, according to which πρῶτος often stands for πρότερος (e.g. Matt. xxi. 28, 36, etc.). The passages are John i. 15, 30; i. 42 Tdf.; xv. 18 (Vulg. prior).

That the wish of certain interpreters to refer Luke ii. 2 also to this head is thoroughly contrary to philology, has of late been sufficiently demonstrated; see the commentaries of de Wette, Meyer, and especially Winer, R.W.B. under Quirinius, and Gram. 244 sq. (229).

THE ARTICLE.

B. § 124, 2; C. § 548 a.; D. p. 348; J. § 659; W. § 117 (111).

Instead of the indefinite article, εἷς without a partitive 1
Gen. following is not infrequently used, as elsewhere also in
later writers (Achil. Tat. 4, 22), — accordingly for τὶς. Thus,
for instance, but in connection with a participle, Matt. xix. 16
and the parallel passage εἷς προςελθὼν εἶπεν (cf. Mark xv. 36) ;
with a substantive, Matt. xxvi. 69 μία παιδίσκη, xxi. 19 συκῆν
μίαν, Mark xii. 42 μία χήρα, etc. Among the variants we
often find for εἷς the reading τὶς, and in the versions *unus* and
quidam.

With this may be compared the Hebrew use of אֶחָד (Sept. εἷς) in
isolated passages, as 1 Kings xx. (xxi.) 13 ; Dan. viii. 3, etc., but it is
unnecessary to assume that it served as the precedent for the N. T.
usage. It is incorrect to refer to this head those passages in which
the idea of unity, in contrast with a (mentioned or unmentioned)
plurality, must have distinctly hovered before the mind of the writer,
as in the Rev. εἷς ἄγγελος xviii. 21 ; xix 17, ἑνὸς ἀετοῦ viii. 13, etc.

The pleonastic combination εἷς τις (but always with a partitive Gen.
following) is found in Luke xxii. 50 ; John xi. 49 (Vulg. *unus*), Mark
xiv. 47 Tdf., without a Gen. following Mark xiv. 51 Tdf. but with
important variants.[1]

THE DEFINITE ARTICLE.

In reference to the definite article the rules and regulations 2
given in the grammars hold good, — so far as in a subject so
delicate as this we can talk of rules. For in the endeavor to 75
lay down fixed laws respecting the use of the article, many
a learned and laborious inquiry has already come to naught;
and the intention ought at length to be abandoned of forcing
the use or the omission of the article under precise regulations,
which find the proof of their nullity and uselessness in the
throng of exceptions which it is necessary to subjoin straightway to almost every rule laid down. For, a writer's sovereign
pleasure does not allow itself to be curtailed, whenever it
seems good to him (or perspicuity, that supreme law of every

---

[1] It is not allowable to compare with this the classic use of εἷς τις, since in the
earlier writers this combination is never used except where it was necessary to
express at the same time unity and indefiniteness united, as is evident
from Soph. Oed. Tyr. 8; Antig. 262, and the other passages, (see Steph. under εἷς
p 289).

intelligent writer or speaker, requires him) to depart even from a well-founded grammatical law. Nevertheless, it is the grammarian's task to settle the nature of the article in its main features, and to elucidate the same by a number of examples, and then to trace back the exceptional uses to their respective principles. It is that of the exegete, to show in every particular passage by what thought the writer was led in one case to use the article, in another and perhaps precisely identical case, to omit it. Accordingly, we shall content ourselves here with selecting from the mass of pertinent material such special cases only as at least approximate to a general use, or rest upon a grammatical basis clearly recognizable.

3 Since the use of the article with Names of Persons is wholly variable in the N. T. also (let the use of the names *Jesus*, *Peter*, *Pilate*, in this respect be traced in the Gospels, and that of *Paul* in the Acts), the matter must be left where the general Grammar places it: viz. by using the article the writer means to designate the person as one known or already mentioned; without the article he wishes simply to give his name. Accordingly, when rather unimportant persons are mentioned for the first time, the article is everywhere omitted unless other reasons render its addition desirable.

Such a reason is the desire to be perspicuous. It will be found, for instance, that indeclinable names often have the article, manifestly only to make the case apparent, especially when the name stands in an oblique case; as, Mark xv. 45 ἐδωρήσατο τὸ πτῶμα τῷ Ἰωσήφ, Rom. xi. 25 πώρωσις ἀπὸ μέρους τῷ Ἰσραὴλ γέγονεν. When the case is plain from the connection, the art. is commonly wanting; as after a Prep., e.g. ἐκ Σιὼν, ἀπὸ Ἰακώβ; with a Gen. after a subst., as Acts xiii. 21 ἔδωκεν αὐτοῖς τὸν Σαοὺλ, υἱὸν Κεὶς, ἄνδρα ἐκ φυλῆς Βενιαμείν

76 etc. That all such rules, however, are only approximately correct, attentive reading will soon teach.

4 It has further been observed, that names of countries have the art. far more frequently than names of cities. This observation is philologically well founded. For the great majority of names of countries are originally adjectives, as ἡ Ἀχαΐα, ἡ Γαλατία, which consequently must be first rendered substantives by the addition of the article; with names of cities, this as a rule is not the case. Again, however, examples of the opposite occur in both cases; and accordingly here, too, the general remarks made in 2 above apply.

On the other hand, it is to be noticed as a constant exception to the above rule, that the common word Αἴγυπτος never has the art. (for in Acts vii. 11 Lchm. [Tdf. Treg.] the art. has another cause); yet probably for no other reason than because the word originally is not an adjective like the rest. And with what has been already said in 3 above, agrees perfectly the fact that names of cities after a prep. (ἐν, εἰς, ἐκ) are connected with the art. very much less frequently than where they stand without a prep., especially in the Nominative.

The names of rivers approximate so much to the nature of appellatives that the addition of the article seems to be almost necessary. In the N. T. the art. is never wanting; see the names Ἰορδάνης, Εὐφράτης, Σιλωάμ in the lexicons.

B. § 124, N. 2; C. § 531; J. § 453 β.

Examples of the use and the omission of the art. with τοιοῦτος 5 and τοσοῦτος are found in the N. T. in sufficient number (cf. e.g. Rom. i. 32; Mark ix. 37; Rev. xviii. 16 with 1 Cor. xi. 16; 2 Cor. iii. 12, etc.) to show that the distinction given in B. l. c. is perfectly observed,(i.e. the prons. are used with and without the art. according as it is either the object so qualified, or the quality as such, that is to be made prominent; and according as reference is made to a description already given, or to one still to be given).

B. § 124, N. 4; H. § 538 c.; C. § 524; D. p. 352; J. § 452.

The use of the art. with possessive prons. is observed by the 6 language of the N.T. so strictly, that no single instance can be adduced of its omission where according to the rule it ought to stand. In the Sept. it is wanting more frequently, but only in certain portions often (e.g. in Prov. σὴν χεῖρα, σὸν οὖς, ἐμῇ σοφίᾳ, etc.), in others never. Where it is wanting in the N. T. the expression is predicative, as then (cf. § 129, 1) the art. must be omitted (e.g. John iv. 34; xiii. 35; xvii. 9; xv. 8, etc.; cf. Luke x. 29, 36; 2 Cor. viii. 23, where, however, the omission of the art. with the following ἀδελφοὶ ἡμῶν is erroneous, see § 127, 27 p. 119), or the art. is brought in afterwards in an attributive limitation that follows; as, Phil. iii. 9 μὴ ἔχων ἐμὴν δικαιοσύνην τὴν ἐκ νόμου. See below § 125, 3 p. 92 sq.

B. § 124, N. 6; D. § 396; J. § 446; W. p. 115 (109).

The definite art. cannot stand for the indefinite — neither 7 in the N. T. nor in any writer who thinks and writes in Greek; although there are passages enough where we, certainly, em- 77 ploy the indefinite art. rather than the definite, or at least might do so. On the contrary, the use of the article has everywhere its positive reason, inasmuch as the writer conceives the object thus designated, as one sufficiently limited, either from its nature, or by the immediate context. In all cases where the definite article appears to stand for the indefinite, the writer has in mind a more closely defining participle or a relative clause, which if added would have been heavy or superfluous. Often by this addition of the article a certain rhetorical emphasis is laid upon the word (cf. § 129, 1, Remark p. 124). In the translation of all such passages we shall do well if, in order to reproduce the intention of the writer, we avail ourselves likewise as far as possible of the definite article, even against our sense of propriety.

Compare in particular with this section the detailed exposition given § 129, 1 p. 123. To elucidate what has here been said, we will select but a few examples: Matt. xiii. 2 Tdf. [ed. 7] ὥστε εἰς τὸ πλοῖον ἐμβάντα καθῆσθαι *he went into the ship* (which was there, stood ready, etc.), on the other hand, Lchm. [Treg. Tdf.], with equal grammatical accuracy, εἰς πλοῖον *into a ship*, John vi. 3 ἀνῆλθεν εἰς τὸ ὄρος (Luther [so A. V.] inaccurately *a mountain*), 1 Cor. iv. 5 ὁ ἔπαινος γενήσεται ἑκάστῳ ἀπὸ τοῦ θεοῦ, deWette *the praise* (*deserved*) ; cf. Rom. iv. 4 ; 1 Cor. ix. 18 ; 2 Cor. i. 17 μήτι ἄρα τῇ ἐλαφρίᾳ ἐχρησάμην ; (where the art. is hard to reproduce in the translation) ; further, in the standing phrase Matt. viii. 12, etc., ἐκεῖ ἔσται ὁ κλαυθμὸς καὶ ὁ βρυγμὸς τῶν ὀδόντων, emphatic · the well-known, the terrible, pains of hell ; so, too, always in the Doxologies e.g. 1 Pet. iv. 11 ᾧ ἔστιν ἡ δόξα καὶ τὸ κράτος etc., Rev. v. 13, etc., see § 129, 22 p. 137. Respecting 2 Thess. iii. 14 see § 125, 2 p. 92.

OMISSION OF THE ARTICLE WITH APPELLATIVES.

B. § 124, N. 7; H. § 530; C. § 533; D. p. 347; J. § 447, 2.

Since in the N. T. the omission of the article is very common in cases where we employ it, and where in strictness it ought to stand in Greek also, Winer gives to this subject in § 19 a thorough examination, distinguished for the clearness and accuracy of its statements. The result he reaches is this: That the usage of the N. T. in this respect follows closely the four points specified in B. under this head [viz. that the Art. is omitted, 1) with general (especially) abstract terms in apothegmatic sentences, 2) in general adverbial adjuncts, 3) with words individualized by the context, 4) with quasi-proper names]; and that likewise the remark there sub-

joined, viz. " that none of these precepts are settled, and consequently in most cases the art. may still be employed,"
is completely applicable to the N. T. We will therefore con- 78
tent ourselves here, with confirming somewhat more in detail,
and completing, the substance of those four rules, by means of
a few examples from the N. T. The article is often wanting,
accordingly,

a) With abstract terms, as δικαιοσύνη, ἀγάπη, πίστις, κακία, πλεονεξία, ἁμαρτία, σωτηρία, also when compound: ζωὴ αἰώνιος, δόξα θεοῦ,
λόγος ζωῆς, etc.; as, 1 Thess. v. 8 νήφωμεν ἐνδυσάμενοι θώρακα πίστεως
καὶ ἀγάπης καὶ περικεφαλαίαν ἐλπίδα σωτηρίας, Gal. v. 5 ἡμεῖς πνεύματι
ἐκ πίστεως ἐλπίδα δικαιοσύνης ἀπεκδεχόμεθα.

b) With such appellatives as approximate to proper names. Thus
with θεός,[1] κύριος, χριστός, πνεῦμα ἅγιον, ἥλιος, γῆ (but not χώρα),
θάλασσα, κόσμος (so e.g. always in the phrase ἀπὸ καταβολῆς κόσμου,
hence also in the synonymous ἀπ' ἀρχῆς κτίσεως), further διάβολος and
σατανᾶς, the last, however, but extremely seldom, and strictly speaking
only in Luke xxii. 3; Acts xiii. 10; for in 1 Pet. v. 8; Rev. xx. 2,
etc., the omission is regular. Lastly, ἀντίχριστος in 1 John ii. 18 with
Lchm. Tdf. [Treg.] according to the oldest mss. [ℵ* also].

c) With such words as commonly seem to be individualized sufficiently by the connection, as πατήρ, μήτηρ (Matt. x. 37; Luke i. 15,
etc.), γονεῖς (Rom. i. 30, etc.), υἱός, ἀνήρ and γυνή in the sense of
husband and wife (Acts xviii. 2 etc.), πόλις, etc. Here belongs also
νόμος to denote the Mosaic law, especially in the Pauline Epp., but
not in the Gospels (cf. d), and θάνατος, e.g. ἄξιος θανάτου, μὴ ἰδεῖν
θάνατον, etc. The combination παῖδες καὶ γυναῖκες also, so common in
the classics, occurs Acts xxi. 5 [σὺν γυναιξὶ καὶ τέκνοις].

d) In general adverbial phrases and standing formulas, especially
when dependent upon prepositions, as κατὰ μεσημβρίαν, ἀπ' ἀνατολῆς,
ἀπ' ἀγορᾶς, ἀπ' ἀγροῦ, ἐν ἀγρῷ, ἐν ὑψίστοις (although an adj., cf. the
note below), πίπτειν ἐπὶ πρόσωπον, κατ' ὀφθαλμούς, ἕως and μέχρι θανάτου,
ἐπὶ θύραις, ἐν μέσῳ, ἀπὸ τρίτης ὥρας, δείπνου γενομένου, ὀψὲ σαββάτων,
πρὸ καιροῦ, ἀπ' ἀρχῆς, ἐγείρειν and ἀναστῆναι ἐκ νεκρῶν,[2] and many
similar expressions. But in one respect the N. T. usage departs

---

[1] Even ὕψιστος, which when it stands for God, though as an adj. it ought to have
the art., is yet used without it in Luke i. 32, 35, 76; vi. 35. Still more extraordinary is Rev. xi. 16 Lchm. εἴκοσι τέσσαρες πρεσβύτεροι for οἱ πρ. (Rec. [T. Tr.]).

[2] Often also ἀνάστασις νεκρῶν, but also on the other hand ἐκ, ἀπὸ τῶν νεκρῶν.
The remark of Winer 123 (117) that the Greeks regularly omit the art. before
νεκροί needs considerable limitation. For example, in Thucyd. the use of the art.
is far more frequent than its omission; and the latter, moreover, occurs for the
most part only in connection with τὰ ναυάγια: 1. 54; 8. 106; 4. 14.

12

manifestly from the classic, viz. eve:. when such adverbial phrases are restricted by a following Genitive to particular cases, and so lose their general character, the art. is frequently wanting; so especially in the Sept. This omission takes place regularly in the Hebraistic circumlocutions for simple prepositions by means of the terms πρόσωπον, χείρ, στόμα, as πρὸ or ἀπὸ προσώπου τοῦ κυρίου, διὰ χειρὸς ἀνόμων, etc. (see § 133, 20 p. 182; § 146, 1 p. 319) ; further ἀπὸ ὀφθαλμῶν σου, ἐν ὀφθαλμοῖς ἡμῶν (Matt. xxi. 42 quotn.), ἔπεσον ἐπὶ πρόσωπον αὐτῶν, ἐξ ἐφημερίας Ἀβιά, ἐν ἡμέραις Ἡρώδου, Νῶε, εἰς ἡμέραν ἀπολυτρώσεως, ἐν ἡμέρᾳ ὀργῆς, εἰς οἶκον αὐτοῦ, ἐν δεξιᾷ αὐτοῦ or τοῦ θρόνου, ἀπ᾽ ἄκρου γῆς ἕως ἄκρου οὐρανοῦ, ἐν βίβλῳ ζωῆς, and many others. Such omissions as belong at the same time to one of the preceding classes (a. b. c.), like the already mentioned πρὸ καταβολῆς or ἀπὸ κτίσεως κόσμου, the Pauline phrase ἐξ ἔργων νόμου, εἰς εὐαγγέλιον θεοῦ, ἐπὶ παροργισμῷ ὑμῶν, κατ᾽ εἰκόνα τοῦ κτίσαντος αὐτόν, εἰς ἔπαινον δόξης αὐτοῦ, ἐν νόμῳ κυρίου (Luke ii. 23, 24), further ἐν γῇ Μαδιάμ, Χαναάν, εἰς πόλιν Δανείδ, ἐκ γῆς Αἰγύπτου, etc., may be justified well enough by the ordinary usage. Cf. on this section § 127, 27, 1) p. 119

USE OF THE ARTICLE WITH MORE CLOSELY DEFINED SUBSTANTIVES.

B. § 125, 1 to N. 5; H. § 531 sqq.; C. § 523; D. §§ 400. 407; J. § 458 sq.

1 As has been already remarked in speaking of the Possess. Prons. § 124, 6 p. 87, the language of the N. T. remained faithful throughout to the general rules of grammar in reference to the position of the article with a substantive having an attributive adjective: That is to say, it either places the adj. between the subst. and art. (τὸ ἅγιον πνεῦμα) ; or after the subst., repeating the art. (τὸ πνεῦμα τὸ ἅγιον) ; even repeating it twice, as Matt. xxv. 41 τὸ πῦρ τὸ αἰώνιον τὸ ἡτοιμασμένον, Rev. viii. 3 ; ix. 13 ; xvii. 1. Hence in John, notwithstanding the frequency with which the phrase ζωὴ αἰώνιος occurs without the art. (agreeably to § 124, 8 a) p. 89), as soon as the art. precedes it the expression is reversed : ἡ αἰώνιος ζωή (xvii. 3), or if the order is retained the art. is doubled (1 John i. 2 ; ii. 25).

It would hardly be possible to adduce examples on the other side, inasmuch as all the instances in which the adj. stands without the art. after a subst. with the art. are either not genuine or find their grammatical explanation in other ways. Since Winer 133 (126) appears to acknowledge the existence of such exceptional cases, we will mention them here. In 1 John v. 20 the reading of the Rec. ἡ ζωὴ αἰώνιος is now set aside on MS. authority and likewise in Luke xii.

12 τὸ γὰρ πνεῦμα ἅγιον. On Mark v. 36 (τὸν λόγον λαλούμενον) see § 144, 16 p. 302. In John v. 36 Tdf. (ἔχω τὴν μαρτυρίαν μείζω τοῦ Ἰωάννου) the word μείζω is predicative, and consequently the example belongs to those given below (5 p. 94). 1 Pet. i. 18 ἐκ τῆς ματαίας ὑμῶν ἀναστροφῆς πατροπαραδότου is quite regular, since the classic Greek authors also are accustomed, after a subst. which already has one attributive, to put a second without the art., as Xen. Ages. 1, 10; Thuc. 6, 31, 5; see other examples of the sort in Bhdy. Syntax p. 323. Accordingly, the common reading also in 1 Cor. x. 3 Tdf. [eds. 2, 7] τὸ αὐτὸ βρῶμα πνευματικὸν ἔφαγον may be defended; but the oldest mss. give [א* simply πνευμ. βρῶμ.] τὸ αὐτὸ πνευματικὸν βρῶμα ἔφαγον [Treg. Tdf.] or ἔφαγον βρῶμα (Lchm.); likewise Gal. i. 4 Tdf.[eds. 2, 7] 80 ἐκ τοῦ ἐνεστῶτος αἰῶνος πονηροῦ, where these mss. [so א*] read ἐκ τοῦ αἰῶνος τοῦ ἐνεστῶτος πονηροῦ (Lchm. [Treg. Tdf.]). Matt. xxiv. 45 τίς ἄρα ἐστὶν ὁ πιστὸς δοῦλος καὶ φρόνιμος a native Greek, to be sure, would perhaps not have written; but it finds its apology in the predicative position of the whole expression. In John xii. 9, 12 the reading ὁ ὄχλος πολύς (B C L [so Tdf. א vs. 9, but in vs 12 he omits the art. with א]) is the only correct one, since ὄχλος πολύς was regarded as but a s i n g l e   w o r d (vulgus, the great mass), and ὁ πολὺς ὄχλος would sound strange, and very likely give another meaning.

The case is different with a d v e r b i a l   a d d i t i o n s   t o   a 2 substantive with the article. According to rule, they also ought always to stand between the art. and the subst., or to be placed after with a repeated art. as is often the case in the N. T.: Rom. vii. 10 ἡ ἐντολὴ ἡ εἰς ζωήν, Acts xv. 23 τοῖς κατὰ τὴν Ἀντιόχειαν καὶ Συρίαν ἀδελφοῖς τοῖς ἐξ ἐθνῶν; see a multitude of similar passages in Winer 133 (126). But the language of the N. T. has liberated itself somewhat from the traditional usage (although the beginnings of such a change can be traced even in good classic authors), in that it also subjoins such adverbial adjuncts w i t h o u t the article.

From the examples belonging under this head, however, we must first except (as analogous to some given in 1 above) all those cases in which the subst. is already furnished with a genitival, adjectival, or adverbial attributive (whether inserted or subjoined); as, Eph. i. 15 τὴν καθ᾽ ὑμᾶς πίστιν ἐν τῷ κυρίῳ, iii. 4 τὴν σύνεσίν μου ἐν τῷ μυστηρίῳ, iii. 13 ταῖς θλίψεσίν μου ὑπὲρ ὑμῶν, vi. 21 ὁ ἀγαπητὸς ἀδελφὸς καὶ πιστὸς διάκονος ἐν κυρίῳ, Phil. i. 26 τῆς ἐμῆς παρουσίας πάλιν πρὸς ὑμᾶς, iii. 14 τῆς ἄνω κλήσεως τοῦ θεοῦ ἐν Χριστῷ Ἰησοῦ, Gal. i. 13 τὴν ἐμὴν ἀναστροφήν ποτε ἐν τῷ Ἰουδαϊσμῷ, Rom. ix. 3 τῶν συγγενῶν μου κατὰ σάρκα, 1 and 2 Thess. i. 1 τῇ ἐκκλησίᾳ Θεσσαλονικέων ἐν Θεῷ, 2 Cor. vii. 7; Col. i. 4, 8, etc. Accordingly, in 2 Thess. iii. 14 the phrase διὰ τῆς ἐπιστολῆς belongs to the preceding τῷ λόγῳ ὑμῶν, and cannot — as the position and the article indicate plainly enough — be referred to σημειοῦσθε following, for thus it would receive an inappropriate emphasis. More surprising, yet absolutely required by the sense (see the recent commentaries and Winer 220 (206)), is the construction of the phrase ἐν δόγμασιν in Eph. ii. 15 with the preceding τὸν νόμον τῶν ἐντολῶν; and still more harsh is the Dative τοῖς δόγμασιν, which belongs to τὸ καθ' ἡμῶν χειρόγραφον, in the parallel passage Col. ii. 14.

But, setting these aside, cases enough are left in which the adverbial adjunct is placed after a subst. limited only by the art., — cases in which exegesis, to be sure, has made manifold attempts to draw the adverbial phrase away from the subst. to other parts of the clause, but in which both position and sense require it to be connected with the subst. Least of all are we compelled to resort to such an apparent grammatical make-shift in cases where the governing subst. is an abstract term whose radical verb is capable of the same adverbial connection; for parallel instances are found even in the earlier prose writers from Herod. and Thucyd. down (see, 81 among others, Poppo on Thucyd. 2, 52; Krüger on Dionys. Historiogr. p. 153), and still more frequently in later authors. From the N. T. e.g. Rom. vi. 4 τὸ βάπτισμα εἰς τὸν θάνατον (cf. vs. 3 εἰς τὸν θάνατον αὐτοῦ ἐβαπτίσθημεν), 2 Cor. ix. 13 ἡ κοινωνία εἰς αὐτούς (agreeably to κοινωνεῖν εἰς in § 132, 8 p. 160; and cf. the examples below, 11 p. 95 sq.). But such adjuncts also occur in the N. T. often enough where at least the more accurate style requires the repetition of the art.; as, 1 Thess. iv. 16 οἱ νεκροὶ ἐν Χριστῷ, 1 Cor. x. 18 βλέπετε τὸν Ἰσραὴλ κατὰ σάρκα, Eph. vi. 5 Tdf. [eds. 2, 7; ed. 8, Treg. cod. Sin. τοῖς κ. σ. κυρίοις] τοῖς κυρίοις κατὰ σάρκα (cf. the parallel passage Col. iii. 22), Eph. iv. 1 ἐγὼ ὁ δέσμιος ἐν κυρίῳ, ii. 11 τὰ ἔθνη ἐν σαρκί. But to give a complete list of all such passages, and in particular to determine when such adverbial adjuncts belong not to the subst. but to the verb or some other part of the proposition, lies quite beyond the limits of grammar, and must be left to the exegesis of the individual passages, since everywhere the context alone can decide. A portion of these doubtful passages are treated by Winer 137 (130). Cf. 11 p. 95.

3 The usage (cf. B. § 125, 3 sub fin.) that, 1) when attributives are placed after with the art., the art. before the subst. is dropped; or, 2) to substantives which (according to § 124, 8 p. 88 sq.) commonly stand without the art., the adjunct, when subjoined, is given with the art., — is quite current in the language of the N. T.

Examples of 1) are Luke xxiii. 49 γυναῖκες αἱ συνακολουθοῦσαι, Acts
i. 12 ἀπὸ ὄρους τοῦ κιλουμένου ἐλαιῶνος, vii. 35 ἀγγέλου τοῦ ὀφθέντος
(cf. vs. 30), 1 Pet. i. 7 χρυσίου τοῦ ἀπολλυμένου, Phil. iii. 9 ἐμὴν δικαιοσύνην τὴν ἐκ νόμου (cf. vs. 6), i. 11 καρπὸν δικαιοσύνης τὸν διὰ Ἰ. Χρ.
Rom. ix. 30 κατέλαβεν δικαιοσύνην, δικαιοσύνην δὲ τὴν ἐκ πίστεως, John
xiv. 27 εἰρήνην ἀφίημι ὑμῖν, εἰρήνην τὴν ἐμὴν δίδωμι ὑμῖν, Acts x. 1, 41;
xxv. 23; Heb. ix. 2, 3, etc.   Examples of 2) are very numerous:
Rom. viii. 33 θεὸς ὁ δικαιῶν, Gal. i. 1 θεοῦ πατρὸς τοῦ ἐγείραντος αὐτόν,
ii. 20 ἐν πίστει ζῶ τῇ τοῦ υἱοῦ, Luke v. 36 Lchm. ἐπίβλημα τὸ ἀπὸ τοῦ
καινοῦ, Mark viii. 27 Καισαρείας τῆς Φιλίππου; cf. Acts xxvi. 22;
1 Tim. i. 4; iii. 13; iv. 8; 2 Tim. i. 13, 14; ii. 10, etc. etc.

REMARK.   Winer's observation 139 sq. (132, cf. ed. 5 p. 159) that
in such cases the substantive is strictly speaking always conceived
indefinitely, and that the limitation following is equal to an
abbreviated relative clause, is at least not to be extended
to the above passages; probably, however, there are passages to which
it applies.   That is to say, since (as we have already seen § 123, 5
p. 78, and as will be shown at length § 144, 9 p. 294) the participle with the art. often takes the place of a relative clause,
such a participle may stand not only after indefinite pronominal expressions, like τὶς, ἕτερος, ἄλλος, πολύς (§ 144, 9 f) p. 295), but in general
also after indefinite and consequently anarthrous substantives, as well
as after such as are predicative and on this account (according to
§ 129, 1 p. 123) also dispense with the article; e.g. Jude 4 παρεισ-
έδυσάν τινες ἄνθρωποι, οἱ πάλαι προγεγραμμένοι εἰς τοῦτο τὸ κρίμα
ἀσεβεῖς; cf. Luke xviii. 9; Gal. i. 7; Col. ii. 8; Luke vii. 32 ὅμοιοι
παιδίοις τοῖς ἐν ἀγορᾷ καθημένοις, John v. 2 [Lchm. Treg.] ἔστιν ἐν τοῖς
Ἱεροσολ. κολυμβήθρα, ἡ ἐπιλεγομένη Βηθεσδά, Acts xx. 19 μετὰ δακρύων 82
καὶ πειρασμῶν τῶν συμβάντων μοι, Rom. ii. 14 ἔθνη τὰ μὴ νόμον ἔχοντα,
ix. 30; Gal. iii. 21 εἰ ἐδόθη νόμος ὁ δυνάμενος ζωοποιῆσαι, ὄντως ἂν ἦν
etc Jas. iv. 14 ἀτμίς (pred.) ἐστε, ἡ πρὸς ὀλίγον φαινομένη, Acts xix. 11
δυνάμεις τε οὐ τὰς τυχούσας ἐποίει etc.; and with the omitted participle
of εἶναι: Phil. ii. 9 ἐχαρίσατο αὐτῷ ὄνομα τὸ ὑπὲρ πᾶν ὄνομα sc. ὄν.   Cf.
besides, the examples given in § 144, 9 f) p. 295.

B. § 125, N. 2; H. § 559 d.; C. § 523 c.; S. p. xxxiii. sq.

That the partitive genitive (which, however, frequently ap-   4
pears in a resolved form, see § 132, 6 p. 158) is not inserted between
the subst. and art. is plain from many examples, as τῇ πρώτῃ τῶν
ἀζύμων, τῇ μιᾷ τῶν σαββάτων, οἱ πρῶτοι τοῦ λαοῦ, τὸ πλῆθος τῶν μαθητῶν,
τῆς πόλεως, etc.   Yet discrimination by means of position between the
partitive and the ordinary Gen. is almost wholly at an end in the
N. T., since in the Gospels and in the Rev. there hardly exists an

instance of insertion (of the ordinary Gen.), and in the Acts and the
Epp. also the modern position grows more and more frequent, as ἡ
ἐκπλήρωσις τῶν ἡμερῶν τοῦ ἁγνισμοῦ (Acts xxi. 26), ὁ νόμος τοῦ πνεύματος τῆς ζωῆς ἐν Χριστῷ (Rom. viii. 2), etc.

B. § 125, N. 4; H. § 535; C. § 523 b.; D. p. 360; J. § 458, Obs. 2.

5   An adjective without the art., standing either before or
after a substantive with the art., is predicative.

Examples (besides John v. 36 adduced under 1 p. 91) are Mark
viii. 17 πεπωρωμένην ἔχετε τὴν καρδίαν ὑμῶν, Heb. vii. 24 ἀπαράβατον
ἔχει τὴν ἱερωσύνην, 1 Pet. ii. 12 τὴν ἀναστροφὴν ὑμῶν ἔχοντες καλήν, iv.
8; Heb. v. 14; 1 Cor. xi. 5 ἀκατακαλύπτῳ τῇ κεφαλῇ, Acts xxvi. 24
μεγάλῃ τῇ φωνῇ φησίν, xiv. 10 Tdf. [eds. 2, 7]; Eph. i. 18 πεφω-
τισμένους τοὺς ὀφθαλμούς, on which passage compare also § 145, 6
p. 317.

B. § 125, N. 5; H. § 536 sq.; C. § 523; D. § 444; J. § 459.

6   Examples of the predicative position in the case of ὅλος are
countless, see the lexicons; but in the case of the other adjs. mentioned
(ἄκρος, μέσος, ἔσχατος) none occur, because the later language is wont
to employ them no longer as adjectives but as substantives, and hence
to frame its expressions by means of the Neuter of the adj. with a
Genitive following; as, τὸ ἄκρον τοῦ δακτύλου or τῆς ῥάβδου, ἐν μέσῳ
τῆς αὐλῆς (not ἐν μέσῃ τῇ αὐλῇ) or αὐτῶν or τῶν πρεσβυτέρων, ἕως
ἐσχάτου τῆς γῆς, Heb. i. 1 ἐπ᾽ ἐσχάτου τῶν ἡμερῶν (Rec. ἐσχάτων). On
the other hand, with the last-mentioned word (ἡμέρα) the common
adjectival position is often found, but in the other sense: ἐν τῇ ἐσχάτῃ
ἡμέρᾳ not at the end of the day, but on the last day; so τὸν ἔσχατον
κοδράντην, ἡ ἐσχάτη πλάνη, etc.

ARTICLE IN LIEU OF A SUBSTANTIVE, OR WITH A SUBSTANTIVE TO BE
SUPPLIED.

B. § 125, 5; H. § 563; C. § 527; D. p. 356; J. § 436.

7   In the N. T., besides the common omission of son and
daughter when the art. is followed by a Genitive (cf. § 123,
8 p. 81 sq.), that of μήτηρ is also to be noticed, Mark xvi. 1;
Luke xxiv. 10 Μαρία ἡ τοῦ Ἰακώβου, Mark xv. 47 Μαρία ἡ
Ἰωσῆτος (complete in Matt. xxvii. 56; Mark xv. 40); of
γυνή, Matt. i. 6 ἐκ τῆς τοῦ Οὐρίου; probably also of ἀδελφός,
Luke vi. 16; Acts i. 13 Ἰούδας Ἰακώβου (cf. Jude 1; Winer,
R.W.B. under Judas, I. p. 632; Credner, Einl. p. 613; on the
other hand, Meyer in ll. cc.), and of πατήρ in the passage
Acts vii. 16 Tdf. [eds. 2, 7] (cf. Gen. xxxiii. 19; xxxiv. 6, etc.).

The designation, so frequent especially in the later profane literature, 83
of a person in a broad sense by the phrase οἱ περί τινα, strictly 8
speaking does not occur in the N. T.   For in Acts xiii. 13 οἱ περὶ
Παῦλον plainly means, *Paul and his companions* (Vulg. *Paulus et
qui cum eo*) ; in xxi. 8 the expression has been discarded ; and John
xi. 19 is doubtful : Tdf. πρὸς τὰς περὶ Μάρθαν καὶ Μαριάμ (Lchm. [Treg.,
cod. Sin.] πρὸς τὴν M. κ. M.).   In Mark iv. 10 ; Luke xxii. 49 οἱ περὶ
αὐτόν is to be understood quite literally, *they that were about him.*

On the other hand, the art. οἱ with a following Genitive
is often found in the sense of 'the people, adherents, etc., of a person,'
as Rom. xvi. 10, 11 οἱ Ἀριστοβούλου, οἱ Ναρκίσσου, 1 Cor. i. 11 οἱ Χλόης,
Acts xvi. 33 αὐτὸς (ὁ δεσμοφύλαξ) καὶ οἱ αὐτοῦ, for which in vs. 32 we
have οἱ ἐν τῇ οἰκίᾳ αὐτοῦ ; and transferred to the followers of Christ,
1 Cor. xv. 23 ; Gal. v. 24 οἱ τοῦ Χριστοῦ.   But in Luke v. 33 μαθηταί
is to be supplied from what precedes, and in Mark ii. 18 οἱ Φαρισαῖοι
is the better reading [so Tdf. Treg., after א etc.].

REMARK.   Respecting the (doubtful) combinations εἰς ᾅδου, ἐν
Αἰγύπτου, see § 132, 27 p. 171.

B. § 125, N. 6; H. § 563; C. § 528; D. p. 357; J. p. 111 sq.

In general, the designation of persons and things by the 9
simple article (οἱ, τό, τά) with a Genitive or an adverbial
limitation following, is by no means uncommon ; and the examples from the classics may be matched in abundance from
the N. T.   Thus with a Gen. following : τὰ Καίσαρος, τὰ τῆς
σαρκός, τὰ τοῦ πνεύματος, τὰ τοῦ πατρός μου, τὰ τῆς αὔριον, τὸ
τῆς συκῆς, τὸ τῆς ἀληθοῦς παροιμίας, τὰ ἑαυτῶν ζητοῦσιν, etc. ;
with an adverbial adjunct following : οἱ ἐν τῇ Ἰουδαίᾳ, ἀπὸ
Κιλικίας, ἀπὸ Ἰταλίας, ἐκ τῆς Καίσαρος οἰκίας, ἐν τῇ οἰκίᾳ · οἱ
ἐκ περιτομῆς, ἐκ πίστεως · τὰ περὶ ἐμέ, πρὸς τὴν χρείαν, κατὰ
τὸν Παῦλον, διὰ τοῦ σώματος · τὸ ἐκ μέρους (1 Cor. xiii. 10 [A.V.
that which is in part], Luth. *Stückwerk*), τὸ ἐξ ὑμῶν (cf. § 128,
2 p. 123), τὰ πρὸς τὴν θύραν (Mark ii. 2 *the entrance-hall*), etc.

B. § 125, 6 and 7; H. § 492; C. § 526; D. § 400; J. § 456.

The same holds true in reference to the use of adverbs with 10
the art. in lieu of adjectives, as ἐν τῷ νῦν καιρῷ, ὁ τότε κόσμος,
ὁ ἔσω ἄνθρωπος, τῇ ἐξῆς ἡμέρᾳ, ἡ ἄνωθεν σοφία, etc., and with
the omission of the substantive : ὁ πλησίον, οἱ ἔξω, εἰς τὸ πέραν,
τὰ ὀπίσω, τῇ σήμερον, ἐπαύριον, ἐξῆς, etc.

REMARK.   Far more rarely will adverbs or adverbial phrases be 11
found joined to a subst. that is not provided with the article or

another attributive, in particular a participle. Such combinations the
language sought to avoid in order to preclude possible misunder-
standings, to which in the other case, by the insertion of the adverbial
qualification between the art. and the subst., the author was not exposed. Yet such combinations have been occasionally permitted,
where the context is of such a nature as to exclude in advance every
ambiguity ; as, for example, in 2 Cor. xi. 23 sq., where κίνδυνοι ἐκ γένους,
ἐν ἐρημίᾳ, ἐν θαλάσσῃ, ἐν νηστείαις πολλάκις, ἐν κόποις περισσοτέρως,
84 stand in the relation spoken of. But elsewhere, also, especially in the
Epistles, the interpreter has often found himself compelled to refer
adverbial limitations of this sort away from the predicate, and to connect them immediately with preceding or following substantives
destitute of both art. and attributive, — substantives which for the
most part are either abstract terms (that according to § 124, 8 p. 89
often stand without the art.), or verbals whose stem-verb is capable
of a similar construction (cf. 2 p. 92). This procedure must be
regarded as the more permissible in the N. T., as we have seen above
(2 p. 91) there are so many combinations likewise grammatically
loose in which the adverbial adjunct is subjoined to the subst. without
the repetition of the article. Thus Mark (i. 23) says briefly ἄνθρωπος
ἐν πνεύματι ἀκαθάρτῳ a man (afflicted) with an unclean spirit, in 1 Cor.
xii. 31 καθ᾿ ὑπερβολὴν ὁδόν is explained by an excellent way, Eph. vi. 23
ἀγάπη μετὰ πίστεως, Gal. v. 5 πνεύματι ἐκ πίστεως, 1 Tim. ii. 7 διδάσκαλος
ἐθνῶν ἐν πίστει καὶ ἀληθείᾳ (cf. § 131, 6 p. 149), Rom. xiv. 17 χαρὰ ἐν
πνεύματι ἁγίῳ (according to § 133, 23 p. 185), etc.

B. § 125, N. 8; H. § 552 a.; C. § 529; D. p. 502; J. § 456.

12   Besides the adverbial expression τὸ λοιπόν (Matt. xxvi. 45, etc.),
λοιπόν, also, without the art. is often used adverbially; see § 128, 2
p. 123. The following also stand adverbially: τὸ καθ᾿ ἡμέραν Luke
xix. 47; Acts xvii. 11 Tdf. [eds. 2, 7], τὸ πλεῖστον 1 Cor. xiv. 27, τὸ
ἐξ ὑμῶν Rom. xii. 18, τὰ πολλά xv. 22.

THE ARTICLE BEFORE ENTIRE SENTENCES.

B. § 125, N. 9; C. § 491; D. § 400; J. § 457.

13   The practice of introducing entire clauses by the neuter
article τό is not uncommon in the N. T. It occurs, 1) before
passages quoted in full or in part, which in this way are made
parts of the sentence ; and, 2) before indirect interrogative
clauses, especially in Luke.

Examples of 1) are Matt. xix. 18 τὸ Οὐ φονεύσεις, οὐ μοιχεύσεις etc.,
Gal. v. 14 ὁ νόμος ἐν ἑνὶ λόγῳ πεπλήρωται, ἐν τῷ Ἀγαπήσεις etc., Rom.
xiii. 9 ; Eph. iv. 9 (τὸ ἀνέβη), Heb. xii. 27 (τὸ ἔτι ἅπαξ), Luke xxii.

37 Tdf. [Treg., cod. Sin.] ;   of 2) Luke i. 62 ἐνένευον τῷ πατρὶ τὸ τί ἂν θέλοι καλεῖσθαι αὐτό, ix. 46 ; xix. 48 ; xxii. 2 ἐζήτουν τὸ πῶς ἀνέλωσιν αὐτόν, xxii. 23, 24 ; Acts iv. 21 ; v. 24 (τὸ τί γένοιτο, according to Sin.), xxii. 30.   Cf. also Rom. viii. 26 ; 1 Thess. iv. 1.   See the commentaries respecting the extremely difficult passage Mark ix. 23, which according to Lchm. (praef. I. p. 44 ; II. p. 7) needs emendation, and is left dubious by the MSS.

THE ARTICLE WITH SEVERAL SUBSTANTIVES CONNECTED BY CONJUNCTIONS.

B. § 125, 10 ; C. § 534 ; J. 359, 9 ; cf. S. p. xv.

It will probably never be possible, either in reference to 4 profane literature or to the N. T., to bring down to rigid rules which have no exception, the inquiry when with several substantives connected by conjunctions the article is repeated, and when it is not.   Nevertheless, it is the business of the grammarian to set forth certain established linguistic principles 85 as the foundation of grammatical usage, and to trace back deviations even, as far as possible, to their analogies.

From this fact alone it follows, that in view of the subjective and arbitrary treatment of the art. on the part of individual writers (cf. § 124, 2 p. 85), it is very hazardous in particular cases to draw important inferences, affecting the sense or even of a doctrinal nature, from the single circumstance of the use or the omission of the article ; see e.g. Tit. ii. 13 ; Jude 4 ; 2 Pet. i. 1 and the expositors of these passages, and cf. 17 c) below, p. 100.   Such inferences are the more precarious, as, moreover, amid the conflict of variations, the reading often can hardly be settled as yet ; and the recent editors, therefore, differ very much on this point.

1) If the connected substantives are of the s a m e gender and 15 number and w i t h o u t a t t r i b u t i v e s, it holds as a general rule that, a) when the substantives may be regarded as parts of one whole, as terms belonging together and related or complementary, it is enough to use the article but o n c e ; but, b) if they denote contrasted, or at least independent, objects or notions, to be conceived of as separate, the article is r e p e a t e d. Nevertheless, the language is by no means bound by this rule, well founded though it is in the nature of things.   The explanation of this, however, lies not in the negligent style of the writers, but in the impossibility, as a matter of fact, of drawing a sharp boundary between the two cases.   In particular, (a) in the first case we often find the article repeated, because the

13

writer, even when the identity is almost complete, may, if he
will, mention the members as members, consequently each by
itself, without incurring the danger of being ambiguous. In
point of fact, at least half of the examples adduced by Winer
p. 128 (122) consist of such cases, where similar ideas are connected and yet each has the article. On the other hand, (b)
in the second case, i.e. with members which are necessarily to
be thought of as separate, we but very rarely find only a single
article used, since in such circumstances the mind demands
the repetition of the article, and its omission can only take
place where the following term, viewed by itself, may also
for some reason be used without the art.

The remarks which have been made will be elucidated by
the following examples :

86   on a). That with terms of kindred nature the art. is now omitted,
now repeated, even by one and the same writer, is seen in the numerous combinations of the words ἀρχιερεῖς, γραμματεῖς, πρεσβύτεροι,
Φαρισαῖοι, in the Gospels. Thus they occur, for instance, in Matt.
(according to the text of Lchm.) with but a single art. in ii. 4; xvi. 21 ;
xx. 18; xxvi. 47; xxvii. 3, 41, with a repetition of the art. in xxi.
15, 23, 45 ; xxvi. 3; xxvii. 1, 12, 20, 62; and so, too, in the other
Gospels. Further, in Luke xv. 6 we read συγκαλεῖ τοὺς φίλους καὶ
τοὺς γείτονας, but directly afterwards in vs. 9 τὰς φίλας καὶ γείτονας
(where Rec. adds a second τὰς) ; likewise also with associated proper
names, Acts xv. 22 σὺν τῷ Παύλῳ καὶ Βαρνάβᾳ, but in xiii. 43 etc. τῷ
Π. καὶ τῷ Β. Other instances of the repetition of the art. with
words which are manifestly related or belong together are Mark vi. 21 ;
xiii. 17 ; Luke i. 53; xi. 39, 42; xii. 11 ; xx. 20 ; John ii. 14 (cf. Luke
xix. 45 Lchm.) ; Acts xv. 4, 6 (cf. xv. 2) ; Rom. vi. 19 ; Col. ii. 3 Tdf.
([but ed. 8] Lchm.[Treg. א] om. second τῆς) ; Rev. vi. 15 ; vii. 12, etc.

on b). On the other hand, that in the second case the art. is almost
indispensable, we see plainly from Acts xxvi. 30 ἀνέστη ὁ βασιλεὺς καὶ
ὁ ἡγεμών, where if the second art. were omitted we should think of
but a single person. Or if we look at 1 Cor. iii. 8 ὁ φυτεύων καὶ ὁ
ποτίζων ἕν εἰσιν, or compare Mark xi. 9 οἱ προάγοντες καὶ οἱ ἀκολουθοῦντες
with 2 John 9 ὁ προάγων καὶ μὴ μένων ἐν τῇ διδαχῇ, we recognize the
difference between the two forms of expression instantly. See more
instances of the legitimate repetition of the art. in this case in Winer
128 (122), many of which, however, belong to 1 p. 90.

16   REMARK. Where several terms are predicated of one and
the same object, the article of necessity can only be used once,
because otherwise uncertainty would arise respecting the meaning.

This appears further from the phrases, ὁ θεὸς καὶ πατὴρ Col. iii. 17;
Eph. i. 3; Phil. iv. 20; 2 Cor. i. 3; 1 Pet. i. 3; Jas. iii. 9, etc.; τοῦ
κυρίου καὶ σωτῆρος 2 Pet. ii. 20 Tdf. [Treg.]; iii. 2, etc., Mark vi. 3
ὁ υἱὸς Μαρίας καὶ ἀδελφὸς Ἰακώβου, Acts iii. 14 τὸν ἅγιον καὶ δίκαιον
ἠρνήσασθε, Tit. i. 15, etc.   Likewise with participles used substantively, John xxi. 24 ὁ μαρτυρῶν περὶ τούτων καὶ γράψας ταῦτα, Gal. i. 7
οἱ ταράσσοντες ὑμᾶς καὶ θέλοντες etc., Phil. iii. 3 οἱ ... λατρεύοντες καὶ
καυχώμενοι, 1 Tim. iv. 3; Luke vi. 49; 2 John 9; see other examples
belonging to this head under 17 and 18 below.   This is the case, also,
even with contrasted predicates (with ἀλλά) 2 Thess. ii. 12.   On the
other hand, Acts xvii. 18; 2 Thess. iii. 2; 1 Tim. iv. 7, etc., may be
regarded simply as the insertion of two adjectives.

2) If the connected members are of the same gender and   **17**
number, and a) one of them, no matter which, is provided with
an attributive limitation which is to be referred to the
two (or more) members, as a rule the article is not repeated;
or b) if the attributive is connected with one of the members
and not to be referred to the other, the art. is used with each
member; or c) if each member is provided with its own attributive, the case is essentially the same as that above in 15, and
the art. is either repeated or dropped, under the same circum-   **87**
stances as there.   Since, however, examples to the contrary are
not wanting under a) and b) also, it is plain that all rules of
this sort, though grammatically well-founded, are not altogether
unyielding; but that, over and above them, the law of perspicuity, or the writer's desire in a particular case to render
more perceptible either the independence of the members or
their similarity and connection, has great influence over the
use and the omission of the article.

What has been said will be rendered clear by the following
examples:

on a) Without the repetition of the art.: Rom. i. 20 ἥ τε ἀΐδιος
αὐτοῦ δύναμις καὶ θειότης, 2 Cor. i. 6; Heb. iii. 1; Phil. i. 19, 20 κατὰ
τὴν ἀποκαραδοκίαν καὶ ἐλπίδα μου, 1 Thess. ii. 12; iii. 7 ἐπὶ πάσῃ τῇ
ἀνάγκῃ καὶ θλίψει ἡμῶν διὰ τῆς ὑμῶν πίστεως, 1 Pet. ii. 25; 2 Pet. i. 10,
11; ii. 20 Lchm. [Tdf.], Eph. iii. 5 Tdf. [eds. 2, 7], etc.   Exceptions:
Eph. iii. 10 ταῖς ἀρχαῖς καὶ ταῖς ἐξουσίαις ἐν τοῖς ἐπουρανίοις, iii. 12;
1 Cor. xi. 27 τοῦ σώματος καὶ τοῦ αἵματος τοῦ κυρίου, Acts xxv. 15;
Rev. xiii. 10.   In the account of the expulsion of the traders from
the temple we read in Matt. (xxi. 12), according to the rule, τοὺς
πωλοῦντας καὶ ἀγοράζοντας ἐν τῷ ἱερῷ; on the other hand, in **Mark xi.**

15 τοὺς πωλοῦντας καὶ τοὺς ἀγοράζοντας ἐν τῷ ἱερῷ; in Luke xix. 45 Lchm. again, according to the rule, τοὺς πωλοῦντας ἐν αὐτῷ καὶ ἀγορά- ζοντας; but in John ii. 14 τοὺς πωλοῦντας βόας καὶ πρόβατα καὶ περιστερὰς καὶ τοὺς κερματιστὰς καθημένους, where καθημένους manifestly belongs to both classes, but perspicuity required the repetition of the article.

on b) With the repetition of the art.: when the attributive limi- tation is used with the first member; Mark vi. 21 τοῖς μεγιστᾶσιν αὐτοῦ καὶ τοῖς χιλιάρχοις, 1 Cor. i. 28; v. 10 (where with four members the art. quite regularly is repeated only once, since the limiting genitive τοῦ κόσμου τούτου belongs by position only to τοῖς πόρνοις, although according to the sense it may be referred to the following members also, which again, as expressing kindred ideas, have the art. in common), Acts vi. 13. When the attributive limitation stands with the second member; Luke i. 58 οἱ περίοικοι καὶ οἱ συγγενεῖς αὐτῆς, viii. 24; Acts vi. 4; xiii. 43; 1 Tim. iv. 6 τῆς πίστεως καὶ τῆς καλῆς διδασκαλίας, 2 Cor. xiii. 2 τοῖς προημαρτηκόσιν καὶ τοῖς λοιποῖς πᾶσιν. Exceptions (respecting which cf. the Remark, 16 above): Col. ii. 8 τῆς φιλοσοφίας καὶ κενῆς ἀπάτης, 2 John 9. Respecting Acts xv. 23 Lchm. [Tdf. Treg.], see Meyer. It is apparent, moreover, that ambiguity is in every instance avoided by the position of the attributive limitation (either before or after the subst.).

on c) (With all which the examples in 15 are to be compared) — with the repetition of the art.: Mark xi. 15 τὰς τραπέζας τῶν κολλυ- βιστῶν καὶ τὰς καθέδρας τῶν πωλούντων, 1 Thess. iii. 11; 1 John iv. 6 τὸ πνεῦμα τῆς ἀληθείας καὶ τὸ πνεῦμα τῆς πλάνης, Rev. xi. 4; without the repetition of the art.: 2 Thess. i. 12 τοῦ θεοῦ ἡμῶν καὶ κυρίου Ἰ. Χρ. cf. 2 Pet. i. 1, etc.; Tit. ii. 13 (see 14 p. 97), Phil. i. 19 (because ὑμῶν is to be referred to both members), iii. 10 Lchm. [Treg.] (where the addition of τὴν is not at all necessary, at least grammatically), Jude 4 (see 14 p. 97), 2 Cor. i. 3 ὁ πατὴρ τῶν οἰκτιρμῶν καὶ θεὸς πάσης παρακλήσεως (according to 16 p. 98 sq.), 1 Tim. vi. 15 (cf. 16 p. 98 sq.).

88　3) If the connected nouns differ in gender, the article
18　is as a rule repeated, since in such a case for two (or more) nouns, whether kindred or dissimilar, one article is no longer sufficient; thus, Eph. vi. 2 τίμα τὸν πατέρα σου καὶ τὴν μητέρα, Luke x. 21 κύριε τοῦ οὐρανοῦ καὶ τῆς γῆς, xiv. 26; Rom. viii. 2 νόμος τῆς ἁμαρτίας καὶ τοῦ θανάτου, xvi. 17; Col. iv. 1; Tit. i. 15, etc., and there ought properly to be no deviation from this usage.

Only in very rare cases does the language take the liberty to deviate, viz. where it makes a decided gain in perspicuity by omitting the article, as with substantives so closely united as to make almost a unity (ὁ μὲν σωφρονῶν καὶ σωφρονοῦσα Plato), or when according to 2) a. an attributive limitation is to be referred to both nouns, or further, where the addition of the art. would have occasioned inconvenience in some way, as Luke xiv. 23 εἰς τὰς ὁδοὺς καὶ φραγμούς, Mark xii. 33 πάντων τῶν ὁλοκαυτωμάτων καὶ θυσιῶν (where the addition of τῶν after the Rec. is positively wrong, on account of πάντων which is manifestly to be referred to both), Luke i. 6; Col. ii. 22 κατὰ τὰ ἐντάλματα καὶ διδασκα- λίας τῶν ἀνθρώπων, Rev. v. 12 τὴν δύναμιν καὶ πλοῦτον καὶ σοφίαν καὶ ἰσχύν etc., Acts xxi. 25 τό τε εἰδωλόθυτον καὶ αἷμα καὶ πνικτὸν καὶ πορνείαν (cf., on the other hand, xv. 20 Tdf.).

4) If the connected nouns differ also in n u m b e r, the genius of the language renders the repetition of the article still more necessary (Col. ii. 13 ἐν τοῖς παραπτώμασιν καὶ τῇ ἀκροβυστίᾳ τῆς σαρκὸς ὑμῶν, Eph. ii. 3, etc.), and no examples to the contrary are found in the N. T. That 1 Cor. iv. 9 establishes no exception, Winer 127 (121), deWette, and others have already observed.[1]

The Article (Prepositive and Postpositive) as a Demonstrative.

B. § 126, 2 and 3; H. § 525; C. § 518; D. p. 345; J. § 444.

The use of the prepositive article standing alone as a de- monstrative, which was always rather poetic, and accordingly restricted in ordinary prose to single phrases, is still more rare in the N. T., and, strictly speaking, appears there only in the combinations ὁ μέν and ὁ δέ, (for the poetic quotation in Acts xvii. 28 cannot be taken into account). But even these com- binations, also, have been retained only where they take the place of the subject, and moreover are in the Masc. or Fem.

[1] On this whole subject cf. Jatho, Brief an d. Phil. Exc. IV., who, however, has arranged all the examples under the single classification of union and separation of ideas. Important and influential as this distribution in itself considered is, it is nevertheless always an erroneous and one-sided procedure to group the phe- nomena of speech o n l y according to such abstract classifications, — a procedure which is the more detrimental to grammar as, owing to their elasticity, it is easy to succeed in bringing under them the great majority of phenomena. Form and substance have always, with the N. T. authors as well as with profane writers, at least an e q u a l share in the structure of discourse ; and to deny the effect of all the more external influences upon the choice of expressions would be to deprive authors of the instincts of speech. But to lay down the above classification as the only one leads to a disregard of the f o r m a l principle ; a disregard which betrays itself, among other ways, in the above-mentioned essay in this : that the author (on p. 79) unhesitatingly lays down the principle that in applying this rule it does not make the l e a s t difference whether the nouns to be connected are of the same or different gender, (why not, then, number also ?).

ὁ, ἡ, οἱ, αἱ ; so that all the cases beginning with τ (τό and τα included) must be left out of view. In the oblique cases, as well as in the Nom. neuter, the form of the postpositive, more usual in later prose, everywhere makes its appearance ; so that now all these combinations begin with the rough breathing : ὁ δέ, οἱ μέν (Heb. xii. 10), ἃ μέν (Matt. xiii. 4), ὃ μέν ... ὁ δέ (ib. 8), ὅν, ᾧ, οὓς μέν, etc.

The only exception, and that, too, more apparent than real, is Eph. iv. 11 (ἔδωκεν τοὺς μὲν ἀποστόλους, τοὺς δὲ προφήτας etc.) ; for in Mark xii. 5 the reading τοὺς μέν is now set aside by MS. authority [Sin. also]. In the Nom. Masc. the form of the postpositive sometimes appears instead of that of the prepositive, e.g. ὃς μὲν ... ὃς δέ Matt. xxii. 5 ; Rom. xiv. 5, 2 ; 1 Cor. xi. 21, or the MSS. vary, as in 1 Cor. vii. 7 ; John v. 11 Lchm. [Treg.].

B. § 126, 4; H. § 525 γ.; C. § 518 e.; D. § 390; J. § 444.

2   Examples of this use (of ὁ δέ alone as a connective in narration in reference to an object already named) can be brought forward in great number, yet only from the historical writings of the N. T. Let it be noticed, too, that in this case only the forms of the prepositive (ὁ, ἡ, οἱ, αἱ) are chosen, hence the exception (John v. 11 Lchm. [Treg.] ὃς δὲ ἀπεκρίθη) appears suspicious ; even here cod. Sin. has ὁ δέ as usual ; on the other hand, in one other passage (Mark xv. 23 [Tdf. Treg.]) both the oldest MSS. give ὃς δέ, but in opposition to [nearly] all other MS. authorities. The combination καὶ ὅς, καὶ οἵ (B. § 126, 5) does not occur.

B. § 126, N. 4; H. § 525 a.; C. § 518; D. p. 576; J. § 764.

3   Of the variations usual in classic Greek instead of ὁ μέν ... ὁ δέ, the following are found in the N. T. : Matt. xvi. 14 Lchm. οἱ μέν ... οἱ δέ (Tdf. [Treg.] ἄλλοι δέ) ... ἕτεροι δέ, John vii. 12 Lchm. [Treg.] οἱ μέν ... ἄλλοι δέ (Tdf. ἄλλοι, see § 149, 13 b) p. 366) cf. 1 Cor. xii. 8 ; Acts xvii. 18 τινές ... οἱ δέ, Mark iv. 4 ὃ μέν ... καὶ ἄλλο, Luke viii. 5 ὃ μέν ... καὶ ἕτερον. On 1 Cor. xii. 28 see § 149, 12 b) p. 365.

Further, under this head belong the various and rather Hebraistic
90 constructions with εἷς (אֶחָד ... אֶחָד Exod. xvii. 12 ; 1 Sam. x. 3), of which the following approximate most nearly to Greek usage : ὁ εἷς ... ὁ δὲ ἕτερος Luke vii. 41 cf. Acts xxiii. 6 ; less so : ὁ εἷς ... καὶ ὁ ἕτερος Matt. vi. 24 ; Luke xvi. 13 ; xvii. 35 Lchm., etc. ; without the art. εἷς ... καὶ ὁ ἕτερος Matt. vi. 24 ; Luke xvi. 13 ; xvii. 34 Tdf. [Treg.] etc., μία [ἡ μία Tdf., cod. Sin.] ... ἡ δὲ ἑτέρα xvii. 35 Tdf. [eds. 2, 7] ; also ὁ εἷς ... ὁ ἄλλος (but in reference to the last two of seven) Rev. xvii. 10 ; cf. § 127, 33 p. 122. Those constructions seem to come nearest to the Hebrew usage in which εἷς is repeated. As, however,

according to recent editors the article in this case is always
dropped, and the expression is employed in reference to more than
two members, its origin may quite as well be found in that mode of
speech, natural to common people, which arises from a simple enumeration of the several members (just as in German); as, εἶς ... καὶ εἶς
Matt. xx. 21; xxiv. 40; Mark xv. 27; John xx. 12; Gal. iv. 22;
compare with this the circumlocution for ἀλλήλων p. 31.   Luke uses
this combination only in the single passage ix. 33 (as in the parallel
passages Matt. xvii. 4; Mark ix. 5), in an enumeration of more than
two members.   After what has been said, the reading of Grsb. Lchm.
etc. in that passage of critical difficulty Mark iv. 8, 20 — according to
which in both verses the word ἔν (without the art.) is thrice repeated —
gains much in intrinsic probability, [Tdf. Treg. cod. Sin. give εἶς thrice
in vs. 8, ἐν in vs. 20]; see p. 30.   Lastly, in Gal. iv. 24 the enumeration, begun with μία μὲν, is continued in vs. 26 by another and similar
construction which connects closely with what precedes.

PRONOUNS.

οὗτος AND ὅδε, ἐκεῖνος.

B. § 127, 1 b.; H. § 679; C. § 544; D. p. 379; J. § 657 sq.

The difference spoken of between οὗτος and ὅδε (that οὗτος
refers *ordinarily* to what *precedes*, ὅδε to what *follows*), although
individual cases in support of it might be adduced from the
N. T. (Rev. ii. 1, 8, 12, etc.), has lost there its general validity,
inasmuch as the use of ὅδε (τοιόσδε, τοσόσδε) is quite isolated,
in fact doubtful (Luke xvi. 25 Grsb.; Acts xv. 23 Grsb.; 2 Cor.
xii. 19 Grsb.).   The N. T. language employs in all cases
almost exclusively the other demonstrative forms οὗτος, τοιοῦτος,
etc.

In James iv. 13 σήμερον καὶ αὔριον πορευσόμεθα εἰς τήνδε τὴν
πόλιν, according to the interpreters τήνδε has the force of an indefinite:
this or that.   As proof of this use, a passage is cited from Plut. Symp.
1, 6, 1 where τήνδε τὴν ἡμέραν is thought to have this signification.
Such, however, is not the case; on the contrary, in Plutarch, as
everywhere in Greek authors, the pronoun has its full
demonstrative force.   Accordingly we are not warranted in this single
biblical passage in taking the pronoun in any other than the demonstrative sense.   The apostle intended, to be sure, any city at option,
yet in thought he could point it out definitely; very much as we, too,
say in a similar case: into this city here (Germ. *in diese Stadt da*).

The familiar Latin usage, according to which, when two
objects are spoken of, whatever be the position of the words,

hic refers to that which at the moment is nearest the thought of the writer and *ille* to the more distant substantive, is quite applicable in Greek prose to the two demonstratives οὗτος and ἐκεῖνος. In the N. T., however, there are but few passages where both demonstrative pronouns make reference in one and the same proposition to two different ideas previously mentioned (see Luke xviii. 14; John v. 38, and cf. Jas. iv. 15). In these passages, as well as in others where οὗτος and ἐκεῖνος occur alone, it can be plainly seen that οὗτος always refers to the leading subject directly under discussion, and ἐκεῖνος to another, ordinarily more distant. Yet the writer in using οὗτος does not allow himself to be disturbed by the accidental proximity of another substantive, especially when the connection manifestly excludes every false reference ; and on the other hand, he can for the same reason safely make reference by means of ἐκεῖνος to an object which as respects the thought is subordinate, though as respects position it is nearer. Cf. my Article on ἐκεῖνος in the Stud. u. Krit. for 1860 pp. 505 sqq., and the supplement in Hilgenfeld's Zeitschr. Bd. V. pp. 204 sqq.

In Acts vii. 19; 2 John 7, οὗτος does not occasion the slightest doubt or ambiguity. In 1 John v. 20, also, an impartial interpreter can refer οὗτος only to θεός, and αὕτη in Acts viii. 26 only to ἡ ὁδός (for this is the subject of discourse, not Γάζα which is used merely to designate the way more precisely). Just as plainly does ἐκεῖνος in Acts iii. 13 refer to Pilate, and in Matt. xvii. 27 to στατήρ. Acts iv. 10 sq. may serve to prove how little is to be conceded to the external position, and how, when the connection is plain of itself, the author confides in the reader's good sense. Here there was occasion enough for perspicuity's sake to use the two demonstratives alternately ; yet οὗτος stands three times in succession: first (ἐν τούτῳ) referring to ὀνόματι Ἰησοῦ (although ὁ θεός just precedes), then (οὗτος) to the lame man, and the third time (οὗτος) again to Ἰησοῦς.

4 There is an analogy to the familiar Latin use of *hic* also in specifications of time (ante hos quinque annos) in Acts i. 5 οὐ μετὰ πολλὰς ταύτας ἡμέρας *after not many days from this*; where, moreover, the position of the words (instead of μετ' οὐ πολλάς) is to be noticed. Similar instances are found in the (later) Greek writers, see Winer 161 (152).

B. § 127, 1 d.; H. § 810; C. § 551 f.; J. § 817, 4.

5 The omission of the demonstrative before the relative is so common in the N.T., that it is hardly worth while to adduce examples

of this general custom.   That in this respect the writers have made
the classic usage quite their own may be seen from the following
passages (the examples where attraction occurs besides, will be found
§ 143, 10 p. 286): John xviii. 26 συγγενὴς ὢν οὗ ἀπέκοψεν Πέτρος τὸ   32
ὠτίον, Mark xv. 12 Tdf. τί θέλετε ποιήσω ὃν λέγετε τὸν βασιλέα τῶν
Ἰουδαίων (respecting the Acc. after ποιεῖν see § 131, 6 p. 149); and
when the Cases differ: Luke vii. 47 ᾧ δὲ ὀλίγον ἀφίεται, ὀλίγον ἀγαπᾷ,
John xi. 3 ἴδε ὃν φιλεῖς ἀσθενεῖ, Rom. iv. 7 μακάριοι ὧν ἀφέθησαν αἱ
ἀνομίαι; or are dependent, variously, upon prepositions: 2 Cor. xi. 12
ἵνα ἐν ᾧ καυχῶνται εὑρεθῶσιν καθὼς καὶ ἡμεῖς (for ἐν τούτῳ ἐν ᾧ, see § 133,
23 p. 185), Rom. x. 14 πῶς ἐπικαλέσωνται εἰς ὃν οὐκ ἐπίστευσαν (for
τοῦτον εἰς ὅν), John vi. 29 ἵνα πιστεύσητε εἰς ὃν ἀπέστειλεν (for εἰς τοῦτον
ὅν), Heb. vii. 13 ἐφ᾽ ὃν λέγεται ταῦτα, φυλῆς ἑτέρας μετέσχηκεν (for
οὗτος ἐφ᾽ ὅν) etc.   On Rom. vi. 21 cf. § 143, 4 b) p. 282.   In this way
many Relative conjunctional phrases have arisen, as ἀνθ᾽ ὧν because (of
this) that, ἐξ οὗ since (the time that), ἀφ᾽ οὗ, ἐν ᾧ, etc., see § 147 under
the several prepositions.

Before Relative adverbs, also, the demonstratives are frequently dropped: and that, too, not only when they express similar
relations (there ... where, etc.) e.g. John xx. 19 τῶν θυρῶν κεκλεισμένων,
ὅπου ἦσαν οἱ μαθηταί, 1 Cor. xvi. 6 ἵνα με προπέμψητε οὗ ἐὰν πορεύωμαι
(for οὗ here answers to the question whither, see p. 71), but also dissimilar (thither ... where) — a case which with the N. T. authors was
very common, in consequence of the want of precision just mentioned
in the use of adverbs of place (cf. besides § 151, 2 p. 377); as, John
xi. 32 ἦλθεν ὅπου ἦν, vi. 62 ἀναβαίνοντα ὅπου ἦν, Mark v. 40 εἰσπορεύεται
ὅπου ἦν i.e. ἐκεῖσε (or ἐκεῖ) ὅπου.

Respecting attraction in such cases see § 143, 12 p. 287.

B. § 127, 1 e.; J. 657, 2.

Οὗτος is often used redundantly, or rather in reference to what   6
follows, before propositions introduced by ὅτι; as, John iii. 19 αὕτη
ἐστὶν ἡ κρίσις, ὅτι τὸ φῶς ἐλήλυθεν etc. Rom. ii. 3 λογίζῃ δὲ τοῦτο ...
ὅτι ἐκφεύξῃ τὸ κρίμα; 2 Cor. i. 12, etc.   Likewise before ἵνα, — respecting which in its connection § 139, 45 p. 240.   On the introductory
τοῦτο before infinitive clauses see § 140, 7 and 9 pp. 262 sq.

CONSTRUCTIO AD SYNESIN WITH THE DEMONSTRATIVES, ESPECIALLY WITH
αὐτός.

The constructio ad synesin as respects gender and number   7
takes place, as with the relative (see § 143, 4 p. 281), so, too,
of course with the demonstrative.   As this usage harmonizes
completely with the genius of the Greek language (B. § 143, 5;

14

H. § 523 ; C. § 498 sq.; D. p. 362 ; J. § 378 sqq.), it is sufficient
here to refer to examples : Matt. i. 21 (λαὸν ... αἰτῶν), xiv.
14 and Mark vi. 46 (ὄχλον ... αὐτοῖς), Matt. xxviii. 19 (ἔθνη
... αὐτούς), Rom. ii. 14 (ἔθνη ... οὗτοι), Mark v. 41 (παιδίον
... αὐτῇ), 2 Cor. v. 19 (κόσμον ... αὐτοῖς), Col. ii. 15 (τὰς
ἀρχὰς καὶ τὰς ἐξουσίας ... αὐτούς), 3 John 9. (ἐκκλησία ...
αὐτῶν), Rev. xvii. 16 (τὰ κέρατα καὶ τὸ θηρίον ... οὗτοι) ;
1 John v. 21 (τεκνία ... ἑαυτούς Tdf. [eds. 2, 7] ἑαυτά Lchm.
[Tdf. Treg.]) is doubtful. Respecting John xvii. 2 (πᾶν ...
αὐτοῖς) see § 128, 1 p. 122.

8   REMARK. It is an extension of the above usage (an extension which
93 occurs likewise with the relative), to employ the most general of the
demonstratives (αὐτός) in reference to a substantive not expressly
mentioned but only s o f a r a s t h e s e n s e i s c o n c e r n e d contained in what precedes. Thus John viii. 44 ψεύστης ἐστὶν καὶ ὁ πατὴρ
αὐτοῦ sc. τοῦ ψεύδους,[1] Rom. ii. 26 ἡ ἀκροβυστία ... αὐτοῦ sc. τοῦ ἐν ἀκρ.
ὄντος, Eph. v. 12 τὰ γινόμενα ὑπ᾽ αὐτῶν sc. the children of darkness, to
be supplied from σκότος and τέκνα φωτός preceding, John xv. 6 where
we find συνάγουσιν αὐτά, owing to the neut. κλῆμα and the plurality
suggested in τὶς, Gal. iii. 12 ὁ ποιήσας αὐτά sc. τὰ τοῦ νόμου.   Not
less customary is it to employ the P l u r a l αὐτοί in referring to the
inhabitants of a place or country already mentioned, e.g. 2 Cor. ii. 12 sq.
(Τρωάδα ... αὐτοῖς), Matt. iv. 23 (Γαλιλαίᾳ ... αὐτῶν), ix. 35 ; Acts
viii. 5 (Σαμαρείας ... αὐτοῖς), xx. 2 ; 1 Thess. i. 9 ; so that at length
the plur. αὐτοί comes to denote in an indefinite way the general idea
of *people*, and the reader is left to judge for himself according to the
connection what persons or classes of men stand in necessary relation
to the substance of the statement.   So e.g. in 1 Pet. iii. 14 τὸν φόβον
αὐτῶν μὴ φοβηθῆτε, where αὐτῶν means the many suggested in τίς ὁ
κακώσων ὑμᾶς ; cf. Heb. iv. 8 ; viii. 8 ; xi. 28 ; Acts iv. 5 τοὺς ἄρχοντας
αὐτῶν viz. of the Jews, Matt. xii. 9 τὴν συναγωγὴν αὐτῶν viz. of the
Galileans (see deWette on iv. 23), Acts x. 10 παρασκευαζόντων αὐτῶν
viz. the inmates of the house, Matt. xix. 2 ὄχλοι πολλοί, καὶ ἐθεράπευσεν
αὐτούς viz. τοὺς ἀρρώστους αὐτῶν according to xiv. 14 ; cf. xii. 15 ; Luke
v. 17.   According to this usage, too, the indefinite interpretation of
αὐτῶν in Matt. xi. 1, and of αὐτοῖς in viii. 4 ; Mark i. 44 ; Luke v. 14,
seems to be perfectly justified. On the other hand, in Acts xii. 21

---

[1] This is the current interpretation according to the well-established reading.
Yet even ancient expositors took exception to it, and Lachmann, following them,
proposes (Vol. II. p. vii of Preface) to read ὃς ἄν for ὅταν.   Then the meaning
would be somewhat altered as follows : *whoever speaketh a lie* (cf. Ignat. Ep. interp.
p. 283 ed. Dressel ἐάν τις Χριστὸν ἀρνῆται υἱὸν εἶναι Θεοῦ) speaketh his own peculiar
language, *because his father also* (ὁ διάβολος) *is a liar.*

ἐδημηγόρει πρὸς αὐτούς means definitely to the Tyrians and Sidonians (vs. 20).

The Use of the Pronoun αὐτός.

B. § 127, 2 and N. 1; H. § 668; C. § 540 i.; D. p. 375; J. § 656.

No pronoun appears more frequently in the Scriptures of   9 the Old and New Testaments than αὐτός ; indeed, this pronoun is employed to such excess (cf. 26 below p. 118, and § 129, 12 p. 131, § 130, 2 p. 142, § 145, 1 p. 314), that it contributes essentially to the peculiar character which distinguishes biblical from classical Greek.

As respects the pronoun's signification, the ordinary rules (B. p. 307 ; H. § 669 ; C. § 540 sq. ; D. p. 462 ; J. § 656) hold good in the main ; but in the N o m i n a t i v e there is a notice-able departure from classic usage. Winer 150 (141 sq.), Fritzsche (ad Matt. p. 47), and others assert, indeed, that (as in the classics) αὐτός in the Nominative never stands for the unemphatic *he*, inasmuch as then it is used, either 1) for Jesus in contrast with his disciples, or 2) with a certain emphasis, or 3) only in definite antithesis to other objects. Although it is true that the majority of passages allow themselves to be distributed among these three classes, yet we have not, by doing this, demonstrated the agreement of the biblical use   14 with the classical ; and besides, there are passages enough where there is absolutely no hint of emphasis or of antithesis and common classic prose would in no case have employed αὐτός, — an assertion which can be made also even of most of the passages where αὐτός represents Christ.

We will endeavor to make what we have said plain by a number of examples from the Gospels, especially from Luke, with whom the Nom. is most frequent.   The language of Luke i. 22 respecting Zach-arias : καὶ αὐτὸς ἦν διανεύων αὐτοῖς, in the classics could only mean *he also* or *he himself*. It is, however, the simple continuation of the narrative.   And should any one wish to assume an antithesis because other persons were previously spoken of, the antithesis is only such a one as the Greek language ordinarily conveyed by ὁ δέ; otherwise we should be compelled to maintain that there is such an antithesis every-where, in every narrative, provided only several persons are spoken of.   Further in ii. 28, where it is said of Simeon καὶ αὐτὸς ἐδέξατο αὐτό etc., καὶ αὐτός might be omitted altogether.   In xvi. 24, where it is said of the rich man καὶ αὐτὸς φωνήσας εἶπεν etc., either ὁ δέ or simply καί might have been used ; for just before, too, he was the subject,

and the mention of Lazarus involves no antithesis. Luke xix. 2
Lchm. [Treg.] καὶ ἰδοὺ ἀνὴρ καλούμενος Ζακχαῖος, καὶ αὐτὸς ἦν ἀρχιτελώ-
νης, καὶ αὐτὸς ἦν πλούσιος, καὶ ἐζήτει etc., where otherwise we should
have had either twice a simple apposition, or at most the participle ὤν
with ἀρχ. and πλούσ. The peculiarity of the language consists precisely in its being thus dissected into many individual propositions, in
which αὐτός is a simple unemphatic repetition of the antecedent subject.

Compare, now, with such sentences, those in which αὐτός or καὶ
αὐτός really is emphatic, as vi. 42 πῶς δύνασαι λέγειν· Ἀδελφέ, ἄφες
ἐκβάλω . . . , αὐτὸς τὴν δοκὸν οὐ βλέπων etc., v. 37 ῥήξει ὁ οἶνος τοὺς
ἀσκούς, καὶ αὐτὸς ἐκχυθήσεται καὶ οἱ ἀσκοὶ ἀπολοῦνται; vi. 3 ὃ ἐποίησεν
Δαυείδ, ὅτε ἐπείνασεν αὐτὸς καὶ οἱ μετ’ αὐτοῦ, xv. 14; xvii. 16; xix. 9,—
although in such passages even it does not seem to be always necessary
to employ the pronoun, e.g. iii. 15; vi. 35.

Further, if we look at the passages in which αὐτός stands for Christ
(some thirty times, more or less, in Luke), we shall find that, in by
far the greater number, the mode of expression or the connection of
clauses is at variance with ordinary usage; as, iii. 16, 23; iv. 15;
v. 1, 14, 16, 17; vi. 8, 20; viii. 1, 22, 37, 54; ix. 51; x. 38; xi. 17,
28; xvii. 11; xxii. 41; xxiii. 9; xxiv. 25, 28, in all which cases
either no pronoun would have been used, or οὗτος or ὁ δέ. On the
other hand, it is used with emphasis apparently only in iv. 30; x. 1;
xviii. 39; xxiv. 39, in which passages it accords with Greek usage.
The weakened force of αὐτός is clearly perceptible in those passages
where it is several times repeated; as, xxiv. 36 ταῦτα δὲ αὐτῶν λαλούν-
των αὐτὸς ἔστη ἐν μέσῳ αὐτῶν καὶ λέγει αὐτοῖς, xxiv. 31 αὐτῶν δὲ διηνοί-
χθησαν οἱ ὀφθαλμοὶ καὶ ἐπέγνωσαν αὐτόν· καὶ αὐτὸς ἄφαντος ἐγένετο ἀπ’
αὐτῶν. Cf. John ii. 24; Mark iii. 31 sq.; Acts xxiii. 9, etc.

Similar observations may be applied to the other books, especially
the historical, e.g. Matt. iii. 11; v. 4; xiv. 2; xvi. 20, etc. In reference also to a preceding or following R e l a t i v e, αὐτός is used in the
sense of *he, the one*, instead of οὗτος or ἐκεῖνος which alone is customary
in such cases in Greek prose, (where αὐτός before a relative always
has its proper meaning, *self*); as, Mark xiv. 44 ὃν ἂν φιλήσω, αὐτός
ἐστιν, Matt. xii. 50 ὅστις ἂν ποιῇ τὸ θέλημα . . . , αὐτός μου ἀδελφός etc.
Matt. xxvi. 48, etc.; so, too, when a participle stands instead of the
relative clause, according to § 125, 3 p. 93, as Luke xxiv. 21 ἠλπί-
ζομεν ὅτι αὐτός ἐστιν ὁ μέλλων λυτροῦσθαι etc.

What has now been taught in reference to the Nom. Masc.
αὐτός, must of course be applied consistently to all other forms
of the Nominative, both Sing. and Plur.

Thiersch (de Pentat. vers. Alex. p. 98) asserts that in the Sept.
αὐτός is used for *he*, but for the Feminine the demonstrative αὕτη is

regularly employed. This seems to be the case also in the N. T.; at
any rate, the numerous examples of αὐτός cannot be matched with a
single indubitable instance of αὐτή, still less of αὐταί. Nevertheless.
the state of the matter may have been different, since in the case of
αυτη and αυται it depended only on the accent to make the one form
or the other; and in point of fact, the readings often fluctuate (Mark
xii. 31; Luke ii. 2; vii. 12; Rom. vii. 10; xvi. 2). Further, if we
look at the several passages where at present αὕτη stands, we find
many which are quite like those with αὐτός given above; to take examples again from Luke: ii. 36 Lchm. [Tdf. Treg.] ("Αννα) αὕτη ...
ζήσασα μετὰ ἀνδρὸς ..., καὶ αὕτη (Tdf. [Treg.] αὐτὴ) χήρα etc., vii. 12
Lchm. [Treg.] τῇ μητρὶ αὐτοῦ, καὶ αὕτη ἦν χήρα (Tdf. om. ἦν [in eds.
2 and 7, not in ed. 8]), viii. 42; 1 Cor. vii. 12, etc. But since in all
these and similar passages the Vulgate has *haec*,[1] while αὐτός it always
reproduces (and on account of all absence of doubt respecting the
form cannot do otherwise) by *ipse*, and αυτη also where it is indubitably
the Fem. of αὐτός by *ipsa* (e.g. Luke i. 36; Rom. viii. 21; xvi. 2;
1 Cor. xi. 14; Rev. xviii. 6), recent editors in the above instances
have for the most part acquiesced in the form αὕτη.

Respecting the Neuter αὐτό, Thiersch (as above) likewise de-   **11**
clares that in the Sept. it does not, after the manner of οὗτος, stand
for *it*, but that τοῦτο is always used instead. Certainly where *it* (as
the Subject) refers to purely abstract ideas, the form τοῦτο may
alone have been in use; but that in the more concrete instances
(which, however, from the nature of the case cannot occur frequently)
the form αὐτό straightway makes its appearance again, is shown once
more by a passage from Luke (xi. 14): ἦν ἐκβάλλων δαιμόνιον, καὶ
αὐτὸ ἦν κωφόν.

Of the Masc. Plur., again, a number of indubitable passages may
be adduced, as for example the αὐτοί common in the Sermon on the
Mount (Matt. v. 4, 5, 6, 7, 8, 9, cf. 3, 10), further Mark ii. 8 Tdf.
[eds. 2, 7] (where Tdf. [7th ed.] remarks correctly, *vox ista αὐτοί
delenda videri poterat, non item addenda*), Luke ii. 50; ix. 36; xiii. 4,
etc. This use becomes more frequent in later authors, presumably
through Roman influence.

B. § 127, 2, iii.; H. § 502 b.; C. § 540 d.; J. § 656.

Of the combination αὐτὸ τοῦτο *id ipsum* a considerable number of   **12**
instances may be brought forward, all of them, too, from the Epistles,
viz. Rom. ix. 17; xiii. 6; 2 Cor. v. 5; vii. 11; Gal. ii. 10; Eph. vi.   **96**
22; Phil. i. 6; Col. iv. 8; doubtful is 2 Pet. i. 5; once also τοῦτο αὐτό

---

[1] Yet the versions do not always agree in this particular; see e.g. Täf.'s note
on Luke ii. 36.

occurs, 2 Cor. ii. 3 ([cod. Sin. also], see the variants). The Masc. αὐτοί
οὗτοι occurs in Acts xxiv. 15, 20.

REMARK. Respecting the quiescing αὐτός in relative clauses
(ὃν ... αὐτόν) after the example of the Hebrew, see § 143, 1 p. 280.

THE REFLEXIVE PRONOUN.

B. § 127, 3 and N. 3; H. § 670 sq.; C. § 537 sq.; J. § 653 sq.

13   In the use of the reflexive pronoun the language of the
N. T. has departed essentially from Attic correctness. It retained, indeed, a knowledge of the difference between the
reflexives and the simple personal pronoun, for it never uses the
reflexive where according to the rule it ought not to stand, e.g.
John viii. 18 ἐγώ εἰμι ὁ μαρτυρῶν περὶ ἐμαυτοῦ, καὶ μαρτυρεῖ
περὶ ἐμοῦ ὁ πέμψας με πατήρ, cf. v. 31, 32; Rom. xvi. 2 αὐτὴ
προστάτις πολλῶν ἐγενήθη καὶ ἐμοῦ αὐτοῦ, but it very frequently neglects it, and contents itself with the simple
personal pronoun instead of the usual reflexives.

To make this plain first in reference to pronouns of the First and
Second Pers. (Sing. and Plur.) : the simple personals take the place
of the reflexives not only, a) in those cases which rest upon the analogy
of ordinary Greek usage, that is to say in which the reference to the
leading subject is rendered difficult by the intervention of subordinate
clauses with a different subject, especially participial and infinitive
clauses, e.g. Luke viii. 46 ἔγνων δύναμιν ἐξελθοῦσαν ἀπ' ἐμοῦ, Acts xxii. 7
ἤκουσα φωνῆς λεγούσης μοι, xxvi. 13; Rom. vii. 23; Col. i. 29; Rev.
x. 9 ἀπῆλθα, λέγων αὐτῷ δοῦναί μοι τὸ βιβλ., Matt. xiv. 28 (cf. also the
subject-acc. with the Infin. expressed by με, σε, etc., instead of ἐμαυτόν,
etc., § 141, 4 p. 274) ; or, b) in those which find a natural apology in
the fact that other personal pronouns are coupled with them, as Matt.
xvii. 27 λαβὼν δὸς αὐτοῖς ἀντὶ ἐμοῦ καὶ σοῦ, Rom. i. 12 (ὑμῶν τε καὶ
ἐμοῦ), Matt. xviii. 15 ; or, c) where the reference to some other term
in the clause, even though it may be merely the article, was more convenient than reference to the subject, as in Gal. i. 17 ἀπῆλθον πρὸς
τοὺς πρὸ ἐμοῦ ἀποστόλους, Phil. ii. 23 ὡς ἂν ἀφίδω τὰ περὶ ἐμέ, — hence
uniformly σου, μου, instead of σεαυτοῦ, etc., when the personal pronouns
are used in place of the possessives (see 19 below, p. 115) ; but
also, d) where the reflexive force of the pronoun goes back directly to
the subject, — yet particularly, only where the oblique case is preceded
by a preposition, as βάλε ἀπὸ σοῦ, μὴ σαλπίσῃς ἔμπροσθέν σου,
παράλαβε μετὰ σοῦ, ἄρατε ἐφ' ὑμᾶς, etc. (Matt. v. 29, 30; xviii. 8, 9 ;
vi. 2; xviii. 16; xi. 29, etc.) ; but the regular construction also occurs
especially in John : ἑλκύσω πρὸς ἐμαυτόν, περὶ σεαυτοῦ μαρτυρεῖς, ἄγε

μετὰ σεαυτοῦ, etc.   But where the case is governed immediately b y
the verb, the reflexive forms in the Singular are constantly 97
used, as βάλε, σῶσον, δεῖξον σεαυτόν, ἔπεχε σεαυτῷ, ἁγιάζω ἐμαυτόν, ἔκρινα
ἐμαυτῷ τοῦτο,—even ἔδοξα ἐμαυτῷ *mihi videbar* (Acts xxvi. 9), although
among the Greeks themselves the expressions δοκῶ μοι and μοι δοκῶ
were common enough (see Steph. sub voce) ; in the Plural, on the
other hand, the forms of the reflexive of the 3d Pers. ἑαυτοῖς, ἑαυτούς,
etc. (respecting which see 15 below, p. 113) are almost always used
in this case, and such instances as Matt. vi. 19, 20 (μὴ θησαυρίζετε
ὑμῖν θησαυρούς), Eph. iv. 22 (see § 141, 4 p. 274) are extremely rare.

As respects the reflexive pronoun of the Third Person, 14
it is to be noticed first of all, that according to the more recent
collations it exists only in the fuller form ἑαυτοῦ, -ῆς, etc. (not
αὑτοῦ, etc.).   It has, accordingly, been assumed that in all
cases where the forms αυτου, αυτω, αυτον, etc. (not εαυτου)
appear, they must be marked with the smooth breathing, and
consequently the reflexive is not used.   This procedure was
occasioned by observing the usage of the Sept., and has been
confirmed, 1) by observing that of the 2d Pers., also, only the
fuller form σεαυτοῦ, etc., has been preserved ; and, 2) that the
reflexive forms of the 1st and 2d Pers. began to be used with
considerably less frequency (see the preceding section) ; 3)
by the usage of ordinary prose, in which (B. § 127, N. 3) a
marked vacillation began likewise to show itself in the employment of the forms αὐτοῦ and αὑτοῦ, etc. ; 4) by the
difference in position commonly observed in connection with
the two forms (αυτου and εαυτου) in a possessive relation (see
on this point 20 below, p. 116) ; 5) by noticing that before
the forms αυτου, etc., when decidedly reflexive in sense, the
prepositions ἐπί, κατά, etc., are never aspirated after elision, see
Tdf. praef. ad Vet. Test. p. xxxiii [ed. 3] ; ad N. T. xxvi. [ed.
2 ; lviii sq. ed. 7] ; Winer 152 (143).

If, now, we compare together the cases in which the forms αὐτοῦ,
etc., and those in which ἑαυτοῦ, etc., are given, we shall find what was
just now said in reference to the first two persons to be in the main
substantiated in reference to the third also, inasmuch as αὐτοῦ, etc.,
are used almost exclusively in a possessive relation (therefore for *suus*),
and in general in all the cases given above (13 p. 110) where immediate reflex reference to the verb is in any way obstructed. If,
however, especial emphasis made the reflexive form necessary, — that
is to say, 1) if in specifications of possession not merely the notion *his*

(*suus*), but his *own* (*suum ipsius*, etc.), was to be expressed; 2) in
case of the emphatic repetition of the subject after verba dicendi in
the construction of Acc. with Infin. (see § 141, 4 p. 274) ; ånd 3) if
the case of the reflexive was governed immediately by the verb
(often also after a preposition), — the fuller forms ἑαυτοῦ, etc., (so far
as we can be sure about the MSS. in this matter) made their appearance

98   EXAMPLES. 1) Of αὐτοῦ, etc. : in a possessive relation, Matt. x. 3ՙ
ὁ εὑρών, ὁ ἀπολέσας τὴν ψυχὴν αὐτοῦ, Luke ii. 7 ἔτεκεν τὸν υἱὸν αὐτῆς,
and so on times without number ;   in immediate dependence on a
participle, Mark x. 32 ἤρξατο λέγειν τὰ μέλλοντα αὐτῷ συμβαίνειν, Acts
ix. 4 ἤκουσεν φωνὴν λέγουσαν αὐτῷ, Heb. xii. 2, etc.,   or on an infinitive,
Eph. i. 4 ἐξελέξατο ἡμᾶς ... εἶναι ἡμᾶς ἁγίους κατενώπιον αὐτοῦ;   as
subject of the Infin. after verba dicendi — a case which can occur but
seldom, since according to rule in Greek the reflexive subject is
separately expressed only for the sake of emphasis, and then ἑαυτόν
must be used, Acts xxv. 21 τοῦ Παύλου ἐπικαλεσαμένου τηρηθῆναι αὐτόν
(where there is no emphasis, and yet the repetition of the subject was
necessary, cf. § 141, 4 p. 274) ;   after prepositions, John ix. 21 αὐτὸς
περὶ αὐτοῦ λαλήσει, Acts xv. 22 ἐκλεξαμένους ἄνδρας ἐξ αὐτῶν, xvi. 3 τοῦτον
ἠθέλησεν σὺν αὐτῷ ἐξελθεῖν, Heb. xiii. 21; Mark ix. 16 τί συνζητεῖτε
πρὸς αὐτούς (cf. i. 27) ; — with unaspirated consonants preceding, Matt.
iii. 16 ἐρχόμενον ἐπ᾽ αὐτόν, Luke vi. 3, 4; Rev. ix. 11 (where Grsb.
and Rec. give ἐφ᾽ αὐτῶν, a correction ; [cod. Sin. ἑαυτῶν]).

   2) Of ἑαυτοῦ, etc., for *his own* : Luke xiii. 34 ὄρνις τὰ ἑαυτῆς νοσσία,
xi. 21 τὴν ἑαυτοῦ αὐλήν, Matt. viii. 22 τοὺς ἑαυτῶν νεκρούς, etc., cf. 20
below, p. 116 ;   as subject after verba dicendi, see for examples § 141,
4 p. 274;   in immediate dependence on the leading predicate, with
and without a preposition, ἀπαρνησάσθω ἑαυτόν (Matt. xvi. 24 ; Mark
viii. 34), ποιεῖν ἑαυτὸν βασιλέα (John xix. 12), ταπεινοῦν (Matt. xviii.
4, etc.) ὑψοῦν (Matt. xxiii. 12, etc.) ἀπολέσαι (Luke ix. 25) εὐνουχίζειν
(Matt. xix. 12) ἑαυτόν, ἀγαπᾶν τὸν πλησίον ὡς ἑαυτόν (Mark xii. 33),
ἵνα ἀγοράσωσιν ἑαυτοῖς (Matt. xiv. 15), βασιλεία μερισθεῖσα καθ᾽ ἑαυτῆς
(Matt. xii. 25), ἀνέστη ἐφ᾽ ἑαυτόν (Mark iii. 26), etc.; to this last class
there are but few exceptions.[1]

---

[1] These seem to be John ii. 24 ἐπίστευεν αὐτόν (Grsb. ἑαυτόν), xix. 17 βαστάζων
αὐτῷ τὸν σταυρὸν ἐξῆλθεν (yet with both the other forms as variants ; [Tdf. ℵ ἑαυτῷ],
Grsb. τὸν σταυρὸν αὐτοῦ), Acts xiv. 17 Lchm. [Tdf. Treg. ℵ] οὐκ ἀμάρτυρον αὐτὸν
ἀφῆκεν (Tdf. [eds. 2, 7] ἑαυτόν), Rev. viii. 6 Lchm. [T.Tr.ℵ] ἡτοίμασαν αὐτούς(Tdf.
[eds. 2, 7] ἑαυτούς, cf. xix. 7), xviii. 7 ἐδόξασεν αὐτήν (Grsb. ἑαυτήν).   Since in this
single class of cases the reflexive is used almost without exception with the first
and second Persons also (13 p. 111), consistency seems to require that in these
passages too, the reflexive, i.e. the aspirated form, be retained, unless we choose to
restore the fuller form ἑαυτόν, etc., which is that presented, as a rule, by MSS.
(Matt. xv. 30 does not belong here.)

B. § 127, N. 5; H. § 672; C. § 539; J. § 654, 2 b.

It is now universally acknowledged, that in authors of every 15
age, prose writers as well as poets, the reflexive of the 3d
Person often takes the place of the reflexive of the 1st or 2d
Person. In the N. T. this occurs especially with the Plural
reflexives. The following seems to be the account of the
matter: Since the pronoun αὐτός as a reflexive had lost its
proper sense of *self* and all emphasis, ἐμαυτόν, σεαυτόν, etc.,
only signifying *me, thee*, etc. (like the English *myself, thyself*),
it became necessary in the Sing., if the precise idea *my* etc.
self was to be expressed, to write the words separately ἐμὲ, 99
σὲ αὐτόν or αὐτὸν σέ, etc. This was not the case in the Plural,
where the two senses *us* (reflex.) and *ourselves*, etc., could
not be distinguished so well as in the Singular; on the contrary,
the separation of the two pronouns would naturally suggest to
the mind the meaning *us* etc. *ourselves*. Accordingly the
usage gradually grew up, after the unquestionable precedent
of the earlier writers (see, for instance, in prose, Thuc. 1, 82
τὰ αὑτῶν ἐκποριζώμεθα, Demosth. Phil. p. 52 εἴπερ μὴ ἑαυτῶν
ἀπεγνώκατε, de Cor. p. 252, 14; 282, 2; Chers. p. 95, 5; Plat.
Phaed. p. 78 δεῖ ἡμᾶς ἀνερέσθαι ἑαυτούς), in case the reflexive
of the 1st or 2d Pers. Plur. was to mean simply *us, you*, without
emphasis, to employ the form of the reflexive of the 3d Pers.
Plur. consisting likewise of a single word, especially as by
doing so no ambiguity could arise in any way. In the N. T.
this usage has already become so thoroughly established that
the disjoined forms (ἡμᾶς αὐτούς, etc.) are no longer used as
mere reflexives, but when they occur have manifestly the force
of *us ourselves*, etc.

Instances of the Plural are very numerous and completely established
by the MSS.; that is to say,

Of the 2d Pers., Matt. iii. 9 μὴ δόξητε λέγειν ἐν ἑαυτοῖς, xvi. 8; xxiii.
31 μαρτυρεῖτε ἑαυτοῖς, xxv. 9 ἀγοράσατε ἑαυταῖς, xxvi. 11 ἔχετε μεθ᾽ ἑαυτῶν, Mark ix. 50; xiii. 9 βλέπετε ὑμεῖς ἑαυτούς, xiv. 7; Luke xii. 1, 33,
57; xvi. 9 etc.; John v. 42; vi. 53 etc.; Acts v. 35; xiii. 46 etc.;
Rom. vi. 11, 13, 16 etc.; 1 Cor. vi. 7, 19 etc. On the other hand,
Acts xx. 30 ἐξ ὑμῶν αὐτῶν ἀναστήσονται ἄνδρες (not reflexive); 1 Cor.
vii. 35 πρὸς τὸ ὑμῶν αὐτῶν σύμφορον *for your own profit;* xi. 13 ἐν
ὑμῖν αὐτοῖς κρίνατε *judge by yourselves*.

Of the 1st Pers., Acts xxiii. 14 ἀνεθεματίσαμεν ἑαυτούς, Rom. viii. 23
αὐτοὶ ἐν ἑαυτοῖς στενάζομεν, xv. 1 ὀφείλομεν ... μὴ ἑαυτοῖς ἀρέσκειν,

1 Cor. xi. 31 ; 2 Cor. i. 9 (twice), iii. 1, 5, etc. On the other hand,
2 Thess. i. 4 ὥστε ἡμᾶς αὐτοὺς ἐν ὑμῖν ἐνκαυχᾶσθαι so that we o u r s e l v e s
boast.

REMARK. Of the S i n g u l a r, it is true, hardly an unquestionable
and satisfactory instance can be adduced from the N. T. In Gal. v.
14 Tdf. [ed. 2] reads again with the Rec. ἀγαπήσεις ... ὡς ἑαυτόν, but
by far the greater number of the ancient MSS. [א also] and authorities
give σεαυτόν (Lchm. Grsb. [Tdf. eds. 7, 8, Treg.]). In John xviii. 34,
again, the most important MSS. ([א] B C L) have ἀπὸ σεαυτοῦ λέγεις
(Lchm. [Treg.]), instead of ἀφ᾽ ἑαυτοῦ (Grsb. Tdf.). On the other
hand, examples are common in the apocr. writings, e.g. Protev. 9, 1 ;
Thom. 7, 2 ; Nicod. 3, 2 ; Ep. Ignat. ad Trall. 3, etc. It is noticeable
that in the classics, also, when the Sing. forms, ἑαυτοῦ etc., appear to be
so used, there is almost always considerable variation in the readings,
but not in the case of the Plural; see e.g. the variants on Xen. Mem.
1, 4, 9 (where almost all the oldest and more important MSS. give
σεαυτοῦ); 2, 1, 7. 30; 2, 6, 35 ; Anab. 6, 6, 15 ; 7, 5, 5 ; Cyr. 1, 6, 35.
44; 5, 1, 20 ; Plat. Phaed. p. 91 C.; Protag. p. 312 A.; Amat. p. 136 D.;
100 Alcib. II. p. 143 C. etc. Since it is often the inferior and later MSS.
which offer the 3d Pers., we may assume thus much at least as certain :
that the usage was in later times pretty generally (in the Plural almost
exclusively) prevalent, and that it must have been very familiar to
the coypists; hence Apollon. Synt. 3, 2 (p. 195 B) expressly instructs
us οὐ γάρ φαμεν ἑ α υ τ ὸ ν ὕβρισα ἢ ἑ α υ τ ὸ ν ὕβρισας, ἑαυτοὺς δὲ ὑβρί-
σαμεν. Consequently, the common assumption (see e.g. Kühner on
Mem. 1, 4, 9 ; Meyer on Gal. 5, 14) that the copyists out of ignorance
changed the 3d Person into the 1st or 2d, may be given up as erroneous,
if not in all, at least in many, passages of ancient authors, and certainly
in the two from the N. T. given above. See besides, Bhdy. Synt.
p. 272, and the copious references on the subject in Matth. p. 1088 ;
Ellendt, Lex. Soph. I p. 272.

THE PRONOUNS τὶς, τίς, ὅστις.

B. § 127, 4; H. § 683; C. § 548; D. § 412; J. § 659.

16   The Indef. Pron. τὶς, τὶ in the pregnant sense of a man of
i m p o r t a n c e, something g r e a t, or merely of the emphatic
something in opposition to *nothing* (see Herm. ad Vig. nott. 112,
113), is not unknown in the N. T.

E.g. Acts v. 36 Θευδᾶς λέγων εἶναί τινα ἑαυτόν (viii. 9 in full: εἶναι
τινα ἑαυτὸν μέγαν) ; Gal. vi. 3 εἰ δοκεῖ τις εἶναί τι μηδὲν ὤν (just as in
Plat. Apol. p. 41 E.), ii. 6 ; vi 15, etc. Cf. on this head § 129, 5 p. 127

B. § 127, 5; H. § 682; C. § 566; D. p. 382; J. § 872.

Instances of the combination of two questions into one **17** (indirect) interrogative clause, are rare. Such appear to be Mark xv. 24 βάλλοντες κλῆρον τίς τί ἄρῃ, Luke xix. 15 ἵνα γνοῖ τίς τί διεπραγματεύσατο.

REMARK. For the use of τίς, τί sometimes instead of the simple relative (or of the indirect interrogative clause instead of the relative clause), see § 139, 58 p. 251. It likewise takes the place of πότερος (e.g. Matt. xxi. 31) in reference to two, like ὁ εἷς for ὁ ἕτερος c.'. p. 30.

B. § 127, N. 10; H. § 681 b.; C. § 550; J. § 816.

The looser use of the relative pron. ὅστις, in so far as it refers to **18** precisely-defined objects, is constantly gaining ground in the later language (see Steph. Paris ed. sub voce p. 2309) and also in the N. T., as numerous examples show : Luke ii. 4 εἰς πόλιν Δαυεὶδ, ἥτις καλεῖται Βηθλεέμ, Rom. xvi. 6, 12 ἀσπάσασθε Μαριὰμ, ἥτις πολλὰ ἐκοπίασεν εἰς ὑμᾶς, Luke xxiii. 18 τὸν Βαραββᾶν, ὅστις ἦν . . . βεβλημένος εἰς φυλακήν, Gal. iv. 26 ἡ ἄνω Ἱερουσαλὴμ . . . ἥτις ἐστὶν μήτηρ ἡμῶν. See besides, Matt. xxi. 33 ; Acts xvii. 10 ; Rom. xi. 4 ; Eph. i. 23 ; iii. 13 ; 2 Tim. ii. 18 ; Rev. xii. 13, etc. That besides, and indeed in by far the majority of cases, ὅστις has its legitimate general force, it is not necessary to state.

PERIPHRASIS FOR THE POSSESSIVES BY MEANS OF THE PERSONAL PRONOUNS, THE REFLEXIVES, AND ἴδιος.

B. § 127, 7, 1); H. § 675; D. p. 352 sq.; J. § 652, 3.

The substitution of the genitives μου and σου for the pos- **19** sessives of the 1st and 2d Pers. Sing. predominates in the New Testament as in the Old — (the adjectives ἐμός and σός are **101** employed oftenest by John) ; and the ear had already become so accustomed to this mode of expressing *mine* and *thine*, that (according to 13 p. 110 above) it was everywhere [1] resorted to, even when classic Greek would have been obliged to employ the reflexive pronouns ἐμαυτοῦ and σαυτοῦ. Their position is uniformly according to the rule : that is, they either precede the article or follow the noun.

Examples : ὁ ἀδελφός σου, μου τοὺς λόγους, σου τὴν κλίνην, μου ὑπὸ τὴν στέγην (Matt. viii. 8, according to § 147, 31 p. 343) ;   for reflexives : John viii. 49 τιμῶ τὸν πατέρα μου, Rom. i. 8 εὐχαριστῶ τῷ θεῷ μου, Matt. v. 24 ἄφες τὸ δῶρόν σου . . . διαλλάγηθι τῷ ἀδελφῷ σου . . . καὶ πρόσφερε τὸ δῶρόν σου, vii. 4, 5, etc.

[1] The only contrary example, 1 Cor. x. 33 τὸ ἐμαυτοῦ σύμφορον, finds its explanation from § 132, 23 p. 169 as an objective, not possessive, genitive, and from the antithesis to τῶν πολλῶν.

B. § 127, 7, 2); H. § 538; C. § 523 sq.; D. p. 353; J. § 452.

20   On distinguishing between the forms αὐτοῦ and ἑαυτοῦ, etc.,
in the place of the Poss. Pron. of the 3d Pers. see 14, p. 111
above. As to their p o s i t i o n, with substantives which have
the article it is, in the main, the regular one, see e.g. Mark
viii. 35 (Vat. Sin.) ; yet here and there (as in classic authors
also, see B. § 127, N. 12) instances to the contrary are found :

1) Of αὐτοῦ, -ῆς, etc. Those instances have a foundation in usage
where αὐτοῦ, etc., get an intermediate position because there are already
o t h e r attributive limitations between the art. and the subst., as Matt.
xxvii. 60 ἐν τῷ καινῷ αὐτοῦ μνημείῳ, Acts iii. 21 τῶν ἁγίων ἀπ᾽ αἰῶνος
αὐτοῦ προφητῶν, 1 Pet. i. 3 κατὰ τὸ πολὺ αὐτοῦ ἔλεος, ii. 9 ; v. 10 ; 2 Pet.
i. 9 τῶν πάλαι αὐτοῦ ἁμαρτιῶν. The intermediate position of αὐτοῦ is
also justifiable when it has a reflexive sense, as Tit. iii. 5 κατὰ τὸ
αὐτοῦ ἔλεος, Heb. ii. 4 κατὰ τὴν αὐτοῦ θέλησιν, Rom. iii. 25. Yet
instances where it is not reflexive are Rom. xi. 11 τῷ αὐτῶν παραπτώματι, iii. 24 ; Jas. i. 18 ; 1 Thess. ii. 19 ; Heb. vii. 18 διὰ τὸ αὐτῆς
ἀσθενές. In the Gospels there are no examples of the sort.

2) Of the irregular position of ἑαυτοῦ, -ῆς, etc.: Matt. xviii. 31 τῷ
κυρίῳ ἑαυτῶν, xxv. 1, 4, 7 ; Luke xii. 36 ; xv. 5 ; xvi. 5 ; xxii. 66 ; Gal.
vi. 4, 8 (elsewhere, however, Paul always has the regular position :
Eph. v. 28, etc.) ; Matt. xxi. 8 ἑαυτῶν τὰ ἱμάτια, Luke xxiii. 48 Lchm.
ἑαυτῶν τὰ στήθη, Acts xxi. 11.

B. § 127, 7, 3); H. § 675 sq.; C. § 538; J. § 652.

21   To express the possessives of the 1 s t and 2 d P e r s o n s
P l u r a l, again, the periphrasis with ἡμῶν and ὑμῶν is incomparably more frequent than the adjective pronouns. Thus, for
instance, *our* in the Gospels is rendered o n l y by ἡμῶν, *your* in
102 Matt. and Luke in like manner only by ὑμῶν ; in Luke ὑμέτερος
occurs only twice (vi. 20 ; xvi. 12), but not in connection with
a subst. ; in John against two passages with ὑμέτερος there are
some thirty with ὑμῶν, and so on.

As respects p o s i t i o n, ἡμῶν and ὑμῶν, just as is the case with
αὐτοῦ, never in the historical books occupy the intermediate place, (but
always stand either before the art. or after the subst.) ; in the other
books this position is also comparatively rare, and indeed there is (as
in 20 above) no deviation from Greek usage when in addition another
adjective or adverbial limitation stands between the art. and subst. ;
e.g. Rom. vi. 6 ὁ παλαιὸς ἡμῶν ἄνθρωπος, 2 Cor. iv. 16 ὁ ἔξω ἡμῶν
ἄνθρωπος, v. i ; Rom. vi. 12 ; 1 Pet. i. 18 ; v. 9 τῇ ἐν κόσμῳ ὑμῶν
ἀδελφότητι. 2 Pet. i. 10 Lchm.; iii. 15 ; Jude 3 Lchm. [Tdf. Treg.].

20 ; but only such examples depart from usage as Rom. xvi. 19 ἡ ὑμῶν ὑπακοή, 1 Cor. ix. 12 τῆς ὑμῶν ἐξουσίας. Yet this intermediate position is peculiar only to the style of the Apostle Paul ; see besides, 2 Cor. i. 6 ; vii. 7 (three times) ; viii. 13, 14 ; xi. 8 ; xii. 19 ; xiii. 9 ; Phil. i. 19, 25 ; ii. 30 ; Col. i. 8 ; 1 Thess. iii. 7, — (all with ὑ μ ῶ ν).

B. § 127, N. 12; D. p. 353; J. § 652, 2.

The non-enclitic form of the 1st Person ἐμοῦ is never used in 22 dependence on substantives except when it stands i n c o n n e c t i o n w i t h o t h e r g e n i t i v e s (in which case σου also must retain the accent) ; as, Rom. i. 12 πίστεως ὑμῶν τε καὶ ἐμοῦ, xvi. 13 τὴν μητέρα αὐτοῦ καὶ ἐμοῦ. Hence in Matt. xvi. 23 we are not to read σκάνδαλον εἶ ἐμοῦ (Lchm. [Tdf. Treg. אᵃ]), but, according to good authorities, either μου (Tdf. [eds. 2, 7]) or the Dative ἐμοί (cod. D). The accent is also retained of course when the pronoun is strengthened by αὐτοῦ, -ῆς : Luke ii. 35 καὶ σοῦ δὲ αὐτῆς τὴν ψυχήν, Rom. xvi. 2.

B. § 127, N. 13; C. § 538; D. p. 353, 372; J. § 656, 4.

The peculiar classic usage of strengthening the possessive 23 a d j e c t i v e pron. by the Genitive of the s u b s t a n t i v e pron. αὐτοῦ, -ῶν, etc. (Lat. *suum ipsius*, etc.) to express the idea of *own*, no longer appears in the language of the N. T.[1] As a substitute for it, the language in expressing this idea avails itself very commonly of the simple adjective ἴδιος ; which thus, when it has no special emphasis, frequently takes the place of the reflexive used possessively, particularly of the 3d Person.[2]

Accordingly ἴδιος stands in the reflexive-possessive sense of the 103 F i r s t Pers. (*my* etc. *own*) 1 Cor. iv. 12,　　 of the S e c o n d Pers. (*thy* etc. *own*) Luke vi. 41 ; Eph. v. 22 ; 1 Thess. ii. 14 ; 2 Pet. iii. 17, of the T h i r d Pers. (for ἑαυτοῦ, etc.) very frequently in all parts of the N. T. (never in the Rev.) ; see among other passages Matt. xxii. 5 ; Luke vi. 44 ; John i. 42 ; Acts i. 25 ; Rom. x. 3 ; 1 Cor. iii. 8 etc. ; 1 Tim. iii. 4, 5 ; Heb. iv. 10 ; Jas. i. 14 : 1 Pet. iii. 1, 5 ; Jude 6, etc.

---

[1] As analogous may be noted Paul's τῇ ἐμῇ χειρὶ Παύλου, at the end of several Epistles.

[2] That ἴδιος is in fact used quite in the sense and stead of ἑαυτοῦ etc. is manifest not only from the variants and parallel passages, as in Luke ii. 3 εἰς τὴν ἑαυτοῦ πόλιν Lchm. [Tdf. Treg.], τὴν ἰδίαν πόλιν Tdf. [eds. 2, 7] (cf. vi. 41 ; Mark xv. 20, etc.), but also from the fact that the expressions are exchanged one for the other without any sensible difference, as in 1 Cor. vii. 2 ; Eph. v. 22, 28, and in 2 Pet. ii. 22 the proverb (Prov. xxvi. 11 κύων ... ἐπὶ τὸν ἑαυτοῦ ἔμετον) is reproduced κύων ἐπιστρέψας ἐπὶ τὸ ἴδιον ἐξέραμα. The Latin versions also frequently translate ⁺t simply by *suus*.

It is noticeable that in the following passages the Genitive αὐτῶν is added to this ἴδιος to strengthen it, just as in Greek it is added to the Possessives : Acts i. 19 τῇ ἰδίᾳ διαλέκτῳ αὐτῶν, Tit. i. 12 τὶς ἴδιος αὐτῶν προφήτης, 2 Pet.[1] iii. 3, 16 κατὰ τὰς ἰδίας αὐτῶν ἐπιθυμίας, πρὸς τὴν ἰδίαν αὐτῶν ἀπώλειαν.

24   Hence ἴδιος with the article used substantively (οἱ ἴδιοι, τὰ ἴδια) takes the place of the constructions current in ordinary classic usage : οἱ ἑαυτοῦ, τὰ ἑαυτοῦ, etc.; as, John i. 11; viii. 44, etc.; Acts xxi. 6; 1 Thess. iv. 11; 1 Tim. v. 8, and with the addition of αὐτοῦ (cf. 23 above) Acts xxiv. 23. It stands likewise for τὰ ἡμῶν αὐτῶν : Luke xviii. 28 ἡμεῖς ἀφέντες τὰ ἴδια.

25   Ἴδιος appears to be used more in its strict sense (proprius) in such passages as John vii. 18 ζητεῖ τὴν δόξαν τὴν ἰδίαν, x. 3, 4; Acts iii. 12; xxviii. 30; Gal. vi. 9; Rom. viii. 32; Heb. ix. 12, etc. Thus Capernaum as the city in which Jesus dwelt and taught (Matt. iv. 13; Mark ii. 1, etc.) is called in reference to him ἡ ἰδία πόλις Matt. ix. 1.

B. § 127, 8; H. § 527 d.; C. § 530 e.; D. p. 353.

26   It is to be noticed as a prominent peculiarity of N. T. usage, that where classic Greek, even in later (post-Christian) authors, manifestly avoids adding possessive limitations, as superfluous, indeed offensive, they are nevertheless subjoined in by far the majority of cases. This usage was occasioned, without doubt, by the language of the Septuagint; which, in consequence of the literal translation of the Hebrew original, contains manifold constructions of the sort, as a comparison of the Sept. with the Hebrew text shows on almost every page.

The following examples may serve to illustrate this very frequent (pleonastic) use : Matt. xxiii. 5 πάντα τὰ ἔργα αὐτῶν ποιοῦσιν πρὸς τὸ θεαθῆναι, xiii. 44 ἀπὸ τῆς χαρᾶς αὐτοῦ ὑπάγει καὶ πωλεῖ πάντα, John ii. 23 θεωροῦντες αὐτοῦ τὰ σημεῖα ἃ ἐποίει, Matt. ii. 15 (quotn.) ἐκάλεσα τὸν υἱόν μου, ix. 18 ἐπίθες τὴν χεῖρά σου, Luke iv. 11 (quotn.) ; x. 27 (quotn.) ; xi. 46 ἑνὶ τῶν δακτύλων ὑμῶν οὐ προσψαύετε τοῖς φορτίοις, Matt. xvii. 8; xviii. 8, etc. If in anything syntactical, it is in precisely this uncommonly frequent employment of the possessives μου, σου, αὐτοῦ, etc. in which, throughout the Greek of the Bible, the Hebrew

104 tinge becomes apparent. Yet instances are not wanting of genuine Greek constructions, as e.g. Matt. xxvii. 24 λαβὼν ὕδωρ ἀπενίψατο τὰς χεῖρας, Mark viii. 1 Tdf. [Treg.] προσκαλεσάμενος τοὺς μαθητάς (cf.

---

[1] With the author of this Ep. the predilection for the expression with ἴδιος seems, to judge from the little that is left us, to have completely suppressed the other mode of expression by means of ἑαυτοῦ, etc

Matt. xv. 32), etc.; and in this particular undoubtedly much may be set down to the account of scribes accustomed to this form of speech, when we consider that the cod. Vat. especially is devoid of an innumerable multitude of these superfluous adjuncts. Cf. with this idiom the excessive use of the pron. αὐτός 9 above, p. 107, and the Hebraism οὖ ... αὐτοῦ in § 143, 1 p. 280.

Finally, as respects the article, the language of the N. T. is not so consistent in the case of possessive limitations consisting of the Gen. of the subst. pron., as in those that are adjectival (§ 124, 6 p. 87); inasmuch as it omits the article not only, 1) where the omission is allowable according to the rules given § 124, 8 p. 88, but also, though far less frequently, 2) where according to general rules the art. is demanded.

Examples of 1), as well when the possessive limitation is a substantive pron. as when it is an actual subst., are comprised among those already given in § 124, 8 p. 88 ;

Of 2) Matt. xix. 28 ἐπὶ θρόνου δόξης αὐτοῦ, xxv. 31 ; Luke i. 72 μνησθῆναι διαθήκης ἁγίας αὐτοῦ, ii. 32 δόξαν λαοῦ σου Ἰσραήλ, Jas. i. 26 Tdf. [Treg. cod. Sin.] μὴ χαλιναγωγῶν γλῶσσαν αὐτοῦ ἀλλὰ ἀπατῶν καρδίαν αὐτοῦ (Lchm. ἑαυτοῦ), v. 20 ἐκ πλάνης ὁδοῦ αὐτοῦ. (Passages like Luke xiii. 19 εἰς κῆπον ἑαυτοῦ, xv. 29 οὐδέποτε ἐντολήν σου παρῆλθον, 1 Cor. iv. 14 ὡς τέκνα μου can at all events, according to the principles laid down B. § 124, N. 4, be so interpreted that the substantives dispense with the article because not limited.)   This omission takes place sometimes also where the possessive limitation is a substantive, as 1 Cor. x. 21 οὐ δύνασθε τραπέζης κυρίου μετέχειν καὶ τραπέζης δαιμονίων, 1 Tim. v. 10 εἰ ἁγίων πόδας ἔνιψεν, 1 Pet. iii. 12 ὀφθαλμοὶ κυρίου ... καὶ ὦτα αὐτοῦ ... πρόςωπον δὲ κυρίου, Rev. ii. 1, 8, 18 Lchm.

In a manner quite analogous the article sometimes falls away also, where according to ordinary Greek usage it is apparently necessary, in the possessive limitation expressed by ἴδιος (23 p. 117) ; e.g. 2 Pet. ii. 16 ἔλεγξιν ἔσχεν ἰδίας παρανομίας, i. 3, 20 ; 1 Cor. vii. 7 ; Tit. ii. 9 δούλους δεσπόταις ἰδίοις ὑποτάσσεσθαι.   In other passages the omission of the article is according to rule, as in the adverbial limitations (§ 124, 8 d) p. 89) κατὰ ἰδίαν πρόθεσιν, καιρῷ ἰδίῳ, καιροῖς ἰδίοις, κατ' ἰδίαν ; or in sentences like John v. 18 πατέρα ἴδιον ἔλεγεν τὸν θεὸν (where it is a predicate).   In 1 Cor. xv. 38 the mss. fluctuate between ἴδιον σῶμα (Lchm. [Treg. Tdf. ℵ*]) and τὸ ἴδ. σ. (Tdf. [eds. 2, 7]).

POSITION OF οὖτος, ἐκεῖνος, πᾶς, ETC., WITH THE ARTICLE.
B. § 127, 9; H. § 537 sq.; C. § 524; D. § 398; J. § 453 sq.; S. pp. xviii. sq.

The usage in this matter had become so established, that offences against it do not occur in the N. T.   Hence we find

105 invariably either αὕτη ἡ πόλις, ἀμφότερα τὰ πλοῖα, πᾶς ὁ ὄχλος, or ἡ γῆ ἐκείνη, τὰ ῥήματα ταῦτα, etc. Though πᾶς does appear frequently without an article (πᾶσα σάρξ, πᾶν δένδρον, μετὰ πάσης προθυμίας, πάντες ἄνθρωποι, Ἀθηναῖοι δὲ πάντες, etc.), yet this is quite according to analogy, because the statements are general and unqualified, or they fall under the class of cases treated of in § 124, 8 p. 88. Whenever the number is presented as limited, the article is never missing; hence πάντες οἱ μαθηταί, πάντας τοὺς προφήτας, αἱ θύραι πᾶσαι, etc.

The insertion of πᾶς, too, b e t w e e n the article and substantive rests upon classic precedent: Acts xix. 7 ἦσαν δὲ οἱ πάντες ἄνδρες ὡσεὶ δώδεκα i.e. the whole number of the men was twelve (cf. xxvii. 37), xx. 18 μεθ’ ὑμῶν τὸν πάντα χρόνον ἐγενόμην *throughout the whole time* (more emphatic than πάντα τὸν χρόνον), Gal. v. 14 ὁ πᾶς νόμος ἐν ἑνὶ λόγῳ πεπλήρωται the law in its entire compass and contents, 1 Tim. i. 16 τὴν ἅπασαν μακροθυμίαν the entire fulness of his longsuffering.

30   REMARK. Although ἕκαστος, which is commonly used substantively, always appears without the art. in the few passages in which it is conjoined to a subst. as an adjective, yet no exception from ordinary usage can be established on this fact, since all the passages may be brought under the same rules which applied above to πᾶς without the art.: Luke vi. 44 ἕκαστον δένδρον, John xix. 23 ἑκάστῳ στρατιώτῃ (the number of the soldiers has not been previously mentioned), Heb. iii. 13 καθ’ ἑκάστην ἡμέραν, Rev. xxii. 2 κατὰ μῆναν ἕκαστον. So we find in Thucyd. κατὰ τὸν ὁπλίτην ἕκαστον, καθ’ ἑκάστην τὴν ἡμέραν used interchangeably with καθ’ ἑκάστην χάρακα, κατὰ ἔτος ἕκαστον; in Herod. ἐπ’ ἡμέρας ἑκάστης and τὸν δήμαρχον ἕκαστον, etc.

The common phrase εἷς ἕκαστος is likewise found in the classics also: Thuc. 1. 77; 2. 60, etc. Respecting ἀνὰ εἷς ἕκαστος see p. 30.

B. § 127, N. 15; H. § 538; C. § 524 c.; D. p. 352; J. § 453, Obs. 1.

31   Further, the article is regularly w a n t i n g, when the demonstrative takes the place of the p r e d i c a t e, or the substantive following must be taken as a predicate and separated from the demonstrative.

Of this rule there are many good examples in the N. T.: Rom. ix. 8 ταῦτα τέκνα τοῦ θεοῦ sc. ἐστίν, Gal. iii. 7 οὗτοι υἱοί εἰσιν Ἀβραάμ, iv. 24; 1 Thess. iv. 3 τοῦτο γάρ (sc. ἀπέχεσθαι ἀπὸ τῆς πορνείας) ἐστιν θέλημα τοῦ θεοῦ, Luke i. 36; xxi. 22. As an objective clause: John iv. 54 τοῦτο πάλιν δεύτερον σημεῖον ἐποίησεν *this was the second sign which* etc., ii. 11 ταύτην ἐποίησεν ἀρχὴν τῶν σημείων. With ἐκεῖνος: John viii. 44 ἐκεῖνος ἀνθρωποκτόνος ἦν, x. 1; and in an objective clause, x. 35

εἰ ἐκείνους εἶπεν θεούς. Here belongs also the much debated passage
Luke ii. 2 Lchm. [Treg.] αὕτη ἀπογραφὴ πρώτη ἐγένετο ἡγεμονεύοντος τῆς
Συρίας Κυρίνου [Tdf. א* ἐγένετο πρώτη] ; and therefore the addition
of the article is by no means necessary (Winer, R.W.B. under
Quirinius).

PERIPHRASTIC FORMS OF THE NEGATIVES.   106

Instead of the negatives οὐδείς and μηδείς, weakened as they   32
were by daily use, the N. T. language employs several more
emphatic modes of expression, effected by resolving these negatives into their component parts, viz.

1) The phrase, current among the Greeks also, οὐδὲ εἷς (B. § 70),
as Matt. xxvii. 14 πρὸς οὐδὲ ἓν ῥῆμα, John i. 3 χωρὶς αὐτοῦ ἐγένετο οὐδὲ
ἓν ὃ γέγονεν, Acts iv. 32 ; Rom. iii. 10 οὐκ ἔστιν δίκαιος οὐδὲ εἷς (still
stronger vs. 12 οὐκ ἔστιν ἕως ἑνός, after Ps. xiv. 1, 3).

2) The simple separation of the two parts of οὐδείς (i.e. οὐ and εἷς,
see B. § 70, 1), but reversing their order, thus : εἷς (μία) ... οὐ ; as,
Matt. v. 18 ἰῶτα ἓν ἢ μία κεραία οὐ μὴ παρέλθῃ, x. 29 ἓν ἐξ αὐτῶν οὐ
πεσεῖται, Luke xi. 46 ; xii. 6, etc.

3) The expression, imitated from the Hebrew or borrowed from
the Septuagint, οὐ (μή) ... πᾶς, but always written separately, so
that the negative comes immediately before the predicate (just as in
the Heb. לֹא ... כָּל e.g. Exod. xx. 10 ; Judg. xiii. 4 ; 2 Sam. xii. 3, etc.) :
Matt. xxiv. 22 οὐκ ἂν ἐσώθη πᾶσα σάρξ, Luke i. 37 ; Acts x. 14 οὐδέποτε ἔφαγον πᾶν κοινόν, 1 Cor. i. 29 ὅπως μὴ καυχήσηται πᾶσα σάρξ, Gal.
ii. 16 ; Rev. xxi. 27. The Greeks would have preferred to express
themselves by means of a double negation, or to use τὶ instead of πᾶν,
— both which expressions also are common enough in the N. T. e.g.
Matt. xxii. 16 ; Mark xiv. 60, etc. ; viii. 26 ; Rom. ix. 11 ; Rev. vii. 1
μήτε ἐπί τι (Rec. [Tdf. א] πᾶν) δένδρον.

Similar in meaning, but probably of a different origin, is the opposite
arrangement of the two words, πᾶς ... οὐ (μή), in the following
passages : Rev. xviii. 22 πᾶς τεχνίτης οὐ μὴ εὑρεθῇ ἐν σοὶ ἔτι, xxii. 3 ;
2 Pet. i. 20 ; Eph. v. 5 πᾶς πόρνος ... οὐκ ἔχει κληρονομίαν, iv. 29 πᾶς
λόγος σαπρὸς ἐκ τοῦ στόματος ὑμῶν μὴ ἐκπορευέσθω. This mode of
expression had its origin, we may suppose, in the circumstance that
when the writer began his sentence an affirmative predicate was
hovering before his mind, as is plain in passages where an affirmative
predicate follows the negative one immediately : [1] John iii. 16 ἵνα πᾶς

---

[1] Whether the celebrated passage 1 Cor. xv. 51 Tdf. [Treg. Alf.] — (on the
origin of Lchm.'s reading see Rückert in loc. This greatly interpolated passage
ran, as we may suppose, originally thus : πάντες ... κοιμηθησόμεθα [μὲν] οὔ, πάντες
δὲ ἀλλαγησόμεθα ; cf. cod. Sin.) — is to be explained in the same way is doubtful,

ὁ πιστεύων μὴ ἀπόληται ἀλλ' ἔχῃ ζωὴν αἰώνιον (cf. vs. 15), vi. 39 ἵνα πᾶν
... μὴ ἀπολέσω ἐξ αὐτοῦ, ἀλλὰ ἀναστήσω αὐτό etc. (on the order see
107 § 151, 4 p. 379), which affirmat. ve predicate, too, in other passages must
be supplied from the negative, as in John xii. 46 ; 1 John ii. 21 ; iii. 15.

Somewhat anomalous, but referable to the above rule, are Rev. vii.
16 ; ix. 4 (οὐδὲ πᾶν καῦμα, etc.), where the preceding predicates (οὐ
μὴ πέσῃ, μὴ ἀδικήσουσιν) must for substance be supplied after the negative οὐδὲ ; on ix. 4 cf. besides § 148, 8 p. 352.

The difference in meaning provided that the negative comes immediately before πᾶς and belongs to it is made plain by such passages
as Matt. vii. 21 ; xix. 11 ; John xiii. 10, 11, 18 ; Acts x. 41, etc.
Compare besides the adverbial expressions οὐ πάντως and πάντως οὐ in
§ 151, 19 p. 389.

B. § 127, 10 ; H. § 538 e. ; D. p. 463 ; J. § 454, 3.

33   That ἄλλος with the article is exchanged, without difference
of meaning, with ὁ ἕτερος (the other of two), we have already
seen in noticing the expressions substituted for ὁ μέν ... ὁ δέ,
§ 126, 3 above, p. 102. Other instances, also, not connected
with this combination are pretty frequent, as Matt. v. 39 ὅστις
σε ῥαπίζει εἰς τὴν δεξιὰν σιαγόνα σου, στρέψον αὐτῷ καὶ τὴν
ἄλλην, xii. 13 ; John xix. 32 ; xx. 3, 4, 8, etc.

NEUTER ADJECTIVES.
B. § 128, 3 ; H. § 496 ; C. § 507 ; D. p. 388 ; J. § 436, 2.

1   In accordance with the familiar metonymy by virtue of
which abstracts are used in a concrete sense (thus in the N.T.
frequently e.g. ἡ περιτομή, ἡ ἀκροβυστία Rom. ii. 26 ; iii. 30 ;
Gal. ii. 7 etc., αἰχμαλωσία Eph. iv. 8), the neuter Singular of
a d j e c t i v e s and p a r t i c i p l e s also is employed to set forth a
plurality of concrete objects in their union.

Examples : John xvii. 2 ἵνα πᾶν ὃ δέδωκας αὐτῷ, δώσῃ αὐτοῖς ζωὴν
αἰώνιον (respecting the arrangement see § 151, 4 p. 379), vi. 37 ;
1 John v. 4 ; Heb. vii. 7 τὸ ἔλαττον ὑπὸ τοῦ κρείττονος εὐλογεῖται (where
ὑπό with the Gen. makes reference to an author, § 147 p. 340).

<hr/>

and has been disputed particularly by Meyer among recent writers, — whom
Winer 555 (517) agrees with. Yet the earlier interpretation (Olsh., deWette,
Rückert, etc.) ought not to be held to be " a make-shift opposed by the context
and without warrant or example " in view of the similarity of the above two passages from John, even notwithstanding the repetition of πάντες. At least the
difficulty does not lie in the grammatical construction (respecting the omission of
μέν cf. the two passages from John and § 149, 11 p. 364, and especially § 148, 14
p. 355), but in the obscure contents of the (repeated) πάντες. In interpreting the
passage, 1 Thess. iv 15–17 is to be specially compared.

Similar is 2 Thess. ii. 6 καὶ νῦν τὸ κατέχον οἴδατε, for which subsequently vs. 7 the Masc. ὁ κατέχων is used; see deWette's excursus on the passage p. 132.   For examples of the Neuter Plural in a concrete personal sense see 1 Cor. i. 27, 28; Gal. iii. 22.   The (good classic) use of the Neuter Participle instead of the simple Substantive (kindred in sense or in derivation) is found especially in Luke; as, τὸ εἰωθός or εἰθισμένον for ἔθος (iv. 16; ii. 27), τὸ γεννώμενον i. 35, etc. See Credner, Einl. p. 135.

B. § 128, N. 4; H. § 552 a.; C. § 509; D. p. 388 sq.; J. § 436, 2.

That the Neuter Sing. and Plur. with the article is often used 2 adverbially has already been remarked § 125, 12 p. 96.   The remark holds true also of the Neuter Sing. and Plur. without the art., e.g. λοιπόν henceforth, for the future, and (in the Epistles) as a conjunction : (8 consequently, furthermore, ergo ceterum : Mark xiv. 41; Acts xxvii. 20; 2 Cor. xiii. 11; 2 Tim. iv. 8; μέσον in the midst, Phil. ii. 15 (Grsb. ἐν μέσῳ); πολλά multum (i.e. both sæpe and vehementer) Matt. ix. 14 [Treg.]; Mark v. 23, etc. (see Wahl, under πολύς).   On the phrase εἶναι ἴσα θεῷ see § 129, 11 p. 131.

REMARK. An isolated Hebraism is the use of the Fem. Sing. in 3 a quotation from the O. T. for the Neuter: Matt. xxi. 42; Mark xii. 11 (παρὰ κυρίου ἐγένετο αὕτη καὶ ἔστιν θαυμαστή etc.) — taken from Ps. cxviii. 23 and originating in the literal translation of the Fem. (as Neut.) זֹאת. See Gesen. Lehrgeb. p. 661 [Gr. § 105, 3]. On πρώτη πάντων ἐντολή see § 150, 6 p. 374.

THE NOUN IN CONSTRUCTION.

SUBJECT AND PREDICATE.

B. § 129, 2; H. § 535; C. § 534; D. § 394; J. § 460.

The Predicate, if it is a noun, naturally dispenses with the 1 article so far forth as it is to be affirmed of the subject merely as an idea, i.e. when taken as a general and unlimited conception; as, John iv. 24 πνεῦμα ὁ θεός, Rom. x. 4 τέλος γὰρ νόμου Χριστός, Acts xix. 26 οὐκ εἰσὶν θεοὶ οἱ διὰ χειρῶν γινόμενοι where, therefore, οἱ γινόμενοι sc. θεοί is the subject.   Yet the article is admissible as soon as the predicative idea is limited, i.e. restricted to something conceived as within definite limits, or assumed as known, or as previously mentioned or designated.   In the N. T. its use is frequent, especially in John (Winer adduces in § 17 [5th ed.; of. 7th ed. § 18, p. 114 (109)] alone more than eighty instances of the sort, and the number could be easily increased); and on comparing them, the admissibility, indeed necessity, of the article is everywhere perceptible, for they can be conveniently distributed into the three following classes :

a) The predicate, a substantive, contains an idea (generally known or previously mentioned) definitely limited.   To make the distinction clear, compare the above passage from John (iv. 24) with 2 Cor. iii. 17 ὁ δὲ κύριος τὸ πνεῦμά ἐστιν, viz. the Spirit of which we are speaking, which emanated from Christ and is operative in his church; or Rom. vii. 7 ὁ νόμος ἁμαρτία (ἐστίν;) with 1 John iii. 4 πᾶς ὁ ποιῶν τὴν ἁμαρτίαν καὶ τὴν ἀνομίαν ποιεῖ, καὶ ἡ ἁμαρτία ἐστὶν ἡ ἀνομία;   or compare Matt. xii. 23 μήτι οὗτός ἐστιν ὁ υἱὸς Δαυείδ; is this the son of David! and xiv. 33 ἀληθῶς θεοῦ υἱὸς εἶ thou art truly God's Son (cf. John i. 34, 50; 1 John iv. 15);   or Acts ii. 7 οὐχ οὗτοί εἰσιν οἱ λαλοῦντες Γαλιλαῖοι and Mark vi. 3 οὐχ οὗτός ἐστιν ὁ τέκτων, ὁ υἱὸς τῆς Μαρίας, etc.   Hence everywhere σὺ εἶ- ἐγώ εἰμι- οὗτός ἐστιν- ὁ 109 Χριστός, ὁ προφήτης, i.e. spoken of in the Scriptures, etc., e.g. Matt. xvi. 16; Mark viii. 29; Luke iv. 41 etc.; John i. 20, 21, 25 etc.; Acts ix. 22; 1 John v. 1 etc.   See further John i. 1 ἐν ἀρχῇ ἦν ὁ λόγος . . . καὶ θεὸς ἦν ὁ λόγος (where, accordingly, the predicate has the art. although the subject dispenses with it; yet the passage is also differently interpreted, see the Comm.), i. 4, 8; viii. 12; ix. 19, 20; x. 7, 14; xi. 25; xiv. 6; xv. 1, 5; xviii. 33; Matt. v. 13; Mark xv. 2; Acts iii. 25; 1 Cor. x. 4; 2 Cor. iii. 2; Phil. iii. 3, 19 (where ὁ θεός is the Pred.), Rev. xviii. 23; xix. 10 etc.   In many of these passages the predicate is already more closely defined by an adjective (as in John xv. 1) or a Genitive (hence John viii. 44 ψεύστης ἐστὶν καὶ ὁ πατὴρ αὐτοῦ), in others it allows itself to be more closely limited by a relative or equivalent participial clause (§ 125, 3 p. 92 sq.) which is understood, and indeed such a clause very often actually follows; e.g. Matt. iii. 17; Mark ix. 7; 2 Pet. i. 17; 1 John ii. 22, etc.

b) The predicate is an adjective or participle rendered substantive by means of the art., i.e. raised to a definitely limited, objective, idea; as, John vi. 69 σὺ εἶ ὁ ἅγιος τοῦ θεοῦ not a holy one of God but the holy one of God, "the one whom God has consecrated (x. 36) and on whom he has set the seal (vi. 27) of sanctity," see deWette in loc. Accordingly in 1 Cor. xii. 6 θεὸς ἐνεργῶν ἐστιν τὰ πάντα ἐν ἡμῖν would only declare simply God works in us; but ὁ ἐνεργῶν signifies it is God (alone) who (in point of fact) works, etc. — substantially, indeed, the same idea, but differing in conception, in energy of expression.   See besides Matt. x. 20; John i. 33; v. 39; vi. 33, 63; viii. 18; ix.8; xiv. 21; Acts ix. 21; 1 John v. 6, 7; Rev. i. 17; ii. 23; iii. 17.

REMARK.   That with s u b s t a n t i v e predicates also the passage often gains in force by the addition of the article, may be seen from 1 Cor. xi. 3 θέλω ὑμᾶς εἰδέναι ὅτι παντὸς ἀνδρὸς ἡ κεφαλὴ ὁ Χριστός

ἐστιν, κεφαλὴ δὲ γυναικὸς ὁ ἀνήρ, κεφαλὴ δὲ τοῦ Χριστοῦ ὁ θεός, where
the omission of the art. would not, to be sure, have altered the meaning, but would have weakened its expression ; Eph. ii. 14 αὐτός ἐστιν
ἡ εἰρήνη ἡμῶν *he is our* (only, true) *peace;* without the art. the proposition would assert of Christ merely in a naked way that he is our
peace ; John xv. 1 ἐγώ εἰμι ἡ ἄμπελος ἡ ἀληθινή, etc. Cf. § 124, 7
p. 87 sq.

c) The proposition is one in which subject and predicate stand in
such a relation to each other that one expression is meant to be merely
explained, elucidated, amplified by the other, as 1 Cor. xv. 56 ποῦ σου,
θάνατε, τὸ κέντρον; τὸ δὲ κέντρον τοῦ θανάτου ἡ ἁμαρτία, etc.   So regularly in explaining the parables : e.g. Matt. xiii. 37 sq. ὁ σπείρων τὸ
καλὸν σπέρμα ἐστὶν ὁ υἱὸς τοῦ ἀνθρώπου, ὁ δὲ ἀγρός ἐστιν ὁ κόσμος etc.,
vi. 22 ὁ λύχνος τοῦ σώματός ἐστιν ὁ ὀφθαλμός.   Cf. the example from
1 John iii. 4 in a) above, and deWette in loc. This holds true in
particular of many passages in which a p r o n o u n, as ἐγώ, οὗτος,
ἐκεῖνος, ὅς, etc., takes the place of the subject; as, Matt. xxvi. 26 τοῦτό
ἐστιν τὸ σῶμά μου, 28 τοῦτό ἐστιν τὸ αἷμά μου, and in the exposition
of the parables : Matt. xiii. 19, 20, 22 etc. See, besides, John i. 19 ;
v. 35 ; vi. 14, 50, 51, 58 ; Acts iv. 11 ; vii. 32 ; viii. 10 ; xxi. 28, 38 ;
Eph. i. 23 ; iv. 15 (cf. v. 23) ; Rev. iv. 5 ; v. 6, 8 ; xx. 14, etc. It is
further to be noticed, that in these instances also the predicative substantive is, as a rule, more closely defined by an adjective, a genitive,
a relative or participial clause.

AGREEMENT OF SUBJECT AND PREDICATE IN NUMBER AND GENDER.   **110**

B. § 129, 3; H. § 515; C. § 569; D. p. 399; J. § 384 sq.

Although the MSS. vary very much, it is nevertheless certain **2**
that the N. T. writers proceed rather arbitrarily in reference
to the use of the Singular and Plural where t h e S u b j e c t is
a N e u t e r P l u r a l. For not only is the S i n g u l a r verb
found where animate and even human beings are the subject,
e.g. Luke xiii. 19 ; Mark iv. 4 (πετεινά, on the other hand in
Matt. vi. 26 the Plural), Luke iv. 41 (δαιμόνια), 1 John iv. 1
(πνεύματα), iii. 10 (τέκνα, moreover in a contrast of two),
Rom. ix. 8 ; 1 Cor. vii. 14,[1] or where the plurality is made
prominent, as Matt. xii. 45 ; Luke viii. 2 (ἑπτὰ πνεύματα,
δαιμόνια), Matt. xviii. 12 (ἑκατὸν πρόβατα), Luke viii. 30
(δαιμόνια πολλά) ; — but also the P l u r a l where inanimate
objects are the subject, as Matt. vi. 28 (κρίνα), John vi. 13

[1] Hence in 1 Tim. ii. 15 it is quite inconsiderate to supply τέκνα, from the
preceding τεκνογονίας, for μείνωσιν.

(κλάσματα), xix. 31 (σκέλη); and abstracts, as Luke xxiv. 11
(ῥήματα), 1 Tim. v. 25 (ἔργα); and even the Neut. Plur. of
a pronoun (very rarely), John xvii. 7 (codd. Vat. Sin.), Rev.
i. 19; 1 Cor. x. 11 Lchm.;[1] and, indeed, both numbers
stand side by side in the same connection : John x. 27 (τὰ
πρόβατα ... ἀκούει ... καὶ ἀκολουθοῦσίν μοι), Rev. i. 19;
(1 Cor. x. 11). In general, however, it is not to be overlooked,
that the majority of instances of the use of the Plural occur
with animate objects; the majority of instances of the Singular,
with inanimate, abstract, and almost always with pronominal,
expressions.

REMARK. As an anomaly is to be noticed Rev. ix. 12 Tdf. [so
Lchm. Treg. א] : ἰδοὺ ἔρχεται ἔτι δύο οὐαί, for οὐαί is Feminine
(ἡ οὐαί ἡ μία). The precedence of the predicate (cf. the following
paragraph) may have led to the introduction of the Singular.

B. § 129, 4 and 5; H. § 511; C. § 570; D. p. 400; J. § 392.

3   Where there are several subjects united by copulative
conjunctions, the Predicate usually stands in the Plural
when it follows, and the first Pers. is preferred in such cases
to the 2d and the 3d : Luke ii. 48 ὁ πατήρ σου κἀγὼ ἐζητοῦμέν
σε, 1 Cor. ix. 6. On the other hand, when the Predicate precedes, either a) the Plural is used, Mark x. 35; Luke viii.
111 19; Acts iv. 27 etc., or b) the Singular, the predicate being
in form restricted to a single object; and this occurs, too,
not only with abstract and impersonal objects, as in Matt. v.
18 ἕως ἂν παρέλθῃ ὁ οὐρανὸς καὶ ἡ γῆ, 1 Tim. vi. 4, but even
with Persons: John xii. 22 ἔρχεται Ἀνδρέας καὶ Φίλιππος
καὶ λέγουσιν τῷ Ἰησοῦ; cf. i. 35; ii. 2, 12; xviii. 15; xx. 3;
Matt. xii. 3; Luke vi. 3; xxii. 14; Mark iii. 33 Lchm. [Treg.
Tdf.]; Acts xi. 14; xxvi. 30; Philem. 23. Sometimes the Predicate stands between the subjects, and then it conforms to
that which precedes: Luke viii. 22 αὐτὸς ἐνέβη εἰς πλοῖον καὶ
οἱ μαθηταὶ αὐτοῦ, Matt. xxii. 40; John iv. 12; Rev. xxi. 22.

[1] In this passage the harshness of the Plural is essentially abated by the adoption (with Tdf. [eds. 2, 7]) of the reading τύποι (standing as it does between
ταῦτα and the verb συνέβαινον) instead of τυπικῶς. The adoption of the reading
τυπικῶς requires the restoration of the Singular [so Treg. Tdf. ed. 8] the more,
inasmuch as it is precisely the *same* MSS. [so א] which exhibit both this word and
the Sing. (as, on the contrary, others exhibit the Plural and τύποι), and the Singular follows again immediately afterwards.

REMARK. Analogous is Acts v. 29 ἀποκριθεὶς δὲ Πέτρος καὶ οἱ ἀπόστολοι εἶπαν, where, notwithstanding the Plur. εἶπαν, the Participle is
referred to Peter alone as the spokesman in the words that follow,
and consequently stands in the Sing. More surprising and harsh,
however, are Luke ii. 33 ἦν ὁ πατὴρ αὐτοῦ καὶ ἡ μήτηρ θαυμάζοντες and
Matt. xvii. 3 ὤφθη αὐτοῖς Μωυσῆς καὶ Ἡλίας συλλαλοῦντες μετ᾽ αὐτοῦ
(Rec. ὤφθησαν), on account of the Participles which immediately follow
in the Plural; cf. Mark iii. 31 ([Tdf.] ℵ G D). With these instances
may be compared the similar constructions in Greek authors, e.g.
Herod. 5, 12; Thuc. 4, 37; App. B. Civ. 1, 32.

With disjunctive conjunctions the Singular is used
by far the most frequently, as well when the predicate precedes
as when it follows; since the assertion, although it may hold
good of the two (or more) members, always applies to the
several objects separately, not to both simultaneously or in
union: e.g. Gal. i. 8 ἐὰν ἡμεῖς ἢ ἄγγελος εὐαγγελίζηται ὑμῖν,
1 Cor. vii. 15 οὐ δεδούλωται ὁ ἀδελφὸς ἢ ἡ ἀδελφή, Matt. v. 18;
xii. 25; Mark iii. 33 Tdf. [eds. 2, 7]; Luke xiv. 5; Eph. v. 5,
etc. In Acts xxiii. 9 and similar passages nothing but the
Sing. is to be thought of.

A rare instance of the Plural is Jas. ii. 15 ἐὰν δὲ ἀδελφὸς ἢ ἀδελφὴ
γυμνοὶ ὑπάρχωσιν καὶ λειπόμενοι τῆς τροφῆς, where the Sing. would have
caused ambiguity, on account of the difference of sex.

B. § 129, 8; H. § 522; C. § 502; D. p. 398; J. § 381.

Examples of the usage here spoken of (the Neuter Sing. 4
of the predicate adj. when the subject is to be conceived of as
thing, χρῆμα or τὶ) are found, though rarely, in the N. T. also:
Matt. vi. 34 ἀρκετὸν τῇ ἡμέρᾳ ἡ κακία αὐτῆς, 2 Cor. ii. 6 ἱκανὸν
... ἡ ἐπιτιμία αὕτη.

B. § 129, N. 8; H. § 683 c.; C. § 507 e.; J. § 381, Obs. 3.

Far more frequently are the Neuters οὐδέν, μηδέν used in ref- 5
erence to Masc. and Fem. subjects, if they blend with the copula
εἶναι into a single idea: *nothing* i.e. of no worth, in contrast with
τὶ εἶναι (see § 127, 16 p. 114); as, 1 Cor. vii. 19 ἡ περιτομὴ οὐδέν ἐστιν
καὶ ἡ ἀκροβυστία οὐδέν ἐστιν, xiii. 2; 2 Cor. xii. 11 οὐδέν εἰμι, John viii.
54; Gal. vi. 3 εἰ γὰρ δοκεῖ τις εἶναί τι μηδὲν ὤν. (But Matt. xxiii. 16, 18
belongs under § 143, 14 p. 288.) Analogous to this usage is 1 Cor.
xi. 5 (γυνὴ) ἓν γάρ ἐστιν καὶ τὸ αὐτὸ τῇ ἐξυρημένῃ, and that of 112
πλεῖον, ἔλαττον when (quite as in the classics) treated almost like
indeclinable words: Matt. vi. 25; Luke xii. 23 ἡ ψυχὴ πλεῖόν ἐστιν

τῆς τροφῆς, ix. 13 οὐκ εἰσὶν ἡμῖν πλεῖον ἢ πέντε ἄρτοι, (on the other
hand, the Plural is used Acts xxiii. 13, 21 ; xxv. 6) ; with this compare
1 Tim. v. 9 ἔλαττον ἐτῶν ἑξήκοντα γεγονυῖα.

B. § 129, 9; H. § 513; J. § 381, Obs. 1.

6   Pronouns, when, at the beginning of a clause, they are not
only subjects, but refer at the same time to the following predicate, are in the ancient languages, as is well
known, put in the same gender with the predicate. Of this
usage there are a great many examples in the N. T. also:
Mark iv. 15 οὗτοί εἰσιν οἱ παρὰ τὴν ὁδόν, Matt. xxii. 38 αὕτη
ἐστὶν ἡ μεγάλη ἐντολή, Mark xii. 28 ; Luke ii. 2 ; Rom. xi. 15
τίς ἡ πρόσλημψις, εἰ μή etc. Eph. i. 18 ; vi. 2 ; Phil. i. 28 ἥτις
ἐστὶν αὐτοῖς ἔνδειξις ἀπωλείας, 1 Cor. iii. 17 (ὁ ναός) οἵτινές
ἐστε ὑμεῖς, etc.

Yet passages are not wanting which appear to approximate to our
(German) usage of employing the Neuter in such a case, as 1 Pet.
ii. 19 τοῦτο γὰρ χάρις etc., where, however, τοῦτο rather prepares the
way for the following clause with εἰ as containing the proper subject
for the predicate χάρις ; cf. vs. 20 where τοῦτο refers back to what
precedes. Nevertheless, in both cases the Vulgate translates, in accordance with ancient usage, *hæc* est gratia.   Here belong, in particular, a number of passages where a preceding, and generally a
foreign, word is interpreted, or even directly translated,
by a relative clause beginning with the Neuter ὅ. If the word to be
explained is itself a Neuter, as in Col. i. 24 σῶμα αὐτοῦ, ὅ ἐστιν ἡ
ἐκκλησία, the Neuter form of the relative was required by that;[1] and
if the predicate of the relative clause is a Neuter, as in Mark xv. 16
τῆς αὐλῆς, ὅ ἐστιν πραιτώριον, Eph. vi. 17 τὴν μάχαιραν τοῦ πνεύματος,
ὅ ἐστιν ῥῆμα θεοῦ, such cases may be regarded as instances of the rule
laid down § 143, 3 p. 281. But there are passages in which neither
of these suppositions is the case and yet the Neuter ὅ is used, —
passages, therefore, in which (according to B. § 125, 8, 2) the word
to be explained is to be taken merely as such, i.e. as a term destitute of gender. We distinguish three cases : a) most frequently the
word to be explained is a foreign word and precedes the relative
clause, as Matt. xxvii. 33 τόπον λεγόμενον Γολγοθᾶ, ὅ ἐστιν κρανίου τόπος
λεγόμενος (a harsh combination, for which Mark xv. 22 more
classically ὅ ἐστιν μεθερμηνευόμενον etc.), Mark iii. 17 Βοανηργές,
ὅ ἐστιν υἱοὶ βροντῆς, John i. 42 (Μεσσίας), 43 (Κηφᾶς), ix. 7 (Σιλωάμ,

---

[1] On τοῦ μυστηρίου, ὅ ἐστιν Χριστός which follows (i. 27 Lchm. [Treg.]) see
§ 143, 3 p. 281, and on ii. 17 see c) below.

see No. 18 p. 21), Acts iv. 36 (Βαρνάβας), Heb. vii. 2 (Σαλήμ) ;　b) the
case is similar when the foreign word fills the place of the predicate
in the relative clause, as Mark xii. 42 λεπτὰ δύο, ὅ ἐστιν κοδράντης,
John xix. 17 κρανίου τόπον, ὃ (Grsb. and Rec. ὅς) λέγεται Ἑβραϊστὶ
Γολγοθᾶ;　c) the term to be explained is a common Greek word
(Masc. or Fem.), as Col. iii. 14 ἀγάπη, ὅ ἐστιν σύνδεσμος τῆς τελειότητος 113
(Grsb. Rec. ἥτις in opposition to the MSS. [Sin. ὅς]), Rev. xxi. 8
λίμνη, ὅ ἐστιν ὁ θάνατος ὁ δεύτερος.[1]

REMARK. All that has been said does not apply, of course, to clauses
in which the pronouns do not refer directly to the predicate, but, as
substitutes for objects previously mentioned, simply constitute the
subject respecting which something is predicated, — and consequently
there can be no thought of a change of gender ; as, Acts viii. 10 οὗτός
(sc. Σίμων) ἐστιν ἡ δύναμις τοῦ θεοῦ, Eph. iv. 15 εἰς αὐτὸν, ὅς ἐστιν ἡ
κεφαλή, Χριστός, i. 23 etc.; see other examples 1, a) and c) above, p. 124.

B. § 129, 10;　H. § 511;　C. § 490 sq.;　J. § 391.

When there are several subjects, if the predicate is in the
Plural the Masc. is preferred to the Fem., as in Luke ii. 33
(ὁ πατὴρ καὶ ἡ μήτηρ θαυμάζοντες), 48 (ὀδυνώμενοι), Jas. ii.
15 etc.　The other case, in which, namely, the adjective etc.
refers as respects gender in form to only one of the subjects,
occurs especially with attributives: Luke x. 1 εἰς πᾶσαν
πόλιν καὶ τόπον, 1 Thess. v. 23 ; Heb. iii. 6 Lchm. [Treg. Tdf.,
Sin.] τὴν παρρησίαν καὶ τὸ καύχημα ... βεβαίαν, ix. 9 δῶρά τε
καὶ θυσίαι, μὴ δυνάμεναι etc.

CONSTRUCTIO AD SYNESIN IN THE PREDICATE.

B. § 129, 11;　H. § 523;　C. § 499;　D. p. 398 sq.;　J. § 378.

The construction known by this name, characteristic as it　8
is more or less of all languages, establishes itself especially in

---

[1] Harsher than any of the above instances is the reading Eph. v. 5 Lchm. [T. Tr.]
πλεονέκτης, ὅ ἐστιν εἰδωλολάτρης, and not analogous to them, because no ἑρμηνεία
of the word πλεονέκτης occurs here.　Moreover, since the origin of this reading,
which in its complete form only B [now א also] exhibits, may be satisfactorily
traced (see Tdf.'s crit. note), the older reading ὅς has been restored by Tdf. [eds.
2, 7] with reason.　Incomparably better accredited is Col. ii. 10 ὅ ἐστιν ἡ κεφαλή,
and preferred by Lchm., as being the more difficult reading, to the equally attested
ὅς ἐστιν [א also] ; but exegesis opposes the reference (in that case necessary) of ὅ
to πλήρωμα, and the putting of the words καὶ ἐστὲ ἐν αὐτῷ πεπληρωμένοι in a
parenthesis.　On the other hand, in Col. ii. 17 the well-attested reading ὅ ἐστιν, as
the more difficult, may be well sustained against the other ἅ ἐστιν [א also], inasmuch as all that has been previously mentioned, grouped together under the
unifying term ὅ, is designated as σκιὰ τῶν μελλόντων in contrast with the
σῶμα Χριστοῦ, [yet Tdf. Treg. prefer ἅ.

17

the unconstrained popular language, which is averse to grammatical punctiliousness; hence examples of it begin with
114 Homer, and come down to the latest Greek, the N. T. included.
As the subject is rendered familiar enough by the general
grammars, examples are subjoined at once; these cannot be
omitted here, since (in connection with those catalogued in
§§ 123, 7 p. 80 ; 127, 7 p. 105 ; 143, 4 p. 281) they constitute
an essential element of the N. T. language.   And in order not
to distract the attention by too many classes of passages, those
in which the construction appears in participial clauses,
whether predicative or attributive, are included.

a) The predicate stands in the Plural, instead of the Singular,
with collectives : most frequently with the terms ὄχλος and πλῆθος,
e.g. John vii. 49 ὁ ὄχλος οὗτος ... ἐπάρατοί εἰσιν, xii. 12 ; Matt. xxi. 8 ;
Mark ix. 15 ; Luke vi. 19 Tdf. [Treg. א], ix. 12 ; xix. 37 ; xxiii. 1 ;
Acts v. 16 ; xxi. 36 ; Rev. vii. 9 ; also with στρατιά Luke ii. 13
(πλῆθος στρατιᾶς ... αἰνούντων), with οἰκία (family) 1 Cor. xvi. 15 ;
Rev. xix. 1, and the collective limitations τὸ τρίτον τῶν ἀνθρώπων, τῶν
πλοίων Rev. ix. 18 ; viii. 9.   Both Sing. and Plur. united : John vi. 2
ἠκολούθει ὄχλος ... ὅτι ἐθεώρουν, xii. 9, 18 ; Luke i. 21 ἦν ὁ λαὸς προσδοκῶν ... καὶ ἐθαύμαζον, Acts xv. 12, and in the Genitive Abs. (cf. τοῦ
στόλου ... πλεόντων in Demosth. Mid. § 45) Mark viii. 1 πολλοῦ ὄχλου
ὄντος καὶ μὴ ἐχόντων.

b) The predicate follows the natural gender of the subject.
Of this the examples are most numerous in the Apocalypse, in accordance with the style of the author (see § 123, 7 p. 80).   Thus iv.
1 ; ix. 13 ; xi. 15 φωνὴ ... λέγων, φωναὶ ... λέγοντες as the author
thought at once, instead of the voice, of the angel uttering it, vii. 4
χιλιάδες ἐσφραγισμένοι (§ 123 p. 78), v. 12 χιλιάδες ... λέγοντες (cf.
§ 144, 13 a) p. 298), iv. 8 Tdf. [2, 7, 8, Treg.; cf. Sin.] ζῷα, ἓν καθ' ἓν
ἔχων ... λέγοντες (cf. θηρίον § 123 p. 80), xix. 14 στρατεύματα ... ἐνδε-
δυμένοι, xvii. 3 Lchm. [Tdf., Sin.] (see § 123 p. 80).   Examples from
other authors are, Mark xiii. 14 (respecting which see p. 81 above),
Luke x. 13 Τύρῳ καὶ Σιδῶνι ... πάλαι ἂν ... καθήμενοι (Grsb. and Rec.
-ναι) μετενόησαν, Acts xxviii. 26 (λέγων) Tdf. [Treg. so cod. Sin.],
Gal. i. 23 (see 14 below, p. 133), Eph. iv. 17, 18 τὰ ἔθνη ... ἐσκοτω-
μένοι.   (But in 1 Cor. xii. 2 ἀπαγόμενοι does not depend immediately
upon ἔθνη, and in Mark ix. 20 ἰδών does not refer to τὸ πνεῦμα, see
§ 144, 13 c) p. 299.)

In almost all the passages cited under a) and b) it will be found
that the employment of the natural gender and number imparts to
the expression a much more unconstrained character than would have
resulted from strict grammatical correctness.

B. § 129, N. 12; H. § 514 b.; C. § 501; D. p. 399; J. § 478.

Instances of the P l u r a l with ἕκαστος and the like are Acts ii. 6 ἤκουον εἰς ἕκαστος, xi. 29, etc.   The first hand reading of cod. Vat. in Acts iv. 32 οὐδὲ εἶς ἔλεγον (Sin. and others ἔλεγεν) is probably not a clerical error.   Similarly 1 Cor. iv. 6 ἵνα μὴ εἷς ὑπὲρ τοῦ ἑνὸς φυσιοῦσθε κατὰ τοῦ ἑτέρου.

B. § 129, N. 14; H. § 518 d.; C. § 499 b.; D. p. 399; J. § 390 d.

The employment of the so-called *Pluralis Majestaticus* is everywhere **10** common in the Epistles, agreeably to the general character of their contents, as Rom. i. 5 ; 2 Cor. i. 8 sqq.; Heb. xiii. 18, etc.   Whether the 1st Pers. Plur. occurring here and there in the Gospels in the discourses of Jesus is to be understood in the same way, is disputed ; see the interpreters on Matt. iii. 15 ; John iii. 11.   On the plural in such passages as Mark iv. 30 (τίνι ὁμοιώσωμεν etc.) see § 139, 4 p. 209.

ADVERBS IN LIEU OF THE PREDICATE.   115
B. § 129, 13; C. § 706; D. p.454; J. § 375, 3.

The power of adverbs to be employed as predicative limita- **11** tions is far greater in the Greek language than, for example, in the Latin, owing to the readiness with which adverbs in Greek, without further change of form, can be turned into adjectives and substantives (§ 125, 10 p. 95).

In the N. T. the following adverbs among others are found so used: ἐ γ γ ύ ς, e.g. ὁ καιρός μου, τὸ πάσχα, τὸ ῥῆμα ἐγγύς ἐστιν Matt. xxvi. 18 ; Rom. x. 8 (a quotn.), ἐ γ γ ύ τ ε ρ ο ν xiii. 11 ; π λ η σ ί ο ν, e.g. Luke x. 29, 36 τίς ἐστίν μου πλησίον *who is my neighbor?* (without the Art. according to § 124, 6 p. 87) ; π ό ρ ρ ω, Luke xiv. 32 αὐτοῦ πόρρω ὄντος ; ο ὕ τ ω ς, Matt. i. 18 ἡ γένεσις οὕτως ἦν, xxiv. 27, 37 ; xix. 10 εἰ οὕτως ἐστὶν ἡ αἰτία (*if the case is so*), Rom. iv. 18 (a quotn.) οὕτως ἔσται τὸ σπέρμα σου (viz. as the stars of heaven), 1 Pet. ii. 15, etc.   In this way is to be explained also the phrase τὸ εἶναι ἴσα θεῷ Phil. ii. 6 ; on the adverbial use of ἴσα see Pape.

B. § 129, 14; H. § 667; C. § 536; D. § 409; J. § 652.

The addition of the personal pronouns ἐγώ, etc., to the verb **12** takes place, as usual, wherever emphasis, and in particular sensible antithesis to other subjects, renders them necessary ; see, for example, 1 Cor. xv. 36 σὺ ὃ σπείρεις, οὐ ζωοποιεῖται etc. (cf. § 151, 17 p. 388), but subsequently on repetition (vs. 37) merely ὃ σπείρεις, John vii. 34, 36 ; i. 19, 22, etc.

Yet it is not to be overlooked that, — agreeably to what has been elsewhere brought forward respecting the immoderate use of the pronouns, and in particular relative to αὐτός as subject (see § 127, 9 p. 107, 26 p. 118, § 130, 2 p. 142), — the personal pronouns were frequently employed where no reason of importance is obvious, and a native Greek, at least, would certainly have contented himself simply with the form of the verb. We mistake the character of the N. T. language, and should misapprehend many passages, should we attempt in this matter to apply the classic standard and assume in all cases a rhetorical reason for the use of the pronoun, — a procedure which would do injustice to the homely and simple narrative style, especially of the Gospels. Compare on this point such passages as Matt. xiv. 16 ; x. 16 ; Mark vi. 37 ; xiv. 30 ; Rom. ii. 3 ; Gal. ii. 19 ; 2 Cor. xi. 29, etc., or look up the numerous passages in which John avails himself of the personal pronoun as the subject of a finite verb. Accordingly we encounter here also, as we did above for instance in the case of the Possessives (αὐτοῦ etc. § 127, 26 p. 118), a continual variation in the documents ; as some of the scribes, accustomed to the usage of the N. T., often added the pronouns, while others proceeded more according to classic principles and omitted the pronouns where they seemed to them superfluous. See, for example, simply in reference to ἐγώ the various readings on Mark i. 2 ; Luke vii. 27 ; John v. 36 ; vi. 40 ; xii. 50 ; xvi. 17 ; xvii. 19 ; xviii. 37, etc.

116　　　　　B. § 129, N. 15; H. § 506; C. § 394; D. p. 372; J. § 467, 3.

13　An instance of apposition to the omitted pronoun implied in the verbal ending, is 1 Pet. v. 1 παρακαλῶ ὁ συμπρεσβύτερος καὶ μάρτυς. This occurs most commonly with appositives in the form of a participle (taking the place of a relative clause), examples of which are given § 144, 9 c) p. 295.

UNEXPRESSED SUBJECT (Germ. *man*, etc.).
B. § 129, 15; J. §§ 373. 893.

14　Although the language of the N. T. is far more liberal in its use of pronouns than the ordinary literary language (see 12 above), yet frequently, when there is an abrupt change of the subject in a minor clause (co-ordinate or subordinate), there is found, as in the classics, no corresponding pronoun, where the connection is evident ; e.g. Mark i. 27 τοῖς πνεύμασιν ἐπιτάσσει, καὶ ὑπακούουσιν αὐτῷ sc. τὰ πνεύματα, 1 Cor. vii. 36 οὐχ ἁμαρτάνει, γαμείτωσαν (var. γαμείτω), where any more precise specification would have been heavy, in fact intolerable.

Thus Luke, relying on the inevitable suggestions of the context, felt no hesitation in writing, xv. 15 ἐκολλήθη ἑνὶ τῶν πολιτῶν, καὶ ἔπεμψεν (sc. ὁ πολίτης) αὐτὸν εἰς τοὺς ἀγρούς, Acts vi. 6 οὓς ἔστησαν ἐνώπιον τῶν ἀποστόλων, καὶ ... ἐπέθηκαν (sc. οἱ ἀπόστολοι) αὐτοῖς τὰς χεῖρας. Luke iv. 39; xvii. 2 are still more simple and obvious; but Acts xvii. 2 κατὰ τὸ εἰωθὸς τῷ Παύλῳ εἰσῆλθεν sc. ὁ Παῦλος is harsh, and hardly Greek, on account of the subject of the leading clause being supplied from a subordinate adjunct; and Acts viii. 7 πολλῶν τῶν ἐχόντων πνεύματα ἀκάθαρτα, βοῶντα (sc. τὰ πνεύματα) φωνῇ μεγάλῃ ἐξήρχοντο, where the subject of the leading clause is identical with the object of the preceding participial clause (on the other reading, Lchm. [Tdf. Treg. cod. Sin.], see p. 380), is anacoluthic, or to be explained by the blending of two constructions (§ 151, 10 p. 383). Examples from Paul's Epistles, are, Gal. i. 23 ἤμην ἀγνοούμενος ταῖς ἐκκλησίαις ..., μόνον δὲ ἀκούοντες ἦσαν viz. the members of the Jewish churches (see b) under 8 p. 130 above); 1 Cor. vii. 17 εἰ μὴ, ἑκάστῳ ὡς ἐμέρισεν ὁ κύριος ..., οὕτως περιπατείτω sc ἕκαστος (on the hyperbaton see § 151, 18 p. 389). See, besides, other similar examples § 151, 10 p. 383.[1]

B. § 129, N. 16; J. §§ 373. 893.

Sometimes the unexpressed subject of a clause is also not to be found in what precedes, although a definite subject was in the writer's mind. In such cases, as a rule it (a) may either be gathered from the necessary connection, or (b) is assumed to be sufficiently known to the readers, e.g. in quotations, which in fact are so often given by hint and in a fragmentary form.

Examples of (a) are Heb. xi. 12 διὸ καὶ ἀφ' ἑνὸς ἐγεννήθησαν viz. the posterity of Abraham, Rom. ix. 11 μήπω γεννηθέντων μηδὲ πραξάν-

---

[1] 1 John v. 16 ἐάν τις ἴδῃ ([so ℵ]; Lchm. εἰδῇ) τὸν ἀδελφὸν αὐτοῦ ἁμαρτάνοντα ..., αἰτήσει, καὶ δώσει αὐτῷ ζωήν etc. is a case hard to decide. Winer (p. 427 5th ed. [cf. 7th ed. p. 523 (487)]) holds the interpretation of deWette and others (who, comparing Jas. v. 14 sqq., would retain the same subject) to be harsh, which is by no means the case, since it has the grammatical sequence in its favor. It is opposed, however, by the use of the word διδόναι in the sense of *acquire, procure*, a circumstance which early induced ancient expositors to assume a new subject, viz. God. And the parallel passage from James, notwithstanding its similarity, is not quite in point: in the first place, because there the predicate is σώσει, and secondly, because the causal relation between the two terms ἐπιστρέψαι and σῶσαι is different from that between αἰτῆσαι and δοῦναι. For the σῶσαι is included in the ἐπιστρέψαι and the ἐπιστρέψας is thereby at the same time a σώσας. The other explanation of the passage in John (that of Winer, Lücke, etc.) is manifestly the harsher, not so much on account of the rapid change of subject, as because the subject understood (ὁ θεός) is also previously to be supplied as the object of αἰτήσει. Nevertheless, taking into consideration the usage given above, and in particular vs. 14 (ἐάν τι αἰτώμεθα ... ἀκούει ἡμῶν), it seems to be the more probable; and the identity of the verbal forms (αἰτήσει ... δώσει Mey. [i.e. Huther]) is no obstacle in the way of this construction; cf. Acts vi. 6 etc. above.

On the double Dative (αὐτῷ, ἁμαρτάνουσι) see § 133, 13 p. 179.

των τι viz. Esau and Jacob (vs. 13), Luke xvi. 4 ἵνα δέξωνταί με εἰς
τοὺς οἴκους αὐτῶν viz. the debtors subsequently mentioned, John
xii. 5 διὰ τί τὸ μύρον οὐκ ἐπράθη ... καὶ ἐδόθη πτωχοῖς viz. the proceeds,
Rom. iv. 3, 22 ; Gal. iii. 6 ; Jas. ii. 23 (a quotation) ἐπίστευσεν Ἀβραὰμ
τῷ θεῷ, καὶ ἐλογίσθη αὐτῷ εἰς δικαιοσύνην sc. τὸ πιστεύειν. Hence it
harmonizes perfectly with the genius of the N. T. language to supply
in John vii. 51 as subject of ἀκούσῃ, not νόμος itself, but 'he who is
administering the law,' and in Heb. x. 38 the general term man educed
from δίκαιος (according to § 151, 23 d) p. 392). This latter passage
Bleek takes otherwise ; cf. also Hab. ii. 4, where the order of the
clauses is reversed.

Examples of (b) : John vi. 31 (a quotation) ἄρτον ἐκ τοῦ οὐρανοῦ
ἔδωκεν αὐτοῖς φαγεῖν, 2 Cor. ix. 9 (a quotation) ἐσκόρπισεν, ἔδωκεν τοῖς
πένησιν · etc.

B. § 129, 16; H. § 504 c.; C. § 571; D. § 381 b.; J. § 373, 2. 3.

16 The case is different with apparently impersonal predicates,
such as σαλπίζει, etc., with which it is usual to supply a verbal
concrete, as σαλπιγκτής, etc. : 1 Cor. xv. 52 σαλπίσει γὰρ, καὶ
οἱ νεκροὶ ἀναστήσονται.

Quite in accordance with this usage, the predicates λέγει or φησίν
are often found in the N. T. in quotations, ὁ θεός or even merely ἡ
γραφή being always to be supplied as subject; as, 1 Cor. vi. 16 ; 2 Cor.
vi. 2 ; Gal. iii. 16 ; Eph. iv. 8 ; v. 14 ; Heb. viii. 5 ; iv. 3 (εἴρηκεν).
Those subjects are also expressed, as in Gal. iv. 30 ; 1 Tim. v. 18, or
to be supplied from the preceding context, as in Heb. i. 5 sqq. Similarly with εὐδόκησεν in Col. i. 19 ὁ θεός is to be supplied, which is
expressed in 1 Cor. i. 21 ; Gal. i. 15 (doubtful). Respecting ἀρξάμενον (Luke xxiv. 47) see § 150, 7 p. 374.

B. § 129, 17; H. § 504; C. § 571 (d); D. § 381 b.; J. § 373.

17 Among the examples of this section respecting an unexpressed and
118 indefinite subject (where in English we use it e.g. προσημαίνει, ἔσεισε,
ἐδήλωσε) may be reckoned Acts ii. 3 ὤφθησαν αὐτοῖς διαμεριζόμεναι
γλῶσσαι ὡσεὶ πυρὸς, καὶ ἐκάθισεν ἐφ᾽ ἕνα ἕκαστον αὐτῶν, where the
subject of ἐκάθισεν (πῦρ or γλῶσσα or πνεῦμα) has been designedly
left obscure, on account of the mysterious and wonderful nature of the
occurrence. More difficult grammatically is Luke xxiv. 21 τρίτην
ταύτην ἡμέραν ἄγει σήμερον, ἀφ᾽ οὗ ταῦτα ἐγένετο. The insertion of
a definite personal subject viz. Ἰησοῦς (Meyer) cannot be justified by
later usage ; for in this, ἄγειν when connected with an object, as
ἡμέραν, ἔτος etc., either has the special signification to celebrate, solem-
nize, a day (Dion. Hal. de comp. verb. in.), or is an imitation of the
Latin use of agere annum (i.q. natum esse, to be old, Galen) ; see

Stephanus sub voce. Moreover, the assumption of a personal subject would only be allowable in case the following relative clause (ἀφ' οὗ, etc.) also contained the same subject, or at least continued the narration of occurrences relating to the same subject. Still more strange does it seem to supply Ἰσραήλ as subject from the preceding τὸν Ἰσραήλ (Bornem.). The majority of interpreters (deWette, etc.) have accordingly taken the expression ἄγει τὴν ἡμέραν as impersonal (pretty nearly equivalent to ἡ ἡμέρα ἄγεται), which not only gives the simplest and most natural meaning, but agrees best with the following relative clause, which is likewise without a personal subject. Although this supposition seems no less than the other to have the o r d i n a r y usage against it, so that we must regard the expression in this sense as a ἅπαξ ῥηθέν, yet it finds its analogue in the use (likewise of isolated occurrence) of ἀ π έ χ ε ι (Mark xiv. 41) *it is enough*, more closely *it is completed, all is over*.[1] All these terms (ἄγει, ἀπέχει, ἐκάθισεν) are, however, to be carefully distinguished from the s t r i c t impersonals of the following section, since they stand out of all connection with verbal constructions. The meaning of ἄγει in the passage before us is given unequivocally in the ancient versions: *tertius dies est, agitur*. Cf. further on this subject § 130, 4 p. 144.

B. § 129, 18; H. § 494; C. § 571 e.; D. § 381 c.; J. § 373, Obs. 1.

To the ordinary impersonal verbs (δεῖ, πρέπει, etc.) a few must be **18** added which are manifestly imitations of the Hebrew idiom or borrowed from the language of the Septuagint. Foremost among these are the common καὶ ἐγένετο or ἐγένετο δέ (וַיְהִי), on the varied construction of which see § 141, 6 p. 276, and the phrase ἀνέβη ἐπὶ καρδίαν (עָלָה עַל לֵב see Gesenius) 1 Cor. ii. 9 (cf. Luke xxiv. 38), which is used quite after the manner of impersonal verbs in Acts vii. 23 ἀνέβη ἐπὶ τὴν καρδίαν αὐτοῦ ἐπισκέψασθαι etc.

B. § 129, 19; H. § 504 c.; C. § 571 c.; J. § 373, 7.

The common modes of expressing the indefinite personal **19** subject (English *one*, Germ. *man*) are by means of the 3d Pers. Plur. Act. or Mid. (even Luke xii. 20 is to be taken thus) and the 3d Pers. Sing. Pass., without any sensible difference; hence both modes of expression are united in a single sentence in Luke xii. 48 πολὺ ζητηθήσεται παρ' αὐτοῦ ... καὶ περισ- **119** σότερον αἰτήσουσιν αὐτόν.

That the 3d Pers. Sing. of the A c t i v e was thus used, the in-

---

[1] See on this passage my detailed exposition in the Stud. u. Krit. for 1858 3d Heft, and cf. the similar use of περιέχει (equiv. to περιέχεται) in 1 Pet. ii. 6 Tdf. [Treg. cod. Sin.]; see p. 144 note.

definite τὶς being omitted (cf. B. § 129, N. 17), can reasonably be held only of 2 Cor. x. 10, in case we read φησίν with Rec., Grsb., Tdf [Treg., א] etc.: αἱ μὲν ἐπιστολαί, φησὶν, βαρεῖαι etc. (φασὶν certainly looks like a correction, and the translation of the Vulgate *inquiunt* like an interpretation, — suggested as it was by common usage). That with both these verbs, however, this usage, in parenthesis, is by no means unknown to Greek and Latin authors is seen e.g. in Demosth. c. Aristocr. p. 150; Plut. Mor. p. 119 F.; Liv. 6. 40; Cic. de fin. 1. 2; 4. 24, etc.

Other passages, which are referred to this head, see under 15 a) p. 133 sq.

OMISSION OF THE COPULA.
B. § 129, 20 and N. 18; H. § 508 a.; C. § 572; D. § 419; J. § 376.

20   The omission of the copula in the 3d Pers. Sing. of the Iudicative is very common in all parts of the N. T., in fact it may be said, particularly in the Pauline Epistles, to be preferred often throughout entire paragraphs. See a great multitude of such passages in Winer 584 (544).

This omission takes place 1) in aphorisms, sententious propositions, and proverbial phrases, as πιστὸς ὁ θεός, οὐ πάντων ἡ πίστις, ἓν σῶμα καὶ ἓν πνεῦμα, εἷς κύριος, πάντα καθαρὰ τοῖς καθαροῖς, τοῖς δὲ ἀπίστοις οὐδὲν καθαρόν ;   2) in questions, and exclamations in an interrogative form, as τί σοι ὄνομα ; τίς ἡ ὠφέλεια τῆς περιτομῆς ; ποῦ οὖν ἡ καύχησις ; τὸ σκότος πόσον (Matt. vi. 23), ὡς ἀνεξερεύνητα τὰ κρίματα αὐτοῦ, etc. 3) in the customary formula ᾧ (οὗ) ὄνομα or ὄνομα αὐτῷ (αὐτοῦ), as Mark xiv. 32 χωρίον οὗ τὸ ὄνομα (Lchm. ᾧ ὄνομα) Γεθσημανεί, Luke i. 5 γυνή, καὶ τὸ ὄνομα αὐτῆς Ἐλισάβετ, 26, 27 ; ii. 25 ; viii. 41 ; xxiv. 13, 18, etc., also when unconnected or parenthetic, as John i. 6 ἄνθρωπος, ὄνομα αὐτῷ Ἰωάννης, iii. 1 ἄνθρωπος, Νικόδημος ὄνομα αὐτῷ ; 4) especially with certain predicates (as indeed in Greek authors, see B. § 129, N. 18; D. § 419 (b) ; J. § 376 c.), — for instance, with the notions *necessary, possible, impossible* with an Infinitive following, or to be supplied : Rom. xiii. 5 διὸ ἀνάγκη ὑποτάσσεσθαι, Heb. ix. 16, 23 ; vi. 4, 18 ἐν οἷς ἀδύνατον ψεύσασθαι θεόν, x. 4 ; xi. 6, 19 Tdf. [cod. Sin. ; Treg.], Gal. iv. 15 εἰ δυνατόν sc. ἦν ; with *hard :* Acts xxvi. 14 σκληρόν σοι πρὸς κέντρα λακτίζειν ; with *righteous :* 2 Thess. i. 6 εἴπερ δίκαιον ἀνταποδοῦναι, etc.   5) before the Relative when the demonstrative correlate is also dropped, as μακάριος ἀνήρ, οὗ οὐ μὴ λογίσηται κύριος ἁμαρτίαν Rom. iv. 8 ; Jas. i. 12, etc.; on this cf. § 151, 24 c) p. 395.

That no such rules as these, however, are invariable is obvious. Respecting other phrases, in part established formulas, such as δῆλον ὅτι, ἵνα τί, τί ὅτι, μικρὸν ὅσον ὅσον, κεφάλαιον δὲ, etc., see the references in the Index, and § 151, IV. Ellipsis, pp. 390 sqq.

Of the other Persons, that most frequently omitted is the **21** 3d Pers. Plural εἰσίν, as in 1 Cor. xvi. 9; Rom. iv. 7, etc., **120** particularly in the course of such statements and deductions as (according to the preceding paragraph) are generally delivered with the omission of the copula; as, Rom. iv. 14; xi. 16; 1 Cor. i. 26; xiii. 8; Heb. ii. 11, etc.

In the first and second Persons the omission more rarely occurs, — as a rule, only when the person is expressly designated by means of the personal pronoun, as in John xiv. 11 πιστεύετε ὅτι ἐγὼ ἐν τῷ πατρὶ καὶ ὁ πατὴρ ἐν ἐμοί, Mark xii. 26 ἐγὼ ὁ θεὸς 'Αβραάμ, 2 Cor. x. 7 καθὼς αὐτὸς Χριστοῦ, οὕτως καὶ ἡμεῖς, John xvii. 23 ἐγὼ ἐν αὐτοῖς καὶ σὺ ἐν ἐμοί; sometimes also where the person is readily suggested by the context, and in other respects no ambiguity arises, as 2 Cor. xi. 6 εἰ δὲ καὶ ἰδιώτης τῷ λόγῳ (sc. εἰμί) ἀλλ' οὐ τῇ γνώσει, Rev. xv. 4 τίς οὐ μὴ φοβηθῇ, κύριε· ... ὅτι μόνος ὅσιος sc. εἶ.

Also when the construction requires the Subjunctive, or **22** the Optative (in wishes), or the Imperative, we find the copula omitted; yet here again but rarely.

The Subjunctive: 2 Cor. viii. 13 οὐ γὰρ ἵνα ἄλλοις ἄνεσις, ὑμῖν δὲ θλῖψις sc. ᾖ or γένηται which is subsequently used vs. 14; viii. 11 ὅπως, καθάπερ ἡ προθυμία τοῦ θέλειν, οὕτως τὸ ἐπιτελέσαι ἐκ τοῦ ἔχειν. The Optative is omitted, particularly in certain very current phrases which have become standing formulas for expressing a wish, as ἵλεώς σοι sc. θεός Matt. xvi. 22, εἰρήνη ὑμῖν, ἡ χάρις μεθ' ὑμῶν, ὁ θεὸς τῆς εἰρήνης μετὰ πάντων ὑμῶν, etc. The Imperative, particularly in connection with preceding imperatives or demands, so that the form to be supplied is necessarily suggested, as Col. iv. 6 (περιπατεῖτε ...), ὁ λόγος ὑμῶν πάντοτε ἐν χάριτι, Heb. xiii. 4, 5; Luke i. 28; Rom. xii. 9 sqq. Respecting μηδὲν σοί etc., see 23 below.

REMARK. Whether in the doxologies (Rom. xi. 36; xvi. 25 sq.; Gal. i. 5; Jude 25; Rev. i. 6, etc.) and in the opening formulas, as εὐλογητὸς ὁ θεὸς καὶ πατήρ 2 Cor. i. 3; Eph. i. 3; 1 Pet. i. 3 (cf. the song of praise in Matt. xxi. 9), we are to supply εἴη or ἔστω, or the Indicative ἐστίν, may be doubtful. Yet in view of Rom. i. 25; 2 Cor. xi. 31 and particularly 1 Pet. iv. 11 (cf. the various readings on Matt. vi. 13) the Indicative ἐστίν decidedly deserves the preference.

Strictly speaking, every case of the omission and insertion **23** of a verbal idea ought to be treated in the chapter concerning Ellipsis. Since, however, a sharp discrimination in terms the supply of which is left solely to our own judgment is quite impossible, it seems to be expedient to treat in this place also

18

of the case where the verb to be supplied is a general term, closely allied to the copula, as παρεῖναι, γενέσθαι, ἐλθεῖν, ai d the like.   In every instance it will be found that the supply of the absent verbal idea (expressed as it is by us in various ways) is facilitated by other parts of the sentence, in particular 121 by a Dative (as the verb's regimen) or a relation indicated by Prepositions.

Here belongs primarily the Hebraistic formula (2 Chron. xxxv. 21; 2 Sam. xvi. 10; xix. 22), which, however, is not unknown to the Greeks (Arr. Epict. 1, 1, 16, etc.), that occurs in the Gospels : τί ἐμοὶ καὶ σοί, Matt. viii. 29 ; Mark i. 24; v. 7 ; Luke iv. 34; viii. 28 ; John ii. 4 [A.V. *what have I to do with thee*] so Luther, (cf. Schweigh. on Herod. 5. 33), — even when the connection requires an Imperative, as Matt. xxvii. 19 μηδὲν σοὶ καὶ τῷ δικαίῳ ἐκείνῳ.   Also the phrase (quite classic) τί πρὸς σέ; τί πρὸς ἡμᾶς; Lat. *quid hoc ad me* [A.V. *what is that to thee*] Luther *was gehts dich an* (Herm. de ellip. p. 111), Matt. xxvii. 4 ; John xxi. 22, 23 ; similarly 1 Cor. v. 12 τί γάρ μοι τοὺς ἔξω κρίνειν ; Other phrases with the Dative are 1 Cor. vi. 13 τὰ βρώματα τῇ κοιλίᾳ καὶ ἡ κοιλία τοῖς βρώμασιν (*exist for* etc.), Rom. xi. 11 τῷ αὐτῶν παραπτώματι ἡ σωτηρία τοῖς ἔθνεσιν (*has come*), iv. 13 οὐ γὰρ διὰ νόμου ἡ ἐπαγγελία τῷ Ἀβραάμ.

In connection with Prepositions: Heb. vi. 8 ἧς τὸ τέλος εἰς καῦσιν, 1 Cor. xv. 21 δι᾽ ἀνθρώπου θάνατος καὶ δι᾽ ἀνθρώπου ἀνάστασις νεκρῶν, Acts x. 15 φωνὴ πρὸς αὐτόν sc. ἐγένετο (cf. vs. 13), 1 Cor. iv. 20 οὐκ ἐν λόγῳ ἡ βασιλεία τοῦ θεοῦ ἀλλ᾽ ἐν δυνάμει, 2 Cor. iv. 15 τὰ πάντα δι᾽ ὑμᾶς, Rom. iv. 9 ὁ μακαρισμὸς οὗτος ἐπὶ τὴν περιτομήν etc. (*refer to*)[1] Matt. xxvii. 25 τὸ αἷμα αὐτοῦ ἐφ᾽ ἡμᾶς, Acts xviii. 6 ἐπὶ τὴν κεφαλὴν ὑμῶν sc. γενέσθω or ἔλθοι (cf. Matt. xxiii. 35).   And with an Adverb instead : Heb. x. 18 ὅπου ἄφεσις τούτων, οὐκέτι προσφορὰ περὶ ἁμαρτίας. Without any adjunct : 1 Cor. xv. 40 καὶ σώματα ἐπουράνια καὶ σώματα ἐπίγεια (i.e. *there are*, after the analogy of i. 26, etc.).

The numerous passages in which the predicate is only to be supplied from the preceding context, are not noticed further here.

With this whole section compare § 151, IV. pp. 390 sq.

THE CASES.

NOMINATIVE AND VOCATIVE.

B. § 129 a.; H. §§ 541-43; C. § 401; J. §§ 476 sqq.

1   The instances in which the Nominative stands instead of other Cases are chiefly occasioned by Anacoluthon (Noms. Absol.) or by loose construction, and will accordingly be treated of elsewhere.

[1 Cf. p. 394.]

Respecting the Nom. in appositional adjuncts see § 123, 5 p. 78 ; — for the Acc. in instances of two Acc., § 131, 8 p. 151 ; — in participial clauses and instances of Nom. Absol. in general, § 144, 4 sqq. p. 291, 13 p. 298 ; § 151, 4 sqq. p. 379, and numerous examples in § 151, 10 p. 383.

The interjection ἰδού and (especially in John) even ἴδε, like the Latin *ecce* and *en*, are followed by a Nominative. (The frequent occurrence of these interjections, both in narration and in argument, is probably derivable not merely from the O. T. alone, but from the popular language in general ; hence they appear more and more frequently in the later period, after Christ.) See numerous examples of ἰδού particularly in Matt., Luke, and the Apocalypse ; of ἴδε with a Nom. following, in Mark iii. 34 Tdf. [Treg. cod. Sin.], xvi. 6 ; John i. 29, 36, 48 ; xix. 5 [ἰδού Tdf. Treg. cod. Sin.], 14, 26, 27, — in these passages, therefore, it is an interjection ; on the other hand, when connected with the Acc. it is the ordinary Imperative of εἶδον, as in John xx. 27.

Peculiar to the Apocalypse is the frequent combination εἶδον καὶ ἰδού likewise followed by a Nom., as in iv. 1 ; vi. 2, 5, etc. Yet the author sometimes allows himself the syntactic liberty of letting both cases (Nom. and Acc.) follow interchangeably, so that εἶδον again governs the Acc. although the Nom. has preceded ; as, xiv. 14 εἶδον καὶ ἰδοὺ νεφέλη λευκή . . . καὶ καθήμενον etc. Cf. iv. 1–4, and vii. 9 which is spoken of in § 123, 5 p. 78 above.

The Nominative stands quite absolutely and as an incomplete parenthesis, where it is employed as a closer limitation of the predicate, — hence adverbially.

It is so used in temporal limitations, in Luke ix. 28 ἐγένετο μετὰ τοὺς λόγους τούτους, ὡσεὶ ἡμέραι ὀκτώ, καὶ παραλαβὼν etc., Matt. xv. 32 σπλαγχνίζομαι . . . , ὅτι ἤδη ἡμέραι τρεῖς προσμένουσιν ; in modal limitations, Mark vi. 40 ἀνέπεσον πρασιαὶ πρασιαί (see p. 30) ; in vs. 39 the construction of Acc. with Infin. requires us to take συμπόσια συμπόσια as Accusative (cf. Luke ix. 14). With this use of the Nom. we may connect the (Johannean) parenthesis ὄνομα αὐτῷ spoken of § 129, 20, 3) p. 136, for which other writers employ either the Accusative adjunct τοὔνομα (§ 131, 12 p. 153), or most commonly the Dative ὀνόματι followed by that case of the proper name which the construction requires, as Acts x. 1 ἀνήρ τις ὀνόματι Κορνήλιος, Matt. xxvii. 32 εὗρον ἄνθρωπον ὀνόματι Σίμωνα, Acts xxvii. 1 ἑκατοντάρχῃ ὀνόματι Ἰουλίῳ, etc.

Respecting a second Nom. and the periphrasis with εἰς for the predicate-Nom. see in connection with § 131, 7 p. 150.

The remark (B. § 129 a. 1) that the Vocative in classic Greek commonly takes the interjection ὦ before it, does not hold in the N. T.   On the contrary, not only is this sign of the Voc. in itself rare (used only sixteen times in all), but in most of these instances it is more than a mere sign of the Voc., inasmuch as the expression generally has an emphatic character, and so contains rather an exclamation than a simple address.

For example, Matt. xvii. 17 (and parall. pass. Mark ix. 19; Luke ix. 41) ὦ γενεὰ ἄπιστος, Rom. xi. 33 ὦ βάθος πλούτου, Luke xxiv. 25; Gal. iii. 1 ὦ ἀνόητοι, Acts xiii. 10 ὦ πλήρης παντὸς δόλου.   As a simple address in classic style it occurs, strictly speaking, only in the Acts (i. 1; xviii. 14; xxvii. 21), for even 1 Tim. vi. 20; Matt. xv. 28; Rom. ii. 1, 3; Jas. ii. 20 are not without a certain emphatic accent.

5   Even when the Vocative has its own form, that of the Nominative is not unfrequently chosen (as in the classics).   The 123 Voc. of the 2d declension in ε is still found most frequently, as κενὲ ἄνθρωπε, δοῦλε πονηρέ, υἱέ, κύριε (this last word always in this form if it has not the article, see below), even θεέ μου (cf. p. 12).   In the 3d declension, with the exception perhaps of those nouns which are often used in the Vocative, as πάτερ, βασιλεῦ, the Nominative is ordinarily used; in Luke xii. 20, also, and 1 Cor. xv. 36, most of the MSS. [Sin. also] give ἄφρων instead of ἄφρον (Grsb.).

The language of the N. T., like that of the Old, differs, however, essentially from the ordinary literary language in this: that the Vocative, besides taking the form of the Nom., very often takes the Article besides (ὁ, οἱ, etc.);[1] cf. 6 p. 141.   Examples abound: Matt. xi. 26 ναί, ὁ πατήρ, Mark v. 41 τὸ κοράσιον, ἔγειρε (although the preceding Aramaic word, ταλιθά, has no article), Luke xviii. 11, 13 ὁ θεός, ἱλάσθητί μοι, John xx. 28 ὁ κύριός μου καὶ ὁ θεός μου, Rom. viii. 15 ἀββᾶ, ὁ πατήρ, Col. iii. 19 οἱ ἄνδρες, ἀγαπᾶτε, Jas. v. 1 ἄγε νῦν, οἱ πλούσιοι, κλαύσατε, Rev. xv. 3 δίκαιαι αἱ ὁδοί σου, ὁ βασιλεὺς τῶν ἐθνῶν. Also in quotations: Acts xiii. 41; Heb. i. 8, 9; x. 7, etc.

[1] That this use is not a mere Hebraism (cf. Gesen. Lehrgeb. p. 654; Gr. § 107, Rem. 2) but rooted in the popular and colloquial language of the Greeks is expressly recognized by Bernhardy (Syntax p. 67), who cites in support of it many examples from Aristophanes and the Dialogues of Plato (Ar. Pac. 466 · Plat. Symp. p. 218 B).

B. § 129 a. 2; H. § 533; C. § 401, 3; D. § 407; J. §§ 467. 476.

A number of the passages in which the Nom. with the article seems   6
to be used as Voc. may also be suitably taken as those in which
adjuncts in apposition with the Voc., and even additions subjoined with καί, take the form of the Nom. with the article,
according to well-known laws of the Greek language. This is the
case when particular persons are expressly designated: Luke xi. 39
ὑμεῖς οἱ Φαρισαῖοι, Rom. xiv. 4 σὺ τίς εἶ, ὁ κρίνων; ii. 1 etc.; even if
the preceding pronoun stands in a different case — an irregularity
sufficiently explained by § 123, 5 p. 78: Luke vi. 25 οὐαὶ ὑμῖν, οἱ
ἐμπεπλησμένοι. In the case of adjuncts with καί: Acts xiii. 16
ἄνδρες Ἰσραηλῖται καὶ οἱ φοβούμενοι etc., 26; Rev. xviii. 20 οὐρανὲ καὶ
οἱ ἅγιοι. In particular we may refer to this head (in accordance
with § 144, 9 d) p. 295) participial adjuncts with the Imperative, which frequently occur in the N. T., as Matt. vii. 23 ἀποχωρεῖτε
οἱ ἐργαζόμενοι, xxvii. 40; Mark xv. 29; Gal. iv. 21, 27 (a quotn.),
Eph. v. 14; Jas. iv. 13; Rev. xii. 12; xvi. 5.

THE OBLIQUE CASES IN GENERAL.

B. § 130, 1-4; C. §§ 397 sq.; D. §§ 148. 469; J. §§ 471 sq.

The settlement of the fundamental signification of the   1
oblique cases forms a leading subject of general Greek grammar, and in particular of philosophic researches in syntax.
But to institute such investigations in a special grammar like
the present would not only be a departure from its aim, but **124**
would lead to but meagre or even incorrect results, since the
language of the N. T. is already far removed from the primary
and formative period of the Greek tongue. In this particular
the process of development in the language must be regarded
as completed, and the results attained in the general grammar
as respects prose usage must accordingly be assumed as already
established, and valid in the main also as respects the N. T.
language. Since, however, with the decline of a nation a
decline is wont as a rule to appear in its language also, we
shall naturally find, in the writings of the N. T. as well as of
the later writers generally, the syntactic combinations, and
consequently the cases also, no longer employed with such
precision and clearness of reference as prevailed in the earlier
language. Hence we shall see many verbs construed with different cases from those used in the earlier language; and
in particular, the more analytic and decomposed language of

later writers will often use prepositions with their cases, where the earlier language was satisfied with the simple cases. Instances of this sort, as matters belonging strictly to the province of N. T. grammar, we shall naturally have to treat with special prominence in the course of the following paragraphs; yet completeness of specification, as respects the cases and other constructions, in reference to every individual verb, it does not fall (as has been already intimated in the preface) within the limits of N. T. grammar to give.

B. § 130, 5 and N. 1; H. § 505; J. §§ 893. 894.

2   Such an essential departure, as has been alluded to, from the ordinary usage, we encounter at once in the application of the general principle that the ancient languages often neglect to designate the object (immediate or remote), where it is already sufficiently clear from the connection; and in particular, are wont to express it but once if two verbs in any way connected have an object in common, — thereby avoiding a multitude of those pronouns that often so encumber modern languages.

The language of the N. T., however, especially that of Luke and of the Ep. to the Heb., is not so far removed from the ordinary Greek as not to avail itself of this advantage; as may be seen from a considerable number of examples: Matt. xiii. 44 θησαυρῷ, ὃν εὑρὼν ἄνθρωπος ἔκρυψεν, xxvii. 65 ἀσφαλίσασθε sc. τὸν τάφον, Mark vi. 5 ἀρρώστοις ἐπιθεὶς τὰς χεῖρας ἐθεράπευσεν, Luke xiv. 4 ἐπιλαβόμενος ἰάσατο αὐτὸν καὶ ἀπέλυσεν, John x. 29 ὁ πατήρ, ὃς δέδωκέν μοι sc. αὐτά, Acts xiii. 3 ἐπιθέντες τὰς χεῖρας αὐτοῖς ἀπέλυσαν, Eph. v. 11 μὴ συγκοινωνεῖτε τοῖς ἔργοις τοῖς ἀκάρποις, μᾶλλον δὲ καὶ ἐλέγχετε, Heb. xi. 19 ἐκ νεκρῶν ἐγείρειν δυνατὸς ὁ θεός, 1 Cor. x. 9; 1 Tim. vi. 2, etc.

But far more frequently than is the case even in still later Greek prose writers, we find (in accordance with the great preference for pronominal constructions often mentioned already) the object expressed by a pronoun, especially αὐτός; so that here, too, the influence of Oriental usage is unmistakable, (cf. § 127, 9 sqq. p. 107 sq., 26 p. 118, § 129, 12 p. 131 sq.) ; as, Mark x. 16 ἐναγκαλισάμενος αὐτά, τιθεὶς τὰς χεῖρας ἐπ᾽ αὐτὰ κατευλόγει αὐτά [Tdf. Treg. ἐναγκ. αὐτ. κατευλόγει τιθεὶς τὰς χεῖρας ἐπ᾽ αὐτά after codd. Sin. Vat.; cf. § 127, 26 p. 119], Luke xvi. 2 φωνήσας αὐτὸν εἶπεν αὐτῷ, Matt. xviii. 2 προσκαλεσάμενος παιδίον ἔστησεν αὐτὸ ἐν μέσῳ. (But in John xv. 2 there are other reasons for the repetition by means of the pron. αὐτό, see § 151, 4 p. 380.) Col. ii. 13 ὑμᾶς νεκροὺς ὄντας ... συνεζωοποίησεν ὑμᾶς.

To the same origin is to be attributed the repetition of the same
object in several clauses connected by conjunctions (cf. e.g. Josh. xxiii.
2; xxiv. 20; Neh. ix. 34; 1 Macc. i. 6, etc.), as Luke xxiv. 50 ἐξήγαγεν
αὐτοὺς ... καὶ εὐλόγησεν αὐτούς, cf. Matt. xxii. 37 (and its parallel
Mark xii. 30), Rev. ix. 21, etc.;   also the un-Greek constructions
in which to the Participle, with and without the art., the pronoun
αὐτός (not οὗτος or ἐκεῖνος, on which see § 144, 21 p. 306) is subjoined
in the same case quite without emphasis,[1] — as Matt. v. 40 τῷ
θέλοντί σοι κριθῆναι ... ἄφες αὐτῷ καὶ τὸ ἱμάτιον, iv. 16; Rev. vi. 4;
Jas. iv. 17 εἰδότι καλὸν ποιεῖν καὶ μὴ ποιοῦντι, ἁμαρτία αὐτῷ ἐστίν, — yes,
even when it has already been used with the Participle, is repeated
again (cf. Col. ii. 13 above), as Matt. xxvi. 71 ἐξελθόντα αὐτὸν εἰς τὸν
πυλῶνα, εἶδεν αὐτὸν ἄλλη, viii. 23 ἐμβάντι αὐτῷ εἰς τὸ πλοῖον, ἠκολούθησαν
αὐτῷ, and also frequently elsewhere in Tdf.'s text [eds. 2, 7] cf. Matt.
viii. 1, 5, 28; xxi. 23; Mark ix. 28, etc.;[2]   and lastly, the practice
(also anomalous), in constructions with the Gen. absol. and sometimes
also with the Acc. and Infin., of expressing the subject by means of a
pronoun, although it has already been given in the leading clause; see
on this in its place § 141, 4 p. 274, and § 145, 1 sqq. p. 314 sq.

REMARK. In Matt. xxi. 41 κακοὺς κακῶς ἀπολέσει αὐτούς the pronoun 3
αὐτούς was formerly held to be a superfluous addition. Modern ex- 126
egesis, however, has acknowledged αὐτούς to be the true object, so
that κακούς is the word which ought to be held to be the rhetorical
addition, made out of fondness for paronomasia, just as was often
the case in Greek authors; as, Lucian, Pisc. κακοὺς κακῶς ἀποτρίψομεν.
That the Latin versions and church fathers seem to take no notice of
αὐτούς is solely owing to the impossibility of reproducing both words
in their foreign idiom (as in our own also); and to take αὐτούς par-
titively quite contradicts the sense of the passage.

[1] Isolated instances of this use adduced from Greek authors do not suffice to
stamp it as an ordinary Greek construction. Where we find something similar
occasionally even in later Greek writers, other causes (generally rhetorical) as
perspicuity, emphasis, the separation by parentheses of words belonging together,
etc., have occasioned the repetition of the pronoun; whereas the frequent
occurrence of this construction in the N. T., considering its small extent, warrants
us in inferring a formal usage.

[2] We see from this that the assumption that all such cases as these last named
are examples of the so-called Dative absolute (§ 145, 5 p. 316) is quite
erroneous. On the contrary, the dative is everywhere governed by the verb of the
leading clause. The abnormal addition of αὐτῷ etc. in the leading clause led to
this false assumption, and probably also often in ancient times to the alteration
(of the mss.) into the Gen. absol., which in fact is itself not according to rule. Cf.
besides § 145, 2 p. 315. [Tdf. ed. 8 adopts the Gen. Abs. (with Treg. Lchm.) in
all except the first.]

B. § 130, N. 2; H. § 684; C. § 577; D. § 430; J. § 359.

4   The remark that verbs originally transitive, by the frequent
omission of an easily supplied object or of a reflexive pronoun,
assume in the Active voice a neuter signification, is so well
established and applies so commonly to all languages, that it
seems to be quite sufficient simply to give a list here of a
number of verbs so used in the N. T. ; the usage is so wide-
spread that we must desist from attempting to give a complete collection of the passages where it occurs, as well as
from referring to analogous instances of the use of the same
verbs by other writers. We find the following used thus
intransitively :

ἄγειν, particularly in the summons ἄγε, ἄγωμεν (on ἄγει in Luke
xxiv. 21 see § 129, 17 p. 134),— together with the compounds
ὑπάγειν (very frequent, especially in the Gospels, where it seems to
take the place of the wanting ἰέναι, see § 137, 10 a) p. 204), παράγειν
to pass by, pass on, ἐπανάγειν to return or merely to put off (Matt.
xxi. 18; Luke v. 3, 4), διάγειν to pass, περιάγειν to go about (Acts
xiii. 11), in this sense it then (according to the analogy of those Middle
verbs that, having acquired a new, transitive, sense, take an object
of their own, cf. B. § 135, 5) takes after it a new object, viz. of the
place, as κώμας, ὅλην τὴν Γαλιλαίαν (Mark vi. 6 etc.), προάγειν to
go before (Mark xi. 9), likewise with a new object when used in this
sense — a use of this verb peculiar to the N. T., and particularly to
Matt. and Mark, as προῆγεν αὐτούς went before them Matt. ii. 9 etc.
(so προέρχεσθαι with the Acc. of a person Mark vi. 33 ; Luke xxii.
47, perhaps after the Latin) ;

ἔχειν, for example καλῶς, ἐσχάτως, (as in colloquial Latin bene habet);
thus ἔχειν κατά τινος means to have something against any one, be angry
with him, Rev. ii. 4, 20; cf. Hermæ pastor, Mandatum 2 (Sin.), —
together with the compounds ἀπέχειν to be at a distance (on ἀπέχει
sufficit see § 129, 17 p. 135), ἐπέχειν to stay, both literally (Acts xix.
22) and in a tropical sense, sc. νοῦν, to direct the mind to something
(Acts iii. 5 ; 1 Tim. iv. 16), in which sense προσέχειν especially is
current, ὑπερέχειν præesse, valere, and with a new object superare,
præstare, ἐνέχειν to watch, be on the watch for any one, insidiari,
περιέχει it runs, stands written 1 Pet. ii. 6 Tdf. [Treg.],[1] ἐν γαστρὶ
ἔχειν to be with child ;

[1] Περιέχει must be taken intransitively in this passage whether we read with
Rec. and others [cod. Sin. also ἐν (τῇ) γραφῇ, or with Lchm. ἡ γραφή (sc. οὕτως
or τόνδε τὸν τρόπον, cf. 2 Macc ix. 18; xi. 16; 1 Macc. xv. 2; Joseph. Antt. 12,
4, 10, etc.). To which of these two readings we ought to give the preference it is

βάλλειν *to storm against, rush upon*, of the wind (Acts xxvii. 14), 127 and the compounds ἐπιβάλλειν of the waves (Mark iv. 37), in the signification *to fall* to Luke xv. 12,[1] προβάλλειν *to sprout* (Luke xxi. 30), συμβάλλειν in various senses (see the lexicons);

κλίνειν *to incline*, together with the compound ἐκκλίνειν;

στρέφειν *to turn (away) one's self* (Acts vii. 42) together with the compounds ἀναστρέφειν, ἐπιστρέφειν;

ἀπορρίπτειν *to throw one's self off*;

παραδοῦναι *to offer, to present itself*[2] (Mark iv. 29);

ἐνισχύειν transitive and intransitive in Luke (see Wahl);

ἀναλύειν *to go away, depart*, also *to return* i.e break up, rise from, a meal (Luke xii. 36) in order to go home (οἴκαδε μετὰ δεῖπνον ἀναλύειν Plut. Tib. Gracch. 14); καταλύειν *to put up* as at an inn (common in later writers in this sense); — not to mention many others, whose intransitive signification has always been in use side by side with the transitive, as αὐξάνειν (p. 54), σπεύδειν, προκόπτειν, διατρίβειν, τελευτᾶν, etc., or whose object was almost uniformly omitted because involved in the signification of the verb, as ἀνοίγειν, ἀνακάμπτειν, γαμεῖν, etc.

In other cases the omission of the object is not a result of the usage **5** by virtue of which the verb comprises the objective relation in itself,

hard to decide, since the balance of authority is in favor of the latter, but other and internal considerations favor the former. See my Essay in the Stud. u. Krit. for 1858 p. 509.

[1] In Mark xiv. 72 καὶ ἐπιβαλὼν ἔκλαιεν, the verb ἐπιβάλλειν has received the most diverse interpretations; see the commentaries. The interpretation common formerly (Luther, *he began to weep* [Tyndale, Cranmer, A.V. margin]) is supported, indeed, by the ancient versions, the variant ἤρξατο κλαίειν, and the gloss of Suidas ἐπέβαλε ἤρξατο; but is both too weak for the tenor of the passage, and also philologically inaccurate, since ἐπέβαλε, as even the addition (ἐπεχείρησεν) in Suidas shows, may mean *conatus est*, but not *coepit*. It would harmonize best with the connection, considering the parallel narratives (ἔκλαυσεν πικρῶς Matt. xxvi. 75; Luke xxii. 62), to take ἐπιβαλών adverbially in the sense of ὑπερβαλλόντως (cf. the Hebrew הַגְבִּיל in 1 Sam. xx. 41; see Gesen. under גָּדַל); but such a use cannot be proved. The most satisfactory interpretation **philologically** is that ἐπιβαλὼν (sc. τὸν νοῦν) is equivalent to ἐννοήσας *considering* i.e. taking to heart, in case it is designed to intensify the preceding ἀνεμνήσθη. See a number of very appropriate precedents for this signification in Wetstein in loc.

[2] The 2d Aor. παραδοῦναι, in analogy with other (syncopated) 2d Aor. forms, is found in the Sept. also with this purely intransitive meaning, e.g. Isa. xlvii. 3. Hence in 1 Pet. ii. 23 (πάσχων οὐκ ἠπείλει, παρεδίδου δὲ τῷ κρίνοντι δικαίως), it appears to be not only more in accordance with the sense but with philology also to supply with the **Imperfect** (παρεδίδου) an object like τὰ ἑαυτοῦ (or κρίσιν) from the context (with Luther et al.), not ἑαυτόν (deWette). The passage cited by deWette, Josh. xi. 19 (not ii. 19), runs quite different y in the Vat. ms. On παραδιδόναι in the sense of *permitto*, also with the object (a thing) omitted, see Stephanus (Paris ed.) sub voce p. 247.

but the objects are easily supplied from the context: as e.g.
αἴρειν sc. ἄγκυραν Acts xxvii. 13, σκάπτειν sc. γῆν Luke xiii. 8,
ἀφανίζειν, κλέπτειν sc. χρήματα Matt. vi. 19, διορύσσειν sc.
τεῖχος Matt. vi. 19, ῥῆξον (sc. φωνὴν see Wetst.) καὶ βόησον Gal. iv.
27, στρῶσον σεαυτῷ sc. κλίνην Acts ix. 34, κατὰ κεφαλῆς
128 ἔχων sc. κάλυμμα or simply τὶ 1 Cor. xi. 4, ἑτοιμάζειν sc. κατάλυμα
Luke ix. 52, συλλαμβάνειν and συλλ. ἐν γαστρί sc. υἱόν Luke
i. 24, 31 ;   or the objects to be supplied are altogether general
terms, as ἀποστέλλειν, πέμπειν sc. τινὰς, ἀκούσας sc. ταῦτα,
σὰρξ καὶ αἷμα οὐκ ἀπεκάλυψέν σοι viz. that of which I am speaking
Matt. xvi. 17 ;   or are intentionally left in the dark by the writer
on account of the variety of notions it is possible to supply, and the
choice among them is referred to the reader, as Jas. iv. 2, 3 ; Col. ii. 21.

Respecting the omission of the object (or of the whole) with partitive statements, see § 132, 6 p. 158.

THE ACCUSATIVE.
B. § 131, 2 ; H. § 544 a. ; C. § 472 f. ; D. § 464 ; J. § 544.

1   Among the verbs which by governing the Acc. depart as a
rule from English and German usage, the following in the
N. T. deserve special mention :

Those signifying to speak well or ill (defame): καλῶς, κακῶς
λέγειν, as usually with the Acc., but only used by Luke in vi. 26 ; Acts
xxiii. 5 (quotn.). The common verb for *defame* is βλασφημεῖν, likewise used with the Acc., as well of the person Matt. xxvii. 39 (or instead
ὄνομα Jas. ii. 7 ; δόξας Jude 8) as of the thing Mark iii. 28, sometimes
also with εἰς Mark iii. 29 ; Luke xii. 10, with ἐν 2 Pet. ii. 12 ἐν οἷς
ἀγνοοῦσιν βλασφημοῦντες (see § 143, 10 p. 287), which, however, designates rather the sphere *within* which the evil speaking occurs.
Respecting ὀνειδίζειν, καταρᾶσθαι, see § 133, 9 p. 177 ;   to do well :
εὖ and καλῶς ποιεῖν with the Dat. : Luke vi. 27 ; Mark xiv. 7 Lchm.
[Treg.] (yet cf. Tdf. ed. 7 in loc.), Matt. v. 44 Grsb. The use of
ποιεῖν with the Acc. of a word expressing time, as χρόνον, τρεῖς μῆνας,
ἐνιαυτόν etc. for our *spend* (commorari) is peculiar, e.g. Acts xv. 33 ;
xviii. 23 ; xx. 3 ; 2 Cor. xi. 25 ; Jas. iv. 13, (elsewhere also in later
writers) ;   to flee : φεύγειν in its strict sense (to run away) is
construed only with ἀπό (in Rev. xx. 11 hebraistically ἀπὸ προσώπου),
particularly with persons, ἀπ᾽ αὐτοῦ, ἀφ᾽ ὑμῶν, and with abstracts
instead, as ἀπὸ κρίσεως, ὀργῆς, εἰδωλολατρείας, Luke iii. 7 ; Matt. xxiii.
33 ; 1 Cor. x. 14 (purely local, Mark xvi. 8) ; in the signification *to
avoid, abstain from*, with the Acc. (of the thing) e.g. ταῦτα, τὴν πορνείαν, etc. Heb. xi. 34 (ἔφυγον στόματα μαχαίρης) is an exception. The
compound ἐκφεύγειν takes only the Acc. or is used absolutely, see

Wahl, (ἐκ purely local in Acts xix. 16); on ἀποφεύγειν see § 132, 5 p. 158; to swear: ὀμνύειν, with the Acc. only in Jas. v. 12; elsewhere with a preposition, and after the example of the Hebrew (cf. Gesen. under שָׁבַע) most frequently by far with ἐν, sometimes with κατά and the Gen. Heb. vi. 13, 16, with εἰς (after a preceding ἐν, cf. § 147 under εἰς and ἐν) Matt. v. 34 sq. Ὁρκίζειν and ἐνορκίζειν (1 Thess. v. 27) to adjure, always with two Accs., see Wahl; on the other hand, ἐξορκίζειν with κατά Matt. xxvi. 63. Cf. § 151, 24 b) p. 394.

REMARK. With νικᾶν the objective limitation is connected once by ἐκ — quite unique, yet not so surprising in the language of the Apoc. abounding as it does in solecisms — (as it were, to win the victory over, Lat. victoriam ferre ex): Rev. xv. 2 τοὺς νικῶντας ἐκ τοῦ θηρίου, Vulg. qui vicerunt bestiam.

B. § 131, N. 3; H. § 544 c.; C. § 472 b.; J. § 489, Obs. 2.

On the construction of verbs expressing an emotion of the mind 2 see § 133, 23 p. 185. Only those are connected with the Acc. of the 129 person, which, like ἐλεεῖν, οἰκτείρειν, are pure transitives. On εὐδοκεῖν with the Acc. see as above.

B. § 131 N. 4; H. § 764 b.; C. § 598 a.; J. § 669, 1.

The Impersonal δεῖ (and δέον ἐστίν Acts xix. 36) is followed only 3 by the Acc. and Infin. or, in general sayings, by the Infin. alone. Cf. § 132, 12 p. 164. Χρή occurs but once, likewise with the Infin.: Jas. iii. 10.

B. § 131, 3; H. § 544; C. § 577; D. § 430; J. § 359.

To the verbs whose signification is originally or predom- 4 inantly intransitive, but which are rendered transitive by the addition of an object, belong, among others from the N.T., the following: μαθητεύειν to be a disciple (verbs in εύω formed from nouns and expressing the state or action of their primitives, B. § 119, 3 a.), τινά Matt. xxviii. 19 etc., θριαμβεύειν to hold a triumph, τινά (Plutarch) Col. ii. 15; 2 Cor. ii. 14; also ἐμπορεύεσθαί τινα 2 Pet. ii. 3, πεινᾶν, διψᾶν δικαιοσύνην Matt. v. 6, θλίψεις με μένουσιν (me manent) Acts xx. 23 — according to a later and rather poetic use of the word.

On the other hand, κλαίειν and πενθεῖν are found but once with the Acc. of the object (Matt. ii. 18; 2 Cor. xii. 21), elsewhere always with ἐπί and the Acc. or the Dat. see § 147 p. 336 sq.; προσκυνεῖν is joined to the Dative uniformly by Paul, and predominantly by the other writers (or to ἐνώπιόν τινος § 133, 3 p. 172); in the Apocalypse it is construed with both the Dat. and the Acc. (as in the Septuagint) without the slightest difference. Its synonym γονυπετεῖν is always followed by the Acc. (or ἔμπροσθεν) ; εὐαγ-γελίζεσθαι is connected indiscriminately now with the Dat., now with the Acc., of the person (see more below, nos. 5, 6) ; hence in the Passive πτωχοὶ εὐαγγελίζονται Matt. xi. 5 ; Luke xvi. 16; Heb. iv. 2, 6, etc., (the Act. εὐαγγελίζειν occurs only in the Apocalypse).

B. § 131, 4; H. § 547; C. § 477; D. § 466; J. § 548, 2.

5   The construction by which an intransitive verb takes the Acc. of its kindred abstract noun (μάχην μάχεσθαι, ὑβρίζειν ὕβριν, etc.) rendered more definite by an adjunct, is not only current in the N.T., but, — fostered as it was by the analogous Hebrew usage (see Gesen. Lehrg. p. 809 sq. [Gr. § 135, Rem. 1.]) and consequently by the Sept. also, — was taken up eagerly and even extended.

Thus we find the following constructions used, and with the re-quisite closer limitation : αὔξειν αὔξησιν, ἁμαρτάνειν ἁμαρτίαν, θαυμάζειν θαῦμα, ὁμολογεῖν ὁμολογίαν, κρίσιν κρίνειν, στρατεύεσθαι στρατείαν, ἀγωνί-ζεσθαι ἀγῶνα, χαίρειν χαράν, φόβον (also πτόησιν 1 Pet. iii. 6) φοβεῖσθαι ; and in the Passive βάπτισμα βαπτισθῆναι Mark x. 38 etc., ἐνδεδυμέ-νος ἔνδυμα γάμου Matt. xxii. 11, καυματίζεσθαι καῦμα μέγα Rev. xvi. 9,— where βάπτισμα, ἔνδυμα, καῦμα are the Accusatives of the object retained in the change of the verb to the Pass. (Mid.) ; see B. § 134, N. 2.

Different from the above are those expressions in which the Ac-cusative takes the place of a simple object, and therefore the closer limitation is either wanting, or at least unnecessary, grammatically considered, (as in the Homeric κτέρεα κτερείζειν, etc.) ; thus διδόναι δόματα, αἰχμαλωτεύειν αἰχμαλωσίαν ducere captivos (after Ps. lxvii. 19), μαρτυρεῖν μαρτυρίαν, διδάσκειν διδασκαλίας, εὐαγγέλιον εὐαγγελίσασθαι, 130 ἰδεῖν ὅραμα, διατίθεσθαι διαθήκην, φυλάσσειν φυλακάς, σπείρειν σπόρον (see still other examples in 6 below, and respecting δεῖν δεσμάς see 7 p. 150). The difference between these constructions and the pre-ceding is plain from this, that when the verb is changed into the Passive, the Accusative, as the natural object, passes into the subject Nominative, as Acts xvi. 9 ὅραμα τῷ Παύλῳ ὤφθη, Mark xv. 26 ἡ ἐπιγραφὴ ἦν ἐπιγεγραμμένη, Gal. i. 11 τὸ εὐαγγέλιον τὸ εὐαγγελισθὲν ὑπ' ἐμοῦ ; and in this way is to be explained 2 Cor. i. 11 ἵνα τὸ εἰς ἡμᾶς χάρισμα ... εὐχαριστηθῇ.

A further extension of this general usage is afforded not only by the phrases (current elsewhere also) ἐλθεῖν ἡμέρας ὁδόν, δέρειν πολλάς sc. πληγάς (§ 134, 6 p. 189) and moreover in several of the examples of the double Accusative which follow in 6 below, but also in such Relative constructions as John xvii. 26; Eph. ii. 4 ἀγάπην ἣν ἠγάπησάς με (cf. 6 sub fin.), Jude 15 περὶ τῶν ἔργων ἀσεβείας ὧν ἠσέβησαν (see § 143, 11 p. 287), Rom. vi. 10 ὃ γὰρ ἀπέθανεν, τῇ ἁμαρτίᾳ ἀπέθανεν· ὃ δὲ ζῇ, ζῇ τῷ θεῷ (i.e. mortem, vitam suam), Gal. ii. 20 ὃ δὲ (i.q. τὴν ζωὴν ἣν) νῦν ζῶ ἐν σαρκί etc.

B. § 131, 5; H. § 553; C. § 480; D. § 465; J. § 582 sq.

Deviations from the construction of the d o u b l e A c c u s a - ℓ t i v e (with the verbs given in the grammars, cf. J. § 583) are either rare or are founded in the analogy of common usage.

Thus δ ι δ ά σ κ ε ι ν is always joined with two Accs. (on Heb. v. 12 see § 140, 13 p. 268) except in Rev. ii. 14 ἐδίδασκεν τῷ Βαλὰκ βαλεῖν etc. (cf. Ev. Nicod. 16, 2; Thom. 4, 2); this exception either follows Hebrew precedent (cf. Job vi. 24, etc., and Gesen. under בְּרִי), or, as is more probable, is due to the circumstance that διδάσκειν here has more the signification of συμβουλεύειν, παραινεῖν (see deWette). The adjunct ἐν πάσῃ σοφίᾳ Col. i. 28; iii. 16 does not denote the object but the mode of teaching, cf. i. 9; κ ρ ύ π τ ε ι ν and ἀ π ο κ ρ ύ π τ ε ι ν are used with the Acc. of the nearer and ἀπό with the Gen. of the more remote object, Matt. xi. 25 ἔκρυψας ταῦτα ἀπὸ σοφῶν, Luke x. 21, etc., hebraistically ἀπὸ προσώπου τινός Rev. vi. 16, ἀπ᾽ ὀφθαλμῶν σου Luke xix. 42 (cf. § 146, 1 p. 320); ἀ φ α ι ρ ε ῖ ν and ἀ φ α ι - ρ ε ῖ σ θ α ί τι ἀπό τινος (according to § 132, 5 p. 157) Luke x. 42; xvi. 3, etc.; likewise α ἰ τ ε ῖ ν and ἀ π α ι τ ε ῖ ν τι ἀπό τινος Matt. xx. 20; Luke vi. 30; xii. 20. But constructions like αἰτεῖν τι π α ρ ὰ θεοῦ, ἀφαιρεῖν τ ι ν ί τι, ἐπερωτῆσαί τινα π ε ρ ὶ τοῦ ῥήματος are perfectly regular; π ο ι ε ῖ ν is found with two Accs. according to the rule only in Matt. xxvii. 22 τί οὖν ποιήσω Ἰησοῦν, Mark xv. 12 Lchm. Treg. τί θέλετε ποιήσω τὸν βασιλέα τῶν Ἰουδαίων (also according to the other reading [ποιήσω ὃν λέγετε etc. Tdf. cod. Sin.], see § 127, 5 p. 105), elsewhere always with the D a t i v e of the person — Matt. xxi. 40; Luke xx. 15; Acts ix. 13, etc. (in many passages the Dative would have been used, too, in ordinary prose, e.g. Mark vii. 12; x. 36, 51, etc.), or a Preposition instead, as Matt. xvii. 12 ἐποίησαν ἐν α ὐ τ ῷ ὅσα ἠθέλησαν (cf. Mark ix. 13), John xv. 21 ταῦτα πάντα ποιήσουσιν εἰς ὑ μ ᾶ ς (Grsb. ὑμῖν). Cf. further the double Accusative in 10 p. 152.

The following are more or less peculiar to the N. T.: π ε ρ ι β ά λ λ ε ι ν τινά τι (in the classics commonly construed otherwise, see Dind. in Steph. Thes. sub voce), as John xix. 2 ἱμάτιον πορφυροῦν περιέβαλον αὐτόν, cf. Luke xxiii. 11 var. (but τινί τι in xix. 43 [where Tdf. (with א) now reads παρεμβαλοῦσιν]); and in combination with the construction mentioned in 5 p. 148: π ο τ ί ζ ε ι ν τινὰ γάλα, ποτήριον Mark ix. 41; 1 Cor. iii. 2, φ ο ρ τ ί ζ ε ι ν τινὰ φορτία Luke xi. 46, χ ρ ί ε ι ν τινὰ ἔλαιον ἀγαλλιάσεως Heb. i. 9 (quotn.) and ἐ γ χ ρ ί ε ι ν τοὺς 131

ὀφθαλμοὺς κολλούριον Rev. iii. 18, ἀγαπᾷν ἀγάπην τινά (see 5 p. 148 sq.),
Εὐαγγελίζεσθαι also is found once with two Accs. according to
later usage (see Pape's Lex.) in Acts xiii. 32—(a passage which is not
to be explained by § 151, 1 p. 376), but elsewhere always, if attended
by two nouns or pronouns as objects, with the Dat. of the Pers. and
the Acc. of the thing announced; as, Luke i. 19; Acts viii. 35;
2 Cor. xi. 7, etc. Respecting ὁρκίζειν see above, 1 p. 147.[1]
On the construction with the Passive see § 134, 5 p. 188.

B. § 131, 6; H. § 556; C. § 480; D. § 465; J. §§ 375, 6; 625.

With verbs denoting to *make* or *hold for* anything, and those
of kindred signification, we find, besides the common construction of two Accusatives, the combination τινὰ εἰς τι
after the example of the Hebrew (Gesen. Lehrg. p. 814) or
the Septuagint. Ποιεῖν, and also καθιστάναι, τιθέναι, have,
indeed, in the N. T. regularly two Accs., but in the O. T.
commonly εἰς: Gen. xii. 2 ποιήσω σε εἰς ἔθνος μέγα, Ezek. iv.
9; 2 Chron. xi. 22 κατέστησεν εἰς ἄρχοντα Ἀβιά, Deut. xxviii.
13, etc. In analogy with these examples are the following:
Acts xiii. 22 ἤγειρεν τὸν Δαυεὶδ αὐτοῖς εἰς βασιλέα, vii. 21
ἀνεθρέψατο αὐτὸν ἑαυτῇ εἰς υἱόν, xiii. 47 τέθεικά σε εἰς φῶς
ἐθνῶν (after Isa. xlix. 6 Alex.), Matt. xxi. 46 εἰς προφήτην
αὐτὸν εἶχον (cf. vs. 26). In Matt. xiii. 30 the MSS. vary between
δήσατε αὐτὰ εἰς δεσμάς Lchm. [Tdf. cod. Sin.] and δεσμάς
Tdf. [eds. 2, 7]. [Treg. gives εἰς in brackets.]

This Hebraistic mode of expression occurs more frequently still
where the construction requires the d o u b l e N o m i n a t i v e, especially
with εἶναι and γενέσθαι; for example in the repeated quotations ἔσονται
εἰς σάρκα μίαν (after Gen. ii. 24), ἐγενήθη εἰς κεφαλὴν γωνίας (after Ps.
cxvii. 22). Cf. Luke iii. 5 (quotn.), xiii. 19 ἐγένετο εἰς δένδρον μέγα,
John xvi. 20 ἡ λύπη εἰς χαρὰν γενήσεται, Rom. xi. 9 (quotn.), 1 Cor.
xv. 45 (quotn.), 2 Cor. vi. 18 ἔσομαι ὑμῖν εἰς πατέρα καὶ ὑμεῖς ἔσεσθέ μοι
εἰς υἱούς (as in 2 Sam. vii. 14 etc.), Heb. i. 5; viii. 10; 1 John v. 8;
Rev. viii. 11. Yet not all the passages of the sort are to be forcibly
brought under this class, since there are many which can be satisfactorily explained by Greek usage (for γενέσθαι εἰς τι is a Greek phrase
also), and where the application of the above Hebraism would be
erroneous and disturbing to the sense; as, 2 Cor. viii. 14; Col. ii. 22;

---

[1] Formerly πείθειν also was numbered among the verbs that take two Accs.
on account of Acts xix. 8; xxviii. 23; recent editors, however, have expunged
τά in both passages, [restored in xix. 8 by Tdf. with cod. Sin.]. The Acc. with
the Passive (Heb. vi. 9, etc.) is explainable by no. 10 below, p. 152.

Jas. v. 3 (εἰς φθοράν, εἰς μαρτύριον ἔσται *tend, redound* to *destruction, prove* a witness), Rev. xvi. 19, etc.   Similarly λαμβάνειν (τὶ εἴς τι): Heb. xi. 8 τόπον ὃν ἔμελλεν λαμβάνειν εἰς κληρονομίαν, and probably Acts vii. 53 also.

REMARK.   Likewise borrowed from the language of the Septuagint and a departure from classic usage (for Xen. Cyr. 3, 1, 33 and the like are not parallel) is the current combination λογίζομαι εἴς τι in the signification *to be reckoned* or *set to the account of, as* etc., for example, in the oft-repeated quotation ἐλογίσθη αὐτῷ εἰς δικαιοσύνην (after the Sept. of Gen. xv. 6.   That the Hebr. חָשַׁב is 132 capable of the same construction, see 1 Sam. i. 13 and Gesen. sub voce), and further in the phrases εἰς οὐδὲν λογισθῆναι, ἡ ἀκροβυστία εἰς περιτομὴν λογισθήσεται, τὰ τέκνα λογίζεται εἰς σπέρμα Acts xix. 27; Rom. ii. 26; ix. 8.   But the phrases with ὡς, Rom. viii. 36 ἐλογίσθημεν ὡς πρόβατα (after the Sept. of Ps. xliii. 23, Hebr. כ), or with μετά and the Gen. Luke xxii. 37 (for which the Sept. in Isa. liii. 12 use ἐν τοῖς ἀνόμοις), have a different meaning and are not opposed to Greek usage.

According to a construction not unknown to the Greeks also 8 (see Bhdy. Synt. p. 66; Matth. § 308; Lob. ad Phryn. p. 517; Schaef. in Schol. Apoll. Rhod. p. 209) the predicative term with verbs of *naming* sometimes stands in the Nominative instead of any other case : John xiii. 13 φωνεῖτέ με ὁ διδάσκαλος καὶ ὁ κύριος (cf. 1 Sam. ix. 9), Rev. ix. 11 ὄνομα ἔχει Ἀπολλύων. On τὸ ὄρος τὸ καλούμενον Ἐλαιών see p. 22.

From the Hebrew usage (קָרָא אֶת־שְׁמוֹ Gen. iv. 25, 26; v. 2, 3, etc.) or from the Sept. are borrowed the (pleonastic) expressions καλέσεις τὸ ὄνομα αὐτοῦ Ἰησοῦν, Ἰωάννην, — also in the Pass. ἐκλήθη τὸ ὄνομα αὐτοῦ Ἰησοῦς Matt. i. 21; Luke i. 31; ii. 21; Rev. xix. 13, etc.; for the classic use of καλεῖν ὄνομα (B. § 131, N. 11; J. § 588, 1) is manifestly of a different nature.[1]

---

[1] Quite isolated is the reading of cod. Vat. in Matt. x. 25 εἰ τῷ οἰκοδεσπότῃ Βεελζεβοὺβ [Βεεζεβοὺλ ed. Tdf.; so Sin.] ἐπεκάλεσαν, πόσῳ μᾶλλον τοῖς οἰκιακοῖς αὐτοῦ, which has been adopted by Lchm.   It belongs to those which without MS. support from other quarters will hardly succeed in gaining the general approval of critics against the entire mass of remaining authorities [cod. Sin. also].   Yet it is very improbable that it should be the emendation of a grammarian who took ἐπικαλεῖν here in the sense of *reproach with* (Meyer).   Ἐπικαλεῖν here, at least in ancient times, was taken in no other signification than *to name*, or more accurately to give the *surname, cognomentum daemonis addiderunt* (as Hilary expressly translates the passage).   Too little attention, however, to the composition with ἐπί naturally led to the result that the Latin versions rendered in accordance with their idiom, *patrem* vocaverunt; and this, again, in the Greek MSS. not only led to the easy alteration of the Dative into the Acc., but also — what is very significant — to the

133

9 B. § 131, 7; H. § 549; C. § 481; J. § 579.

The Acc. of limitation with adjectives and other predicative terms, known under the name of the Greek Acc., has
passed in the N. T. pretty much out of use. Single instances
are Heb. ii. 17 πιστὸς ἀρχιερεὺς τὰ πρὸς τὸν θεόν, Rom. xii. 18
etc. cf. § 125, 12 p. 96. For the most part the Dative, or a
Prep. like κατά, is substituted for it ; as, Luke xxiv. 25 βραδεῖς
τῇ καρδίᾳ, Mark vii. 26 ; Acts iv. 36 Κύπριος τῷ γένει, xviii. 3
σκηνοποιοὶ τῇ τέχνῃ ([so cod. Sin.], Grsb. τὴν τ.), and the
expressions ἀπὼν τῷ σώματι, παρὼν τῷ πνεύματι, σοφοὶ ...
συγγενεῖς ... κύριοι κατὰ σάρκα, ταπεινὸς κατὰ πρόσωπον, etc.
On the other hand, with the Passive (Middle) the Acc. is
much in use, see §§ 134 and 135.

B. § 131, 8 and N. 12; C. § 478 a.; J. § 579, 6.

10 Instances of the pronominal Accusative neuter with
verbs which otherwise govern a different case, are : Luke ix. 45
αἴσθωνται αὐτό, Matt. xix. 20 τί ὑστερῶ (§ 132, 22 p. 169),
2 Cor. xii. 13 ὃ ἡττήθητε (ἡσσώθητε), Acts xxv. 8 τι ἥμαρτον,
μεριμνᾷν τὰ τοῦ κυρίου 1 Cor. vii. 32 etc., even οὐδὲν χρείαν
ἔχω Rev. iii. 17 (cf. § 129, 5 p. 127). Examples of cases in
which the verb is connected with two Accusatives in consequence of this usage only are : Luke iv. 35 μηδὲν βλάψαν αὐτόν,
Matt. xxvii. 44 τὸ αὐτὸ ὠνείδιζον αὐτόν, Acts xxv. 10 ; Gal. iv.
12 οὐδέν με ἠδικήσατε, Mark viii. 36 ; Gal. v. 2 etc. ὑμᾶς οὐδὲν
ὠφελήσει. With the Passive: πείθεσθαι οὐδέν, τὰ κρείττονα
Acts xxvi. 26 ; Heb. vi. 9.

Respecting Acts xiii. 2 see § 147, 30 p. 342.

B. § 131, 9; H. § 550; C. § 482; D. p. 498; J. § 548 g., cf. § 905, Obs. 2, 7.

11 The use of the Accusative in giving the duration of time
and the measure of distance agrees with the ordinary use.
It is seldom employed in the more definite specifications of

change of ἐπικαλεῖν into the simple καλεῖν (see the various readings). To this it
must be added : that another leading authority, the cod. Alex., is wanting here, and
the saying is one of those preserved by the evangelist Matt. alone; and in particular, the circumstance that the construction of ἐπικαλεῖν with the Dat. in consequence
of the ἐπί in composition (B. § 147, N. 9) can not only be established grammatically,
but the employment of the Dative in this connection is so natural that it would be
most likely to suggest itself to an author of little practice, writing in the language of
the people. Moreover, compare the altogether analogous example of ἐπονομάζειι
with the Dat. in Greek authors in Steph. sub voce, Heind. on Plato's Phaedr. 30
and οᵘ καλεῖν ὄνομα τινί in B. § 131, N. 11 ; Heinⅰ. on Plato's Crat. 6.

time, — as John iv. 52 for which in vs. 53 ἐν with the Dat. is used, yet with a slight difference.

Further, mention deserves to be made of the peculiar position (which originated perhaps through the influence of the Latin usage, and frequently occurs also in writers of the κοινη, as Plutarch, Lucian, Appian, Josephus) of the prepositions ἀπό and πρό in specifications of place and time; as, John xi. 18 ἦν Βηθανία ἐγγὺς τῶν Ἱεροσολύμων ὡς ἀπὸ σταδίων δεκαπέντε some fifteen stadia distant *from Jerusalem*, xxi. 8; Rev. xiv. 20; John xii. 1 πρὸ ἓξ ἡμερῶν τοῦ πάσχα ἦλθεν six days *before* the Passover (cf. Amos i. 1; iv. 7, and the corresponding 134 (Latinizing) use in Plutarch e.g. Philop. 4; Oth. 11, and in Appian e.g. 1. 15; 2. 115, etc.). Together with these constructions the common one is in use, Luke xxiv. 13, etc. Cf. Zumpt, Gr. § 396.

B. § 131, 10; H. § 552; C. § 483; D. p. 502; J. § 579.

The Acc. as an adverbial adjunct of the mode, etc., 12 as τὴν ἀρχήν, τὸν ἀριθμόν *as respects number*, τοὔνομα *by name* (Matt. xxvii. 57), μακράν sc. ὁδόν, has its foundation in ordinary usage. But ἀκμήν in the sense of *adhuc* (Matt. xv. 16) is un-Attic (see Pape). On the Hebraism ὁδὸν θαλάσσης (דֶּרֶךְ הַיָּם) Matt. iv. 15 see Meyer in loc.

B. § 131, NN. 13, 14; H. § 547 d.; C. § 481 b.; D. § 467; J. § 580.

Analogous to the use of the Acc. in classic Greek as if in 13 apposition to a clause, and before proverbs, quotations, etc., is its varied employment also in the N. T. in certain abbreviated and parenthetic adjuncts, — appositive limitations, as it were, of the preceding or following thought (not of single words, — a case in which the Nominative sometimes appeared contrary to the rule, § 123, 5 p. 78). When such adjuncts are in the Neuter, it is hardly possible to say positively whether they are to be taken as Nominatives or as Accusatives.

Examples: a) referring to what precedes, Rom. xii. 1 παρακαλῶ ὑμᾶς παραστῆσαι τὰ σώματα ὑμῶν θυσίαν ζῶσαν ..., τὴν λογικὴν λατρείαν ὑμῶν — an adjunct which can neither be regarded as in apposition to θυσίαν alone, nor as an object dependent immediately on παρακαλῶ. 2 Thess. i. 5 ἔνδειγμα τῆς δικαίας κρίσεως and Rev. xxi. 17 μέτρον ἀνθρώπου may also be taken as Accusatives. Further, Acts x. 36 Tdf. [cod. Sin. Treg.] τὸν λόγον, ὃν ἀπέστειλεν τοῖς υἱοῖς Ἰσραήλ etc., for with ὑμεῖς οἴδατε (vs. 37) begins a new paragraph, so that τὸν λόγον does not belong to that as object (Meyer). The omission of ὃν (Lchm.) has probably been occasioned by the unusual character

20

of the construction. In Rev. i. 20 τὸ μυστήριον may be construed simply as the object of the preceding γράψον;   b) referring to what follows, Rom. viii. 3 τὸ γὰρ ἀδύνατον etc., Heb. viii. 1 κεφάλαιον δέ etc.; yet these two Neuter adjuncts may be taken unhesitatingly as Nominatives also, according to § 151, 6 p. 381.

B. § 131, N. 16; H. § 545; C. § 476; J. § 579, 3.

14   An Acc. of exclamation might be found in Rev. xii. 12 which according to Lchm.'s text [so Tdf. Treg.; Sin. gives οὐαὶ εἰς etc.] runs οὐαὶ τὴν γῆν καὶ τὴν θάλασσαν, Vulg. vae terrae et mari. But since οὐαί (differing from the exclamation of astonishment οὐά Mark xv. 29) neither in the Apocalypse nor anywhere else is otherwise construed than either with the Dative or with the Vocative instead (in which case the Dative can be omitted, Rev. xviii. 10, 16, 19), and the woe is aimed at the *inhabitants* of the earth as is plain from the following ὑμᾶς and the context, it is necessary to educe the idea τοῖς κατοικοῦσιν (which the Rec. has adopted) out of the preceding σκηνοῦντες and to let the Acc. depend on that. Compare under this head the examples in § 151, 23 d) p. 392 sq.

135   THE GENITIVE.
B. § 132, 1; H. § 558; C. § 444 g.; D. p. 482; J. § 464.

1   Assuming the distinction between the subjective Genitive and the objective to have been made plain by the general grammar, we remark here:

1) That the union of substantives, especially abstract terms, by the Genitive relation is employed with fondness by some of the N. T. writers, particularly by Paul in his doctrinal argumentations and by the author of the Apocalypse, so that two, three, yes four, Genitives stand in immediate dependence one upon another. Such an accumulation of Genitives is manifestly avoided by the native Greeks, because it easily begets ambiguity (see e.g. 1 Thess. i. 3; Rom. xi. 33, etc.).

2) That exegetes, especially where dogmatic interests come in, differ very much in interpreting a Genitive, whether as subjective or objective; and yet the settlement of the matter is properly left to them, because grammar, from *its* point of view, must concede in most cases the possibility of both opinions; cf. Winer 186 (175). As the subject, however, is one of weighty importance for the understanding of Scripture, and the decision in all disputed cases necessarily presumes thorough investigation of the usage of individual writers, ex-

position of the internal connection in every passage, comparison of parallel expressions, and the like, it well deserves a separate and systematic treatment of its own.

The mode of expression mentioned under 1) we will illustrate in a number of instances. The ambiguity easily occasioned by accumulating Genitives it was sought to avoid as follows:

a) If the Genitives depend one on another, they stand, as far as possible, in the o r d e r in which they depend on one another;

b) If, however, two Genitives depend on o n e a n d t h e s a m e substantive, this fact is also, at least as a rule, indicated by the p o s i t i o n (before and after the governing substantive).

Examples under a)　　Of t w o Genitives: Col. ii. 2 τὸ πλοῦτος τῆς πληροφορίας τῆς συνέσεως, ii. 11 ἡ ἀπέκδυσις τοῦ σώματος τῆς σαρκός, Rom. xi. 33 ὦ βάθος πλούτου καὶ σοφίας καὶ γνώσεως θεοῦ (where, grammatically viewed, it may be doubtful whether σοφίας and γνώσεως depend together with πλούτου upon βάθος, or both together upon πλούτου; the context favors the former opinion, see Mey. in loc.) etc. Of t h r e e Genitives, — then as a rule the last is a personal (possessive) 1 36 term which easily unites with its predecessor into one whole: 2 Cor. iv. 4 τὸν φωτισμὸν τοῦ εὐαγγελίου τῆς δόξης τοῦ Χριστοῦ, Col. i. 13 τὴν βασιλείαν τοῦ υἱοῦ τῆς ἀγάπης αὐτοῦ, 1 Thess. i. 3 (μνημονεύοντες ὑμῶν ...) τῆς ὑπομονῆς τῆς ἐλπίδος τοῦ κυρίου ἡμῶν Ἰησοῦ Χριστοῦ — where the five Genitives are to be so arranged that τοῦ κυρίου ἡμῶν Ἰησοῦ Χριστοῦ is taken as a whole and governed by ἐλπίδος, which together with ὑμῶν (according to b) below) is governed by ὑπομονῆς, and this by the verb μνημονεύοντες, Eph. i. 19 κατὰ τὴν ἐνέργειαν τοῦ κράτους τῆς ἰσχύος αὐτοῦ, iv. 13 (twice); i. 6; Heb. v. 12, etc.　　Of f o u r Genitives: Rev. xix. 15 πατεῖ τὴν ληνὸν τοῦ οἴνου τοῦ θυμοῦ τῆς ὀργῆς τοῦ θεοῦ τοῦ παντοκράτορος, cf. xvi. 19; xiv. 8.　　The O. T. also offers examples of the sort.

Examples under b): Rev. vii. 17 ἐπὶ ζωῆς πηγὰς ὑδάτων (cf. § 147, 31 p. 343), Acts v. 32 Tdf. [eds. 2, 7 ; not 8] ἐσμὲν αὐτοῦ μάρτυρες τῶν ῥημάτων τούτων, 2 Cor. v. 1 ἡ ἐπίγειος ἡμῶν οἰκία τοῦ σκήνους, Phil. ii. 30 τὸ ὑμῶν ὑστέρημα τῆς λειτουργίας, 1 Thess. i. 3, see under a).　　Further, position requires us in Rev. iii. 10 (τὸν λόγον τῆς ὑπομονῆς μου) to make μου depend on ὑπομονῆς, in Heb. vi. 1 τοῦ Χριστοῦ on τῆς ἀρχῆς, not on λόγον; and in 2 Pet. iii. 2 τοῦ κυρίου is hardly to be carried over ἐντολῆς and connected with ἀποστόλων, which according to the mss. [Sin. also] has already the Gen. ὑμῶν (not ἡμῶν Rec. Grsb. and the translation).　　The passages where, besides, the Genitive is separated from its substantive, as 1 Thess. ii. 13; 2 Cor. iii. 6: 1 Pet.

iii. 21, etc., are of a different sort, and hardly admit of a doubt as respects the meaning; see respecting them in connection with § 151, 13,
14 p. 387.   The reference of σου, however, in Rev. xviii. 14 is doubtful
(even according to the MSS. [א puts it before τῆς ἐπιθ.]).

2   REMARK.   Exegetical works on the N. T., particularly the older,
often speak of a periphrasis of the Genitive (subjective and
objective) by means of prepositions, especially κατά with the Acc.
Winer 193 (182), Fritzsche, Meyer, and others, have declared themselves as decidedly opposed to this expression; and in truth, as
respects the origin and philosophy of the matter, with entire correctness, since we cannot speak of the two modes of expression as grammatically i d e n t i c a l, and in general, caution must be exercised in the
application of such terms.   The simplicity and intelligibleness of
grammatical exposition would suffer, however, should we insist in
practice upon carrying this caution too far; for the rigorous application
of this principle would affect also many other phenomena which in
grammatical discourse we are wont to meet with under the title
"Periphrasis."   We do not take offence when grammars speak of a
periphrasis of the partitive genitive by means of prepositions, as ἐξ, ἐν,
in Latin *ex, de, inter ;* just as little should we in the present case.   The
only important point is that we connect the right views with grammatical terminology.   (Cf. in § 151 the chapter on Ellipsis pp. 390 sqq.)

That is to say, since it was at all times easy (in comparison, for
example, with the Latin) for the Greek language by virtue of its
arrangement of words, which was in this particular rigidly prescribed
(cf. § 125), to make prepositional phrases dependent i m m e d i a t e l y
u p o n s u b s t a n t i v e s, it is in perfect analogy with the development
of language to assume, that the later language (of prose), agreeably
to its analytic nature, carried the application of this usage further and
further, and employed prepositional expressions even where the earlier
137 language still preferred the simple case.   So that, strictly speaking,
the case was not periphrased, but the prepositional phrase d i s p l a c e d
the simple case, or, as Bernhardy (Synt. p. 241) aptly describes it, was
employed i n t h e s e n s e o f t h e Genitive.   Just as we, instead of
'your faith,' might also say 'the faith among you' i.e. the faith existing among you, so too, we find in the N. T. instead of the usual
ἡ πίστις ὑμῶν the phrase ἡ καθ' ὑμᾶς πίστις (Eph. i. 15), and in other
writers οἱ καθ' ὑμᾶς ῥήτορες (Longin. 15. 8) instead of the ordinary
οἱ ῥήτορες ὑμῶν (cf. Acts xvii. 28).   Now if such an instance as this
occurs often, and shapes itself into a species of u s a g e, as was un-
deniably the case in the later language with κατά and the Acc. (e.g.
ἡ κατὰ τὴν ἀρχὴν ἀπόθεσις, ἡ κατὰ τὸ σῶμα ῥώμη Diod. Sic., ἡ κατ' αὐτὸν
ἀρετή Ael., αἱ κατ' Ἀννίβαν πράξεις, ἡ κατὰ τὸν ἥλιον ἀνατολή, . . . πορεία,

τὰ κατὰ τὰς πλατείας διαστήματα Polyb., etc.), the grammarian is perfectly authorized to call this, for brevity's sake, as is done in so
many other cases, a periphrasis for the Genitive in the sense above
defined.

Lastly, it is in no wise agreeable to the nature of these expressions
to supply everywhere in explaining them (as is so frequently done)
an omitted verbal idea (as ὤν, γενόμενος, etc.) ; just as we do not
deem it necessary also to supply such an ellipsis with the periphrasis
for the partitive Genitive. On the contrary, the verbal idea is either
already included in the governing substantive, as (to take an example
from the N. T.) in Phil. i. 5 ἡ κοινωνία ὑμῶν εἰς τὸ εὐαγγέλιον (see 8
p. 160), or is naturally suggested by the context, or by the force of
the preposition, as Mark v. 26 τὰ παρ' αὐτῆς πάντα (otherwise τὰ ἑαυτῆς),
2 Cor. viii. 7 ἡ ἐξ ὑμῶν ἀγάπη, Acts xxiii. 21 ἡ ἀπὸ σοῦ ἐπαγγελία (thy
promise, consent). That in this sense also we can call the super-
scriptions (which without doubt are very ancient) εὐαγγέλιον κατὰ
Ματθαῖον, etc., (precisely, *gospel according to* the understanding,
apprehension, of *Matthew*) circumlocutions instead of the Genitive, is
plain. In a manner quite similar, as we shall see below, 10 p. 161,
attributes (with substantives) which we regularly reproduce by
a d j e c t i v e s are expressed both by the Gen. of a subst. and also by
κατὰ with the Acc.

B. § 132, N. 1; H. § 677; C. § 538 d.; D. p. 482; J. § 652, Obs. 6.

Examples of the use of the P o s s e s s i v e pronoun instead of the 3
o b j e c t i v e G e n i t i v e of a personal pronoun are Luke xxii. 19 ;
1 Cor. xi. 24 τοῦτο ποιεῖτε εἰς τὴν ἐμὴν ἀνάμνησιν, Rom. xi. 31 τῷ
ὑμετέρῳ ἐλέει, 1 Cor. xvi. 17 τὸ ὑμέτερον ὑστέρημα, xv. 31 Tdf. [so
Lchm. Treg. cod. Sin., etc.] νὴ τὴν ὑμετέραν καύχησιν. In John xv. 9
the idea of mutual love seems to predominate.

B. § 132, 2; H. § 559 b.; C. § 418 a.; D. p. 482 sq.; J. § 542, vi. b.

The Genitive of the c o u n t r y in the mention of cities is 4
found in Matt. xxi. 11 ; Mark i. 9 Ναζαρὲτ τῆς Γαλιλαίας, John
ii. 1 etc. Κανᾶ ... Βηθσαϊδὰ τῆς Γαλ. ; moreover Τάρσος τῆς
Κιλικίας, Πέργη τῆς Παμφυλίας, etc.

B. § 132, 3. 4 and N. 2; H. § 579 sq.; C. § 405; D. § 451; J. §§ 529, 530.

That the genitive as the *whence*-case, in particular the 5
G e n i t i v e o f s e p a r a t i o n with the corresponding predicates,
is very frequently elucidated or periphrased by the addition
of the prepositions ἀπό and ἐκ (ἐκ χειρός § 133, 20 p. 182)
does not need to be detailed ; see the lexicons under αἴρειν, 138

ἀφαιρεῖν and ἀφαιρεῖσθαι,[1] ἐλευθεροῦν, καθαρίζειν, λούειν (to bathe, cleanse from), λύειν, λυτροῦν, ῥύεσθαι, σώζειν, χωρίζειν, the adjectives ἄσπιλος (Jas. i. 27), καθαρός (Acts xx. 26), ἀθῷος (Matt. xxvii. 24), etc.   Cf. § 147 under ἐκ pp. 326 sq., and ἀπό pp. 322 sqq.

With other words this insertion of the preposition occurs less frequently; e.g. παύειν 1 Pet. iii. 10, ἀναπαύεσθαι ἐκ τῶν κόπων Rev. xiv. 13 rest from (after) their labors, ὑστερεῖν Heb. xii. 15, κωλύειν Luke vi. 29.   In general, the Hebrew use of מִן with these and similar terms (see e.g. 2 Sam. iii. 28, also the Sept. ἀθῷος ἀπό) may not have been without influence.

Other verbs are, perhaps accidentally, connected only with the Genitive; see the lexicons under διαφέρειν, ἀποστερεῖσθαι (respecting Jas. v. 4 see § 147, 6 p. 326), παύεσθαι.   Ἀποφεύγειν, as a transitive construed commonly with the Acc. (2 Pet. ii. 20), also takes by virtue of its composition the Genitive (2 Pet. i. 4).   On κρύπτειν and its compounds see § 131, 6 p. 149, and on ἁμαρτάνειν see § 133, 3 Rem. p. 173.

B. § 132, 5; H. § 559; C. § 415 sq.; J. § 533, cf. § 893 e.

6   Agreeably to what was said above (2 p. 156), instead of the partitive Genitive we far more frequently find a periphrasis by means of prepositions.   Thus particularly (as in Latin) εἰς, δύο, τινὲς, πολλοὶ ἐξ αὐτῶν, or with ἐν (corresponding to the Latin inter) as Jas. v. 13, 14, 19 ἐάν τις ἐν ὑμῖν πλανηθῇ, etc., and with εἶναι Matt. ii. 6; Rom. i. 6, etc.   The language of the N. T. goes further, too, in that it not infrequently o m i t s the indefinite part (τινές), so that there then remains merely the whole in the Genitive, with or without ἐκ; and this Genitive then takes in the sentence the place of the subject, or of the object.   (On this point compare the earlier Greek usage in B. p. 484 note, 21st Germ. ed.; p. 497 note, 22d ditto.)

Examples: Acts xxi. 16 συνῆλθον καὶ τῶν μαθητῶν σὺν ἡμῖν, John xvi. 17 εἶπον οὖν ἐκ τῶν μαθητῶν αὐτοῦ πρὸς ἀλλήλους, Rev. xi. 9 βλέπουσιν ἐκ τῶν λαῶν (sc. πολλοί) ... τὸ πτῶμα αὐτῶν, Matt. xxiii. 34

---

[1] Καθελεῖν, also, in the signification to take down is used with ἀπό (Acts xiii. 29), but in the signification to destroy, always with the Acc. of the object. Hence in Acts xix. 27 (the text of which is very uncertain) the Accusative τὴν μεγαλειότητα (Tdf. [eds. 2, 7]) is more simply taken as Subject-Acc. of καθαιρεῖσθαι (without αὐτῆς it might according to § 134, 7 p. 189 be taken as the Object-Acc.).   On the other reading (which is the more difficult, and is supported by the most important mss. [א also]) τῆς μεγαλειότητος αὐτῆς (Lchm. Tdf. Treg.) the Genitive must be explained according to what is said below, 7 p. 159.

ἐξ αὐτῶν ἀποκτενεῖτε ... καὶ ἐξ αὐτῶν μαστιγώσετε, Luke xxi. 16; Rev.
ii. 10; Matt. xiii. 47 ἐκ παντὸς γένους (sc. τὶ) συνάγειν. Hence, too,
the participial limitations that follow can be subjoined in the
Nominative or the Accusative: John vii. 40 ἐκ τοῦ ὄχλου οὖν,
ἀκούσαντες τῶν λόγων, ἔλεγον (Grsb. adds πολλοί), Acts xxi. 16;
2 John 4 εὕρηκα ἐκ τῶν τέκνων σου περιπατοῦντας ἐν ἀληθείᾳ.
Similar to these examples is Acts xv. 7 ἐν ὑμῖν ἐξελέξατο ὁ θεὸς etc.
Isolated instances of the sort occur even in classic authors; as, 139
Xen. An. 3, 5, 16; Ages. 1. 22, etc. Cf. the following paragraph.

REMARK. Examples of the use of the whole with ὁ μέν ... ὁ δέ in
the same case with the part, do not occur. But similar to Anab.
5, 5, 11 is Eph. v. 33 ὑμεῖς οἱ καθ᾽ ἕνα ἕκαστος ... ἀγαπάτω etc.

B. § 132, 5 c); H. § 572 a.; C. § 421 sq.; D. p. 473 sq.; J. § 533.

The beginnings of the usage treated of above (in 6) appear   7
in the connection (so frequent in the classics) of the partitive
Genitive immediately with verbs, principally with εἶναι
(with which it is usual to supply τίς, τὶ for explanation); as,
Acts xxiii. 6 τὸ ἓν μέρος ἐστὶν Σαδδουκαίων, τὸ δὲ ἕτερον Φαρι-
σαίων, 1 Tim. i. 20 ὧν ἐστιν Ὑμέναιος (on the Gen. with εἶναι
see in its place, 11 below, p. 162 sq.) — and when the Gen. is
resolved by ἐκ: John xviii. 17 καὶ σὺ ἐκ τῶν μαθητῶν εἶ, Luke
xxii. 58, etc. But the whole without any specification of part
is commonly enough found also in connection with words of
complete predication, as διδόναι, λαμβάνειν, ἐσθίειν, etc.; yet
here again there is this difference, that the whole does not as
in the earlier Greek writers stand in the simple Genitive (with
the exception of Rev. ii. 17), but depends on an intervening
preposition (ἐξ, ἀπό).

Examples: Luke xx. 10 ἀπὸ τοῦ καρποῦ τοῦ ἀμπελῶνος δώσουσιν
αὐτῷ, 1 John iv. 13 ἐκ τοῦ πνεύματος αὐτοῦ δέδωκεν ἡμῖν, Matt. xxv. 8;
Mark xii. 2 ἵνα λάβῃ ἀπὸ τῶν καρπῶν, Rev. xviii. 4; John xxi. 10
ἐνέγκατε ἀπὸ τῶν ὀψαρίων, Acts ii. 17 ἐκχεῶ ἀπὸ τοῦ πνεύματός μου; and
particularly often with the words φαγεῖν and πιεῖν, Matt. xv. 27 τὰ
κυνάρια ἐσθίει ἀπὸ τῶν ψιχίων, 1 Cor. xi. 28 ἐκ τοῦ ἄρτου ἐσθιέτω, Luke
xxii. 18 οὐ μὴ πίω ἀπὸ τοῦ γεννήματος τῆς ἀμπέλου, John iv. 14 ἐκ τοῦ
ὕδατος, vi. 50; 1 Cor. ix. 7, etc. By this construction are also to be
explained Acts v. 2 ἐνοσφίσατο ἀπὸ τῆς τιμῆς i.e. a part of the price,
Rev. v. 9 ἠγόρασας ἐκ πάσης φυλῆς sc. πολλούς (for ἡμᾶς [so cod. Sin.]
is a later addition).

REMARK. (B. § 132 5 b.; H. § 589; C. § 420; J. § 527). Examples
of partitive specifications of time with adverbs are Matt. xxviii.
1 ὀψὲ σαββάτων, Luke xviii. 12 δὶς τοῦ σαββάτου. Cf. Col. ii. 16

B. § 132, 5 d); H. § 574; C. §§ 424, 427; D. p. 472 sq.; J. § 585.

8   Among the verbs of partaking, etc., we may notice, κληρονομεῖν only with the Acc.; μεταδιδόναι with the Dat. of the person and Acc. of the thing; λαγχάνειν with the Acc. (see Wahl), respecting the Gen. see § 140, 16 a) p. 269; μετέχειν once also with ἐκ (for the simple Gen.) 1 Cor. x. 17, μέρος ἔχειν μετά τινος (of the person) John xiii. 8, and ἔν τινι (of the thing) Rev. xx. 6; κοινωνεῖν only once with the Gen. (Heb. ii. 14), elsewhere always with the Dative, as well of the thing (Rom. xii. 13, etc.) as also of the person, 140 in which case the Dat. of the thing (in which) is expressed by a circumlocution with ἐν Gal. vi. 6 (see Mey.), or even with εἰς Phil. iv. 15 οὐδεμία μοι ἐκκλησία ἐκοινώνησεν εἰς λόγον δόσεως etc. *let me take part in the account* etc.

The Substantive κοινωνία is often construed with εἰς (cf. 2 above) 2 Cor. ix. 13; Phil. i. 5, also with πρός 2 Cor. vi. 14; κοινωνίαν ἔχειν with μετά 1 John i. 3, 6, 7. The Adjective κοινωνός is commonly construed with the Gen. (of the person and the thing); the person is also put in the Dat. (Luke v. 10), and the thing construed with ἐν (Matt. xxiii. 30).

B. § 132, 5 e) and N. 10; H. § 574 b.; C. § 426; D. p. 483 sq.; J. § 536.

9   Verbs signifying to lay hold of, to touch, are sometimes construed with the Genitive, and sometimes also, inasmuch as from their nature they easily assume a purely transitive signification, with an object-Accusative.

Among the compounds of λαμβάνεσθαι the verb ἐπιλαμβάνεσθαι, which governs as well the Gen. of the person as of the thing, is connected with both Genitives at the same time by Luke in xx. 20, 26. But that it is said in the Middle to govern also an Accusative of the person, arises from a misapprehension of the construction. Nowhere (not in Greek authors even) does such an Acc., where it seems to occur, depend on the verb ἐπιλαμβάνεσθαι alone, but it in all cases stands connected with another transitive verb, so that the Acc. is dependent on both predicates together (by the σχῆμα ἀπὸ κοινοῦ; cf. § 133, 11 note[1] p. 178). The examples of this use (quite classic in cast) are, moreover, all from Luke's writings: Acts ix. 27 ἐπιλαβόμενος αὐτὸν ἤγαγεν, xvi. 19 ἐπιλαβόμενοι τὸν Παῦλον εἵλκυσαν, xviii. 17 ἐπιλαβόμενοι Σωσθένην ἔτυπτον — passages which are to be construed like Luke xiv. 4 ἐπιλαβόμενος ἰάσατο αὐτόν. Further, ἀντιλαμβάνεσθαι always has the Genitive. On the other hand, προσλαμβάνεσθαι agreeably to its composition and signification (*take to one's self, take*

up, take aside) is uniformly joined to the Accusative (of the person) :
Matt. xvi. 22 ; Acts xvii. 5 ; Philem. 17, etc.   The Gen. of the thing
(τροφῆς Acts xxvii. 36) may be explained either by 7 p. 159, or 19
p. 167 ; (but in vs. 34 προσλαβεῖν is a false reading instead of
μεταλαβεῖν).

To ἔχεσθαι (Heb. vi. 9) we may add the compounds ἀντέχεσθαι
and ἀνέχεσθαι which always have the Genitive ; (in 2 Thess. i. 4
the Dative is to be explained by attraction, but cod. B has the very
important variant ἐν ἑχεσθε).

Κρατεῖν which in the N. T. has become for the most part a perfect
transitive *to lay hold of, hold fast* (κρατήσας τὸν Ἰωάννην, κρατεῖν τὴν
παράδοσιν, τὴν διδαχήν, κράτει ὃ ἔχεις, οἱ ὀφθαλμοὶ ἐκρατοῦντο Luke xxiv.
16, etc.), in a figurative sense is connected sometimes also with the
Genitive, Acts xxvii. 13 (τῆς προθέσεως), Heb. iv. 14 ; vi. 18 (ὁμολογίας,
ἐλπίδος), and likewise in the proper signification *to lay hold of, to touch*
viz. τῆς χειρός with Gen. of person following and dependent on this,
Matt. ix. 25 ; Luke viii. 54 (Mark ix. 27 Lchm. [Tdf. Treg.]).   But
the combination current in later writers τινὰ τῆς χειρός occurs only in
Mark ix. 27 Tdf. [eds. 2, 7 ; Grsb.], cf. i. 31 ; analogous to this is
πιάζειν, Acts iii. 7 πιάσας αὐτὸν τῆς δεξιᾶς χειρός.

B. § 132, N. 12; H. § 568; C. § 437 d.; D. p. 482; J. § 435 c.

The use of a substantive in the Genitive as a peri- 10
phrasis for an Adjective, which is mentioned as a poetic
peculiarity among the Greeks, is found not infrequently in 141
the N. T. ; at any rate, there are numerous genitives that can
hardly be reproduced by us otherwise than by means of their
corresponding adjectives.   In this peculiarity the influence of
the genius of the Oriental tongues is unmistakable, for they
were especially addicted to this more poetic mode of expression.
See respecting the Hebrew, Gesen. Lehrg. p. 644 [Gr. § 104].

The following may serve as examples : Luke xvi. 8 ὁ οἰκονόμος τῆς
ἀδικίας *the unjust steward*, xviii. 6 ὁ κριτὴς τῆς ἀδικίας *the unjust judge*,
iv. 22 λόγοι τῆς χάριτος *gracious words*, Rom. i. 26 πάθη ἀτιμίας *dis-
honoring passions*, xii. 20 ἄνθρακες πυρός, Heb. xii. 15 ῥίζα πικρίας
(after the Alex. reading of Deut. xxix. 18), Matt. xxiv. 31 μετὰ
σάλπιγγος φωνῆς μεγάλης *with a loud-sounding trumpet* (not, *with the
loud sound of a trumpet*, see § 147, 31 p. 343 ; cf. τρία μυστήρια κραυγῆς
the three loudly-proclaimed mysteries, Ign. ad Eph. 19).

Under this head belong in particular the numerous phrases formed
by means of the substantive υἱοί or τέκνα followed by the Gen. of
an abstract (cf. the Heb. בֶּן־ and אִישׁ־מְרִי, and the like ; see Gesen.

21

Lex. under בְּ) e.g. τέκνα φωτός, κατάρας, ὑπακοῆς, υἱοὶ ἀπειθείας, φωτός, ἡμέρας, νυκτός, σκότους, ὁ υἱὸς τῆς ἀπωλείας, etc., 1 Thess. v. 5; 2 Pet. ii. 14; 1 Pet. i. 14, etc.

Yet on the whole this use of the Genitive is by no means so general as to warrant the laying down of a special rule — (the Hebrew Genitive of material, for example, is even in the Sept. regularly rendered by adjectives, as χρυσοῦς, ξύλινος, ὀστράκινος, λίθινος, etc., sometimes by ἐκ as in Rev. xviii. 12 but with an adj. subjoined), and many of the cases otherwise referred to this head, in particular those in which the Gen. is more closely defined by an attributive (e.g. a pronoun) and the expression thus loses its general character, are in translation more suitably reproduced literally. Hence in Col. i. 13 υἱὸς τῆς ἀγάπης αὐτοῦ deWette translates *Son of his love* (Luther [so A.V.] *his beloved Son*), Heb. i. 3 ῥῆμα τῆς δυνάμεως αὐτοῦ *the word of his power*, Acts v. 20 τὰ ῥήματα τῆς ζωῆς ταύτης *the words of this life*, cf. xiii. 26; Rom. vii. 24, etc. On the other hand, those phrases (especially Pauline) in which the governing substantive also is an abstract idea are of a general rhetorical nature; as, 2 Cor. iv. 7 ὑπερβολὴ τῆς δυνάμεως (equiv. to ὑπερβάλλουσα δύναμις), Rom. vi. 4 καινότης ζωῆς, ἀδηλότης, βάθος πλούτου, etc.

REMARK. Quite in accordance with the exposition given in 2 p. 156, qualitative limitations are often expressed by κατά with the Acc. instead of by the Gen., as 2 Cor. vii. 10 ἡ κατὰ θεὸν λύπη *godly sorrow*, Rom. xi. 21 οἱ κατὰ φύσιν κλάδοι *the natural branches*, ix. 11 ἡ κατ᾽ ἐκλογὴν πρόθεσις (see Mey.); also without the article, καθ᾽ ὑπερβολὴν ὁδόν (see § 125, 11 p. 96). But they are seldom expressed by κατά with the Genitive (see § 147, 20 p. 334).

THE GENITIVE WITH εἶναι (γίνεσθαι).

B. § 132, N. 13; H. § 572; C. §§ 421 sq. 437; D. p. 473 sq.; J. § 518.

11
142 Although the N. T. use of the Genitive with εἶναι arose from common classic usage, and agrees in general with that of Greek authors, yet the subject is so important that it seems expedient to review that usage once more here in its special application by the N. T. writers.

In an examination of it we must first of all set aside those passages in which, viewed formally, a substantive found in the same sentence is to be repeated, although as respects sense they may belong to one of the classes given below; as, Luke xx. 38 θεὸς οὐκ ἔστιν (sc. θεὸς) νεκρῶν ἀλλὰ ζώντων, 1 Cor. xiv. 33 οὐκ ἔστιν ἀκαταστασίας ὁ θεὸς, ἀλλὰ εἰρήνης, 2 Cor. ii. 3 ἡ ἐμὴ χαρὰ πάντων ὑμῶν (sc. χαρά) ἐστιν, 1 Pet. iii. 3 ὧν (sc. κόσμος) ἔστω οὐχ ὁ ἔξωθεν ... κόσμος, 1 Thess. v. 5, 8, etc.

But in Jas. v. 12 ὑμῶν depends immediately on τὸ ναί, and ἤτω is the copula.

I. If the limiting Genitive with εἶναι is p e r s o n a l, the phrase signifies, a) most commonly *property, possession* — as well external or proper, Luke iv. 7 ἔσται σοῦ πᾶσα, John xix. 24 λάχωμεν περὶ αὐτοῦ, τίνος ἔσται, Luke xx. 14 ἵνα ἡμῶν γένηται ἡ κληρονομία, Mark xii. 7 ; Matt. v. 3 ; xxii. 28 ; Luke xx. 33 ; John x. 12 ; Acts xxi. 11 ; 1 Cor. iii. 21 ; — as also tropically that of ideal connection and dependence, as θεοῦ εἶναι, Χριστοῦ εἶναι Mark ix. 41 ; Acts xxvii. 23 ; Rom. viii. 9 ; xiv. 8 ; 2 Cor. x. 7 ; 2 Tim. ii. 19 (πνεύματος Luke ix. 55 Grsb.), Παύλου ... Ἀπολλώ 1 Cor. i. 12, οὐκ ἐστὲ ἑαυτῶν vi. 19. Analogous in structure to these examples is the elliptical phrase τῆς ὁδοῦ εἶναι sc. κυρίου or σωτηρίας Acts ix. 2 ; [1] also b) *duty* or right, power, Acts i. 7 οὐχ ὑμῶν ἐστιν γνῶναι χρόνους (cf. Matt. xx. 23), Rom. ix. 16 οὐ τοῦ θέλοντος ..., ἀλλὰ τοῦ ἐλεῶντος θεοῦ sc. ἐστίν, Heb. v. 14 τελείων ἐστὶν ἡ στερεὰ τροφή ; and c) pure *causality*, 2 Cor. iv. 7 ἵνα ἡ ὑπερβολὴ τῆς δυνάμεως ᾖ τοῦ θεοῦ καὶ μὴ ἐξ ὑμῶν. But

II. If the limiting Genitive is a t h i n g, it is to be taken in a qualitative sense ; and it may then denote, either a) a *permanent* quality — a use which in ordinary Greek prose is as rare (see B. p. 335) as the similar use spoken of in the preceding paragraph (10 p. 161), as Heb. xii. 11 πᾶσα παιδεία οὐ δοκεῖ χαρᾶς εἶναι ἀλλὰ λύπης, x. 39 οὐκ ἐσμὲν ὑποστολῆς εἰς ἀπώλειαν, ἀλλὰ πίστεως, 2 Pet. i. 20 πᾶσα προφητεία ἰδίας ἐπιλύσεως οὐ γίνεται (is of such a nature that, etc.) ; or b) one that is *transient*, as in Greek, ἦν ἐτῶν δώδεκα Mark v. 42 ; Acts iv. 22, ὅτε ἐγένετο ἐτῶν δώδεκα Luke ii. 42.

REMARK. Apparently this last idiom underlies the specifications of size in Rev. xxi. 16 sq. ἐμέτρησεν τὸ τεῖχος αὐτῆς ἑκατὸν τεσσεράκοντα τεσσάρων πηχῶν, and still more anomalously ἐμέτρησεν τὴν πόλιν τῷ καλάμῳ ἐπὶ σταδίους δώδεκα χιλιάδων sc. σταδίων ; as though they arose from the simple statements τὸ τεῖχος ἦν ἑκατὸν τεσσ. τεσσ. πηχῶν, ἡ πόλις ἦν δώδεκα χιλιάδων.

B. § 132, 10 a); H. § 575; C. § 414; D. p. 468; J. § 539.

The extension of the causal Genitive with words of p l e n t y, **12** b e i n g f u l l, by means of the prepositions ἐκ and ἀπό is frequent in the N. T. ; and that, too, not only with Pass. and Neut. verbs like **143** χορτασθῆναι, πληρωθῆναι, γέμειν (cf. § 147 under ἀπό p. 323, and ἐκ p. 327), as Matt. xxiii. 25 (cf. vs. 27) Tdf. [cod. Sin.], John xii. 3 ; Luke xvi. 21 ; Rev. xix. 21, but also after the transitive γεμίσαι,

---

[1] Quite similar is the use of ὄνομα absolutely, with the obvious ellipsis of κυρίου, as Acts v. 41 ; in Jas v. 14 also cod. Vat. omits τοῦ κυρίου (certainly not by accident).

Luke xv. 16 ἐπεθύμει γεμίσαι τὴν κοιλίαν ἀπὸ τῶν κερατίων.   More in accordance with our usage, and yet not unknown to the Greeks also, is the construction of these words with the (instrumental) Dative, Rom. i. 29 ; 2 Cor. vii. 4, to which Dative according to N. T. usage (§ 133, 17 p. 181) ἐν is frequently added, particularly with περισσεύειν ; see Wahl.

The Impersonals δεῖ and χρή (§ 131, 3 p. 147) are no longeɪ construed with nouns. The place of these verbs in the sense of *to need* is supplied by personal constructions, e.g. with χρήζειν, χρείαν ἔχειν (cf. § 140, 3 note p. 259), προσδεῖσθαι with the Gen. ; see also ὑστερεῖν in 22 p. 169. Δεῖσθαι which only occurs in the sense of *to ask for, entreat*, is likewise accompanied uniformly by the Gen. of the person, but takes the thing in the Acc. (2 Cor. viii. 4; x. 2).

REMARK. The Accusative (of a neuter word) with γέμειν, Rev xvii. 3, and in close proximity to another word in the Genitive (vs. 4) is most simply explained by the analogy of the Accusative after Passives, as πληροῦσθαι § 134, 7 p. 189.

B. § 132, 10 c); H. § 578; C. § 431; D. p. 478 sq.; J. §§ 519. 520.

13   The prepositions used to characterize more precisely the Genitive with verbs of b u y i n g and s e l l i n g are ἐκ Matt. xxvii. 7 (whose force is apparent from the construction in i. 18) and ἀντί Heb. xii. 16. Peculiar is the phrase ἀγοράζειν τιμῆς in the pregnant signification '*dearly* bought' 1 Cor. vi. 20 ; vii. 23, and the Gen. δηναρίου without a verb Rev. vi. 6 ; also the expressions συμφωνεῖν δηναρίου and ἐκ δηναρίου Matt. xx. 2, 13, as it were : make a contract *for* a denarius.

B. § 132, 10 d); H. § 576; C. § 432 b. and c.; D. p. 484 sq.; J. §§ 493. 515 Obs.

14   Πειράζειν *to try, put to the test*, commonly in a bad sense, in later writers and in the N. T. is wholly transitive; πειρᾶσθαι does not occur connected with a noun. Μνημονεύειν is construed as well with the Gen. as with the Acc., without any sensible difference of signification; see Wahl. The Acc. with the Middle ἀναμιμνήσκεσθαι (2 Cor. vii. 15) is explained by § 135, 5 p. 193.

B. § 132, 10 e); H. §§ 576. 577; C. § 432 d.; J. § 496.

15   To verbs signifying *to care for, be anxious*, must be added from the N. T. the newly formed word σπλαγχνίζεσθαι *to have compassion* from τὰ σπλάγχνα (i.q. רַחֲמִים Prov. xii. 10) ; it is construed sometimes absolutely, sometimes with the Gen. (Matt. xviii. 27) or περὶ with the Gen. (ix. 36), but commonly with ἐπί and the Dat. or Acc. Μέλει μοι occurs with the Gen. only in 1 Cor. ix. 9, elsewhere always with περί. On the construction of μεριμνᾶν and other similar verbs, as μακροθυμεῖν, θαυμάζειν (which is no longer ever construed

with the Gen.) see under verbs of emotion § 133, 23 p. 185 and
25 p. 186.   On the other hand, φείδεσθαι and (in accordance
with their composition) καταγελᾶν and καταφρονεῖν are construed only with the simple Genitive whether of the person or of the
thing. In 1 Tim. iv. 12 neither the sense nor usage (cf. 9 p. 160 and
17 note p. 167) prevents our making both Genitives depend
immediately on καταφρονεῖν.

REMARK In Gal. v. 26, where with φθονεῖν both the Dative
and the Accusative (ἀλλήλους) have manuscript authority, in the
absence of other passages in support of the Acc. of the person the
reading ἀλλήλοις [so Sin.] deserves the preference.

B. § 132, 10 g) and N. 16, 17; H. § 577 b.; C. § 431 c. d.; D. p. 479; J. § 501.   144

To verbs of accusing and the like, belongs καταμαρτυρεῖν 16
followed by the Gen.: Matt. xxvi. 62, etc. Moreover κατηγορεῖν, with the Gen. of the person, has once also κατὰ
repeated from the verb (Luke xxiii. 14), and once contrary to
usage (and hence not without var.[Sin. too]) the person in the
Acc. Rev. xii. 10; the thing it takes, as commonly, in the Acc.
Καταδικάζειν is used with the Acc. of the person Matt.
xii. 7; Jas. v. 6, κατακρίνειν (like κρίνειν) also always
with the Acc. of the person (by metonymy also τὴν ἁμαρτίαν
Rom. viii. 3); but the punishment to which the person is
condemned is put (by the Greeks commonly in the Acc.,
sometimes in the Gen.) in the Dative, because (as is supposed)
this construction was the prevalent one with the verb ζημιοῦν,
as θανάτῳ Matt. xx. 18; Mark x. 33 (in this way 2 Pet. ii. 6
is to be explained), or expressed periphrastically: ἔνοχον εἶναι
θανάτου Mark xiv. 64.

The thing or the offence of which one is accused, etc., never
stands in the Genitive alone; for whenever it seems to occur thus, it
is to be explained by the law of Attraction (§ 143, 8 sq. p. 285) as an
Accusative — as in Acts xxiv. 8; xxv. 11; Luke xxiii. 14 (on ἐγκαλεῖσθαι στάσεως see § 133, 9 p. 177), — or the common circumlocutions
with prepositions appear, especially περί τινος, and also ἐπί τινι. Cf.
Acts xxiii. 6; xxiv. 21 and xxvi. 6.   On the phrase ἐκδικεῖν τι ἔκ
τινος see § 133, 20 p. 182.

B. § 132, 10 h.; H. § 576; C. § 432; D. p. 469; J. § 485.

Among the verbs of perception (physical and mental) 17
none is more common than ἀκούειν, — the representative, so
to speak, of all other similar verbs. The constructions of this

verb in the N. T. are exceedingly various; yet they connect themselves closely with those preserved in ordinary Greek.

In the first place, as respects its construction with n o u n s (on its construction with verbs see § 144, 16 p. 301) the p e r s o n, so far as he is the author of the (*immediately* perceived) sound or speech, uniformly stands only in the G e n i t i v e, never in the Accusative; [1] the t h i n g either in the A c c u s a t i v e, so far forth as the speech or sound is the natural object of the hearing, or (but only with substan-

145 tives which denote a sound, etc.) in the G e n i t i v e, in so far as by metonymy (cf. 16 above, p. 165) instead of the speaking etc. person, the thing i.e. the speech, the sound itself, is introduced; as, ἀκούει τῶν λόγων αὐτοῦ equiv. to αὐτοῦ λέγοντος. Examples are: Matt. ii. 9· ἀκούσαντες τοῦ βασιλέως (at the same time with the collateral idea of obeying), Mark vi. 20 ἡδέως αὐτοῦ ἤκουεν, Luke ix. 35, etc.; xi. 31 τὴν σοφίαν Σολομῶνος, xxiii. 6 Γαλιλαίαν (i.e. the *word Galilee*; ἀκούειν Γαλιλαίας could only mean *Galilee*, i.e. to hear the Galileans speak), Acts vii. 34 (quotn.) ἤκουσα τοῦ στεναγμοῦ αὐτῶν i.e. αὐτῶν στεναζόντων, so in John x. 3 τῆς φωνῆς αὐτοῦ, Luke xv. 25 συμφωνίας καὶ χορῶν, etc. It is hardly possible to express in translation the difference in signi- fication between φωνήν and φωνῆς ἀκούειν, λόγων and λόγους ἀκ., since both expressions are used side by side e.g. John v. 25, 28, 37; Acts ix. 4, 7; Rev. xiv. 2, 13, etc., and as respects the sense, therefore, it is a matter of indifference whether we read in Mark xiv. 64 ἠκούσατε τὴν βλασφημίαν (Lchm.) or τῆς βλασφημίας (Tdf. [Treg. cod. Sin.]), in John vii. 40 ἀκούσαντες τῶν λόγων (Lchm. Tdf. [Treg. cod. Sin.]) or τὸν λόγον (Grsb.), only the Genitive as a causal case is more forcible than the Object-Acc.

Frequently b o t h limitations — that of the person and that of the thing — are found dependent alike upon t h e v e r b. Then a threefold construction occurs: 1) the thing is put in the Acc., the person in the Gen., as Acts i. 4 τὴν ἐπαγγελίαν, ἣν ἠκούσατέ μου, and perhaps also such sentences as Matt. vii. 24, 26 ὁ ἀκούων μου τοὺς λόγους, see p. 167 note;   2) the thing in the Acc., the person in the Gen. but with a p r e p o s i t i o n intervening, as ἐκ, παρά and (contrary to ordinary usage) sometimes ἀπό, as Acts x. 22 ἀκοῦσαι ῥήματα παρὰ σοῦ, John viii. 40 ἀλήθειαν ἣν ἤκουσα παρὰ τοῦ θεοῦ, 2 Cor. xii. 6 Tdf. [eds. 2, 7; ed. 8, Treg. Lchm. cod. Sin. om. Acc.] ἀκούει τι ἐξ ἐμοῦ, 1 John i. 5·

---

[1] When sometimes the person alone is found in the Acc. with ἀκούειν, he is not the author of the sound, but the o b j e c t of the hearing, and strictly speaking to be regarded always as the beginning of an Infinitive construction (with the Acc.); as, Eph. iv. 21 εἴγε αὐτὸν ἠκούσατε etc., not *if ye have heard him* (personally), but *if ye have heard him that he is Christ* etc., hence briefly *if ye have heard* OF *him.* See similar examples in Greek authors in Ar. Pac. 603, Thesm. 164; Xen. Cyr. 1 1, 4; and cf. my Essay in the Easter programme, Potsdam. 1855, p. 5.

ἀγγελία, ἣν ἀκηκόαμεν ἀπ᾿ αὐτοῦ; with this case may be reckoned also
those sentences where the object (a thing) is periphrastically expressed
by an entire clause or by περί and the Gen. (Acts ix. 13, etc.) or must
be supplied e.g. John vi. 45 ὁ ἀκούσας παρὰ τοῦ πατρὸς καὶ μαθὼν (A
adds τὴν ἀλήθειαν) ἔρχεται πρός με, i. 41;   3) both the limiting
nouns are put in the Genitive; as, John xii. 47 ἐάν τίς μου ἀκούσῃ τῶν
ῥημάτων, xviii. 37; Luke vi. 47; Acts xxii. 1 ἀκούσατέ μου τῆς πρὸς
ὑμᾶς ἀπολογίας.[1]

With the other verbs of perception, such as πυνθάνεσθαι, μανθάνειν, 14ε
συνιέναι, the o b j e c t of the perception always stands in the Accusative,
the person in the Genitive connected by means of a prep., especially
παρά,(μανθάνειν almost always with ἀπό see § 147,5 p 324).   Ἅπτεσθαι
to touch uniformly has the Gen., both of the person and of the thing.

REMARK. Acts ix. 1 Σαῦλος ἔτι ἐ μ π ν έ ω ν ἀπειλῆς καὶ φόνου is an   18
imitation of ὄζειν, πνεῖν μύρων (B. § 132, 10 h.), and has the stronger
signification of breathing, panting.

B. § 132, 10 i); H. § 576; C. § 432 a.; D. p. 470; J. § 537.

Among verbs signifying to taste, to enjoy, to have an advan-   19
tage, γεύεσθαι has commonly the Genitive, yet is also joined as
transitive to the Accusative, John ii. 9; Heb. vi. 5; κορέννυσθαι,
χορτάζειν (cf. 12 p. 163), ὀνίνασθαι take the Genitive.   On the
phrase προσελάβοντο τροφῆς (Acts xxvii. 36) see 9 p. 161.

B. § 132, N. 20; H. § 586; C. § 511 b.; D. p. 391 sq.; J. § 781.

Of the familiar classic breviloquence by which in comparisons the   20

---

[1] We may be in doubt whether in this last case we ought not rather to make
the Gen. of the person depend immediately upon the Gen. of the thing, and in
this way to reduce the two limitations to a single one, as is indubitably the case in
such sentences as ἤκουσα τοῦ στεναγμοῦ αὐτῶν, etc.   The question, however, comes
to be a mere dispute about words, since according to both constructions the resultant sense is the same.   Yet since 1) the construction with a double G e n i t i v e
cannot be any more surprising than that with a double Acc. and a double Dat.
(§ 133, 27 p. 165), and is unquestionably found in Greek usage, e.g. with κατηγορεῖν
Aesch. Ctes. p. 61 τῶν τεττάρων καιρῶν κατηγορῶ σου, ib. p. 84; Dem. Mid. in.,
with καταγελᾶν Plat. Soph. 239 E. cf. ἐπιλαμβάνεσθαι above 9 p. 160 and καταφρονεῖν
15 p. 165; cf. also the double Gen. with δεῖσθαι, χρήζειν, B. § 132 N. 14; C. § 414 c;
J. § 529 Obs. 1; and 2) the personal Genitive in this case so often precedes the
other substantive, or is even separated from it by a word (although position alone
would not decide the matter, cf. Luke xiv. 24, etc.), — the grammarian is fully
authorized to make both the limiting nouns in the above passages depend on
ἀκούειν.   From the circumstance, perhaps not accidental, that the personal limitation always precedes the other substantive if ἀκούειν also stands before it, and
on the other hand, if ἀκούειν follows it the personal adjunct also is placed after it
(John x. 16, 27; Heb. iii. 7, 15, etc.), we may infer at least a close connection
between the personal Genitive and the verbal idea.

w h o l e of the object compared is substituted for a part, or a single substantive takes the place of an entire clause (see the examples in the grammars and cf. Herm. ad Vig. no. 55 and § 133, 10 p. 177 below), the N. T. exhibits a few indubitable instances : Matt. v. 20 ἐὰν μὴ περισσεύσῃ ἡ δικαιοσύνη ὑμῶν πλεῖον τῶν γραμματέων instead of τῆς δικαιοσύνης τῶν γραμ., John v. 36 Tdf. [cod. Sin.] ἔχω τὴν μαρτυρίαν μείζω τοῦ Ἰωάννου for τῆς τοῦ Ἰωάννου or ἢ ὁ Ἰωάννης ἔχει. But 1 Cor. i. 25 does not belong here (see Meyer).

B. § 132, N. 21; H. § 660 d.; C. § 511 c.; D. p. 393; J. § 780, Obs. 1.

21 Examples of the o m i s s i o n o f ἤ without change of case (as in Latin) in connection with the idea *more* (*plus*) are the following: Matt. xxvi. 53 παραστήσει μοι πλείω δώδεκα λεγεῶνας ἀγγέλων (where ἤ is an explanatory addition) ; and in like manner according to later usage in connection with ἐπάνω, 1 Cor. xv. 6 ὤφθη ἐπάνω πεντακοσίοις ἀδελφοῖς. In Acts xxiii. 13, 21; xxiv. 11; xxv. 6 (iv. 22) the case is not evident; yet these passages, beyond all doubt, must be so construed, and in Mark xiv. 5 the Genitive is required on other grounds also. Rarely ἤ is expressed : Luke ix. 13.

REMARK. That the Gen. of comparison can be used with Positives also if they include the idea of a comparative (B. § 132, N. 24) is illustrated in the N. T. by π ε ρ ι σ σ ό ς and the adverb ὑ π ε ρ ε κ π ε ρ ι σ σ ο ῦ, as Matt. v. 37; Eph. iii. 20. Cf. with this the similar construction with παρά § 147, 27 p. 339. On the Gen. of comparison with the Superlative, see § 123, 14 p. 84.

B. § 132, 12; H. § 581; C. § 406 sq.; D. p. 476; J. § 504 sq.

22 Among the verbs which contain the idea of a c o m p a r i s o n,
147 π λ ε ο ν ε κ τ ε ῖ ν, according to the usage of later writers (see Pape's Lex.), is connected as a simple transitive only with the Accusative, after the analogy of many other verbs; see Wahl. Hence the Passive πλεονεκτεῖσθαι (2 Cor. ii. 11), as also in the earlier writers (Xen., Dem.) according to B. § 134, 5. Respecting διαφέρειν see above, 5 p. 158; respecting ἐλαττοῦν, -οῦσθαι, see under παρά § 147, 27 p. 339.

The Dative with ἡ τ τ ά ο μ α ι in 2 Pet. ii. 19 ᾧ τις ἥττηται, τούτῳ καὶ δεδούλωται is an instrumental Dat. ; but it may also be regarded as the Dat. of the Person with a Passive (§ 134, 2 p. 187), since ἡττάω in later writers (Polyb., Diod.) has become a pure transitive, like δουλόω.

ὑστερεῖν, -εῖσθαι, commonly construed with the Genitive, occurs once also with ἀπό, see § 147, 2 p. 322. In the sense cf the Latin *desum alicui* it is joined to the Dative in the Sept. (Neh. ix. 21; Eccl. vi. 2), once also to the Acc. in the sense of the impersonal δεῖ (Ps. xxii. 1 οὐδέν με ὑστερήσει), and this is the reading also of some of the oldest MSS. [Sin. also] in Mark x. 21 (ἕν σε ὑστερεῖ), which reading Tdf. has adopted instead of the former σοι; on the Acc. of the thing (ἕν, τί) see § 131, 10 p. 152. ὑπερέχειν is construed with the Gen. in Phil. ii. 3, with the Acc. in iv. 7. περισσεύειν by its chief signification, *to have plenty, abundare*, (e.g. ἄρτων, ἐν ἐλπίδι) belongs to no. 12 above p. 163. The derived signification *to surpass, superare*, it acquires, strictly speaking, only by the addition of μᾶλλον (Phil. i. 9; 1 Thess. iv. 1, 10), yet it is uniformly used absolutely i.e. without the Gen. of the object surpassed (respecting Matt. v. 20 see 20 above, p. 168), for which the periphrasis of παρά with the Acc. is used in Eccl. iii. 19, ὑπέρ in 1 Macc. iii. 30. Of the verbs of *ruling* βασιλεύειν is joined most frequently to ἐπί with the Acc., Rom. v. 14, etc., more rarely to ἐπὶ with the Gen. Rev. v. 10; Matt. ii. 22 Tdf. [eds. 2, 7; ed. 8 om. prep. with Lchm.]. On the other hand, ἄρχειν and ἡγεμονεύειν always have the Genitive (as has cod. B also [so Sin.] with βασιλεύειν in Matt. ii. 22), and likewise ἡγεῖσθαι, but only with ὁ ἡγούμενος used substantively. Further, from the N. T. belong here also κυριεύειν, καταδυναστεύειν, ἀνθυπατεύειν (Acts xviii. 12 Tdf. [eds. 2, 7; but ed. 8 ἀνθυπάτου ὄντος, with Lchm. Treg. cod. Sin. etc.], αὐθεντεῖν,—all with the Genitive. ἄρχεσθαι in the sense of *to begin* is construed only with ἀπό.

B. § 132, N. 26; H. cf. § 509; C. of. § 444; D. p. 388; J. § 436 a.

Since every adjective, participle, verbal adjective, can be 23 rendered a substantive by its position in the sentence (not merely by the article), it can in such circumstances also be construed with the Genitive instead of the constructions, casal (or adverbial), which otherwise properly belong to it.

Examples are frequent: ὁ ἀγαπητός μου in the address ἀγαπητοί μου (1 Cor. x. 14 etc.), ἐν γεννητοῖς γυναικῶν (Matt. xi. 11; Luke vii. 28), οἱ εὐλογημένοι τοῦ πατρός μου (Matt. xxv. 34), τὸ ἐμαυτοῦ ... τὸ ὑμῶν αὐτῶν σύμφορον (1 Cor. vii. 35 etc.), ἄνομος and ἔννομος θεοῦ (1 Cor. ix. 21), κλητοὶ Ἰησοῦ Χριστοῦ (Rom. i. 6), διδακτοὶ θεοῦ (John vi. 45), σύμμορφοι τῆς εἰκόνος τοῦ υἱοῦ (Rom. viii. 29), and likewise also σύμφυτοι τῆς ἀναστάσεως Rom. vi. 5 (see deWette). Cf. with these the expression θεοῦ (not θεῷ) ὑποτασσόμενοι in Ign. ad Eph. 5. Hence ὁ δέσμιος Ἰησοῦ Χριστοῦ (Eph. iii. 1 etc.) in brief for, 'a prisoner *for the cause of* Christ (cf. iv. 1).

B. § 132, N. 27; H. § 587 e. § 584 b.; C. § 446 b.; D. p. 478; J. § 507 sq.

24
148 But even when the parts of speech just mentioned retain their adjectival nature (in connection with substantives therefore) they can be construed with the Genitive so far forth as it subjoins the n e c e s s a r y complement of the idea of quality i n c o m p l e t e l y expressed in the adjective, etc.

1 Cor. ii. 13 οὐκ ἐν διδακτοῖς ἀνθρωπίνης σοφίας λόγοις, ἀλλ' ἐν διδακτοῖς πνεύματος, 2 Pet. ii. 14 καρδία γεγυμνασμένη πλεονεξίας ([so cod. Sin.], Rec. -αις), Jas. i. 13 θεὸς ἀπείραστος κακῶν not *inexperienced* (that would be ἄπειρος) *in evil*, but *untempted by evil*, — agreeably to the parallelism of the passage and the derivation from the N. T. πειράζειν.[1] Accordingly ἔ ν ο χ ο ς is construed either (as commonly) with the Dative, Matt. v. 21, 22,[2] or with the Genitive, Matt. xxvi. 66, etc. (so also Herm. Mand. 2) ; in the same way we have ἐ γ γ ὺ ς τινί (for which also ἐπί with the Dat. is used) and τινός.   But whether ὅ μ ο ι ο ς was also connected in this way with the Genitive (like *similis* in Latin) is doubtful, and rests only on John viii. 55 [so cod. Sin.] where Lchm. [so Treg.] has given the preference to ὑμῖν.   In Heb. iii. 12 καρδία πονηρὰ ἀπιστίας, the Gen. is rather to be regarded as dependent on the whole expression καρδία πονηρά.

B. § 132, N. 28; cf. D. p. 483 sq.; J. § 540, Obs.

25 To the examples (given in B. note) of a free use of the Genitive with verbs (λοῦσαι ποταμοῖο, etc.) may be added from the N. T.: βάπτειν τὸ ἄκρον τοῦ δακτύλου ὕδατος Luke xvi. 24, cf. Arat. 650, 858, 951 (Lev. xiv. 16), συμφωνεῖν δηναρίου (see above 13 p. 164).

B. § 132, 14; H. §§ 590, 591; C. § 433; D. § 452; J. §§ 522, 523.

26 a) Examples of the Genitive in general s t a t e m e n t s of T i m e are χειμῶνος, νυκτός (especially in connection with ἡμέρα: νυκτὸς καὶ ἡμέρας and the reverse), μεσονυκτίου, ἀλεκτοροφωνίας (Mark xiii. 35), τοῦ λοιποῦ

---

[1] Similar is the Genitive καρδίας in Acts vii. 51 with ἀπερίτμητοι in cod. Vat. after the analogy of other verbals compounded with a privative (Grams. as above). But the adjunct καὶ τοῖς ὠσίν immediately following agrees badly with this Genitive. The supposition is much more probable that the Vat. reading arose merely by ᾳ clerical error from the Dat. Plur. καρδίαις, and accordingly this very old and well-attested [by cod. Sin. also] reading deserves decidedly the preference over the other (τῇ καρδίᾳ Rec.). On ἄσπιλος, ἀθῷος ἀπό see above, 5 p. 158.

[2] The construction with εἰς which also occurs in this passage (ἔνοχος εἰς τὴν γέενναν) hardly rests on a usage of the word ἔνοχος, nor is a verbal idea (βληθῆναι after v. 29, 30; xviii. 9, etc.) to be supplied here outright.   It is rather — agreeably to the character of the Biblical Greek — a vivid, concrete, c i r c u m l o c u t i o n for the D a t i v e (§ 133, 2. 3 p. 172), called out by the concrete term γέεννα, in antithesis to the preceding abstract term κρίσει and the word συνεδρίῳ used in a similar sense.

(Gal. vi. 17). But it is never used in definite specifications; hence in Matt. xxiv. 20 quite regularly μὴ γένηται ἡ φυγὴ ὑμῶν χειμῶνος μηδὲ σαββάτῳ, and likewise idiomatically ὀψὲ ... δὶς τοῦ σαββάτου (see 7 above, Rem. p. 159). (The Accusative τὸ μὲν σάββατον Luke xxiii. 56 is used according to § 131, 11 p. 152.) In connection with adjectives or participles the above described specifications of time pass over into the Gen. absol.; as, μέσης νυκτός, ... ἡμέρας Matt. xxv. 6; Acts xxvi. 13; ὄρθρου βαθέως Luke xxiv. 1 etc.

b) The Genitive in general specifications of Place is more 149 rare, — as in the classics. Here only two examples from Luke can be adduced: v. 19 μὴ εὑρόντες ποίας (sc. ὁδοῦ) εἰσενέγκωσιν αὐτόν, and xix. 4 ἐκείνης ἤμελλεν διέρχεσθαι.

In both the preceding cases (a. and b.) expressions with prepositions most commonly appear, even as the received text adds διά in both the passages just quoted.

B. § 132, N. 30; H. § 509 β.; C. § 438; D. § 399 β.; J. § 436, 1 b.

The word ᾅδης is found construed in Greek fashion (εἰς ᾅδου) but 27 once, Acts ii. 31 Lchm. [Treg.], although even here the important authority of codd. Vat. and Sin. (followed by Tdf.) opposes this construction. Elsewhere the word has directly the signification underworld, hell, and is construed accordingly; thus εἰς ᾅδην Acts ii. 27 (quotn.), ἐν τῷ ᾅδῃ Luke xvi. 23; πύλαι, κλεῖς ᾅδου, etc. Hence that even in the phrase ἕως ᾅδου (Matt. xi. 23; Luke x. 15) it is not to be taken otherwise is plain.

REMARK. Very extraordinary for the language of the N. T. would be the ellipsis — after the analogy of the above εἰς ᾅδου — of γῆ in Heb. xi. 26 Lchm. τῶν ἐν Αἰγύπτου θησαυρῶν, and probably hardly to be regarded as anything more than a clerical error of cod. A, (cod. Clarom. [Sin. also] omits ἐν, and the Vulg. translates Aegyptiorum.)

THE DATIVE.
B. § 133; H. § 594; C. § 448; D. § 455; J. § 586.

As in the general Grammar, we take as the basis of our treatment of the Dative the two leading distinctions in the same, viz. the Dative of the Person or of the Object affected (the Dative proper), and the Dative of the Thing (the Ablative).

A. DATIVE OF THE PERSON OR OF THE OBJECT AFFECTED.

In this use it coincides in general with the Dative of other 1 languages, and the grammarian, therefore, can conveniently pass over all those instances which need no explanation, such as δοῦναι, παραδοῦναι, λέγειν τινί, πείθεσθαι τῇ ἀληθείᾳ, ἀκολουθεῖν τινι etc., and likewise those in which we, to be sure, generally avail ourselves of prepositions, yet the identity of which with the examples just given is at once obvious; as, ἀπολογεῖσθαί τινι to defend oneself *before* any one Acts xix. 33 etc., προθυμίαν, ἣν ὑπὲρ ὑμῶν καυχῶμαι Μακεδόσιν *to* the Macedonians 2 Cor. ix. 2, ψεύσασθαι ἀνθρώποις, τῷ θεῷ Acts v. 4, προσαναλῶσαι τὸν βίον ἰατροῖς *on* physicians Luke viii. 43, λαλεῖν τινι *to talk to* [Germ. *zu*] one.

2
150   As everywhere, so especially in the N. T., for the Dative of the Person various periphrases with prepositions are substituted: the language bringing to view the manifold internal and ideal significations of the Case by the more concrete terms of relationship, viz. the prepositions, (in English by ' to,' ' for,' ' towards,' etc.). Inasmuch as here also the grammarian must proceed upon the views set forth § 130, 1 p. 141 and § 132, 2 p. 156, he must restrict himself to exhibiting this general usage in those examples which are peculiarly characteristic of the N. T.

3   The most common circumlocutions which are used instead of, or in the sense of, the Dative of the object affected, are formed by means of the prepositions εἰς (of which a few examples have been already given, § 131, 6 p. 149 and § 132, 24 p. 170 note), πρός with the Acc. (as in λέγειν τινί and πρός τινα), μετά with the Gen. (as in λαλεῖν τινί and μετά τινος John iv. 26, 27) σύν more rarely ἐν and ἐπι with the Dat. — as will appear from the contents of this entire section.

More peculiar are the periphrases by means of the prepositions ὀπίσω, ἔμπροσθεν, and the Hebraistic ἐνώπιον (לִפְנֵי). Thus we often find ὀπίσω instead of the Dative (or the more classic μετά Rev. vi. 8; xiv. 13) with ἀκολουθεῖν (see Wahl), with which compare Luke xix. 14 ἀπέστειλαν πρεσβείαν ὀπίσω αὐτοῦ, Acts xx. 30 ἀποσπᾶν τινα ὀπίσω αὐτῶν (*after them* i.e. to attract to themselves) and 22 below, p. 184; ἔμπροσθεν and ἐνώπιον (κατενώπιον): Matt. v. 16 (τὸ φῶς) λαμψάτω ἔμπροσθεν τῶν ἀνθρώπων, xi. 26 οὕτως ἐγένετο εὐδοκία ἔμπροσθέν σου, xviii. 14 οὐκ ἔστιν θέλημα ἔμπροσθεν τοῦ πατρός μου, x. 32, 33; xi. 10; xxiii. 14, etc., προσκυνεῖν (§ 131, 4 p. 147) ἐνώπιόν τινος Luke iv. 7; Rev. xv. 4 (and so the Sept. after the Hebrew: Ps. lxxxv. 9; Isa. lxvi. 23); further Luke viii. 47 ἀπήγγειλαν ἐνώπιον παντὸς τοῦ λαοῦ, xv. 10 γίνεται χαρὰ ἐνώπιον τῶν ἀγγέλων, xxiv. 11 ἐφάνησαν ἐνώπιον αὐτῶν (likewise φανερωθῆναι and the adj. ἀφανής, 2 Cor. vii. 12; Heb. iv. 13),

Acts vi. 5 ἤρεσεν ὁ λόγος ἐνώπιον τοῦ πλήθους — and in accordance
with this also the verbals ἀρεστός, εὐάρεστος, ἀπόδεκτος, ἐνώπιόν τινος
1 John iii. 22; Heb. xiii. 21 etc., ἄμωμος, ἀνέγκλητος κατενώπιόν τινος
Eph. i. 4; Col. i. 22 (cf. 14 below, p. 179, and § 134, 3 p. 188)
Corresponding to καυχᾶσθαι τινί above (1 p. 172) we have καυχᾶσθαι
ἐνώπιον τοῦ θεοῦ 1 Cor. i. 29, to θύρας μοι ἀνεῳγμένης (2 Cor. ii. 12),
θύραν ἐνώπιόν σου ἀνεῳγμ. Rev. iii. 8, to the common ὁμολογεῖν τινί
the construction with ἔμπροσθεν (7 p. 176) and with ἐνώπιον Rev. iii.
5, etc.

In all the above passages the Dative might be used just as well, but
the adverbial periphrasis is more lively, pictorial, and suited to the
Oriental way of looking at things; hence it is added as a sort of complement even to a preceding Dative, as Luke i. 75 λατρεύειν αὐτῷ . . .
ἐνώπιον αὐτοῦ.

REMARK. ἁμαρτάνειν also, which in the N. T. retains only the
secondary signification *to fail towards one (to sin)*, ought strictly to
have been joined to the Dative of the person, as indeed is frequently
the case in the Sept. (Judg. xi. 27; 2 Chron. xix. 10, etc.); yet
everywhere the periphrasis with εἰς appears instead (as frequently
also even in classic writers, see Pape), Matt. xviii. 21 etc. So in the
O. T. also, where too ἐναντίον, ἔναντι are connected with ἁμαρτάνειν.

The constructions, in part very diversified, of the following 151
verbs, πιστεύειν, πεποιθέναι, ἐλπίζειν, ὁμολογεῖν, 4
deserve a special and comprehensive exposition, since these
words as respects their signification also were used often in a
decidedly different sense after the introduction of the new
religion from that which they anciently bore.

Πιστεύειν. Passing over all those passages where it is used in
the ordinary sense (*give credit to, put faith in*) and construed as
usual, we notice its appearance

1) Absolutely, equivalent to πίστιν ἔχειν (Mark ix. 42 Tdf. [cod.
Sin.]) i.e. trustfully (μὴ διακριθέντα, cf. Matt. xxi. 21, 22; Jas. i. 6) to
cleave to the new dispensation of grace with faith in God the Redeemer:
Mark xvi. 16; Luke viii. 12, 50; John iv. 53, etc.; also in the Passive,
Rom. x. 10.

2) With the Dative, and that a) of the Person, which is
indeed the common construction, but in the majority of cases is applied
also to this new idea; as, Μωυσεῖ John v. 46, Ἰωάννῃ Matt. xxi. 26,
32; Mark xi. 31 etc., τῷ Ἰησοῦ Matt. xxvii. 42 Lchm.; John v. 46;
viii. 31 etc., τῷ πέμψαντί με John v. 24, τῷ κυρίῳ Acts v. 14; xviii. 8,
τῷ θεῷ xvi. 34; Rom. iv. 3 (quotn.); Tit. iii. 8 etc. The gradual
transition into the above special N. T. signification is to be explained

by the common ellipsis of a clause, as ὅτι εἰμὶ, εἶ, ἐστὶν Χριστός etc.
b) Instead of the Dative of the Person who is believed, frequently
by metonymy an a b s t r a c t in the Dative is substituted, as τῇ γραφῇ
καὶ τῷ λόγῳ John ii. 22, γράμμασιν, ῥήμασιν v. 47, τοῖς γεγραμμένοις
Acts xxiv. 14, τοῖς ἔργοις (μου) John x. 38, ἀκοῇ xii. 38 (quotn.),
ἀληθείᾳ 2 Thess. ii. 12, ὀνόματι Ἰησοῦ 1 John iii. 23.

3) Exclusively pertaining to the n e w s i g n i f i c a t i o n of the
word is its construction — very frequent, particularly in John —
with εἴς τινα to believe on (in) any one, and here again a) with
the Acc. of the P e r s o n : Matt. xviii. 6; Mark ix. 42 Lchm.;
John ii. 11; iii. 16, 18 etc.; Acts x. 43 etc.; Rom. x. 14; Gal. ii. 16;
Phil. i. 29; 1 Pet. i. 8 — everywhere in reference to God or the
person of Christ; and alternating with the Dative 1 John v. 10;
b) by metonymy with the Acc. of an a b s t r a c t — again in John,
especially εἰς τὸ ὄνομα Ἰησοῦ i. 12; ii. 23; iii. 18; 1 John v. 13, also
εἰς τὸ φῶς John xii. 36, εἰς τὴν μαρτυρίαν 1 John v. 10.   That in this construction the ellipsis of a clause is, logically considered, no longer
demanded, is obvious; hence the word in its new sense, when connected
with nouns, g r a d u a l l y s e t t l e d u p o n t h i s c o n s t r u c t i o n.

4) Far more rare is the construction ἐπί τινα, instead of that
with εἰς, and in the same sense.   Thus ἐπὶ τὸν κύριον Acts ix. 42; xi.
17; xvi. 31, cf. xxii. 19; Rom. iv. 5, 24.   This use is uncertain in
the gospels: Matt. xxvii. 42 (cod. B [ℵ Tdf. Treg.]), John iii. 15 Lchm.

5) The construction with ἐπί and the D a t i v e o f t h e P e r s o n
seems to belong more to the O. T.; hence in the quotation from
Isaiah (xxviii. 16 Alex.) in Rom. ix. 33; x. 11; 1 Pet. ii. 6, cf. 1 Tim.
i. 16.   Matt. xxvii. 42 Tdf. [ed. 7] is doubtful.   The construction
with ἐπί and the D a t i v e o f t h e T h i n g (Luke xxiv. 25; Rom. iv.
18) rests upon the Greek use of the preposition ἐπί with the Dat.,
see § 147, 24 p. 336.

6) The rarest construction is with the p r e p o s i t i o n ἐν, — unquestionably supported only in Mark i. 15, and there with the Dat. of the
thing: ἐν τῷ εὐαγγελίῳ.   Respecting its force (whether to believe in
. . . , trust in . . . , believe through, by virtue of, the gospel) interpreters differ; and it is the more difficult to arrive at anything certain
on this point, as in the other passage (John iii. 15) the MSS. and
editors also disagree (Lchm. ἐπ' αὐτόν [ℵ εἰς], Tdf. [Treg.] ἐν αὐτῷ).
The Seventy, in accordance with the Hebr. original (cf. Gesen. under
יאמן Hiphil, and Fritzsche on Mark p. 26), employ the construction ἐν
τινι frequently in the sense 'to trust in,' e.g. Jer. xii. 6; Ps. lxxvii. 22;
1 Sam. xxvii. 12 Alex.

The (Pauline) formula πιστὸς ἐν κυρίῳ, ἐν Χριστῷ Ἰησοῦ (Eph. i. 1;
Col. i. 2, etc.) did not originate in the verbal construction, cf. 5 and
6 p. 175.

7) The construction with the object-A c c u s a t i v e (of the thing) in the sense ' to believe *something*,' as ἔργον Acts xiii. 41 ([so cod. Sin.]; Grsb. ᾧ), πάντα 1 Cor. xiii. 7, ἀγάπην 1 John iv. 16 (hence in the Passive: τὸ μαρτύριον ἡμῶν 2 Thess. i. 10, cf. 1 Tim. iii. 16). Further, the Acc. of the object with πιστεύειν in the sense of *to entrust, confide*, as αὐτὸν or ἑαυτόν τινι John ii. 24, and the allied construction of the Acc. with the Passive (πιστεύομαί τι, see § 134, 7 p. 189) find their basis in the ordinary Greek usage.

Π ε π ο ι θ έ ν α ι *to trust* admits in the main of the same constructions, being joined 1) with the D a t i v e, as in Greek writers, e.g. ἑαυτῷ, δεσμοῖς, ὑπακοῇ, 2 Cor. x. 7; Phil. i. 14; Philem. 21; 2) w i t h ε ἰ ς, but only once, εἰς ὑμᾶς Gal. v. 10; 3) with ἐ π ί and the A c c. of the P e r s o n, Matt. xxvii. 43 Tdf. [Treg. cod. Sin.]; 2 Cor. ii. 3; 2 Thess. iii. 4; 4) with ἐ π ί and the D a t i v e, — and that both of the person, Luke xviii. 9; 2 Cor. i. 9; Heb. ii. 13 (quotn.), doubtfully in Matt. xxvii. 43 (B), and also of the thing, Luke xi. 22 (πανοπλίᾳ), Mark x. 24 (χρήμασιν).

In the phrase πεπ. ἔ ν τ ι ν ι the expression with ἐν, if a personal Dative follows, is more an abverbial adjunct designating the g r o u n d of the trust; hence it is commonly connected with one of the above constructions or with a clause introduced by ὅτι, as Gal. v. 10; 2 Thess. iii. 4; Phil. ii. 24 (ἐν κυρίῳ), cf. 6 below and 23 p. 185. But it is otherwise with the Dative of the thing, as πεποιθέναι ἐν σαρκί Phil. iii. 3, 4 (a periphrasis for the Dative above: *to trust in the flesh;* cf. 21 and 22 p. 183).

Ἐ λ π ί ζ ε ι ν *to hope*, in the earlier Greek prose uniformly prefers,   6 with the exception of the object-Accusative (ἀγαθά Xen. βούλησιν Thuc., also τὶ παρά τινος Dem.), the verbal construction (with the Infin. etc.). The connection with the Dative in Thuc. 3. 97 τῇ τύχῃ ἐλπίσας (but in the following clause with ὅτι, where τύχη is the subject) gives ἐλπίσας the sense of πεποιθώς, *trusting fortune*, parallel to the preceding τούτοις πεισθείς — a sense in which ἐλπίδα ἔχειν also is often construed by the Greeks with ἐν and ἐπί with the Dat. On the other hand, as early as in the Sept., where the Hebr. words יָחַל‎, חָסָה‎, and בָּטַח‎ are generally all translated by ἐλπίζειν, the construction with nouns has become by far the predominant one, in fact almost the only one in use, and from thence passed also into N. T. usage. The construction most current in the Sept. (in consequence of the above Hebrew verbs being joined with אֶל‎ and עַל‎) is w i t h ἐ π ί — both with persons and abstract terms — and likewise also in the N. T.; that is to say, 1) with ἐ π ί and the A c c u s a t i v e, frequent in the O. T., in the N. T. indubitably only in 1 Tim. v. 5; 1 Pet. i. 13 (iii. 5); but 2) most commonly with ἐ π ί and the D a t i v e, Rom. xv. 12

153 (quotn.), 1 Tim. iv. 10 ; vi. 17, cf. 1 John iii. 3 ;   3) with εἰς (rare
in the Sept. e.g. Isa. li. 5), as εἰς ὅν John v. 45 ; 2 Cor. i. 10, εἰς θεόν
1 Pet. iii. 5, cf. i. 21 also Acts xxiv. 15 ἐλπίδα ἔχων εἰς θεόν (but with
Acc. and Infin. following) ;   4) with ἐν (likewise rare in the Sept.,
Ps. xxxii. 21 ; 2 Kings xviii. 5, since there the Hebr. בְּ also is commonly rendered by ἐπί, e.g. with חָסָה in Ps. v. 12 ; vii. 2 ; xxv. 20,
etc.), 1 Cor. xv. 19. Respecting Phil. ii. 19 (ἐλπ. ἐν κυρίῳ followed
by the Acc. and Infin.) cf. the similar use in 5 p. 175 and 23 p. 185.

Only in one passage (Matt. xii. 21) does it appear with the simple
Dative, and that, strange to say, a quotation from the O. T. (Isa.
xlii. 4), where the Sept., which Matt. seems to follow here, gives the
common construction ἐπὶ τῷ ὀνόματι. Fritzsche and others have
therefore taken offence at this Dative ; on account, however, of the
almost unanimous authority [Sin. also] in its favor, it is retained by
the editors, and must be explained by the analogy of the construction
πεποιθέναι τινί. Of the remaining constructions those with ἐν and ἐπι
with the Dative adhere most closely to classic usage, those with εἰς
and ἐπί with the Accusative belong exclusively to the later (biblical)
Greek.

7   Ὁμολογεῖν is connected   1) in the signification to confess, as
commonly, with the Dative of the person and Accusative of the thing,
as Matt. vii. 23 ; Acts xxiv. 14, etc.   2) in the signification to praise
(equiv. to ψάλλειν) ὁμολογεῖν, commonly ἐξομολογεῖσθαι, is likewise
connected with the Dative of the person or of the personified object
(ὀνόματι) ; but the use is borrowed from the Sept.[1] where the Hiphil
הוֹדָה is regularly translated thus ; hence in the quotations from the
O. T. in Rom. xiv. 11 ; xv. 9, cf. Heb. xiii. 15 ; Matt. xi. 25 ; Luke
x. 21 ;   3) in connection with the Accusative of the person
Jesus (Rom. x. 9 ; 1 John ii. 23) it acquires the specific N. T. signification to confess Jesus (as Redeemer, etc.), and the expression is
then to be taken, in analogy with πιστεύειν τινί above, as an abbreviated
clause (with a participle), such as appears in full in 1 John iv. 2
ὁμολογεῖν Ἰησοῦν Χριστὸν ἐν σαρκί ἐληλυθότα, 2 John 7. The change
into the Passive occurs Rom. x. 10.   4) The construction with
ἕν τινι in the same sense is peculiar to Matthew and Luke ; as,
Matt. x. 32 ἐν ἐμοί (Vulg. me), ἐν αὐτῷ (Vulg. eum D αὐτόν), Luke
xii. 8. But this is not a Hebraism, see Fritzsche ad Matt. p. 386.
5) The person before whom as witness, or in whose presence, the
confession is given, is expressed by means of the preposition ἔμπροσθεν in the last two passages quoted, by ἐνώπιον in Rev. iii. 5.
Cf. above, 3 p. 173.

      [1] Hence the Apocalypse connects even αἰνεῖν with the Dative (xix. 5)
according to a less common usage of the Sept. (Jer. xx. 13 ; 1 Chron. xvi. 36
2 Chron. xx. 19, etc.).

B. § 133, 2 a and b; H. § 602; C. § 450; D. p. 489; J. §§ 592. 601.

With all verbs (both simple and compound) whose signification can be traced back to the idea of union or approach in a friendly or a hostile sense, manifold periphrases by means of prepositions make their appearance, as elsewhere, instead of the Dative. **8**

Thus for example we have μάχεσθαι, διακρίνεσθαι, διαλέγεσθαι, ὁμιλεῖν **154** τινί and πρός τινα, μιγνύειν μετά τινος and ἔν τινι, πολεμεῖν μετά τινος, κρίνεσθαι (to contend) τινί and μετά τινος Matt. v. 40; 1 Cor. vi. 6; with other verbs there is no circumlocution, as ἐπιτίθεσθαι, προσέχειν, καταλλάττειν, διαλλάττεσθαί τινι, etc. Notice, in particular, with the Dative: διακατελέγχεσθαί τινι by controversy to convince Acts xviii. 28; ἑτεροζυγοῦντες ἀπίστοις in a peculiar sense, see the lexicons; γαμηθῆναι (of the woman, p. 55) τινί after the Latin nubere, 1 Cor. vii. 39; Mark x. 12 Tdf. [ed. 7]. Respecting προσέχειν ἀπό see § 147, 3 p. 323.

B. § 133, 2 c. d.; H. § 605; C. § 452; D. p. 489 Obs.; J. § 589.

Among verbs (mostly compounded with a preposition) of exhorting and requesting the following deviate from the usual construction: παραινεῖν with the Acc., Acts xxvii. 22; εὔχεσθαί τινι and πρός τινα (2 Cor. xiii. 7); καταρᾶσθαι with the Acc. Mark xi. 21; [Luke vi. 28 Lchm. Treg. Tdf. cod. Sin.]; Jas. iii. 9, with the Dative Luke vi. 28 Tdf. [eds. 2, 7]. Among those of censuring and reproaching ὀνειδίζειν has uniformly the Acc., both of the person and of the thing, Matt. v. 11 etc.; hence in the Passive, 1 Pet. iv. 14; ἐγκαλεῖν τινί and κατά τινος (Rom. viii. 33), — the thing always with περί and the Gen. Acts xxiii. 29; xxvi. 2 (according to § 147, 30 p. 341), xxvi. 7; in xix. 40 also στάσεως, as the following article τῆς shows, still depends on περί (cf. 18 below, p. 181); μέμφεσθαι with the Acc., Heb. viii. 8 (where, however, according to Bleek the reading αὐτοῖς and the connection of the same with λέγει are to be preferred). Other verbs, as ἐμβριμᾶσθαι, ἐπιτιμᾶν, are uniformly construed only with the Dative. **9**

B. § 133, 2 f. and N. 4; H. § 603; C. § 451; D. p. 490; J. § 594.

An example of the Dative with ὁ αὐτός is found in 1 Cor. xi. 5. Of the brachylogy already mentioned (§ 132, 20 p. 167 sq.) and peculiar to the ancient languages — (comparison with the whole instead of the part) — see several examples in the Apocalypse: ix. 10 ἔχουσιν οὐρὰς ὁμοίας σκορπίοις, xiii. 11 κέρατα δύο ὅμοια ἀρνίῳ. Similar is Jude 7 and the construction with ἰσότιμος 2 Pet. i. 1. In a solitary instance, in a quotation, ὡς with the Nominative is loosely used with ὁμοιοῦν instead of the Dative, Rom. ix. 29 (after the Sept., not the Heb.). **10**

23

THE DATIVUS COMMODI AND RELATED DATIVES.

B. § 133, 2 g.; H. § 597; C. § 453; D. § 458; J. § 595 sqq.

11　To the Dative known under the designation Dativus commodi et incommodi, many and in part very peculiar constructions and phrases with the Dative may be referred.

Thus μαρτυρεῖν τινι means *to give testimony in one's favor*, as Luke iv. 22, etc.; by metonymy it is construed also with the Dative of the thing, as τῇ ἀληθείᾳ John v. 33 cf. Luke xi. 48 etc., for which also the circumlocution with περί and the Gen. is often used. On the other hand we find καταμαρτυρεῖν τινός according to § 132, 16 p. 165. Notice further Matt. xiii. 14 ἀναπληροῦται αὐτοῖς ἡ προφητεία τοῦ Ἡσαΐου,[1] 1 Cor. vii. 28 θλῖψιν τῇ σαρκὶ ἕξουσιν, 2 Cor. ii. 13 οὐκ 155 ἔσχηκα ἄνεσιν τῷ πνεύματί μου (not equiv. to ἐν τῇ σαρκί, ἐν τῷ πνεύματι), 2 Cor. ii. 1 ἔκρινα ἐμαυτῷ, etc.

12　In this way is to be explained the use of the Dative in various connections which is especially characteristic of the Apostle Paul, and rests on profound views of language.

Thus, after the analogy of the common phrase ζῆν τῷ θεῷ, κυρίῳ (Rom. vi. 10, 11; xiv. 8; ἑαυτῷ xiv. 7; 2 Cor. v. 15), the expression ἀποθανεῖν τινί in the same passages is formed; and this verb is used by metonymy with the Dat. of the abstract, τῇ ἁμαρτίᾳ Rom. vi. 2, 10, 11, τῷ νόμῳ Gal. ii. 19 cf. Rom. vii. 4. In the same way in the 1st of Peter (ii. 24) in contrast with τῇ δικαιοσύνῃ ζῇ the word ἀπογενέσθαι alsc, which according to its composition ought to have the Genitive, is construed with the Dative ταῖς ἁμαρτίαις. Paul connects the same view with other predicates in order to express the ideal reference of an ordinary and every-day act to God or any individual, or even to a (substituted) abstract term; see the entire argument in Rom. xiv. 4–8, where, besides the verbs above-named, also φρονεῖν, ἐσθίειν, οὐκ ἐσθίειν, στήκειν,[2] πίπτειν stand in the same construction. In Gal. v. 1 τῇ ἐλευθερίᾳ (ᾗ) ἡμᾶς Χριστὸς ἠλευθέ-

---

[1] By comparison with this passage the Dative in Luke xviii. 31 is explained most satisfactorily, τελεσθήσεται πάντα τὰ γεγραμμένα διὰ τῶν προφητῶν τῷ υἱῷ τοῦ ἀνθρώπου; here the Dative depends on both predicates by virtue of the σχῆμα ἀπὸ κοινοῦ (as in § 132, 9 p. 160 the Accusative with ἐπιλαβέσθαι), although externally it belongs rather to the former (τελεσθήσεται). The simple resolution of the Dative into περὶ τοῦ υἱοῦ is thoroughly unphilological, and the Vulgate's translation (*de filio*) according to the above exposition is only to be defended in a general way. The Dative if referred to γεγραμμένα alone, must at least have been preceded by ἐπί, as in John xii. 16. [Yet cf. 3 Macc. vi. 41.]

[2] In 2 Cor. i. 24 (τῇ γὰρ πίστει ἑστήκατε) the assumption of this Dat. would impart to the passage too high an oratorical coloring. It is more probable that τῇ πίστει here is to be taken in the sense of the phrase στήκειν ἐν τῇ πίστει which elsewhere occurs (1 Cor. xvi. 13), see Meyer and 19 below, p. 182.

ρωσεν etc., τῇ ἐλευθερίᾳ is according to both readings equally to be taken as a Dat. com. (see especially Meyer pp. 256, 259). The Dative in Rom. vi. 20 ἐλεύθεροι ἦτε τῇ δικαιοσύνῃ is peculiar and hard to reproduce ; it is called out by the parallelism of δουλωθέντες τῷ θεῷ in vs. 22 (and to be rendered perhaps *towards, in relation to*, but not *from*).

B. § 133, N. 5; H. § 599; C. § 462 e.; D. § 459; J. § 600, 2.

The softer Dat. com., commonly designated by the gram- 13 marians the Dativus ethicus, is not a mere peculiarity of the earlier language, but a genuine product of the language of the people, whence it has found its way so frequently into the poems of Homer, the writings of Herodotus, Plato, etc. Accordingly the assumption of such a Dative in the N. T. is quite in accordance with the genius of its language. Cf. the note on § 129 a, 5 p. 140.

Here belong : Rev. ii. 16 ἔρχομαί σοι ταχὺ καὶ πολεμήσω μετ' αὐτῶν, 5 ἔρχομαί σοι καὶ κινήσω τὴν λυχνίαν ;[1] probably also 1 John v. 16 if, 156 according to § 129, 14 note p. 133, we assume ὁ θεός as subject for δώσει and refer αὐτῷ as Dat. eth. to the person αἰτήσας ; and, according to many interpreters, also the critically and hermeneutically difficult passage Heb. iv. 2 (according to the more ancient reading [so א] — received also by Tdf. [eds. 2, 7, 8] — μὴ συγκεκραμένος τῇ πίστει τοῖς ἀκού-σασιν i.e. *the word which in the hearers was not mixed with faith*, see Mey. [i.e. Lünemann] in loc. On the other hand, for Lchm.'s reading [so Treg.] see Bleek II. p. 501 sqq.). Simpler and easily intelligible is the Dat. in John vi. 13 ἃ ἐπερίσσευσαν τοῖς βεβρωκόσιν. Finally, the Dative in ἀποτάξασθαί τινι *to dismiss any one*, bid him farewell, literally *to withdraw one's self for one;* this phrase is quite un-Attic, in fact solecistic (ἔκφυλον πάνυ Phryn.), and first made its appearance in the Alexandrian age (Josephus, Philo), but later became pretty general : Mark vi. 46 ; Luke ix. 61, etc.

B. § 133, N. 7; H. § 601; C. § 462; D. § 459; J. § 600, 1.

Also of the Dative of subjective judgment — closely re- 11 lated to the preceding — there are several unquestionable examples : in particular, Acts vii. 20 ἦν ἀστεῖος τῷ θεῷ (*in the sight of God*), 2 Cor. x. 4 ὅπλα δυνατὰ τῷ θεῷ (Luth. *mächtig vor Gott,* [A.V. m rg. *to God*]) ; 2 Pet. iii. 14 is doubtful (see § 134, 2 p. 187). From the

---

[1] DeWette differently, — taking σοι in the sense of *to thee.* But the appeal to ἥκειν τινί Plut. Aem. Paul. 16 is not in point, since there the Dative depends on the expression ἧκε μηνύων. In Philostr. Vit. Apoll. 2. 14 ἥκειν τινί has quite another sense, and in Matt. xxi. 5 (Zech. ix. 9) σοι is a literal translation of the Hebr. לָךְ. [This note, as respects de Wette, seems to be founded in a mistake.]

O. T. cf. Jonah iii. 3 πόλις μεγάλη τῷ θεῷ. But it corresponds more with N. T. usage (cf. 3 above p. 172) to periphrase this Dative by means of a preposition, and none was better suited to this purpose than ἐνώπιον (Hebr. לִפְנֵי, Eng. *before* i.e. in the sight of) e.g. δίκαιος, βδέλυγμα ἐνώπιον τοῦ θεοῦ, μέγας ἐνώπιον κυρίου (Luke i. 6 Lchm. 15 ; xvi. 15 ; Acts iv. 19, etc.), πολυτελὲς ἐνώπιον θεοῦ 1 Pet. iii. 4 (cf. the analogous use of ἐνώπιον with the so-called Dativus Passivi § 134, 3 p. 188), as well as ἔναντι, ἐναντίον, which is often interchanged with ἐνώπιον in the various readings, Acts viii. 21 ; Luke i. 6 Tdf. [Treg.], xxiv. 19, and the compound κατενώπιον see 3 p. 173.

B. § 133, 2 h.; H. § 595 d.; C. §§ 454 e. 464 c.; J. § 588.

15   Some relics of the construction (formerly pretty extended, and called by the old grammarians σχῆμα Κολοφώνιον) of the D a t i v e in immediate d e p e n d e n c e upon s u b s t a n t i v e s, particularly those whose stem-verb permits the same construction (as βροτοῖς δοτήρ Aesch.) have been preserved in 2 Cor. ix. 11, 12 (where in both cases τῷ θεῷ is best made to depend on εὐχαριστία), and in 2 Cor. xi. 28 Lchm. [Treg. Tdf.] according to the reading ἐπίστασίς μοι. Respecting the signi-fication of this expression interpreters differ. If the Dative is genuine (which, according to the authorities [א* also] and the rendering of cod. Claromont. *in me*, is hardly to be doubted) ἐπίστασις cannot sig-nify *attention*, because then the Dative would not stand in the relation of v e r b a l regimen to the substantive. The most probable assump-tion is that as ἀπόστασις (from ἀφίστασθαί τινος) signifies defection, so ἐπίστασις (from ἐφίστασθαί τινι) signifies accession, uprising (Acts xxiv. 12), and ἐπίστασίς μοι denotes *concourse, thronging, to me* (ἐπίστασις occurs in the sense of *thronging* also in App. B.C. 4, 129), more precisely *my being encompassed, beleaguered*, and the detention caused thereby, with which the Dative is as necessary as the Gen. is with ἀπόστασις, ἀφίστασθαι. Cf. Rückert in loc.   The Dative with
157 participles and adjectives used substantively is still more plainly an effect of the verbal power of both these parts of speech, and needs no further confirmation by means of examples.

B. § 133, 3 and N. 10; H. § 605; C. § 699 f. g.; J. § 622, Obs. 1; § 623, Obs. 4; § 635, Obs.

16   That c o m p o u n d v e r b s, particularly those compounded with σύν, ἐν, ἐπί, are joined to the Dative, see § 147, 33 p. 344. In John ix 6 ἐπέχρισεν αὐτοῦ τὸν πηλὸν ἐπὶ τοὺς ὀφθαλμούς the Genitive indeed seems to depend on ἐπέχρισεν (according to B even on ἐπέθηκεν), somewhat after the analogy, therefore, of verbs of *touching*. This however is not the case ; on the contrary, the Gen. αὐτοῦ (cf. vs. 15) is to be connected by Hyperbaton with ὀφθαλμούς, and the addition

τοῦ τυφλοῦ to be expunged, with Lchm. Tdf.[1] [Treg.].　See more ex-amples of the sort from the classics in B. § 133, N. 10 and from the N. T. in the section on Hyperbaton § 151, 13 sqq. pp. 387 sqq.

B. Dative of the Thing (instrument, etc.).

B. § 133, 4; H. § 606 sq.; C. § 465 sq.; D. § 457; J. § 607 sq.

That the Dative of the Thing comprises most of the relations **17** of the Latin Ablative does not need to be shown at length. But the language of the N.T. departs a little from the ordinary usage in that the preposition ἐν is prefixed to this Dative with uncommon frequency.[2]　Although a similar use is here and there to be found even in Greek writers also (see the grammars under ἐν), yet this N. T. peculiarity is hardly an extension of those isolated instances in the classics, but mani-festly a result of the frequent occurrence of the preposition in the Sept. (after the example of the Hebr. בְּ), as is apparent from countless examples from the Old T. and New, see 19 p. 182. And in general, through the influence of the Oriental manner of expression, both the compass and contents of the signification of this preposition became essentially modified, see § 147, 9 sq. p. 328 sq.

B. § 133, 4 a.; H. § 607 a.; C. § 466 b.; D. p. 491; J. § 591, Obs. 2.

With χρῆσθαι, elsewhere in the N. T. always construed with the **18** Dative, the Accusative is given to us by the oldest MSS. [Sin. also] in one passage, 1 Cor. vii. 31 οἱ χρώμενοι τὸν κόσμον ὡς μὴ καταχρώ-μενοι.　The instance is so isolated that recent editors were the first to venture to put it in the text.　The construction is indeed an erroneous one (the appeal to Xen. Ages. 11, 11 is inadmissible as the Acc. there was set aside long ago, and still less ought we to argue back from the usage of later Byzantines), but finds its apology in the use of the compound καταχρῆσθαι with the Acc. by later writers, as Lucian, and **158** Plutarch (see Steph. Thes. sub voce), so that the Acc. in the above passage is governed to a certain extent ἀπὸ κοινοῦ (§ 132, 9 p. 160; 133, 11 note[1] p. 178) by the καταχρώμενοι also immediately following; see another example of such retro-action in 9 above, p. 177 (Acts xix.

---

[1] The phrase τοῦ τυφλοῦ, taken up again by Tdf. in his [7th] edition of 1859, has been expunged once more in his [8th] edition of 1869 (after cod. Sin.).

[2] Many, particularly of the earlier commentators, believed therefore that ἐν was a sort of sign of the Dative in the N. T., and was added even to a personal Dative without altering the sense.　The error of such a view Winer 217 (204) has sufficiently shown by examples.

40). Certainly native Greek writers would hardly have allowed themselves to employ constructions of the sort.

19 Examples of the addition of ἐν to the instrumental Dative, where the Greeks decidedly would have used the simple Dative only, are the following: ἐν τίνι ἁλισθήσεται (Matt. v. 13), ἐν ᾧ μέτρῳ μετρεῖτε (Matt. vii. 2), ἀγαπᾶν ἐν ὅλῃ τῇ καρδίᾳ etc. (in Matt. xxii. 37 closely after the Hebr., cf. the parallel passage Mark xii. 30), καταπατεῖν ἐν τοῖς ποσίν (Matt. vii. 6), ἀποκτείνειν ἐν μαχαίρῃ (Rev. xiii. 10), ἀπολέσθαι ἐν μαχαίρῃ (Matt. xxvi. 52), διαφέρειν ἐν δόξῃ (1 Cor. xv. 41), etc. Further, examples where ἐν is alternately used and omitted, often close together, are ὑγιαίνειν ἐν τῇ πίστει (Tit. i. 13) and τῇ πίστει (ii. 2) cf. 12 above, note[2] p. 178, ἐν τῷ στόματι and στόματι ὁμολογεῖν, ἐν τῇ καρδίᾳ and τῇ καρδίᾳ πιστεύειν (Rom. x. 9 etc. where, however, the change from the Act. to the Pass. construction has, perhaps, not been without influence), βαπτίζειν ὕδατι (Luke iii. 16 etc.) and ἐν ὕδατι (not *in* water, Matt. iii. 11 etc.), β. ἐν πνεύματι, β. ἐν πυρί (e.g. Acts i. 5 Ἰωάννης ἐβάπτισεν ὕδατι, ὑμεῖς δὲ ἐν πνεύματι βαπτισθήσεσθε), etc. That ἐν can stand even with Persons so far forth as they serve as the means of an action, see § 147, 10 p. 329.[1]

20 REMARK. Otherwise, when Persons are the means, διά with the Gen. is employed as usual. As a special peculiarity, however, is to be noticed the Hebraistic periphrasis for it (which really is not rare) by means of the Substantive χείρ, and that both in the form διὰ χειρός (בְּיַד), even with a Gen. Plur. following, and also διὰ χειρῶν: e.g. Mark vi. 2 δυνάμεις αἱ διὰ χειρῶν αὐτοῦ γινόμεναι, Acts ii. 23 διὰ χειρὸς ἀνόμων, xi. 30 διὰ χειρὸς Βαρνάβα καὶ Σαύλου, xiv. 3; xix. 11 etc.; rarely ἐν χειρί, Gal. iii. 19 — (this is frequent in the Sept., as Gen. xxxviii. 20 etc.).

Many other periphrases expressive of simple relations are formed with the word χείρ after Hebrew precedent; for example, of the Dative with παραδιδόναι by means of εἰς χεῖρας (בְּיַד), Matt. xxvi. 45; Mark ix. 31 etc.; ἐκ χειρός (מִיַּד) is used with verbs of *separation, liberation*, instead of the Gen. or the simple ἐκ. John x. 39 ἐξῆλθεν ἐκ τῆς χειρὸς αὐτῶν, Acts xii. 11; Rev. xix. 2 ἐξεδίκησεν τὸ αἷμα ἐκ χειρὸς αὐτῆς (like 2 Kings ix. 7; 1 Sam. xxiv. 16 etc.) for which in Rev. vi. 10 we have merely ἐκδικεῖς ἐκ τῶν κατοικοῦντων (cf. xviii. 20; Luke xi. 50, 51), and σὺν χειρί, as Acts vii. 35 ἀγγέλου

---

[1] By this addition of ἐν to the instrumental Dat. it is possible for the language of the N. T. to make instrumental limitations depend, without a participle, immediately upon substantives. Several instances of the sort have already been treated of § 125, 2 p. 92 and 11 p. 96, — instances some of which indeed have their foundation in the analogy of ordinary Greek usage, but some are destitute of such analogy, and belong tc the peculiar language of the N. T.

by the hand, under the protection, of an angel. All these phrases, like
the trope χεὶρ κυρίου (Acts xi. 21), plainly bear an Oriental stamp, and
are not to be identified with isolated, analogous (poetic), modes of
expression in Greek authors. Cf. in general Gesen. under יָד. 159·

With the idea of *speaking*, instead of χεὶρ the term στόμα is substituted, hence διὰ στόματος Acts i. 16; iv. 25, etc.; also with a
Plural following, iii. 18, 21 (and likewise in the Sept., 2 Chron. xxxvi.
21, etc.). See more respecting these and similar periphrases under
prepositions § 146, 1 p. 319.

B. § 133, 4 b.; H. § 608 sq.; C. § 467; D. p. 487 sq.; J. § 603.

The Dative of the mode or manner (ablativus modi), as 21·
well as the Dative of complement and closer limitation
(in which case it often takes the place of the similarly used
Accusative in Greek writers, see § 131, 9 p. 152), is only a
phase of the foregoing Dative; as, ταπεινὸς τῇ καρδίᾳ, βραδὺς
τῇ καρδίᾳ, ἀδύνατος τοῖς ποσίν, περιτέμνεσθαι τῷ ἔθει *after the
custom* (Acts xv. 1), προφητεύειν τῷ σῷ ὀνόματι *by virtue of
(by) thy name* (Matt. vii. 22). In its stead we frequently find
of course, as in Greek authors, periphrases by means of such
prepositions as κατά, διά, ἐν; and in particular, with ἐν
many adverbial expressions of mode and manner are formed —
likewise after Greek precedent; as, ἐν ἀληθείᾳ, ἐν παραβολῇ,
ἐν πραΰτητι, ἐν μέρει, ἐν τάχει, etc. On all these, as well as
respecting the common construction ποιεῖν τι ἐν ὀνόματί τινος,
see § 147, 10 p. 329; and respecting ἔρχεσθαι, πορεύεσθαι ἐν in
particular, the following paragraph under b).

As an extension of this Dative, mention may here be made 22·
of two genuine biblical uses of this case, which, since they are
manifestly indebted to Oriental phraseology for their origin,
must have appeared more or less alien to the Greek idiom:

a) The Hebrew usage of subjoining to a finite verb the form of the
Infin. absolute (מוֹת יָמוּת, etc.) to strengthen the verbal idea in divers
aspects (see Gesen. Lehrg. p. 778 sq. [Gr. § 128, 3]) is commonly
translated in the Sept. by the Dative of the abstract derived
from the verb (or even by the Participle of the same verb, on
which see § 144, 30 p. 313); as, διαμαρτυρίᾳ μεμαρτύρηται Gen. xliii. 2,
ἐπιθυμίᾳ ἐπιθυμήσεις xxxi. 30, θανάτῳ ἀποθανεῖσθε ii. 17, φθορᾷ φθα-
ρήσεται Isa. xxiv. 3, κλαυθμῷ ἔκλαυσεν xxx. 19, ἰάσεται ἰάσει xix. 22,
ἀκοῇ ἀκούσετε vi. 9, χάρητε χαρᾷ lxvi. 10, ἀφῇ ἀφθήσεται Jer. xxxi.
(xlviii.) 9, φυγῇ ἔφυγον xxvi. (xlvi.) 5, κακίᾳ κακοποιήσετε 1 Sam. xii. 25,

and many others.   Analogous expressions, in part new formations,
are found in the N. T.: ἀκοῇ ἀκούειν Matt. xiii. 14 (quotn.), ἐπιθυμεῖν
ἐπιθυμίᾳ Luke xxii. 15, χαρᾷ χαίρειν John iii. 29 (but with a limiting
adjective added in Greek fashion ἐχάρησαν χαρὰν μεγάλην Matt. ii. 10),
ἀπειλῇ ἀπειλεῖν Acts iv. 17 Tdf. [eds. 2, 7], παραγγελίᾳ παρηγγείλαμεν
v. 28, ἀναθέματι ἀνεθεματίσαμεν xxiii. 14 (Deut. xiii. 15; xx. 17),
προσευχῇ προσηύξατο Jas. v. 17.   Similarly θανάτῳ τελευτάτω Mark vii.
10 (quotn.), ἀποκτεῖναι ἐν θανάτῳ Rev. ii. 23; vi. 8.   That this usage,
notwithstanding the various similar phrases from earlier and later
writers which Lobeck, Parall. p. 523 sqq., adduces (γάμῳ γεγαμηκώς
160 Dem., φύσει πέφυκεν Hippocr., παιδιᾷ παίζειν Plut., also φυγῇ ἔφυγον
Plat., in Latin *occidione occidere*), is not an outgrowth of Greek
phraseology, but solely derived from the Hebrew (or Alexandrian)
idiom, this same scholar shows clearly and convincingly by a comparison of examples on both sides.

b) Not less peculiar is the Dative which is subjoined to verbs
of going (πορεύεσθαι, στοιχεῖν, περιπατεῖν), when taken tropically
(cf. our *walk*), to designate the way i.e. the manner of walk.   So
in particular with ὁδῷ, ὁδοῖς (after the Hebr., see Gesen. under דֶּרֶךְ),
which is used indeed in the O. T. in the proper sense (1 Sam. xv. 20),
but often enough also in the figurative (Ps. lxxx. 14; Tob. iv. 5), in
the N. T. Acts xiv. 16 εἴασεν πορεύεσθαι τοῖς ὁδοῖς αὐτῶν, Jude 11 τῇ
ὁδῷ τοῦ Κάϊν ἐπορεύθησαν; ὁδῷ πορεύεσθαι is often found also in
Hermas.   Analogous is στοιχεῖν ἴχνεσιν in Rom. iv. 12.   After the
same model many other constructions are formed, instead of ὁδός
some other abstract term being added in the Dative, e.g. περιπατεῖν
τοῖς ἔθεσιν to *walk in, after, the customs* Acts xxi. 21, πνεύματι Gal. v.
16, πορεύεσθαι τῷ φόβῳ τοῦ κυρίου Acts ix. 31, εἰ ζῶμεν πνεύματι, πνεύματι καὶ στοιχῶμεν Gal. v. 25, κανόνι vi. 16, also merely τῷ αὐτῷ sc.
κανόνι (see the various readings) Phil. iii. 16.

That in this case also, instead of the simple Dative periphrases
with prepositions appear, follows as a matter of course after all
that has been said above;— particularly with ἐν and κατά, as ἐν ἀγάπῃ,
ἐν ἀληθείᾳ, κατὰ ἀγάπην, σάρκα, ἄνθρωπον πορεύεσθαι etc., see the Lex.
Ὀπίσω also (see 3 above, p. 172) belongs here in the two parallel
passages 2 Pet. ii. 10; Jude 7 ὀπίσω σαρκὸς πορευόμενοι, ἀπελθοῦσαι,
literally to *walk after the flesh* (the lusts), Germ. *dem Fleische nach-
gehen.*   The familiar Hebrew formula of adieu (1 Sam. i. 17
etc.) runs in Greek either πορεύου, ὕπαγε εἰς εἰρήνην or ἐν εἰρήνῃ (Mark
v. 34; Luke vii. 50; Acts xvi. 36 etc.),—differing in conception but
not in sense.   The phrase ἔρχεσθαι ἐν ὀνόματι κυρίου (Matt. xxi. 9)
is also quoted from the O. T.

B. § 133, 4 c.; H. § 611; C. § 456 sq.; D. p. 491; J. § 607.

Among verbs expressing e m o t i o n, the verb ἀγαλλιᾶσθαι (see **23**
p. 51) *to rejoice*, which did not come into use till the time of the
Sept., has acquired especial currency in the Bible: sometimes, as in
the Sept., with ἐν; sometimes with ἐπί and the Dat. Further, the
verb εὐδοκεῖν *to be well pleased*, used also by later profane writers
(Polyb. Diod.), is employed again most commonly with ἐν (rarely εἰς
2 Pet. i. 17) after Alexandrian precedent; also with the simple Acc.
of the thing, Heb. x. 6, 8 ὁλοκαυτώματα . . . οὐκ ηὐδόκησας (for which
in Ps. xxxix. 7 the Alex. text reads ἐζήτησας). Whether it was also
joined to the Acc. of the p e r s o n (Gen. xxxiii. 10) is doubtful; in
Matt. xii. 18 Tdf. in ed. 7 [so 8] has returned to the original and
better attested reading εἰς ὅν [א* B ὅν]. The verb κ α υ χ ᾶ σ θ α ι *to
boast* is especially used by Paul, — most frequently again with ἐν
(Jer. ix. 23), also with ἐπί and the Dat. (Ps. v. 12) and with the Acc.
of the thing, see Wahl; on the other hand, the Gen. with κατακαυ-
χᾶσθαι (Rom. xi. 18) is to be explained by the altered signification
of the verb, after the analogy of the syntactical use of καταφρονεῖν,
καταγελᾶν (§ 132, 15 p. 165). Ξ ε ν ί ζ ε σ θ α ι (Luther, *sich befremden
lassen*, [A.V. *think strange*]) is used with the simple Dative and with
ἐν, 1 Pet. iv. 4, 12.   Among other more common verbs θ α υ μ ά ζ ε ι ν
is no longer, as in the classics, joined to the Genitive, but most commonly, yet quite idiomatically, to ἐπί with the Dat. (not to ἐν, on Luke
i. 21 see below § 140, 9 p. 263), περί with the Gen. Luke ii. 18, in **161**
a peculiar, pregnant, sense to ὀπίσω Rev. xiii. 3; moreover it is
several times used with the simple Accusative — not only of the thing
(τὸ γεγονός, τὸ ὅραμα), but also once of the person Luke vii. 9.
Ε ὐ α ρ ε σ τ ε ῖ ν and -εῖσθαι (only in the Ep. to the Heb.) is used
with the simple Dative. Χ α ί ρ ε ι ν commonly with ἐπί and the
Dative, sometimes also with ἐν (Luke x. 20; Phil. i. 18; Col. i. 24).
But in the Pauline phrase χαίρειν ἐ ν κ υ ρ ί ῳ the words ἐν κυρίῳ (as
above in 5 p. 175) are an adverbial adjunct designating the mode or
nature of the joy; hence e.g. in Phil. iv. 10 the object of the joy is
added in a clause with ὅτι. So with the substantive, χαρὰ ἐν πνεύματι
ἁγίῳ Rom. xiv. 17 (cf. § 125, 11 p. 96). On the diversified constructions of the other verbs of emotion, such as μακροθυμεῖν, εὐφραίνεσθαι,
ὀργίζεσθαι, λυπεῖσθαι, συλλυπεῖσθαι, ἐκπλήττεσθαι, μεριμνᾶν, etc., see the
lexicons.

REMARK. To set up a special class (as is often done) under the **24**
title Dative of the e n d (consilii) is unnecessary either in reference
to general or to N. T. usage, since all the examples brought under
this head may be referred to the idea of the preceding Dative (motive,
occasion, *propter* not *causa*), — whether such a Dative stands with

24

strict Passives (Rom. xi. 20 *propter* infidiam, Gal. vi. 12 *propter* crucem), or sometimes elliptically with Active or Neuter verbs a Passive idea being supplied (cf. the Lat. *metu, odio, studio* for propter metum, etc., Zumpt § 454) ; as, Rom. iv. 20 οὐ διεκρίθη τῇ ἀπιστίᾳ, 1 Cor. viii. 7 τινὲς δὲ τῇ συνειδήσει ... ἐσθίουσιν, 2 Cor. i. 15 ταύτῃ τῇ πεποιθήσει ἐβουλόμην ἐλθεῖν.

B. § 133, 4 c. note; C. § 472 e.; J. §§ 495. 607.

25   To the examples adduced from Greek authors of verbs whose idea is capable of such varied reference that they can be construed with all three cases, may be added from the N. T. the verb μεριμνᾶν: according to 11 p. 178 it is construed with the Dative (τῇ ψυχῇ, τῷ σώματι Matt. vi. 25 etc.), takes after it the object of the care as usual in the neut. Acc. (τὰ τοῦ κυρίου 1 Cor. vii. 32 ; τὰ περὶ ὑμῶν Phil. ii. 20), and finally in one passage according to recent editors [so cod. Sin.] is connected with the Genitive (like other verbs of caring § 132, 15 p. 164), viz. Matt. vi. 34 μεριμνήσει ἑαυτῆς.   Moreover, it is used with περί, ὑπέρ, see Wahl.

B. § 133, 4 e.; H. § 613; C. § 469; D. p. 487; J. § 606.

26   In reference to Time, the Dative is used to specify a) a definite point of time ; b) the space of time (*within*, for which the Acc. is also used, see § 131, 11 p. 152) ; c) periodically returning portions of time.

In cases a) and b) ἐν is often added to the Dative (as in Lat. *in, during*); in c) we find besides κατά with the Acc. also (cf. p. 30).

Examples : of a) ταύτῃ τῇ νυκτί, τῇ τρίτῃ ἡμέρᾳ, etc. ; of b) ἱκανῷ χρόνῳ; πολλοῖς, αἰωνίοις χρόνοις ; ἑτέραις γενεαῖς ; τεσσεράκοντα καὶ ἓξ ἔτεσιν, Acts viii. 11 ; Rom. xvi. 25 ; Eph. iii. 5 ; John ii. 20, etc.   The reading varies between the Dat. and the Acc. in John xiv. 9 ; Acts xxviii. 12, also with the Nom. Matt. xv. 32 (on which see § 129 **a.** 3 p. 139), now with and now without ἐν John ii. 20 ; of c) τοῖς σάββασιν, τῇ ἑορτῇ, ἐν σαββάτῳ, Matt. xii. 2, 5 ; Luke ii. 41 etc., κατὰ ἑορτήν Matt. xxvii. 15 etc.

B. § 133, 5; cf. H. § 500 b.; J. § 611, Obs. 1.

162   The possibility of the combination of two Datives in the N. T.
27 according to the σχῆμα καθ᾿ ὅλον καὶ μέρος is as little to be denied as the construction of two Accs. (§ 131, 6 p. 149) and of two Gens. (§ 132, 17 note p. 167).   Yet the compass of the N. T. books is so limited that the opportunity for the construction was rare. 2 Cor. xii. 7 ἐδόθη μοι σκόλοψ τῇ σαρκί plainly belongs here. Elsewhere we find two different Datives united in one construction, but not after

the above schema: 1 John v. 16 and Heb. iv. 2 (on which see 15
above, p. 179).　Rom. vii. 25 τῷ νοΐ δουλεύω νόμῳ θεοῦ grammatically
viewed presents no difficulty.

THE VERB.

THE PASSIVE.

B. § 134, 1-3;　H. § 693;　C. § 586;　D. § 431;　J. II. p. 21.

The most common mode of designating the personal 1
author of a passive state is, in the N. T. as in the classics,
by means of ὑπό with the Gen. ; in certain cases also by means
of παρά with the Gen., ἐκ and even ἀπό.　Respecting all this
see the Prepositions.

The personal m e d i u m is likewise designated as usual by διά with
the Gen., as τὸ ῥηθὲν διὰ Ἡσαΐου, Ἱερεμίου, τὸ ῥηθὲν ὑ π ὸ τοῦ κυρίου δ ι ὰ
τοῦ προφήτου λέγοντος etc., or hebraistically by διὰ χειρός, στόματος,
according to § 133, 20 p. 182.

B. § 134, 4;　H. § 600;　C. § 461;　D. pp. 431, 492;　J. § 611.

Instead of the prepositions, the D a t i v e a l o n e, according 2
to an ancient usage, is employed to designate the personal
author (the Dat. *rei* coincides with the Dat. *instrumenti*),
especially with the Perfect and Aorist Pass., as Luke xxiii. 15
οὐδὲν ἄξιον θανάτου ἐστὶν πεπραγμένον αὐτῷ.　Yet this use in
Greek is by no means so general that we can assume that it
can be substituted indifferently in any and every case for ὑπό
with the Gen.　On the contrary, it is restricted, at least in
prose, to certain predicates and phrases, to which this Dative
imparts a somewhat m o d i f i e d signification corresponding
to the force of the Dative.　Cf. with this the Latin phrase
alicui probare, and the like, in Lat. prose ; Zumpt § 419.

Thus the Dative in the common phrase ὀφθῆναί τινι (cf. Eur. Bacch.
912) imparts to ὀφθῆναι the simple neuter force, *to appear to one* (cf.
p. 52), and the same holds true more or less of the phrases (likewise
often recurring) εὑρεθῆναι and γνωσθῆναί τινι; as, Rom. x. 20 (quotn.)
εὑρέθην τοῖς ἐμὲ μὴ ζητοῦσιν, ἐμφανὴς ἐγενόμην τοῖς ἐμὲ μὴ ἐπερωτῶσιν,
Luke xxiv. 35 ; 2 Cor. xii. 20 ; Phil. iv. 5 γνωσθήτω πᾶσιν ἀνθρώποις
(*become known*).　In 2 Pet. iii. 14 αὐτῷ, as the very position indicates,
is best referred ἀπὸ κοινοῦ to both terms (ἀμώμητοι and εὑρεθῆναι), 163
since it stands in equally close relation to both, (respecting the Dative
with ἀμώμητος see § 133, 14 p. 179).

Formerly many other Datives also were taken in the same sense
(as Dats. of the author), but incorrectly (e.g. Matt. v. 21 ; Heb. iv. 2);

for in general the assumption of such a Dative, particularly in the
N. T., seems only to be warranted where analogy and usage render
its presence manifest.

3   REMARK. As a periphrasis for this Dative, i.e. to render it vivid or
to approximate it to the Oriental style of thought, the preposition
ἐνώπιον is employed (agreeably to the closely related cases in § 133,
14 p. 180) ; as, Luke xii. 6 ἓν ἐξ αὐτῶν οὐκ ἔστιν ἐπιλελησμένον ἐνώπιον
τοῦ θεοῦ by him, i.e. concretely, in his sight, *before* him ; Rom. iii. 20
οὐ δικαιωθήσεται πᾶσα σὰρξ ἐνώπιον αὐτοῦ, with which may be compared
παρὰ τῷ θεῷ δικαιοῦται Gal. iii. 11, cf. Rom. ii. 13 ; 2 Thess. i. 6.

B. § 134, 5; H. § 694; C. § 586; D. p. 431 sq.; J. II. p. 22.

4   Since even the earlier authors did not hesitate to construe
in the Passive, like pure transitives, verbal ideas which
take their limiting object in another case than the Accusative,
the N. T. authors also, particularly the better writers among
them, made this good classic usage their own, — recommended
as it was by facility of construction.

Thus we find κατηγορεῖσθαι in Matt. xxvii. 12 ; Acts xxv. 16,
κατεγνωσμένος in Gal. ii. 11, ἐγκαλεῖσθαι in Acts xix. 40 etc., μαρτυρεῖ-
σθαι (testimony is given me, I get the witness) frequently in the Acts
and the Ep. to the Heb. (see Wahl), — a liberty which John (in his
third Ep. vs. 12 Δημητρίῳ μεμαρτύρηται ὑπὸ πάντων) did not avail
himself of, perhaps because it was unknown to him. Further,
εὐαρεστεῖσθαι Heb. xiii. 16, διακονηθῆναι Mark x. 45. Χρηματίζειν τινί
to give a response to one (Jos. Antt. 10, 1, 3 etc.) undergoes as a rule
the same change into the Passive : χρηματίζομαι it is revealed *to me,
divinitus edoceor* (Matt. ii. 12 etc.; Acts x. 22 ; Heb. viii. 5 etc.);
only in Luke ii. 26 is the other (impersonal) construction found, ἦν
αὐτῷ κεχρηματισμένον (but D gives ἦν κεχρηματισμένος as usual). See
still other examples in 7 below, p. 189.

With other verbs the personal mode of expression is quite universal
because they were in general by later writers connected rather with
the Accusative, i.e. regarded as transitives. Thus particularly πλεονεκτεῖσθαι according to § 132, 22 p. 168, εὐαγγελίζεσθαι in the Passive
§ 131, 4 p. 148.

B. § 134, 6; H. § 553 a.; C. § 587; D. § 465; J. § 545, 3; also p. 256, Obs. 3.

5   The retention of the Accusative of the thing as the
object of the Passive, with verbs which govern two Accs.,
is found with διδάσκειν, 2 Thess. ii. 15 cf. Gal. i. 12 ; and with
ποτίζειν according to the present reading in 1 Cor. xii. 13 (ἐν
πνεῦμα ἐποτίσθημεν).

The anomalous passive construction with such verbs as κρύπτεσθαι, ἀποκρύπτεσθαι, ἀφαιρεῖσθαι ἀπό τινος (Col. i. 26 ; Luke xviii. 34 ; x. 42) rests on the construction of these verbs with ἀπό, — more usual even in the Active, see § 131, 6 p. 149. Respecting the Gen. ἀπεστερημένος τῆς ἀληθείας (1 Tim. vi. 5) see § 132, 5 p. 158.

B. § 134, N. 2; H. § 555 a.; D. § 466; J. § 548, cf. p. 245.

That in the constructions treated of in § 131, 5 p. 148 (αὔξειν αὔξησιν etc.) the Acc. of the abstract is in like manner retained when the verb is changed into the Passive, has already been illustrated by examples under that head. Of the same origin is the elliptical phrase (cf. § 123, 8 p. 82) in Luke xii. 47 δαρήσεται π ο λ λ ά ς, ὀ λ ί γ α ς sc. πληγάς, and the construction (formed regularly after παιδευθῆναι παιδείαν) ἐπαιδεύθη πᾶσαν σοφίαν in a (rejected) reading of cod. D Acts vii. 22.

B. § 134, 7; H. § 595; C. § 587; D. p. 432; J. § 584, 2.

But not only when the verb is capable of being construed with two nouns in the Accusative is it followed by an Acc. in the Passive; the A c c. of the t h i n g (often expressed, according to § 131, 10 p. 152, by a pron. or adj. of the neuter gender) or of the a b s t r a c t is also subjoined to the Passive predicates of many other verbs. That this use stands in the closest relation to the so-called Greek Accusative treated of in § 131, 9 p. 152, has already been remarked there. It is to such a degree characteristic of the Greek tongue above all others, and was so firmly rooted, too, in the phraseology of the people, that it not only did not disappear from the later language and in particular that of the N. T., but was employed with decided preference by all the N. T. writers nearly to the same extent. The Latins also borrowed it, as is well known, from the Greek.

As the subject itself has been rendered sufficiently familiar by general Greek grammar, we may adduce here briefly (in order to exhibit the extension of the usage in the N. T.) the examples only, among which are to be included the instances where the p e r s o n a l S u b j e c t implied in the verb has arisen from the D a t i v e or the G e n i t i v e in the Active (4 p. 188): ζημιοῦσθαι τὴν ψυχήν Matt. xvi. 26; Mark viii. 36, δεδεμένος τοὺς πόδας καὶ τὰς χεῖρας John xi. 44, διεφθαρμένος τὸν νοῦν 1 Tim. vi. 5, ῥεραντισμένος τὰς καρδίας, λελουμένος τὸ σῶμα Heb. x. 22, πληροῦσθαι καρπὸν δικαιοσύνης, τὴν ἐπίγνωσιν Phil. i. 11; Col. i. 9 (Eph. i. 23 must be taken as Middle i.e. actively), περίκειμαι (equiv. to περιτέθειμαι according to B. § 109 p. 198) ἅλυσιν

Acts xxviii. 20, ἀσθένειαν Heb. v. 2, κεκαυτηριασμένος τὴν συνείδησιν
1 Tim. iv. 2, κατηχούμενος τὸν λόγον Gal. vi. 6, particularly πιϲτεύεσθαι
(to be entrusted with) e.g. τὸ εὐαγγέλιον, τὸ κήρυγμα, τὴν οἰκονομίαν, τὰ
λόγια, Tit. i. 3 ; 1 Cor. ix. 17 ; Rom. iii. 2 ; Gal. ii. 7, etc. (but 2 Thess.
i. 10 ; 1 Tim. iii. 16 belong to § 133, 4, 7) p. 175). The following
are very free and brachylogic, after Paul's style : 2 Cor. iii. 18 τὴν
αὐτὴν εἰκόνα μεταμορφούμεθα are changed *to* the same image, vi. 13
τὴν αὐτὴν ἀντιμισθίαν πλατύνθητε καὶ ὑμεῖς expand yourselves (your
hearts), as I do, after my example, for the recompense. See the
other (Pass.-Mid.) examples under the Middle § 135; and respecting
πείθεσθαι τὰ κρείττονα, οὐδέν see § 131, 6 note p. 150, and 10 p. 152.

REMARK. Luke (in Acts xxi. 3) peculiarly and without similar
precedent in other writers has written, instead of ἀναφανείσης τῆς
Κύπρου . . . ἐπλέομεν, exchanging the subjects, ἀναφανέντες τὴν Κύπρον
appeared before Cyprus, as it were *after we had allowed Cyprus to
appear to us* i.e. had come in sight of it. Yet the reading of the Vat.
MS. ἀναφάναντες (confirmed now by cod. Sin.) deserves perhaps
the decided preference ; [so Tdf.].

VERBAL ADJECTIVES.

B. § 134, 8–10; H. § 804 sq.; C. §§ 458. 682; D. p. 190 sq.; J. §§ 613. 383; G. § 114.

165　　Of the two verbal adjectives (in -τέος and -τός) the form in -τέος is
8　　rare. The word βλητέον occurring in Luke v. 38 ; Mark ii. 22
Lchm. has the Active construction (τὸν οἶνον). Adjectives in -τός
include the idea of possibility in an Active and Passive sense (cf. p. 42),
corresponding to Germ. adjectives in -*lich* and -*bar* [Eng. -*ly* and -*ble*],
as ὁρατός, δυνατός, θνητός, παθητός, ἀνεκλάλητος, ἀμάραντος, ἄπταιστος,
etc.; often also without the collateral notion of power (as among the
Greeks, too), as ἀγαπητός, γεννητός, γνωστός, ἔκθετος, ἄνιπτος, etc.

Adjectives in -τός are no longer capable of the verbal construction ;
hence, for example, ἀγαπητός is only connected with the Gen.
(ἀγαπητοί μου, θεοῦ), never with the Dative. On the Dative with
ἀμώμητοι (2 Pet. iii. 14), see no. 2 above, p. 187 ; and in like manner
the Dative with γνωστός, ἀρεστός, δυνατός, ἀποδεκτός, etc., depends
not on the form but on the signification of the word. Most of
them, consequently, have become as respects their signification and
construction completely adjectives (or substantives, as ὁ χριστός,
οἱ ἀγαπητοί), just as the ending -τος in other cases also is a common
formative syllable of adjectives e.g. αἰχμάλωτος, ἀθέμιτος, ἀγράμματος,
τὰ ἑρπετά, etc.

Hence it is not improbable that, with the disappearance of the
verbal use of the verbal adjectives, the N. T. writers, to designate a
participle corresponding to the Latin in -*ndus*, have followed Hebrew

precedent (see Gesen. Lehrg. p. 791; [Gr. § 131, 1]) and frequently
taken other participles in this sense. Yet we have a right to assert
this probably only of the Future Part. (Heb. iii. 5 εἰς μαρτύριον τῶν
λαληθησομένων), or of the Present in which according to § 137, 11
p. 206 the notion of futurity or of *conatus* is already included, — most
plainly in Heb. xii. 18 προσεληλύθατε ψηλαφωμένῳ (ὄρει) καὶ
κεκαυμένῳ πυρί; (see the other examples ibid.). Other participles, as
κατεγνωσμένος Gal. ii. 11, ἐβδελυγμένος Rev. xxi. 8, ἐκριζωθέντα Jude
12, which are also so explained sometimes, are to be taken strictly
according to their form as Past Part., and to be translated accordingly.

THE MIDDLE.

B. § 135, 1-3; H. §§ 687 sq. 694 c.; C. § 578 sqq.; D. § 432 sq.; J. § 362 sq.

That Middle verbs, if translated by us reflexively or intran-   1
sitively, give the preference in the N. T., as in later writers
generally, to the Passive form of the Aorist rather than
the Middle, has already (p. 51 sq.) been taught. The number
of these Passive Aorists (for the most part to be translated
intransitively) is very great; and examples, therefore, are to
be found everywhere in multitudes. With many verbs, nevertheless, the Middle form of the Aorist had already come into
such universal use (e.g. with φυλάσσεσθαι, κομίζεσθαι, αἰτεῖσθαι,
ἔχεσθαι and all its compounds), that even in the N. T. no
contrary examples of the Aorist formation are extant.

B. § 135, 4; H. § 533 a.; D. p. 434; cf. J. § 583.

Instances of the Object-Accusative with verbs which in the 166
Active admit the construction of two Accusatives, are found most   2
frequently with ἐν- and ἐκδύεσθαι, — and that both in the proper
sense (χιτῶνα, ἔνδυμα, τρίχας καμήλου) and in the tropical (Ἰησοῦν, τὸν
νέον ἄνθρωπον, ἀφθαρσίαν, τὸν θώρακα τῆς δικαιοσύνης), — ἐνδιδύσκεσθαι ἱμάτιν, πορφύραν, περιβάλλεσθαι (according to § 131, 6
p. 149) ἱμάτιον, στολάς, etc. often in the Apocalypse, and according to
the same analogy περιζώννυσθαι as well with the Acc. of the
girding object (ζώνην) as of the girded (ὀσφύν), and likewise ὑποδεῖσθαι
σανδάλια and πόδας. On all these see the lexicons. Exceptions are
rare; only ἀμφιέννυσθαι and περιβάλλεσθαι permit (like our *to wrap
one's self in, clothed with*) the construction with ἐν: Matt. xi. 8;
Luke vii. 25; Rev. iii. 5 (without ἐν iv. 4 Lchm.).

B. § 135, 5; H. §§ 544 a. 687; C. § 579; D. p. 436; J. § 549 sq.

The number of verbs which in the Middle acquire a new   3
transitive sense, and accordingly govern also a new Object-

Accusative, is likewise very considerable. The following
deserve notice in this respect as peculiar:

ἐπαισχύνεσθαί τινα to be ashamed of (shame one's self before)
any one Mark viii. 38, etc., analogous to which ἐντρέπεσθαι also
in the same sense (which arose from the signification of the Active
to make ashamed, intimidate, abash, 1 Cor. iv. 14) as in later writers
(Polyb.) is regularly joined to the Acc. Matt. xxi. 37, etc.; in earlier
writers the Middle is current in the sense *to give heed to*, and accordingly in connection with the Genitive (see Pape); ἀποστραφῆιαί
τινα *to turn one's self away from one*, shun him, 2 Tim. i. 15; φυλάσσεσθαι (*to be on one's guard against*) is indeed as usual joined to
the Acc. in Acts xxi. 25; 2 Tim. iv. 15, but more in accordance with
N. T. usage, as with the Active φυλάσσειν in the sense of *to preserve*
from etc. (2 Thess. iii. 3 θεὸς ὑμᾶς φυλάξει ἀπὸ τοῦ πονηροῦ) and other
verbs of similar meaning (see § 147, 3 p. 323), is the construction
with ἀπό, as Luke xii. 15 φυλάσσεσθε ἀπὸ πάσης πλεονεξίας, for which
we have in 1 John v. 21 φυλάξατε ἑαυτοὺς ἀπὸ τῶν εἰδώλων. In the
signification *to observe* it is used in the Active, even in the N. T.
Matt. xix. 20; Mark x. 20 Lchm.; Luke xviii. 21, in which passages
formerly the Mid. was read, as is done still by Tdf. [Treg.] in Mark
after the majority of MSS. [cod. Sin. also]. Φοβεῖσθαι is almost
always connected with the Acc., but sometimes (after § 147, 3 p. 323)
with ἀπό, Matt. x. 28; Luke xii. 4; αἰσχύνεσθαι ἀπό in 1 John
ii. 28.

B. § 135, 6; H. § 689 sq.; C. § 582; D. p. 436 sq.; J. § 362, 2.

4   The remark that the Greeks employ the Middle form to
designate an action that takes place in some connection with
the subject, is performed for his own advantage or disadvantage,
in general, stands in some close relation to him, — is in the
main applicable to the N. T. also.

Among the numerous examples of this signification of the Middle
in its broader application we may mention — besides the verbs named
above (2 p. 191) denoting an action done to one's own body (to
which yet others are to be added, as νίπτεσθαι τὰς χεῖρας; ἀλείψασθαι,
κείρασθαι τὴν κεφαλήν) — such as the following: σπάσασθαι μάχαιραν;
προσ- εἰσκαλεῖσθαί τινα; ἐπικαλεῖσθαι θεόν, Καίσαρα; ἐπι- προσλαμβάνεσθαι; περιποιεῖσθαι; ἐνδείκνυσθαι; σημειοῦσθαι; κομίζεσθαι;
167 ἔχεσθαι together with its compounds; further, among those compounded with ἀπό and ἐκ (B. p. 354), ἀπωθεῖσθαι, ἀποτίθεσθαι, ἀπο-
λύεσθαι, ἀπομάσσεσθαι, ἀποδίδοσθαι, ἀπείπασθαι, ἐξαγοράζεσθαι, ἐκτρέπεσθαι, etc.

B. § 135, N. 3; C. § 585; D. p. 438 sq.; J. § 363, 3. 4. 6.

How exactly the N. T. language could still make the distinction [5]
between the Active and the Middle forms of o n e a n d t h e s a m e
verb, can be seen clearly in many cases. Let any one compare in
this respect in the lexicons the examples of νίπτειν and νίπτεσθαι,
λούειν and ἀπολούεσθαι, κείρειν and κείρεσθαι, φυλάττειν and φυλάττεσθαι
(see 3 above, p. 192), ἀποκαλύπτειν and ἀποκαλύπτεσθαι, and of those
verbs whose Middle is used in a signification essentially altered : ἐπιτιθέ-
ναι and ἐπιτίθεσθαι, ἀποδιδόναι and ἀποδίδοσθαι, κρίνειν and κρίνεσθαι (διακρίνεσθαι), αἱρεῖν and αἱρεῖσθαι, ποιεῖν and ποιεῖσθαι — the last only in
a mental reference, as in the phrases μνήμην, λόγον, σπουδὴν ποιεῖσθαι,[1]
etc. Yet instances are not wanting in which the A c t i v e, as the
generic form, stands for the Middle and alternates with it without any
sensible difference (cf. B. § 135, 6 ; J. § 363, 3 and Obs. 2). Thus we
find in particular α ἰ τ ε ῖ ν and αἰτεῖσθαι, even in close proximity, as Jas.
iv. 3 αἰτεῖτε καὶ οὐ λαμβάνετε, διότι κακῶς αἰτεῖσθε, 1 John v. 15 (αἰτώμεθα
... ἠτήκαμεν), Matt. xx. 20 and 22, Mark vi. 23 and 24 ; σ υ γ κ α λ ε ῖ ν
and συγκαλεῖσθαι Luke xv. 6, 9 Lchm. [Treg.], Acts v. 21 and x. 24,
etc. ; δ ι α τ ά σ σ ε ι ν and διατάσσεσθαι ; for σπάσασθαι μάχαιραν (Mark,
Acts) Matt. says, xxvi. 51, ἀ π έ σ π α σ ε ν τὴν μάχαιραν ; ε ὑ ρ ί σ κ ε ι ν
occurs in the sense of εὑρίσκεσθαι in Matt. x. 39 (ὁ εὑρὼν τὴν ψυχὴν
αὑτοῦ) ; ἐ ν ε ρ γ ε ῖ ν and ἐνεργεῖσθαι, — although between these forms
this distinction has been observed by Paul (see Fr. on Rom. vii. 5 ,
Winer 258 (242)) : that with the Active the operating subject is
personal,[2] with the Middle (in 1 Thess. ii. 13 also) non-personal ; see
the numerous passages in Wahl. But ποιεῖν often stands in the
phrases before designated where, at least in the classic style, the Middle
alone was usual ; as, συμβούλιον ποιήσαντες ; ποιῆσαι ἔλεος, πρόθεσιν, etc.

But on the other hand the Middle is, strictly speaking, never used
without some sort of reference to the subject ; (in Acts ix. 39 this
reference is still intimated, but only very feebly it is true, in the μετ'
αὐτῶν that follows). In single cases it involves at least a different
signification from the Active (a tropical or mental) ; particularly in
certain c o m p o u n d s, which, because they were used almost exclusively in the Middle form, have almost become complete Deponents.
Thus Paul has written in 2 Cor. xi. 2 ἡρμοσάμην ὑμᾶς Χριστῷ, instead
of the ordinary ἥρμοσα, in order to express the idea of s p i r i t u a l
espousal to Christ, iii. 18 τὴν δόξαν κυρίου κατοπτριζόμενοι (to view in

---

[1] In Acts viii. 2, therefore, the reading of the oldest MSS. [Sin. also] ἐποίησαν
κοπετόν is to be preferred with Lchm. [Tdf. Treg.] to the Middle form.

[2] That with σ υ ν ε ρ γ ε ῖ also, in Rom. viii. 28, πάντα was not formerly taken as
Subject is proved by the important (although probably only explanatory) addition
ὁ θεός (A R Lchm.).

a mirror), Heb. xi. 40 τοῦ θεοῦ προβλεψαμένου, Col. ii. 15 ἀπεκδυσά-
μενος τὰς ἀρχὰς καὶ τὰς ἐξουσίας (deWette, *to disarm*), and many of the
168 most current compounds, as ἐπαγγέλλεσθαι, ἀποκρίνεσθαι, ἀντιλαμβάνεσθαι,
ἐπιτίθεσθαι, etc.[1]

B. § 135, N. 4; H. § 688 a.; C. § 583; D. p. 435; J. § 363, 2.

6   A deviation from ordinary usage consists, as has already been
intimated § 127, 26 p. 118, in the practice of often expressing again
separately the P o s s e s s i v e and R e f l e x i v e limitations strictly
speaking already comprised in the Middle form; as, συγκαλεσάμενος
τοὺς συγγενεῖς α ὐ τ ο ῦ (αὐτ.); ἀπέθεντο τὰ ἱμάτια α ὐ τ ῶ ν (Acts vii. 58),
διαλογίζεσθε ἐν ταῖς καρδίαις ὑ μ ῶ ν (Mark ii. 8, etc.), ὅπως ἐνδείξωμαι
τὴν δύναμίν μ ο υ (Rom. ix. 17), etc. Where, however, especial
e m p h a s i s required the addition of the *reflexive* pron. to the Middle.
N. T. usage harmonizes with the ordinary usage; as, διεμερίσαντο
ἑαυτοῖς John xix. 24 (quotn.), ἀνεθρέψατο αὐτὸν ἑαυτῇ Acts vii. 21,
σεαυτὸν παρεχόμενος Tit. ii. 7.

(THE MIDDLE.)

B. § 136, NN. 3, 4; H. § 415; C. §§ 575 sq. 588; D. § 350; J. § 365, 3.

That the Perfect of middle and deponent verbs shares the middle
(A c t i v e) signification of the verb hardly needs mention, since the
usage is sufficiently established, see e.g. 2 John 8 [?]; Acts xiii. 47; also
in the periphrastic form with εἶναι (§ 144, 24 p. 308), Acts xx. 13
διατεταγμένος ἦν. That single tenses, however, — especially the Aor.
and Perf. Pass. — of these verbs are also used in the P a s s i v e sense,
see on p. 52.

THE TENSES.

B. § 137; H. §§ 695 sqq.; C. §§ 590 sqq.; D. §§ 422 sq.; J. §§ 394 sq.; G. §§ 8 sqq.

1   Among all known ancient languages none distinguishes the
manifold temporal (and modal) relations of the verb so accurately as the Greek. It is conceivable that under the
prolonged dominion of the Greek language and culture, per-
meating as they did the concerns of a l l classes, the knowledge
of the signification of these forms of speech (so essential in
making one's self understood) was not only not lost by the
less cultivated portion even of the Greek people, but also
became the possession of those f o r e i g n populations and

---

[1] Only ἠμύνατο Acts vii. 24 seems to stand completely for the Active. But we
must consider that the Active form ἀμύνειν is pre-eminently poetic and the Middle
came in later prose into such general use that it must be regarded as having become a Deponent, — as well in the signification *to repel from one's self*, as *to defend*
(another), *to avenge* (*ulcisci*). See Lucian, Dial. Mort. 13, 6 ; Jup. trag. 37.

individuals that made the Greek tongue their own. Had the
Jews and others become acquainted with this foreign tongue 169
only through the medium of the written langcage, not through
contact with people who spoke Greek themselves, or had the
adoption of the language taken place suddenly and not before
the time when the N. T. books were composed, instead of
gradually and centuries earlier, there would be greater reason
than there is for the assertion that the N. T. writers in the
use of the Greek tenses labored under a degree of uncertainty,
fostered by the well-known poverty of the Hebrew tongue in
this respect; or even if they had employed exclusively only
certain Greek temporal forms and avoided others, we might
assume at all events the possibility of such a supposition. We
see, however, that the N. T. writers, even those less practised
in the use of language, avail themselves with great assurance
of the whole treasure of the Greek temporal forms — Active,
Passive, and Middle. Obscurity and uncertainty of thought
occasions necessarily a diminished facility in the employment
of the corresponding forms of speech. That this is the case,
for example, with respect to the Moods, particularly the
Optative and the Tenses connected with ἄν, will appear from
the exposition given below. But in the use of the Tenses
the N. T. writers are by no means deficient in the requisite
skill. Consequently the so-called Enallage Temporum
or Interchange of Tenses, which was applied by some of the
older interpreters of Scripture often and indiscriminately, is
to be opposed on behalf of the N. T. language at the outset,
and discarded on principle. Still less does the observation
that other languages — particularly we ourselves in translating — frequently employ different temporal relations, give
us any right to assume that the writer in Greek connected
with a tense any other conception than that residing in the
tense.

  Accordingly, whenever our mode of conception departs from the
tense employed, it is our business to transfer ourselves to the position
of the writer, and take pains in every case to apprehend the temporal
relation which corresponds to the tense he used, and, if possible,
to reproduce it. This, too, thanks to the more recent judicious
criticism and thorough philological study, has already been done by
most modern interpreters; and thus a multitude of absurdities have

been removed from the interpretation of the N. T.   We can accordingly dispense here with an extended refutation of those grammatical errors the more readily, as the scientific treatment of the
Greek language adopted at the present day universally in the schools
secures at the outset the inexperienced (and consequently still impartial)
reader of the N. T. from errors of the sort.   Whoever, therefore, out
of professional interest wishes to obtain a closer acquaintance with
them, must be referred to the commentaries or to the ample
170 collection of them in Winer § 40.   Yet no one will be disposed to
insist that consistency in the maintenance of this position be carried
so far as to forbid us to recognize the least inaccuracy in expression
or deviation from ordinary usage; on the contrary, to exhibit such
anomalies is especially the object of this section; only we shall see
in them, rather, a product of the unconstrained p h r a s e o l o g y o f
t h e p e o p l e or an illegitimate extension of a Greek form of thought,
and not an (immediate) influence of a foreign idiom.

B. § 137, 1 and 2; C. § 605 d.; J. § 399, 2 sq.; G. § 17.

2   The distinction established in the general Grammars between
the Perfect, as a tense having a present reference, and the
Aorist, as a narrative tense, holds completely in the N. T., as
every attentive reader can convince himself by comparing the
verbal forms which occur on every page.   It may suffice here,
therefore, to adduce a few passages in which both tenses have
clearly preserved their proper force when united in a single
sentence: Col. i. 16 ἐν αὐτῷ ἐκτίσθη τὰ πάντα . . . εἴτε θρόνοι
εἴτε κυριότητες . . . · τὰ πάντα δι᾽ αὐτοῦ καὶ εἰς αὐτὸν ἔκτισται,
καὶ αὐτός ἐστιν πρὸ πάντων etc., 1 John i. 2 ἡ ζωὴ ἐφανερώθη,
καὶ ἑωράκαμεν καὶ μαρτυροῦμεν, Mark xv. 44 Πιλάτος ἐθαύμασεν
εἰ ἤδη τέθνηκεν, καὶ . . . ἐπηρώτησεν (τὸν κεντυρίωνα) εἰ
πάλαι ἀπέθανεν, Acts xxi. 28 Ἕλληνας εἰσήγαγεν εἰς τὸ
ἱερὸν καὶ κεκοίνωκεν τὸν ἅγιον τόπον τοῦτον, John viii. 40 (ζητεῖτέ
με ἀποκτεῖναι) ὃς τὴν ἀλήθειαν ὑμῖν λελάληκα, ἣν ἤκουσα παρὰ
τοῦ θεοῦ.   See more examples of the sort in Winer 272 (255).

If, nevertheless, Perfects are sometimes used in a p u r e l y
A o r i s t i c f o r c e, that is something which not only took place in
Greek authors (Bhdy. p. 379), but has its natural foundation   1) in
the well-known usage by virtue of which P r e s e n t s so frequently
take the place of the Aorist in narration (see B. § 137, N. 7; H. § 699;
C. § 609; D. p. 405; J. § 395, 2; G. p. 6, and as examples of this
Present from the N. T. John i. 44; xx. 4–6; Acts x. 11, etc.),
and   2) in the deterioration of the later language, in which (per-

haps in consequence of the influence of the Latin) the use of the
Perfect as an historic tense, even by poets, becomes more and more
frequent; see the list from Plutarch in Wytt. adnot. p. 412 sq.,
from Nonnus in Lehrs quaest. epp. p. 274. The examples from the
N. T. which belong here are, however, almost all of such a nature
that the Perfects stand in connection with (preceding) Aorists, so
that a narrative character was thereby impressed upon the passage as
it were in advance: (cf. Dem. Hal. p. 84 ἐψηφίσαντο καὶ ὡμολογήκασιν,
Ach. Tat. p. 100, 33 ed. Jacobs; Luc. Deor. dial. 19. 1, etc.) Rev. v. 7
καὶ ἦλθεν καὶ εἴληφεν (τὸ βιβλίον), viii. 4 sq. καὶ ἀνέβη ὁ καπνὸς ...
καὶ εἴληφεν ... καὶ ἐγέμισεν, 2 Cor. xi. 25; Heb. xi. 28; also with the
participle: Matt. xxv. 24 ὁ τὸ ἓν τάλαντον εἰληφώς, for which previously
(vs. 20) λαβών was used.

It is therefore more correct certainly, in many passages of the kind,
not to seek out laboriously any subtile distinction in the temporal
reference of these two tenses, as in Jas. i. 24 where in ἀπελήλυθεν 171
some have wanted to assume a protracted stay in contrast with κατενόησεν and ἐπελάθετο (see further on this passage in 8 below, p. 202),
Luke iv. 18 where ἀπέσταλκεν in contrast with ἔχρισεν is said to sig-
nify continuance to the present time; nor is it allowable in Heb. xi.
17 to find in the Perf. προσενήνοχεν (in contrast with the Aorists in
vss. 4, 5, 7, 11, etc.) the expression of an act not yet completed,
which would agree least of all with the Perfect; see de Wette.

B. § 137, 3; H. § 706; C. § 605; D. p. 419; J. § 404; G. p. 25.

That on the other hand the Aorist may stand for the 3
Perfect, has been denied indeed by many grammarians in
reference to ordinary Greek usage, and by Winer 276 (259)
in reference to the N. T. also; yet with too little qualification.
As in so many other instances (cf. § 132, 2 p. 156) the question
depends simply upon our connecting the correct idea with the
grammatical terminology. That is to say, inasmuch as the
relation of time expressed by the Perfect is compounded, as it
were, of that of the Aorist and that of the Present — the action
having its beginning in the past (Aorist) but extending either
itself or in its effects down to the time being (Present), — in
cases where the Aorist is used in the sense of the Perfect we
must take this view of the matter: that the Aorist was not
intended to express both relations of the Perfect at once, but
that the writer for the moment withdraws from the present
and places himself in the past, consequently in the position of
a narrator. This position is uniformly the most natural for the

act of composition ; and from it there results of itself, if not a
positive aversion to the Perfect, yet a greater preference for
the Aorist.   The continuance of the action, therefore, and its
working down to the present time, resides, not indeed in
the tense, but in the connection; and the necessary
insertion of this relation is left in every case to the hearer.

The following may serve as examples : Matt. xxiii. 2 ἐπὶ τῆς Μωνσέως
καθέδρας ἐκάθισαν οἱ γραμματεῖς καὶ οἱ Φαρισαῖοι seated themselves (and
still sit), Heb. viii. 1 ἔχομεν ἀρχιερέα ὃς ἐκάθισεν ἐν δεξιᾷ etc. (cf.
x. 12); the common O. T. quotation (Matt. iii. 17 etc.) οὗτός ἐστιν . . .
ἐν ᾧ εὐδόκησα.   In Mark iii. 21 ἐξέστη corresponds closely to the
Presents following (ἔχει, ἐκβάλλει), so that certainly we are not to think
of a merely transient ἔκστασις ; Col. i. 21 νυνὶ δὲ ἀποκατήλλαξεν
(ἀποκατηλλάγητε Lchm.), deWette : hat etc. versöhnet, [A.V. now hath
he reconciled].   In John xv. 8 ἐν τούτῳ ἐδοξάσθη ὁ πατήρ μου, ἵνα καρπὸν
φέρητε, even ancient interpreters explained ἐδοξάσθη by δοξάζεται, see
Lücke ; xiii. 31 νῦν ἐδοξάσθη ὁ υἱὸς etc. (prophetic Aorist, for δοξάσει
follows, cf. 4 below).   Another example is the common ἔγραψα in
letters : not merely in reference to previous letters but also to the one
just written, at its close (1 Pet. v. 12, etc.) ; or, in reference to single
172 sections of it, at the end of that section (1 Cor. ix. 15, etc.).   In fact
the Present γράφω often stands in its stead (1 Cor. iv. 14, etc.), and
even the two forms alternate, 1 John ii. 12 sq., at the most with the
difference that γράφω is employed rather in reference to the entire
letter, ἔγραψα to that portion of it thus far written (deWette).   But
even this distinction is perhaps too delicate, when we take into consideration the ancient use of ἔπεμψα (Acts xxiii. 30 ; Phil. ii. 28 ; Philem.
11) and of the Latin misi, litteras dedi (Krüger § 451) ; so that the
change of tense in the 1st Ep. of John probably arose solely from the
need of variety in connection with the sixfold repetition of the verb.
Respecting Eph. v. 29 and other similar Aorists in aphorisms, etc., see
8 below, p. 201.

4   There is still another case in which the two preterite forms
are interchanged in a way which, as respects the sense at least,
is perfectly indiscriminate, viz. in an impassioned apodosis
after a conditional clause with ἐάν or εἰ — the proleptic
Perfect or Aorist.   This case has caused certain expositors
even to assume an enallage of these tenses and the Future.
This use, however, is of such a general, rhetorical, nature that
it belongs not only to every age (see among others Joseph. B.J.
4, 3, 10 and more examples in Mtth. Gr. § 500), but also to
every language (see, for the Latin, Krüger § 444 Rem. 1).

The natural tense in such clauses is the Perfect; as, 1 Cor. xiii. 1 ἐὰν ταῖς γλώσσαις τῶν ἀνθρώπων λαλῶ ... γέγονα χαλκὸς ἠχῶν etc., Rom. iv. 14 εἰ γὰρ οἱ ἐκ νόμου κληρονόμοι, κεκένωται ἡ πίστις καὶ κατήργηται ἡ ἐπαγγελία, xiv. 23 ὁ διακρινόμενος ἐὰν φάγῃ, κατακέκριται, 2 Pet. ii. 20, and with a Participle taking the place of the conditional clause Rom. xiii. 8.   On the other hand, the Aorist is used in John xv. 6 ἐὰν μή τις μένῃ ἐν ἐμοί, ἐβλήθη ἔξω ὡς τὸ κλῆμα καὶ ἐξηράνθη, καὶ συνάγουσιν αὐτά etc. (see further on this in 8 below, p. 202), Rev. x. 7 ὅταν μέλλῃ σαλπίζειν, καὶ ἐτελέσθη τὸ μυστήριον, 1 Cor. vii. 28 ἐὰν γαμήσῃς, οὐχ ἥμαρτες.   A difference between the two forms exists only in so far as in the Perfect the continuous and in the Aorist the momentary nature of the action comes into prominence.

REMARK. With this obliteration of the difference between the two 𝟝 tenses, which later increased more and more, it does not excite surprise that the MSS. in many passages fluctuate between the two forms. With no verb is this more frequently the case than with δίδωμι, owing to the similarity of the two forms.   Since, too, the context almost everywhere permits both forms to seem admissible, according as the momentary act of giving or the resultant continuous possession is intended to receive prominence, a decision is often difficult, indeed positively impossible; and hence the recent editors, as a matter of fact, often disagree.   Thus, for example, in John v. 36; vi. 32; vii. 19; xvii. 6, 7, 22, 24, Lchm. has decided for ἔδωκα [so Treg. in vi. 32; vii. 19; xvii. 6], Tdf. [with cod. Sin.] for δέδωκα [but in xvii. 6 Tdf. has now adopted ἔδωκα after cod. Sin. etc.]; see besides, the various readings on iv. 12; vii. 22; xii. 49; xiii. 3, 15; xvii. 4, 8, 9, 14; xviii. 9, 11; 1 John iii. 1; iv. 13; v. 20.   Yet here it is to be noticed particularly, that where the sense necessarily requires the pure Aoristic time (e.g. John xviii. 22; xix. 9, etc.), no fluctuation of the 𝟙𝟟𝟛 sort occurs in the MSS.

B. § 137, N. 1; H. § 706; C. § 605; D. cf. p. 420 sq.; J. § 404; G. p. 25.

The use of the Aorist instead of the (Latin, German, 𝟞 English, etc.) Pluperfect in subordinate clauses, especially temporal and relative, is so generally acknowledged, that it is hardly necessary to adduce passages in proof of it from the N. T.; see e.g. Luke vii. 1; John xi. 30, etc.

In leading clauses the case is different.   Here, since the relation of time could not be regarded as adequately defined either by an explanatory conjunction or by immediate connection with other parts of the sentence (as is the case with subordinate clauses), the form of the Pluperfect is incomparably more necessary; and, as matter of fact, the use of the Aorist is found then in Greek authors far more rarely

(see the Grammars as above). Hence, in interpreting the N. T.—
the language of which had already become completely wonted to the
somewhat cumbrous form of the Pluperfect (as is evident from numerous examples) — we shall proceed more safely if we assert such a use
of the Aor. at the most only where the temporal reference is obvious
from the immediate context. Yet here, too, it must hold as a rule,
after the analogy of the exposition given in 3 p. 197, that the author
where he reports in the Aorist facts that have previously occurred (see especially Matt. xiv. 3 sq.) has at once transferred himself
as a narrator to the time then being, leaving his hearer to supply the
temporal relation for himself; as is manifest, for example, in the
passage adduced, from the fact that the writer alternates between the
Aorist and the Imperfect (cf. 7 below). See besides John xviii. 24
(and Lücke in loc.), vi. 22 sq. It is an uncritical procedure, however, when certain interpreters avail themselves of this circumstance
(very precarious as it is, and suggestive of arbitrary interpretation)
in order by its aid to remove all the discrepancies which occur
in different authors relative to the sequence of the events narrated.
For it is far more probable that the writers, in cases where the temporal reference of the Pluperfect is absolutely necessary to
intelligibility, would have made use of it, since the Pluperfect
form was thoroughly current with them. See in this respect particularly Matt. xxvii. 37 (and deWette on the passage), John xviii. 12;
Mark iii. 16 (compared with the narratives of other Evangelists,
John i. 43 cf. Matt. xvi. 18), and still other examples in Winer 275
(259).

B. § 137, 4–6; H. §§ 696 b. 701. 716; C. § 592; D. §§ 426. 427; J. §§ 401, 3. 405; G. pp. 7, 8, 24.

7   The established grammatical distinction between the Aorist
as a purely narrative tense (expressing something momentary)
and the Imperfect as a descriptive tense (expressing something contemporaneous or continuous) holds in all its force in
the N. T., as is plain from many passages e.g. Matt. xxi. 8 sq.;
Mark xi. 15 sqq., etc. But since every writer must be left to
decide to which conception he in narrating the facts will give
the preference, it is quite profitless to adduce all the examples
where an Imperfect appears according to our conception to
be used instead of the Aorist, or, on the other hand, an Aorist
instead of the Imperfect (see e.g. Matt. xxvi. 26 ἔκλασεν ...
174 ἐδίδου ... ἔδωκεν). And it would be still more futile, in
matters which the caprice of the writer alone decides, to try to
establish a general difference of usage.

What has been said respecting the Indicative of the tenses mentioned, holds, of course, also for their respective moods (to wit, those of the Aorist and of the Present). The use of the Participles, however, is in so far more precise, that with the Present Part. to the idea of continuance that of incompleteness or of contemporaneousness (with other predicates) must necessarily be added, and with the Aorist Part. that of the completed (real or imaginary) past has sovereign control, whether the action be momentary or fill the duration of an entire period. (For details see B. § 137, 6; W. § 45, 1.)

For an example of the Imperfect with the force of to be wont, see Mark xv. 6; and of the Imperf. ἐκέλευον, which the Attics prefer to use in the sense of the Aorist, see Acts xvi. 22. Respecting the Imperfect *de conatu* see below, 10 c) p. 205.

The Gnomic Aorist.

B. § 137, N. 5; H. § 707; C. § 606; D. p. 412; J. § 402; G. § 30.

Respecting this Aorist, commonly designated in the grammars the Aorist of habitude[1] with the sense of the Present (in contrast with the Imperfect), it is necessary to make a few general preliminary remarks, as the brief notices hitherto given in the grammars do not suffice to make it understood.

According to Moller's exposition (Philol. Bd. viii. 1) this Aorist, used alike by poets and prose writers of every age, can indeed express habitualness, but just as well and still more frequently the necessity or universality of an action or state; which does not, like habitualness, permit of exceptions. Since now this Aorist was employed for the most part in general propositions deduced from experience, propositions whose contents are valid not only for the past but also for the present and the future, the title "Gnomic Aorist" designates more correctly its essential nature. Its use in Greek occurs not only in similitudes, propositions involving comparisons (as so often in Homer), and ideal pictures (Plato, Phaedr. p. 246 sq.), but also in abstract, maxim-like declarations founded in practical observation (see the examples from Thucyd. and Demosth. given by Moller). The Present (strictly *non-preterite*) nature of this Aorist appears not only from its frequent and immediate connection with Presents (and Perfects), but also from the employment with it of the Subjunctive with ἄν in subordinate clauses (according to B. § 139, 9), especially temporal and relative clauses (e.g. frequently in the above passage of Plato, moreover in Hom. Il. π. 690; Hesiod. ἔργ. 738, etc.)

[1] [In German, *Aorist des Pflegens;* English, *Iterative Aorist.*]

When, then, Winer 277 (260) asserts that the Aorist never in the
N. T. expresses what is habitual, the assertion is well founded so far
forth as the peculiarity of the Aorist in question is not adequately
175 described by the feature cf habitualness; but the occurrence of the
Gnomic Aorist, according to the above description of it, ought at the
same time not to be denied.   For the objection that the whole idiom
presumes too nice an observance of the laws of classic Greek and
greater familiarity with them than can be supposed in the N. T.
authors, may perhaps be decisive for a portion of them, but not for
all.   On the contrary, the employment of the Aorist, as the most
common historic tense, corresponds perfectly to the character of
popular expression, which so gladly endeavors to break away from
the form of abstract presentation and spontaneously falls into the tone
of narration (cf. 3 p. 197).   Observe the form of the Homeric comparisons, or the description of the shield in the Iliad (where moreover
Imperfects and Aorists continually alternate in the narrative).

In the N. T. this is the view to be taken of the comparisons in Jas. i.
10 sq. καυχάσθω ὁ πλούσιος ἐν τῇ ταπεινώσει αὐτοῦ, ὅτι ὡς ἄνθος χόρτου
παρελεύσεται.   ἀνέτειλεν γὰρ ὁ ἥλιος σὺν τῷ καύσωνι καὶ ἐξήρανεν
τὸν χόρτον, καὶ τὸ ἄνθος αὐτοῦ ἐξέπεσεν καὶ ἡ εὐπρέπεια τοῦ προσώπου
αὐτοῦ ἀπώλετο· οὕτως καὶ ὁ πλούσιος ... μαρανθήσεται.   Similar is
1 Pet. i. 24 πᾶσα σὰρξ ὡς χόρτος, καὶ πᾶσα δόξα αὐτῆς ὡς ἄνθος χόρτου·
ἐξηράνθη ὁ χόρτος, καὶ τὸ ἄνθος αὐτοῦ ἐξέπεσεν.   Further Jas. i. 23
ἔοικεν ἀνδρὶ κατανοοῦντι τὸ πρόσωπον ... ἐν ἐσόπτρῳ· κατενόησεν γὰρ
ἑαυτὸν καὶ ἀπελήλυθεν (see 2 p. 197) καὶ εὐθέως ἐπελάθετο ὁποῖος ἦν.
From the same source, viz. the requirements of historic presentation,
proceed the Aorists in Paul's doctrinal analysis in Rom. viii. 29 οὓς
προέγνω, καὶ προώρισεν· ... οὓς δὲ προώρισεν, τούτους καὶ ἐκά-
λεσεν· καὶ οὓς ἐκάλεσεν, τούτους καὶ ἐδικαίωσεν· οὓς δὲ ἐδικαίωσεν,
τούτους καὶ ἐδόξασεν; hence it is not necessary to assume that the
last Aorist (ἐδόξασεν) differs in force from all the rest (cf. Eph. ii. 5 sq.).
Finally, the two Aorists in John xv. 6 quoted in 4 above, p. 199, may
also, in part at least, be included under the head of the Gnomic Aorist,
inasmuch as the thought contains an experimental truth set forth
figuratively, in which the two momentary acts (ἐβλήθη, ἐξηράνθη)
come into manifest antithesis to the continuous one denoted by the
Present (συνάγουσιν).   In Eph. v. 29 οὐδείς ποτε τὴν ἑαυτοῦ σάρκα
ἐμίσησεν, ἀλλὰ ἐκτρέφει καὶ θάλπει αὐτήν, the preterite force is retained
indeed by the particle ποτέ, yet in such a way (as the Presents
following show) that the validity of the statement for the time now
current is, at the same time, included (cf. 3 above p. 197).   A like
reference in James ii. 6 (with ἠτιμάσατε) is at least not excluded.
In John x. 18 αἴρει is probably an early correction for the original

ἦρεν (the first-hand reading of the Vat. and the Sin. MSS.) and the latter word, therefore, probably ought to have been adopted by Tischendorf in his 8th ed.

If, then, it is evident from the exposition given, that the N. T. writers, so far forth as their writings philologically viewed are products of G r e e k modes of thought,[1] must have been led by the very nature of the popular language to use this Aorist as a matter of course when occasion occurred — (and the cases would certainly be 176 more numerous if the compass of the books were greater, since with the present compass they are already pretty numerous), it is also a settled truth on the other side, that where the genius of the Greek language had no opportunity to develop itself freely, the assumption also that this Aorist is used seems to be inadmissible. Hence the Aorists in quotations from the O. T., as Heb. i. 9; x. 5, 6, are not to be brought under this head, since in the Sept. translation the foreign idiom has exercised, particularly in the choice of the Greek T e n s e, too considerable and unmistakable an influence. On the Aorist εὐδόκησα in quotations, see 3 p. 198.

B. § 137, N. 8; H. § 698; C. § 612; D. p. 405 sq.; J. § 396; G. p. 5.

Of the P r e s e n t s which include at the same time a P e r f e c t 9 force (i.e. are translated by us commonly by the Perfect), ἥκω and ἀκούω occur frequently (Luke ix. 9; xvi. 2; 1 Cor. xi. 18; John ii. 4, etc.); ἀπέχειν in the signification *to have received already* (Luther, *dahin haben* Matt. vi. 2 etc., cf. Herm. Vis. 3, 13) is likewise to be found even in Greek authors, see Pape. That in Matt. ii. 4, however, γεννᾶται is not to be taken after the analogy of the (poetic) use of τίκτειν, γεννᾶν (see B. l.c.) in the sense of the Perfect, but as a pure Present, the context shows; see Fritzsche in loc.

B. § 137, N. 10; H. § 699 a.; C. § 609; D. p. 405; J. § 397; G. p. 6.

Lastly, that the Present frequently stands where things still 10 future are spoken of — consequently that the Present comprises within itself the F u t u r e f o r c e of the verb, is a phenomenon so common in all ages and all languages, that in order to describe it we least of all need the unp'ilosophic designation *enallage temporum.*

In order to set the cases in the N. T. which belong under this head in the right light, we will distribute them into the following classes:

[1] That this, as respects style, holds quite peculiarly also of the Epp. of J a m e s and P e t e r, has often, and with reason, been emphasized by the interpreters.

a) The idea of the verb is of such a nature that of itself it includes the force of the Future. This holds (as in our language) pre-eminently of two verbal ideas: that of *coming*, ἔρχεσθαι, together with its synonymes ὑπάγειν, πορεύεσθαι, etc., and that of *becoming*, γίνεσθαι. As in ἥκω (see No. 9) there inheres a Perfect force (I *have come, am present*), so in ἔρχομαι a Future (I *come, shall appear*). For both ideas the language contents itself with the form of the Present, as that which, participating alike in both temporal relations, stands midway between both, including in itself the termination of the one and the beginning of the other. That the Present ἔρχομαι in all the Moods takes the place of εἶμι (which by the Attics was commonly employed in a Future sense, but in the N. T. as a simple verb is not used) has already been mentioned (p. 50) and is plain from innumerable examples; as, John iv. 23 ἔρχεται ὥρα καὶ νῦν ἔστιν, xiv. 3 ἐὰν ἑτοιμάσω τόπον ὑμῖν, πάλιν ἔρχομαι καὶ παραλήμψομαι ὑμᾶς, i. 30 ὀπίσω μου ἔρχεται ἀνήρ etc., especially in the Part. ὁ ἐρχόμενος of the Messiah Matt. iii. 11 etc., the formula in the Apocalypse ὁ ὢν καὶ ὁ ἦν καὶ ὁ ἐρχόμενος of God, τὰ ἐρχόμενα (John xvi. 13), ὁ αἰὼν ὁ ἐρχόμενος (Mark x. 30, etc.) of the future. By the Future
177 ἐλεύσομαι (Matt. ix. 15 ἐλεύσονται ἡμέραι etc., 1 Cor. iv. 19; xvi. 12, etc.) the beginning of the future action is placed at a distance, by the Present it is placed more in the present (to be sure, not always in the immediate present of which the senses take cognizance as John xxi. 3, but also proleptically in the imaginary present of prophetic vision); see under b).

For ἔρχεσθαι in the sense of to go i.e. *to go away*, especially in the Gospels and the Rev. (never in the Acts, by Paul, or in the Ep. to the Heb.; also not in the Sept.), the provincial (cf. the Egyptian papyrus in Mullach's Vulgarspr. p. 20) ὑπάγειν is a favorite word. This word is often used in the future sense — in the Indicative most frequently by John, also in connection with ἔρχεσθαι e.g. viii. 14 πόθεν ἦλθον καὶ ποῦ ὑπάγω· ... πόθεν ἔρχομαι καὶ ποῦ ὑπάγω, cf. xxi. 3; xiv. 28. Πορεύεσθαι also is found in the Present like ἔρχεσθαι and used in company with it, e.g. John xiv. 2, 3, 12; xvi. 28; Acts xx. 22; Rom. xv. 25, etc.; likewise ἀναβαίνειν Matt. xx. 18 etc.; John vii. 8; xx. 17; προάγειν Matt. xxi. 31.

It is hardly worth while to adduce examples of γίνεσθαι — a word in which a future force still more evidently resides; as, Luke xii. 54 sq. λέγετε ὅτι ὄμβρος ἔρχεται, καὶ γίνεται οὕτως· ... λέγετε ὅτι καύσων ἔσται, καὶ γίνεται, cf. xi. 26; xv. 10; Mark xi. 23, etc. Similarly ἐγείρεται John vii. 52.

b) The Future force follows inevitably from the context. In this case the Present as the more common and simple verbal form perfectly takes the place of the Future in all languages, and a multitude of instances can be adduced from the N. T. where not only the Present alone has the future force, as 1 Cor. xv. 32 αὔριον γὰρ ἀποθνήσκομεν,[1] but also where (especially in John) Presents alternate with Futures without a sensible difference, or where (in parallel passages) one writer employs the Present, the other the Future; as, John x. 4, 5, 12–16, 18; xvi. 15, 16, the discourses and similitudes of Jesus in the 14th and 15th chapters; Matt. vii. 8 Tdf.; Gal. ii. 16 (δικαιοῦται ... δικαιωθήσεται), Matt. xxiv. 40 compared with Luke xvii. 34. Further, see those Presents (with the circumflex on the last syllable) which have already been adduced (p. 38) in connection with the Attic formation of the Future, and still others below, § 139, 3 p. 209; 39 p. 235; 61 p. 255. If there is any difference between the two forms, it is that—but only taken quite in the general—which has been already given under a) viz. that the Present is rather used if either the commencement of the future action falls in the present, or (in general maxims, comparisons, etc.) the statement has equal validity for the present as well as the future; the Future, on the other hand, is used with actions whose beginning is projected to a (definite or indefinite) distance (e.g. John xvi. 13 sq.; 20 sq., etc.), or whose occurrence is not definitely to be expected till after the accomplishment of others (expressed perhaps by such general Presents; as, John xvi. 19). Yet this criterion is only an approximate one, since the author certainly allowed himself in many cases to be guided merely by feeling (cf. p. 38); and, for example, even in reference to actions purely future seems designedly to have chosen the Present, in **178** order to portray the more impressively their closely impending occurrence, as in Matt. xxvi. 2.

c) Finally, under this head belongs the familiar antique usage (see B. l. c.; H. § 702; C. § 594; D. p. 409; **J.** § 398, 2; G. pp. 5, 7; and, for the Latin, Krüger § 446 Anm. 2) by which the Present, and consequently in narration the Imperfect, designates the will, the mere intention, to perform an act; or, according to grammatical terminology, is used *de conatu:* so the Pres. in John x. 32 (διὰ τί) λιθάζετέ με; xiii. 6 σύ μου νίπτεις τοὺς πόδας; the Imperf. in Luke i. 59 ἐκάλουν αὐτὸ Ζαχαρίαν (cf. 60), Acts vii. 26 συνήλλασσεν αὐτούς (cf. 27). In Matt. iii. 14, however, in διεκώλυεν the idea of the verb actually passed into execution, and consequently the Imperf. is used in the ordinary sense. That the same holds true of other passages also (as Gal. i. 13; Heb. xi. 17), Winer 269 (253) has already noticed.

As the Participles uniformly reproduce the temporal **11**

---

[1] After Isa. xxii. 13, where, although the Heb. text has the Future, the Sept. (like the German) gives the Present.

reference of their respective Indicatives (see above, 7 p. 201),
so the Present Part. also participates in the nature of the
Present that has just been unfolded, inasmuch as, including
within itself a future force, it often stands for the Future Part. ;
and thus the number of actual Future Parts. in the N. T. has
been greatly diminished.

If then a Present Part. stands in connection with an actual Future,
from the idea of contemporaneousness resident in the Pres.
Part. the notion of futurity results of itself; as, 2 Pet. iii. 10 στοιχεῖα
δὲ καυσούμενα λυθήσονται, Luke i. 35 τὸ γεννώμενον ἐκ σοῦ ἅγιον
κληθήσεται υἱὸς θεοῦ, etc. But Present Participles are frequently
used in a future sense also when not thus connected, particularly if
the future action they designate takes its beginning in the real or
imaginary, the absolute or the relative, present, — if the statement,
therefore, has a validity quite universal. In this sense food is called
in John vi. 27 unqualifiedly ἡ ἀπολλυμένη; gold, in 1 Pet. i. 7, τὸ
ἀπολλύμενον (perishable); the hardened and believers are called by
Paul so often οἱ ἀπολλύμενοι, οἱ σωζόμενοι, 2 Cor. ii. 15 etc.; mortal
men οἱ ἀποθνήσκοντες, Heb. vii. 8 cf. 2 Cor. vi. 9. The blood of Christ
is spoken of as τὸ περὶ πολλῶν ἐκχυννόμενον, Matt. xxvi. 28 (Mark xiv.
24; Luke xxii. 20); all things (ταῦτα πάντα) in the above passage
from 2 Pet. (iii. 11), directly after the Fut. λυθήσονται, are straightway declared to be λυόμενα. To the general proposition in 1 Cor.
xv. 32 (αὔριον ἀποθνήσκομεν) corresponds precisely Matt. vi. 30 τὸν
χόρτον ... αὔριον εἰς κλίβανον βαλλόμενον. To these may be added
also the Present Participles (so far forth as used de conatu) spoken
of in § 144, 11 p. 297. In other cases still, the future force resides
in the signification of the verb, as in the above ὁ ἐρχόμενος, τὰ
ἐρχόμενα, τὰ ἐπερχόμενα (10 a) p. 204), Luke ii. 45 ὑπέστρεψαν ἀναζη-
τοῦντες, 1 Cor. ii. 1 ἦλθον καταγγέλλων, Acts xxi. 2 εὗρον πλοῖον διαπερῶν
(on the passage) εἰς Φοινίκην, 1 Cor. iv. 14 οὐκ ἐντρέπων ὑμᾶς γράφω
ταῦτα.   Cf. with the entire contents of this section the sparsely
occurring examples of the actual Future Participle in § 144, 10 p. 296.

B. § 137, NN. 12, 13; C. §§ 599. 643 h.; J. II. p. 64; G. p. 21.

12   Instances of the Perfect Subjunctive, and still more of the Perfect
and Future Optative (rather rare, moreover, in Greek authors), no
longer occur in the N. T.

Of the Imperatives Passive, besides the Present, that of the
Perfect is in use in the 2d Person (ἔρρωσο, ἔρρωσθε, μέμνησθε,
179 πεφίμωσο), but commonly that of the Aorist in all Persons (ἄρθητι,
βλήθητι, ἁγιασθήτω, γνωσθήτω, φοβήθητε, etc.).

The Moods.

B. § 139; H. §§ 719 sqq.; C. §§ 613 sqq.; D. §§ 509 sqq.; J. §§ 410 sqq.; G. Chap. I.

While as respects the Tenses the language of the N. T. does **1**
not, in the main, depart from the general usage of the Greeks,
but, on the contrary, a few minor irregularities excepted, has
known how to conform to it perfectly, it falls manifestly far
behind that usage in the employment of the relations of Mood.
It would be very hasty, however, to draw a conclusion from
the inferior facility in the use of the Moods respecting the
N. T. use of the Tenses also. For, exact discrimination in
the use of tenses is, as has been already remarked, not only
quite indispensable to mutual intelligibility, but it is far easier
for the mind of a common man, that is to say, one little trained
and taught in literature and language, to become familiar
with a system of temporal forms ready to his hand, even though
diversified, than to master the Modal forms, regulating and
presupposing, as the latter do, a more delicate and cultivated
linguistic sense. The wealth and charm of the Modal expressions, as they appear especially at the flourishing period of
Attic prose in the writings of Thucydides, Plato, Xenophon,
exhibits the complete impress of the literary and refined
genius of the Athenian people. The finer shades of Modal
relation disappear more and more the further the language
departs in time and space from this focus of Greek culture.
Only the zealous study of the language of Hellenic culture,
the aspiration after intellectual development in the Hellenic
sense, could render it possible for later authors, such as Lucian,
Plutarch, Arrian, etc., to acquire a beauty and finish of diction
approximating, although never attaining, to that of the
flourishing period. Since the N. T. authors were far from
indulging in any such endeavor, but on the contrary, as the
repositories of a new intellectual movement found themselves
almost in direct antagonism to it, they were little concerned with the acquisition (toilsome at the best) of Greek
phraseology in its more refined development; — all the less as
they were primarily interested only in rendering themselves **180**
plain and intelligible to their own countrymen, who, as a
whole, were certainly far removed at that time from such
culture. Foreign influences, — partly the general influence
of the Latin language upon the Greek, partly that of the

Hebrew, and in particular of the translation of the Bible (which is extremely restricted in its use of the Moods) into the language of the N. T. writers, — certainly contributed here also to the far greater imperfection of expression which characterizes the N. T. ; for, as respects the Moods, it presents no inconsiderable contrast to the language of contemporary — in fact, much later — profane writers, and even of ecclesiastical writers also.   Again, however, L u k e's language, particularly in the Acts, is that which employs the Modal relations with more certainty and precision.

The Subjunctive and Optative in Simple Sentences.

B. § 139, m. 2; H. § 720 c.; C. § 647; D. § 516; J. § 417; G. § 88.

The Conjunctivus dubitativus or deliberativus. This Subjunctive is found sometimes standing quite alone in all three Persons; sometimes, as occurs so often in Greek and Latin, in immediate connection (i.e. without the intervention of conjunctions) with the Indicatives βούλει, θέλεις.

Examples of the 1st Person are, Rom. vi. 1 ἐπιμένωμεν τῇ ἁμαρτίᾳ; 15 ἁμαρτήσωμεν; 1 Cor. iv. 21 ἐν ῥάβδῳ ἔλθω; vi. 15 ποιήσω; xi. 22 τί εἴπω ὑμῖν; ἐπαινέσω ὑμᾶς ἐν τούτῳ; οὐκ ἐπαινῶ, John xviii. 11 οὐ μὴ πίω αὐτό;   of the 2d Person : Matt. xxiii. 33 πῶς φύγητε ἀπὸ τῆς κρίσεως;   of the 3d Person : Luke xxiii. 31 ἐν τῷ ξηρῷ τί γένηται; Matt. xxvi. 54 πῶς οὖν πληρωθῶσιν αἱ γραφαί; Rom. x. 14 Lchm. [Treg.; Tdf. ℵ* bis].   In connection with βούλει etc. it is frequent: θέλεις εἴπωμεν (Luke ix. 54), θέλεις συλλέξωμεν (Matt. xiii. 28), τί θέλετε ποιήσω ὑμῖν (Matt. xx. 32 etc.), τίνα θέλετε ἀπολύσω ὑμῖν (Matt. xxvii. 17, 21 etc.), βούλεσθε ἀπολύσω ὑμῖν τὸν βασιλέα τῶν Ἰουδαίων (John xviii. 39), etc.   (Cf. the similar construction with ἀφεῖναι in 4 p. 210.)

That instead of this Subj·· nctive the F u t u r e should be substituted (hence frequently found also as a variant, Rom. vi. 15 ; Matt. xiii. 28 ; xxvi. 17 ; Mark xiv. 12 ; Luke xxii. 9 ; xi. 5, etc.) is, considering the internal and external affinity of the two forms, perfectly grammatical ; as, John v. 47 πῶς πιστεύσετε; Acts iv. 16 Lchm. τί ποιήσομεν; Rom. x. 14 Tdf. ℵ* πῶς ἀκούσονται; Cf. besides, with interrogative clauses, 61 p. 254, and Lob. Phryn. 734.   Respecting the addition of ἵνα after θέλεις etc. see 41 p. 236.

3   REMARK. Since the Subjunctive in this sense was quite current in N. T. Greek, it may be doubted whether in the N. T. the form of the I n d i c a t i v e P r e s e n t instead of the Subjunctive is admissible, or the Indicative if thoroughly established critically can be taken in this

way.   Here belongs the consideration of John x.. 47 τί ποιοῦμεν, ὅτι
οὗτος ὁ ἄνθρωπος πολλὰ ποιεῖ σημεῖα; This sentence is in form and
substance almost identical with those above, so that it seems rather
too artificial to assume with Winer 284 (267) a difference in s i g n i f i - 181
c a t i o n between this τί ποιοῦμεν and the ordinary τί ποιήσομεν or
ποιήσωμεν (Acts iv. 16) ; on the contrary, the simplest interpretation
(which corresponds also to the popular usage, *was thun wir* equiv.
to *was sollen wir thun*, [*what do we* equiv. to *what are we to do*]) is
not only adequate, but may be justified by usage also.   For we must
consider here 1) that the first stages of this use in free conversational
style are found even in the earlier writers (see Bhdy. p. 396) ;
2) that in later writers, or those who had no positive need of accuracy
of expression, the usage doubtless extended itself still more ; [1] and
3) that the form ποιοῦμεν belongs to those c i r c u m f l e x e d Presents
(treated of above, p. 38) which are represented in the vers. Ital. by
the Future (*faciemus*, in the Vulg. on the other hand *facimus*, cf.
ποιῶ in Matt. xxvi. 18 var.).   Therefore ποιοῦμεν here is nothing more
or less than a Present, which, according to § 137, 10 b) p. 204 sq., includes the force of the Future ; and as a trustworthy witness of the
mode of expression current among the people ought not to be called in
question.

Quite in the same way was the word π α ρ α ζ η λ ο ῦ μ ε ν in 1 Cor. x.
22 taken by a portion of the ancient translations (*æmulemur* not
æmulabimur),— an interpretation which appears to be in no wise
unsuited to the sense of the passage, although the more recent expositors (though not Rückert) reject it.   Cf. further the Indic. Pres.
with ἐάν, ὅταν, ἵνα below, 23 p. 222, 39 p. 234.

B. § 139, m. 3; H. § 720 a.; C. § 628; D. § 516; J. § 416; G. § 85.

Conjunctivus adhortativus.   This Subjunctive also 4
is very common, especially in the 1st Pers. Plural, as ἄγωμεν,
φάγωμεν καὶ πίωμεν, γρηγορῶμεν καὶ νήφωμεν, ἐπὶ τὴν τελειό-
τητα φερώμεθα etc. ; rare in the 1st Pers. Singular, Acts vii. 34
(after Exod. iii. 10) νῦν δεῦρο ἀποστείλω σε.   The relationship
between this Subjunctive and a declaration expressed by the
Fut. Indic. is obvious ; hence both verbal forms are united
with almost the same force in Rev. xix. 7.   And in many
passages where the sense admits of both acceptations the MSS.

[1] Cf. the completely analogous τί ποιοῦμεν in Pseudo-Luc. Asin. 25, (as several
MSS. give in Luc. Pisc. 10 also) ; τί δρῶμεν ; φεύγομεν ἢ μένομεν ; Alciphr. 1, 11
Mein. ; Arr. Exped. 7, 11, 2 (where Krüger rashly emends πράττωσιν and λέγωσιν);
Lucian 38, 16 ; 44, 53 ; 47, 4. 14 ; Acta Petr. et Paul. 45, and the quite common
use (noticed also below § 148, 10 p. 353) of the Indicative with μήποτε.

27

(and editions) waver between the two forms, — as particularly
in the above passage from Acts, where formerly ἀποστελῶ was
read ; and, on the other hand, the Subjunctive was read where
now we have Futures: Jas. iv. 13 ; Heb. vi. 3.

Also in the much-debated passage (see Winer 286 (268 sq.)) Jas.
iv. 15, the text of which is very uncertain, the Future seems in both
cases to deserve the preference (ζήσομεν ... ποιήσομεν [so Tdf. Treg.
cod. Sin.]) ; but there are other difficulties besides, see § 149, 8 d)
p. 362.

Peculiar to this Subjunctive is the almost pleonastic prefixing
of the Imperative ἄφες *let* (analogous to the Latin *fac, cave*
182 before Subjunctives, and similar to the use of θέλεις, βούλει in 2
p. 208), supposed to be a provincialism current in the colloquial
language of those regions.

Its use is, therefore, especially characteristic of the Synoptists (cf.
ὑπάγω in § 137, 10 a) p. 204), and is found as well with the 1st Pers.
S i n g u l a r of the Subjunct. following, ἄφες ἐκβάλω *let me pull out*
Matt. vii. 4 ; Luke vi. 42, as with the 1st Pers. P l u r a l ἄφες ἴδωμεν
Matt. xxvii. 49, for which in Mark xv. 36 we find the Impera. also in
the Plur. ἄφετε ἴδωμεν. Cf. ἄγε etc. p. 70.   On the force of the
verb ἀφεῖναι for ἐᾶσαι (the two verbs are interchanged in the MSS. in
Acts v. 38) and the common construction with the Infin., see the
lexicons and § 140, 1 p. 258.

5   REMARK. That for t h i s Subjunctive also the I n d i c a t i v e
P r e s e n t could be substituted, even in the more negligent popular
language, is hardly conceivable : because 1) the proposition would
then be destitute of any intimation how the Indicative is to be taken
(which with the deliberative Subjunc. was still given by the interrogative form) ; and because 2) here the middle term, as it were, is
wanting, viz. the Fut. Indic., for which in such cases the Pres. Indic.
is first wont to appear, see 3 p. 209, 23 p. 222, 39 p. 234. For even
the Future cannot directly take the place of this Subjunct., since it
imparts to the sentence at once instead of the Imperative force the
character of a direct assertion. Hence Lchm. in Gal. vi. 10 in his
larger edition instead of ἐ ρ γ α ζ ό μ ε θ α has restored the Subjunct.
[Treg. Tdf.] ; yet the Indic.[1] also, in the p r o p e r force of the Pres.
Indic., gives a sense not to be rejected, see Mey. p. 306. The Pres.
ἐρχόμεθα, however, in John xxi. 3 rests on the principle in § 137, 10 a)
p. 204 ; so too ἐρχόμεθα, πορευόμεθα, often in the Apocrypha.

[1] To the ἐργαζώμεθα in codd. Vat. and Sin. (so frequently are ο and ω interchanged) the less importar.ce is to be attached, as both MSS. just before give ἔχωμεν
instead of ἔχομεν which is alone correct.

B. § 139, m. 4; H. § 720 b.; C. § 628; D. p. 413; J. § 120, 3; G. § 86.

The limitations in reference to the **negative Imperative** **6**
and the **Aorist Subjunctive** as its substitute (viz. that
the former expresses a continued or repeated, the latter a single
or momentary, prohibition, etc.) are observed in the N. T. very
rigidly and without exception; see e.g. the Sermon on the
Mount throughout.   Consequently in the Present only the
Imperative is used: μὴ γράφε, μὴ κρίνετε, μὴ φοβοῦ, μὴ
φοβεῖσθε; in the Aorist in the Second Pers. only the
Subjunctive: μὴ νομίσῃς, μὴ νομίσητε, μὴ ἀποστραφῇς, μὴ
κριθῆτε, μὴ φοβηθῆτε (not φοβήθητε, cf. Matt. x. 26 and 28)
etc.; but in the Third Pers. the Imperative in both instances:
μὴ χωριζέτω, μὴ ἐσθιέτω, μὴ γνώτω, μὴ καταβάτω, μὴ ἐπιστρε-
ψάτω.

B. § 139, mm. 5, 6; H. § 845; C. § 627; D. § 544; J. § 748; G. § 89.

Owing to the great external similarity between the form of   **7**
the (Aorist) Subjunctive and that of the Future, and the affinity
of the two modes of expression, there occurred, as is well
known, very early (see the examples from Homer in B. l.c.) an
interchange or intermingling of the two forms.   In the classic
period that followed, indeed, the use of these forms was settled;
but in later writers considerable vacillation in the employment
of them is again discernible.   Hence the frequent combination **183**
of the Subjunctive and the Future to form a single proposition
or thought in the O. T. as well as the New;[1] hence the fluctuation, recurring every where (and already remarked in 2
and 4 above), between the two forms as preserved by the MSS.,
especially where only the change of a letter is involved (ο and
ω, ε and η, see 8 below); hence the reproduction and explanation of a Future form by the Subjunctive in the ancient
exegetical writings, glossographies, etc.(see Lob. Phryn. p. 723).

Thus, then, the two forms alternate without the slightest
difference in signification (cf. 2 p. 208) after the combined particles οὐ μή, a combination which is very common in all parts
of the N. T. (occurring close upon one hundred times).   Yet, ·
on the whole, here the Subjunctive is the prevalent form;

___

[1] E.g. Lev. x. 6; Deut. xxix. 13; Isa. vi. 10; Matt. vii. 6; xiii. 15 quotn., Luke
i. 15; viii. 17; xi. 5, 7 Tdf.; xii. 58; xxii. 17 sqq.; xxii. 30; John vi. 37; x. 28;
xii. 40 quotn.; Phil. ii. 11 Tdf.; Rev. iii. 9; ix. 5, 6; xv. 4; xix. 7; xxii. 14,—a
portion of these, however, allow themselves to be construed and explained according
to the analogy of the usage treated of § 151, 9 p. 382.

and, moreover, in those cases where the (Aor.) Subjunctive differs essentially in form from the Future (ἔλθῃ, πίω, συνῆτε, εὑρεθῇ, κλεισθῶσιν, etc.), is handed down for the most part without any variation; far less frequently (and often only as an isolated variant) the Future.

As the Future is often used in the exegetical writings of the Church Fathers instead of the Subjunctive preserved in the N. T. text, all the doubtfully transmitted Future forms awaken the suspicion that they originally served (either as marginal glosses or elsewhere) only to explain the Subjunctives, and then subsequently passed over into a portion of the mss. Such passages are Mark x. 15 εἰσέλθῃ (D εἰσελεύσεται), xiii. 2 καταλυθῇ (var. καταλυθήσεται [so Sin. without μή]), Luke xxii. 16 φάγω (D φάγομαι), 1 Thess. v. 3 ἐκφύγωσιν (var. ἐκφεύξονται). The Future form is firmly established only in Matt. xvi. 22 οὐ μὴ ἔσται without var.; has preponderant authority in Luke xxi. 33 παρελεύσονται [so Sin.]; while the authorities are equally divided between the two forms [Sin. gives Fut.] in Mark xiii. 31; Heb. x. 17 (cf. Jer. xxxviii. 34), Rev. ix. 6; xviii. 14.[1] Cf. besides the examples in the following paragraph.

The identity in signification of the Subjunctive and the Future after οὐ μή is established unquestionably: not only by quotations from the O. T. like Matt. xiii. 14 ἀκούσετε καὶ οὐ μὴ συνῆτε, βλέψετε καὶ οὐ μὴ ἴδητε (where after the example 184 of the Sept. the Hebr. Future is rendered by the Subjunctive), but also by such passages as Matt. xxiv. 21 οἵα οὐ γέγονεν, οὐδ᾽ οὐ μὴ γένηται, John x. 28 οὐ μὴ ἀπόλωνται ... καὶ οὐχ ἁρπάσει τις, xi. 26 οὐ μὴ ἀποθάνῃ εἰς τὸν αἰῶνα, Matt. xxiv. 35 (παρελεύσεται ... οὐ μὴ παρέλθωσιν) cf. with Luke xxi. 33; Heb. x. 17 Lchm. [Treg. Tdf. cod. Sin.] cf. with viii. 12; Luke i. 15; xxi. 18; John vi. 37 (viii. 12); Rev. xv. 4. Hence the ancient versions give the Future almost uniformly — for which, indeed, the (synonymous) Pres. Indicative often appears as a variant, and the Subjunctive without var. only in the passages designated in 18 below, p. 218.

That the N. T. writers employed this construction with οὐ μή also to designate that form of statement which classic Greek expressed rather by means of οὐ and the Optative with ἄν — see 18 p. 218.

---

[1] In other passages still the Future is sufficiently attested, but not the particles. Thus in Matt. xxiv. 2 οὐ καταλυθήσεται [so Sin.] has been restored instead of οὐ μὴ καταλ.; and so ought we to read likewise in John x. 28 (οὐχ ἁρπάσει [Sin. οὐ μὴ ἁρπάσῃ]), and w th Tdf. [Treg.] also in Luke xxii. 34 (οὐ φωνήσε. [so Sin.]).

Lastly, it is to be noticed particularly, that in the N. T. only
the Aorist Subjunc. (and the Second Aor. as well as the
First, see 8) is used after οὐ μή, and not a single instance of
the Subjunc. Present is found. For in Heb. xiii. 5 the
variant ἐγκαταλείπω [Tdf. cod. Sin.] cannot establish itself
against the received reading (-λίπω [Treg. also]).

B. § 364, m. 6 and p. 376 Note; C. § 627 a.; J. § 748, Obs. 3; G. p. 79 sq.

The much contested canon of Dawes, which, however, Bern- 8
hardy (Syntax p. 402) among recent writers adheres to,
with certain limitations, and defends, — (according to which
only the Subjunc. of the Second Aor. can stand after οὐ μή
and ὅπως in the Active and Middle, otherwise always the
Future) — can hardly be carried through as respects ordinary
Greek usage, least of all, however, in the N. T.

Bernhardy maintains the admissibility of the First Aor. Subjunc.
only in cases where it differs essentially from the Future as respects
form (see 7), consequently in liquid verbs, or where the Future has
the Middle form (ἀκούσομαι etc.), or the circumflexed form (κομῶ etc.):
consequently, everywhere except when the two forms differ externally
only in the vowel of the Mood. But these are the very cases
where in all MSS., as well those of profane literature as of the Old and
New Testaments, the greatest uncertainty occurs in the readings; so
that by the way of criticism, and owing to the great internal and external affinity of the two forms, absolutely no sure result can be
attained either in favor of the one or of the other. Hence indubitable and well-attested Subjunctives of the 1st Aorist,
such as ἀπολέσῃ, ἀπαγγείλῃς, ἀφορμίσῃ, ἐκπλεύσῃς, δείσῃς, ἀπολαύσωμεν,
ought to be allowed to pass as proof of the admissibility of this Subjunctive. In the N. T. also, in almost all cases where the 1st Aor.
Subjunc. and the Future differ only in the Mood-vowel, there occurs
so great a degree of variation in the readings, that there was no other
course left here to the editors, except to follow the authorities, and
put now one form in the text and now the other. Accordingly at 185
present we read after οὐ μή

1) The Future: Matt. xv. 5 τιμήσει; xxvi. 35, Mark xiv. 31
ἀπαρνήσομαι [in Mk. Tdf. -ωμαι, so cod. Sin.]; Mark ix. 41 ἀπολέσει
[Tdf. -σῃ, so Sin.]; Luke x. 19 ἀδικήσει; John iv. 14 διψήσει; x. 5
ἀκολουθήσουσιν [-ωσιν cod. Sin.].

2) The 1st Aorist Subjunctive: Matt. x. 23, Gal. v. 16
τελέσητε; Matt. x. 42 ἀπολέσῃ; xvi. 28 (Mark ix. 1; Luke ix. 27)
γεύσωνται; Matt. xxv. 9 ἀρκέσῃ [Tdf. μήποτε οὐκ ἀρκ., so cod. Sin.];

Mark xvi. 18 βλάψῃ; Luke xviii. 7 ποιήσῃ; Luke xxii. 67, Acts xiii. 41 πιστεύσητε; John viii. 12 περιπατήσῃ; John viii. 51 θεωρήσῃ [-σει cod. Sin.], 52 γεύσηται; xiii. 8 νίψῃς, 38 φωνήσῃ; Rom. iv. 8 λογίσηται; 1 Thess. iv. 15 φθάσωμεν; Heb. viii. 11 διδάξωσιν; 2 Pet. i. 10 πταίσητε; Rev. xviii. 23 φάνῃ.   In almost all these passages, indeed, the other spelling (as Future) is also found, but for the most part far more feebly attested, frequently by single or insignificant MSS.; several times, however, (e.g. in 1 Thess. iv. 15; 2 Pet. i. 10; Acts xiii. 41, etc.) no trace even of a Future form is found among the variants.   Hence in all these cases both Lchm. and Tdf. [so Treg.] have adopted the Subjunctive form.

3) The passages in which — the authorities being pretty equally divided — the editors disagree, seem to be the following: John vi. 35 (πεινάσει Lchm. -σῃ Tdf. [Treg. cod. Sin.], διψήσει Lchm. [Tdf. Treg. cod. Sin.] -σῃ Tdf. [ed. 2]), Gal. iv. 30 (κληρονομήσει Lchm. [Treg. Tdf. cod. Sin.], -σῃ Tdf. [eds. 2, 7]).   Cf. besides Luke xxii. 34, 68; John x. 28, and the Lat. verss. on Rev. ix. 6; xviii. 14.

REMARK. If then, according to the evidence above given (7 and 8), the Future with οὐ μή as a rarer form must be recognized along with the Subjunctive, yet after ὅπως the Subjunctive has decidedly supplanted the Future; inasmuch as, in all the passages (some fifty) with the exception of one (Matt. xxvi. 59), the Subjunctive is given by the authorities almost without the least variation. The Future is found in the MSS. as an isolated reading in Mark v. 23; Acts ix. 12; Rom. iii. 4; ix. 17; 1 Cor. i. 29; and in the above passage Matt. xxvi. 59 also there are still authorities enough [cod. Sin. among them] for the Subjunctive (the reading of cod. Vat. moreover is uncertain [Tdf. gives it as -σωσιν]), so that even here its restoration seems to be required.

Cf. in general respecting the fluctuation of the MSS. in reference to both forms, besides Nos. 2 and 4 above, Nos. 22, 23, 31, 38, 61.

B. § 139, m. 7; H. § 721, 1; C. § 638; D. p. 548; J. § 418, b.; G. § 82.

9   The Optative, which is somewhat rare in the N. T. (see 11), is still used most frequently, agreeably to its name, in expressing a wish, desire; as, Heb. xiii. 21; 1 Thess. v. 23; 2 Thess. ii. 17, etc.

Instead of the Optative the Future is once found, yet with the particle of wishing ὄφελον, Gal. v. 12.

B. § 139, m. 8; H. § 721 b.; C. § 638; D. § 517; J. § 418 Obs. 1; G. § 83.

10   There are also a few examples of the Indicative of a Preterite with a particle of wishing (ὄφελον) to express a wish

which has now become impossible, or, under the existing circumstances, is seen in advance to be incapable of fulfilment: 1 Cor. iv. 8 ὄφελόν γε ἐβασιλεύσατε had ye but attained to lordship (by which the ironical character of what precedes is brought out), Rev. iii. 15 ὄφελον ψυχρὸς ἦς ἢ ζεστός (previously, οὔτε ψυχρὸς εἶ οὔτε ζεστός), 2 Cor. xi. 1 ὄφελον ἀνείχεσθέ μου ... ἀφροσύνης Vulg. *utinam sustineretis* (not *sustineatis*), hence the following ἀλλὰ καὶ ἀνέχεσθέ μου is to be taken correctively (see Meyer); cf. ὄφελον ἐμιμοῦντο Ign. ad Smyrn. 12.

Peculiar is the periphrasis by means of a clause with θέλω εἰ followed by the Aor. Indic., Luke xii. 49 ; see below, 52 p. 246. But that clauses with εἰ without an apodosis following (such as Luke xix. 18 f. 42 etc.) are not clauses of wishing, see § 151, 26 p. 396.

B. § 139, m. 9; H. § 728 sq.; C. § 617; D. § 513 sqq.; J. § 797; G. § 31 sq.

The most considerable departure from ordinary usage as 11 respects the Moods, consists in the fact that the N. T. hardly puts the Optative in use any longer as a Mood of dependence in indirect discourse, particularly after an historic tense. It sometimes employs instead the Indicative in independent discourse, and that, too, far more extensively than was the case among the Greeks ; sometimes it includes the dependent form of statement which the classic language had assigned to the Optative under the form of the Subjunctive. The first of these substitutes was essentially favored by the circumstance, that in accordance with the character of popular language discourses are almost always quoted directly (as in Heb. and the Sept.), and a protracted recital in oblique discourse hardly occurs (§ 141, 1 p. 272). The second, viz. the greater prominence given to the Subjunctive at the expense of the Optative (gradually quite disappearing), may have been a consequence of the general influence of Latin on the later Greek. The proofs of these statements will not only be found in great number below, where we treat of the several forms of dependent clauses, but by the reader who notices the point will be met with everywhere, particularly in the historic writings.

The Optative as a dependent Mood appears most frequently in the writings of Luke ; its use even here, however, is unmistakably on the decrease. In the apocryphal writings of the N. T. it has almost completely disappeared. Cf. 63. p. 256.

B. § 139, m. 10 sqq.   H. § 873; C. § 618; D. § 501; J. § 424; G. § 86.

12   The use of the Particle ἄν (so important in expressing
modal relations) had already become so thoroughly established
in the literary language, that all that is taught in the general
grammar respecting its force holds completely in reference
to the N. T., although in its employment the N. T. is
more sparing, and several of the more delicate constructions
(like the ἄν with the Participle and the Infin. 20 p. 219) are
no longer met with. The following points may be noticed
respecting the use of this particle in the N. T. :

B. § 139, m. 12 a); H. § 704; C. § 616 b.; D. § 515; J. II. 93; G. § 30. 2.

13   Examples of ἄν with an Indicative Preterite to denote repetition,
though not numerous, are completely established: Mark vi. 56 ὅπου
187 ἄν [ἐὰν Tdf. cod. Sin.] εἰσεπορεύετο ... ἐτίθεσαν τοὺς ἀσθενοῦντας · καὶ
ὅσοι ἄν ἥπτοντο [ἥψαντο Lchm. Tdf. Treg. cod. Sin.] αὐτοῦ ἐσώζοντο,
Acts ii. 45 ; iv. 35 καθότι ἄν τις χρείαν εἶχεν. This principle appears to
explain also 1 Cor. xii. 2 (ὡς ἄν ἥγεσθε), see more at length in § 151,
10 p. 383.

B. § 139, m. 12 b); H. §§ 746, 752; C. § 636; D. p. 539 sq.; J. II. 93; G. § 37, 3.

14   The ordinary force of a Preterite Indicative with ἄν,
so far forth as it denotes the non-existence or impossibility of
fulfilment of the declaration contained therein, occurs as a
rule (just as in Greek authors) in the apodosis of the fourth
case of hypothesis (cf. below, 25 p. 224).

Yet there are also several examples of this Mood without the
customary protasis, which in such case is either reserved in
the mind or finds expression in a different form: Luke xix. 23 κἀγὼ
ἐλθὼν σὺν τόκῳ ἄν αὐτὸ ἔπραξα, where the protasis is contained in the
preceding interrogative clause διὰ τί οὐκ ἔδωκας etc.; similar is Matt.
xxv. 27, see the following paragraph; Heb. x. 2 ἐπεὶ οὐκ ἄν ἐπαύσαντο
(cf. ix. 26 in No. 15) where the unfulfilled condition to be supplied in
thought lies in the ἐπεί (for otherwise, sc. εἰ ἐδύνατο, see § 149, 5 p. 359).

B. § 139, m. 13; H. §§ 703, 745 a.; C. § 632; D. pp. 541, 411; J. §§ 398, 3; G. p. 97 sqq.

15   The case here mentioned of the (apparent) omission of
ἄν with predicates such as ἔδει, ἀνῆκεν, ἐδύνατο, etc., is by no
means rare in the later language (nurtured perhaps by the
analogous use of the Latin, debebam, poteram, etc.), or in the
N. T. also. But it is very erroneous grammatically, and a

supposition prompted solely by our modern ideas of idiom, to think that the particle in such cases is only o m i t t e d. On the contrary, we are to conceive of the matter thus : that there is no addition whatever of ἄν to the form of statement, since not the necessity or possibility of the fact is denied (that would be expressed by ἔδει ἄν etc.), but the fact itself.

Very instructive examples from the N. T. may be added to those given in the grammar ; as, Matt. xxv. 27 ἔδει σε βαλεῖν τὸ ἀργύριόν μου τοῖς τραπεζίταις, καὶ ἐλθὼν ἐγὼ ἂν ἐκομισάμην τὸ ἐμὸν σὺν τόκῳ where the addition of ἄν was as necessary in the second clause, as the simple Imperfect in the first, Acts xxiv. 19 οὓς ἔδει ἐπὶ σοῦ παρεῖναι, εἴ τι ἔχοιεν πρὸς ἐμέ (therefore, as the Optative shows, not the fourth form of hypothesis).   See besides, ἔ δ ε ι in Matt. xviii. 33 ; xxiii. 23 ; Acts xxvii. 21 ; 2 Cor. ii. 3 ; Heb. ix. 26 ; ἀνῆκεν in Eph. v. 4 Lchm. [Tdf. Treg. cod. Sin.] ; Col. iii. 18 ; κ α θ ῆ κ ε ν Acts xxii. 22 ; ὤ φ ε ι λ ο ν 1 Cor. v. 10 ; 2 Cor. xii. 11 ; ἠ δ ύ ν α τ ο Acts xxvi. 32 ; John ix. 33, — on which last two passages and some others 27 c) p. 226 below is also to be compared.

A similar difference between our mode of expression and the Greek idiom occurs in connection with the ideas *to wish, be willing, like ;* as, ἐ β ο υ λ ό μ η ν (our *I should like*), Acts xxv. 22 ἐβουλόμην τοῦ ἀνθρώπου ἀκοῦσαι, Philem. 13 ; η ὐ χ ό μ η ν, Rom. ix. 3 ηὐχόμην ἀνάθεμα εἶναι . . . ὑπὲρ τῶν ἀδελφῶν μου etc., (in these passages the addition of ἄν weakens the sense, since then the existence, the possibility, of the w i s h i t s e l f is put in question) ; — and with the predicates κ α λ ὸ ν ἦ ν, 188 κ ρ ε ῖ τ τ ο ν ἦ ν (cf. the Latin *melius, aequum fuit,* Krüger § 463) : Matt. xxvi. 24 ; Mark xiv. 21 (see 27 c) p. 226), 2 Pet. ii. 21 κρεῖττον ἦν αὐτοῖς μὴ ἐπεγνωκέναι ἢ etc.   See Herm. de Part. ἄν p. 60.   Paul, according to his custom (§ 129, 20 p. 136), omits in these cases the copula altogether, as 1 Cor. ix. 15 καλὸν γάρ μοι μᾶλλον ἀποθανεῖν ἢ etc.

B. § 139, m. 14 ; H. § 757 ; C. § 619 ; D. p. 544 ; J. § 428 ; G. § 36, 2.

The Particle ἄν (after Relatives ἐάν also, see p. 72) is used 16 in the N. T. by far most frequently with the S u b j u n c t i v e. On the character of this form of statement — (the particle belonging rather to the p r o n o u n etc. than to the verb), see the general grammars ; and on its employment, see below, under dependent clauses.

B. § 139, m. 15 ; H. § 722 ; C. § 636 ; D. § 504 ; J. § 425 ; G. § 39.

On the other hand, the O p t a t i v e with ἄν (the Mood 17 formerly employed so frequently to express subjective opinion

28

or softened assertion, which Attic urbanity so readily substitutes in place of the most positive affirmations), has passed almost entirely out of use.

In general, this Mood bears so decidedly the peculiar impress of Greek diction that most of the N. T. writers seem hardly any longer to be acquainted with it (even John does not, for in xiii. 24 the Optative is no longer read), and it is still found only in the writings of Luke, who approximates nearest to the classic Greek style: — in the Gospel (according to the older editions) five times, and eight times in the Acts, which small number recent criticism has again diminished (see for example Luke xv. 26; xviii. 36; Acts ii. 12 Lchm. [Tdf. Treg.], xvii. 20 Lchm. [Tdf. Treg.], xxi. 33 Lchm.). This Mood is described in the grammar as a modification of the independent form of statement; hence even in Luke it never stands after conjunctions or relatives. It commonly appears in (direct and indirect) interrogative clauses, in which it was especially favorite with the Greeks also (see H. below p. 254); in a non-interrogative direct clause it is found but once, Acts xxvi. 29.

18   REMARK. As a substitute for this characteristic Greek Mood the Future is introduced in positive sentences, e.g. in a supposed case (Lat. dicat, dixerit aliquis) 1 Cor. xv. 35; Jas. ii. 18 ἐρεῖ τις, Rom. ix. 19; xi. 19 ἐρεῖς οὖν, v. 7 μόλις γὰρ ὑπὲρ δικαίου τις ἀποθανεῖται; further, very commonly in direct and indirect questions, 1 Cor. xv. 29 ἐπεὶ τί ποιήσουσιν; Rom. iii. 6 ἐπεὶ πῶς κρινεῖ ὁ θεός; (sc. εἰ ἄδικος εἴη, see § 149, 5 p. 359), vi. 1 τί οὖν ἐροῦμεν; Mark iv. 13 οὐκ οἴδατε ... πῶς πάσας τὰς παραβολὰς γνώσεσθε; etc. In many such and similar passages the Greeks would probably have used the Optative with ἄν; although it cannot be denied also that the mode of expression with the Future has foundation in usage, and strictly nothing more can be inferred from the above examples than a certain aversion (or ignorance) on the part of the N. T. language as respects this form of statement, where the possibility of employing it lay so close at hand.

In negative clauses the substituted mode of expression has taken on a more recognizable form, inasmuch as for οὐκ ἄν with the Optative following (according to 7 p. 212) the Subjunctive (or the Future) with οὐ μή appears, — a construction which, as is well known (cf. B.

189 § 139, 6), was interchanged with the other even by the Greeks. As examples of this, may be set down especially those passages where the ancient versions either unanimously or in part employ the Lat. Subjunctive: Mark xiii. 2 οὐ μὴ ἀφεθῇ λίθος ἐπὶ λίθῳ, ὃς οὐ μὴ καταλυθῇ (Vulg. destruatur), Matt. xxv. 9 μήποτε οὐ μὴ ἀρκέσῃ ἡμῖν καὶ ὑμῖν (Vulg. sufficiat), Luke xviii. 29 οὐ μὴ λάβῃ (Vulg. recipiat), John xi. 56 οὐ μὴ ἔλθῃ (Vulg. veniat. veniet).

B. § 139, m. 16; H. § 760; C. § 617 d.; J. §§ 405, 2; 829; G. § 20, N. 1 sq.

The rule, carefully observed in good prose, that in relative **19**
and other subordinate clauses, whenever the leading thought
falls in the future, the action which precedes and is completed
before it is expressed by the Aorist Subjunc. with ἄν (and
likewise in Latin by the Fut. exactum, or Pluperf. Subjunc.
in its stead), is but seldom disregarded in the N. T. also.

Examples of the regular construction, especially after relatives
(ὅς ἄν, ὅσα ἄν, ὅπου ἄν) as well as after conjunctions compounded with
ἄν (ἕως ἄν, ἐάν, ὅταν), are found abundantly in all parts of the N. T.
That the freer usage also, that is to say the simple Future and even
the Present Indic., is found in such clauses is to be expected, since
instances of it can be pointed out even in Greek and Latin writers;
e.g. after ὅστις Matt. v. 39 Tdf. [eds. 2, 7] ὅστις σε ῥαπίσει . . .
στρέψον αὐτῷ etc. (Lchm. [Tdf. Treg. cod. Sin.] ῥαπίζει), 41 ; vii. 24
πᾶς ὅστις ἀκούει μου τοὺς λόγους καὶ ποιεῖ αὐτοὺς ὁμοιώσω αὐτὸν etc.,
x. 32 ὅστις ὁμολογήσει . . . ὁμολογήσω κἀγὼ etc.

A different liberty, viz. the dropping of ἄν with the Subjunctive, is
spoken of below: 31 p. 228, 33 p. 230.

B. § 139, m. 17 sq.; H. §§ 783, 803; C. § 658 a.; D. p. 543; J. § 429; G. § 41, cf. § 42, 3 NN. 1, 2.

The more delicate use of the particle ἄν, by which when **20**
joined to the Infinitive and Participle it imparts to
these verbal forms the modal force of an Optative or Indicative
with ἄν, is altogether unknown to the N. T.

It is likewise not found with the Infin. after the verbs δοκεῖν, ἐλπίζειν,
etc. (see § 140, 2 p. 259), and hardly can the solitary instance of the
sort which actually occurs (2 Cor. x. 9) be regarded as a remnant of
the ancient construction after δοκεῖν. Rather, in the words μὴ δόξω
ὡς ἄν ἐκφοβεῖν ὑμᾶς the expression ὡς ἄν (which two words were so
often heard, and by later writers used more and more frequently, in
immediate connection; see the examples from Lucian in Du Mesnil,
Stolper Progr. 1867, p. 24) has become for the apostle, as it were, a
single word with the signification *quasi*, just as in Greek ὡσπερανεί,
later ὡσανεί (B. § 151, IV. 3), is used in the same sense. In further
confirmation of this interpretation, compare 1 Cor. vii. 5 μὴ ἀποστερεῖτε
ἀλλήλους, εἰ μήτι ἄν ἐκ συμφώνου πρὸς καιρόν, where ἄν also stands
without any verb. To supply here the Optative, such as γένοιτο,
in order to connect ἄν with it (as similar phenomena in a few passages
of the Greek poets are to be explained, see Hartung II. p. 330)
militates with the apostle's usage (see 17 p. 217). Hence we must
supply, either the Indicative after the analogy of 2 Cor. xiii. 5 εἰ μήτ

ἀδόκιμοί ἐστε), or the Subjunctive according to Luke ix. 13 (εἰ μήτι ...
190 ἀγοράσωμεν), and combine ἄν, again in the sense of *somehow, perchance,*
with the restrictive particle εἰ μήτι so as to form one whole.[1]

A r e p e t i t i o n of ἄν in lengthened sentences, or after the insertion of parenthetic thoughts, nowhere occurs.

A. Conditional Sentences.

Since the various forms of conditional sentences rest upon
the general basis given above and in the grammars, it may
suffice here to assume that the four chief forms of these sentences are familiar, and to point out the d e v i a t i o n s from the
same which occur in the writings of the N. T.

B. § 139, m. 22-24; H. § 745 sqq.; C. § 631 sq.; D. § 502; J. § 851; G. § 47 sq.

21   The f i r s t t w o forms of hypothesis (εἰ with the Indicative,
ἐάν with the Subjunctive) are by far the most frequent, and
the distinction given in the grammars is in general applicable
to them in the N. T. But the majority of the writers were so
much accustomed to these two modes of stating an hypothesis,
that they (in harmony with the general observation made in
11 p. 215) manifestly avoided the third case, εἰ with the
Optative, preferring to substitute for it one of the first two (cf.
22 below.)

See the more extended treatment of this point, and the few instances
of εἰ with the Optative still extant, in 24 below, p. 223. Examples of
the first two species, however, are found everywhere. The difference
between them (described in the grammars) is plainly to be recognized
in sentences where both are used in close proximity; as, Gal. i. 8, 9,
where the hypothesis expressed in the 8th verse by ἐάν with the Subjunctive is resumed or repeated in the 9th with greater energy and
definiteness by εἰ with the Indicative. So in Acts v. 38, 39.

B. § 139, m. 25; H. § 747 b.; D. cf. § 513; J. § 854, Obs. 1; G. § 50, 1 NN. 2 and 3.

22   Since the later common Greek writers are pretty negligent
in discriminating between the two particles εἰ and ἐάν and we

---

[1] Possible, however, and not at variance with the character of the N. T. ellipses,
or of Paul's style in particular, is the assumption that ἄν here is to be taken in
the sense of ἐάν and (according to § 151, 23 b. p. 392, 24 b. p. 394, and § 129,
23 p. 137) its predicate to be supplied in an altered form from what precedes
(accordingly here ἀποστερῆτε, or the more general γένηται). The only objection
to this is the extremely rare use of ἄν for ἐάν (see p. 72). As respects the
meaning of the passage, however, it remains a matter of indifference whether we
choose to explain the origin of the ellipsis (which certainly exists here) gram
matically in the one way or the other.

often find in them εἰ with the Subjunctive and ἐάν with the 191
Indicative (see the references in Winer 295 (277)), we might
expect beforehand that the N. T. writers also would not keep
themselves free from such inaccuracies. Of the first case, the
use of εἰ with the Subjunctive, we find, to be sure, accidentally
(for cf. 31 p. 228 and 33 p. 230) no example which is quite
certain ; for in some of them the readings vary, some are set
aside by the MSS. (as Rev. xi. 5 [but cod. Sin. θελήσῃ the
second time]), some are capable of a special interpretation.

The most probable is 1 Cor. ix. 11 εἰ ... ἐσπείραμεν, μέγα εἰ ἡμεῖς
ὑμῶν τὰ σαρκικὰ θερίσωμεν. So Tdf. reads [eds. 2, 7] with the
majority of the MSS. instead of the former Future [Tdf. Treg. cod.
Sin. also] which is found so often as a variant of the Aor. Subjunct.
(see 8 p. 213). Since strictly considered the Greek Optative would
be in place here, in point of fact the Subjunctive as its substitute
(21 p. 220) seems to deserve the preference even on grammatical
grounds. Further, Luke ix. 13 οὐκ εἰσὶν ... εἰ μήτι πορευθέντες ἡμεῖς
ἀγοράσωμεν βρώματα. The Subjunct. here is not only thoroughly
established by the MSS. [cod. Sin. also], but as a *conjunct. dubitativus*
(described above, 2 p. 208) is not at variance with the sense (*unless
perhaps we are to buy*). In classic Greek, however, the Fut. Indic.
would have been used here in preference (see B. § 139 m. 23, and the
example from Xen. An. 4, 7, 3). In 1 Thess. v. 10 (οὐκ ἔθετο etc.) ἵνα,
εἴτε γρηγορῶμεν εἴτε καθεύδωμεν, ἅμα σὺν αὐτῷ ζήσωμεν the Subjunct.
stands rather by the attraction of the Subjunct. of the final clause, to
which it is parenthetic (cf. the quite similar examples in 24 p. 224) ;
and the frequent use of the double conjunction εἴτε ... εἴτε, especially
by Paul (see the Lexx.), caused it, like an unchangeable particle (corresponding to the Latin *sive* ... *sive*), to appear even where out of
regard to the Subjunct. following ἐάντε ought to have stood.[1] The
same holds true of the formula ἐκτὸς εἰ μή, which in like manner
became so established in the signification *except, unless* (1 Tim. v. 19;
1 Cor. xv. 2, see on these § 148, 13 p. 355) that it remained unaltered
even with the Subjunctive : 1 Cor. xiv. 5 ἐκτὸς εἰ μὴ διερμηνεύῃ. Lastly,
in Phil. iii. 12 (εἰ ... καταλάβω) εἰ means *whether*, and belongs under
62 p. 255.

[1] The use of ἐάντε ... ἐάντε in Rom. xiv. 8 might seem to contradict this. But
how little we are warranted in expecting from the N. T. authors accuracy, or
even uniformity, in the employment of the conjunctions as well as of the adverbs
and prepositions, is a point on which probably there is hardly a doubt any longer
among N. T. critics. Compare, for instance, the following paragraph, and also
the detailed statements made above on p. 70 sq., and the chapter below on Particles.
Prepositions, etc.

23   On the other hand, the second case, ἐάν with the Indicative, is given so frequently, that it is to be eliminated as little from the writings of the N. T. as of the Old. See Tdf. N. T. Praef. p. xxvi [ed. 7 p. lvii].

192   It is, indeed, not to be denied that the instances in question almost disappear amid the multitude of those that are grammatically regular, and suspicion may also be raised by the circumstance that hardly a single passage with the Indicative is completely beyond question critically. Yet when we consider that in countless passages with the Subjunctive not the smallest variation is found (which would not be the case if the Indicative were chargeable solely to the copyists), it is far more probable that, where a diversity of readings occurs in such a number of instances, this fact results from the circumstance that the copyists, commentators, etc., early altered the Indicative which gave them offence. When we add to this, that in pretty nearly as many passages ὅταν with the Indicative occurs, and moreover the circumstance that the Latin versions, which render the Aor. Subjunc. very consistently by the fut. exactum, have the first Future in many of these questionable passages, and that the ancient grammarians expressly admit the existence of the usage by their censure of it (see Bekk. An. p. 144; Thom. Mag. p. 132 ed. Ritschl), it is no longer to be disputed that that lax use of the particles ἐάν, ὅταν etc., had at least begun to be practised at the time when the apostles wrote. How far we are authorized to set down merely to the account of the copyists offenses of the kind in the writings of authors who, in earlier or later times, were educated by Greek literature and wrote with Greek models before their eyes, is considered by Klotz ad Devar. II. 468 sqq. and 690.

The decision when the Indicative is to be received into the text, depends, of course, less upon internal grounds, than upon the weight which is attached in every instance to the authorities; and hence the more recent editors differ much in this respect.

To avoid repetition elsewhere we will include here at the same time the passages with ὅταν and the Indicative:

The probability of the Indicative is the greatest in the case of the Future, which according to 8 p. 213 is so often interchanged with the Aor. Subjunct. The most certain instances are Luke xix. 40 ἐὰν σιωπήσουσιν [so Sin.], Rev. iv. 9 ὅταν δώσουσιν [Sin. -ωσιν]; less certain are Luke xi. 12 Tdf. [eds. 2, 7] ἐὰν αἰτήσει [but ed. 8 drops ἐὰν, so Treg. cod. Sin.] (Vulg. petierit), Acts viii. 31 Tdf. [Treg.] ὁδηγήσει (after codd. Vat. and Sin.), 1 Tim. v. 11 Tdf. [eds. 2, 7] ὅταν καταστρηνιάσουσιν [-σωσιν Tdf. Treg. cod. Sin.] (Vulg. *luxuriatae fuerint*); cf. also Matt. vii. 9, 10 Tdf. ed. 7 [ed. 8 drops ἐάν with Lchm. Treg. cod. Sin.]. The Future is well attested besides, though not received, in Matt. x. 19 ὅταν παραδώσουσιν [-ῶσιν Sin.] (*tradent*). Cf. Herm. Vis. 1, 4 (μετανοήσουσιν) ; 2, 2 etc.

If the examples with the Future, owing to the internal affinity between this tense and the Subjunctive, still maintain a certain analogy to Greek usage (cf. the examples from the classics quoted by Klotz as above), the same no longer holds true of the Present, the employment of which (or rather of the particle in connection with it), in the N. T. at least, must be accounted for solely by the indifference beginning to prevail in reference to grammatical precision of expression.   Thus, firmly established are 1 John v. 15 ἄν (i.e. ἐάν) οἴδαμεν [ἴδωμεν Sin.], Mark. xi. 25 ὅταν στήκετε [στῆτε Sin.]; strongly attested are Luke xi. 2 Tdf. [ed. 7] ὅταν προσεύχεσθε [-χησθε ed. 8, so Treg. cod. Sin.], Rom. xiv. 8 Lchm. ἐάντε ἀποθνήσκομεν, Luke vi. 34 Tdf. [eds. 2, 7; Treg.] ἐὰν δανείζετε [δανίσητε Tdf. ed. 8, so cod. Sin.] (Lchm. δανείσητε) ; less so Mark xiii. 7 Tdf. [eds. 2, 7] ὅταν ἀκούετε ['ex errore de B', yet so Treg.; Tdf. ed. 8 ἀκούσητε, so cod. Sin. Lchm.], Rom. ii. 14 var. ὅταν ποιοῦσιν.

Lastly the Preterite. Indubitable instances of this are found only **193** with ὅταν owing to its prevalent temporal force, so that it stands then completely for ὅτε (*cum*), as ἐάν stands for εἰ ; from this it follows that in such fixed compounds the original force of the particle ἄν begins gradually to disappear in the N. T. (cf. 20 p. 219). Thus, firmly established are Mark iii. 11 ὅταν ἐθεώρουν, Rev. viii. 1 ὅταν ἤνοιξεν [ὅτε cod. Sin.]; and hardly to be doubted is Mark xi. 19 Tdf. [Treg. cod. Sin.] ὅταν ἐγένετο, (Lchm. ὅτε).

The Indicative is found besides in isolated instances with both particles, especially in codd. D and E ; as, Matt. v. 11 ; x. 23 ; Mark xiii. 4 ; Luke xi. 21 ; xiii. 28 ; John viii. 36 ; Acts viii. 31 (Vulg. *ostenderit*). Examples from the Sept. are Ex. viii. 21 ; Lev. i. 14 ; 1 Sam. xvii. 34 ; Job xxii. 3 ; Ps. xlvii. 4 (Alex.) ; cxix. 7 ; cxviii. 32, and there are innumerable instances in the Apocrypha in which the particle ἄν has lost all force.

B. § 139, m. 26; H. § 748; C. § 631 d.; D. p. 539; J. § 855; G. § 50, 2.

That the use of the third form of hypothesis, εἰ with the **24** Optative, is but very limited has already been remarked, 21 p. 220.   Of the case in its fully developed form (in the protasis εἰ with the Opt., in the apodosis the Opt. with ἄν), not even a single instance is found ; on the contrary, in the only passage where the Opt. with ἄν stands in the leading clause, and consequently there was opportunity for the full construction, this form of hypothesis was nevertheless not employed.

The instance (otherwise quite regular grammatically, see B. § 139, 30 a) is Acts viii. 31 πῶς γὰρ ἂν δυναίμην, ἐὰν μή τις ὁδηγήσῃ με. Even when dependent on historic tenses, the Second form of hypothesis almost always makes its appearance (pursuant to the general remarks 11 p. 215 and 63 p. 256); as, John ix. 22 συνετέθειντο, ἵνα ἐάν τις αὐτὸν ὁμολογήσῃ Χριστόν, ἀποσυνάγωγος γένηται, xi. 57 δεδώκεισαν, ἵνα ἐάν τις γνῷ etc., Acts ix. 2 ᾐτήσατο, ὅπως, ἐάν τινας εὕρῃ, ἀγάγῃ etc. Cf. 1 Thess. v. 10 above, 22 p. 221. When the Optative occurs, it appears rather in short, fragmentary, parenthetic clauses, as εἰ τύχοι 1 Cor. xiv. 10; xv. 37, εἴ τι ἔχοιεν Acts xxiv. 19, εἰ δύναιντο xxvii. 39 Lchm. [Tdf. Treg. cod. Sin.], εἰ δυνατὸν εἴη (Tdf. [eds. 2, 7] ἦν) xx. 16 Lchm. [Tdf. Treg. cod. Sin.], εἰ θέλοι τὸ θέλημα τοῦ θεοῦ 1 Pet. iii. 17. Both forms of hypothesis, viz. the 2d and the 3d, occur close together, but grammatically, in 1 Pet. iii. 13, 14. In all other passages εἰ with the Optative has the meaning *whether, if perhaps,* and belongs then under H. below p. 255 sq. In many of the books (in all four Gospels, for example) the case is no longer extant.

B. § 139, m. 28; H. § 746; C. § 631 b.; D. p. 539 sq.; J. § 856; G. § 49, 2.

25 On the other hand, the fourth form of hypothesis, regularly framed (εἰ with the Pret. Indic., and in the apodosis a Pret. with ἄν), comes into use pretty frequently, — as well with the Imperf. Luke vii. 39, etc., as Aorist Matt. xi. 21, 23 etc., and Pluperf. John xiv. 7 etc.; and with different tenses in the two clauses, John xviii. 30; Gal. iii. 21; Heb. iv. 8; 1 John ii. 19. Examples of the Imperfect (to express *duration,* B. N. 4) in the protasis, in place of the Pluperf., are John xi. 21, 32, cf. Matt. xxiii. 30.

B. § 139, m. 30 b.; H. § 746 a. b.; C. § 631 f.; cf. § 615; D. p. 540 sq.; J. § 856; G. § 49, cf. 54.

26 The form of the fourth case of hypothesis is so sharply
194 defined, that the N. T. writers have in the main adhered strictly to the grammatical model; for, an alteration of it would have caused ambiguity, and have disturbed at once the character of the hypothetical statement. Nevertheless, d e v i a t i o n s are found here and there: — and that as well 1) in the Protasis, as 2) in the Apodosis.

1) In the Protasis. Once, when the apodosis is formed regularly, εἰ with the Present is the construction given in the protasis: John viii. 39 Lchm. εἰ τέκνα τοῦ Ἀβραάμ ἐ σ τ ε, τὰ ἔργα τοῦ Ἀβραὰμ ἐποιεῖτε

ἄν [Tdf. Treg. omit ἄν; so cod. Sin.]. Most of the interpreters and editors, indeed, have taken offence at this reading, and have adopted into the text instead the very weakly-attested ἦτε (and thus restored the construction to the ordinary form), explaining to themselves the origin of ἐστέ in various ways (see Lücke). But ἐστέ is not only the correct reading, and perfectly suited to the character of this particular passage, but is founded also in actual usage. This usage, however, has sometimes not been duly noticed; and sometimes, owing to the rarity of its occurrence, it was probably obliterated by correction very early by the copyists and commentators. In the N. T. there are, in particular, three other passages where the Present is given by the most important MSS. viz. John xiv. 28; Luke xvii. 6 [so cod. Sin. Tdf. Treg.]; Heb. xi. 15 [so cod. Sin. Tdf. Treg.]. In all these, indeed, the Imperfect (which is likewise found) has been generally received into the text; and yet they, particularly the first two, have (in comparison with the other regularly constructed passages) an unmistakable similarity in character to the above passage from John.[1]

2) In the Apodosis, — inasmuch as the particle ἄν is 27 omitted with the preterite. Winer, 305 (286), is inclined to the opinion, that this omission occurs merely in consequence of negligence peculiar to the later writers. This is the case, indeed, elsewhere (see e.g. 31 p. 228), but not in the fourth class of conditional sentences. On the contrary, such an omission is allowable only in fixed cases, which are observed also in the N. T., and may be reduced to the four classes that follow.

That is to say, the omission of ἄν occurs

a) When ἄν has already been expressed previously in the same connection with another predicate. This instance, which often occurs in the classics and is founded in the nature of the case, is accidentally not to be met with in the text of the N. T.; but it occurs once only as a various reading of cod. A in Luke xvii. 6 (ὑπήκουσεν).

b) When the predicate (or the copula) to which it belongs is also dropped, as 1 Cor. xii. 19 εἰ δὲ ἦν τὰ πάντα ἓν μέλος, ποῦ τὸ σῶμα; — agreeably to which vs. 17 also is to be completed; and as an important 195 variant in Gal. iii. 21.

c) Where the apodosis contains such a predicative term as ἔδει, καλὸν ἦν, ἠδύνατο etc. The omission here (as was explained above,

---

[1] To show all this requires a more extended examination than can be given here. Such an examination, therefore, I have endeavored to give in another place (theol. Stud. u. Krit. for 1858, 3d No., pp. 474 sqq.); to this, accordingly, I refer the reader.

15 p. 216) is so necessary according to Greek habits of thought, that it is only by way of concession to our usage that we can speak of supplying ἄν. That even the copyists of the N. T. books felt no need here of supplying the particle, is plainly to be seen from the fact that ἄν is no longer found even as a variant. Examples are (cf. 15 p. 217) Matt. xxvi. 24; Mark xiv. 21 καλὸν ἦν αὐτῷ, εἰ οὐκ ἐγεννήθη ὁ ἄνθρωπος ἐκεῖνος,[1] John ix. 33 εἰ μὴ ἦν οὗτος παρὰ θεοῦ, οὐκ ἠδύνατο ποιεῖν οὐδέν, Acts xxvi. 32 ἀπολελύσθαι ἠδύνατο ὁ ἄνθρωπος οὗτος, εἰ μὴ ἐπικέκλητο Καίσαρα.

d) Lastly, ἄν is dropped for r h e t o r i c a l reasons: where, though the fact itself is impossible or improbable, the orator in the vivacity of his thought desires to represent it as actually having occurred, or at least, as almost taken place. This case (which, as is familiar, is not unknown to the Latin writers also, cf. Zumpt § 519, b.) belongs rather to the more delicate Greek usage (see the examples from the classics in Hermann, de part. ἄν p. 70 sq.), yet it is discoverable also in a few indubitable instances in the N. T.; most plainly in Gal. iv. 15 μαρτυρῶ ὑμῖν, ὅτι, εἰ δυνατὸν (sc. ἦν), τοὺς ὀφθαλμοὺς ὑμῶν ἐξορύξαντες ἐδώκατέ μοι, Rom. vii. 7 τὴν ἐπιθυμίαν οὐκ ᾔδειν, εἰ μὴ ὁ νόμος ἔλεγεν etc., perhaps also in Gal. iii. 21 (see the var.). 2 Cor. xi. 4; Acts xi. 17 do not belong here; in both these passages nothing more than the first form of a conditional sentence is to be sought for.[2] Moreover, ἄν is wanting here and there in the MSS.; as, John viii. 19; ix. 41; Acts xviii. 14; Heb. iv. 8; xi. 15.

28   REMARK. As an appendix to this Section respecting Conditional Sentences, mention may be made here of another and peculiar mode of expressing the hypothetical relation of two clauses: viz. without conjunctions, by the a s y n d e t i c   j u x t a p o s i t i o n of the clauses. The clause containing the hypothesis stands then in the I n d i c a t i v e, and by Lchm. [Tdf. Treg.] is commonly (though unnecessarily, see Herm. de Ellip. p. 180) distinguished by a mark of interrogation; as, 1 Cor. vii. 18 περιτετμημένος τις ἐκλήθη · μὴ ἐπισπάσθω, 21 δοῦλος ἐκλήθης · μή σοι μελέτω, 27 δέδεσαι γυναικί · μὴ ζήτει λύσιν, Jas. v. 13 κακοπαθεῖ τις ἐν ὑμῖν · προσευχέσθω κ.τ.λ. On the other hand, in Rom. xiii. 3 the first clause really contains a question.

---

[1] The relationship of the statement — put forth as it is here with perfect positiveness (hence οὐκ, according to § 148, 3 d) p. 347) — to the f i r s t form of conditional sentences is so close, that this last in fact appears in plain shape Mark ix. 42 καλόν ἐστιν αὐτῷ μᾶλλον, εἰ περίκειται etc.

[2] Commonly two passages more, from the Gospel of John (xv. 22, 24 and xix. 11), are reckoned among the examples of the omission of ἄν. See respecting them both, and also respecting the omission of ἄν in John viii. 39 (26 above, p. 224 sq.), as well as on the entire subject, my exposition in the Stud. und Krit. as above, pp. 485 sqq.

To be compared with this construction is the prefixing of the hypothesis in the form of an Imperative, in which case the con- **196** clusion is always subjoined by means of καί; as, John ii. 19 λύσατε τὸν ναὸν τοῦτον, καὶ ἐν τρισὶν ἡμέραις ἐγερῶ αὐτόν, Jas. iv. 7 ἀντίστητε τῷ διαβόλῳ, καὶ φεύξεται ἀφ' ὑμῶν, Eph. v. 14. That all such cases belong to the popular language (which likes to resolve periodic structures into single independent members), and consequently find their analogies in all languages, is obvious. Cf. the periphrasis or resolution by which Participles become leading clauses, § 144, 2 p. 290.

B. Relative Sentences.

B. § 139, m. 82; H. §§ 755 sq.; C. §§ 640 sq.; J. §§ 826 sq.; G. §§ 58 sq.

On the general statements respecting the Moods in Relative **79** sentences — [viz. a clause with the Indic. either refers back to a demonstr. or is of a general nature ; in a clause with the Subjunct. ἄν associates itself with the relative, and the clause is always general ; a clause with the Optative without ἄν corresponds to a conditional sentence of the third class, and contains a subjective complement to the leading thought ; ἄν is added to the Optat. if the relation of thought spoken of in 17 p. 217 is to be expressed ; the historical tenses in the Indic. with ἄν are used where they would be used in simple clauses], — we need only remark, that the addition of ἄν (or ἐάν, see p. 72) in clauses with the Subjunctive is at least the rule even in the N. T., as is apparent from numerous examples. Relative clauses with the Optative as a mood of dependent statement are no longer to be met with ; but we find instead, in intermediate clauses in the oratio obliqua or after historic tenses, either (as so frequently in Greek) the Indicative (Mark vi. 45 etc.), or the Subjunctive with ἄν (according to 11 p. 215 above).

If this last case after historic tenses is rare, the reason is solely to be found in the fact that the occasion for using it seldom occurred in the N. T. writings, in consequence of the choice almost everywhere of the direct mode of introducing discourse in the historical books, and of the predominantly concrete contents of the Epistles. Examples of the Subjunctive with ἄν thus used are, Matt. xiv. 7 ὡμολόγησεν αὐτῇ δοῦναι, ὃ ἂν αἰτήσηται (instead of the regular ὃ αἰτήσαιτο or αἰτήσειεν), 1 Thess. ii. 7 sq. ὡς ἐὰν τροφὸς θάλπῃ τὰ ἑαυτῆς τέκνα, οὕτως ... εὐδοκοῦμεν etc. (for εὐδοκοῦμεν is — as the context teaches, the Vulg. translates, and cod. Vat. by the augment ηὐδ. intimates — only to be taken as the Imperfect) ; cf. the similar cases in 24 p. 224, and Rev xiii. 15.

Less surprising, and in accordance with the usage given 37 p. 233 and 33, 3) p. 230, is the simple Subjunctive in relative clauses which contain also the purpose after historical tenses, as Acts xxi. 16 συνῆλθον ... ἄγοντες παρ᾽ ᾧ ξενισθῶμεν Μνάσωνι, see below, 32 p. 229.

30   REMARK. The Indicative Present is given us once with ὅπου ἄν, and has been adopted by Lchm. [Tdf. 7, Tr.] : Rev. xiv. 4 οὗτοι οἱ ἀκολουθοῦντες τῷ ἀρνίῳ, ὅπου ἂν ὑπάγει. Although this construction conflicts with the usage of the N. T. elsewhere, it is yet conceivably correct, especially in the Apocalypse, and finds analogies in the examples (quoted in 23 p. 222 sq.) of the Indicative after ἐάν and ὅταν. The employment also (so frequent in Greek authors as well as in Latin) of the Indicative in general relative clauses (B. § 139 m. 32 ; J. §§ 826, 4 ; 827 c. ; G. § 62 N. 1) may have been not without influence. Cf. further 22 p. 221 above, with the note. The Indicative, moreover, is often found as a variant, e.g. Mark iv. 25 ; xi. 24 (Grsb.), Luke x. 22 ; John ii. 5 ; 1 Cor. xvi. 2 ; 2 Cor. viii. 12 ; Col. iii. 23.

197   B. § 139, m. 33; H. § 759; C. § 619 d.; J. § 828, 2; G. § 63, 1.

31   Corresponding to the lax construction of the Subjunctive with εἰ (spoken of in 22 p. 220 above), is the employment (far more frequent) of the simple Subjunctive without ἄν in general relative clauses, — a construction not uncommon also in the earlier poets (see reff. above). As, however, it was not allowable in ordinary prose, and at the most appears as a rare exception to a usage otherwise fixed (see Poppo on Xen. Cyr. 2, 2, 25), we should err, certainly, in wishing to identify it with that poetic construction ; especially since it stands in so obvious analogy with other cases in the N. T. (cf. 33 p. 230), and contains. moreover, in itself its adequate grammatical justification. That is to say, since ἄν falls away only after the compound relative ὅστις, just as after ὅσος, πᾶς ὅς, etc., and not after the simple ὅς (which first acquires a general force by means of ἄν), we discover plainly that the N. T. authors omitted ἄν whenever universality was already sufficiently indicated by the pronoun, and consequently the addition of ἄν might seem to them to be superfluous.

Here again we find, however, as in all similar cases, considerable fluctuation in the readings — (ἄν besides occurring almost everywhere as a variant, and still more frequently the interchange, already of.en alluded to, of the Subjunctive with the Future taking place, even where ἄν has been left standing) ; so that the critical editions often disagree, and we shall probably never succeed altꝰgether in reaching certainty on this point. As examples we may take Jas. ii. 10 ὅστις τηρήσῃ, Matt. x. 33 Lchm. [Treg.] ὅστις ἀρνήσηται (Tdf. [so cod. Sin.] inserts ἄν), John xvi. 13 Lchm. ὅσα ἀκούσῃ (Tdf. [ed. 2] ἄν, [ed. 7 ὅσα ἀκούσει without ἄν, so Treg.; ed. 8 ὅσα ἀκούει, so cod. Sin.]), Matt. xii. 36 πᾶν ὃ λαλήσωσιν (Tdf. [Treg. cod. Sin.] -σουσιν); and as examples of various readings, Matt. v. 41; x. 32; xviii. 4; John v. 19, etc. An example of the Subjunct. and the Fut. together is Luke viii. 17 Tdf. [eds. 2, 7]; of the Fut. with ἄν, Acts vii. 7 Tdf. [Treg.] (Rev. xi. 6 var.). The Future often occurs as a variant where the Subjunct. is received: Matt. v. 19; xvi. 25; xviii. 19; Mark viii. 35; ix. 41; x. 11, 35; Luke xii. 8, etc. Now, though here and there the reading which offends against general usage is perhaps to be set down to the account of the copyists, yet this much is certain: that the great fluctuation in the MSS. would not exist if there had been no mistakes in this respect on the part of the authors themselves. For it is particularly to be noticed, that there are cases in abundance where it is the anomalous modes of expression which are found in the earlier MSS., and the regular that occur in the later; consequently the suspicion arises that the latter are later corrections.

Respecting the very common Subjunctive after ἕως ὅτου and similar conjunction-like phrases, as ἄχρις οὗ, ἄχρι ἧς ἡμέρας, see 33 p. 230.

B. § 139, m. 34; H. § 756; C. § 642; J. § 836, 4; G. § 65.

Instances of relative sentences (whether with the Future **32** or with the Subjunctive) which at the same time contain an intimation of p u r p o s e are rare in the N. T., since it employs for this end the express statement by means of the final par- **198** ticle ἵνα almost invariably.

John ix. 36 τίς ἐστιν, ἵνα πιστεύσω εἰς αὐτόν, v. 7 ἄνθρωπον οὐκ ἔχω, ἵνα βάλῃ με εἰς τὴν κολυμβήθραν, 2 Cor. xii. 7 ἐδόθη μοι σκόλοψ ... ἵνα με κολαφίζῃ, ἵνα μὴ etc. Rev. xix. 15 ἐκπορεύεται ῥομφαία, ἵνα ἐν αὐτῇ πατάξῃ τὰ ἔθνη; especially after ἀποστέλλω and the like, as Gal. iv. 5 ἐξαπέστειλεν τὸν υἱὸν αὐτοῦ, ἵνα τοὺς ὑπὸ νόμον ἐξαγοράσῃ, ἵνα etc. Yet we may with confidence (guided even by the position) take as relative clauses including the expression of a purpose, the example in 29 p. 228 ἄγοντες παρ' ᾧ ξενισθῶμεν Μν. (see § 143, 7 p. 284), and also Luke vii. 4 ἄξιός ἐστιν ᾧ παρέξῃ τοῦτο (cf. the construction with ἵνα after ἄξιος in 46 below, p. 240), Matt. xxi. 41 γεωργοῖς, οἵτινες ἀποδώσουσιν etc.

It is to be noticed further, that instead of the regular relative clause after such predicates as οὐκ ἔχω (non habeo quod followed by the Subjunct.) e.g. Luke xi. 6 οὐκ ἔχω ὃ παραθήσω αὐτῷ, the form of an Indirect Question is commonly substituted, see 58 below, p. 251. On Acts xix. 40 see § 151, 29 note p. 400.

C. Temporal Sentences.

B. § 139, m. 37; H. cf. § 758; C. § 641 d.; D. p. 578 sqq.; J. §§ 840 sqq.; G. §§ 58 sqq.

33   As the constructions in temporal sentences agree in their general principles with those in relative sentences, because the temporal conjunctions themselves were mostly relatives originally (ὡς, ὅτε, ἕως, ἐξ οὗ, etc.), all the deviations from classic usage touched on above in connection with relative sentences will repeat themselves here.

1) The O p t a t i v e as a dependent Mood no longer occurs except in a single instance, either the Indicative or the Subjunctive (with and without ἄν, see 3 below) being substituted for it, as above. The instance of the Optative used in classic fashion is again from Acts (xxv. 16) ἀπεκρίθην, ὅτι οὐκ ἔστιν ἔθος ... πρὶν ἤ ἔχοι etc.

2) Corresponding to the use of ὅπου ἄν and ἐάν with the Indicative, ὅ τ α ν also is sometimes joined to the I n d i c a t i v e; see more on this point, together with examples, in 23 above, p. 222. Respecting ἕως ἄν with the Fut. see the following paragraph (3).

3) Temporal particles which express a l i m i t or g o a l (our till, until), ἕως, μέχρι, ἄχρι, together with all their extensions, as ἕως οὗ, ἕως ὅτου, etc., if they are joined to the Subjunctive, take (as being originally relatives) according to rule the particle ἄν: Matt. xxiii. 39; xxiv. 34, etc. Still more commonly, however, they are construed, agreeably to their signification, after the analogy of the final particles ἵνα and ὅ π ω ς below: that is to say, with the simple Subjunctive with-out ἄ ν, even after historical tenses.

Examples are very numerous, and are in the main also thoroughly established critically, while in ordinary Greek prose the construction with the simple Subjunctive can be regarded only as an isolated and doubtful exception. In order to get a view of the great extent to which this usage is carried in the N. T., we give here a list of the passages. Thus we find with the Subjunctive, ἕως in Matt. xviii. 30; 34 Lchm.; Mark xiv. 32; Luke xv. 4; xvii. 8; xxii. 34; 2 Thess. ii. 7; Heb. x. 13 (after a Pret., but with reference to the Present, see § 137, 3 p. 197); Jas. v. 7 Tdf. [Treg.]; Rev. vi. 11; ἕως οὗ in Matt. xiv. 22; xviii. 34 Tdf. [Treg.]; xvii. 9; xxvi. 36 Tdf. [Treg.]; Luke xii. 59 [Tdf. Treg. cod. Sin. om. οὗ]; xxiv. 49; John xiii. 38; Acts xxiii. 12 (after an historical tense), 14, 21; xxv. 21 (after an historical tense); 2 Pet. i. 19; ἕως ὅτου Luke xii. 50; xiii. 8; xv. 8 [οὗ Treg.

cod. Sin.]; xxii.16,18 [οὗ Treg. cod. Sin.];   μέχρι Eph. iv.13 ; μέχρις
οὗ Mark xiii. 30 ;   ἄχρι Rev. vii. 3 ; xv. 8 (after an historical tense) ;
xx. 3, 5 (after an historical tense) ;   ἄχρις οὗ Luke xxi. 24 ; Rom.
xi. 25 ; 1 Cor. xi. 26 ; xv. 25, [Tdf. in Lk. Cor. -ρι οὗ with cod. Sin.] ;
Gal. iii. 19 ; iv. 19 [μέχρις οὗ Treg. Tdf. cod. Sin.] ;   ἄχρι ἧς ἡμέρας Luke
i. 20 ;   and finally, also after πρὶν ἤ Luke ii. 26 [π. ἤ ἄν Tdf., π. ἄν
Treg., ἕως ἄν cod. Sin.], (and in xxii. 34 as a variant for ἕως).   It is
noticeable that here the Subjunctive does not, as in so many similar
cases, alternate with the F u t u r e ; but the Future, with the exception
perhaps of the passage Rev. xvii. 17 (itself uncertain) and a few
various readings, is well nigh excluded.   That this usage stands in
closest connection with the N. T. structure of final clauses, appears
on comparing the respective paragraphs (37 and 38 p. 233 sq.).   And
since also the omission of ἄν with the S u b j u n c t i v e in all clauses
which contain the expression of a purpose has its foundation in classic
usage (see B. § 139, m. 45 and m. 47), much less here can we think
of the retention of ἄν with the F u t u r e (cf. 23 p. 222 and 31 p. 228),
— an instance of which, in point of fact, hardly occurs even as a
variant, with the exception of a very doubtful case in Luke xiii. 35
Lchm. (see fine print under 4) ; cf. ἕως ἄν with the Future in Act.
Petr. et Paul. 63.

On the other hand, the connection of all these particles with the
I n d i c a t i v e   P r e s e n t is not in the least anomalous, since as
temporal conjunctions, particularly in the signification *as long as, until*
(cf. the Lat. *dum, donec*, etc.), they can be construed also as such,
consequently with the Indicative ; as, Matt. v. 25 ἴσθι εὐνοῶν . . . ἕως
ὅτου εἶ μετ᾽ αὐτοῦ ἐν τῇ ὁδῷ, Heb. iii. 13 παρακαλεῖτε ἑαυτούς, ἄχρις οὗ
τὸ σήμερον καλεῖται, John ix. 4 ἕως ἡμέρα ἐστίν, xxi. 22, 23 ; 1 Tim. iv.
13 ἕως ἔρχομαι, Mark vi. 45 ἕως ἀπολύει, Acts xxi. 26, — these last two
passages are at the same time examples of the Indic. instead of the
Optat. in an intermediate clause to express an indirect statement
(11 above, p. 215).

4) With all other particles of time which contain no specification of a limit, if the construction with the Subjunctive
occurs, the p a r t i c l e ἄν (ἐάν) is a d d e d regularly and
almost without exception.   Hence, always ἡνίκα ἄν, ὁσάκις ἐάν,
ἀφ᾽ οὗ ἄν, with the Subjunctive following ; and ὅτε, ἐπεί in
such cases become as usual ὅταν, ἐπάν, as Matt. ii. 8 ; Luke
xi. 22, etc.

Only in a single passage (Luke xiii. 35) is the construction of ὅτε
with the Subjunctive extant and received : οὐ μὴ ἴδητέ με, ἕως ἥξει ὅτε
εἴπητε.   Yet the Subjunctive εἴπητε here as respects its f o r c e man-

ifestly depends rather on the idea of end contained in ἕως, as is plain from the sense or from a comparison of the parallel passage Matt xxiii. 39 (ἕως ἂν εἴπητε), and ἥξει ὅτε forms a parenthetic insertion quite superfluous for the sense (and hence omitted also by MSS. of repute [cod. Sin. among them]).

5) A faulty construction is that of ὡς in a temporal sense (cum Luke xii. 58) with the Subjunctive and ἄν, since in this case, at 200 least in Attic prose, it either has a thoroughly telic force (but is never so used in the N. T.), or signifies as, and then, as introducing a relative clause, takes ἄν according to rule; so in the N. T. in 1 Thess. ii. 7 (see 29 above, p. 227). Three times, however, ὡς ἄν with the Subjunctive occurs decidedly in a temporal signification (as soon qs): most clearly in 1 Cor. xi. 34 τὰ λοιπὰ ὡς ἂν ἔλθω διατάξομαι (Vulg. cum venero), Phil. ii. 23 ὡς ἂν ἀφίδω (Vulg. ut venero), and probably also Rom. xv. 24 (see § 144, 7 p. 294); cf. Joseph. B. J. 2. 14; 3. 8; Prov. i. 27; Clem. Ep. 1. 12 (ὡς ἐάν). For examples of ὡς ἄν with the Indic. in the Sept. see Winer 309 (290).

B. § 139, m. 39; H. § 760 c.; C. cf. § 641; D. § 580; J. § 843; G. §§ 60, 62.

34   The employment of the Optative in temporal clauses, and corresponding relative clauses, to denote repetition is unknown in the N. T. The N. T. language employs for this purpose, either the Indicative with ἄν according to 13 p. 216 (see the examples there), or the Subjunctive with ἄν, as, for instance, with ὁσάκις 1 Cor. xi. 25, 26; Rev. xi. 6. The proper particle of repetition, ὁπότε, ὁπόταν, is never used in the N. T.; and even in Luke vi. 3 (where Lchm. [so Treg.] has given ὅτε after the best MSS. [Sin. also]), if ὁπότε is preferred with Tdf., it would not have the iterative force.

B. § 139, m. 41; H. § 878; C. § 703 d.; D. § 583; J. § 848; G. § 67.

35   The rule laid down in reference to the use of πρίν or πρὶν ἤ is observed in the N. T. most accurately: — the Subjunct. and Optat., where they occur, appearing in every case after a preceding negation (Luke ii. 26; xxii. 34 var.; Acts xxv. 16); whereas in all the passages with the Infinitive, the main clause contains no negation. Of the Indicative after πρίν there is no example extant.

D. CAUSAL SENTENCES.

B. § 139, m. 42–44; D. §§ 615 sqq.; J. §§ 801 sqq.; G. §§ 80, 81.

36   In the construction of causal sentences there is no deviation from ordinary usage (viz. that the Indic. is employed when the cause is represented as external or objective, the Optat. when it is subjective), farther than that they are treated only as inde-

pendent sentences, i.e joined to the Mood of independence. Also, when s u b j e c t i v e reasons are specified, the N. T. language, even in the Acts, employs (according to the general remarks in 11 p. 215) instead of the Optative only the I n d i c a t i v e ; as, Acts vi. 1 ἐγένετο γογγυσμὸς τῶν Ἑλληνιστῶν, ὅτι παρεθεωροῦντο αἱ χῆραι αὐτῶν, x. 45 ἐξέστησαν, ὅτι . . . ἐκκέχυται etc.

The most common causal particles are ὅτι, διότι, ἐπεί, ἐπειδή, less frequently ὡς. These particles are often used as co-ordinating particles, and then are to be translated by *for* (Germ. *denn*), as Rom. iii. 6 ἐπεὶ πῶς κρινεῖ ὁ θεός ; In the compounds διό and διόπερ the co-ordinating force is the prevalent one ; hence their frequent construction with the Imperative, or the Subjunctive in its stead: διὸ εὐθυμεῖτε (Acts xxvii. 25), διόπερ φεύγετε (1 Cor. x. 14), διὸ ἔχωμεν χάριν (Heb. xii. 28), etc.

E. Final Sentences.

201

B. § 139, m. 45 ; H. p. 275 sq. ; C. § 624 ; D. p. 597 sq. ; J. § 805 ; G. §§ 43 sq.

The two particles of design ἵνα and ὅπως (never, ὡς)—nega- 37 tively ἵνα μή, ὅπως μή, or even simply μή (μήποτε, μήπως, etc.) — are joined almost uniformly to the S u b j u n c t i v e, rarely to the Future (38 p. 234). At the same time it is to be noticed, that the practice (beginning to show itself even in old classic authors, e.g. Thucydides) of using instead of the Optative the Subjunctive, even after h i s t o r i c t e n s e s and in the midst of narration, as the Mood especially suited to the expression of a purpose striving to become actual (see B. l. c.), has become the established rule in the N. T., as may be seen from innumerable examples : thus, after ἵνα, Matt. xiv. 36 παρεκάλουν ἵνα ἅψωνται, xii. 10 ; xix. 13 ; Acts xxvii. 42 βουλὴ ἐγένετο, ἵνα . . . ἀποκτείνωσιν, μή τις διαφύγῃ (Rec. -γοι), John iv. 8 after the Pluperf. ἀπεληλύθεισαν ἵνα ἀγοράσωσιν ; after ὅπως, Acts viii. 15 ; ix. 2, 24 ; xxv. 3 παρεκάλουν . . . ὅπως μεταπέμψηται etc.

Of the O p t a t i v e not an example is any longer found ; and that γνοῖ, παραδοῖ (also after historic tenses) accordingly are not Optatives, but Subjunctives, has already been remarked on p. 46 ; e.g. Mark v. 43 διεστείλατο ἵνα γνοῖ, ix. 30 ; xiv. 10 ἀπῆλθεν ἵνα παραδοῖ (cf. vs. 11), Luke xix. 15 ; John xiii. 2. Only in Eph. i. 17 and iii. 16 has Tdf. [eds. 2, 7] adopted the Optative δώῃ after ἵνα ; yet even the acceptance of these Optatives would not touch the rule,[1] since 1) here the Optat.

[1] Lchm. has in both passages the Subjunctive (once in the form δάῃ, and once in the form δῷ, [Treg. Tdf. ed. 8 with cod. Sin.? in i. 17 δώῃ, in iii. 16 δῷ]) ; and thus

30

stands in both cases after leading tenses, and 2) the Optat. in both
passages should be explained as the Optative in the proper sense, viz.
of a wish (not as the Mood of a dependent statement), and therefore
be taken rather as independent, very much as in one passage the
Imperative even is used after ἵνα, viz. in a quotation given without
verbal change : 1 Cor. i. 31 ἵνα ... ὁ καυχώμενος ἐν κυρίῳ καυχάσθω.

The addition of ἄν to ὅπως has likewise passed almost com-
pletely out of use, it being found only in a few passages by Luke
(Gosp. ii. 35; Acts iii. 19) and solitary quotations from the O. T.:
Acts xv. 17 (after Amos ix. 12 Alex.) ; Rom. iii. 4.

B. § 139, m. 47; H. § 756; C. § 624 b.; J. § 811, 2; G. p. 68; W. 289 (271).

38 The rule which holds in classic usage, that the Future
202 Indicative can stand only after ὅπως, never after ἵνα, is not
applicable at all to the N. T.: since 1) according to 8 above, p.
213, ὅπως is joined to the Subjunctive almost without exception ; and 2) after ἵνα itself the Future is given (and accepted)
several times indubitably. See Thom. Mag. p. 186, ed. Ritschl.

The most frequent and unquestionable use of the Future after ἵνα
is in the Apocalypse (cf. 33, 3) p. 231) — where it was for the most
part displaced by the Rec. — frequently in immediate connection with
a Subjunct. (agreeably to 7 note, p. 211) ; as, iii. 9 ἵνα ἥξουσιν καὶ
προσκυνήσουσιν ... καὶ γνῶσιν, xxii. 14 ἵνα ἔσται ... καὶ εἰσέλθωσιν, vi.
4, 11, etc. But it occurs elsewhere also, as Luke xx. 10 (δώσουσιν),
Acts xxi. 24 where accordingly γνώσονται can be also included as a part
of the final clause, just as in Luke xxii. 30 ἵνα ἔσθητε καὶ πίνητε ... καὶ
καθίσεσθε (Vulg. et sedeatis), Mark xv. 20 (σταυρώσουσιν), iii. 2 (κατη-
γορήσουσιν [not Tdf.]), John xii. 20 (προσκυνήσουσιν), 1 Cor. ix. 15 Tdf.
[eds. 2, 7; not 8] (κενώσει), xiii. 3 Tdf. (κανθήσομαι), Gal. ii. 4 (κατα-
δουλώσουσιν), 1 Pet. iii. 1 (κερδηθήσονται), Luke xiv. 10 Tdf. [Treg.
cod. Sin.] (ἐρεῖ, al. εἴπῃ), Phil. ii. 11 Tdf. (κάμψῃ καὶ ἐξομολογήσεται, al.
[so Treg. cod. Sin.] -σηται), and besides as a variant John xvii. 2 etc.

39 REMARK. A few examples also are extant of ἵνα with the Indicative Present, as above, in the case of ἐάν and ὅταν. Since, however, the relation expressed by the Subjunctive or the Future is incomparably more important in clauses indicating purpose than after ἐάν,
ὅταν, etc. (cf. the Latin constructions after cum, si, ut), all such cases,
if other considerations do not sustain them or the text is not certain,
give rise to a suspicion of clerical error in later times, when, as is

harmonizes with the ordinary construction of verbs of entreating etc., according to
42 p. 237. But in this case the restoration of the spelling of the Vat. ms. (δῷ
in both instances) deserves preference. Cf. 62 p 256.

well known, the Modal relations underwent a constantly increasing corruption. Lchm. has taken the Indic. Present into his text in three passages only : it is the almost unanimous reading in 1 Cor. iv. 6 (φυσιοῦσθε [so Tdf. Treg. cod. Sin.]), Gal. iv. 17 (ζηλοῦτε [so Tdf. Treg. cod. Sin.]), less certain in 2 Pet. i. 10 ἵνα ποιεῖσθε (Tdf. ποιεῖσθαι [so Treg. cod. Sin.] cf. 42 p. 237). Perhaps it is no accident that in all three passages the Present has the circumflexed form, and so they can be reckoned among the cases (described on p. 38, in § 137, 10 b) p. 205, and in 3 above, p. 209) where the Present on account of its having the circumflex on the last syllable takes the place of the Future. Tdf., moreover, has adopted the Present in several other instances also : John xvii. 3 (ἵνα γινώσκουσιν [so Treg.]), Gal. vi. 12 (διώκονται), Tit. ii. 4 (σωφρονίζουσιν [with א*; so Treg.]), Rev. xiii. 17 (δύναται [eds. 2, 7]) ; cf. Acta Petr. et P. 58, 81 ; P. et Thecl. 11 etc. Yet the Subjunctive has everywhere weighty authorities in its favor, especially cod. Vat. [and in the last four bibl. passages, except Tit. l.c., cod. Sin. also], and is consequently to be preferred to the Indicative, especially in the last three passages, where the idea of purpose is predominant. Only in the passage from John (xvii. 3) has the Indic., in addition to the emphatic external attestation, some internal probability also in its support ; since, as the following section will show, John is much less rigorous than others in his employment of the particle ἵνα, and its original telic force is often obscured by him, as in fact in the above passage : αὗτη δέ ἐστιν ἡ αἰώνιος ζωὴ, ἵνα γινώσκουσιν σὲ etc. Cf. 45 p. 240.

On the Force of the Particle ἵνα in the N.T.

As ἵνα is one of those particles used most frequently and peculiarly in the N.T., it seems to be necessary to give a complete survey here of the N.T. use of the same.[1]

It is not to be denied, that the use of this conjunction increased steadily the farther the Greek language departed from the classic period, but especially in the popular dialect; and that gradually a multitude of relations were expressed by it for which in the literary language other particles or other constructions were employed. An indication of the facts is afforded even by an external comparison of the Acts or the Ep. to the Heb., composed as they are in the spirit of classic Greek, with

[1] Compare with this the expositions given by Winer 457 sqq. (426 sqq.) [cf. 334 sqq. (314 sqq.)] ; Fritzsche, Excurs. ad Matt. pp. 836 sqq. ; [see also Jelf § 803 ; Green, N. T. Gram. pp. 170 sq. ; Ellicott on Eph. i. 17 ; Sophocles, Glossary etc. §§ 88 sq. and Lexicon sub voce].

one of the Gospels written more in the popular phraseology, particularly the Gospel of J o h n . This Gospel employs the particle ἵνα nearly a hundred and fifty times (his Epp. twenty-five times), whereas in the much more extensive book of the Acts it appears only sixteen times, and in the Ep. to the Heb. twenty times. The Acts still uses now ἵνα now ὅπως ; but in John, with the exception of a single passage (xi. 57, where ἵνα immediately precedes), the other final particle has wholly disappeared.

41   On a general survey of the clauses introduced by ἵνα, we find the principal deviation from classic usage to consist in the fact, that the particle makes its appearance, not only as usual after c o m p l e t e predicates — so that the clause as a s u p e r a d d e d statement of design stands in a certain external independence as respects the leading predicate (*in order that, to the end that*), but also after so-called i n c o m p l e t e predicate ideas (e.g. θέλειν), and serves to subjoin to them their n e c e s s a r y complement. In good prose, as is well-known, the Infinitive is used in this latter case ; or after certain predicates (as παρακαλεῖν, etc., see B. § 139, m. 45) ὅπως also, never (or at least but very seldom) ἵνα. This classic use of ὅπως just mentioned may be regarded as the commencement of the later prevalent resolution or periphrase of the Infinitive by means of Particles. In the place of ὅπως (by which the clause at least still preserved the form of an indirect question) appeared first of all with such predicates as παρακαλεῖν etc. (see 42) the pure particle of design ἵνα. Gradually, however, the number of the (incomplete) predicates after which the Infinitive — formerly the o n l y construction used — was re-
204 solved by a clause with ἵνα, increased more and more ;[1] so that the proper telic force of the particle constantly receded further, or was blended with the senses of other particles (as ὅτι, ὥστε) ; see below. Even in the language of the majority of the N. T. writers this use is by no means still in its initial stage, but has already become considerably extended, as will appear from the following paragraphs.

42   Thus much, however, is still to be laid down as respects the

[1] In modern Greek the Infinitive has at length completely disappeared, and is only expressed by the particle νά (which came from ἵνα) with a Subjunctive following ; as, νὰ φάγω, νὰ γράφῃ. See Mullach, Vulgarspr. S. 373.

N. T. : that ἵνα cannot as in the later Greek arbitrarily take the place of every Infinitive (and so even of ὅτι after verba dicendi), but the predicates after which it stands are still in the main of such a nature that the dependent clause can be regarded as a statement **akin to a specification of purpose.**

This is the case, in the first place, with all predicates which can be referred to the notion of a **wish, request, command, admonition.**

These are in particular the following: θέλειν, παρακαλεῖν, διαστέλλε-σθαι, εἰπεῖν,[1] παραγγέλλειν, ἀπαγγέλλειν, (e.g. 2 Thess. iii. 12 ἵνα ἐσθίωσιν, for which previously, in vs. 10, ὅτι with the Imperative had been used: ὅτι . . . μηδὲ ἐσθιέτω, cf. 51 p. 245), κηρύσσειν, γράφειν (e.g. Mark xii. 19 where the ὅτι before ἵνα is superfluous, or rather the two kinds of statement residing in γράφειν are intimated by ὅτι and ἵνα, ix. 12, etc.), προσεύχεσθαι and the substantive προσευχή (e.g. Eph. vi. 19 ; Phil. i. 9 ; respecting the Optative with it see 37 p. 233, above), δεῖσθαι and ἐρωτᾶν in the sense of *beseech*, ἐντέλλεσθαι, ἐντολὰς διδόναι and λαμβάνειν, αἰτεῖσθαι. Here belong, also, all those passages where the sense requires us to supply the idea of entreaty etc. suggested by ἵνα, e.g. κάμπτειν γόνατα Eph. iii. 16, συνιστάναι *commendare* Rom. xvi. 2, διαμαρτύρεσθαι 1 Tim. v. 21, ἀνασείειν τὸν ὄχλον *to stir up* and entice Mark xv. 11; Luke xx. 10 ἀπέστειλεν δοῦλον, ἵνα δώσουσιν *with the order that* etc.; and often in clauses where the demand is expressed by the form of the sentence, to wit, by the **Imperative,** e.g. βλέπε ἵνα πληροῖς (Subjunct.) Col. iv. 17, σπουδάσατε ἵνα ποιεῖσθε (see 39 p. 234), πληρώσατέ μου τὴν χαρὰν ἵνα τὸ αὐτὸ φρονῆτε Phil. ii. 2, ζητεῖτε ἵνα περισσεύητε 1 Cor. xiv. 12, etc.

For the same reason ἵνα connects itself readily with the ideas *to counsel, admonish, threaten, adjure,* as βουλὴ ἐγένετο, συνεβουλεύσαντο ἵνα ἀποκτείνωσιν αὐτούς, ἐπετίμησεν αὐτοῖς ἵνα μηδενὶ λέγωσιν, ἐξορκίζω σε ἵνα ἡμῖν εἴπῃς, συνετέθεικτο ἵνα, etc., and in general occurs after many other predicates and constructions, in so far as by the action contained in them something is to be striven for or averted, — hence after the ideas *to exert one's self, to seek, to equip one's self, to prepare, to be on one's guard,* etc., as ζητεῖν, παρατηρεῖν, διώκειν, ζηλοῦν, ἑτοιμάζειν, ζητεῖν εὐκαιρίαν, φυλάσσεσθαι, etc.

---

[1] Εἰπεῖν and other verba dicendi acquire in this way the force of κελεύειν, as Matt. xx. 21 εἰπὲ ἵνα καθίσωσιν, Mark iii. 9 etc., and it is remarkable that this latter verb, κελεύειν, is never joined to ἵνα, but always to the Infinitive. The influence of the Latin construction with *jubere* may have contributed to this; hence also the (unclassic) construction with the Infin. Pass., see § 141, 5 p. 275.

43   Further, ἵνα is used after many predicates in order to designate the effect contained in the dependent clause as one
designed, one included within the province of the subject's
vo li tio n.   In this way the force of ἵνα approximates essentially to that of the (apparently opposite) particle ὥστε.

Consequently, when lexicographers and commentators adduce among
the significations of ἵνα those of ὥστε also, they are by no means to be
condemned as holding erroneous philological views.   For every effect
or consequence, so far forth as it is to be regarded not as one which
is merely external and resulting as a matter of fact, but as intended
and striven after by the subject, falls thereby under the idea of finality.
Hence, not only do the Latin writers employ for both purposes one
and the same particle (*ut*), but also in Greek ὥστε when it governs
the Infin. is reckoned with reason by many grammarians (see e.g.
Bäumlein, Schulgr. § 590 sq. [cf. D. p. 597]) among the final particles;
and there are cases enough where the final reference in ὥστε is so
predominant that we can only translate it by *in order to* (see below,
50 Rem. p. 244; Bäumlein, as above; Matth. Gr. § 531, Anm. 2).   In
point of fact the majority of the predicates adduced in this and the
following section are in Greek writers predominantly connected with
ὥστε.   Accordingly ἵνα is connected frequently with the ideas *to effect,
to make, to compel, to persuade, to admit, to confer,* etc.: as, π ο ι ε ῖ ν
Mark iii. 14; Luke xviii. 41 τί σοι θέλεις ποιήσω; ὁ δὲ εἶπεν · ἵνα
ἀναβλέψω, Rev. xiii. 15 Lchm.;[1] τ ι θ έ ν α ι John xv. 16 ἔθηκα ὑμᾶς ἵνα
ὑμεῖς ὑπάγητε καὶ καρπὸν φέρητε;   δ ι δ ό ν α ι, especially in the Apocalypse in the common construction ἐδόθη αὐτῷ ἵνα etc., further in ἐξουσίαν
διδόναι, Acts viii. 19 δότε κἀμοὶ τὴν ἐξουσίαν ταύτην, ἵνα ... λαμβάνῃ,
Mark xi. 28 τίς σοι τὴν ἐξουσίαν ταύτην ἔδωκεν, ἵνα ταῦτα ποιῇς; ἀγγα-
ρεύειν Matt. xxvii. 32;   πείθειν Matt. xxvii. 20;   ἀφιέναι Mark xi. 16;
εἰς τὴν καρδίαν βάλλειν (τινί) John xiii. 2, etc.

44   There remain still a great number of predicates and constructions in which the idea of purpose decidedly re c e d e s
206 into the background, and ἵνα indicates solely a reference
to something fu tu re and still to be realized, and often the
dependent clause contains also merely the completion of the
statement given incompletely in the predicate : — in brief, then,
cases where the clause with ἵνα serves as a periphrasis for the
I n fi n i ti v e (with or without ὥστε) alone in use in ordinary

---

[1] The omission of ἵνα in this passage in the text of Tdf. [eds. 2, 7, 8; so cod. Sin.]
so that the simple Subjunctive ἀποκτανθῶσιν would depend immediately on ποιήσῃ,
somewhat as in Latin the Subjunct. without *ut* after *fac, sine,* etc., is very improbable.
Cf. 49 note p. 243.

prose; particularly for the Infin. Future, which hardly continues to be employed in the N. T., or for the Infin. with τοῦ which is much in use there (and with which it often alternates after the same predicates and in the same sense; see § 140, 12 sqq. pp. 266 sqq.).

This is the freest use of ἵνα in the N. T. And although it never stands in the strict ecbatic sense (for ὥστε with the finite verb), it has nevertheless here reached the very boundary line where the difference between the two relations (the telic and the ecbatic) disappears and it is nearer to the ecbatic sense than to its original final sense. Necessary as the demand is, that in a systematic inquiry into the use of the particle, even within a comparatively restricted field, we should always make its original telic force, which is the only force it has in earlier Greek writers, our point of departure, and trace out thence the transitions to its diverse shades of meaning; the interests of exegesis would gain very little, if in every individual passage of the N. T. even (the language of which has already departed so far from original classic Greek usage) we should still take pains, at the cost of the simple and natural sense and by a recourse to artificial means, always to introduce the telic force. In our language, as a rule, the particle *that* (which in like manner unites in itself both reference;) is an adequate translation; but there are instances where we approximate more nearly to the intention of the writer if we translate it most simply and in a way which corresponds best to the sense of the passage, viz. by the mere Infinitive, even with *so that, so as* (i.e. ὥστε with the Infin.). All this will be plain from the

EXAMPLES: John viii. 56 Ἀβραὰμ ἠγαλλιάσατο, ἵνα ἴδῃ τὴν ἡμέραν τὴν ἐμὴν equiv. to ὅτι ὄψοιτο not *that he saw* but *that he should see*, like Rev. xiv. 13 μακάριοι οἱ νεκροὶ ... ἵνα ἀναπαήσονται, John xv. 13 μείζονα ἀγάπην οὐδεὶς ἔχει ἵνα τις τὴν ψυχὴν αὐτοῦ θῇ (equiv. to ὥστε θεῖναι) which impels him to etc., 1 Thess. v. 4 οὐκ ἐστὲ ἐν σκότει, ἵνα ἡ ἡμέρα ὑμᾶς ὡς κλέπτης καταλάβῃ *so that the day could surprise you*, John ix. 2 τίς ἥμαρτεν, ἵνα τυφλὸς γεννηθῇ no external consequence, but designating the internal causal connection, ordained by a higher power, between sin and malady: *so that he should* (must) *be born blind*, Luke ix. 45 ἠγνόουν τὸ ῥῆμα καὶ ἦν παρακεκαλυμμένον ἀπ᾽ αὐτῶν, ἵνα μὴ αἴσθωνται αὐτό not *in order that* etc. but *so that they could not understand it*, John v. 20 μείζονα ἔργα δείξει, ἵνα ὑμεῖς θαυμάζητε (not *in order that*, but) *so that ye will wonder*, Matt. x. 25 ἀρκετὸν τῷ μαθητῇ, ἵνα γένηται ὡς ὁ διδάσκαλος equiv. to τὸ γενέσθαι, Gal. v. 17, etc. That, however, many passages were taken by the (earlier) interpreters in the ecbatic sense where the final is altogether admissible, in fact necessary (e.g. John vii. 23, etc.), has been shown by Winer 457 (426) by a number of examples.

207
45
In accordance now with the foregoing section, we find in the N. T. the following predicates joined to this comparatively ecbatic ἵνα, where the Greek literary language certainly would have used either ὥστε with the Infin. or quite a different construction : συμφέρειν Matt. v. 29; 30, etc. ; ἀρκεῖν John vi. 7 ; ἀρκετὸν εἶναι (see 44 p. 239), ἱκανὸν εἶναι Matt. viii. 8 ; Luke vii. 6 ; χρείαν ἔχειν John ii. 25, etc. ; συνήθειά ἐστιν John xviii. 39 ; μισθός ἐστιν 1 Cor. ix. 18 ; καλόν ἐστιν 1 Cor. ix. 15 Tdf. [eds. 2, 7; not 8] ; ἐμοὶ ἐλάχιστόν ἐστιν 1 Cor. iv. 3 ; ἡ ὥρα ἔρχεται, ἐλήλυθεν John xvi. 32 (on the other hand vs. 25 ἔρχεται ὥρα, ὅτε οὐκέτι λαλήσω etc.) ; ἔδωκα χρόνον Rev. ii. 21 ; ἐμὸν βρῶμά ἐστιν ἵνα ποιῶ τὸ θέλημα etc. John iv. 34; μειζοτέραν οὐκ ἔχω χαρὰν ἵνα ἀκούω 3 John 4 ; and when referring to a preparatory demonstrative preceding : πόθεν μοι τοῦτο ἵνα ἔλθῃ πρός με Luke i. 43 (cf. Protev. 12. 2 ; Acta Andr. 6, — this last Apocryphal book was written early, is a decided imitation of the canonical writings, and exhibits several instances of the ecbatic ἵνα), τοῦτό ἐστιν τὸ ἔργον, ἵνα πιστεύσητε John vi. 29, αὕτη ἡ ζωὴ ἵνα γινώσκουσιν (see above, 39 p. 235) John xvii. 3, αὕτη ἡ ἀγάπη ... ἵνα τὰς ἐντολὰς τηρῶμεν 1 John v. 3 (cf. iv. 17). Yet it always remains for the interpreter to decide which reference in ἵνα, agreeably to the most obvious sense, predominates in every individual case.

46
That all the above prescriptions in reference to the signification and use of ἵνα are not rigidly fixed, and cannot be, in consequence of the wide difference in style of the several authors in this particular, has already been intimated, 40 p. 235. Often the example given above is the only one of the kind in the N. T. ; many of the predicates mentioned admit quite as often, sometimes still more frequently, some of them even commonly, of the construction with the Infinitive (with and without τοῦ), as θέλειν, ζητεῖν, ποιεῖν, πείθειν, ἀφεῖναι, ἱκανὸν εἶναι, χρείαν ἔχειν, etc.

The complete equivalence of the construction with the Conjunction and that with the Infinitive is evident from many passages : — particularly from parallel passages, as Matt. xxvi. 17 ποῦ θέλεις ἑτοιμάσωμέν σοι φαγεῖν and Mark xiv. 12 ποῦ θελ. ἑτ. ἵνα φάγῃς, John i. 27 ἄξιος ἵνα λύσω τὸν ἱμάντα and Acts xiii. 25 ἄξιος λῦσαι τὸ ὑπόδημα ; — or from those in which both constructions are dependent immediately upon a single predicate and united into a single sentence, as 1 Cor. ix. 15 Tdf [eds. 2, 7 ; not 8] καλόν μοι μᾶλλον ἀποθανεῖν ἢ τὸ καύχημά μου ἵνα τις κενώσει, Rev. vi. 4 ἐδόθη αὐτῷ λαβεῖν τὴν εἰρήνην ἐκ τῆς γῆς καὶ ἵνα ἀλλή-

λους σφάξουσιν; — or where the MSS. are divided between the two
constructions, as 2 Pet. i. 10.

REMARK. In conclusion, mention may be made here of the rather　47
frequent elliptical constructions with ἵνα (ἀλλ᾽ ἵνα etc.). One species
of them, where the governing idea is implicitly given in the predicate
of the leading clause, has already been treated of above in 42 p. 237.
Often an entire clause, or some such thought as 'this happened' etc.,
is suppressed, as it either is easily to be supplied from the context, or
if added would have been cumbersome and prejudicial to the simplicity
of the sentence, which is sufficiently intelligible without it (cf. the
similar instances § 151, 24 c) p. 395); as, Mark xiv. 49 καθ᾽ ἡμέραν
ἤμην . . . καὶ οὐκ ἐκρατήσατέ με · ἀλλ᾽ ἵνα πληρωθῶσιν αἱ γραφαί, John ix.
3 οὔτε οὗτος ἥμαρτεν, οὔτε . . . , ἀλλ᾽ ἵνα φανερωθῇ etc., xv. 25 ; 1 John 208
ii. 19, cf. John xiii. 18 ; xiv. 30. Similarly Luke xvii. 2 λυσιτελεῖ
αὐτῷ εἰ λίθος περίκειται . . . ἢ ἵνα σκανδαλίσῃ than if he lives to etc.,
Gal. ii. 9, 10 δεξιὰς ἔδωκαν ἐμοὶ καὶ Βαρνάβᾳ ἵνα ἡμεῖς εἰς τὰ ἔθνη . . . ·
μόνον τῶν πτωχῶν ἵ ν α μ ν η μ ο ν ε ύ ω μ ε ν.

Further, we shall find that by means of such elliptical constructions
with ἵνα — very much as in the case of the rare Infin. Fut. (according
to 44 p. 239) — the far more rare P a r t i c i p l e F u t u r e (see § 144,
10 p. 296), which the classic language likes so much to employ to
express a purpose, was avoided, or even periphrased, as appears from
the following examples: Rev. vi. 2 ἐξῆλθεν νικῶν καὶ ἵ ν α ν ι κ ή σ ῃ,
John i. 8 οὐκ ἦν ἐκεῖνος τὸ φῶς, ἀλλ᾽ ἵνα μαρτυρήσῃ περὶ τοῦ φωτός, Eph.
v. 27 τὴν ἐκκλησίαν, μὴ ἔχουσαν σπίλον ἢ ῥυτίδα, ἀλλ᾽ ἵνα ᾖ ἁγία καὶ
ἄμωμος (dependent as respects construction on παραστήσῃ).

Lastly ἵνα is used (quite as in classical writers the elliptical ὅπως
B. m. 46 ; H. § 756 a. ; C. § 626 ; D. § 611 ; J. § 812, 2 ; G. § 45 N. 7)
as a c i r c u m l o c u t i o n f o r t h e I m p e r a t i v e : either after a
preceding verbum dicendi, as in Mark v. 23 λέγων ὅτι τὸ θυγάτριόν μου
ἐσχάτως ἔχει · ἵ ν α ἐλθὼν ἐπιθῇς τὰς χεῖρας αὐτῇ, ἵνα σωθῇ ;　　　or
without such antecedent, as in 2 Cor. viii. 7 ἀλλ᾽, ὥσπερ περισσεύετε . . . ,
ἵνα καὶ ἐν ταύτῃ τῇ χάριτι περισσεύητε ;　or in continuation of a foregoing Imperative, as Eph. iv. 29 πᾶς λόγος σαπρὸς μὴ ἐκπορευέσθω,
ἀλλ᾽ εἴ τις . . . ἵνα δῷ χάριν, v. 33 ἕκαστος ἀγαπάτω τὴν ἑαυτοῦ γυναῖκα, ἡ
δὲ γυνὴ ἵνα φοβῆται τὸν ἄνδρα.

The r e s t r i c t i v e c o n c l u s i o n with ἵνα μὴ, as Philem. 19 ἵνα
μὴ λέγω σοι ὅτι . . . προσοφείλεις (cf. 2 Cor. ii. 5 ἵνα μὴ ἐπιβαρῶ), corresponds to the Latin constructions ne dicam and the like.

───────────

B. § 139, m. 50 ; H. § 720 ; C. § 624 ; D. § 538 ; J. § 814 ; G. § 46.

After verbs of f e a r i n g etc. (φοβεῖσθαι, εὐλαβεῖσθαι) our　48 *that* is rendered, as in the classics, by μή; (*that not*, Lat. *ne non*, by μὴ οὐ according to § 148, 11 p. 354). Of the dependent moods only the Subjunctive (agreeably to the use in final clauses) is still employed after μή, even after historic tenses; as, Acts xxvii. 17 φοβούμενοι μὴ ... ἐκπέσωσιν, ἐφέροντο, 29 ; xxiii. 10 φοβηθεὶς μὴ διασπασθῇ ἐκέλευσεν. After leading tenses: 2 Cor. xi. 3 ; Heb. iv. 1, etc. ; Subjunctive in connection with the Future, 2 Cor. xii. 20, 21.

In Acts v. 26 Lchm. [Treg.] ἐφοβοῦντο γὰρ τὸν λαόν, μὴ λιθασθῶσιν, the subordinate clause does not seem to be dependent on ἐφοβοῦντο, but to belong as a telic specification (for ἵνα μὴ λιθ. as Tdf. et al. actually read, after A) to what precedes, since if it depends on ἐφοβοῦντο, it ought, according to the analogy of the familiar construction (οἶδά σε ὅτι), to have been so framed that τὸν λαόν might have been its Subject, as in Thuc. 4, 108 τοὺς ξυμμάχους ἐφοβοῦντο, μὴ ἀποστῶσιν. Yet it is more probable that the sentence, when compared with the similar passage Gal. iv. 11 (φοβοῦμαι ὑμᾶς, μή πως εἰκῇ κεκοπίακα εἰς ὑμᾶς), contains a blending of two constructions (ἐφοβ. τὸν λαόν, and ἐφοβ. μὴ λιθασθῶσιν) ; or rather, that after the analogy of the instances given in § 151, 10 p. 383 there is a bound from the Active construction over into the Passive (consequently for μὴ λιθάσῃ or λιθάσωσιν ἡμᾶς). Further, the reading μὴ λιθ. is not only the better attested (codd. Vat. Sin. etc.), but the other (ἵνα μὴ λιθ.) would rather appear to be a correction of it than vice versa ; cf. besides, Ep. Barn. 6 and the quite similar instance in Thuc. 4, 8, 7. More difficult is it to explain by the same analogy the change in the passage from the Ep. to the Gal. (iv. 11), if we avail ourselves merely of the recorded words. But the thought which was in the mind of the apostle when he began the sentence (φοβοῦμαι ὑμᾶς) was something like, 'I fear that ye may render futile my endeavors'; for which by a change of construction the thought at once was presented, 'that I have labored for you in vain.' On the use of the Indic. Perfect (κεκοπίακα) in order to set forth the object of fear as an already existing fact, as it were, or to anticipate it, cf. Hermas Mand. 12, 5 ; Protev. 14. 1, the corresponding examples from Greek authors in B. l.c., and below, § 148, 10 p. 353.

REMARK. The two verbs βλέπειν and ὁρᾶν are often used tropically, in the sense of φυλάσσεσθαι, to be on one's guard, *take heed*. Hence they take also the same constructions as this verb, viz. either a noun with ἀπό and the Gen. (see § 147 under ἀπό p. 323), or a verb with μή (not ἵνα μή; for in 2 John 8 βλέπετε ἑαυτούς, ἵνα μὴ ἀπολέσητε etc. the first clause forms a complete thought, and the clause which follows is a subjoined specification of end). Now since both these verbs always immediately precede the clause negatived by μή in the

Imperative form, they appear almost like a pleonastic addition, after the fashion of the very similar constructions in Latin with *vide*, *cave ne* etc.   The Mood is as usual in sentences expressing apprehension and warning the Aorist Subjunct., as Matt. xviii. 10 ὁρᾶτε μὴ καταφρονήσητε ἑνὸς τούτων, xxiv. 4 βλέπετε μή τις ὑμᾶς πλανήσῃ, Mark xiii. 5 ; Luke xxi. 8 βλέπετε μὴ πλανηθῆτε, Acts xiii. 40 ; 1 Cor. x. 12 ; 1 Thess. v. 15 ; Heb. xii. 25 ; yet the Future also, which so frequently alternates with this Subjunct., may take its place, as Col. ii. 8 βλέπετε μή τις ἔσται, Heb. iii. 12.[1]

Finally, there are a few passages where those Imperatives (ὅρα, ὁρᾶτε) must really be regarded as thoroughly pleonastic additions, they being prefixed to another Imperative (or Subjunctive in its place) negatived by μή, and even to a positive Imperative without anything intervening (cf. § 151, 32 p. 402) ; as, Matt. ix. 30 ὁρᾶτε μηδεὶς γινωσκέτω, viii. 4 ὅρα μηδενὶ εἴπῃς, Mark viii. 15 ὁρᾶτε βλέπετε ἀπὸ τῆς ζύμης τῶν Φ. ; hence also in Matt. xxiv. 6 (ὁρᾶτε μὴ θροεῖσθε) the form θροεῖσθε is not to be taken as Indicative (for the Future), but as Imperative.

The case is different with the actual Indicative in Luke xi. 35 σκόπει οὖν μὴ τὸ φῶς τὸ ἐν σοὶ σκότος ἐστίν.   Since, that is to say, σκοπεῖν is never used in the sense of φυλάσσεσθαι, like the above two verbs (hence in Gal. vi. 1 the clause with μὴ is to be construed as a pure telic clause, for ἵνα μὴ etc.), but uniformly in its proper signification *to look at, regard*, the dependent clause is to be taken as an indirect question in the Indicative (see H. below) : *see to it whether* 210 *the light . . . is not* etc.

On the elliptical ὅρα μή see § 151, 24 b) p. 395.

F. Illative Sentences.

B § 139, m. 52 sqq.; H. §§ 770. 771; C. § 671 d.; D. § 596; J. § 863; G. §§ 65, 3; 98.

As respects sentences expressing consequence, the N. T. 50 writings depart but little from the general rules.   With ὥστε, so far forth as at the beginning of a clause it is the co-ordinating particle (*itaque*), the Indicative is joined (Matt. xii. 12, etc.).   And even when the Subjunctive follows (1 Cor. v. 8 ὥστε ἑορτάζωμεν etc.) the particle is co-ordinating, since the Subjunct. here is the Conjunct. adhortativus described in 4 above, p. 209, and therefore only takes the place of the

---

[1] The positive injunction rendered by the Future after ὅρα in Heb. viii. 5 (ὅρα ποιήσεις etc., a quotn.) is not to be explained by the omission of ἵνα, but results solely from the literal translation of the Hebrew, and is founded consequently upon no N. T. usage.

Imperative, which after ὥστε is pretty frequent, *e.g.* 1 Cor. iii. 21; iv. 5; x. 12; xi. 33, etc.

But whenever it is the subordinating particle (*ita ut*), the construction with the Infinitive (Acc. with Infin.) is almost the only one in use: and that, too, both when the dependent clause contains the purely natural consequence of the leading action,[1] as Matt. viii. 24; xiii. 2, etc.; and when it is a designed consequence, as Matt. x. 1; xii. 22; Acts xiv. 1, etc.   See the Remark.

Of the use of ὥστε in the sense of *so that* with the Indicative (which then of course represents the consequence objectively, as a fact accomplished) there are but two instances: once after οὕτως John iii. 16 (οὕτως ἠγάπησεν ... ὥστε τὸν υἱὸν αὐτοῦ ἔδωκεν), and once almost in the co-ordinating sense (*itaque*) Gal. ii. 13.   After τοσοῦτος likewise ὥστε (not ὅσος B. m. 57) is used, and with the Infin. Matt. xv. 33.   Of ὡς with the Infin. instead of ὥστε, according to Greek usage, there is but one example in Acts (xx. 24), which to judge from the copious variants seems to have almost ceased to be intelligible to the copyists, etc. Ὡς occurs as a variant in Luke ix. 52 (supported by א B).

REMARK. Since, as was remarked above (43 p. 238), ὥστε unites in itself both references — that of result and that of design, there are cases where, as in ἵνα the ecbatic (44 p. 238), so in ὥστε the final, force predominates; or at least, while the issue is still future, it is anticipated or represented in thought as if already realized. 211 That in Greek authors also this usage is by no means unknown (see e.g. Lys. or. 19, 16), and hence even in them, too, ὥστε and ὅπως are found after the same predicates, has likewise already been remarked above.   Cf. also εἰς τὸ followed by the Infin. in § 140, 10 p. 264.   The most marked passages of the sort in the N. T. are the following: Matt. xxvii. 1 συμβούλιον ἔλαβον οἱ ἀρχιερεῖς, ὥστε θανατῶσαι αὐτόν (where cod. D explains the ὥστε by ἵνα θανατώσουσιν), — but after the same predicate ὅπως with the Subjunct. as usual stands in Matt. xxii. 15; Mark iii. 6; further Luke iv. 29 ἤγαγον αὐτὸν ... ὥστε κατακρημνίσαι αὐτὸν (where again many MSS. and the Rec. have εἰς τὸ κ.). ix. 52 εἰσῆλθον εἰς κώμην Σαμαρειτῶν, ὥστε ἑτοιμάσαι αὐτῷ, xx. 20 ἵνα

---

[1] This case is by far the more frequent one with ὥστε and the Infin. in the N. T. (and is also common enough in classic writers, see B. m. 53 and 54), because for the second, the designed consequence, the particle ἵνα was employed (according to what was said above, see 40, 43 sqq. pp. 235 sqq.) by many writers, particularly John; hence, as matter of fact, this Evangelist no longer uses ὥστε with the Infin., and even ὥστε with the Indic. (after οὕτω) occurs only once in his writings, see above.

ἐπιλάβωνται αὐτοῦ λόγου, ὥστε παραδοῦναι αὐτὸν τῇ ἀρχῇ.　Matt. xv. 33 also is to be taken most naturally in this sense.

G.　Declarative Sentences (with ὅτι).

B. § 139, m. 58 sqq.; H. §§ 733 sq.; C. §§ 643 sq.; D. §§ 590 sq.; J. §§ 800 sq.; G. §§ 69 sq.

The only particle which belongs under this head is ὅτι; for **51** ὡς is always to be translated by *how*.　The Optative as the Mood of indirect assertion is in this connection completely excluded, because in its stead the Indicative everywhere makes its appearance, as Matt. xvi. 20, 21, etc.　But even this use of the Indicative with ὅτι is frequently not observed, as the N. T. writers (like the Seventy) prefer to introduce discourses in the direct form, even twice or thrice in succession in one and the same sentence.　This is done either without the intervention of a particle (in which case the more recent editions [but not Tdf.'s 8th] begin the clause with a capital letter), or (after a mode in use even by the Greeks, B. m. 61; G. § 79) by means of the particle ὅτι, which is then redundant. (In this case recent editions [except Treg.'s] do not use the capitals,[1] and also put no stop after ὅτι, — a procedure which sometimes where the third Person is used, or the same Person in both the dependent and the leading clause, causes ambiguity.)

Examples occur in great number everywhere: of direct discourse twice in succession, John i. 15 λέγων Οὗτος ἦν ὃν εἶπον Ὁ ἐρχόμενος γέγονεν etc. (see on this § 151, 1 d) p. 377), v. 12 ἠρώτησαν Τίς ἐστιν ὁ ἄνθρωπος ὁ εἰπών σοι Ἆρον καὶ περιπάτει; of both kinds (with and without ὅτι), John x. 36 ὑμεῖς λέγετε ὅτι· βλασφημεῖς, ὅτι (*because*) εἶπον Υἱὸς τοῦ θεοῦ εἰμι (see on this § 141, 1 p. 272); of direct discourse three times, John x. 34 ἀπεκρίθη Οὐκ ἔστιν γεγραμμένον ὅτι· ἐγὼ εἶπα Θεοί ἐστε; further, of ὅτι before the 2d Pers. Sing. of the Imperative, John ix. 11; xiv. 9 (cod. Sin., on which Tdf. remarks, tale ὅτι non inferri sed expelli solet), before the 3d Pers., 2 Thess. iii. 10.

The Subjunctive as the dependent Mood is impossible (because experience has already decided the matter, cf. B. m. 58), and hence where it occurs it must be taken as the Subjunctive in independent clauses (see above, 2 sqq. p. 208), as Rom. iii. 8 φασίν τινες ἡμᾶς λέγειν ὅτι ποιήσωμεν τὰ κακά, ἵνα ἔλθῃ τὰ ἀγαθά (conjunct. adhort. or dubit.; upon the construction see further § 141, 3 p. 274); or it takes **212** the place of the Future, according to N. T. usage, e.g. after οὐ μή:

---

[1] On the other hand, if ὅτι is written with a capital, it belongs to the direct discourse itself, e.g. 1 Cor. xii. 15, etc.　Cf. below, 59 p. 252.

Matt. v. 20 λέγω, ὅτι οὐ μὴ εἰσέλθητε εἰς τὴν βασιλείαν τῶν οὐρανῶν, Mark. xiv. 25 λέγω ὑμῖν, ὅτι οὐκέτι οὐ μὴ πίω, etc.

Respecting ἵνα after εἰπεῖν and other verba dicendi see 42 note p. 237..

B. § 139, m. 59, 60; C. § 639; J. § 804, 8. 9; G. § 113, NN. 7, 9; § 56.

52   After μιμνήσκεσθαι and the like, our *that* is only given in the N. T. by ὅτι (not ὅτε). On the other hand, εἰ is frequently found instead of ὅτι after θαυμάζειν, as Mark xv. 44 Πιλᾶτος ἐθαύμασεν, εἰ ἤδη τέθνηκεν, 1 John iii. 13 μὴ θαυμάζετε, εἰ μισεῖ ὑμᾶς ὁ κόσμος. Similar examples are Luke xii. 49 τί θέλω, εἰ ἤδη ἀνήφθη (see above, 10 p. 215), Acts xxvi. 8 ἄπιστον κρίνεται παρ᾽ ὑμῖν, εἰ ὁ θεὸς νεκροὺς ἐγείρει; Heb.. vii. 15 κατάδηλόν ἐστιν, εἰ ... ἀνίσταται ἱερεὺς ἕτερος (cf. vs. 14).

B. § 139, m. 61; H. § 743 b.; C. § 644; J. § 802, Obs. 8; G. § 79.

53   Among the examples of ὅτι before direct discourse may also be reckoned the case where, instead of a construction by means of the verbal adj. or the Impersonal δεῖ, the Imperative itself makes its appearance, as 2 Thess. iii. 10 παρηγγέλλομεν ὑμῖν, ὅτι εἴ τις οὐ θέλει ἐργάζεσθαι, μηδὲ ἐσθιέτω (cf. the example from Thucyd. in B. m. 36 — m. 61 in the last ed.; the similar case with εἰ μή in § 149, 4 p. 359; and in 42 above, p. 237, the other construction with ἵνα and the Subjunct.).

Respecting the redundant ὅτι before the Acc. with Infin. (Acts. xxvii. 10) see § 151, 10 p. 383.

H. Interrogative Sentences, Direct and Indirect.

B. § 139, m. 62 sqq.; H. §§ 824 sqq.; J. §§ 871 sqq.; G. §§ 68 sqq. 88.

54   The practice just mentioned of quoting language almost exclusively in the direct form, has as its natural consequence that the form of the direct interrogative sentence has become by far the predominant one. In order not to scatter too much our treatment of a topic of great importance for the comprehension of the N. T. writings, we will bring together here into a single summary the entire N. T. usage (in other respects as well as mood) of both kinds of sentence.

Direct interrogative clauses which have not already an interrogative pronoun, as τίς; τί; or an interrogative adverb, as πῶς, ποῦ, etc., at their head, are, as is well known, in both the ancient languages (contrary to the usage of German and other modern tongues) generally introduced by an interrogative particle. But in the popular or colloquial language, which designates interrogative clauses plainly enough merely by the interrogative accent, this aid was slighted, as a rule, even by the Greeks and Romans; and its f r e q u e n t use was probably characteristic rather of the literary language.

Agreeably to what has been said, the language of the N. T. has employed, in by far the majority of cases, the popular mode of introducing interrogative clauses w i t h o u t an i n t e r r o g a t i v e word. And this it has done not only (as happens for the most part in the historical books) immediately after a verbum quaerendi in the fore- 213. going narrative, — as John ix. 19 ἠρώτησαν· οὗτός ἐστιν ὁ υἱὸς ὑμῶν, ὃν λέγετε ὅτι τυφλὸς ἐγεννήθη; v. 6 λέγει αὐτῷ· θέλεις ὑγιὴς γενέσθαι; — but also (as often happens in the epistolary style, in protracted arguments, etc.) without a preceding verbum quaerendi; in which case the presence of an interrogative clause, therefore, is only to be discovered by the connection, as 1 Cor. ix. 11; 2 Cor. iii. 1, etc. Questions which expect an affirmative answer are, at least as a rule, distinguished by a direct negative (οὐ, οὐχί, οὐδέ, οὐδείς, etc.) placed at the very beginning of the clause; as, John xi. 8 οὐχὶ δώδεκα ὧραί εἰσιν τῆς ἡμέρας; vii. 42 οὐχ ἡ γραφὴ εἶπεν ὅτι etc. This form of question is especially characteristic of Paul, who accordingly, assuming tacitly the affirmative answer of the persons addressed, often uses several such interrogative clauses in succession, as 1 Cor. ix. 1 sqq.

The practice of distinguishing the interrogative clause by 55. an i n t e r r o g a t i v e p a r t i c l e, although the less frequent, is yet not an uncommon, practice; but the manner of doing so, or the choice of the particle, deviates more or less from ordinary usage.

The p a r t i c l e ἆρα (formerly employed most frequently), corresponding to the Latin -ne and by no means always expecting a negative answer, appears, at the most, only in Luke's writings (Gospel xviii. 8; Acts viii. 30); for in Gal. ii. 17 εἰ δὲ ... εὑρέθημεν ἁμαρτωλοί, ἄρα Χριστὸς ἁμαρτίας διάκονος the form ἄρα (as invariably with Paul) is with Lchm. and many interpreters to be preferred, but the clause nevertheless to be taken as a question: 'is then, forsooth, after all, Christ' etc.; cf. the quite similar clauses, yet without the interrogative form, in ii. 21; iii. 29; v. 11 etc. 1 Cor. xv. 18, and on the ἄρα, often used thus in questions by Greek authors, Plato, Gorg. p. 477, etc. On the whole, perhaps as respects the N. T. writers the conjecture has considerable probability, that a precise distinction (which moreover even in Greek authors it is hard to carry out, see Ph. Buttm. on Pl. Charm. 15; Ellendt, Lex. Soph. sub voce; Klotz ad Devar. II 160 sqq.) between the two particles has been lost sight of; hence, too, the illative particle so often stands at the beginning, see § 149, 18 p. 371.

Very common, on the other hand, is a question (anticipating a negative answer) by means of the Particle μή (see B. § 148, 5; H. § 829; C. § 687; D. p. 559; J. § 873, 4; G. p. 84) for which μήτι is often used; Eng. *surely not?* or simply, *perhaps, possibly* (spoken in a doubting tone).

Matt. vii. 9, 10 μὴ λίθον ... μὴ ὄφιν ἐπιδώσει αὐτῷ; *surely he will not give him a stone ... a serpent?* Luke xvii. 9 μὴ ἔχει χάριν τῷ δούλῳ; *is he perchance thankful to the bondman?* vi. 39 μήτι δύναται τυφλὸς τυφλὸν ὁδηγεῖν; in reply to which we have again a question, but with οὐχί, *nonne?* Matt. xxvi. 22, 25 μήτι ἐγώ εἰμι, ῥαββί: (although the answer follows, σὺ εἶπας), Mark ii. 19; Acts vii. 28; Rom. iii. 5; Jas. iii. 12; and often in John: iii. 4; vi. 67, etc. (cf. also 62 p. 256). This form of interrogation we must conceive of as having sprung originally from an indirect construction, as 'I hope, am of the opinion, that he surely will not' etc.; and this thought several ancient MSS. suggest immediately after a question of the sort in Luke xvii. 9 by the addition οὐ δοκῶ. Peculiar to Paul is the use, instead of the answer to such questions, of the well-known negatory formula (Gen. xliv. 7; Luke xx. 16) μὴ γένοιτο, as Rom. iii. 4, 6; ix. 14; xi. 1, 11.

If in such questions the predicate is n e g a t i v e d b e s i d e s, that can be done according to the rule (§ 148, 11 p. 354) only by the direct negation οὐ; the question requires then an affirmative answer (*nonne*), as Rom. x. 18 μὴ οὐκ ἤκουσαν; μενοῦνγε etc., 19 μὴ Ἰσραὴλ οὐκ ἔγνω; πρῶτος Μωϋσῆς λέγει etc., 1 Cor. ix. 4, 5, 6; xi. 22.

Quite in the same way arose, from the form of indirect interrogation, the d i r e c t i n t e r r o g a t i v e s e n t e n c e s (particularly frequent in the writings of Luke) w i t h εἰ p r e c e d i n g. Then εἰ is s u p e r f l u o u s, precisely as ὅτι was in the declarative sentences treated of in G. p. 245; and the usage, as in that case, is to be accounted for by the constant tendency to pass over into direct discourse.

The direct nature of such interrogative clauses becomes incontestably evident from sentences like Luke xxii. 49 εἶπαν· κύριε, εἰ π α τ ά ξ ο μ ε ν ἐν μαχαίρᾳ; xiii. 23 κύριε, εἰ ὀλίγοι οἱ σωζόμενοι; Acts i. 6; xix. 2 εἶπεν· εἰ πνεῦμα ἅγιον ἐλάβετε πιστεύσαντες; xxi. 37 Παῦλος λέγει· εἰ ἔξεστίν μοι εἰπεῖν τι πρὸς σέ; xxii. 25; xxiii. 9; Matt. xx. 15 Tdf. (where, however, Tdf. in his 8th ed. has correctly altered εἰ again, with codd. Vat. Sin. etc., into ἤ; the Lat. versions also give uniformly either *an* or *aut*), Mark viii. 23 Tdf. (after cod. Vat.; in his 8th ed. Tdf. reads again βλέπει after cod. Sin.); cf. 56 p. 249. Hence we may probably take without hesitation those clauses also as direct, which externally differ in nothing from the form of the indirect question (with εἰ *whether*), as Acts vii. 1 εἶπεν ὁ ἀρχιερεὺς · εἰ ἄρα ταῦτα οὕτως ἔχει; Matt. xii. 10 ἐπηρώτησαν αὐτὸν λέγοντες · εἰ ἔξεστιν τοῖς σάββασιν θεραπεύειν; xix. 3.   This usage is found, moreover, in the Sept. also, e.g. Gen. xliii. 6; Judg. xiii. 11; 1 Sam. x. 24, etc., which translates in this way the Hebr. הֲ, which likewise stands before direct questions and indirect, see Gesen. sub voce.

The particle οὐκοῦν (B. § 149 m. 18; H. § 866 a.; C. § 687 c.; D. § 535; J. § 791 Obs.) in the single passage in which it occurs (John xviii. 37) is not interrogative, but illative in reference to what precedes; but the clause (as above with ἄρα) is an interrogative clause of the first kind (cf. 54 p. 246): οὐκοῦν βασιλεὺς εἶ σύ; *ergone rex es? thou art then* (according to what thou sayest) *a king?*

Direct double questions (without a material interrog- **56** ative word, as τίς, ποῦ, etc.) are properly marked, as with us, only by the ἤ (*or*) in the second clause, consequently merely by the tone, in the popular fashion spoken of 54 p. 246; as, Matt. xi. 3 σὺ εἶ ὁ ἐρχόμενος, ἢ ἕτερον προσδοκῶμεν; Mark xii. 14 ἔξεστιν δοῦναι κῆνσον Καίσαρι, ἢ οὔ; δῶμεν, ἢ μὴ δῶμεν; Doubtful instances, with the pleonastic εἰ (55 p. 248) at the beginning, are: Luke xiv. 3 Lchm. where Tdf. [Treg.], comparing the parallel passage Matt. xii. 10, have expunged εἰ [Sin. om.], and Luke vi. 9 where all three editors have preferred the form of an indirect question.

From strict double questions (i.e. those whose members mutually exclude each other) those cases are to be carefully distinguished, where to an antecedent question — instead of the answer, or in completion and continuation of the first question — a second is subjoined and **connected by** ἤ. For example: after an interrogative clause **215** of the first kind (with οὐ), Matt. xii. 3 sqq. οὐκ ἀνέγνωτε, τί ἐποίησεν ... ; ἢ οὐκ ἀνέγνωτε ἐν τῷ νόμῳ etc., xx. 15 Lchm. [Tdf. Treg.], (Tdf. [eds. 2, 7] εἰ) ; after a question negatived by μή (55 p. 248), 1 Cor. ix. 8 μὴ κατὰ ἄνθρωπον ταῦτα λαλῶ, ἢ καὶ ὁ νόμος ταῦτα οὐ λέγει; 9 μὴ τῶν βοῶν μέλει τῷ θεῷ, ἢ δι᾽ ἡμᾶς πάντως λέγει; i. 13; Matt. vii. 16, etc.; after a double question, Gal. i. 10 ἄρτι ἀνθρώπους πείθω ἢ τὸν θεόν; ἢ ζητῶ ἀνθρώποις ἀρέσκειν; The same particle (ἤ) stands also, as *an* does in Latin, with a simple **antithetic question** after a preceding categoric clause; as, Matt. xxvi. 53; 2 Cor. xi. 7; xiii. 5; 1 Cor. xiv. 36 (where even the double ἤ involves no double question), etc.

Indirect interrogative clauses are dependent on a **57** verbum quaerendi, dicendi, cognoscendi, etc., which

sometimes must first be educed from the predicate of the leading clause, or supplied ; as, after ἐγένετο φιλονεικία ἐν αὐτοῖς
(Luke xxii. 24), βάλλοντες κλῆρον, τίς τί ἄρῃ (Mark xv. 24),
ἦν τάραχος, τί ἄρα ὁ Πέτρος ἐγένετο (Acts xii. 18). They
divide themselves into two classes, according as they are
introduced

A. by a merely formal interrogative word, pointing out the
interrogative clause as such (num, whether). The interrogative particle uniformly employed with simple, positive, interrogative clauses is εἰ, as Mark xv. 44 ἐπηρώτησεν αὐτὸν, εἰ
πάλαι ἀπέθανεν, xv. 36 ἴδωμεν, εἰ ἔρχεται Ἡλίας, John ix. 25
εἰ ἁμαρτωλός ἐστιν, οὐκ οἶδα ; in negative clauses (whether not,
whether not perhaps) simply μή (μήποτε), as Luke iii. 15
διαλογιζομένων πάντων περὶ τοῦ Ἰωάννου, μήποτε αὐτὸς εἴη ὁ
Χριστός (with which may be compared the μή after βλέπετε,
ὁρᾶτε, in 49 p. 242).

With indirect double questions the full form of interrogation
(usual with Greek writers) by means of the two particles πότερον
... ἤ appears but once viz. John vii. 17 γνώσεται, πότερον ἐκ τοῦ θεοῦ
ἐστιν, ἢ ἐγὼ ἀπ' ἐμαυτοῦ λαλῶ. Elsewhere εἴτε is used instead even
twice, as 2 Cor. xii. 3 εἴτε ἐν σώματι, εἴτε χωρὶς τοῦ σώματος, οὐκ οἶδα,
ὁ θεὸς οἶδεν ; or the question is resolved into two, as 2 Cor. xii. 2
εἴτε ἐν σώματι, οὐκ οἶδα, εἴτε ἐκτὸς σώματος, οὐκ οἶδα. In by far the
majority of double questions, however, the direct interrogative
form is chosen (with the simple ἤ in the second clause), see 56 p. 249.

B. by a material interrogative word, i.e. by a pronoun or
a pronominal adverb of place, time, manner. The language,
as is well known, created interrogative words (in the form of
relatives) for this special purpose, such as ὅστις, ὁποῖος, ὅπου,
ὁπότε, ὅπως, etc., which it employs as substitutes for the simple
relative forms ὅς, οἷος, ὡς, etc., in designating indirect interrogative clauses. As, however, at all times, even in indirect
questions, the direct interrogative pronouns τίς, ποῖος, etc.,
very frequently make their appearance, this is the case in a
still higher degree in the N.T., owing to the strong inclination
of its authors to employ direct forms of statement.

213   Examples of both kinds are found everywhere : as, after οἶδα indirect interrogation, οἶδεν ὧν χρείαν ἔχετε ; ὅπου ἐγὼ ὑπάγω οἴδατε ; εἰδυῖα
ὃ γέγονεν ; οὐκ οἴδατε οἴου πνεύματός ἐστε, etc. direct interrogation, οὐκ
ᾔδει τίς ἐστιν ; τί λέγεις οἷκ οἶδεν ; οὐκ οἶδα ποῦ ἔθηκαν, πόθεν ἦλθον, ποία

ἡμέρᾳ ὁ κύριος ἔρχεται ; and in connection with the familiar construction
(§ 151, 1 p. 377) οἶδά σε τίς εἶ, οὐκ οἶδα ὑμᾶς πόθεν ἐστέ ; with other
predicates, as Matt. vi. 28 καταμάθετε τὰ κρίνα πῶς αὐξάνουσιν, Luke
xii. 36 προσδεχόμενοι τὸν κύριον πότε ἀναλύσῃ etc. Both species are
united in one sentence, as 1 Tim. i. 7 μὴ νοοῦντες μήτε ἃ λέγουσιν μήτε
περὶ τίνων διαβεβαιοῦνται, — a combination which in Greek authors also
is not rare ; see the examples in Lobeck ad Phryn. p. 57 ; Schneidewin
on Soph. Oed. Tyr. 71.

REMARK. It is to be noted as a deviation from the regular usage 58
(which, however, occurs likewise even in Greek authors) that the
preference for the direct interrogative form is so great, that this form
is not only substituted for the ordinary indirect question, but is sometimes chosen even where according to rule only a pure relative
clause is allowed to stand. But this occurs only after predicate ideas
which have a certain affinity with verba sentiendi etc., so that the underlying thought can or must be traced back to the form of an indirect
question. This takes place most frequently both in Greek authors
and in the N. T. after the verb ἔχειν (οὐκ ἔχειν), as Matt. viii. 20 οὐκ
ἔχει ποῦ τὴν κεφαλὴν κλίνῃ (equiv. to he knows not etc.), Mark viii.
1, 2 οὐκ ἔχουσιν τί φάγωσιν, Luke xii. 17 οὐκ ἔχω ποῦ συνάξω τοὺς καρπούς. Cf. 1 Cor. xv. 2 τίνι λόγῳ εὐηγγελισάμην ὑμῖν εἰ κατέχετε. On
the other hand the construction is regular in Luke xi. 6 οὐκ ἔχω ὃ παραθήσω αὐτῷ, Heb. viii. 3 ἔχειν τι ὃ προσενέγκῃ. The indirect question
after this predicate is the more admissible, as ἔχειν is very often construed with the Infinitive, after the manner of verba sentiendi etc.
(οὐκ ἔχουσιν ἀνταποδοῦναί σοι Luke xiv. 14, etc.) ; hence both modes
of expression are united : Acts xxv. 26 ἀσφαλές τι γράψαι οὐκ ἔχω ·
. . . ὅπως σχῶ τί γράψω. After the analogy of this verb still other
verbs are found construed in the N. T., as Matt. x. 19 δοθήσεται ὑμῖν
τί λαλήσετε (equiv. to ye will have etc.), Luke xvii. 8 ἑτοίμασον τί
δειπνήσω (brachylogically equiv. to that I may have what etc.). Cf. on
this topic Bhdy. p. 443 ; and among the passages from Greek authors,
Plut. Mor. p. 606 C. σὺ τί κρέας λέγεις ποιεῖς, οὐ τί νοῦν ἔχων ἄνθρωπος,
Callim. Ep. 30 (and Bentley's note), Schol. on Soph. Oed. Col. 3. In
the Sept. also the usage is not unknown, as Deut. xxix. 18 ; Ps.
xxxix. 6.

Moreover, the following passages come into consideration here :
Matt. xxvi. 62 and Mark xiv. 60 οὐδὲν ἀποκρίνῃ, τί οὗτοί σου καταμαρτυροῦσιν ; Hardly is τί to be taken here in a purely relative sense
(equiv. to ὅ, Vulg. ad ea quae). That something must be supplied
here is obvious, as a direct reference of τί to οὐδέν is impossible. It
is most simple to supply a verbal idea like to hear, so that the abbreviated thought if rendered grammatically complete would run · an-

swerest thou nothing (hearing) what these witness against thee? cf. § 151, 25 p. 395. That the ancients, too, construed the passage in this way is apparent from the manner in which the Evang. Nicod. (Pars I. B) 2. 1 as it were paraphrases the words: λέγει ὁ Πιλάτος· Ἀκούεις τί οὗτοί σου καταμαρτυροῦσιν, καὶ οὐκ ἀποκρίνῃ. Acts xiii. 25 Tdf. [eds. 2, 7] τ ί ν α (Lchm. [Tdf. Treg. cod. Sin.] τί) με ὑπονοεῖτε εἶναι, οὐκ εἰμὶ ἐγώ. Here the first clause in its dependence on the leading clause is decidedly relative, hence according to rule instead of τίνα strictly ὅν ought to have stood; but, instead of this, the first clause has retained the form which it would have had if not in dependence, viz. the form of an interrogative clause. Obviously the placing of the dependent clause before the leading clause occasioned the anomaly. Similar is Jas. iii. 13 τίς σοφὸς καὶ ἐπιστήμων ἐν ὑμῖν, δειξάτω τὰ ἔργα αὐτοῦ etc. Here the first clause is commonly taken as an independent direct question, and accordingly an interrogation mark placed after ὑμῖν. But the disruption of clauses produced in this way, as well as the wholly unprovoked asyndetic transition to δειξάτω without any subject, renders it probable that the two clauses are to be separated (with Lchm.) only by a comma. Then an inversio structurae (cf. § 151, 8–11 pp. 381 sqq.) has taken place here as in the preceding example. The direct interrogative form of the first clause, occasioned by its precedence and retained by the immediate proximity of such a predicate as δειξάτω, passed (owing to the construction that follows) naturally over into the force of the kindred relative clause; (cf. the Germ. *wer* when it precedes). Lastly, Mark xiv. 36 ἀλλ' οὐ τί ἐγὼ θέλω, ἀλλὰ τί σύ is translated in the Vulg. by the relative: *quod volo,* and accordingly a predicate like γενέσθω was as a rule supplied. But neither the meaning nor the form of the sentence permits such an addition. On the contrary, the direct negation (οὐ) as well as the pronoun τί render an ellipsis in harmony with an indirect interrogation (Fritzsche, *quaeritur;* Meyer, *the question is*) apparently more justifiable.

But indubitable instances of the opposite case also occur, viz. in which the R e l a t i v e or i n d i r e c t form of interrogation is employed in a decidedly d i r e c t i n t e r r o g a t i v e s e n t e n c e. To be sure, all constructions of the sort (like most of the preceding examples) are founded in a faulty or negligent treatment of the forms of phraseology established by the literary language; and hence the occurrence particularly of this second case in native Greek writers has been emphatically disputed (see Bhdy. p. 443; Schaef. on Demos. p. 1199). Nevertheless, after what Lobeck (ad Phryn. p. 57) has adduced, all such irregularities in earlier writers can hardly be set aside by arbitrary emendation; and to supply a verbum sentiendi and the like in every individual case, would amount to nothing else than giving the force of

direct question to the R e l a t i v e form (see Ph. Buttm. on Plat. Meno.
6). Thus in the N. T. an instance, textually quite unquestionable, is
Matt. xxvi. 50 εἶπεν αὐτῷ· Ἐταῖρε, ἐφ᾽ ὃ πάρει; (Vulg. *ad q u o d venisti ?*).
Since elsewhere, neither in the N. T. nor, according to Lobeck's express testimony, in profane authors also is any example to be found of
the s i m p l e relative so used (but only of the compound ὅστις), the
interpreters have objected to taking this ἐφ᾽ ὃ in the sense of ἐπὶ τί, and
sought to remove the irregularity of the expression by the assumption
of an aposiopesis; but this here would be likewise irregular (cf. § 151
V. p. 396), and is quite at variance also with the character of the
passage, in which there is no motive for leaving the thought incomplete. We reach the natural and only congruous interpretation of the
words solely by the assumption of the faulty use of ὃ in the sense of
an interrogatory exclamation, — a use, however, which does not seem
to be more faulty than the use of τίς spoken of in 58 p. 251, and in
view of the examples which follow is by no means without analogy.

Ἡλίκος is loosely used in an interrogative exclamatory sense in
Jas. iii. 5 ἰδού, ἡλίκον πῦρ ἡλίκην ὕλην ἀνάπτει. Cf. the Homeric usage
in B. § 139, m. 35 a. p. 373.

In particular, however, is to be traced to the later use of the rel. **218**
pron. ὅστις in direct questions (see Lobeck and cf. Apollon. Adv. p.
550) the fact that often in the N. T. ὅ, τι in the sense of τί or διὰ τί
wherefore? (Tdf. [so Treg.] writes it then without the diastole ὅτι)
stands at the head of a d i r e c t question; see Lchm. praef. p. xliii.;
Epist. Barn. pp. 16, 18, 20 ed. Dress. The passages are the following: Mark ix. 11 ἐπηρώτων λέγοντες· Ὅ, τι λέγουσιν οἱ γραμματεῖς, ὅτι
Ἡλίαν δεῖ ἐλθεῖν πρῶτον; 28 ἐπηρώτων αὐτόν· Ὅ, τι ἡμεῖς οὐκ ἠδυνήθημεν
ἐκβαλεῖν αὐτό (Euthym.: τὸ ὅ, τι ἀντὶ τοῦ διὰ τί etc., which is actually
given by several MSS. see Tdf.'s crit. note), Mark ii. 16 Tdf. [Treg.]
Ὅ, τι μετὰ τῶν ἁμαρτωλῶν ἐσθίει καὶ πίνει; Probably also John viii.
25 εἶπεν ὁ Ἰησοῦς· Τὴν ἀρχὴν ὅ, τι καὶ λαλῶ ὑμῖν; Commonly this
clause is taken not as a question, but by construing ὅτι as a pure relative. But even the ancient Greek interpreters took ὅ, τι here in the
sense of διὰ τί, which best suits the passage; see on the whole passage,
which is exegetically very difficult, Lücke's Com. Ὅ, τι is found
besides as a noteworthy variant in Mark ii. 7. Matt. vii. 14 also must
be taken into consideration. Here Tdf. has restored the original reading of the Vat. codex [and Sin.], confirmed also by Origen, ὅτι στενὴ
ἡ πύλη etc., and has not treated the clause as a question, but taken the
ὅτι as parallel to the first ὅτι in the 13th vs. in the sense of *for.* The
most natural sense, however, is given by the old reading τί [so Lchm.
Treg.] with the force of an exclamation (Vulg. *quam*), although elsewhere, in the N. T. at least, τί is not used in this way; see Meyer. If

the reading ὅτι is genuine, this also (in view of the use just treated of, and that of the Sept. immediately following) may be taken in an exclamatory sense. Yet, owing to the want of precedents from other quarters, a positive decision in this passage cannot be given just yet.

In the Sept. also the use of ὅτι in the sense of διὰ τί is found; as, 1 Chron. xvii. 6 Ὅ,τι οὐκ ᾠκοδομήσατέ μοι οἶκον κέδρινον ; compared with the parallel passage in 2 Sam. (vii. 7) ἵνα τί οὐκ ᾠκοδομήκατε etc. ; and the Heb. מָה, which in 2 Sam. vi. 20 and Cant. vii. 6 is translated by τί (with e x c l a m a t o r y force), is rendered in Jer. ii. 36 by ὅ, τι (in the same signification) : ὅ, τι κατεφρόνησας σφόδρα τοῦ δευτερῶσαι τὰς ὁδούς σου, cf. also Herm. Vis. iii. 10 sub fin., Evang. Nicod. xiv. 3.   On the combination τί ὅτι see § 149, 3 p. 358.

60   As respects M o o d , both with direct and indirect questions the construction with the I n d i c a t i v e is by far the most common.   As this usage, which again springs from the predilection for direct forms of statement (hence the P r e s e n t Indic. is so often used even in narration after historical tenses), is rendered sufficiently familiar by classic Greek, only a few examples need be given here : Luke vi. 7 παρετηροῦντο αὐτὸν, εἰ ἐν τῷ σαββάτῳ θεραπεύει, John x. 6 οὐκ ἔγνωσαν τίνα ἦν ἃ ἐλάλει, ix. 25 ; Acts x. 18 ἐπυνθάνοντο εἰ Σίμων ἐνθάδε ξενίζεται, Mark viii. 23 Lchm. [Tdf. Treg.].   Respecting Luke xi. 35 see above, 49 p. 243.   In dependent discourse, consequently, the Indicative in most of the N. T. authors takes completely the place of the O p t a t i v e, which in this case (according to what 219 was said above, 11 p. 215) still appears only in the writings of Luke : Gospel i. 29 διελογίζετο ποταπὸς εἴη, iii. 15 ; viii. 9 ; xv. 26 ; xviii. 36 ; xxii. 23 ; Acts ii. 12 Sin.; xvii. 11 ; xxv. 20 ; xxi. 33 Lchm. [Tdf. Treg.].   See further 62 below, p. 256.

The mood of subjective opinion which in Greek authors so often comes into use in these clauses, viz. the O p t a t i v e w i t h ἄν, is found (agreeably to 17 p. 217) likewise only in Luke : in d i r e c t question, Acts xvii. 18 ; viii. 31, in i n d i r e c t, Luke i. 62 ; vi. 11 ; ix. 46 ; Acts v. 24 ; x. 17 ; according to Tdf.'s text [eds. 2, 7] also ii. 12 : xvii. 20 ; xxi. 33 ; as a variant in Luke xv. 26 [Treg.] ; xviii. 36.

61   On the other hand, after what has been said in 11 p. 215, and 18 p. 218, it will be easily understood that most of the remaining N. T. writers give admission in these sentences, in addition to the Indicative, to the construction with the S u b - j u n c t i v e ; here therefore in the form of the Conjunct. dubitativus or deliberativus (2 p. 208).   This Subjunctive construc-

tion they employ both with direct and indirect questions; particularly, too, after historical tenses, where classic usage would certainly have availed itself of the Optative with or without ἄν.

That this Subjunctive is interchanged with the Fut. Indicative has already been remarked, 2 p. 208. Still more frequently, however, the fluctuation of the MSS. (and editions), often alluded to, between the forms (externally differing but slightly) of the 1st Aor. Subjunct. and the Fut. Indic., may be observed here also.

As the examples of this Subjunctive in direct questions have already been given in 2 p. 208, we will only exhibit here (by adducing a number of passages) the extent of the usage in indirect interrogation (yet commonly by means of the direct interrogative word):

a) The Subjunctive, after leading tenses: Matt. vi. 25 μὴ μεριμνᾶτε τί φάγητε, xv. 32; viii. 20; Mark vi. 36; viii. 1, 2; xiii. 11; Luke xii. 5, 11, 22, 29; John xii. 49, etc.; after historical tenses: Mark ix. 6; xiv. 1, 11 ἐζήτει πῶς αὐτὸν παραδοῖ (see 37 p. 233), 14, 40; Luke xxii. 2, 4; Acts iv. 21, etc.

b) The Future Indicative, after leading tenses: Matt. xxiv. 3; Mark xiii. 4; 1 Cor. vii. 16; after historical tenses (which takes place again as in 55 p. 248, 60 p. 254, in consequence of the discourse passing over into the direct form): John xxi. 19; Mark iii. 2 [Tdf. reads the Pres.], with which, according to § 137, 10 p. 203, also the passages with ἔρχομαι, ὑπάγω and similar Presents may be reckoned, as Luke xvii. 20; Mark xiii. 35; John iii. 8, etc. Cf. Eph. v. 15; 1 Cor. iii. 10.

c) Both forms in one sentence: Matt. x. 19 [Tdf. Treg. cod. Sin. Subjunct. bis]. The recent editors are divided between the two forms in Mark ix. 6 [yet Treg. Tdf. now Subjunct. with Lchm.; so cod. Sin.], Rom. viii. 26 [all now Subjunct., so cod. Sin.], 1 Cor. vii. 32 sq. [ditto]; and moreover the MSS. vary in many passages, as Matt. viii. 20; x. 19; Mark xi. 18; Luke xii. 36; xix. 48; Phil. i. 22, etc.

The clauses that belong under this head with ὅπως after such predicates as ζητεῖν, συμβούλιον ποιεῖν, παρατηρεῖν, etc., have already been included in the previous sections (8 p. 214, 37 sqq. p. 233 sqq.).

B. § 139, m. 66; J. § 877 Obs. 5; G. p. 156.　　　　220

Sometimes in Greek a clause placed after a leading clause is yet to 62 be regarded as dependent on a verbum sentiendi understood, like the Homeric αἴ κε τύχωμι, αἴ κε πίθηται (see reff.), the prosaic ἐάν πως, the Latin si forte, the Germ. ob etwa, (to see) whether possibly etc.

Several corresponding constructions connected with various conjunctions are found in the N. T., commonly with the S u b j u n c t i v e or
the F u t u r e in its stead, in Luke (after historical tenses) with the
O p t a t i v e also.   An example with εἰ καί and the Subjunct. has
already been mentioned 22 p. 221 : Phil. iii. 12 διώκω, εἰ καὶ καταλάβω ;
further, with εἴ πως : Phil. iii. 11 (συμμορφιζόμενος), εἴ πως καταντήσω
εἰς τὴν ἐξανάστασιν (probably also a Subjunctive), Rom. xi. 14 τὴν δια-
κονίαν μου δοξάζω, εἴ πως παραζηλώσω μου τὴν σάρκα καὶ σώσω τινὰς ἐξ
αὐτῶν, Acts xxvii. 12 (ἔθεντο βουλὴν ἀναχθῆναι), εἴ πως δύναιντο παρα-
χειμάσαι ;   with εἰ ἄρα : Mark xi. 13 ἰδὼν συκῆν ἦλθεν, εἰ ἄρα τι εὑ-
ρήσει ἐν αὐτῇ, Acts xvii. 27 (ἐποίησεν etc.), εἰ ἄρα γε ψηλαφήσειαν αὐτὸν
καὶ εὕροιεν.

Under this head belongs also the clause with the negative interrogative μή ποτε (55 p. 248) and the Subjunct. 2 Tim. ii. 25 δεῖ ἤπιον
εἶναι . . . , μή ποτε δώῃ (better δῷ, Tdf. [Treg. Sin. ?] δῴη ; cf. 37 note
p. 233) αὐτοῖς ὁ θεὸς μετάνοιαν i.e. waiting to see whether God may
not perchance give etc. ; as well as the similar constructions after
δ ε ῖ σ θ α ι to pray : Acts viii. 22 δεήθητι τοῦ θεοῦ, εἰ ἄρα ἀφεθήσεται
σοι etc. Rom. i. 10 δεόμενος, εἴ πως ἤδη ποτὲ εὐοδωθήσομαι.

GENERAL REMARKS ON THE MOODS.
B. § 139, m. 67; H. §§ 728. 729; C. § 617; J. §§ 410–414; G. App. I.

63   From the entire course of the preceding exposition of the
use of the Moods in the N. T., we derive with confidence the
four following particular conclusions :

1) That the law respecting *consecutio temporum* so called,
(in Greek more correctly *modorum*), viz. that in dependent
clauses leading tenses are followed by the Subjunctive, historical tenses by the Optative, does not apply at all to the great
majority of the N. T. writings, and retains but a limited application even in the writings of Luke.   In Luke the O p t a t i v e
is still recognized as the d e p e n d e n t mood after historical
tenses only in certain conditional sentences (24 p. 223), in indirect question (60, 62 p. 253 sq.), and once after πρὶν ἤ (33 p.
231) ; but in all other dependent clauses it is no longer current.

2) That the S u b j u r.c t i v e (or its substitute the F u t u r e)
to a great extent supplies the place of the disappearing or
wanting Optative as a dependent mood, and also of the O p t a-
t i v e w i t h ἄν as the mood of subjective assertion (cf. 7, 8,
11, 18, 21, 29, 33, 34, 37 sqq., 61 sq.).

3) That the inclination, which begins to appear even in
221 classic authors, to substitute the form of direct discourse for

the indirect — (agreeably to which the clauses of transition to indirect discourse often stand in the I n d i c a t i v e of that tense which would have been employed in direct discourse) — has come in the N. T. to possess still more general sway (see 21, 29, 36, 51, 60) ; and further, as the result of this,

4) That the discourse often bounds quite out of the indirect form i n t o t h e d i r e c t (see B. § 139, m. 69), — a transition which strictly speaking involves in every instance a *variatio structuræ*, and hence, with other similar cases, will receive particular consideration again under this heading below, § 151, 11 p. 385. Here belongs the frequent use of direct discourse after ὅτι (51 p. 245), the less common direct interrogation after εἰ (55 p. 248), and the Imperative after ἵνα and ὅτι (37 p. 234, 53 p. 246).

THE IMPERATIVE.

B. § 139, m. 72; H. § 723 cf. 710 a.; C. § 655 cf. 597; D. pp. 549 sqq.; J. § 420 cf. 413, 2; G. §§ 84 sqq. cf. p. 37.

Of the periphrastic modes of expressing the Imperative, the　**61** categoric by means of the F u t u r e I n d i c a t i v e and the direct negative ο ὐ is not uncommon in the N.T. Although a similar construction occurs also in Greek writers, and elsewhere too, owing to the close relationship between the two forms of time (see Fritzsche on Matt. v. 48), yet the usage, so far forth as the Imperative is actually in this way peri-phrased, is in the N.T. at least derived from the Septuagint.

For we must here consider, a) that the construction occurs almost exclusively in literal q u o t a t i o n s from the O. T. ; and b) that the expression in these quotations is for the most part n e g a t i v e, which is solely owing to the circumstance that the Imperative in Hebrew is not negatived, but the Future is used instead (see Gesen. Lehrg. 771 [Gr. § 125, 3 c.]), and this subsequently was literally translated by the Sept. ; e.g. οὐ φονεύσεις, οὐ μοιχεύσεις Matt. v. 27,[1] οὐκ ἐκπειράσεις κύριον, οὐκ ἐπιθυμήσεις, etc. More rarely does this use of the Future occur without a negation : and rather in continuation of other Futures already negatived (e.g. from the Sept. of Lev. xix. 12), as Matt. v. 33 (quotn.) οὐκ ἐπιορκήσεις, ἀποδώσεις δὲ τῷ κυρίῳ τοὺς ὅρκους σου, — or of the Imperative, Matt. xix. 19 τίμα τὸν πατέρα καὶ μητέρα, καὶ ἀγαπήσεις τὸν πλησίον etc. ; or with a certain difference of tone, as Matt. vii. 5 ἔκβαλε πρῶτον . . . , καὶ τότε διαβλέψεις ἐκβαλεῖν etc. (The un-negatived

---

[1] On the other hand, in free reference the common Greek construction is employed : μὴ φονεύσῃς, μὴ μοιχεύσῃς Mark x. 19 ; Luke xviii. 20.

Fifth Commandment is a l w a y s in the Imperative : τίμα τὸν πατέρα
etc., side by side with the other negatived ones in the Future, just as
in the Sept.)

65
222 From this Hebraistic circumlocution for the Imperative we
must carefully distinguish the c l a s s i c G r e e k circumlocution,
externally quite the same, viz. also by means of the Future
negatived by οὐ, but in the form of a q u e s t i o n ; in this way
the Greek expressed not a negative (as in the preceding case),
but a positive command. This circumlocution, favorite with
classic writers (see reff. and B. § 137 N. 6), is found however
but once, and that too in Acts xiii. 10 οὐ παύσῃ διαστρέφων τὰς
ὁδοὺς κυρίου ; *wilt thou not cease?* i.e. *cease.*

On the common periphrasis of the Imperative by means of the Aor.
Subjunct., and that peculiar to the N. T. by means of the elliptical ἵνα,
see 6 p. 211 and 47 p. 241 ; and on the Imperative as a rhetorical
substitute for a hypothetical clause or a participle, see 28 p. 227
above and § 144, 2 p. 290, — after ἵνα, ὥστε, ὅτι, Nos. 37, 50, 53.

THE INFINITIVE.

B. § 140, 1; H. §§ 763, 764; C. § 663; D. §§ 584 sq.; J. §§ 662–666; G. Chap. V.

1   The Infinitive as the subject of a sentence with such predicates
as δεῖ, καλόν ἐστιν, προσήκει, etc., and further as the complement
of an incomplete predicate idea, as after the ideas *to be wont, to
be able, to be willing,* etc., is very common, and needs no further
illustration. As predicates with an Infin. following which
are especially current in the later or biblical language, we may
notice ζητεῖν *to seek, endeavor* (this occurs even in Demosth.,
e.g. Lept. p. 495, 497), ἀφιέναι *to permit* (on the construction with the Subjunctive alone after ἄφες see § 139, 4 p. 210),
δέδοται, ἐδόθη (cf. 4 below, p. 261) αὐτῷ γνῶναι etc., for which
the Apocalypse prefers to let a clause with ἵνα follow, according to § 139, 43 p. 238).

It follows from what was said § 139, 11 sqq. p. 215, that after the
ideas *to request* (with which in the N. T. ἐρωτᾶν belongs), *to command,
to exhort,* and the like, the Infinitive can indeed stand (most frequently
so, always in Greek style, in the writings of Luke; as, with ἐρωτᾶν
Acts iii. 3, δεῖσθαι xxvi. 3, παραινεῖν xxvii. 22, often after παρακαλεῖν,
also in Paul's writings, etc.), but in its stead, agreeably to Hellenistic
or Common Greek usage elsewhere, a periphrasis by means of the
C o n j u n c t i o n ἵνα is wont to make its appearance.

On κελεύειν see § 141, 5 p. 275.

B. § 140, N. 1; H. § 711; C. §§ 598. 660; D. p. 580; J. § 408; G. p. 38.

The Infinitive Future after verbs whose idea has ref- 2
erence to the Future is little used, viz. only a few times after
μέλλειν in the Acts. The N. T. language employed instead
either the Infin. Aorist (so especially after ἐλπίζειν) or the
Infin. Present (so almost always after μέλλειν). Where the
future is to be designated more distinctly, ὅτι with the Indic.
Future regularly makes its appearance.

Examples of μέλλειν with the Present Infin. are found every- 223
where, see the lexx.; with the Future Infin. (ἔσεσθαι) Acts xi. 28;
xxiii. 30 Tdf. [eds. 2, 7]; xxiv. 15 (25 Tdf. [eds. 2, 7]); xxvii. 10;
with the Aorist Infin. Acts xii. 6; Gal. iii. 23; Rev. iii. 2, 16; xii. 4;
Matt. xx. 22 Vat.

Examples of the Aorist Infin. after ἐλπίζειν, and that too (according to § 139, 20 p. 219) uniformly without ἄν, are frequent; see
the lexx. The Future Infin. is found once as a variant of cod. B in
Acts xxvi. 7; on the other hand ὅτι with the Future Indicative occurs
in Acts xxiv. 26; 2 Cor. i. 13; xiii. 6; Philem. 22.

B. § 140, 2; H. § 767; C. § 663 g.; D. § 586; J. § 667; G. § 93.

The simple Infinitive dependent on a substantive or an
adjective belongs to the rarer constructions of the N. T.,
other constructions being as a rule preferred in its stead, e.g.
ἵνα with the Subjunct., ὥστε with the Infin. (see p. 244), εἰς τό
followed by the Infin., the Infin. with τοῦ (see below, p. 266 sq.).

The classic mode of expression with the simple Infin. is found most
frequently in the Ep. to the Heb. (cf. Introd. p. 1 sq.); as, iv. 1 κατα-
λειπομένης ἐπαγγελίας εἰσελθεῖν (Vulg. introeundi) εἰς τὴν κατάπαυσιν
αὐτοῦ, vi. 10 οὐκ ἄδικος ὁ θεὸς, ἐπιλαθέσθαι τοῦ ἔργου ὑμῶν (Vulg. ut
obliviscatur), v. 11 λόγος δυσερμήνευτος λέγειν (Vulg. ininterpretabilis
ad dicendum). Here belongs also the phrase ὦτα ἀκούειν in Mark
and Luke; in Matt. cod. Vat. [and in xiii. 9, 43 cod. Sin. also] omits
the Infin. adjunct; so Tdf. also, [Treg. puts it in brackets].

In other cases when the Infinitive stands after substantives
and adjectives, these latter constitute, together with a verb of
some sort, an incomplete verbal idea of which the Infin. contains the necessary complement (Infin. expletivus).

Thus, for example, χρείαν ἔχω βαπτισθῆναι, ἀπελθεῖν, γράφειν, γράφεσθαι, etc., instead of the common δεῖ, προσήκει followed by the Acc.
and the Infin., Matt. iii. 14; 1 Thess. iv. 9 ¹; v. 1, etc., ἐξῆλθεν δόγμα

¹ In this passage authorities are equally divided between χρείαν ἔχετε (Rec.
Grsb. [Tdf. Treg. ℵ*]), and χρείαν ἔχομεν (Lchm.) γράφειν ὑμῖν. Since the

παρὰ Καίσαρος (equiv. to Κ. ἐκέλευσεν) ἀπογράφεσθαι πᾶσαν τὴν οἰκου-
μένην Luke ii. 1, ἐδόθη ἡ χάρις αὕτη (equiv. to ἐχαρίσθη or simply ἐδόθη
see 1 p. 258) εὐαγγελίσασθαι Eph. iii. 8, ὀφειλέτης ἐστὶν (equiv. to
ὀφείλει) ποιῆσαι Gal. v. 3, ἐγένετο ὁρμὴ τῶν Ἰουδαίων (equiv. to οἱ Ἰουδαῖοι ὡρμήσαντο) ὑβρίσαι Acts xiv. 5, ἀρκετός ἐστιν (equiv. to ἀρκεῖ) ὁ
παρεληλυθὼς χρόνος ... κατειργάσθαι 1 Pet. iv. 3.   Hence the Infin. is
quite common after such predicates as ἐξουσίαν ἔχειν (1 Cor. ix. 4, 5, 6
224 Lchm. [Tdf. Treg.]), καιρὸν ἔχειν, δυνατός εἰμι, ἀδύνατόν ἐστιν, ἱκανός
εἰμι, ἐξουσία (sc. ἐστίν Rev. ix 10), as they all stand for the ideas *to be
able, to be unable, to be in a condition*, etc.   After the same analogy,
but more free, is 1 Cor. vii. 39 (ἡ γυνὴ) ἐλευθέρα ἐστὶν ᾧ θέλει γαμηθῆναι;
further ὥρα ἐστίν with the Infin. in Rom. xiii. 11 ὥρα ἤδη ἡμᾶς ἐξ ὕπνου
ἐγερθῆναι (Vulg. correctly : *hora est surgere*, not *surgendi*), Rev. xiv. 15
ὥρα ἦλθεν θερίσαι · ἕτοιμός εἰμι, ἄξιός εἰμι etc.   After all these predicates,
however, the other and above-mentioned constructions also were wont
more or less to appear instead of the simple Infinitive ; see above.

REMARK. In Greek authors the syntactical license mentioned in
B. note 2 p. 384, viz. of letting a Genitive (a noun) and an Infinitive
(a verb) depend simultaneously upon o n e   a n d   t h e   s a m e substantive, although the noun standing in the Gen. strictly speaking belongs
to the Infin. (and consequently ought to stand in the Acc.), is by no
means rare (see Kühner, ausf. Gr. [ed. 1] II. p. 610 [J. II. p. 642]).
An instance of it occurs in Rev. xi. 18 ἦλθεν ἡ ὀργή σου καὶ ὁ καιρὸς
τῶν νεκρῶν κριθῆναι καὶ δοῦναι etc., consequently for the regular ἦλθεν
ὁ καιρὸς τοῦ τ ο ὺ ς ν ε κ ρ ο ὺ ς κριθῆναι.[1]   Rom. ix. 21 ἔχει ἐξουσίαν τοῦ
πηλοῦ ἐκ τοῦ αὐτοῦ φυράματος ποιῆσαι etc. is of another sort ; here we
can either make τοῦ πηλοῦ depend on φυράματος, or refer both words,
the noun and the verb, to ἐξουσίαν, yet so that the Infin. serves epexe-
getically to explain the substantive.

earlier reading is the more difficult on account of the Active Infin., and a comparison with v. 1 (γράφεσθαι) may easily have occasioned the correction ἔχομεν,
deWette and Tdf. have returned to it.   The use of the Active Infin. for the Passive
is thoroughly established (cf. τὰ δέοντα εἰπεῖν and the like, B. § 140, 2 ; J ξ 667,
obs. 5), and occurs accidentally with the same phrase χρείαν ἔχειν (but followed
by an Infin. with τοῦ) in Heb. v. 12 χρείαν ἔχετε τοῦ διδάσκειν ὑμᾶς (if with the
majority we put a comma after ὑμᾶς, see 13 below, p. 268 note.   As χρείαν ἔχειν
in the signification *to need* (which predominates here as in v. 1; hence in both
instances ἔχετε) according to § 132, 12 p. 164 takes the place of the impersonals
δεῖ etc., it shares with them also the same constructions of nouns and verbs (i.e.
Genitive and simple Infinitive).

1 Very probably, in accordance with the style of the Apocalypse, the absolute
Accusative also which follows according to the mss.[Sin. also] (Lchm. [Treg.]),
τοὺς μικροὺς καὶ τοὺς μεγάλους, is to be referred to the pervasive force of this leading
predicate (*to be punished, judged*) ; since, καιρός being so far off, instead of the
Genitive the subject Accus. (§ 141) could or must now make its appearance.

B. § 140, 3; H. § 765; C. § 663 h.; D. § 607; J. § 669; G. § 97.

After c o m p l e t e predicate ideas also the simple Infinitive 4 (but always alternating with the periphrastic constructions mentioned 3 p. 259) is still employed very frequently in the N. T., as in classic authors, to express the d e s i g n or de- signed r e s u l t (where in Latin the gerundial construction is commonly used).

This occurs most frequently after verbs which express a m o t i o n or d i r e c t i o n w h i t h e r (cf. below, 16 γ) p. 270), as ἤλθομεν προσ- κυνῆσαι Matt. ii. 2, τί ἐξήλθατε ἰδεῖν Matt. xi. 8 sq.; Luke vii. 25 sq., προελεύσεται ἐπιστρέψαι καρδίας πατέρων Luke i. 17, ἦλθον καταλῦσαι Matt. v. 17, βαπτισθῆναι Luke iii. 12, εἰσῆλθεν Χριστὸς ... ἐμφανισθῆναι ὑπὲρ ἡμῶν Heb. ix. 24, τίς ἀναβήσεται ... Χριστὸν καταγαγεῖν Rom. x. 6, 7, ἀνήχθη εἰς τὴν ἔρημον ... πειρασθῆναι Matt. iv. 1, ἀποστέλλει αὐτοὺς κηρύσσειν Mark iii. 14; cf. 1 Cor. i. 17; x. 7 (quotn.) etc.   and similar pre- dicates, as δ ι δ ό ν α ι: ἐδώκατέ μοι φαγεῖν Matt. xxv. 35, ἔδωκαν αὐτῷ πιεῖν ὄξος xxvii. 34 (Pass. εἶπεν δοθῆναι αὐτῇ φαγεῖν Mark v. 43 etc.), καθὼς τὸ πνεῦμα ἐδίδου ἀποφθέγγεσθαι αὐτοῖς Acts ii. 4; λ α μ β ά ν ε ι ν: Mark vii. 4 ἄλλα πολλὰ ἃ παρέλαβον κρατεῖν; but also after those in which the idea of motion recedes more: Acts v. 31 τοῦτον ἀρχηγὸν καὶ σωτῆρα ὕφωσεν ..., δοῦναι μετάνοιαν, xv. 10 τί πειράζετε τὸν θεόν, ἐπιθεῖναι ζυγόν etc., 2 Pet. iii. 2 διεγείρω ὑμῶν τὴν εἰλικρινῆ διάνοιαν, μνησθῆναι (Vulg. ut memores sitis).   Paul, too, avails himself not infrequently of this 225 Infinitive to denote design (cf. 10 below, p. 264); as, 2 Cor. x. 13, 16; xi. 2; Col. i. 22; iv. 6, etc.

B. § 140, N. 4; H. § 772; C. § 665; D. § 607 a. Obs.; J. § 662, 5; G. § 100.

Examples of the use of the Infinitive in parenthetic clauses, — 5 except the phrase ὡς ἔπος εἰπεῖν (once in Heb. vii. 9) borrowed from the rhetorical classic usage, — are not found.

THE ARTICLE (τό) WITH THE INFINITIVE.

B. § 140, 5; H. § 778; C. § 664; J. § 678 cf. 670; G. §§ 90; 96.

The Infinitive may take the A r t i c l e (τό), and it acquires 6 in this way not only the appearance, but to a certain degree also the nature, of a substantive, inasmuch as it is declined, serves as the subject or object of a clause, and sometimes (in addition to the article) is still more closely limited by pronouns; as, 2 Cor. vii. 11 αὐτὸ τοῦτο τὸ κατὰ θεὸν λυπηθῆναι πόσην κατειργάσατο σπουδήν, Heb. ii. 15 διὰ παντὸς τοῦ ζῆν ἔνοχοι ἦσαν δουλείας.   In other respects the Infinitive uniformly re- tains its verbal nature; since, as may be seen from numerous

examples, it does not as in other languages (e.g. Germ. Ital.)
take the attributive adjuncts of a substantive (in the form of
Genitives or Adjectives), but always and without change the
constructions which go with a verb as such, (and placed generally between the Article and the Infinitive).

REMARK. Only the Infin. ζῆν seems to have been early construed
quite as a substantive (like ζωή) ; hence we find it not only connected
with an Adjective in the above passage from Hebrews, and frequently
in the Ep. of Ign. ad Eph. written about A.D. 100 : τὸ ἀληθινὸν ζῆν
(Cap. xi.), ἐκ τοῦ προκειμένου ζῆν (Cap. xvii.), but even with the Genitive : Ep. Ign. ad Magn. I (ἡμῶν), V (αὐτοῦ) ; ad Smyrn. IV τὸ
ἀληθινὸν ἡμῶν ζῆν.

B. § 140, 5 a. and b., and N. 5; H. § 778; C. § 664; J. § 678; G. § 96.

7　The Infinitive, rendered a substantive by means of the
Article, is wont to stand

　　a) As the S u b j e c t of a clause in general sentences ;

Examples are pretty numerous. The predicate is as a rule a noun
(subst., adj., pron.), with or without the copula, as πλεῖον, καλόν,
αἰσχρόν, περισσόν, ἀναγκαιότερον, φοβερόν, Χριστός, κέρδος, τί ἐστιν
(Mark ix. 10 ; Phil. i. 21, etc.), less frequently a verb, as Matt. xv. 20
τὸ ἀνίπτοις χερσὶν φαγεῖν οὐ κοινοῖ τὸν ἄνθρωπον, Rom. vii. 18 τὸ θέλειν
παράκειταί μοι, τὸ δὲ κατεργάζεσθαι τὸ καλὸν οὔ, Phil. i. 29 ὑμῖν ἐχαρίσθη
τὸ . . . πιστεύειν etc.

REMARK. After a preparatory D e m o n s t r a t i v e in the leading
clause the Infin. following stands according to rule (B. § 140 N. 5)
w i t h o u t the Art., the place of which is supplied by the demonstrative ; as, Jas. i. 27 θρησκεία καθαρὰ α ὕ τ η ἐστίν, ἐπισκέπτεσθαι etc., Eph.
iii. 8 (see 3 p. 260), 1 Thess. iv. 3 τοῦτό ἐστιν θέλημα τοῦ θεοῦ . . . ,
ἀπέχεσθαι ὑμᾶς ἀπὸ τῆς πορνείας, εἰδέναι etc., where, however, subsequently (vs. 6) for perspicuity's sake, after the intervention of several
lengthy specifications, the last Infin. again takes the Article : τὸ μὴ
ὑπερβαίνειν etc. Cf. with this the examples in B. l.c. N. 6.

8　　b) As the O b j e c t of the clause, — if the Infinitive is not a
mere complementary predicate of an incomplete verbal idea
226 (e.g. ζητεῖν, βούλεσθαι, etc.), but is to be regarded as the real
object of the predicate in the clause, and consequently serves
as a circumlocution for an abstract substantive, so far forth as
that is the object of the clause.

Examples of this construction also are numerous enough : Matt.
xx. 23 and Mark x. 40 τὸ καθίσαι . . . οὐκ ἔστιν ἐμὸν δοῦναι, Acts xxv.
11 οὐ παραιτοῦμαι τὸ ἀποθανεῖν (death), Rom. xiii. 8 ὀφείλετε τὸ ἀλλή-

λους ἀγαπᾷν (reciprocal love), 1 Cor. xiv. 39 (prophecy, speaking with tongues), 2 Cor. viii. 10, 11 ; Phil. ii. 13 (the willing and the performance), ii. 6 (equality with God), iv. 10 (your care for me). In Phil. i. 22 also the term αἱρήσομαι is to be supplied from what follows. In 2 Cor. x. 2 δέομαι τὸ μὴ παρὼν θαρρῆσαι etc. Paul has employed this mode of expression in a bold, almost violent, yet very expressive way : literally, *I entreat* (viz. of you) *the not being obliged to be severe,* i.e. I pray you not to force me to severe proceedings against you (when I arrive in Corinth). In other passages the text varies, as in 1 Thess. iii. 3 where Lchm. Tdf. Treg. have adopted the Acc. (τό [so cod. Sin.]) in place of the former Dat., so that now τὸ μηδένα σαίνεσθαι depends immediately on παρακαλέσαι ;[1] so in Acts iv. 18 where Lchm. [and Tdf.] (after B [א*]), and in Luke vii. 21 where all three editors omit τό.

REMARK. In *this* case (cf. 7 Rem. p. 262) after a preparatory demonstrative the insertion of the Article with the following Infinitive seems, so far as the few passages will permit us to form a judgment, to have been more usual : Rom. xiv. 13 τοῦτο κρίνατε μᾶλλον, τὸ μὴ τιθέναι πρόσκομμα τῷ ἀδελφῷ, 2 Cor. ii. 1 ἔκρινα ἐμαυτῷ τοῦτο, τὸ μὴ πάλιν ἐλθεῖν etc. But without the Art. in 1 Cor. vii. 37.

B. § 140, 5 c); H. § 779 sq.; C. § 663; D. p. 598 sq.; J. § 678; G. § 94.

The genuine Greek practice (which disappeared gradually in later Greek) of subjoining to a clause adverbial adjuncts (which in other languages are generally given by means of entire subordinate clauses) by means of the Infinitive used substantively and governed by a Preposition, is still in full force in the N. T., at least in the better written portions. This construction is employed most frequently by Luke, as well in the Gospel as in the Acts, by the author of the Ep. to the Heb., also by Paul who has quite mastered it ; very rarely by John (only four times in the Gospel), and never in the Apocalypse. The (old) prepositions thus used are ἀντί, διά, ἐν, εἰς, μετά, πρό, and πρός. In reference to their use we may note the following :

ἀντί, but once : Jas. iv. 15 ἀντὶ τοῦ λέγειν ὑμᾶς *instead of* etc.

διά, only with the Accusative, instead of a subordinate causal clause with *because* (*quia, eo quod*), is very common : Matt. xiii. 5, etc.

ἐν is used in two ways : 1) in a temporal sense, to denote contemporaneousness or duration, *while, during* ; as, Matt. xiii. 4 ἐν τῷ σπείρειν αὐτὸν ἃ μὲν ἔπεσεν etc., 25 ἐν τῷ καθεύδειν αὐτοὺς ἦλθεν etc.,

---

[1] According to Lchm., Reiske, Cobet (Praef. ad N. T. p. 90) we are to read. μηδὲν ἀταίνεσθαι i.q. ἄχθεσθαι, χαλεπῶς φέρειν. [Cf. Valckenaer's Opusc. II. 246 sq.].

Acts xi. 15, etc. In ordinary prose, as in Latin, the construction of the Gen. absolute would have been preferred; hence Luke who uses this Infin. construction most frequently, particularly in connection with ἐγένετο δέ (see § 141, 6 p. 276), unites both modes of expression with 227 the same sense in one sentence, as Luke iii. 21 ἐγένετο δὲ ἐν τῷ βαπτισθῆναι ἅπαντα τὸν λαὸν καὶ Ἰησοῦ βαπτισθέντος ἀνεῳχθῆναι τὸν οὐρανόν;— or the Infin. with ἐν stands instead of an ordinary participial clause, and the mode of expression appears still more strange (see on this especially § 141, 3 p. 274), as Luke x. 35 ὅ, τι ἂν προσδαπανήσῃς, ἐγὼ ἐν τῷ ἐπανέρχεσθαί με (equiv. to ἐπανελθὼν) ἀποδώσω σοι, Acts viii. 6 προσεῖχον οἱ ὄχλοι ... ἐν τῷ ἀκούειν αὐτοὺς καὶ βλέπειν (Vulg. audientes et videntes), Luke xi. 37 ἐν δὲ τῷ λαλῆσαι αὐτὸν (equiv. to ἔτι λαλοῦντα) ἐρωτᾷ αὐτὸν Φαρισαῖος. It is not to be overlooked that the frequent recurrence of this mode of expression in the Gospel of Luke contributes essentially to distinguish its language from that of the Acts, where we meet with it far more rarely. 2) to subjoin to the predicate adverbial adjuncts in which ἐν preserves its proper or instrumental force (in, by), nearly for the Lat. Gerund in the Ablative or with in and the Ablat.; as, Acts iv. 29 δὸς τοῖς δούλοις σου ... ἐν τῷ τὴν χεῖρά σου ἐκτείνειν etc., Heb. ii. 8 (Vulg. in eo quod), viii. 13 ἐν τῷ λέγειν 'καινήν' πεπαλαίωκεν τὴν πρώτην (Vulg. dicendo). In other cases it may appear doubtful (although the sense would be little affected thereby) whether we should allow the instrumental force or the temporal to predominate; e.g. Luke i. 21 ἐθαύμαζον ἐν τῷ χρονίζειν αὐτὸν ἐν τῷ ναῷ (Vulg. mirabantur quod tardaret; the ordinary construction of θαυμάζειν however is with ἐπί, see § 133, 23 p. 185; θαυμάζειν ἐν also occurs in Ev. Thom. 15, 2), Mark vi. 48 βασανιζομένους ἐν τῷ ἐλαύνειν (Vulg. in remigando), cf. Luke xii. 15; Acts iii. 26.

Rarely for the instrumental use of the Infin. we find the simple Dative: 2 Cor. ii. 13 οὐκ ἔσχηκα ἄνεσιν τῷ μὴ εὑρεῖν με Τίτον. Respecting 1 Thess. iii. 3 see 8 p. 263, above.

10 εἰς followed by an Infin., a construction employed by Paul with especial fondness (in Rom. alone seventeen times), serves 1) to state the design, accordingly for ἵνα and like ad with the Gerund in Latin,— either connecting itself immediately with the verb, as Matt. xx. 19 παραδώσουσιν αὐτὸν τοῖς ἔθνεσιν εἰς τὸ ἐμπαῖξαι (Vulg. ad inludendum), xxvi. 2 παραδίδοται εἰς τὸ σταυρωθῆναι (Vulg. ut cruci figatur; for which John, who never employs this construction, says, agreeably to his usage, ἵνα σταυρωθῇ xix. 16; cf. § 139, 40 p. 236), Heb. viii. 3 πᾶς ἀρχιερεὺς εἰς τὸ προσφέρειν δῶρά τε καὶ θυσίας καθίσταται, ix. 28; 1 Cor. xi. 22 οἰκίας ἔχετε εἰς τὸ ἐσθίειν καὶ πίνειν, xi. 33; Acts iii. 19; vii. 19, etc.;— or forming an independent final clause, as Rom. iv. 11, 18; xi. 11; xii. 2; xv. 8, 13; 1 Cor. x. 6; 2 Cor. iv. 4; Gal. ii. 17;

Eph. i. 12, 18 etc., and alternating with ἵνα, as Phil. i. 10; 1 Thess. ii. 16; Heb. ii. 17, particularly if one telic specification is dependent on another, as Rom. i. 11; iv. 16; 1 Cor. ix. 18; 2 Thess. iii. 9.

2) as in classic Greek, statements of design so often include within themselves those of result and *vice versa* (see § 139, 43 sq. p. 238 sq., 50 Rem. p. 244), so εἰς with the Infin. can be employed in stating the result, i.e. the d e s i g n e d c o n s e q u e n c e, accordingly for ὥστε *ita ut ;* hence it occurs sometimes as a variant in the oldest MSS. instead of that final ὥστε (§ 139, 50 p. 243). In this sense many passages are to be taken; as, Rom. i. 20 τὰ ἀόρατα αὐτοῦ τοῖς ποιήμασιν νοούμενα καθορᾶται . . . , εἰς τὸ εἶναι αὐτοὺς ἀναπολογήτους ;[1] see besides vi. 12 ; vii. 4, 5 ; 2 Cor. i. 4 ; viii. 6 ; Heb. xi. 3, etc.

3) it frequently stands also where ordinary usage would have been **228** satisfied with the s i m p l e I n f i n i t i v e (with or without the Art.), and in particular for the Infin. (Pres. or) F u t u r e after predicates whose signification looks forward, such as διδόναι, δεῖσθαι, ἐρωτᾶν, μαρτυρεῖν (*obtestari*) etc., and which for the same reason admit also of the construction with ἵνα (§ 139, 42 p. 237); as, Rom. xv. 16 διὰ τὴν χάριν τὴν δοθεῖσάν μοι, εἰς τὸ εἶναί με λειτουργὸν Ἰησοῦ Χριστοῦ, 1 Thess. ii. 12 μαρτυρούμενοι εἰς τὸ περιπατεῖν ὑμᾶς ἀξίως τοῦ θεοῦ, iii. 10 δεόμενοι εἰς τὸ ἰδεῖν ὑμῶν τὸ πρόσωπον, Phil. i. 23 τὴν ἐπιθυμίαν ἔχων εἰς τὸ ἀναλῦσαι καὶ σὺν Χριστῷ εἶναι, 2 Thess. ii. 2 ἐρωτῶμεν ὑμᾶς εἰς τὸ μὴ ταχέως σαλευθῆναι ὑμᾶς . . . μηδὲ θροεῖσθαι, ὁ νῦν τὸ κατέχον οἴδατε, εἰς τὸ ἀποκαλυφθῆναι αὐτόν ; naturally connected with this use stands

4) the e p e x e g e t i c Infin. with εἰς τό (*in respect to, to* (the intent that), with which is to be compared the Infin. with τοῦ in 14 p. 268); as, 1 Thess. iv. 9 θεοδίδακτοί ἐστε εἰς τὸ ἀγαπᾶν ἀλλήλους, Rom. iii. 26 πρὸς τὴν ἔνδειξιν τῆς δικαιοσύνης αὐτοῦ, εἰς τὸ εἶναι αὐτὸν δίκαιον etc., viii. 29; 2 Thess. i. 5 ἔνδειγμα τῆς δικαίας κρίσεως . . . εἰς τὸ καταξιωθῆναι ὑμᾶς etc., Jas. i. 19 ταχὺς εἰς τὸ ἀκοῦσαι, βραδὺς εἰς τὸ λαλῆσαι, Rom. xii. 3 φρονεῖν εἰς τὸ σωφρονεῖν, 1 Cor. viii. 10, etc. In these cases we likewise put either simply the Infin. with *to*, or the Conjunction *that*.

μ ε τ ά only with the Accusative, and always in a temporal force (*after, after that*), as often in Greek authors also; as, Heb. x. 15, 26 ; Matt. xxvi. 32 ; Mark i. 14 ; Luke, Acts, etc.

π ρ ὸ τ ο ῦ followed by the Infin. — likewise only in a temporal reference — serves frequently as a periphrasis for the conjunction π ρ ί ν with the Infin. (hence after p o s i t i v e sentences) and is interchanged with it : Matt. vi. 8 ; Luke ii. 21 ; xxii. 15 ; John i. 49 ; xvii. 5 ; xiii.

---

[1] That in this passage interpreters have at all periods, even the most recent, diverged in two just opposite directions, the ecbatic and the final, is one proof more that the two relations (as so often with ἵνα and ὥστε) lie undistinguished side by side.

19 πρὸ τοῦ γενέσθαι (for which in xiv. 29 πρὶν γενέσθαι), Acts xxiii. 15 ; Gal. ii. 12, etc.

πρός, used only with the Accusative, means in accordance with its original signification primarily *with reference to* the fact that etc., as Luke xviii. 1 ἔλεγεν παραβολὴν αὐτοῖς πρὸς τὸ δεῖν πάντοτε προσεύχεσθαι, λέγων etc., Matt. xxvi. 12 τοῦτο ἐποίησεν πρὸς τὸ ἐνταφιάσαι με ; then, and interchangeably with εἰς (even in the variants, as Jas. iii. 3), in a final signification : Mark xiii. 22 ; Eph. vi. 11.

Of the other (improper) prepositions, we find used in this way εἵνεκεν (for which commonly the simple Genitive appears) but once : 2 Cor. vii. 12, on account of the preceding εἵνεκεν ; and ἕως, also but once : Acts viii. 40.

THE INFINITIVE WITH τοῦ IN THE N. T.

B. § 140, NN. 10, 11; H. § 781; C. § 664 d.; D. p. 480; J. §§ 492, 678 b.; G. §§ 94 sq.

12
229 This form of expression, which in the earlier Greek writers is on the whole pretty rare but in later writers becomes more and more frequent, belongs to those constructions of which the language as well of the Old T. as of the New is especially fond of availing itself; and which, since the limits of its employment were materially enlarged, contributes much to the peculiar complexion of the biblical diction.   Hence, it is necessary to give here a connected exposition of the entire usage.

The general use of the expression, however, does not prevent the existence of a great diversity in this respect among individual N. T. writers.   John in consequence of his decided predilection for ἵνα (§ 139, 40 p. 236) makes no more use of this construction than of εἰς τό (10 above, p. 264) either in his Gospel or his Epistles.   Matthew uses it often, but Luke the most frequently and with the most varied application (twenty-five times in the Gospel and perhaps about as often in the Acts).   In Paul's and the other Epp. it recedes somewhat before the other and similar construction with εἰς τό.   In Mark and the Rev. we are almost in doubt whether it occurs.   Cf. in general on this subject the extended discussions in Winer, p. 324 sqq. (304 sqq.), and Fritzsche, Com. on Matt. Excurs. II. p. 843 sq.

13 The construction is founded, as its external form shows, in a Genitive relation ; and hence must be understood and explained from the nature of this case.   To facilitate our review of the instances that occur, we will distribute them into the following classes : I. those in which the Infin. with τοῦ is governed immediately by some word contained in the leading clause, — which is either a) a Substantive, or b) an Adjective,

or c) a Verb; II. those in which the Infin. with τοῦ stands more by itself, constituting a clause independent of the leading clause so far as the case is concerned.

I. The Infinitive with τοῦ stands in immediate dependence on a term which is contained in the leading clause, and expresses an incomplete thought, to which it stands in the same relation as the Infin. expletivus in 3 p. 259, above : that is to say, it contains the necessary complement, generally in a final sense, of that incomplete idea. Cf. the similar constructions with εἰς τό in 10, 3) p. 265, and with ἵνα in § 139, 41 sqq. pp. 236 sqq.

In accordance with the general rules respecting the Genitive (B. § 132, 1 and 7) this Infinitive is dependent

a) On a Substantive.

We should much mistake the nature of most of the clauses falling under this head, were we to regard the Infin. with τοῦ (after the fashion of the Lat. gerund in -di) as a Gen. dependent on a noun in such a way that the Infin. takes pretty nearly the place of an abstract substantive in like relation, as *ars scribendi the art of writing.* For the Greeks, with their copious store of abstract substantives, and the facility with which in case of necessity they could at any time form new ones, had almost no need of this mode of expression. On the contrary, the Infin. with τοῦ retains its entire v e r b a l n a t u r e a n d f o r c e, so that it depends merely o u t w a r d l y upon a substantive in the leading clause. This is evident, partly from the fact that it is often accompanied by its o w n S u b j e c t (in the Acc. according to the rules of § 141 pp. 272 sqq.), see the examples subjoined; and partly from the circumstance, that Latin writers in the extant cases either would not, or could not, have used their gerund in -di, as Rom. xi. 8 ἔδωκεν ὀφθαλμοὺς τοῦ μὴ βλέπειν καὶ ὦτα τοῦ μὴ ἀκούειν, in Latin not *oculos non videndi, aures non audiendi,* but *ad non videndum* etc., or, as the Vulg. renders it, *ut non videant, . . . audiant.* It is uniformly necessary, therefore, to· take the substantive on which the Infin. appears to depend and expand it, with a verb either present in the clause or to be supplied, into a verbal predicate idea, upon which the Infinitive adjunct, whether with its subject expressed or understood, is then made to depend, quite in the way in which in c) below it depends on verbs. For example, Luke i. 57 τῇ Ἐλισάβετ ἐπλήσθη ὁ χρόνος τοῦ τεκεῖν αὐτήν not *the time of her delivery was fully come,* but *the full time came that she should be delivered,* cf. ii. 6 ; ii. 21 ἐπλήσθησαν ἡμέραι ὀκτὼ τοῦ περιτεμεῖν αὐτόν Vulg. not literally, as it is in the habit of doing: *circumcidendi eum,* but (Passively, cf. the note below),

230

ut circumcideretur, xxii. 6 ἐζήτει εὐκαιρίαν τοῦ παραδοῦναι αὐτόν (for
which ἵνα is used in the parallel passage Matt. xxvi. 16) ; Acts xiv.
9 ἔχει πίστιν τοῦ σωθῆναι (Vulg. *ut salvus fieret*), xx. 3 ἐγένετο γνώμη
(i.e. *he resolved*, hence the preceding Partic. ποιήσας in the Nom. construed ad synesin according to § 144, 13 b) p. 298) τοῦ ὑποστρέφειν διὰ
M., xxvii. 20 περιῃρεῖτο ἐλπὶς πᾶσα τοῦ σώζεσθαι ἡμᾶς, Rom. viii. 12
ὀφειλέται ἐσμὲν (equiv. to ὀφείλομεν) τοῦ ζῆν etc., xv. 23 ἐπιποθίαν ἔχων
(equiv. to ἐπιποθῶν) τοῦ ἐλθεῖν (cf. Phil. i. 23), 1 Cor. x. 13 ποιήσει τὴν
ἔκβασιν τοῦ δύνασθαι ὑπενεγκεῖν (Vulg. *ut possitis sustinere*), Heb. v. 12
Lchm. χρείαν ἔχετε τοῦ διδάσκειν ὑμᾶς (personal object) τινὰ (subject
Acc.) τὰ στοιχεῖα (material object) τῆς ἀρχῆς etc.,[1] 1 Pet. iv. 17 ὁ
καιρὸς (sc. ἐστὶν) τοῦ ἄρξασθαι τὸ κρίμα (*ut incipiat*). The Infinitive
alone often stands in the same circumstances (as may be seen from a
comparison of the examples in 3 p. 259), and in point of fact in some
instances the τοῦ has now been expunged by the editors as a later
addition, e.g Rev. ix. 10; xiv. 15, and probably also in 1 Cor. ix. 6
Lchm. [Tdf. Treg. ; so cod. Sin.].   The instances which approximate
most closely to the use of the Latin gerund in *-di* are perhaps Luke x.
19 δίδωμι ὑμῖν τὴν ἐξουσίαν τοῦ πατεῖν ἐπάνω ὄφεων, 1 Cor. ix. 10 ἐπ'
ἐλπίδι τοῦ μετέχειν, although even these admit of being easily referred
to the above category.

14   REMARK. On the other hand, the Infin. with τοῦ is often found also
231 (quite in accordance with the examples from classic authors given in
B. § 140 N. 11) as an **epexegetic addition** to an abstract substantive, as though a **verbal** periphrasis and explanation of it (cf. 10, 4)
p. 265) : Rom. i. 24 παρέδωκεν αὐτοὺς ... εἰς ἀκαθαρσίαν τοῦ ἀτιμάζεσθαι
τὰ σώματα αὐτῶν, 2 Cor. viii. 11 ἡ προθυμία τοῦ θέλειν, Phil. iii. 21 κατὰ
τὴν ἐνέργειαν τοῦ δύνασθαι αὐτόν etc., Luke xxi. 22 ἡμέραι ἐκδικήσεως
αὗταί εἰσιν τοῦ πλησθῆναι πάντα τὰ γεγραμμένα, Acts ix. 15 σκεῦος ἐκλογῆς
ἐστίν μοι οὗτος τοῦ βαστάσαι τὸ ὄνομά μου, xiii. 47 (quotn.) τέθεικά σε
εἰς φῶς ἐθνῶν τοῦ εἶναί σε εἰς σωτηρίαν etc.   Only in this way is to be
explained the construction (in other respects also quite anomalous) in
Rev. xii. 7 ἐγένετο πόλεμος ἐν τῷ οὐρανῷ, ὁ Μιχαὴλ καὶ οἱ ἄγγελοι
αὐτοῦ τοῦ πολεμῆσαι μετὰ τοῦ δράκοντος instead of the ἐπολέμησαν of the
Text. Recept., which aims to avoid the harshness, but falls into another
mistake.   The Nominative is used ad synesin with the Infin., since the
latter takes the place, so to speak, of a subordinate clause with a finite verb.

[1] So according to Lchm.; and compare Dem. Lept. 40, where likewise three Accs.
are united.   The other construction, which Tdf. [so Treg.] follows : τοῦ διδάσκειν
ὑμᾶς, τίνα τὰ στοιχεῖα etc. differs but little in sense, and has the interpretation of
Origen (διδάσκεσθαι), the Vulg. (*ut vos doceamini*), the version in cod. Claromon-
tan. (*doceri vos*) et al. in its favor.   Since this construction also harmonizes with
the genius of the language (cf. the example from Luke ii. 21 above, and § 140,
3 p. 259 note) a decision is difficult, indeed from a grammatical point of
view absolutely impossible.   See Bleek.

b) On an **Adjective** contained in the leading clause. As **15** a rule this also constitutes together with the copula the predicate of the clause, and the Infin. with τοῦ contains the necessary complement. Yet, by virtue of the verbal nature inhering in Adjectives, they are also by themselves capable of this construction.

The connection is the simplest when the Adjective already permits of itself the construction with the Genitive, as 1 Cor. xvi. 4 ἐὰν ἄξιον ᾖ τοῦ κἀμὲ πορεύεσθαι, Rom. vii. 3 ἐλευθέρα ἐστὶν ἀπὸ τοῦ νόμου, τοῦ μὴ εἶναι αὐτὴν μοιχαλίδα; but it occurs also with other Adjectives, as Acts xxiii. 15 ἕτοιμοί ἐσμεν τοῦ ἀνελεῖν αὐτόν (cf. with this the Infin. alone in 3 p. 259), Luke xvii. 1 ἀνένδεκτόν ἐστιν τοῦ μὴ ἐλθεῖν τὰ σκάνδαλα, xxiv. 25 ὦ ἀνόητοι καὶ βραδεῖς τοῦ πιστεύειν (cf. the construction with εἰς τό in 10 p. 265).

c) On a **verbal idea** contained in the leading clause. This **16** is by far the most common use of the Infin. with τοῦ. It is essentially identical with the two preceding constructions, and differs only externally in the circumstance that the governing predicate idea here is a verb, there a noun. Further: as in the construction with an Adjective, it is wholly a matter of indifference whether the verb is elsewhere **construed with the Genitive or not**; and that the Infin. with τοῦ stands again in most evident analogy with the similar use of ἵνα, εἰς τό with the Infin., and the Infin. alone, may be seen on comparing the respective sections.

We will classify the examples under the following heads:

α) the construction finds its (rather superficial) occasion in the circumstance that the verb according to general usage is capable of being construed with the Genitive; as, Luke i. 9 ἔλαχεν τοῦ θυμιᾶσαι (in connection with nouns, however, λαγχάνειν in the N. T. is construed only with the Accusative, see § 132, 8 p. 160 and cf. Bhdy. p. 176), Matt. xxi. 32 οὐ μετεμελήθητε τοῦ πιστεῦσαι αὐτῷ, 2 Cor. i. 8 ἐξαπορηθῆναι τοῦ ζῆν.

β) the construction takes place if the verbal idea is of a negative kind and intimates that something is to be *avoided, averted* etc., these predicates (according to B. § 132, 4) being likewise capable of taking **232** the Gen. [Gen. of *separation*]. In this case, moreover, the **negative** μή is as a rule also added to the **Infin**. (cf. § 148, 13 p. 355). Luke iv. 42 κατεῖχον αὐτὸν τοῦ μὴ πορεύεσθαι ἀπ᾽ αὐτῶν, xxiv. 16 οἱ ὀφθαλμοὶ αὐτῶν ἐκρατοῦντο τοῦ μὴ ἐπιγνῶναι αὐτόν, Acts x. 47 μήτι τὸ ὕδωρ κωλῦσαι δύναταί τις τοῦ μὴ βαπτισθῆναι τούτους; xiv. 18 κατέπαυσαν τοὺς ὄχλους τοῦ μὴ θύειν, 1 Pet. iii. 10 (quotn.) παυσάτω τὴν γλῶσσαν ἀπὸ κακοῦ καὶ χείλη τοῦ μὴ λαλῆσαι δόλον, Acts xx. 20, 27 οὐδὲν ὑπεστειλάμην τοῦ μὴ [1] ἀναγγεῖλαι ὑμῖν. The omission of μή is decidedly contrary to the main usage and very rare : Rom. xv. 22 ἐνεκοπτόμην πολλάκις τοῦ ἐλθεῖν πρὸς ὑμᾶς.

γ) after verbs of motion to indicate the purpose of the motion, alternating with the simple Infinitive (see 4 p. 261) : Matt. xiii. 3 ; Luke viii. 5 ἐξῆλθεν ὁ σπείρων τοῦ σπεῖραι (but in Mark iv. 3, according to the recent editors, without τοῦ), Luke xxiv. 29 εἰσῆλθεν τοῦ μεῖναι σὺν αὐτοῖς, Heb. x. 7 (quotn.) ἥκω τοῦ ποιῆσαι τὸ θέλημά σου, Matt. iii. 13 παραγίνεται τοῦ βαπτισθῆναι ὑπ᾽ αὐτοῦ, Luke v. 1 Lchm. ἐπικεῖσθαι αὐτῷ τοῦ ἀκούειν, Acts xviii. 10 ἐπιθήσεταί σοι τοῦ κακῶσαί σε.

δ) also after other words signifying action, which need an additional statement to complete their thought in order to express the purpose or the result designed by the action : accordingly, for ἵνα (which may be, rendered in English that ... should) after the predicates spoken of § 139, 41 sqq. pp. 236 sqq.; as, Jas. v. 17 προσηύξατο τοῦ μὴ βρέξαι (commonly ἵνα), Acts xxi. 12 παρεκαλοῦμεν τοῦ μὴ ἀναβαίνειν αὐτὸν εἰς Ἰ. (commonly ἵνα, ὅπως, or the simple Infin.), xxiii. 20 συνέθεντο τοῦ ἐρωτῆσαί σε (ἵνα John ix. 22 ; Infin. alone Luke xxii. 5), xv. 20 ἐπιστεῖλαι αὐτοῖς τοῦ ἀπέχεσθαι ἀπὸ τῶν ἀλισγημάτων (Infin. alone xxi. 25), Luke iv. 10 (quotn.) ἐντελεῖται αὐτοῖς τοῦ διαφυλάξαι σε. So, moreover, after ποιεῖν (cf. ἵνα § 139, 43 p. 238) Acts iii. 12, κατανεύειν Luke v. 7, κρίνειν Acts xxvii. 1 (cf. 1 Cor. vii. 37 var.), τὸ πρόσωπον ἐστήριξεν Luke ix. 51, διήνοιξεν τὸν νοῦν τοῦ συνιέναι (caused them to understand) xxiv. 45. In an exceptional way the Infin. with τοῦ stands once after ἐγένετο even : Acts x. 25 ὡς δὲ ἐγένετο τοῦ εἰσελθεῖν τὸν Πέτρον (so also Act. Barn. 7), for which elsewhere the simple Infin. is always used (§ 141, 6, c) p. 277). Cf. the Latin ut after fit, etc.

17 II. The other case — that in which the Infin. with τοῦ stands after complete predicates (accordingly for ἵνα in its proper signification, in order that, eo consilio ut), so that it is to be regarded as an independent telic clause — is very common ; and finds adequate explanation in the general use of the Gen. (to express causal departure and direction upon, B. § 132, 8, 9). Hence the assumption of an ellipsis (ἕνεκα, χάριν) is superfluous.

For examples see Matt. ii. 13 ; xi. 1 ; xxiv. 45 ; Luke i. 77, 79 ; ii. 24, 27 ; xii. 42 (Tdf.) ; Acts iii. 2 ; vii. 19 ; xx. 30 ;

---

[1] Classic usage would have demanded in this case the double negative μὴ οὐ, (because the leading verb is itself negative, cf B. § 148 Note 6, 2) p. 427) ; G. p 198.

xxvi. 18; Rom. vi. 6; xi. 10; Gal. iii. 10; Phil. iii. 10; Heb. xi. 5.

REMARK. In the Sept. the use of the Infin. with τοῦ occurs to a **233** still greater extent almost. See a great number of examples (to be found on almost every page) in Winer, p. 325 sq. (305).

B. § 140, 7; H. § 784; C. § 670; D. § 526; J. § 671; G. § 101; W. 316 (296).

Of the Infinitive instead of the Imperative, as it **18** is sometimes used in the classics, there is no single instance wholly unquestionable; since everywhere the leading mark of this Infin., viz. the addition of the Subject in the Nominative, is wanting. The usage, too, is predominantly poetic (see the examples in the Gramms. ll.c., and cf. Bhdy. p. 388). Hence it is more correct grammatically, to regard the Absolute Infinitives which actually occur in this sense as resulting from an elliptical mode of expression; and that is perfectly accordant with the unartificial and popular diction of the N. T.

In explaining them we may assume an ellipsis of the simplest predicate, perhaps λέγω, for which analogous cases enough are to be found also in the N. T. writings; see § 151, 24 b) p. 394. This suggests itself most naturally, in fact necessarily, not only when the subject is at hand in the Accusative, as Tit. ii. 2 πρεσβύτας νηφαλίους εἶναι, σεμνούς, σώφρονας etc. (see the analogous instances from classic authors, B. § 141, N. 6), but authenticates itself elsewhere also, as in the salutation χαίρειν, by the accompanying Dative; see § 151, 24 a) p. 394. The assumption of this ellipsis is amply sufficient in the remaining cases also, and the occasion of the ellipsis may always be discovered from the nature of the individual passage. Thus in Luke ix. 3 we are not to assume with many interpreters a variatio structurae in explaining the Infin. (μήτε ... ἔχειν), — as if the beginning of the discourse after εἶπεν were direct, and then the words μήτε ἀνὰ δύο χιτῶνας ἔχειν depended again in indirect discourse upon εἶπεν, and subsequently in the following verse the discourse continued in the direct form again; on the contrary, the language is to be construed as flowing unbroken in a direct form,[1] and with ἔχειν a predicate like λέγω, the idea of which is easily suggested by the context, is to be supplied. The dependent negative

---

[1] Discourse springs far more naturally from the (unwonted) indirect form over into the almost uniformly employed direct form (see § 151, 10. 11 p. 383 sq.); as is the case in the very passage parallel to the above viz. Mark vi. 9.

(μήτε) was retained, because the Infin. ἔχειν (not λέγω) is negatived, and owing to the Imperatival cast of the entire passage, which is further continued in the following verses.   Further, in Rom. xii. 15 quite absolutely : χαίρειν μετὰ χαιρόντων, κλαίειν μετὰ κλαιόντων. Here, too Imperatives immediately precede, from which, since the connection necessarily requires the Infinitives to be taken in an imperative force, a predicate like λέγω (or even δεῖ) is to be supplied. In supplying some such term here we are the more justified as the entire passage is conspicuous for its great laxity of structure (notice the Participial clauses that precede and follow, standing in like manner absolutely), merely giving the thoughts and leaving the grammatical connection of them entirely to the reader. Cf. other passages of the sort under the head of Anacoluthon below, § 151, 12 p. 386. Finally, Phil. iii. 16 πλὴν εἰς ὃ ἐφθάσαμεν, τῷ αὐτῷ στοιχεῖν occurs likewise between pure Imperatives, and Subjunctives in their stead ; so that the apostle deemed the addition of a governing predicate to be no longer necessary for the understanding of his words.

The Accusative and Infinitive.

B. § 141, 2; H. § 773; C. § 666; D. § 584; J. § 672; G. cf. §§ 73. 105.

It has often been remarked already that in the rather loose style of the N. T., notwithstanding great facility in handling this construction, the substituted conjunctions (ὅτι, ἵνα) are far more frequent. And in particular, lengthy passages given *in sermone obliquo* no longer occur ; because in such cases the direct form of statement (preferred even in the b r i e f e s t statements) takes its place ; see especially § 139 E. pp. 233 sqq., and G. pp. 245 sq. Not infrequently is a protracted oblique discourse avoided by a sudden transition into the form of direct discourse ; respecting this see in its place § 151, 11 p. 385.

John x. 36 affords an example of the great predilection for the direct form of statement ; here, after λέγετε, the direct discourse consisting merely of a single word (βλασφημεῖς) comes in, although the subordinate clause which follows (ὅτι εἶπον etc.) is construed as if ἐμὲ βλασφημεῖν preceded, and the fact too that the entire apodosis begins with a Relative (ὃν ὁ πατὴρ ἡγίασεν) would sooner lead us to expect the Infin. after λέγετε ; moreover, see i. 15 and other examples in § 151, 1 d) p. 377, and § 139, 51 p. 245. Further, under this head belongs the direct discou se (current also in our colloquial speech) after v e r b s o f a s k i n g, th words of the asker himself being at once introduced (consequently in the Imperative) instead of the contents of the request in the Infinitive, as Luke xiv. 18 ἐρωτῶ σε, ἔχε με

παρῃτημένον, Phil. iv. 3; Acts xxi. 39 δέομαί σου, ἐπίτρεψόν μοι etc.,
Luke ix. 38 Lchm. δέομαί σου, ἐπίβλεψον,[1] 1 Cor. iv. 16 παρακαλῶ ὑμᾶς,
μιμηταί μου γίνεσθε. In narration, however, according to custom,
another λέγων is inserted before the direct request: Matt. viii. 31;
xviii. 29; John iv. 31; Acts xvi. 15, etc.

As a peculiarity in the use of this construction it is to be 2
noticed, that the Infinitive in dependent discourse not only takes
the place of the Indicative, but also of the Imperative (or
Subjunctive), so far forth as it would have been employed in
direct discourse; and that consequently the simple Infinitive
often includes the idea of o b l i g a t i o n, n e c e s s i t y, or p e r-
m i s s i o n. This is the case especially after such predicates as
contain a wish, request, or summons (δεῖσθαι, εὔχεσθαι, παρακαλεῖν, παραινεῖν, ἐντέλλεσθαι, etc.); but not infrequently also
after λέγειν, κηρύσσειν, and the like, so far forth as they are
used instead of the more expressive terms *to command* etc. 235
(cf. § 139, 42 note [1], p. 237); further, after the predicates to
believe, to trust, in so far as the idea *to consider one's self as*
authorized etc. is at the same time contained in them. On
this usage, which belongs to classic Greek, cf. Bhdy. p. 371
and the works there referred to.

Although the Infinitive is used in this way not merely of what
happens but of what o u g h t to happen, yet we are not obliged on this
account to s u p p l y δ ε ῖ ν in order to explain it, but the usage results
solely from the general philological principle (see Kühner on Xen.
Mem. 2, 2, 1) that the Infinitive in itself is a verbal form without relation, and that it acquires in every case its more precise signification
from the context. That sometimes (when the governing word is a
general term, such as εἰπεῖν, πιστεύειν) ambiguity is easily occasioned
by this mode of expression cannot be denied; hence in such cases the
decision rests wholly with the reader who carefully examines the context. A few examples of such Infinitives after less expressive predicates, with or without a subject expressed, are the following: Rev.
x. 9 ἀπῆλθα, λέγων αὐτῷ δ ο ῦ ν α ί μοι τὸ βιβλαρίδιον, Acts xxi. 4 ἔλεγον
τῷ Παύλῳ μὴ ἐπιβαίνειν εἰς Ἱεροσόλυμα, 21 λέγων μὴ περιτέμνειν αὐτοὺς
τὰ τέκνα μηδὲ τοῖς ἔθεσιν περιπατεῖν (cf. xv. 24 Grsb.), Rom. xiv. 2 ὃς

---

[1] It is surprising that Tdf. rejects this reading, in spite of its attestation by cod.
Sin., and has adopted ἐπίβλεψαι into his text. Nowhere in all Greek literature
has a Middle form of ἐπιβλέπω (except the Future) been preserved; and even the
Sept. has ἐπίβλεψον more times than can be counted, never ἐπίβλεψαι. The
reading επιβλεψαι (cod. Vat. etc.) is to be accented ἐπιβλέψαι [so Treg.], and is
nothing more than a (Grecizing) emendation of the Imperat. ἐπίβλεψον.

μὲν πιστεύει φαγεῖν πάντα (deWette: *essen zu dürfen, that he may eat*),
ii. 21 ὁ κηρύσσων μὴ κλέπτειν, ὁ λέγων μὴ μοιχεύειν, 2 Cor. iv. 6 ὁ εἰπὼν
ἐκ σκότους φῶς λάμψαι, Eph. iv. 22 ἐδιδάχθητε ἀποθέσθαι ὑμᾶς ... τὸν
παλαιὸν ἄνθρωπον.   So also with the Infin. after ὥστε, 2 Cor. ii. 7 ὥστε
μᾶλλον ὑμᾶς χαρίσασθαι καὶ παρακαλέσαι; the Infin. with τό, e.g. after
κρίνειν 2 Cor. ii. 1; Rom. xiv. 13; and the Nom. with the Infin. 2 Cor.
x. 2, etc.

B. § 141, N. 3; H. § 823; C. § 659   J. 898, 4.

3   An analogous instance to that quoted (B. l.c.) from the Anab. (6, 4,
18) — in which the leading clause is attracted by a parenthetic
verbum dicendi and passes over into a subordinate clause with ὅτι —
is found in Rom. iii. 8 καὶ (supply τί) μὴ, καθὼς φασίν τινες ἡμᾶς λέγειν,
ὅτι ποιήσωμεν τὰ κακά etc., where according to our idiom ὅτι is superfluous.   So likewise Ev. Nicod. 15, 1 (cf. 15, 5).   Cf. § 139, 51 p. 245
and Meyer on Rom. l.c.

B. § 141, N. 4; H. § 775; C. § 667; D. § 588; J. § 673.

4   The omission of the subject in the Infinitive clause when it
is identical with that of the leading clause is commonly
observed in the N. T.   Yet deviations occur : the subject —
and that, too, in the Accusative — being separately
expressed again,

a) after verba dicendi, especially in the 3d Pers. (in which
case, according to § 127, 14 p. 111 sq., the full Reflexive
form ἑαυτόν -ούς etc. is almost always chosen), but for the
most part only when perspicuity and emphasis required the
repetition;

b) in such Infinitive clauses as subjoin to the leading clause
a temporal or causal limitation (§ 140, 9 sqq.), not so much for
236 emphasis' sake as by designating the particular subject to
deprive the clauses of the universal character which they would
otherwise have.

Examples of a) after verba dicendi — in the 3d Pers. (like the
Lat. *se*), Luke xx. 20 ἀπέστειλαν ἐγκαθέτους ὑποκρινομένους ἑαυτοὺς
δικαίους εἶναι, xxiii. 2 λέγοντα ἑαυτὸν Χριστὸν εἶναι, Acts v. 36 Θευδᾶς
λέγων, εἶναί τινα ἑαυτόν viii. 9; xxv. 4; Rev. ii. 2, 9; iii. 9; but
αὐτόν only in Acts xxv. 21 τοῦ Παύλου ἐπικαλεσαμένου τηρηθῆναι αὐτόν;
— in the 2d Pers. Eph. iv. 22 (see 2 above, p. 274) where the separation of the dependent clause from its governing word (ἐδιδάχθητε) by
the parenthetic clause occasioned the repetition of the subject (ὑμᾶς),
2 Cor. vii. 11 συνεστήσατε ἑαυτοὺς (see § 127, 15 p. 113) ἁγνοὺς εἶναι,
Heb. x. 34 Lchm. [Treg. Tdf. Sin.] γινώσκοντες ἔχειν ἑαυτοὺς κρείσσονα

ὕπαρξιν. In classic writers likewise cases of the kind are found, but on the whole far less frequently (see the Gramms. as above).

b) in temporal etc. subordinate clauses (a use which in the Apocryphal writings of the N.T. has become almost universal): Matt. xxvi. 32; Mark xiv. 28 μετὰ τὸ ἐγερθῆναί με προάξω ὑμᾶς, Luke x. 35 ἐγὼ ἐν τῷ ἐπανέρχεσθαί με ἀποδώσω σοι, xxii. 15 (ἐπεθύμησα) πρὸ τοῦ με παθεῖν, John ii. 24 (ἐπίστευεν αὐτὸν) διὰ τὸ αὐτὸν γινώσκειν πάντας, Heb. vii. 24; 2 Cor. ii. 13 (οὐκ ἔσχηκα) τῷ μὴ εὑρεῖν με Τίτον. The case is different in Rom. xv. 16 where the leading subject governing the Infin. clause (εἰς τὸ εἶναί με λειτουργόν) is not ἐγώ but θεός (virtually contained in the Passive clause δοθεῖσαν ὑπὸ τοῦ θεοῦ). Finally, with regard to the fact that in all these passages given under b) the R e f l e x i v e form which according to rule ought to have appeared has not been chosen, see what is said § 127, 13 p. 110.

On the Acc. and Infin. in hortatory sentences see § 140, 18 p. 271.

On the Construction of κελεύειν, and similar Words, with the Infin.

It has already been remarked, p. 237 note [1], that κελεύειν in the N.T. only admits of being construed with the Acc. and Infin., never of being connected with a resolved clause and the particle ἵνα ; and in this respect the language of the N.T. coincides with ordinary usage.[1] But the influence of the Latin use of *jubere* is unmistakable in this particular: that the P a s s i v e Infin. and Acc. is so often connected with κελεύειν instead of the Active usual in ordinary Greek.

As a rule, where nothing but the idea is required, the A o r i s t P a s s . Infin. is chosen; as, Matt. xviii. 25 ἐκέλευσεν αὐτὸν πραθῆναι ... καὶ ἀποδοθῆναι, xiv. 9 ; xxvii. 58, 64 κέλευσον ἀσφαλισθῆναι τὸν τάφον, Luke xviii. 40 ἐκέλευσεν αὐτὸν ἀχθῆναι, Acts xii. 19 ; xxi. 33, 34 ; xxv. 21 (where the change from the Aor. Infin. to the Pres. Infin. is to be noticed, cf. xxv. 4) etc. It may be remarked further, that only 237 M a t t h e w and L u k e employ κελεύειν; but the other writers avail themselves uniformly of other verbs instead, as ἐντέλλεσθαι, παραγγέλλειν, κηρύσσειν, εἰπεῖν, and that, too, either followed by ἵνα, according to

---

[1] Only in one passage, Matt. xv. 35, is the D a t i v e given with Infin. following by a considerable number of MSS.: ἐκέλευσεν τοῖς ὄχλοις ἀναπεσεῖν. This reading Tdf. eds. 2, 7 (even against the authority of B and the express statement of Origen, which Lchm. [so Treg.] followed) has retained, out of regard for other ancient authorities (and especially the parallel passage Mark viii. 6), with Grsb. Rec. etc. (According to the concurrent testimony of codd. Vat. and Sin. however the passage runs καὶ π α ρ α γ γ ε ί λ α ς τῷ ὄχλῳ ἀναπεσεῖν ἐπὶ τὴν γῆν ἔλαβεν; and Tdf. also has rightly adopted this reading in his 8th ed.)

§ 139, 42 p. 236 sq., or the Infinitive construction. But the same unclassic construction with the Aorist Pass. Infin. is found after these predicates also, in so far as they are intended to represent the precise idea of κελεύειν; as, Mark v. 43 εἶπεν δοθῆναι αὐτῇ φαγεῖν, vi. 27 ἐπέταξεν ἐνεχθῆναι τὴν κεφαλὴν αὐτοῦ, Acts v. 21 ἀπέστειλαν ἀχθῆναι αὐτούς, xxv. 21 ἐπικαλεσαμένου τηρηθῆναι αὐτόν (see 4 p. 274), xxii. 24 εἴπας μάστιξιν ἀνετάζεσθαι αὐτόν, 1 Thess. v. 27 (ἐνορκίζω) ἀναγνωσθῆναι τὴν ἐπιστολήν. To the scribes who wrote the MSS. (especially D and B) the construction still seemed rather strange, and hence they often emended it into the Infin. Active; see the variants on Mark v. 43; vi. 27; Acts xxii. 24. Hence it is very probable that in Mark viii. 7 εἶπεν παρατεθῆναι (Lchm.) is the original reading, — as cod. A actually gives and the variant παραθῆναι leads us to conjecture. The reading παρατιθέναι (Tdf. [eds. 2, 7 ; Treg.]), which again is supported particularly by B and D, might easily have arisen by correction owing to the similarity of form, but by its Present form does not agree well with the passage. The same remark holds of Mark x. 49 Lchm. εἶπεν αὐτὸν φωνηθῆναι; so not only by far the greater number of MSS. give the passage, but the Latin versions also render it, which they would not have done if the translators had had before them the other reading (φωνήσατε αὐτόν, Tdf. [Treg.] after [א] B C).

On the Construction of ἐγένετο followed by an Infinitive and a Finite Verb.

6 A conspicuous peculiarity of the historical style in the N. T. (with the exception of John's Gospel) is the frequent occurrence of the Aoristic phrase καὶ ἐγένετο or ἐγένετο δέ, by which the narrative of new events is announced, and at the same time connected with what precedes. It arose from the familiar Hebrew expression וַיְהִי, and passed over from the translation of the Seventy into the narrative language of the N. T. In the first three Gospels, almost without exception immediately after this formula a specification of time is subjoined (likewise after the mode of Hebrew discourse): and that either by an adverbial phrase (ἐν μιᾷ τῶν ἡμερῶν, μεθ' ἡμέρας τρεῖς etc.), or by a clause with ὅτε (in Matt.) or ὡς (in Luke), or by a Genitive Absolute, but ordinarily by an Infinitive clause introduced with ἐν (§ 140, 9 p. 264). The construction which then follows is of three forms; according as

a) The occurrence itself (again after Hebrew precedent) is given in a Finite Verb connected by καί: as

238 Mark ii. 15 καὶ ἐγένετο (Tdf. [Treg.] γίνεται without ἐν τῷ) ἐν τῷ

κατακεῖσθαι αὐτὸν … καὶ πολλοὶ τελῶναι συνανέκειντο τῷ Ἰησοῦ, cf. Luke
v. 1, 12 ; ix. 51 ; x. 38 ; xiv. 1 ; xvii. 11 ; xix. 15 ; xxiv. 4, 15 ; Matt.
ix. 10 καὶ ἐγένετο αὐτοῦ ἀνακειμένου, καὶ ἰδοὺ πολλοὶ … συνανέκειντο,
Luke ii. 15 καὶ ἐγένετο, ὡς ἀπῆλθον … καὶ οἱ ἄνθρωποι εἶπον, v. 17 καὶ
ἐγένετο ἐν μιᾷ τῶν ἡμερῶν, καὶ αὐτὸς ἦν διδάσκων, καὶ ἦσαν etc., viii. 1, 22.
Somewhat different, and departing from the Heb. idiom, is Acts v. 7
ἐγένετο δὲ ὡς ὡρῶν τριῶν διάστημα καὶ ἡ γυνὴ εἰσῆλθεν.   Or

b) The occurrence is given, indeed, in a Finite Verb, but
without καί.   This is the most frequent construction.

Matt. vii. 28 καὶ ἐγένετο, ὅτε ἐτέλεσεν ὁ Ἰησοῦς τοὺς λόγους τούτους,
ἐξεπλήσσοντο, cf. xi. 1 ; xiii. 53 ; xix. 1 ; xxvi. 1 ; Luke i. 23 καὶ ἐγένετο, ὡς ἐπλήσθησαν αἱ ἡμέραι …, ἀπῆλθεν, cf. vs. 41 ; xi. 1 ; xix. 29 ;
Mark i. 9 καὶ ἐγένετο ἐν ἐκείναις ταῖς ἡμέραις, ἦλθεν Ἰησοῦς, cf. Luke i.
59 ; ii. 1 ; ii. 46 ; vi. 12 ; vii. 11 ; ix. 37 ἐγένετο δὲ ἐν τῇ ἑξῆς ἡμέρᾳ,
κατελθόντων αὐτῶν, συνήντησεν αὐτῷ ὄχλος, cf. xi. 14 ; xx. 1 ; Mark iv.
4 καὶ ἐγένετο ἐν τῷ σπείρειν, ὃ μὲν ἔπεσεν etc. cf. Luke i. 8 ; ii. 6 ; viii.
40 ; ix. 18, 33 ; xi. 1, 27 ; xvii. 14 ; xviii. 35 ; xxiv. 30, 51.   It is to
be noticed, moreover, that in these sentences the predicate of the leading clause almost always stands in the first place, i.e. directly
after the specification of time, except in Mark iv. 4 ; Luke xi. 27 ;
xxiv. 30 ; xviii. 35 ; i. 8, where (but generally for perceptible reasons)
this arrangement is departed from somewhat.   Hence, in Luke ix. 57
Lchm. the comma must be put after ὁδῷ ; according to the reading of
Tdf. [Treg., who omit ἐγένετο] the passage does not belong under this
head.   Or

c) The occurrence stands (dependent on ἐγένετο) in the
Acc. with the Infin.   The subsequent facts are then
either subjoined in a finite verb, Mark ii. 23 καὶ ἐγένετο παρα-
πορεύεσθαι αὐτὸν διὰ τῶν σπορίμων, καὶ ἤρξαντο οἱ μαθηταί etc.
cf. Luke vi. 1, 6, or follow likewise in the Infinitive, Luke iii.
21, cf. xvi. 22.

This mode of expression, as that which approximates most nearly to
the genius of the Greek language, is employed almost always by Luke
in the Acts, e.g. xix. 1 ἐγένετο δὲ ἐν τῷ τὸν Ἀπολλὼ εἶναι ἐν Κορίνθῳ,
Παῦλον διελθόντα … ἐλθεῖν, cf. ix. 37 ; xvi. 16 ; xxviii. 17, — he,
besides, divesting the idiom more and more of its strictly Hebraistic
complexion by omitting the clauses specifying time (so even in the
Gospel, xvi. 22 ; further, Acts iv. 5 ; ix. 32, 43 ; xiv. 1 ; xxviii. 8), or
making them precede (ix. 3), and then by rendering ἐγένετο itself
dependent on a conjunction (e.g. xxi. 1 ὡς δὲ ἐγένετο ἀναχθῆναι ἡμᾶς
etc. cf. xxi. 5 ; xxvii. 44), and finally by connecting the Dative with

it (αὐτοῖς xi. 26, μοι xxii. 6).   Cf. Credner, Einl. ins N. T. p. 133.
On the construction with τοῦ and the Infin. see § 140, 16, δ) p. 270.

7   REMARK. Also the analogous formula used in the prophetical books
of the O. T. (וְהָיָה, Sept. καὶ ἔσται followed by the Fut.) is found
unaltered in the N. T., yet only in literal q u o t a t i o n s, and always,
as in the corresponding passages of the O. T., without a following καί ;.
as, Acts ii. 17 ἔσται ἐν ταῖς ἐσχάταις ἡμέραις, ἐκχεῶ ἀπὸ τοῦ πνεύματος
etc. 21 καὶ ἔσται, πᾶς ... σωθήσεται (cf. Rom. x. 13), Acts iii. 23 ἔσται
239 δὲ, πᾶσα ψυχὴ ... ἐξολεθρευθήσεται (a free quotation, after the Heb.,
of Deut. xviii. 19), Rom. ix. 26 (quotn.).

ATTRACTION IN CONNECTION WITH THE INFINITIVE.
B. § 142, 2; H. § 774, 1. 2. 3; C. § 667; D. § 588 sq.; J. § 672 sq.

1   The general rule that predicative and other declinable
adjuncts (Participles, etc.) with the Infin. stand in the N o m -
i n a t i v e if the (omitted) Subject of the Infin. is identical with
that of the leading clause (φάσκοντες εἶναι σοφοί Rom. i. 22,
ἐμαρτυρήθη εἶναι δίκαιος Heb. xi. 4), needs no further illustration ; still less, the rule that such adjuncts stand in the A c c u -
s a t i v e when they refer to a preceding word in the same case
(κατέκριναν αὐτὸν εἶναι ἔνοχον θανάτου Mark xiv. 64).

Of the more refined use of Attraction (which, however, was often
neglected even by the best Greek authors), by virtue of which predicative adjuncts with the Infin. referring to a G e n i t i v e or D a t i v e
in the leading clause are put in the same case (ἔξεστί μοι γενέσθαι εὐδαίμονι etc.), no example can be adduced from the N. T. It occurs only
occasionally in connection with subjoined P a r t i c i p i a l adjuncts,
although even here the Accusative has become more usual. See on
this in its place § 144, 20 b) p. 305.

B. § 142, N. 2; H. § 774 sq.; C. § 667; D. cf. § 589; J. §§ 674. 676; G. cf. § 93 N. 2.

2   Of the Impersonals πρέπει, προσήκει, ἔξεστι, συμβαίνει and the like,
π ρ έ π ε ι (πρέπον ἐστίν) occurs in four constructions :   1) as commonly
with the Dative and the Infin. (Matt. iii. 15) or with the Infin. to be
supplied, Tit. ii. 1 λάλει ἃ πρέπει (sc. λαλεῖν) τῇ etc. ;   2) with the
Dative after πρέπει and a following A c c u s a t i v e adjunct with the
Infin., see the example Heb. ii. 10 in § 144, 20 b) p. 306;   3) the
Dative with πρέπει is attracted by the following Infin. and as its S u b -
j e c t passes over into the Accusative (Acc. and Infin.), 1 Cor. xi. 13
πρέπον ἐστὶν γυναῖκα ἀκατάλυπτον προσεύχεσθαι ;   4) in a personal construction, Heb. vii. 26 τοιοῦτος ἡμῖν ἔπρεπεν ἀρχιερεύς.   Ἔξεστιν
(ἐξόν ἐστιν) has as a rule the Dative and Infin. ; Luke, however, also
uses the Accus. and Infin. in vi. 4 οὓς οὐκ ἔξεστιν φαγεῖν, εἰ μὴ μ ό ν ο υ ς

τοὺς ἱερεῖς, and according to the best MSS. [Sin. also] in xx. 22·
Tdf. [Treg.]; the Acc. occurs, besides, several times as a variant in·
cod. B (Mark ii. 26 [so א also, and now Tdf.]), and in Origen. Both·
these constructions (with the Dat. and with the Acc.) occur also with·
ἐγένετο in the Acts, see § 141, 6, c) p. 277. On the construction of·
δεῖ see § 131, 3 p. 147.

B. § 142, 3. 4; H. § 775; C. § 667; J. § 672, 4.

Examples of a N o m i n a t i v e adjunct with an Infin. used subtan-　3·
tively with the Article, or dependent on a Preposition, are extremely
rare (because in sentences of this kind according to N. T. usage the
Subject of the leading clause, if identical with that of the Infin., is repeated, and then stands in the Acc. according to the rule § 141, 4, b)
p. 274); as, 2 Cor. x. 2 δέομαι δὲ τ ὸ μὴ π α ρ ὼ ν θαρρῆσαι etc. (see on
this § 140, 8 p. 263.

In clauses with ὥστε and πρίν we find no example of the Nominative and Infin.; but only of the Infin. alone, hence without the repetition of the Subject (Matt. xxvii. 1, etc.), and of the Acc. and Infin., 240
but with a new Subject, Matt. i. 18, etc.

B. § 142, N. 3; C. § 667; J. § 672, Obs. 1; 673, 2 sq.

To such an example as ὑπέσχετο α ὐ τ ὸ ς ποιήσειν (in which αὐτός is　4·
not the Subject, otherwise it would have been in the Acc., but only an
attributive adjunct belonging to the omitted Subject of the Infin.)
an analogous instance occurs in John vii. 4 οὐδεὶς γάρ τι ἐν κρυπτῷ
ποιεῖ καὶ ζητεῖ α ὐ τ ὸ ς ἐν παρρησίᾳ εἶναι. For so all the editors (excepting Lchm.) and the commentators read. But we cannot with many interpreters regard αὐτός as merely a resumption of the Subject; in such
cases the language of the N. T. requires under all circumstances the
Accusative (and that, too, of the Reflexive ἑαυτόν etc.). The examples
quoted by Lücke (Com. Vol. II. p. 190), viz. Matt. xii. 50; Mark xv.
43, have no force in proof of the resumptive use of αὐτός with an
I n f i n i t i v e; cf. on the other hand for the opposite use (of ἑαυτόν
etc.) the examples cited in § 141, 4, a) p. 274. On the contrary, αὐτός
here has its original signification *self*, and is nothing more than an
attributive adjunct in the Nominative belonging to the omitted subject;
subjoined by the writer not for antithesis (to τι) or emphasis, but solely
for perspicuity's sake; and hence ought not to receive much stress:
and yet seeks himself to be manifest.[1] Against the other reading αὐτό
(which rests, moreover, only on weak authority) Lücke declares himself most positively, and with reason. According to it ζητεῖν, which

---

[1] For this interpretation see Kling in the Stud. u. Krit. for 1836, p. 153. Lücke
did not assent to it, perhaps only because he objected to the too great prominence
given to an *antithesis*.

everywhere else as an auxiliary verb is joined only to the simple Infin. and the Acc. of the O b j e c t, would be construed like a verbum sentiendi with the Infin. and the Acc. of the S u b j e c t; for this no precedent can be found. That reading could only be justified if instead of εἶναι such a verb as ποιῆσαι followed.

RELATIVE SENTENCES.

B. § 143; H. §§ 511 sqq. 807 sqq.; C. §§ 551 sqq. 562 a.; D. §§ 401 sq.; J. §§ 818 sq. 833 Obs. 2.

1 As a special peculiarity in these sentences mention must first of all be made of an indubitable H e b r a i s m which has passed over from the language of the Old Testament into certain parts of the New.

The Seventy, in translating the original, very commonly imitated the Hebrew mode of expressing the Relative (אֲשֶׁר with a separated Personal pronoun following) in this way: to the Relative Pron., placed at the beginning of the Relative clause, they subjoined (but never i m m e d i a t e l y, and likewise only in the oblique cases as in Hebrew) the Pron. αὐτός in the same case: e.g. the Acc. Lev. xvi. 32 ὃν ἂν χρίσωσιν αὐτόν (אֲשֶׁר־אֹתוֹ), 241 the Gen. Ruth iii. 2 οὗ ἦς μετὰ τῶν κορασίων αὐτοῦ (אֲשֶׁר with suffix following), the Dat. Neh. viii. 12 ἐν τοῖς λόγοις, οἷς ἐγνώρισεν αὐτοῖς (אֲשֶׁר־לָהֶם), 1 Kings xiii. 10 ἐν τῇ ὁδῷ, ᾗ ἦλθεν ἐν αὐτῇ (אֲשֶׁר־בָּהּ); frequently also with the Preposition repeated and with Adverbs, as Ex. iv. 17; Lev. xi. 32, 34; Josh. xxiv. 13, etc. In Greek authors a similar construction only, not the same, is found; see Fritzsche ad Lucian. p. 109.

In the N. T. the Hebraizing language of the Apocalypse most frequently employs this mode of expressing relation, and that without laying in the least any sort of emphasis thereby upon the pronominal adjunct; as, iii. 8 ἣν οὐδεὶς δύναται κλεῖσαι αὐτήν, vii. 2 οἷς ἐδόθη αὐτοῖς, 9; xx. 8; xiii. 12; and likewise with the Relative adverb, ὅπου ... ἐκεῖ xii. 6 Tdf. [so cod. Sin.], 14, ὅπου ... ἐπ' αὐτῶν xvii. 9. In other writers it occurs only as a somewhat rare exception, e.g. Mark vii. 25, and probably rather in certain national sayings, as Matt. iii. 12; Luke iii. 16, 17; Mark i. 7, or in quotations from the O. T., as Acts xv. 17 (ἐφ' οὓς ... ἐπ' αὐτούς), Rom. iii. 14 cod. B, 1 Pet. ii. 24 Tdf. [א*] οὗ ... αὐτοῦ.

But the e m p h a t i c addition of αὐτὸ τοῦτο to ὅ (quod ipsum) Gal. ii. 10 (cf. Lucian. Abd. 6) does not belong here; and αὐτός in the Nominative can in Relative clauses have only the signification self: 1 Pet. ii. 24.

B. § 143, 2; H. § 503 a.; C. § 496; J. § 818.

The general rule, that in Relative clauses which refer back **!**
to the First or Second Person the verb must stand in the
same Person, is not disregarded in the New Testament, (but
commonly a Participle then takes the place of the Relative
clause, see § 144, 9, b) p. 294).   Hence we find in John viii.
40 ἄνθρωπον ... ὃς λελάληκα, because ἄνθρωπον is in apposition with the με preceding.

Rev. ii. 24 ὑμῖν δὲ τοῖς λοιποῖς τοῖς ἐν Θυατείροις, ὅσοι οὐκ ἔχουσιν etc.
is, indeed, a deviation; but the construction is to be referred to the
underlying simple thought, *to those among you* (τοῖς λοιποῖς) *who have
not* etc., hence to be explained as a constr. ad synesin.

B. § 143, 4; H. § 513 b.; C. § 500; D. p. 362; J. § 821, 3.

That the Relative (ὅς, ὅστις) conforms in Gender to the **3**
Substantive of its own clause, instead of that of the preceding clause to which it strictly refers, is a very common construction in the N. T. also, as may be seen from the examples;
with which in general § 129, 6 p. 128, should be compared.

Mark xv. 16 αὐλῆς ὅ ἐστιν πραιτώριον, Acts xvi. 12 Φιλίππους, ἥτις
ἐστὶν πρώτη πόλις, Gal. iii. 16 σπέρματι, ὅς ἐστιν Χριστός, Col. i. 27 Tdf.
and Eph. i. 14 Tdf. [Treg.] (where both readings, ὅς [so ℵ] and ὅ, are
almost equally attested), vi. 17; iii. 13 (but in Col. iii. 5 ἥτις probably
refers only to πλεονεξία), 1 Tim. iii. 15; 1 John ii. 8; Rev. iv. 5 Lchm.
[Tdf. Sin.], v. 8 (if we refer αἵ to θυμιαμάτων).   This construction is
in most cases more natural than the regular one; especially if the
predicate in the Relative clause is a Personal pronoun, as 1 Cor. iii. 17.

CONSTRUCTIO AD SYNESIN WITH THE RELATIVE.   242
B. § 143, 5; H. § 523; C. § 499; D. p. 362; J. § 819.

With the contents of this paragraph must be compared the **4**
detailed statements made previously: §§ 127, p. 105 sq.; 123,
p. 80; 129, p. 129 sq.   What was there said applies in general
in its full extent to Relative sentences also.   Referring, therefore, as respects the general subject to those sections, we give
here at once the examples relating to Relative sentences:

a) The Relative in the Singular refers to an antecedent
Plural; as,

Acts xxiv. 11 οὐ πλείους εἰσίν μοι ἡμέραι δώδεκα ἀφ' ἧς (sc. ἡμέρας)
ἀνέβην; and there is no reason for explaining otherwise the Sing. in
Phil. iii. 20: ἐν οὐρανοῖς ὑπάρχει, ἐξ οὗ (sc. οὐρανοῦ) καὶ σωτῆρα ἀπεκδεχόμεθα, — the license here is the more natural as the preceding Plural

is to be understood only as a Singular and the word (οὐρανός) is used indiscriminately in both numbers ; see p. 24.

b) The Relative in the Plural refers to a collective term in the Singular ; as,

Luke vi. 17 πλῆθος πολὺ, οἳ ἦλθον, Acts xv. 36 κατὰ πᾶσαν πόλιν, ἐν αἷς etc., xxii. 5 πᾶν τὸ πρεσβυτέριον, παρ᾽ ὧν etc.   But in Rom. vi. 21 before ἐφ᾽ οἷς an idea like τοιαῦτα or τοιούτους sc. καρπούς is to be supplied, according to § 127, 5 p. 105.

c) The Relative accords with the natural Gender of its antecedent substantive (cf. § 123, 7 p. 80): — most frequently after τέκνον, τεκνία, stands in the Masculine.

Gal. iv. 19 ; John i. 13 ; 2 John 1 ; Philem. 10.   Further, παιδάριον ἕν, ὅς John vi. 9, ἔθνη οἳ Acts xv. 17; xxvi. 17, cf. Rom. ii. 14 sq., θηρίον ὅς Rev. xiii. 14 (Rec. ὅ [so cod. Sin.]), ὀνόματα οἳ iii. 4 (Lchm. [T. Tr. Sin.] ἅ).   Then in reference to the Person of Christ : κεφαλὴ ὅς Col. ii. 19, and in the celebrated passage 1 Tim. iii. 16 according to the reading now (and indeed by Griesbach) received: μυστήριον, ὅς [so ℵ] ἐφανερώθη etc.; see the commentaries on the passage, and cf. Col. i. 27 ; Eph. i. 14 in 3 p. 281.

REMARK. Under this head also must be brought the case, where the Relative, if referring to material or abstract objects, stands in the Neuter Plural instead of the Masc. or the Fem. (as in the case of the Demonstrative αὐτά § 127, 8 p. 106), having less regard to the grammatical gender of the word, than to the general neuter idea (of things etc.) which it expresses ; cf. § 129, 4 p. 127.   Thus in Acts xxiv. 17 sq. Tdf. [eds. 2, 7], the oldest MSS. [Sin. also, followed by Lchm. Treg. and now Tdf.] give, indeed, ἐλεημοσύνας ποιήσων καὶ προσφοράς, ἐν αἷς etc. ; but this reading betrays more the correcting hand of the copyists than the common reading ἐν οἷς.

d) The Relative refers to a noun which is only implied in the leading clause (cf. § 127, 8 p. 106).

2 Pet. iii. 1 ταύτην δευτέραν ὑμῖν γράφω ἐπιστολὴν, ἐν αἷς etc. where from δευτέραν ἐπιστολήν the term "two letters" is to be educed ; Phil. ii. 15 τέκνα θεοῦ μέσον γενεᾶς σκολιᾶς, ἐν οἷς (ἀνθρώποις τῆς γεν. σκολ.) etc.

B. § 143, 6; H. §§ 243. 525 β.; C. § 557; D. § 392; J. § 834.

243   Relative clauses are naturally and originally subordinate or
5   secondary clauses, and hence strictly ought always to append only subordinate thoughts immediately dependent on the leading clause, or adjuncts of individual members of it.   But the influence of Latin upon the later Greek language is un-

mistakable, in the fact that Relative clauses so often either stand in Latin style quite at the beginning of a sentence, or serve as a continuation of the leading clause; yet in such a way that in b o t h cases they contain l e a d i n g thoughts, and thus assume the relation of c o - o r d i n a t e l e a d i n g c l a u s e s (hence ὅς is equivalent to καὶ οὗτος, *et hic* etc.).

Yet this usage is employed less by those authors who wrote in the popular language, than by those who wrote a literary and periodic style. Hence this mode of expression, though originally the less idiomatic, is found most frequently of all in the writings of L u k e, particularly in the Acts; often also in the Epistles, because these compositions strive after an extended periodic structure. This is less the case in the Evangelists, even in the discourses which occur there. A portion of these clauses still evince their characteristic as s u b j o i n e d leading clauses by inserting immediately after the Relative the additional connective καί (just as in the German sentence *was er auch that*).

Examples are very numerous.   a) W i t h o u t κ α ί: John xix. 17 (but not vi. 21 where εἰς ἦν ὑπῆγον is a s u b o r d i n a t e adjunct to γῆς), Acts v. 16, 36; vii. 20; ix. 35, 39; xi. 28; xiv. 8, 9; xvii. 10; xxvi. 12 (ἐν οἷς), 19 (ὅθεν *quare*), xxviii. 15; Gal. iv. 24, etc. On Acts xxiv. 14 see § 151, 10 p. 383; on Rom. xvi. 27 § 144, 7 p. 293.

   b) W i t h κ α ί: Luke x. 30; Acts i. 11; x. 39; xii. 4; xiii. 22; xxviii. 10; Gal. ii. 10, etc. On Acts xxiv. 6 see § 144, 7 p. 293. Cf. also § 149, 8 f) p. 363. This combination is common in later authors.

B. § 143, 7 b.; H. § 818 Rem. d.; C. § 562; J. § 833. 2.

The usage that when two successive c o - o r d i n a t e Relative **6** clauses have one and the same antecedent the D e m o n s t r a - t i v e (αὐτός) takes the place of the Relative in the second clause, harmonizes so closely with the character of the popular language (hence it is so frequent even in Homer) that in the N. T. also many examples of it are found, as Luke xvii. 31 ὃς ἔσται ἐπὶ τοῦ δώματος καὶ τὰ σκεύη αὐτοῦ ἐν τῇ οἰκίᾳ, μὴ καταβάτω, cf. xiii. 4; John i. 33; Acts iii. 13 Tdf. [ed. 8 omits αὐτόν, so א], 1 Cor. viii. 6; 2 Pet. ii. 3, etc.

A portion of these instances may be fitly traced also to the circumstance that the N. T. writers were familiarized by the O. T. with sudden transitions from relative, participial, and other subordinate clauses to leading clauses (in continuation of the subordinate clauses; cf. on the Hebrew, Gesen. Lehrg. 802), and hence often employed this construction of their own accord; see on this in its place § 151, 8 sq. p. 381 sq.

REMARK. Also of the more delicate construction (cf. B. § 143, 8 ;
J. § 825), when the case of the Demonstrative occurring in a closely
244 connected s u b o r d i n a t e c l a u s e following the Relative is assumed
by the Relative, and, the Demonstrative being dropped, both clauses
are thus blended externally into one (as οἷς ἐάν τις δῷ equiv. to οἷ, ἐάν
τις αὐτοῖς δῷ), an example occurs (so far as the great fluctuation of the
MSS. permits us to discover the text) in Matt. vii. 9 Tdf. [ed. 7; ed. 8
om. ἐάν, so Treg. cod. Sin.]: τίς ἐστιν ἐξ ὑμῶν ἄνθρωπος, ὃν ἐὰν αἰτήσει (i.e. ὅς, ἐὰν αὐτὸν αἰτήσει) ὁ υἱὸς αὐτοῦ ἄρτον, μὴ λίθον ἐπιδώσει αὐτῷ ;
In this case we encounter the additional irregularity that the last
clause, instead of continuing the Relative construction, passes over into
a direct question introduced by μή.   Cf. the parallel passage from
Luke in § 151, 10 p. 384.   According to the other reading (which drops
ἐάν) the Relative construction alluded to disappears.

B. § 143, 12; H. § 809; C. § 554 c.; D. p. 364; J. § 824, II.

7   Examples of Relative clauses where the governing noun (or
antecedent so-called) is i n c o r p o r a t e d i n t o t h e R e l a t i v e
c l a u s e (but without the Article and not immediately after the
Relative) are, Mark vi. 16 ὃν ἐγὼ ἀπεκεφάλισα Ἰωάννην, οὗτος
ἠγέρθη, Luke i. 4 ; xxiv. 1 φέρουσαι ἃ ἡτοίμασαν ἀρώματα, John
vi. 14, etc.   On Phil. iii. 18 ; Philem. 10, etc. see § 123, 3 p.
77 sq.

Slightly anomalous is Acts xxi. 16 συνῆλθον ... ἄγοντες παρ᾽ ᾧ ξενισθῶμεν Μνάσωνί τινι Κυπρίῳ, ἀρχαίῳ μαθητῇ.   According to the above
rule this would express the following thought: ἄγοντες Μνάσωνά τινα
Κύπριον, παρ᾽ ᾧ ξενισθῶμεν ; so in fact it is understood by the Vulgate
(which here is guided by a correct grammatical instinct) and several
expositors.   But the context and probable facts in the case stand
opposed to this, and require the meaning (which Luther, deWette, et al.
express) who led us TO a certain Mnason etc.   Many, among them
Winer 214 (201), have accordingly explained the Dative Μνάσωνι as
a species of l o c a l Dative, made it depend immediately on ἄγοντες, and
resolved it by πρὸς Μνάσωνα.   Not only has this interpretation (as
deWette has remarked) its difficulty, but, apart from the rarity of such
a Dative, the Greek would not be good ; since in this case the words
must of necessity have been arranged thus : ἄγοντες (sc. ἡμᾶς) Μνάσωνί
τινι Κυπρίῳ, παρ᾽ ᾧ etc.   The position of the words, moreover, is the
very thing which forces us to the only correct interpretation (proposed
by Bornemann, Schol. in Luc. p. 177), according to which the words
are indeed to be construed according to the above rule, but as follows :
ἄγοντες (ἡμᾶς) παρὰ Μνάσωνά τινα Κύπριον, παρ᾽ ᾧ etc.   This gives, too,

the sense demanded by the majority of interpreters, and alone suited
to the passage.   The contraction of the two clauses into one is easily
explicable, owing to the similarity of the two adjuncts ($\pi a \rho á$ $\tau \iota \nu a$ and
$\pi a \rho á$ $\tau \iota \nu \iota$), and acquires still more grammatical probability if we substitute in the first place $\pi a \rho á$ with the Dative.   For this use of a Dat.
dependent on a P r e p o s i t i o n with a verb of motion is by no means
unusual, and is found both in Greek authors and in the N. T.; see
§ 147 under $\pi a \rho á$ p. 339.   The omission of the object $\dot{\eta} \mu \hat{a} s$, at which 245
however no one would take offence, occasioned the erroneous assump-
tion (early disseminated by the rendering of the Vulgate) that $\mathrm{M} \nu á$-
$\sigma \omega \nu a$ was the object of $\check{a} \gamma o \nu \tau \epsilon s$.   If this were what Luke had wanted to
say, he would for perspicuity's sake not only have placed $\mathrm{M} \nu á \sigma \omega \nu a$ in
the A c c u s a t i v e immediately with $\check{a} \gamma o \nu \tau \epsilon s$, but probably also have
subjoined a local specification, as $\grave{\epsilon} \kappa \epsilon \hat{\iota} \theta \epsilon \nu$ etc.

ATTRACTION IN RELATIVE SENTENCES.

B. § 143, 13; H. § 808; C. § 554 a. b.; D. § 402; J. § 822.

Of the constructions pre-eminently peculiar to the Greek **8**
tongue, perhaps none became more the usage of all times and
dialects, than that known under the name of A t t r a c t i o n in
Relative sentences.   It is so thoroughly rooted in the craving
for external symmetry inborn in all native Greeks, and in the
general propensity to subordinate grammatical precision of expression to beauty of form, that it passed over also into the
p o p u l a r language and almost suppressed the regular form of
expression.[1]   Hence numerous examples of it, moulded thoroughly in the spirit of the best Greek prose, are found in all
parts of the N. T. : — most frequently, again, in Luke, yet also
not seldom in John and in the Epistles, less prominently in
Matt., Mark, and the Revelation.   In the Sept. also this construction is current (see e.g. Deut. xiv. 23; xv. 18; xvi. 2,
5, 18, etc.).

We will arrange the examples as follows (cf. B. l.c.):

Ordinary examples of the G e n i t i v e (according to the model
$\mu \epsilon \tau a \delta \iota \delta \grave{\omega} s$ $a \grave{\upsilon} \tau \hat{\omega}$ $\tau o \hat{\upsilon}$ $\sigma \acute{\iota} \tau o \upsilon$ $o \hat{\upsilon} \pi \epsilon \rho$ — instead of $o \nu \pi \epsilon \rho$ — $\check{\epsilon} \chi \epsilon \iota s$) : Matt. xviii.
19; Luke v. 9 [Treg. and] B, xv. 16; John iv. 5, 14; vii. 39; xv.

---

[1] In fact examples are not wanting where the regular construction has been
altered into the other by the c o p y i s t s, or at least it is very doubtful which reading was the original one; see below, and the variants on Mark xiii. 19 (Lchm.
[Treg. Tdf. cod. Sin.] $\check{\eta} \nu$), xiv. 72; John ii. 22 (Lchm. [Treg. Tdf. cod. Sin.] $\check{o} \nu$),
iv. 5, 50 (Lchm. [Treg. Tdf.] $\check{o} \nu$), vii. 39; Tit. iii. 5 (Lchm. [Treg. Tdf. Sin.] $\check{a}$),
Rev. i. 20 (Lchm. [T. Tr. Sin.] $o \check{\upsilon} s$) ; cf. the note on 9 p. 286.

20; xxi. 10; Acts i. 1; iii. 21, 25; vii. 17, 45; ix. 36; x. 39; xxii. 10; 1 Cor. vi. 19; 2 Cor. i. 6; x. 8; Eph. i. 8; Tit. iii. 6; Heb. ix. 20 (quotn.), vi. 10; Jas. ii. 5; 1 Pet. iv. 11; 1 John iii. 24; Jude 15.

Ordinary examples of the Dative (according to the model εὖ προσφέρεται τοῖς φίλοις οἷς — instead of οὕς — ἔχει): Matt. xxiv. 50; Mark vii. 13; Luke ii. 20; v. 9; ix. 43; xii. 46; xxiv. 25; John xvii. 5, 11; Acts ii. 22; vii. 16: xvii. 31; xx. 38; 2 Cor. xii. 21; Eph. ii. 10; 2 Thess. i. 4; Rev. xviii. 6.

It is to be noticed that in the majority of the passages referred to 246 there is not the least fluctuation in the text; only cod. D has sometimes (quite alone) the Accusative instead of the other two cases.

B. § 143, 14; H. § 809; C. § 553; D. p. 364 sq.; J. § 824 II.

9 The noun of the antecedent clause is incorporated into the Relative clause (but according to 7 p. 284 not placed immediately after the Relative) and assumes also the case of the Relative; as,

Luke iii. 19 περὶ πάντων ὧν ἐποίησεν πονηρῶν ὁ Ἡρώδης, xix. 37 περὶ πασῶν ὧν εἶδον δυνάμεων, Rom. iv. 17 (see 11 p. 287). Similar is 2 Cor. x. 13 κατὰ τὸ μέτρον τοῦ κανόνος, οὗ ἐμέρισεν ἡμῖν ὁ θεὸς μέτρου, ἐφικέσθαι ἄχρι καὶ ὑμῶν (see de Wette). Here belongs also Acts xxv. 18 if we adopt [so Treg.] the text of B E etc. viz. περὶ οὗ οἱ κατήγοροι οὐδεμίαν αἰτίαν ἔφερον, ὧν ἐγὼ ὑπενόουν πονηρῶν.[1]

B. § 143, 15; H. § 810; C. § 554 N.; J. § 822.

10 The noun or pronoun (τούτων, τούτοις, etc.) in the antecedent clause is wholly omitted so that the Relative stands quite alone in the case which properly does not belong to it, according to the example μεμνημένος ὧν ἔπραξε (i.e. τῶν πραγμάτων, ὧν for ἃ ἔπραξε); also when dependent on a Preposition (cf. § 127, 5 p. 104 sq.): μὴ θορυβεῖτε ἐφ' οἷς ἂν λέγω.

Luke ix. 36 ἀπήγγειλαν οὐδὲν ὧν ἑώρακαν, xxiii. 41 ἄξια ὧν ἐπράξαμεν

---

[1] Whether the last word πονηράν or πονηρῶν, pronounced superfluous by many commentators (condemned also by Tdf. [eds. 2, 7] but given by the oldest MSS. [ℵ* πονηρά]) is to be admitted into the text, is a question on which textual criticism has probably yet to come to a decision. Grammatically viewed there is nothing against the addition in either form. But (in opposition to Meyer [?]) the preference is probably to be yielded to the reading πονηράν (adopted by Lchm. [Tdf.]) as the less common, because here the change of πονηράν into πονηρῶν would take place even more easily than usual, owing to the position of the word; cf. the preceding note, p. 285. The meaning is: *Among all the accusations which they brought forward, there was not, as I surmised, a bad one* (they brought forward no bad one). Both the alteration of the word into πονηρῶν and its omission (since it is contained by implication in ὑπενόουν) may very easily have been the work of correcting copyists or commentators.

ἀπολαμβάνομεν, John vii. 31 πλείονα σημεῖα ποιήσει ὧν οὗτος ἐποίησεν, xvii. 9 (ἐρωτῶ) περὶ ὧν δέδωκάς μοι, Acts viii. 24; xxi. 19, 24 (arising from ἃ κατήχηνται *quae* docentur), xxii. 15; xxv. 18 (see the note on 9 p. 286); Rom. xv. 18; 1 Cor. vii. 1; 2 Cor. xii. 17; Eph. iii. 20; Heb. v. 8 ἔμαθεν ἀφ᾽ ὧν ἔπαθεν τὴν ὑπακοήν, 2 Pet. ii. 12 ἐν οἷς ἀγνοοῦσιν βλασφημοῦντες. Here belong also Acts xxvi. 22 (where the Participle too is drawn into the attraction; see § 144, 20 p. 305), and xxvi. 16 respecting which see 11 below.

All the examples quoted hitherto follow strictly the leading **11** rule of attraction, viz. that the Relative if unattracted would have stood in the Accusative. But so great was the fondness for this construction that it was employed also where, strictly, attraction was not grammatically admissible. For, since by **247** means of it members belonging together could be so joined together as to blend into one externally rounded and recognizable whole, the N. T. writers were unwilling to be deprived of this advantage even in cases where strict usage was opposed to it.

A portion of these cases may, to be sure, be referred to constructions with the Accus., as 2 Cor. i. 4 τῆς παρακλήσεως ἧς παρακαλούμεθα, Eph. i. 6 Lchm. [Treg. Tdf. **א***] τῆς χάριτος αὐτοῦ ἧς ἐχαρίτωσεν ἡμᾶς, iv. 1 τῆς κλήσεως ἧς ἐκλήθητε (cf. 1 Kings viii. 29 τῆς προσευχῆς ἧς προσεύχεται), — all which are founded on the familiar construction treated of § 131, 5 p. 148. More free, yet sustaining a certain analogy to the same usage, are Acts xxiv. 21 φωνῆς ἧς ἔκραξα (cf. Isa. vi. 4 τῆς φωνῆς ἧς ἐκέκραγον) and Jude 15 τῶν ἔργων ἀσεβείας αὐτῶν ὧν ἠσέβησαν. But the following stand out of all analogy: 2 Thess. i. 4 θλίψεσιν αἷς ἀνέχεσθε (see however § 132, 9 p. 161), Acts i. 22 ἕως τῆς ἡμέρας ἧς ἀνελήμφθη (Vulg. *qua* adsumptus est), Rom. iv. 17 κατέναντι οὗ ἐπίστευσεν θεοῦ ante deum, *cui* credidit (since in this sense πιστεύειν τινά is wholly contrary to usage; see § 133, 4 p. 173 sq.), 1 Tim. iv. 6 var., Acts xxvi. 16 μάρτυρα ὧν τε εἶδες ὧν τε ὀφθήσομαί σοι (*quibus* apparebo tibi). In this last passage the first clause ὧν τε εἶδες is perfectly regular, but the second is drawn into the attraction manifestly only for symmetry's sake, which is not readily sacrificed to grammatical strictness by a Greek writer (like Luke)[1]; cf. Jude 15. On Acts xiii. 39, however, see § 147, 30 p. 342.

B. § 143, N. 5; H. § 811 a.; C. § 554 d.; D. p. 364; J. § 822 Obs. 10.

Relative Adverbs also sometimes undergo attraction. Examples **12**

---

[1] The variation of cod. Vat. and sundry versions (ὧν εἶδές με etc.) can only be founded in a misunderstanding of the passage (perhaps cf ὧν for ὡς).

from the N. T. are Matt. xxv. 24, 26 συνάγω ὅθεν (equiv. to ἐκεῖθεν ὅπου) οὐ διεσκόρπισα. Cf. with this § 127, 5 p. 105 and the similar kind of attraction in § 151, 2 p. 377.

B. § 143, 17; H. § 817; C. § 534 c.; D. § 404; J. § 824.

13 Of the so-called *attractio inversa* — (a species of anacoluthon where the antecedent is attracted by the Relative and takes its case; see the details in the general Grammars) — a few wholly unquestionable instances are found.

Thus in the oft-repeated quotation from the O. T. (Ps. cxvii. 22) λίθον ὃν ἀπεδοκίμασαν οἱ οἰκοδομοῦντες, οὗτος ἐγενήθη etc. Matt. xxi. 42, etc.; but in 1 Pet. ii. 7 Lchm. [Treg.] λίθος ὃν [λίθον ὅν Tdf. א*]. Further, Luke i. 73 (διαθήκης), ὅρκον ὃν ὤμοσεν πρὸς Ἀβραάμ etc., 1 Cor. x. 16 τὸν ἄρτον ὃν κλῶμεν, οὐχὶ κοινωνία ἐστὶν etc. On Acts x. 36 Tdf. [א*] see § 131, 13 p. 153 sq. An antecedent general pronominal idea is likewise attracted by the Relative in Luke xii. 48 παντὶ ᾧ ἐδόθη πολύ, πολὺ ζητηθήσεται παρ᾽ αὐτοῦ. Cf. here § 151, 4 p. 379.

B. § 143, 19; H. cf. § 822; 853 b.; 757; C. § 641; J. 836, 6. 7; G. § 60.

14 A general Relative clause (ὃς ἄν etc.) sometimes takes the place of
248 a c o n d i t i o n a l c l a u s e with ἐάν (also a species of anacoluthon);
as, Matt. x. 14 ὃς ἂν μὴ δέξηται ὑμᾶς . . ., ἐξερχόμενοι ἐκτινάξατε τὸν κονιορτὸν etc., xxiii. 16, 18 ὃς ἂν ὀμόσῃ ἐν τῷ ναῷ, οὐδέν ἐστιν. Cf. the opposite case in § 149, 6 p. 360.

THE PARTICIPLE.

B. § 144; H. § 784 D.; C. § 673; J. § 662; G. Chap. vi.

1 With respect to the use of Participles by the several N. T. writers a few general remarks must first be premised. As in course of time Infinitive constructions in the ancient languages were gradually resolved into conjunctional clauses (§ 141, 1 p. 272), the like takes place also with the Participle. Every one conversant with Greek literature knows with what predilection in its classic period participial constructions are employed, and how the entire system of its structure of sentences depends in great part on the employment of these clauses. Yet the artificial periodic structure produced by their aid is rather a product of the refined (rhetorical) literary language and remained pre-eminently a characteristic of it, while the plain popular language of all periods — (read the lively and circumstantial descriptions, narratives, comparisons of Homer) — preferred, instead of lengthy and involved periods, to give,

rather, the individual members as independent clauses with a
finite verb, and to indicate the mode of their connection by
some of the simplest particles. Since, moreover, this analytic
mode of construction suited more the genius of Oriental expression (and accordingly prevails in the books of the O. T.),
it was natural that, particularly in the language of the
Gospels marked especially by the national peculiarities
(Luke's not excepted, cf. § 141, 6 p. 276), the employment of
participial constructions should noticeably recede before the
construction by means of finite verbs, and that numerous combinations by means of conjunctions (especially καί) are preferred where the classic literary language would without doubt
have availed itself of the construction with the Participle, or
of other subordinate dependent clauses.

The following passages will illustrate in general what has been said:
Matt. vii. 27 καὶ κατέβη ἡ βροχὴ καὶ ἦλθον οἱ ποταμοὶ καὶ ἔπνευσαν οἱ
ἄνεμοι καὶ προσέκοψαν τῇ οἰκίᾳ ἐκείνῃ, καὶ ἔπεσεν, καὶ ἦν ἡ πτῶσις αὐτῆς
μεγάλη, viii. 14–16 καὶ ἐλθὼν ὁ Ἰησοῦς etc., Mark i. 12, 13 ; Luke xviii.
32–34 παραδοθήσεται καὶ . . . ἀναστήσεται· καὶ αὐτοὶ οὐδὲν τούτων συνῆ- 249
καν, καὶ ἦν τὸ ῥῆμα τοῦτο κεκρυμμένον ἀπ᾽ αὐτῶν, καὶ οὐκ ἐγίνωσκον τὰ
λεγόμενα, xix. 2, 3 καὶ ἰδοὺ ἀνήρ etc., John iv. 47–50 ; Matt. xxi. 46
compared with the parallel passages, etc. ; see also § 151, 31 p. 401.
A multitude of similar examples may be adduced also from the Apocalypse. On the other hand, Luke in the Acts is removed the farthest
from this form of narration ; the language of this book in its manner
of employing participial constructions approximates quite conspicuously
to the style of the classic Greek writers, and in passages reproduces
completely the traits of the Greek mode of thought and expression
(read in particular the speeches put into the mouth of the persons that
make their appearance, e.g. of Peter in Chaps. ii. and iii., of Paul in
Chaps. xvii. xxii. xxiv. xxvi., of Tertullus in Chap. xxiv., in part also of
Stephen in Chap. vii., or separate historical sections such as iv. 13–24 ;
xvi. 18–23, 27 ; xix. 1–9 ; xxvii. 30, etc.). The Epistolary writings,
particularly those of Paul, and still more the Epistle to the Hebrews,
likewise frequently employ participles, since for the treatment of didactic and dogmatic material no form of expression was better suited than
the philosophic, finished, language of the learned Greeks of that day.
Yet it is not to be denied, that in handling participial constructions
classic dexterity in many respects fails the authors of these Epistles,
and that their periods, on account of the very excess of participles,
relative and other subordinate clauses, parentheses, and changes of
structure, are often deficient in perspicuity and prepare grave difficul-

ties for the interpreter; see, for example, the first chapters of the
Epp. to the Ephesians and the Colossians.

2   One mode of resolving a periodic combination of clauses
into juxtaposed independent clauses has already been spoken
of (§ 139, 28 p. 226) in connection with hypothetic constructions.   Far more extensive would a collection prove to be of
those instances from all parts of the N. T. in which, instead
of Participles (usual in the classic literary language) standing
in some kind of temporal or causal relation to the leading
clause, the finite verb is introduced, to which then the leading
verb is subjoined by καί.

Since an enumeration of all the passages of the sort belongs rather
to a work on N. T. Rhetoric than to a Grammar, it may suffice to
illustrate the usage in separate characteristic examples: Matt. xviii.
21 ποσάκις ἁμαρτήσει εἰς ἐμὲ ὁ ἀδελφός μου καὶ ἀφήσω αὐτῷ; where
certainly every native Greek would have written τῷ ... ἁμαρτήσαντι,
since the first clause stands temporally in a subordinate relation to the second; Luke xxiv. 18 σὺ μόνος παροικεῖς Ἰερουσαλὴμ καὶ
οὐκ ἔγνως τὰ γενόμενα ἐν αὐτῇ; John vii. 4 οὐδεὶς ἐν κρυπτῷ τι ποιεῖ καὶ
ζητεῖ αὐτὸς ἐν παρρησίᾳ εἶναι, vi. 50 οὗτός ἐστιν ὁ ἄρτος ..., ἵνα τις ἐξ
αὐτοῦ φάγῃ καὶ μὴ ἀποθάνῃ, iii. 19 αὕτη ἐστὶν ἡ κρίσις, ὅτι τὸ φῶς
ἐλήλυθεν ... καὶ ἠγάπησαν μᾶλλον τὸ σκότος ἢ τὸ φῶς, Rom. x. 20
ἀποτολμᾷ καὶ λέγει.   Also with an adversative Particle: Rom. vi. 17
χάρις τῷ θεῷ, ὅτι ἦτε δοῦλοι τῆς ἁμαρτίας, ὑπηκούσατε δέ etc.

Here belongs, further, the juxtaposition of two Imperatives of such a sort that the emphasis lies only on one of the
250 commands given.   This likewise is in accordance with a mode
of popular speech (cf. the Latin *divide et impera*, i.e. divide if
thou wilt conquer).

Thus the frequent ἔρχου καὶ ἴδε (instead of the literary ἐλθὼν ἴδε or
ἔρχου ἵνα ἴδῃς) John i. 47; Rev. vi. 1, 5, 7, ἐρεύνησον καὶ ἴδε John vii.
52, still more plainly Eph. iv. 26 (quotn.) ὀργίζεσθε καὶ μὴ ἁμαρτάνετε
where it is impossible to understand the first command as direct (cf.
Mehlh. Schema ἀπὸ κοινοῦ etc. 1833).   Further, the combination of an
Imperative with a following finite verb in the Future; as, ἔρχεσθε
καὶ ὄψεσθε John i. 40 Tdf. [Treg.], αἰτεῖτε καὶ δοθήσεται· κρούετε καὶ
ἀνοιγήσεται Matt. vii. 7 (Luke xi. 9), ἄρατε καὶ εὑρήσετε Matt. xi. 29, etc.

B. § 144, 1; C. cf. § 679; D. cf. §§ 420, 421 Obs. 5; J. cf. §§ 705, 2. 4; 759 Obs. 4; W. 350 sq.
(328 sq.).

3   Participles take the place of subordinate clauses only.
There are many passages, particularly in Paul's Epistles, where

Participles appear to stand independently; and hence it has been frequently asserted that in the N. T. even l e a d i n g c l a u s e s are formed in Hebrew fashion (see Gesen. Lehrg. p. 791; Gr. § 131, 2) by means of Participles. Such an assumption, however, would militate fundamentally with the genius of Greek (prose) usage; (not even the Seventy take this liberty even where they had a Participle before them in the Original). The probability of this assertion, therefore, in Paul's case must be disputed at the outset, since even from the most Hebraistic books of the N. T. no sure instance of such a usage can be brought forward. It would be unreasonable likewise to wish to apply to the language of such a writer as Paul the isolated precedents extant in c l a s s i c G r e e k poets and earlier prose authors (which, besides, are all capable of a proper explanation). On the contrary, all the examples adduced as of this class may be brought substantially under some one of the following heads:

a) The Participle appears to stand independently in incomplete c i t a t i o n s f r o m t h e O. T., or those quoted from memory. **4**

For instance: 1 Cor. iii. 19 ὁ δρασσόμενος τοὺς σοφοὺς ἐν τῇ πανουργίᾳ αὐτῶν. Here it is plain even from the Article that the Participle can only hold the place of a S u b j e c t, and consequently cannot possibly itself be predicate (with ἐστίν understood), but a complete predicate (βουλὴν αὐτῶν ἐξέστησεν according to Job v. 13) is to be supplied, provided Paul designed to give a complete thought here where he was only concerned with the contents of the g i v e n words of the quotation; cf. Heb. i. 7 (after Ps. civ.), Matt. ii. 18 (after Jer. xxxi. 15). In this way we can explain, too, most simply the Participle διδούς in Heb. viii. 10 and x. 16, viz. as a quotation according to the Alexandrian text[1] **251** from Jer. xxxi. (xxxviii.) 33. For to connect it grammatically with διαθήσομαι is so harsh as to seem hardly conceivable, and the connection with ἐπιγράψω is prevented by καί.

b) In p r o v e r b i a l p h r a s e s. **5**

These, as is well known, appear in all languages often as grammatically incomplete sentences (see e.g. Matt. v. 38), since the supply of what is necessary to render the sentence grammatically complete is

---

[1] In cod. Vat. it is given completely διδοὺς δ ώ σ ω etc. The quotations in the Ep. to the Heb., however, agree almost always with the text of the Alexandrian codex, (those in the Pauline Epistles more with the Vatican codex); see Bleek, Heb. Vol. I. p. 369 sqq.

made unconsciously and involuntarily by the hearer himself, and in all such quotations it is the s e n s e only which is important, not the grammatical construction. E.g. 2 Pet. ii. 22 κύων ἐπιστρέψας ἐπὶ τὸ ἴδιον ἐξέραμα · ὗς λουσαμένη εἰς κυλισμὸν βορβόρου.

6 c) The Participle is to have a finite verb s u p p l i e d to it from the context, as was often the case also in Greek authors (see B. § 151, IV. 5, and compare the chapter on Ellipsis below, p. 390) ; and

d) The Participle stands anacoluthically, the sentence for any reason (generally in consequence of parenthetic insertions) following another construction or even breaking off and remaining incomplete (cf. the chapter below on Anacoluthon, p. 378).

To one of these last two heads are almost all Participles apparently standing absolutely to be referred, especially in Paul's writings. But as respects the individual cases, especially if both modes of explanation appear to be grammatically admissible, the opinions of the most reputable interpreters are not infrequently divided. As the number of passages is very considerable; as, further, an evident struggling with expression has often interrupted the grammatical sequence of thought and forced it into the background, and the correct understanding of the several passages for the most part requires a student to enter somewhat thoroughly into the context, not only grammatically, but also doctrinally, historically, rhetorically : the grammarian must restrict himself, at least in *this* connection, to establishing the existence of the two classes of cases described, and to illustrating their nature in a few prominent examples.[1]

Examples of c) are, Rom. v. 10 sq. εἰ γὰρ ἐχθροὶ ὄντες etc. Here not only has καυχώμενοι been taken as a finite verb by many modern interpreters, but the variant καυχώμεθα (as an ancient interpretation) is extant. Nevertheless the Part. must be regarded as a "tardily subjoined" adjunct to σωθησόμεθα; see the comm. of Fritzsche, de Wette, 252 Meyer.   2 Cor. viii. 19 sq. οὐ μόνον δὲ, ἀλλὰ καὶ χειροτονηθεὶς etc., a parenthetic clause (left at the same time incomplete) which, since it stands out of all construction, is to be completed with the aid of the preceding Relative clause as follows : *who not only on this account* (ἐν τῷ εὐαγγ. i.e. as a publisher of the gospel), *but also as one chosen by the churches, is h e l d i n r e s p e c t;* the στελλόμενοι following is connected again most simply with the leading predicate συνεπέμψαμεν.

---

[1] On account of their obvious structural difficulties, such sentences even in ancient times were forced to undergo attempts at emendation of all sorts ; see e.g. the various readings on Rom. v. 11 ; 2 Cor. viii. 21 ; Heb. vii. 1 ; 1 Pet. ii. 11.

In the following verse (21), however, if with Tdf. [eds. 2, 7; not 8, Treg. cod. Sin.] we read προνοούμενοι γάρ, we should be obliged again to take the participial clause parenthetically and supply with it such an idea as, *I do this* etc. (cf. § 151, 24 b) c) p. 394 sq.). Mark xii. 5 where for οὓς μὲν δέροντες, οὓς δὲ ἀποκτέννοντες a predicate like *they maltreated* is to be derived from ἀπέκτειναν (cf. § 151, 23 d) p. 392). See, besides, Heb. vii. 1–3 (according to the difficult reading [so too ℵ], adopted by Lchm. [Treg.], ὅ ς συναντήσας etc., what is necessary to complete it grammatically being given in the second verse), 1 Pet. ii. 18 (οἱ οἰκέται, ὑποτασσόμενοι etc.), iii. 1 (αἱ γυναῖκες, ὑποτασσόμεναι etc.), 7 (οἱ ἄνδρες, συνοικοῦντες etc.) — with all which Participles the appropriate predicates are to be supplied from the context; see the commentaries. Since such Participles absolute often cannot be otherwise t r a n s l a t e d than by finite verbs, too great compliance with our usage has led to the taking as leading clauses of yet many other Participles, the grammatical coherence of which either with preceding or following clauses has been satisfactorily proved by the more sharp and discriminating criticism of recent interpreters; see, for instance, 2 Cor. v. 12; Rom. xii. 6 (where before ἔχοντες δέ none of the larger marks of punctuation is to be placed), xiii. 11 (referring to vs. 8), Heb. xii. 15; 2 Pet. ii. 1 (ἀρνούμενοι, ἐπάγοντες etc.), iii. 5 (where the participial clause begins with ἐξ ὕδατος), etc.

Examples of d) are, 2 Cor. v. 6 θαρροῦντες καὶ εἰδότες etc. Here **7** the Participles are anacoluthic; for after the parenthesis διὰ πίστεως γάρ etc. the sentence, attracted by the predicate of the parenthesis and resuming the initial θαρροῦντες, takes another turn: θαρροῦμεν δέ etc. In 2 Pet. i. 17 (λαβὼν γὰρ παρὰ θεοῦ etc.) the construction is completely broken off with vs. 17; in vs. 18 a different construction follows, the subject changing or rather reverting to the preceding one (in vs. 16), and the grammatically incomplete thought which began with vs. 17 being incorporated as object (ταύτην τὴν φωνήν) into this following clause. John xiii. 1 (ἀγαπήσας ... ἠγάπησεν), where the sentence, begun with πρὸ δὲ τῆς ἑορτῆς etc., led astray by the intervening ἀγαπήσας, suddenly passes over to a conclusion that does not correspond to the first participial clause (εἰδώς etc.). In the following verse the interrupted sentence is not indeed grammatically completed, but continued in the interrupted narrative. In John vi. 22 Rec. the participial clause (ἰδὼν [Lchm. Tdf. Treg. εἶδον, cod. Sin. εἶδεν] ὅτι etc.) is taken up again in vs. 24 by ὅτε οὖν εἶδεν [cod. Sin. καὶ ἰδόντες ὅτι etc.]. Acts xxiv. 5 (εὑρόντες γάρ etc.) where the discourse, instead of giving the leading clause belonging to the Participle, continues in the 6th verse in a Relative construction, just as in Rom. xvi. 25–27; (cf. the doxology in Act. Polycarp. 20, and the similar case

Acts xxiv. 18 in § 151, 10 p. 383). Rom. xv. 23 sq. Lchm. [Tdf.
Treg. א*] (νυνὶ δὲ μηκέτι etc.) where the participial clause ἐπιποθίαν
ἔχων etc., owing to the parenthesis ἐλπίζω γὰρ etc., is left unfinished,
and the discourse returns in vs. 25 to the original νυνὶ δέ of vs. 23,.
see Lchm. vol. II. pref. p. ix, [and Tdf.'s note on vs. 24 in his ed.
8]; the addition ἐλεύσομαι πρὸς ὑμᾶς appears to be (an emendation)
of later origin.   To be sure, on this method of explaining them, the
sentences acquire for the most part a very irregular and anomalous
253 aspect. Yet compare the great multitude of similar changes in construction (a liberty of which the N. T. writers, and foremost among
them Paul, made a very extensive use) with the Participle in 13
p. 298 below, and in different connections § 151, 12 p. 386, § 123, 5
p. 78.

8   REMARK. The former practice of construing even participial clauses
which stand in indubitable connection with finite verbs as leading
clauses, because, strictly taken, they contain not subordinate but rather
co-ordinate adjuncts of the action expressed by the leading verb, rests
upon an oversight of the laws of the Greek language; e.g. Jas. ii. 9
εἰ δὲ προσωπολημπτεῖτε, ἁμαρτίαν ἐργάζεσθε, ἐλεγχόμενοι ὑπὸ τοῦ νόμου
ὡς παραβάται; see also Luke iv. 15 (ἐδίδασκεν . . . δοξαζόμενος), Rom.
iii. 24, etc. Modern exegesis has already shown sufficiently the error
of such an interpretation.

B. § 144, 1 and N. 1; H. § 785; C. § 678; D. §§ 393 b., 492; J. §§ 451. 695; G. § 108.

9   Participles take the place in particular of Relative
clauses; in which case the Participle as a rule has the
Article before it, cf. § 125, 3 Remark, p. 93. This is, to be
sure, a general principle of the Greek language. But since
the N. T. in employing it manifestly goes farther than the
ordinary usage, we will here give a view of the cases by classi-
fying them. The Participle stands in place of a Relative
clause

a) After a Substantive likewise rendered definite by the Art.; as,.
Jas. iii. 6 ἡ γλῶσσα καθίσταται ἐν τοῖς μέλεσιν ἡμῶν, ἡ σπιλοῦσα ὅλον τὸ
σῶμα etc. Yet the substantive can also stand w i t h o u t an Art. in
the cases specified § 125, 3 p. 92; proper names, too, as a rule then
dispense with the article (cf. B. § 124, 3), as 1 Thess. i. 10 Ἰησοῦν, τὸν
ῥυόμενον ἡμᾶς.

b) After Personal Pronouns, since they uniformly take the place
of a definite substantive, as Rom. ix. 20 σὺ τίς εἶ, ὁ ἀνταποκρινόμενος,
xiv. 4; Jas. iv. 12 σὺ τίς εἶ, ὁ κρίνων (for which in the passage from
Jas. the Rec. Grsb. etc. have after several MSS. ὃς κρίνεις), Rom. viii.

4 ἐν ἡμῖν, τοῖς περιπατοῦσιν, Eph. i. 12, 19 ἡμᾶς, τοὺς προηλπικότας, τοὺς πιστεύοντας, 1 Cor. viii. 10 σὲ τὸν ἔχοντα; rarely after the Demons. Pron. αὐτός in place of the 3d Pers., John i. 12 ἔδωκεν αὐτοῖς ἐξουσίαν ... τοῖς πιστεύουσιν.

c) Also when the (1st and 2d) Person is not expressed separately but contained in the verbal ending (on which cf. § 129, 13 p. 132), as Heb. iv. 3 εἰσερχόμεθα εἰς τὴν κατάπαυσιν, οἱ πιστεύσαντες, vi. 18 ἵνα παράκλησιν ἔχωμεν, οἱ καταφυγόντες, 1 John v. 13 ζωὴν ἔχετε αἰώνιον, οἱ πιστεύοντες.

d) In appositional adjuncts to the Vocative, for the same reason. See the examples of this in § 129 a. 6 p. 141.

e) When the Participle takes the place of a Substantive, and accordingly stands alone without referring to an object expressly mentioned. Here the insertion of the article is required, inasmuch as in general, according to B. § 124, 1, the g e n u s is designated (*he who, such a one as*); if, however, the Participle expresses indefinite i n d i v i d u a l s, or those for any reason not more closely designated, either τὶς, τινές is wont to stand with it, or it is used alone w i t h o u t 254 an a r t i c l e.

Examples of this very common usage are, Rom. iii. 11 Tdf. οὐκ ἔστιν ὁ συνιῶν, οὐκ ἔστιν ὁ ἐκζητῶν τὸν θεόν as it were, this class of men is not to be found among them; but in vs. 12 οὐκ ἔστιν ποιῶν [Tdf. ὁ with א] (sc. τὶς) χρηστότητα, Matt. xxv. 29 τῷ ἔχοντι παντὶ δοθήσεται· τοῦ δὲ μὴ ἔχοντος, καὶ ὃ ἔχει ἀρθήσεται ἀπ᾽ αὐτοῦ, 2 Cor. xi. 4 εἰ ὁ ἐρχόμενος ἄλλον Ἰησοῦν κηρύσσει.[1]   Without the article, Mark i. 3 φωνὴ βοῶντος ἐν τῇ ἐρήμῳ, Rev. ii. 14 ἔχεις ἐκεῖ κρατοῦντας τὴν διδαχὴν Βαλαάμ, Rom. iii. 12; Matt. xxiv. 38.   With τὶς, particularly in the periphrasis for a finite verb by means of the Participle with εἶναι (see 24 sqq. pp. 308 sq.), as Mark xiv. 4 ἦσάν τινες ἀγανακτοῦντες etc.

f) Thus far the insertion of the article in the above cases is perfectly regular.   But the N. T. departs somewhat from ordinary usage (although a few scattered examples are found in Greek authors also, see Bhdy. p. 318; Winer 110 (104)) in this respect, that even when the indefinite and general pronominal words (such as τὶς, ἄλλος, ἕτερος, πολλοί) are expressly inserted, the Participle can retain the article; as, Gal. i. 7 τινές εἰσιν οἱ ταράσσοντες ὑμᾶς, Col. ii. 8 μή τις ἔσται ὁ συλαγωγῶν (cf. Ignat. ad Eph. 8 μηδεμία ἔρις ἡ δυναμένη), Luke xviii. 9 εἶπεν πρός τινας τοὺς πεποιθότας, see besides Jude 4 in § 125, 3 Rem.

---

[1] Even if the object which the writer has in mind in using the Participle is subsequently mentioned, the Participle must nevertheless first of all be so construed: for example, John v. 45 ἔστιν ὁ κατηγορῶν ὑμῶν, Μωϋσῆς not, *Moses is he who accuses you*, but, *there is one who accuses you, Moses.*   Cf. with this the case where the Participle with the Art. takes the place of a P r e d i c a t e, in § 129, 1, b) p. 124.

p. 93 ; Acts iv. 12 οὐδὲ γὰρ ὄνομά ἐστιν ἕτερον, τὸ δεδομένον ἐν ἀνθρώποις, John xii. 12 ὄχλος πολὺς ὁ ἐλθὼν εἰς τὴν ἑορτήν, Mark xv. 41 ἄλλαι πολλαὶ αἱ ἀναβᾶσαι, 2 John 7 πολλοὶ πλάνοι ἐξῆλθαν ... οἱ μὴ ὁμολογοῦντες. To these add the other examples in § 125, 3 Rem. p. 93. in which the participle with the article is subjoined to an indefinite substantive or one standing in a predicative relation. In all these cases the article intimates that the Participle is an Adjectival adjunct (and consequently takes the place of a Relative clause), not a limitation pertaining to the verb (and so to be resolved by a Conjunction). Nevertheless the Greeks, however, would even then have preferred the Participle without the article, or a complete Relative clause.

REMARK. On the practice of the Apocalypse to subjoin without alteration the Participle in the Nominative (as an apposition) to other Cases, see § 123, 5 p. 78.

B. § 144, 3; H. § 789 d.; C. § 598 b.; D. p. 599; J. § 811, 3; G. §§ 108, N. 1; 109, 5.

10 The Future Participle (which, moreover, in the N. T. has become a rarity, e.g. with the Article, τὸ ἐσόμενον Luke xxii. 49, ὁ παραδώσων John vi. 64, τὸ γενησόμενον 1 Cor. xv. 37, τὰ λαληθησόμενα Heb. iii. 5) is found as a substitute for a final clause only in the Acts: viii. 27; xxiv. 11 (ἦλθεν etc.) προσκυνήσων, xxiv. 17 ποιήσων, xxv. 13 ἀσπασόμενοι ; and with ὡς (to express the purpose as it exists in the mind of the subject, B. § 144, N. 14; H. § 795 e.; C. § 680; J. § 701; G. § 109, N. 4) in the Ep. to the Heb. xiii. 17 ἀγρυπνοῦσιν ... ὡς λόγον ἀποδώσοντες.

255 Elsewhere to express the purpose the Infinitive is employed, or Conjunctions, even in passages where the use of the Participle would have been more convenient (see the examples in § 139, 47 p. 241 and cf. § 140, 4, 10, 13, 17),— or the Present Participle is used according to the following paragraph.

B. § 144, N. 4; H. § 789 Rem. g.; J. cf. § 897.

11 The Present Participle, besides its ordinary use to express a continuing action and simultaneousness, expresses in the N. T. the following relations also :

1) In connection with the article it is often used without any temporal reference, merely to present the idea of the verb either in the form of a substantive or an adjective, in the same way that the Pres. Infinitive (yet in this case interchangeably with the Aorist) often serves to designate the verb's idea as such. For example,

Eph. iv. 28 ὁ κλέπτων μηκέτι κλεπτέτω, Matt. xxvii. 40 ὁ καταλύων τὸν
ναὸν καὶ ... οἰκοδομῶν, σῶσον σεαυτόν, Rev. xx. 10 ὁ διάβολος ὁ πλανῶν
αὐτούς, 1 Thess. i. 10 Ἰησοῦν, τὸν ῥυόμενον ἡμᾶς etc. Hence in John
(vi. 33, 41, 50, 51) there is a difference between ὁ ἄρτος ὁ καταβαίνων
(a conception) and ὁ ἄρτος ὁ καταβάς (with a temporal reference), see
Lücke.

2) Like the Indicative it often includes in itself the Future force,
and hence is used, especially in connection with ὡς, even to express
the end or object; see on both points § 137, 10, 11 pp. 203 sqq.
and 144, 22 p. 307.

3) Like the Indicative (§ 137, 10 c) p. 205) it is used also of the
intention (de conatu): Matt. xxiii. 13 ὑμεῖς τοὺς εἰσερχομένους οὐκ
ἀφίετε εἰσελθεῖν, Acts xxviii. 23 Παῦλος ἐξετίθετο ... πείθων αὐτοὺς περὶ
τοῦ Ἰησοῦ (whereupon subsequently, οἱ μὲν ἐπείθοντο, οἱ δὲ ἠπίστουν).
So in the evangelic narrative Judas before executing the betrayal is
almost always called ὁ παραδιδούς, e.g. Matt. xxvi. 25 (in Lat. versions
qui traditurus erat), 46, 48; Mark xiv. 42, 44; John xviii. 2, 5 etc.;
but in reference to the betrayal as accomplished ὁ παραδούς, Matt. x. 4;
xxvii. 3 Lchm. [Treg.].

B. § 144, 4; J. § 706; W. § 45, 3.

In sentences which contain two or more Participial clauses, **12**
whether in immediate succession or separated by a finite verb,
we find in general (even in those writers that rather rarely
employ the Participial construction) the rule observed, that
only co-ordinated Participles are connected by καί or τέ;
as, Matt. iv. 23; xxvii. 48; xxviii. 12, etc. Otherwise, particularly if the narrative advances from one fact to another by
means of them, the Participles are placed side by side without
any connective.

Of this genuine classic usage a great many examples are still found:
particularly in the Acts, as xxii. 26 ἀκούσας ὁ ἑκατοντάρχης προσελθὼν
ἀπήγγειλεν λέγων, xvi. 27 ἰδὼν τὰς θύρας ἀνεῳγμένας, σπασάμενος μάχαιραν
ἤμελλεν ἑαυτὸν ἀναιρεῖν, νομίζων etc., xxiv. 5, perhaps also xiii. 27 (if
with Lchm., vol. II. Pref. p. viii, we expunge the καὶ before τὰς φωνάς,
since the passage in its extant form can hardly be defended grammatically); but also in the Gospels, as Matt. iv. 13 καταλιπὼν τὴν
Ναζαρὲθ ἐλθὼν κατῴκησεν etc., 24 (προσήνεγκαν αὐτῷ etc.), xxvi. 44
(ἀφεὶς ... λέγων), Mark v. 15 θεωροῦσιν τὸν δαιμονιζόμενον καθήμενον
ἱματισμένον καὶ σωφρονοῦντα, 26 sq. (πολλὰ παθοῦσα καὶ δαπανήσασα ...
ἀκούσασα ... ἐλθοῦσα), iii. 5; Luke vii. 37, etc.; and in the Epistles,
as 1 Cor. xi. 4; 2 Tim. i. 4; 2 Pet. ii. 1, etc   Sometimes the MSS. **256**
vary, since there are cases enough where in point of fact both inter-

pretations are admissible; see, for example, Matt. ii:. 1 sq. (Lchm. omits καὶ, Tdf. [ed. 7] gives it [ed. 8 omits it, ʒo cod. Sin.]), xxviii. 2, and elsewhere.

B. § 144, N. 5; C. §§ 504 b.; 659; J. §§ 707 sqq.

13 The cases where Participles share in the so-called *constructio ad synesin* or *sensum* with respect to Gender and Number are already to be found in the exposition of this construction given § 129, 8 p. 129 sq. It remains here to make mention of the instances where this construction occurs in reference to Case. These are all either anacoluthic, i.e. have arisen in consequence of a mental change of construction (cf. 7 above, p. 293), or to be explained by the fact that the Participle refers, not to the grammatical, but to the logical Subject of the leading clause. We will arrange the examples according to the Cases; yet it is to be noticed that here only those instances are considered where the Participle stands in the Nominative instead of another Case. For the instances of the Genitive and Accusative belong under the head of absolute cases, consequently to § 145, 6 p. 317.

The Participle, then, (without the Article, cf. § 123, 5 p. 78) is found in the Nominative

a) Where the precise grammatical connection requires the Genitive; these are pure instances of the second class, the Participle being referred to the logical, instead of the grammatical, subject of the preceding or following leading clause: Jude 16 τὸ στόμα αὐτῶν λαλεῖ ὑπέρογκα, θαυμάζοντες (equiv. to λαλοῦσιν etc.), Acts xix. 34 ἐπιγνόντες δὲ ... φωνὴ ἐγένετο μία ἐκ πάντων (equiv. to πάντες ἔκραξαν). Further, see Col. ii. 2 (αἱ καρδίαι αὐτῶν, συμβιβασθέντες), 2 Cor. vii. 5 (σάρξ ἡμῶν ... θλιβόμενοι), ix. 11 and 13 (πλουτιζόμενοι ... δοξάζοντες, making reference to vss. 10 and 12); perhaps also Rev. v. 12 since λέγοντες owing to the Gender can strictly speaking refer only to αὐτῶν (yet according to § 129, 8 b) p. 130 another mode of explanation is also admissible, which gives the same sense), 2 Cor. i. 7 (see Meyer). From the O. T. belongs under this head the frequently occurring ῥῆμα κυρίου ... λέγων, as in Gen. xv. 1; 1 Kings xvii. 8 (Al. text); 1 Sam. xv. 10; 2 Sam. vii. 4, etc.

b) Instead of the Dative, the construction taking a different turn, as Acts xx. 3 ποιήσας μῆνας τρεῖς ... ἐγένετο γνώμη τοῦ ὑποστρέφειν (see § 140, 13 p. 268); or the Participle refers to the logical Subject of the leading clause, as Col. iii. 16 ὁ λόγος τοῦ Χριστοῦ ἐνοικείτω ἐν ὑμῖν ... διδάσκοντες etc. (where we are not with Lchm. to assume a parenthesis), Acts xv. 22 sq. ἔδοξεν τοῖς ἀποστόλοις ... γράψαντες. On the other hand, in Eph. iii. 18 the Participles may (with Lchm.) be suitably referred to the grammatical subject in ἐξισχύσητε (see § 151, 18 p. 389), and likewise in Phil. i. 30 ἔχοντες together with πτυρόμενοι etc. to στήκετε. The first hand reading of cod. Vat., ἔχον, can hardly be founded in a mistake of the copyist, but looks like an emendation occasioned by the extremely great hyperbaton.

c) Instead of the A c c u s a t i v e: — in every instance in consequence of a change of construction, as Mark ix. 20 ἰδὼν αὐτόν, τὸ πνεῦμα εὐθὺς ἐσπάραξεν αὐτόν, where the sentence, instead of continuing in the Passive, suddenly takes an Active turn, and hence the subject changes (cf. the similar examples in § 151, 10 p. 383) ; most naturally after an antecedent Acc. and Infin., since this construction easily and naturally changes in the mind, especially after parenthetic clauses, into a direct 257 statement, as Eph. iv. 2 παρακαλῶ ὑμᾶς περιπατῆσαι (equiv. to περιπατή-σατε), ἀνεχόμενοι etc., 2 Pet. iii. 3 (μνησθῆναι ... γινώσκοντες) and prob-ably also 1 Pet. ii. 11, where, however, several MSS. even (see Tdf.'s crit. note) exhibit the alteration ἀπέχεσθε.

REMARK. The examples from the Revelation where the Participle stands in the Nominative (with or without the Article) and the con-struction requires a different Case, have not been included here, because they in part may be referred to the observation in § 123, 5 p. 78, in part are a consequence of the connection of clauses peculiar to that book, and spoken of § 151, 12 p. 386.

B. § 144, 5 and N. 6; H. cf. §§ 788. 801; C. § 677 e. f.; D. § 578; J. § 693; G. § 112, 2.

The familiar Greek idiom, according to which what with us 14 is a s u b o r d i n a t e c i r c u m s t a n c e is expressed in Greek by the finite verb and the l e a d i n g i d e a by a P a r t i c i p l e dependent on that verb, has in the N. T. in the case of λαν-θάνειν and its associated verbs almost completely disappeared, only a few instances of it being adducible (almost exclusively from Luke and the Ep. to the Hebrews): Heb. xiii. 2 ἔλαθόν τινες ξενίσαντες, Luke xxiii. 12 προϋπῆρχον ἐν ἔχθρᾳ ὄντες, Acts viii. 16 ὑπῆρχον βεβαπτισμένοι, xix. 36 κατεσταλμένοι (cf. 18 p. 304), Matt. xvii. 25 προέφθασεν αὐτὸν λέγων.

What elsewhere admits, with more or less plausibility, of being com-prised under this head (which, however, owes its establishment to our modern linguistic sense) restricts itself to the following: The idea again (πάλιν) is sometimes given by Luke, after Hebrew prece-dent (see Gesen. Lex. sub יָסַף, and Lehrgb. 824; Gr. § 139, 2 and 3 a.) or the Sept. (Gen. iv. 2 ; Ex. x. 28 ; xiv. 13 etc.), by προστί-

θ ε σ θ α ι but with an *Infinitive* following (cf. Ep. Clem. 1, 12), as Luke
xx. 11, 12 προσέθετο ἕτερον πέμψαι δοῦλον (on the other hand in the
parallel passage Mark xii. 4 πάλιν ἀπέστειλεν; so the Seventy sometimes render וַיֹּסֶף by πάλιν, as Gen. viii. 10), Acts xii. 3 προσέθετο
συλλαβεῖν τὸν Πέτρον; and *vice versa* (cf. the Homeric ἆλτο λαθών), as
προσθεὶς εἶπεν παραβολήν Luke xix. 11.   The idea *continuing, per-*
sisting, Luke expresses by ἐ π ι μ έ ν ω with the Participle (cf. John
viii. 7), Acts xii. 16 ἐπέμενεν κρούων, or ο ὐ δ ι α λ ε ί π ω, Luke vii. 45,
after the analogy of παύεσθαι (15 below). The expression ἐ τ έ λ ε σ ε ν
διατάσσων (Matt. xi. 1) also may be fitly translated by the adverb
adequately, sufficiently. On θέλειν followed by the Infin. see § 150, 8.
p. 375 ; cf. also 8 above, p. 294.

B. § 144, 6; H. §§ 796 sq.; C. § 677; D. §§ 591. 592; J. §§ 681 sqq.; G. § 113.

15   On the other hand, the rule according to which certain
verbal ideas, particularly those of internal and external perception, of learning, of ceasing, take after them their c o m -
p l e m e n t a r y   c l a u s e s (which we as a rule express by the
Infin. with *to* or a clause with *that*) in the form of a P a r t i -
c i p l e, is pretty accurately observed by the N.T. writers ; only
that in cases where both constructions, the Participle and the
Infinitive, are admissible (e.g. with ἀκούειν, εἰδέναι), they give
the preference to the latter, but still more frequently introduce
the complementary verbal idea as a subordinate clause, with a
conjunction (ὅτι).

258   The instances that occur, arranged according to Cases, are
the following :

a) The Participle in the N o m i n a t i v e.

Thus with παύεσθαι Luke v. 4, frequently in the Acts, the Ep. to
the Heb., and by Paul, see Wahl ; with φαίνεσθαι Matt. vi. 16, 18
(but not Rom. vii. 13) ; with ὑπάρχειν (only by Luke and in the Epp.,
cf. 14 p. 299 and 18 p. 304) ; with καλῶς ποιεῖν and εὖ πράττειν
Acts x. 33 ; Phil. iv. 14 ; 2 Pet. i. 19 ; 3 John 6 ; Acts xv. 29. Further, οὐ τρέμουσιν βλασφημοῦντες 2 Pet. ii. 10 (after the model of
αἰσχύνεσθαι), μὴ ἐγκακῶμεν τὸ καλὸν ποιοῦντες (like παύεσθαι) Gal. vi. 9 ;
2 Thess. iii. 13.   On the other hand, with verbs of e m o t i o n, as
ἀγαλλιᾶσθαι (Acts xvi. 34), χαίρειν (John xx. 20 ; Phil. ii. 28), Participles stand in the ordinary participial relation, containing as they do
the r e a s o n of the emotion. With εὐχαριστεῖν the statement which
gives the reason or the contents of the thankfulness is almost always
introduced with ὅτι ; hence in 1 Cor. xiv. 18 the former reading λαλῶν
(which arose from the omission of the connective) has now been

changed with reason into the λαλῶ of the mss. [א also].   On 1 Tim.
v. 13, see 17 p. 303.[1]

b) The Participle in the A c c u s a t i v e, or construction of the
Acc. with the Participle ; this occurs most frequently with
verbs of internal and external perception and of learning.

Thus with ἀκούειν (see under c)), ὁρᾶν Mark i. 10 ; Acts viii. 23 ;
Heb. ii. 8 etc., βλέπειν Matt. xv. 31, Mark, Luke, Acts, etc., θεωρεῖν
John vi. 19 ; x. 12, Acts, etc., γινώσκειν Mark v. 30, Luke, Acts, Heb.,
but most frequently with ὅτι,[2] ἐπίστασθαι Acts xxiv. 10 (xxvi. 3 var., on
which see § 145, 6 p. 317), εὑρίσκειν very often, Matt. xx. 6 ; Rev. iii.
2, etc., hence with the Pass. the Particip. is in the Nom. as Matt. i.
18 ; Phil. iii. 9 etc. (cf. 18 p. 304), ὁμολογεῖν 1 John iv. 2 ; 2 John 7.
For the references in all these cases see the Lexicons.   Other verbs
which are frequently so construed in Greek authors, — e.g. besides
εἰδέναι (see note [2]), χαίρειν (see a)), the *verba narrandi* such as ἀν-,
ἀπ-, καταγγέλλειν, λαλεῖν (with the exception of Acts xxvi. 22, see 20
below, p. 305), — are joined almost exclusively to ὅτι, more rarely to
the Acc. with the Infin.

c) The Participle in the G e n i t i v e, only with ἀκούειν.   It **16**
is necessary to bring together here into a single summary the
diversified v e r b a l constructions of this verb, just as in § 132,
17 p. 165 sq. we exhibited its construction with nouns.

Since according to p. 166 the Genitive with ἀκούειν designates the
person whose speech or sound is immediately perceived (instead of
which, however, an abstract substantive indicating a sound often appears
by metonymy),

α) It can only be connected with the G e n i t i v e and Participle **259**
where an immediate hearing or perception occurs ; and the Participle
too must in every instance be the P r e s e n t, owing to the simultaneousness of the two actions of speaking (or sounding) and hearing.
Examples are very numerous : with persons, Mark xii. 28 ; xiv. 58 ;
Acts ii. 6, 11 ; vi. 11, 14 ; viii. 30 etc., Rev. vi. 3, 5 ; viii. 13 etc., and
with φωνῆς (instead of the person himself) Acts xi. 7 ; xxii. 7 ; Rev.
xiv. 13 ; xvi. 1.

On the other hand, the A c c u s a t i v e with ἀκούειν designates simply

---

[1] On the pre-eminently Alexandrian use of εὑρίσκεσθαι with a Participle for εἶναι
with a Participle, which increased more and more as time went on, see Dind. in
Stephanus's Thesaurus sub voce, p. 2418.

[2] Its synonym ε ἰ δ έ ν α ι is never found with the Participle (yet cf. 18 p. 304),
but always either with the Infin. (Luke iv. 41 ; 1 Pet. v. 9), or with ὅτι, or with an
indirect question.   In the last two cases the subject of the dependent clause often
lingers as an object with the leading verb (according to § 151, 1 p. 377) : οἶδά σε
-ίς εἶ, ἔγνων σε ὅτι εἶ, accordingly as if an incipient Participial or Infinitive clause.

the object of the perception. In construction with nouns alone, therefore, strictly speaking only a thing i.e. an abstract, such as λόγον, φωνήν,[1] can be joined to ἀκούειν in the Accusative, see § 132, 17 and the note, p. 166. But if the object of the perception is expanded into an entire clause, ἀκούειν acquires primarily the signification of mediate hearing, or internal perception (learning). Inasmuch as, further, the subject of this dependent clause (which moreover may be any term whatever, person or thing) is attracted to ἀκούειν as object, its predicate (if the clause is not dependent on a conjunction) passes over either

β) into the Infinitive: Acc. and Infin.; or

260 γ) into the Participle: Acc. and Particip.

The difference between these two constructions is the general one (cf. B. p. 402 Note) viz. that the Infin. presents the idea of the verb indefinitely, while the Participle exhibits an action or state in a clear and definite relation to another; — the Infin. names the action generally, the Particip. describes it. Still it hardly allows itself to be reproduced by us in the translation, since we in both cases must employ a resolved construction with the conjunction *that*. The construc-

---

[1] It makes no difficulty that a Present Participle can be added as an apposition to such an object-Accusative, as to any other substantive, without forming the construction of the Acc. with the Particip. which follows under γ) below, inasmuch as ἀκούειν retains its proper signification of *to hear* (not the secondary one of *to learn, be informed*). Several instances of this are actually extant: Acts ix 4; xxvi. 14 (cf. Rev. v. 13) ἤκουσεν φωνὴν λέγουσαν etc. This is in *sense* hardly to be distingnished from ἤκουσεν φωνῆς λεγούσης (so, too, without a Part. ἀκούειν λόγους and λόγων, see p. 166), but yet taken closely is to be translated *he heard a voice which said* etc. Here comes into consideration a passage from Mark (v. 36, "locus perdifficilis," Tdf.): ὁ δὲ Ἰησοῦς ἀκούσας (Tdf. [Treg. cod. Sin.] παρακούσας) τὸν λόγον λαλούμενον λέγει etc. This sentence, too, owing to the signification (*to hear*) cannot be brought under the following construction (γ) of the Acc. with the Participle. But according to the analogy of the examples just mentioned there would result the rather incongruous sense, *as he heard the word which* or *as it was spoken*, — a pleonasm hardly conceivable. For while in the other examples the addition λέγουσαν was necessary, owing to the direct discourse which followed and was immediately connected with it, in this case every occasion of the sort quite disappears. Less surprising and more natural would it be to take the Participle as a simple attributive adjunct to λόγον (just as we say, *the spoken word*). But then N.T. usage (which here can hardly be convicted of the slightest anomaly, see § 125, 1 p. 90) would demand the adjectival position, therefore either τὸν λόγον τὸν λαλ. or τὸν λαλ. λόγον. The corruption of the passage is certainly very ancient, as the variants shew. But it is very significant that the Vatican codex actually exhibits the attributive position mentioned (τὸν λόγ. τὸν λαλ.), and no-less important that cod. D and many (Old Lat.) versions wholly omit the completely superfluous addition λαλούμενον, but have instead simply τὸν λόγον or τοῦτον τὸν λόγον. The original reading, as I think, has been preserved either in these last or in the position of the words in cod. Vat.

tion of the Acc. and Infinitive occurs only in John xii. 18 ἤκουσαν
τοῦτο αὐτὸν πεποιηκέναι, 1 Cor. xi. 18 ἀκούω σχίσματα ἐν ὑμῖν ὑπάρχειν ;
that of the Acc. and Participle is somewhat more frequent : Luke iv.
23 ὅσα ἠκούσαμεν γενόμενα εἰς Καφ., Acts vii. 12 ἀκούσας ὄντα σιτία εἰς
Αἴγ., 2 Thess. iii. 11 ; 3 John 4. The difference between these passages and those with the Acc. and Participle in the preceding note is
obvious : in those ἀκούειν still has the signification *to hear*, here the
mediate sense *to learn ;* in those only the Present Part. was used, after
the style of the examples under α) ; in these any Participle whatever
may be subjoined to the Acc., since the clauses are no longer contemporaneous.

δ) Instead of the two preceding constructions the verbal forms are
most commonly resolved into a c l a u s e w i t h ὅτι; of this examples
are found everywhere, Matt. iv. 12 etc. Finally,

ε) As after every verbum sentiendi, an i n d i r e c t q u e s t i o n takes
the place of the objective clause : Matt. xxi. 16. ἀκούεις τί οὗτοι
λέγουσιν;

That in the last two cases the subject of the subordinate clause can
stand as the object of ἀκούειν follows from § 151, 1 p. 376.

REMARK. Only in a single passage does the Participle (after μανθάνειν) appear to be used in a way opposed to the genius of the language
viz. 1 Tim. v. 13 ἅμα δὲ καὶ ἀργαὶ μανθάνουσιν π ε ρ ι ε ρ χ ό μ ε ν α ι τὰς οἰκίας
etc. According to the general rule, μανθάνω ὤν can only mean *I perceive, notice, t h a t I a m ;* on the other hand, the signification *I l e a r n
t o b e* belongs exclusively to the construction with the Infinitive, and
indeed occurs just before (vs. 4) : μανθανέτωσαν εὐσεβεῖν καὶ . . . ἀποδιδόναι. Now although the Infin. as a more general verbal form can take
the place of the Participle (cf. B. p. 402 (465) note), yet the r e v e r s e
is n e v e r the case. Nevertheless this Participle has been taken in
this sense by the majority of translators (Vulg., Luther, deWette) :
they learn to go about etc. To avoid this grammatical error other
methods of interpretation have been proposed by the interpreters.
Sometimes μανθάνειν has been taken in the sense of *to be accustomed,
in the habit of ;* this meaning, however, μανθάνειν never has, at least in
the Present, and even in the Preterite it would require in this sense
the Infinitive, since a Greek could have had no other idea before his
mind than to h a v e l e a r n e d. At other times ἀργαί has been represented as the word immediately dependent on μανθάνουσιν, so that
by supplying the copula (εἶναι) it would mean, *they learn to be idle* etc.
(Winer, Meyer [i.e. Huther]). Against this supposition, however,
there are — apart from the sense — most weighty objections, viz. 1)
the position, according to which ἀργαί must imperatively be taken as
an attribute of the subject ; 2) the ellipsis of the Infin. εἶναι, since

according to both general and N. T. usage (see 18 below) we are warranted in supplying only the Participle οὖσαι, and the possibility of
taking the passage in the way described is afforded only by the addition of the Infin. εἶναι; 3) usage. For what is adduced from other
writers as a warrant for it, proves on closer examination to be insuf-
ficient. The reference to Plato, Euthyd. p. 276 (οἱ ἀμαθεῖς ἄρα σοφοὶ
μανθάνουσι) is not in place, since there the (perfectly senseless) addition σοφοί has been discarded on MS. authority, and the passage from
Dio Chrys. (or. 55 p. 558 Σωκράτης μὲν παῖς ὢν ἐμάνθανε λιθοξόος τὴν
τοῦ πατρὸς τέχνην) is of quite another sort. Considering the textual
certainty of the Participle in the above passage, and the employment
— elsewhere so absolutely correct — of the Participle on the part of
the N. T. writers, there is hardly any other choice left us than, according to Bengel's proposal, to assume here that the mode of expression is anacoluthic, so as to give rise to the meaning "*discunt quae
obeundo domos discuntur.*" What they περιερχόμεναι τὰς οἰκίας learn
is sufficiently indicated, not grammatically indeed, but as respects the
sense, by the following epithets ἀργαί, φλύαροι, περίεργοι, λαλοῦσαι τὰ
μὴ ὄντα; and the specific thought Bengel supplies (*statum familiarum
curiose explorant*), which perhaps as too gratuitous and far-fetched has
damaged his interpretation somewhat, is not needed.

B. § 144, N. 7; C. § 677 d.; J. § 682, 3 ; G. § 113, N. 5.

18 The omission of the Participle ὤν, ὄντα etc. in these
complementary clauses is usual in the N. T. also, in fact rather
more common than its insertion. Cf. 22 p. 308.

Thus with διατελεῖν, Acts xxvii. 33 ἄσιτοι διατελεῖτε; with φαίνεσθαι, Matt. xxiii. 27, 28 φαίνονται ὡραῖοι, δίκαιοι, 2 Cor. xiii. 7 ;.
Rom. vii. 13; with οἶδα, Mark vi. 20 εἰδὼς αὐτὸν ἄνδρα ἅγιον; with
ἀφεῖναι (*to leave*) Luke x. 30 Lchm. [Treg. Tdf.] ἀφέντες ἡμιθανῆ ;
and very often with εὑρίσκειν, Luke ix. 36; xxiii. 4, 22; Acts v. 10 etc.,
1 Cor. iv. 2; Gal. ii. 17 etc., 2 Pet. iii. 14; Rev. ii. 2; v. 4 etc. (quite
elliptical are Mark xiv. 16 ; 2 Cor. xi. 12). The omission is most
natural with ὑπάρχειν, since this word as a synonym of εἶναι already
includes in itself ὤν: Luke viii. 41; ix. 48; Acts ii. 30; xxi. 20 etc.
See Wahl.

B. § 144, N. 10; J. § 438 Obs.

19 The phrase ὁ καλούμενος, frequently employed in the writings of
Luke (and a few times in the Rev. also), uniformly takes its proper
position (Ptcp. between the Art. and Subst.) : τῇ καλουμένῃ στείρᾳ (Lk.
i. 36), Σίμωνα τὸν καλ. ζηλωτήν (vi. 15), etc. (In Greek writers the
appellation also intervenes between the Art. and the Participle; as,
τῶν δήμων καλουμένων, τοὺς Ῥείτους καλουμένους, Thuc. Xen.). On the

way in which the other N. T. authors express themselves, see § 129, 6
p. 128.

B. § 144, N. 12; C. § 657 d.; J. § 682, 674 sq.

The Participle also (in Greek authors frequently, in the N.T. 20
rarely) suffers attraction.   Three classes of cases occur.
which rest, however, essentially on the same principle :

a) The clause with the Participle is already, as a Relative
clause, attracted ; cf. pp. 285 sqq.   Then the Participle, which as
respects its form belongs to the Relative (and which consequently
had there been no attraction would have stood, like the Relative,
in the Acc.), is changed with it into the same case.

This case occurs in Acts xxvi. 22 οὐδὲν ἐκτὸς λέγων ὧν τε οἱ προφῆται
ἐλάλησαν μελλόντων γίνεσθαι, arising from οὐδὲν τούτων ἃ ... ἐλάλησαν μέλλοντα γίνεσθαι — (a genuine classic example). Cf. § 123, 3
p. 77.

b) The Participle dependent on an Infin., if as a closer
limitation of the same it ought, according to the general rule
(B. § 141, 1), to have stood in the Accusative, is attracted
by a noun which stands in the leading clause (and which at 262
the same time is the subject of the Participle), and assumes the
case of this noun.

This case is a legitimate extension of the familiar construction
ἔξεστί μοι εἶναι εὐδαίμονι (B. § 142, 2).   What the predicate adjective
εὐδαίμονι undergoes here takes place also with entire participial clauses ;
and as in this example both constructions are admissible (εὐδαίμονι and
-μονα), so also in the N. T.   And in fact the remark made above (cf.
§ 142, 1 p. 278) that the N. T. likes to employ the regular and more
simple construction with the Acc., while classic usage prefers the other
case (as a rule the Dative), holds good here also.   An evident instance of attraction is given in 2 Pet. ii. 21 κρεῖσσον ἦν αὐτοῖς μὴ ἐπεγνωκέναι ... ἢ ἐπιγνοῦσιν ἐπιστρέψαι etc. (for which ἐπιγνόντας also
might have stood).   Further, in the Acts (the style of which harmonizes most with this idiom) xv. 25 Lchm. [Treg.] ἔδοξεν ἡμῖν ... ἐκλεξα-
μένοις πέμψαι etc. (where Tdf. [so cod. Sin.] has preferred the other,
just as good Greek, reading ἐκλεξαμένους, which is given in vs. 22
without var.), xxvii. 3 Lchm. [Treg. Tdf. cod. Sin.] ἐπέτρεψεν (sc.
αὐτῷ) ... πορευθέντι τυχεῖν etc. (where Tdf. [eds. 2, 7] reads with the
majority of more recent MSS. πορευθέντα), xvi. 21 ἔθη ἃ οὐκ ἔξεστιν ἡμῖν
παραδέχεσθαι οὐδὲ ποιεῖν Ῥωμαίοις οὖσιν ; see also the example from
xxii. 17 in § 145, 2 p. 315.   Elsewhere the Accusative is always
used : and that not only where the Dative in the leading clause is
omitted (1 Pet. iv. 3), or where the Participle stands after the Infin

(Acts xi. 12 Lchm. [Treg. Tdf.], xxvi. 20, cf. Matt. xviii. 8), but also where the Participle precedes, in which case the Greeks, owing to the proximity of the Participle to the noun in the leading clause, would certainly have preferred attraction ; as, Luke i. 73 sq. τοῦ δοῦναι ἡμῖν ... ῥυσθέντας λατρεύειν, Acts xxv. 27 ἄλογον γάρ μοι δοκεῖ πέμ-ποντα ... σημᾶναι, and especially Heb. ii. 10 ἔπρεπεν αὐτῷ (sc. θεῷ), πολλοὺς υἱοὺς εἰς δόξαν ἀγαγόντα τὸν ἀρχηγὸν ... τελειῶσαι. The reader, therefore, here must not allow himself to be misled by the ordinary classic usage and refer ἀγαγόντα, owing to the identity of case, to the following ἀρχηγόν (instead of to God, αὐτῷ).

c) The Participle, although in signification belonging to the leading clause, is attracted by a different and nearer case (with which of course it must have the same subject) in a subordinate clause.

This case occurs in Rev. xvii. 8 (θαυμασθήσονται οἱ κατοικοῦντες ὧν ... βλεπόντων etc.) where βλέποντες is manifestly a correction. Cf. § 145, 1 sq. p. 314 and the use in B. § 141, N. 3.

B. § 144, 8 and N. 13; J. § 696, Obs. 5; G. p. 218 sq.

21　Particles are employed in connection with Participles. Thus in particular, after an antecedent participial clause, οὕτως serves to resume the same in the leading clause ; as, Acts xx. 11 ἀναβὰς δὲ καὶ κλάσας ... οὕτως ἐξῆλθεν, xxvii. 17 ; cf. John iv. 6. Cf. § 149, 1 p. 357.

Of ἔπειτα in the same sense there is but a single example (and that rejected by the modern editors) : Mark vii. 5 (ἔπειτα ἐπερωτῶσιν according to many mss., see vs. 2).

Of the usage (see B. p. 404 note) by which a Participle, rendered a substantive by means of the Article, is taken up again by an Adjective Pronoun (οὗτος, ἐκεῖνος), there are many examples : 263 Matt. xxiv. 13; Mark vii. 15, 20; Luke ix. 48; John i. 18; v. 11; vii. 18; Acts ii. 22; xvii. 6; xv. 38; Rom. xiv. 14; (on Mark xii. 40 see § 123, 5 p. 79). All these examples are predominantly rhetorical in their nature. The same thing happens often after substantives alone, and after Relative clauses, in order to bring the idea in the leading clause out again with a certain rhetorical emphasis, as John xii. 48; Rom. vii. 15, 19; ix. 6, 8 etc., and after the Infin. used substantively, as Phil. i. 22 (see § 149, 8 d) p. 362). The case is different with the pronoun αὐτός. This, if it stands with the leading verb in the Nominative after a Participle, has its proper sense self, as 1 Pet. v. 10; but if it stands in an oblique case its use is founded in the pleonastic style of the N. T. writers, which has been often alluded to already (see § 130, 2 p. 142), and of which more will be said below, § 145, 2 p. 315 (cf. § 151, 4 and 5 p. 379 sq.).

B. § 144, N. 14; H. §§ 793, 795 e.; C. §§ 598 b.; 675 e.; 680; J. §§ 701 sqq.; G. § 109 N. 4.

No example occurs of the addition of the words ἅτε, οἷα, οἷον to Participles where the latter specify an objective reason. On the other hand, the connection of ὡς with a Participle is very common. We will bring together the cases that occur under the three following heads:

a) The participial limitation is to be conceived of as uttered from the mind of the speaking or acting subject, no matter whether the statement it contains rests on a matter of fact or merely on a supposition, (*quippe qui, as* [Germ. *als*] one who etc.).

For example, 1 Pet. ii. 13, 14 ὑποτάγητε τῷ βασιλεῖ ὡς ὑπερέχοντι etc. (subjective motive), Luke xvi. 1 διεβλήθη ὡς διασκορπίζων etc. (statement of the people), 1 Cor. vii. 25 γνώμην δίδωμι ὡς ἠλεημένος etc. (personal conviction), 2 Cor. vi. 9, 10 (general notion, which however is straightway corrected in the following clauses; cf. on the contrary the objective statements in vss. 3, 4), Rom. vi. 13; Heb. xii. 27; xiii. 3, etc. The understanding of such clauses is commonly facilitated by expanding them into participial clauses like εἰδότες, νομίζοντες, λέγοντες ὅτι followed by a finite verb (cf. Acts xxvii. 30 προφάσει ὡς μελλόντωι etc.).

b) The limitation rests on a comparison, whether with given or only supposed facts, objects, views, (*perinde ac, velut, quasi, tanquam, as* [Germ. *wie*] one who etc.).

For example, Acts iii. 12 ἡμῖν τί ἀτενίζετε, ὡς ἰδίᾳ δυνάμει πεποιηκόσιν etc., xxiii. 15 ὡς μέλλοντας διαγινώσκειν (Vulg. *tanquam cognituri*), 20; 1 Cor. iv. 7 τί καυχᾶσαι ὡς μὴ λαβών (*quasi non acceperis*), v. 3; 2 Cor. x. 14; Col. ii. 20; Heb. xi. 27.

c) It contains, when the Participle stands in the Future, a statement of purpose, uttered in the spirit of the acting or speaking subject.

This case occurs (since Future Participles are so rarely used, see 10 p. 296) but once: Heb. xiii. 17 ἀγρυπνοῦσιν ὡς λόγον ἀποδώσοντες. But since the Present, both in the Indic. and in the Participle (according to 11 above p. 296, and § 137, 10. 11 pp. 203 sqq.), so often contains telic and other statements having reference to the future, we may unhesitatingly bring under this head also Rom. xv. 264 15 ἔγραψα ὑμῖν, ὡς ἐπαναμιμνήσκων ὑμᾶς etc., 1 Thess. ii. 4 οὕτως λαλοῦμεν, οὐχ ὡς ἀνθρώποις ἀρέσκοντες ἀλλὰ θεῷ.

REMARK. It is to be noticed besides, that examples of the participial structure with ὡς are found in all four cases, and have been given above (on ὡς before the Gen. absol. see particularly § 145, 7 p. 318); further, that the Participle is sometimes to be supplied from the context, as Eph. vi. 7 μετ᾽ εὐνοίας δουλεύοντες, ὡς τῷ κυρίῳ καὶ οὐκ ἀνθρώποις, Col. iii. 23; 1 Pet. iv. 11, etc.; but particularly, that according to N. T. usage (see 18 p. 304) the Participle ὤν, ὄντος etc. is regularly dropped, so that the (predicative or adverbial) adjunct thereto pertaining is left standing alone with ὡς: 1 Pet. ii. 12 καταλαλοῦσιν ὑμῶν ὡς κακοποιῶν sc. ὄντων, Rom. xiii. 13 ὡς ἐν ἡμέρᾳ (sc. ὄντες) εὐσχημόνως περιπατήσωμεν, John vii. 10 etc. See in general Wahl under ὡς.

B. § 144, N. 15; H. § 795 f.; C. § 674 f.; D. §§ 621. 622; J. § 697 d.; G. § 109, N. 5.

23   That Participles are to be taken in a restrictive sense (*although*) is sometimes indicated simply by the connection, as Matt. xxvi. 60 οὐχ εὗρον, πολλῶν προσελθόντων ψευδομαρτύρων; but commonly by the addition of the particles καίπερ and καίτοι, especially in the Ep. to the Heb. (iv. 3; v. 8; vii. 5, etc.). The anticipatory position of ὅμως, which as respects the sense is not expected until later, occurs in 1 Cor. xiv. 7 ὅμως τὰ ἄψυχα φωνὴν διδόντα, where a καίπερ is to be derived from the ὅμως for the Participle διδόντα, Gal. iii. 15 ὅμως ἀνθρώπου κεκυρωμένην διαθήκην οὐδεὶς ἀθετεῖ (where ὅμως is antithetic to the idea ἀνθρώπου κεκ. διαθ.).

CIRCUMLOCUTION FOR SIMPLE TENSE-FORMS BY MEANS OF THE PARTICIPLE WITH εἶναι (γίνεσθαι).

B. § 144, 9; H. § 797; C. § 679; J. § 375; W. p. 348 (326 sq.)

24   It has been remarked in general, that the farther ancient languages become removed from their origin, the more their formations both in the department of nouns and of verbs are gradually resolved into their component parts; accordingly we find periphrases (not only of unusual tenses and those difficult of formation, but also of very common tense-forms) by means of εἶναι (γίνεσθαι) and Participles becoming more and more common in the later language. To be sure, a similar periphrastic mode of expression is found at all periods, and in the best writers, both of poetry and of prose; since in many instances it is entitled to preference above the common mode. Yet even a superficial comparison shows that the above-named construction appears incomparably more frequently in the N. T. writings than elsewhere, indeed that it is of such prominence as to impart to individual portions of the N. T. a

certain distinctive character which distinguishes their style from others.   As it would be uncritical and erroneous amid the innumerable phrases of the sort found in the N. T. to discern in all cases solely a periphrasis for a simple tense-form, so 265 on the other hand it would be a false and fruitless endeavor to claim that in every single instance they differ syntactically from the simple tense.   In our attempt now to classify the cases, regardless of the question whether a given construction is to be taken in the periphrastic or the proper sense (for a strict separation of them into these two classes is neither theoretically nor practically feasible), the number of examples is so copious that we must at the outset disclaim any attempt at completeness in details.   We remark

1) That only those passages can be taken into consideration where the Participle has no Article, since when connected with the Art. the Participle must at once be construed as standing by itself i.e. as a part of the sentence separate from the copula, whether it be as subject (ἀληθές ἐστιν τὸ γινόμενον, τίς ἐστιν ὁ παραδιδούς σε, etc.), or as predicate noun (σὺ εἶ ὁ ἐρχόμενος, ὑμεῖς ἐστε οἱ λαλοῦντες, see § 129, 1 p. 123 sq.), or as an attributive (οὗτός ἐστιν ὁ ἄνθρωπος ὁ διδάσκων etc.) ; and

2) That a combination of the verb εἶναι (γίνεσθαι) with the anarthrous Participle in a periphrastic sense can only take place if the Participle is of the Present or the Perfect tense ; since, as will appear from the exposition that follows, a circumlocution with the anarthrous Aorist Part. does not and cannot occur.[1]

[1] The correctness of this statement is at once apparent on a comparison of parallel passages.   Thus the sentence τίς μου ἥψατο; (Mark v. 30) cannot be resolved into τίς ἦν ἁψάμενος, but can only be rendered τίς (ἦν or ἐστιν) ὁ ἁψάμενος (Luke viii. 45) ; for τίς σοι ἔδωκεν τὴν ἐξουσίαν ταύτην (Matt. xxi. 23 ; Mark xi. 28) we find not τίς ἐστιν δούς σοι, but τίς ἐστιν ὁ δούς σοι τὴν ἐξουσίαν ταύτην (Luke xx. 2) ; and for the Aorist ἰδόντες οἱ μαθηταὶ ἠγανάκτησαν (Matt. xxvi. 8) not ἦσαν ἀγανακτήσαντες, but only ἦσαν ἀγανακτοῦντες (Mark xiv. 4). Accordingly, where the Aorist Part. occurs in connection with εἶναι it always has the article : οὗτός ἐστιν ὁ ῥηθείς (Matt. iii. 3), ὁ γενόμενος ἐν τῇ ἐκκλησίᾳ (Acts vii. 38), ὁ πορθήσας (Acts ix. 21), ὁ παρὰ τὴν ὁδὸν σπαρείς (Matt. xiii. 19), ὁ σπείρας ἐστὶν ὁ διάβολος (xiii. 39), τίς ἐστιν ὁ παίσας σε (Matt. xxvi. 68 ; Luke xxii. 64) etc.   Hence in Luke xxiii. 19, where the MSS. are divided between ἦν βληθείς (Tdf. [Treg.]) and βεβλημένος (Lchm.), from a grammatical point of view the second reading is certainly the preferable one ; and its existence in the oldest MSS. proves at least that offence was early taken at the unusual character of the other verbal

The combination, then, of the verb εἶναι with a Present or a
Perfect Part. without the article is employed

266   a) If the writer wants to have the predicate of the sentence
25 taken more in a substantial and qualitative than in a
verbal sense, i.e. if not the idea of the action expressed by the
verb as such — as it is contained in a finite verb — holds the
place of the predicate, but the idea of the verb exhibited
participially in the form of a noun (whether substantive or
adjective).

Thus the sentence ἀνακρινόμεθα, ἐν τίνι οὗτος σέσωσται (Acts iv. 9)
plainly differs from χάριτί ἐστε σεσωσμένοι (Eph. ii. 5) in this: that
the predicate of the first is purely verbal (*by what means he has been
recovered*), that of the other nominal (*ye are recovered* persons, saved
ones). Further, John v. 7 ἄλλος πρὸ ἐμοῦ καταβαίνει (*comes down
before me*) is different from Jas. i. 17 πᾶν δώρημα τέλειον ἄνωθέν ἐστιν
καταβαῖνον (*is one coming down from above*, this is its attribute; cf.
iii. 15 οὐκ ἔστιν ἄνωθεν κατερχομένη, ἐπίγειος, ψυχική etc.). The distinction is the same when we say, *the hairs of your head have been
numbered* (ἠρίθμηνται Luke xii. 7), and *are* (things) *numbered* (ἠριθμη-
μέναι εἰσίν Matt. x. 30), or between *I live* (ζῶ Rev. iii. 1) and *I am
living* (i.e. the living one ζῶν εἰμι i. 18).

Among the numerous examples of this sort we select — with the
Perfect Part., κεκαλυμμένος (*hidden, dark*), μεμεστωμένος (*filled,
full*), πεπωρωμένος (*hardened*), γεγονώς (*old, natus,* cf. p. 55 s.v.),
τετελειωμένος, εὐηγγελισμένος, ἡγιασμένος, ἀπηλλοτριωμένος, ἠλπικότες, etc.;
with the Present Part. ποιοῦν καρπόν, καρποφορούμενον *of such a
nature that it bears fruit, fruitful*), λόγον ἔχον (*rational*), ἔχων κτήματα
πολλά (*rich* Matt. xix. 22; Mark x. 22, instead πλούσιος σφόδρα in
Luke xviii. 23), ἦν ὑποτασσόμενος (*subject*), ἴσθι εὐνοῶν, ἴσθι ἐξουσίαν
ἔχων, etc. In consequence of this adjectival nature of the Participles,
they can occasionally with the aid of the Part. ὤν enter into a new
participial formation, as Eph. iv. 18; Col. i. 21 ὄντες ἀπηλλοτριωμένοι,
ἐσκοτισμένοι.

26   b) Although the idea of duration resides in the simple
tense-forms of the Present and Imperfect, it does not belong
to them invariably,[1] but does to the periphrases with the

form. But it is still more probable that both βληθείς and βεβλημένος are later
additions (hence the variation), and in point of fact cod. Sin. omits both.

On the periphrasis for the various tenses by means of εἶναι and a Participle
(particularly also with the doubtful or poetic Aorist Part.) see Dind. in Steph.
Thesaur. sub εἰμί pp. 258, 259; Cobet, Nov. Lect. 307, 621; var. Lect. 322; Porson,
Adv. 294 (260).

[1] Hence instead of the Moods of the Pres. (which, in contrast with the Moods

Participle and the Pres. or Imperf. of εἶναι; hence the latter are pre-eminently suited to denote c o n t i n u o u s a c t i o n s or s t a t e s.

Accordingly ἑστώς, προσδεχόμενος, προσδοκῶν εἰμι, γίνου γρηγορῶν (Rev. iii. 2), ἦν πειραζόμενος (Mark i. 13), ἦσαν δ ι ὰ π α ν τ ὸ ς αἰνοῦντες καὶ εὐλογοῦντες (Luke xxiv. 53) are more expressive than ἕστηκα, προσδοκῶ, γρηγόρει, ἐπειράζετο, etc.; ἦσαν νηστεύοντες (Mark ii. 18), καπηλεύοντες ἐσμέν (2 Cor. ii. 17) more emphatic than ἐνήστευον, καπηλεύομεν, etc.   In the F u t u r e, which in its simple form does not discriminate between the two ideas of duration and instantaneousness, 267 the periphrasis is the only expedient by which to express definitely the idea of duration.   Thus everybody feels the difference between ἔσεσθε μισούμενοι (Matt. x. 22 etc.), ἔσῃ σιωπῶν (Luke i. 20), ἀνθρώπους ἔσῃ ζωγρῶν (Luke v. 10), Ἱερουσαλὴμ ἔσται πατουμένη ὑπὸ ἐθνῶν (Luke xxi. 24) and μισηθήσεσθε, ζωγρήσεις, etc.   Both species of Future are united in Mark xiii. 25 (ἔσονται πίπτοντες ... σαλευθήσονται).   Also the Perfect Part. with ἔσομαι by no means always forms a periphrasis for the Futurum exactum, but on the contrary serves to transfer to the future as continuous the qualitative idea expressed by the Participle; as, Matt. xvi. 19 ὃ ἂν δήσῃς (Fut. exact.), ἔσται δεδεμένον, ὃ ἂν λύσῃς, ἔσται λελυμένον (not, *will have been bound*, but *will r e m a i n bound* etc.), xviii. 18; Luke vi. 40, and in connection with the simple Future in Luke xii. 52.

R e m a r k. It is not to be overlooked, that with many predicates in frequent use this mode of expressing continuance has become almost the established usage and suppressed the simple forms of the verbs. Thus the already mentioned use of ἦν καθήμενος for ἐκαθήμην (see p. 56), γεγραμμένον ἐστίν for the ordinary γέγραπται, ὅ ἐστιν λεγόμενον, μεθερμηνευόμενον, ἅ ἐστιν ἀλληγορούμενα, etc.   Hence ἦν διδάσκων, ἦν (ἐγένετο) κηρύσσων, βαπτίζων, means simply *he was teaching, preaching, baptizing*, not *he was a teacher, a baptizer* etc., as may be seen from the additional adjuncts appended (e.g. the object, Matt. vii. 29; Mark i. 22; adverbial qualifications, Mark i. 39; John i. 28; iii. 23).

c) In both the former cases (a) and b)) the emphasis always 27 rests upon the Participle as the proper predicate, and εἶναι is simply a copula.   But often it was of importance for the writer to give more prominence to the idea of b e i n g, e x i s t e n c e, residing in the verb, than is done by the simple tense-form. This is accomplished likewise most naturally by joining the Participle to εἶναι (generally preceding).

of the Aor., denote duration pre-eminently; cf. p. 201) the periphrasis is manifestly avoided, indeed hardly occurs. Hence in Jas. ii. 15 Lchm. ὦσιν is certainly a later addition.

The Participle in such cases is either itself the subject of εἶναι, as Matt. xxiv. 38 ἦσαν ἐν ταῖς ἡμέραις τρώγοντες καὶ πίνοντες, γαμοῦντες καὶ ἐκγαμίζοντες, Rom. iii. 12 οὐκ ἔστιν ποιῶν χρηστότητα; or commonly an attributive to the expressed subject, as Acts xxv. 14 ἀνήρ τίς ἐστιν καταλελειμμένος ὑπὸ Φήλικος δέσμιος, xxi. 23 εἰσὶν ἄνδρες τέσσαρες εὐχὴν ἔχοντες. In particular, under this head belongs the popular (oriental) manner of narrating, as the narrator at the beginning of his narrative, or as often as a new person or object is introduced, by means of the Imperf. ἦν or ἦσαν lingers as it were a moment on the object which is to be discoursed about, and then with a Participle following the subject continues his account, quite after the mode in which new events are introduced by ἐγένετο δέ etc. (§ 141, 6 p. 276). Examples are found especially in the Gospels: Matt. viii. 30 ἦν δὲ μακρὰν ἀπ᾽ αὐτῶν ἀγέλη ... βοσκομένη, xxvii. 55 ἦσαν γυναῖκες ... θεωροῦσαι, 61; Mark ii. 6; iii. 1 Tdf. [Sin.] (cf. Matt. xii. 10 where ἰδού takes the place of the ἦν), v. 11; xv. 40; Luke ii. 8; John ii. 6; xi. 1, etc.

28   d) Also, after deducting all the cases already mentioned,
268 there are still a great many examples remaining, where the union of the Pres. Part. with the 3 d Person of the Imperf. ἦν, ἦσαν, stands in narration simply for the historical Imperfect (alone in use in such cases in Greek authors) as distinguished from the momentary Aorist. These instances we are the more justified in taking pre-eminently for periphrases in the strict sense, as there are two writers especially who have a decided preference for employing them, viz. Mark and Luke.

The following may pass for examples of such periphrases in the midst of a narrative. In mentioning them we will cite at the same time those parallel passages where, instead of the periphrasis, the simple Imperfect or the Aorist or another construction, e.g. a subordinate participial clause, makes its appearance. From Mark: ἦν καθεύδων (iv. 38, ἐκάθευδεν Matt. viii. 24), κράζων (v. 5), κατακόπτων (v. 5), ἦσαν συλλαλοῦντες (var. συνελάλουν, ix. 4; cf. Matt. xvii. 3; Luke ix. 30), ἀναβαίνοντες (x. 32, cf. Matt. xx. 17), ἦν προάγων (x. 32), ἦσαν ἀγανακτοῦντες (xiv. 4, for which the Aorist in Matt. xxvi. 8, see note on 24 p. 309), ἦν συγκαθήμενος (xiv. 54, ἐκάθητο Matt. xxvi. 58; Luke xxii. 55). From Luke: ἦν προσευχόμενον (i. 10), διανεύων (i. 22), ἦν θαυμάζοντες (ii. 33), ἦσαν ἀτενίζοντες (iv. 20), ἦν συνεχομένη (iv. 38, cf. Matt. viii. 14), ἦν ἑστώς (v. 1, cf. Matt. iv. 18), ὑποχωρῶν (v. 16), ἦσαν κατακείμενοι (v. 29, συνανέκειντο Matt. ix. 10), ἦν διανυκτερεύων (Luke vi. 12), ἐκβάλλων (xi. 14, ἐθεράπευσεν Matt. xii. 22), ἦσαν παρατηρούμενοι (xiv. 1), ἐγγίζοντες (xv. 1), ἦν θέλων (xxiii. 8), ἦσαν πορευόμενοι (xxiv. 13), ἦν καιομένη (xxiv. 32); and quite as frequently in the Acts: i. 10, 14; ii. 2; viii. 1, 28, etc.

e) Lastly, it can only be regarded, grammatically, as a cir- **29**
cumlocution, that in the Perfect and Pluperfect Passive
(sometimes also Active), where in the ordinary language a
periphrasis was already in general use in individual forms
(as the 3d Pers. Plur. of the Pass., the entire Subjunct. and
Opt.), the periphrastic forms with the Perfect Part. have
become very prevalent also in the remaining Persons of
the Indicative, perhaps in consequence of the influence of
Latin upon the later language. The majority of instances
of the sort are, moreover, from Mark and Luke again.

Thus, for example, the Pluperfect appears periphrased in Mark
i. 33; xv. 26 ἦν ἡ ἐπιγραφὴ ἐπιγεγραμμένη, Luke ii. 26 ἦν αὐτῷ κεχρηματισμένον ὑπὸ τοῦ πνεύματος, iv. 16, 17; v. 17; viii. 2; xxiii. 19 (see
24 note, p. 309), 38, 51, 53, 55; Acts i. 17; xiv. 26; xvi. 9 Lchm.
[Tdf. Treg.], xxii. 20; xviii. 25; xix. 32; xx. 13; xxi. 29; xxii. 29,
and so also by other writers, e.g. Paul, but on the whole more rarely.

REDUNDANT PARTICIPLES.

B. § 144, N. 19; H. § 788; C. § 674; J. cf. § 696 Obs. 1; 705, 4; G. § 109 N. 8.

Here mention must be made of an acknowledged Hebraism, **30**
particularly of the Greek O. T. The Seventy, namely, often
added to a finite verb the Participle (Present or Aorist) of the
same verb, always placing it close beside, indeed as a rule, **269**
before the finite verb. That in this way a special emphasis
was not always aimed at, but that the combination is solely an
imitation of the Hebrew construction with the Infin. absol., has
already been remarked in connection with the similar case in
§ 133, 22 p. 183. Thus we find in the Sept. μισῶν ἐμίσησα,
ἀναβάντες ἀναβησόμεθα, πατάξας πατάξω, ἔφαγεν ἔσθων, βασι-
λεύων βασιλεύσεις, κυριεύων κυριεύσεις, ἀγείροντες ἤγειραν,
ἐξαίρων ἐξῆρεν, πορευομένη πορεύομαι, μαχόμενος ἐμαχέσατο
and many others, even when the Heb. text presents no similar
construction; as, Exod. xxiii. 26 (Piel), Gen. xix. 17.

To the language of the N. T. this construction is strictly
speaking foreign, since it is found only in quotations, viz.
Acts vii. 34 ἰδὼν εἶδον, Matt. xiii. 14 βλέποντες βλέψετε, Heb.
vi. 14 εὐλογῶν εὐλογήσω σε καὶ πληθύνων πληθυνῶ σε.

This species of pleonasm must have appeared still more strange to
a native Greek, hence as a matter of fact nothing altogether similar is
found in classic literature; see the exposition of the subject by Lobeck
40

in his Paralipomena p. 532, and the examples quoted there. Of a different sort, on the other hand, (as results from the very position of the Participle), and belonging to G r e e k usage, are such examples in the narrative style as ἐλάλησεν αὐτοῖς λέγων Matt. xiv. 27 etc., Luke xxiv. 6; John viii. 12; Acts viii. 26 etc. (cf. xxvi. 14), Rev. xvii. 1 etc. (for which in Mark vi. 50, according to 1 and 2 above pp. 288 sq., we find ἐλάλησεν ... κ α ὶ λέγει), εἶπεν ... λέγων Mark xii. 26; Luke xx. 2, ὥστε γινώσκοντες Eph. v. 5. But in Acts xiii. 45 the disagreeable, indeed un-Greek, tautology (ἀντέλεγον ... ἀντιλέγοντες), which is especially surprising in the Acts, is not confirmed by the oldest MSS.

31   REMARK. On the common transition from participial clauses into the finite verb as a c o n t i n u a t i o n of a participial clause, see § 151, 8 p. 382.

CASES ABSOLUTE.

B. § 145, 2. 3; H. §§ 790, 791 c.; C. §§ 675, 658 b.; D. p. 485 sq.; J. § 695, 2 b.; G. §§ 110, 111.

1   In the N. T. also Passive Genitives Absolute are pretty rare (e.g. Matt. i. 18; Rom. ix. 11, etc.), and in no wise formed like the Passive Ablativi consequentiæ in Latin (see particularly the instance in Heb. ix. 19, which is neither Latin nor Greek). In general, however, the N. T. writers are thoroughly conversant with the employment of the absolute construction according to the laws of the G r e e k language; only they go farther in this respect, that they disregarded grammatical accuracy (m o r e f r e q u e n t l y than Greek 270 writers allowed themselves to do so) by employing this construction even when the subject of the participial clause was not only present in the governing clause in an oblique case, but even as its subject. Most of these instances, however, find their natural explanation in the circumstance (cf. reff. above) that the Gen. absol. p r e c e d e s, and so the influence of the leading clause at the beginning of the sentence was still somewhat in the background. That in this way often an (un-Greek) a c c u m u l a t i o n of P r o n o u n s must result, has already been remarked § 130, 2 p. 142.

In reference to the text we find here again such noticeable disagreement in the MSS. (and consequently in the recent editions also) that a decision is often difficult: on the one hand, because it might just as easily happen that copyists of Greek education, taking offence at the inaccurate construction, should seek to remove it by alterations (for the most part trifling), as that others, once accustomed to a construction employed on the whole so often, or in order to produce identit·

of expression in parallel passages, should write it even where originally
the regular idiom had been employed; and because, on the other hand,
the compass of the writings is not considerable enough to establish
accurately the usage of the individual writers in this respect. Cf. the
similar observation in § 127, 26 p. 118. We arrange the examples
under the two heads:

a) The Genitives absolute precede their leading clause,
which already contains the subject of the participial clause;
and that

α) In an oblique case: — hence either in the Dative, as Matt.
ix. 18 ταῦτα αὐτοῦ λαλοῦντος αὐτοῖς, ἰδοὺ ἄρχων εἷς ἐλθὼν προσεκύνει
αὐτῷ, ix. 10; xviii. 24; xxiv. 3; xxvi. 6; xxvii. 17, besides also v. 1
Tdf. [Treg.], viii. 1, 5, 28 Lchm. [Treg. Tdf.], xxi. 23 Lchm. [Treg.
Tdf.], Mark xiii. 1; Luke xii. 36 (see 4 p. 316), xiv. 29; xvii. 12;
xxii. 10 εἰσελθόντων ὑμῶν εἰς τὴν πόλιν συναντήσει ὑμῖν, John iv. 51
Acts iv. 1 (xx. 18 Lchm.); or in the Accusative, as Matt. xviii. 25
μὴ ἔχοντος αὐτοῦ ἀποδοῦναι, ἐκέλευσεν αὐτὸν ὁ κύριος πραθῆναι, Mark
v. 18; ix. 28 Lchm. [Treg. Tdf.], x. 17; xi. 27; xiii. 3; Luke ix. 42;
xv. 20; xviii. 40; xxii. 53; John viii. 30; Acts xix. 30; xxi. 17;
xxv. 7; xxviii. 17; 2 Cor. xii. 21 μὴ πάλιν ἐλθόντος μου ταπεινώσει με
ὁ θεός μου.   But if it is present in the leading clause as a Genitive,
the employment of the Gen. absol. with the subject expressed
is even more irregular than with the Dative and Accusative, because
it might easily have been avoided, but especially because in this way
an accumulation (to a Greek ear far more disagreeable still) of
altogether identical pronouns must often arise. Since, however, precisely the same thing occurs with participial clauses in the
Dative and Accusative (ἐμβάντι αὐτῷ ἠκολούθησαν αὐτῷ etc., see the
examples in § 130, 2 p. 143), the genuineness of sentences of this
kind also is not to be doubted: Matt. vi. 3 σοῦ δὲ ποιοῦντος ... μὴ
γνώτω ἡ ἀριστερά σου, v. 1 Lchm., xxvii. 19; Mark ix. 28 Lchm.
[Treg. Tdf. cod. Sin.] (where the Acc. may have arisen from emendation
as easily as the Gen.), xiii. 1; Luke xv. 20; John iv. 51 αὐτοῦ κατα-
βαίνοντος, οἱ δοῦλοι αὐτοῦ ὑπήντησαν αὐτῷ.[1]   271

β) Likewise as subject, so that leading clause and subordinate
both have the same subject; as, Matt. i. 18 μνηστευθείσης τῆς
μητρὸς αὐτοῦ ... εὑρέθη ἐν γαστρὶ ἔχουσα, where the harshness of the
construction is moderated by the parenthesis (πρὶν ἤ etc.). In Acts
xxii. 17 all three oblique cases in direct succession are in this way

[1] Of the opposite case also, viz. that the subject of the leading clause is
contained in the antecedent Gen. absol. in an oblique case (Genitive), an instance
occurs in Heb. ix. 19 λαληθείσης πάσης ἐντολῆς ὑπὸ Μωυσέως, λαβὼν (sc Μωυσ
τὸ αἷμα. . ἐράντισεν.

united in a single sentence: ἐγένετο δέ μοι ὑποστρέψαντι εἰς Ἰερ. καὶ προσευχομένου μου ἐν τῷ ἱερῷ γενέσθαι με ἐν ἐκστάσει.

3   b) The Genitives absolute **follow** the governing clause. Since the anomaly of this structure is too conspicuous, and grammatically is even hardly to be justified, but few such examples are found.

2 Cor. iv. 18 κατεργάζεται ἡ μ ῖ ν, μὴ σκοπούντων ἡ μ ῶ ν τὰ βλεπόμενα, probably in order to connect the participial clause more independently with the **e n t i r e** leading clause, not merely with the single word ἡμῖν. Heb. viii. 9 (quotn.) ἣν ἐποίησα ἐν ἡμέρᾳ ἐπιλαβομένου μου τῆς χειρὸς αὐτῶν etc. after a perfectly un-Greek construction in the Sept., so that the instance can hardly be reckoned as belonging to the Gen. absol. construction. For, apart from the grammatical error of employing the Gen. absol. where the subjects are identical, a native Greek could not possibly add the temporal adjunct (ἐν ἡμέρᾳ) besides, since this is already contained in the very construction, and the words if immediately dependent on ἐν ἡμέρᾳ must have run, ᾗ ἐπελαβόμην (as Justin Mart. cum Tryph. 11 p. 228 actually writes; cf. Lam. iii. 57 ; Ps. xvii. 1 ; Lev. vii. 35), or at least with the Infin. τοῦ ἐπιλαβέσθαι με. Consequently the construction employed (which occurs also Baruch ii. 28) is nothing more than a thoughtless imitation of the original Hebrew (בְּיוֹם הֶחֱזִיקִי, cf. Gesen. 320), of which no other similar example is to be found in the N. T.   On Rev. xvii. 8 (θαυμασθήσονται . . . βλεπόντων) see § 144, 20, c) p. 306.

B. § 145, 4; H. § 791 a.; C. § 676 a.; J. § 695 Obs. 1; G. § 110, 1 N. 2.

4   It is rare that an instance occurs where the Participle (if its subject is obvious from the context) stands **a l o n e** in the absolute case, — owing to the propensity of the N. T. writers to insert the pronouns everywhere (§ 130, 2 p. 142).

Luke xii. 36 ἵνα ἐλθόντος καὶ κρούσαντος εὐθέως ἀνοίξωσιν αὐτῷ (cf. 2 a) a p. 315), Acts xxi. 10 ἐπιμενόντων δὲ (Grsb. Rec. add ἡμῶν [cod. Sin. αὐτῶν]) κατῆλθέν τις etc. Rom. ix. 11 (see § 129, 15 p. 133 sq.). Cf. besides Luke viii. 20 Tdf. (ἀπηγγέλη αὐτῷ λεγόντων [eds. 2, 7]) and the various readings on Matt. xvii. 14, 26 (Lchm. [Treg. Tdf. cod. Sin.]).

B. § 145, 5; J. § 699.

5   On the pretended **D a t i v e s   a b s o l u t e** for the Gen. abs. see § 130. 2 note[2] p. 143. The state of the case is different if the subject of such an apparent Dative absol. contains itself the notion of time or instru-272 ment; in this case the employment of the Dative with the Participle is not only admissible (see the examples in the Gram.), but even if the N. T. is now restored, after MSS. [Sin. also], with perfect confidence instead of the former Genitive, Matt. xiv. 6 γενεσίοις δὲ γενομένοις τοῦ Ἡρώδου ὠρχήσατο etc.

B. § 145, NN. 4, 6, 7; H. §§ 792 sq.; C. § 675 d. sq.; J. §§ 700 sq.; G. § 110, 2 sq.

Nominatives and Accusatives absolute. The **6** instances in the N. T. which may be brought under the head of Nom. absol. have already, so far forth as the Participle is used as such (i.e. without an article), been quoted and treated of in full above, under § 144, 6, 7 p. 292 sq. and 13 p. 298; but in so far as it is used with the article, the examples fall under § 123, 5 p. 78 and § 151, 4 sq. p. 379 sq. Hence it remains for us here to speak of the possible occurrence of an Accusative absolute. The peculiar classic use, however, of the Accus. absol. viz. with ὡς preceding (ἐσιώπα, ὡς πάντας εἰδότας *he was silent as if all knew* i.e. because he thought all knew) does not occur in the N. T. Hence, whatever else of the sort is found there, must, like most Nominatives absol. according to p. 298 above (cf. B. § 145 N. 6), be explained as anacoluthic.

The construction, however, can be pointed out with confidence only in a single instance: Acts xxvi. 3 ἥγημαι ἐμαυτὸν μακάριον ἐπὶ σοῦ μέλλων ἀπολογεῖσθαι, μάλιστα γνώστην ὄντα σε πάντων etc. That the clause is actually an Accus. absol. is proved by the express insertion of the Subject (σε) with ὄντα, whereby all connection of the participial clause with some other portion of the sentence is prevented. It is to be explained as having arisen from a construction altered while in the mind, probably in view of what precedes, so that the intended thought was *I esteem myself happy that thou art appointed my judge.*[1] Moreover, several interpreters would discover an Accus. absol. also in Eph. i. 18 (ἵνα δῷ ὑμῖν πνεῦμα σοφίας ..., πεφωτισμέ-νους τοὺς ὀφθαλμοὺς τῆς καρδίας ὑμῶν), the Participle not being referred to ὀφθαλμούς but to the persons addressed. That it cannot be such, follows from the fact that the subject, hence in the form ὑμᾶς, is not expressed (as it is in the preceding passage). Consequently the Accusative must be connected by anacoluthon immediately with the preceding Dative ὑμῖν. But in opposition to that, too, it may be remarked, 1) that such a license, although perhaps it might be defensible in classic authors (especially poets), in the N. T. at least — even in Luke — can only be shown to occur with the Nominative, as

---

[1] Cf. with this the very similar sentence in the Act. Andr. (the style of which often reminds one of Luke) § 13 : οὐδ' ἄν σοι πιστεύσω, ἴδιόν μου σαυτὸν λέγοντά σε.

the case whose construction is the loosest, see the exposition in § 144, 13 p. 298; 2) that the choice of the Accusative of the Participle (without an expressed subject) would be the more surprising here, as the employment of the regular Dative (πεφωτισμένοις) referring to the preceding ὑμῖν was so natural. Hence, on grammatical grounds the other explanation (see § 125, 5 p. 94) unhesitatingly deserves the preference, as the more probable; the more so as the sense also is by no means opposed to it.

B. § 145, N. 7; H. § 793; C. § 675 d.; J. § 701 sq.; G. § 113, N. 10.

7 Analogous to the examples of ὡς with the Participle (§ 144, 22 p. 307) is the appearance of the same particle in a similar sense before the construction of the Gen. absol. (Of **273** the Acc. absol. with ὡς there is no example, as was said in the preceding paragraph.)

1 Cor. iv. 18 ὡς μὴ ἐρχομένου μου πρὸς ὑμᾶς, ἐφυσιώθησάν τινες, 2 Cor. v. 20 πρεσβεύομεν, ὡς τοῦ θεοῦ παρακαλοῦντος, 1 Pet. iv. 12 (ὡς ξένου συμβαίνοντος), 2 Pet. i. 3 ὡς πάντα τῆς θείας δυνάμεως δεδωρημένης etc.,— all which are to be taken as s u b j e c t i v e motives of the following main action, and therefore, as on p. 307 above, to be resolved by εἰδότες ὅτι, or even simply by νομίζοντες, λέγοντες ὅτι ...

B. § 145, N. 10; H. § 792; C. § 675 b.; J. § 700; G. § 110, 2.

8 I m p e r s o n a l s in an absolute participial construction stand, as is well-known, in the A c c u s a t i v e. No instance, however, occurs in the N. T., except that Paul, instead of the short parenthetic clause εἰ τύχοι (used a few times, 1 Cor. xiv. 10; xv. 37), employs in 1 Cor. xvi. 6 the neuter Acc. τυχόν. This τυχόν, however, is used nearly in an adverbial sense even in classic writers, as Xenophon, Plutarch, et al. (see Pape under τυγχάνειν), and ought not to be taken otherwise here, since the leading mark of an Impersonal used verbally, viz. the dependent clause, is wanting: πρὸς ὑμᾶς, τυχὸν (if it so chances, perhaps), παραμενῶ καὶ etc. With ἐξόν however (Acts ii. 29; 2 Cor. xii. 4) ἐστίν is always to be supplied. Respecting ἀρξάμενον (Luke xxiv. 47) see § 150, 7 p. 374.

§ REMARK. A peculiar, but genuine Greek, example of the b l e n d i n g of two very current constructions, the absolute Participle and the Acc. and Infin., is found in Acts xxiii. 30 μηνυθείσης δέ μοι ἐπιβουλῆς εἰς τὸν ἄνδρα μέλλειν ἔσεσθαι, ἐξαυτῆς ἔπεμψα πρὸς σέ, which arose from the underlying grammatical combination μηνυθέντος (or μηνυθέν, see B § 145 N. 10) μοι, ἐπιβουλὴν εἰς τὸν ἄνδρα μέλλειν ἔσεσθαι. See on this topic (of blended constructions) in general § 151, 10 below, p. 383.

ADVERBS.

B. § 146, 4; H. § 588 sq.; C. § 703, 1; D. § 488; J. § 526 sq.

The number of Adverbs which being joined to the Genitive 1
have acquired almost the force of Prepositions, and hence
are often employed as periphrases of the ordinary prepositions,
may be increased from the N. T. The particulars here which
are of importance grammatically, are the following:

From the old preposition ἀντί arose by composition and derivation
(besides the common ἐναντίον *towards, in presence of,* and ἀντικρύ *over
against*), ἔναντι *before (coram),* ἀπέναντι and κατέναντι *over
against, in presence of,* also *against* in a hostile sense (Acts xvii. 7);
from ἀνά the common ἐπάνω with the force of ὑπέρ with the Acc. in
a local and immaterial sense *above, over,* in a numerical sense *more
than* (see the constr. in § 132, 21 p. 168) Mark xiv. 5; 1 Cor. xv. 6.
A preposition, unknown to the earlier writers (and that probably first
arose in the East), with which principally the Seventy render the 27 ↑
Heb. לִפְנֵי and בְּעֵינֵי, is ἐνώπιον in various constructions, to which for
the most part our prep. *before* i.e. *in conspectu, ante oculos* corresponds,
and often in circumlocutions for the Dative, see § 133, 3 sqq. p. 172 sq.;
also compounded κατενώπιον, in the same signification. The
adverbs ἔμπροσθεν *before, ante,* and ὀπίσω *back, behind,* even for
ἀπό (Matt. xvi. 23, where immediately afterwards it is employed in
altogether a different sense), are used in various peculiar constructions
and significations; also in circumlocution for simple cases (see e.g.
pp. 172, 176, 184). The word ἕως, *until,* rarely used elsewhere as
a prep., is frequently found in the N. T. connected with the Gen. as
well in a local as a temporal reference, particularly in Matt. and Luke.
As a conjunction connecting clauses it stands as often in connection
with the Relative οὗ, ὅτου, as without it; (so μέχρι, ἄχρι). Ἕως can
also be prefixed to other prepositions (and adverbs, see 4 p. 320, and
cf. the Germ. *bis*); as, ἕως εἰς (πρὸς) Βηθανίαν, ἕως ἐπὶ τὴν θάλασσαν,
ἕως ἔξω τῆς πόλεως. The neuter μέσον is once found used quite like
a prep. in the sense of μετά or μεταξύ: Phil. ii. 15.

Still more diffuse, and more or less Hebraistic, circumlocutions for simple prepositions are formed by means of the
substantives πρόσωπον (פָּנִים), χείρ (יָד), στόμα (פֶּה),
ὀφθαλμός (עַיִן).

For example: πρὸ προσώπου for the simple πρό, commonly with
persons, once even metonymically in a temporal reference, Acts xiii. 24
(πρὸ προσώπου τῆς εἰσόδου αὐτοῦ); ἀπὸ προσώπου (מִפְּנֵי) for the
simple ἀπό (Acts, Rev.); further, ἐν προσώπῳ, κατὰ πρόσωπον, εἰς
πρόσωπον followed by the Genitive, see the Lexx. With χείρ par-

ticularly the instrumental διὰ χειρός and διὰ χειρῶν ; see on these and
other phrases with χείρ § 133, 20 p. 182.   With στόμα, the analogous
διὰ στόματος, see ibid.[1]   With ὀφθαλμός : Matt. xxi. 42 ; Mark xii.
11 (quotn.) ἔστιν θαυμαστὴ ἐν ὀφθαλμοῖς ἡμῶν, Luke xix. 42 ἐκρύβη ἀπὸ
ὀφθαλμῶν σου etc.

B. § 146, N. 2 ; H. § 626 ; D. pp. 526, 572 ; J. §§ 529, 2 ; 773 Obs. 4.

2   Instead of the ordinary ἄνευ, Luke uses twice the poetic ἄτερ :
xxii. 6, 35. Πλήν except, when it is to serve as the connective of
clauses, is commonly in the earlier writers joined with other conjunctions (εἰ, ἀλλά, ὅτι, etc.).   In the N. T. however, as in general in later
writers from Aristotle on, it often stands alone as an adversative
conjunction. Cf. ἕως.

B. § 146, N. 3 ; cf. W. § 81, 3.

3   Substantially under this head (of the D a t i v e with adverbs) belong
such examples as Matt. viii. 34 ; John xii. 13 ἐξῆλθεν εἰς ὑπάντησιν τῷ
Ἰησοῦ, where the Dative is governed by the entire verbal idea (equiv.
to ὑπήντησεν) ; on the other hand, in Matt. xxv. 1 the Gen. τοῦ νυμφίου
depends immediately on the Substantive ὑπάντησιν.

275

PREPOSITIONS BEFORE ADVERBS.

4   The facility with which prepositions connected themselves
with other words, or were employed in composition, or were
themselves, especially in the earlier language, used adverbially
(cf. B. § 147, N. 5 ; H. § 615 ; C. §§ 703 b., 706 ; J. §§ 640, 644),
occasioned a great multitude of constructions or compositions
in part entirely new, — a d v e r b s c o m i n g t o d e p e n d o n
p r e p o s i t i o n s just like substantives.

Analogous to the above (1 p. 319) mentioned combinations w i t h
ἕ ω ς (viz. ἕως εἰς, ἕως ἐπί, etc.), we find also not only the regular expressions, with article prefixed, ἕως τοῦ νῦν, ἕως τῆς σήμερον, but also
without an article and in direct connection, ἕως ἄρτι, ἕως πότε, ἕως κάτω,
ἕως ἔσω εἰς (Mark xiv. 54), ἕως ὧδε, ἕως σήμερον, ἕως ἑπτάκις (as we too
say until now, to here, etc.) ; likewise ἅ μ α, in the expression ἅμα
πρωΐ, Matt. xx. 1.   Further, of the old prepositions we find ἀ π ό
thus used (it corresponding then entirely to our since), — in the phrases
ἀπὸ τότε from (since) then, ἀπὸ πέρυσι since a year ago, ἀπὸ πρωΐ ἕως
ἑσπέρας, ἀπ᾽ ἄρτι ; on the other hand with the article, ἀπὸ τοῦ νῦν, —

---

[1] Hebraistic, also, is the construction ἐπὶ στόματος δύο μαρτύρων (on the statement of two witnesses, Matt. xviii. 16 ; 2 Cor. xiii. 1, cf. Deut. xix. 15), and the
expression — an imitation of the ἐν στόματι ῥομφαίας used very often by the Sept. —
πεσοῦνται στόματι μαχαίρας, Luke xxi. 24 ; cf. Heb. xi. 34 (ἔφυγον στόματα μαχαίρης)
and Gesen. sub פֶּה no. 3.

and ἐπί before adverbs of number without affecting their meaning, ἐπὶ τρίς, ἐφ᾽ ἅπαξ. Hence combinations of the sort were regarded also as actual compositions, and accordingly written in one word, as ἀπάρτι, ἐφάπαξ, ἀντιπέρα[1]; further ὑπερλίαν, ὑπερεκπερισσοῦ, ὑπεράνω (Lchm. writes even ὑπερεγώ as one word in 2 Cor. xi. 23), ὑποκάτω, ἔκπαλαι, παραυτίκα.

In general, however, this use takes place only to a limited extent and rather in certain customary and established phrases. That it reaches back to pretty early times, may be seen from Kühner, ausf. Gr. § 620 [Jelf § 644]; Krüger, Sprachl. § 66, and the examples for the entire language in Lobeck ad Phryn. p. 45 sq.

Respecting the pleonastic·combinations ἀπὸ μακρόθεν etc. see p. 70.

PREPOSITIONS.

B. § 147; H. §§ 614 sqq.; C. §§ 688 sqq.; D. § 470 sq.; J. §§ 472. 614 sqq.

An acquaintance with prepositions, as respects their use and **1** their signification, is of great and pervading importance for the understanding of the N. T., since they, in the first place, were so often substituted for the constructions by case usual elsewhere (cf. p. 142), and secondly, deviate in their signification, both as respects its contents and its compass, not unessentially from the ordinary usage. But to give an exhaustive exposition of the subject would far transcend the limits of this grammar (indeed the complete exhibition of the N. T. use of the two prepositions ἐν and εἰς alone would require perhaps the space of a book); and the grammarian may the more readily desist from the undertaking, as the **276** subject has already found minute consideration in the special lexicons.[2] Here, as everywhere, he must confine himself merely to pointing out the prominent and distinguishing peculiarities of usage.

Prepositions with the Genitive.

'ANTI. In the signification of this preposition (*instead of, for*) no deviation occurs from ordinary usage; as, John i. 16 χάρις ἀντὶ χάριτος *grace for grace*.

'AΠO is one of the prepositions most frequently used as **2**

---

[1] This, and not ἀντιπέραν, almost all the MSS. [Sin. also] have in Luke viii. 26. This (otherwise poetic, see Stephanus, Thes.) form in -α is found as early as Polybius. Tdf. accentuates it, after MSS., ἀντίπερα; yet the accentuation according to analogy deserves the preference, since " nulla est in accentibus codicum auctoritas."

[2] See in particular the clear and well-arranged separate articles in Wahl's clavis minor.

well in the O. T. as in the New, and often in a manner deviating from the ordinary usage.   Its fundamental signification,
viz. departure from the exterior of an object, is of course
the prevalent one in the N. T. also.   Yet this, as well as all
those delicate shades in the signification of ἀπό which the N. T.
has in common with classic Greek, remains excluded from our
exposition; and even those individual instances where the
preposition is used in a pregnant or especially characteristic
sense, referrible nevertheless to its fundamental meaning, we
must leave to the exegete,[1] turning our attention at once to

---

[1] This mode of proceeding — the only one which suits the scientific criticism of
the present day — has, as matter of fact, come into general use now among recent
commentators, and thus a multitude of absurd assertions in reference to individual
senses of this preposition (and others) have been expelled from the province of
N. T. exegesis.   On this account, respecting such details in the use of the prepositions we refer to the commentaries.   For since such passages are by no means
few in number, a detailed explanation and tracing out of the sense from the
fundamental signification in every individual case, however instructive such a
treatment might be for an acquaintance with the grammatical handling of these
prepositions on the part of the N. T. writers, would carry us much too far.   To
render this evident once for all, we will here treat as briefly as possible of a
number of such instances in the case of the prep. ἀπό: Acts viii. 22 (cf. Heb. vi. 1)
μετανόησον ἀπὸ τῆς κακίας σου ταύτης for in the idea of μετανοεῖν is included at the
same time that of turning one's self away (Luther renders it very freely
repent for etc., similarly deWette on account of etc.), 2 Thess. ii. 2 σαλευθῆναι ἀπὸ
τοῦ νοός to be thrown into violent mental agitation so as to lose one's senses,
Acts xvi. 33 παραλαβὼν αὐτοὺς ... ἔλουσεν ἀπὸ τῶν πληγῶν, the Vulg. renders
freely lavit plagas, but literally to wash away the blood or the dust from the
wounds, 2 Tim. i. 3 λατρεύω τῷ θεῷ ἀπὸ προγόνων from my forefathers i.e. in the
way inherited from my forefathers, as they did, Col. ii. 20 ἀπεθάνετε σὺν Χριστῷ
ἀπὸ τῶν στοιχείων τοῦ κόσμου, 2 Cor. xi. 3 φοβοῦμαι μὴ φθαρῇ τὰ νοήματα ὑμῶν ἀπὸ
τῆς ἁπλότητος, Rev. xviii. 14 πάντα τὰ λαμπρὰ ἀπώλετο ἀπὸ σοῦ, — in these last
three passages the idea of turning away or of separation is plainly to be perceived in
the verbal idea itself (in the case of ἀποθανεῖν and ἀπόλλυσθαι in their very outward
composition), Rom. ix. 3 ηὐχόμην ἀνάθεμα εἶναι ἀπὸ τοῦ Χριστοῦ to be accursed and
thus fall from fellowship with Christ, Heb. xii. 15 ὑστερῶν ἀπὸ τῆς χάριτος τοῦ
θεοῦ keeping aback i.e. at a distance from grace, Rom. vii. 2, 6 etc. καταργεῖσθαι
ἀπὸ τοῦ νόμου, τοῦ Χριστοῦ, i.e. the law, Christ, has no influence on a man, and consequently he is released from the law, from Christ, Matt. xviii. 7 οὐαὶ τῷ κόσμῳ
ἀπὸ τῶν σκανδάλων on account of temptation, i.e. the woe comes upon it from etc.,
Heb. v. 7 εἰσακουσθεὶς ἀπὸ τῆς εὐλαβείας on account of, in consequence of, his piety
(see the recent comm.), Acts xx. 9 κατενεχθεὶς ἀπὸ τοῦ ὕπνου in consequence of, as a
result of, the sleep (cf. d) above), Matt. xi. 19; Luke vii. 35 ἐδικαιώθη ἡ σοφία ἀπὸ
τῶν τέκνων αὐτῆς is justified on or in her children, i.e. taking her children as our
point of departure (considering their works) we perceive wisdom to be justified,
exalted above the calumniation of mockers; but otherwise in Acts xiii. 39 ἀπὸ
πάντων ὧν (i.e. ἀφ' ὧν) οὐκ ἠδυνήθητε δικαιωθῆναι ἐν νόμῳ Μωυσέως justified and
thereby freed from all etc., likewise in Luke v. 15; viii. 2 τεθεραπευμένος ἀπὸ
πνευμάτων healed and freed from spirits; similarly Rom. vi. 7; Heb. x. 22.   In

those respects in which the usage of the N. T. (and essentially also that of the Old) differs from common usage, viz. in that the prep. ἀπό is employed where native Greeks would have preferred,[1] a) a case alone, b) the prep. ἐκ, c) the prep. παρά, d) the prep. ὑπό.

a) That the language of the N. T. often employed the prep- 278 osition ἀπό (extended ἀπὸ προσώπου, see p. 319) where the 3 earlier Greek was satisfied with the Genitive alone may be seen from § 130, 1 p. 141; § 132, 2. 5. 7. 12. 17 etc. pp. 156 sqq.; and that with verbs which otherwise ordinarily were joined with two objects-Accusative, one of the nouns by virtue of a different conception of the thought is construed with ἀπό, see § 131, 6 p. 149 and § 134, 5 p. 189.   Here we must attend to still another and altogether analogous use of ἀπό, which like-wise has already been incidentally mentioned: viz. the ideas *to be on one's guard*, *to protect*, *to be ashamed*, *to fear*, and the like, as φυλάσσειν, φυλάσσεσθαι, φοβεῖσθαι, αἰσχύ-νεσθαι, βλέπειν, προσέχειν, προσέχειν ἑαυτῷ (in the O. T. also ἐκστῆναι, πτοηθῆναι, στέλλεσθαι, etc.), frequently take after them the object of the fear etc. in the Genitive with ἀπό.

See the examples above in § 135, 3 p. 192, and in the lexicons, under the several words.   Compare also ἐκ below, and on Acts v. 35 (προσέχειν ἑαυτῷ ἐπὶ τοῖς etc.) under ἐπί p. 337.   This construction might be regarded as an expansion of the classic use of φυλάσσειν (Xen. Hell. 7, 2, 10; Cyr. 1, 4, 7); but more probably it grew to such an extent under the influence of foreign idioms, viz. of the Latin (cf.

specifications of time often merely the name of the person is used, brachylogically, as ἀπὸ Ἀβραάμ since the time of Abraham; metonymically ἀπὸ αἵματος Ἀβελ, etc.

[1] We expressly say *preferred*, and thereby admit that even in Greek authors occasionally the mode in which the N. T. writers are wont to express themselves can be met with as an isolated phenomenon. Yet it would be very rash to insist on inferring a general usage on account of isolated passages in classic authors (how often an author in the moment of writing creates new constructions!); and indeed the bringing together of parallel passages, often from out of the way and sometimes from extremely heterogeneous writings by profane authors, has in many cases done more harm than benefit to the interpretation of the N. T.   To be sure, the beginnings of a corruption may be sometimes pointed out in native authors; then to establish the peculiarity of the N. T. usage it is absolutely neces-sary to show how what in Greek authors remained an isolated phenomenon, without influence on the general (or more correctly, the literary) usage, became in the N. T. customary and not infrequently the rule.   Far more frequently, however, the N. T. usage has quite another origin than phenomena, externally similar, in classic writers; and then the explanation of it, and of the particular passages in which it occurs, must be derived from other sources than the classics.

the constructions cavere, timere, tueri, *ab* aliquo) on the later Greek, and of the Hebrew use of מִן and מִפְּנֵי upon the language of the Old and N. T. particularly; (cf. Gesen. under יָרֵא, חָתַת, שָׁמֵר, בּוֹשׁ). Examples of the same construction in the Sept. are of *ἀπό*, Jer. x. 2; xii. 13; xxxi. 13; ii. 36; Ps. cxx. 7; Josh. vi. 18; Deut. i. 29; Ecclus. xvii. 14, etc. of *ἀπὸ προσώπου* (מִפְּנֵי), Jer. i. 17; Ezek. ii. 6; iii. 9; Mal. ii. 5; Josh. xi. 6; Eccl. viii. 12, etc.

4   b) *ἀπό* stands where a more exact designation of the relation would have required *ἐκ*. Of this the following passages may serve as examples:

Matt. vii. 16 *ἀπὸ τῶν καρπῶν ἐπιγνώσεσθε*, where *ἐκ* would have been the more precise expression (cf. the variants on vii. 20 Lchm.), Heb. xi. 34 *ἐδυναμώθησαν ἀπὸ ἀσθενείας*, Rev. xiv. 3, 4 *ἀγορασθῆναι ἀπὸ τῆς γῆς, ἀπὸ τῶν ἀνθρώπων*. Also in the periphrases for the partitive Gen. 279 with *πίνειν, ἐσθίειν, χορτάζεσθαι, γεμίζειν* ordinary usage would certainly have preferred *ἐκ* (see § 132, 12 p. 163), likewise in such phrases as *οἱ ἀπὸ τῆς ἐκκλησίας* Acts (xii. 1), *οἱ ἀπὸ τῆς αἱρέσεως* (xv. 5), *ἔχειν τὸ ἔνδυμα ἀπὸ τριχῶν καμήλου* Matt. (iii. 4, cf. *λάρναξ ἀπὸ σιδήρου* App. B. C. 4, 44), *ἄνδρες εὐλαβεῖς ἀπὸ παντὸς ἔθνους* Acts (ii. 5), etc. In specifications of descent, *ἀπό* in Greek writers designates rather the more remote and general, *ἐκ* the more immediate and special, origin. Nevertheless in the N. T. the combinations *ὁ ἀπὸ Ναζαράθ, ὁ ἀπὸ Ἀριμαθαίας, οὐδεὶς ἀπὸ τῆς φυλῆς, ἣν Φίλιππος ἀπὸ Βηθσαϊδά* (John i. 45, although *ἐκ τῆς πόλεως* immediately follows in apposition) are quite as frequent as the regular *οἱ ἀπὸ Κιλικίας*, etc. Both prepositions occur in their proper relation in Luke ii. 4 *ἀνέβη Ἰωσὴφ ἀπὸ τῆς Γαλιλαίας ἐκ πόλεως Ναζαράθ*.

5   c) where usage would have preferred *παρά*.

Thus mention has already (§ 132, 17 p. 166) been made of the thoroughly unclassical construction of *ἀπό* with *ἀκούειν*. It occurs far more commonly still with *μανθάνειν*, — and that not only when it has the signification to learn *on* (i.e. *from* the case of) a person or thing, as Mark xiii. 28 etc. *ἀπὸ τῆς συκῆς μάθετε τὴν παραβολήν*, Matt. xi. 29 *μάθετε ἀπ᾽ ἐμοῦ*, but also in the signification to be informed, cognoscere, hence for *παρά*, as Gal. iii. 2 *τοῦτο θέλω μαθεῖν ἀφ᾽ ὑμῶν*, Col. i. 7 *καθὼς ἐμάθετε ἀπ᾽ Ἐπαφρᾶ* (on the other hand, *παρά* in 2 Tim. iii. 14), — and with other verbal ideas, as *λαμβάνειν* and its compounds,[1] Matt. xvii. 25, 26; 1 Cor. xi. 23; Col. iii. 24; Heb. vi. 7; 3 John 7, *δανείσασθαι* Matt. v. 42; further, in constructions like

---

[1] Yet the construction with *παρά* is likewise frequent with these verbs, and in particular is always used when the recipient takes a thing from the giver immediately; see the exposition in Winer p. 370 (347) note.

ὸ ἔπαινος γενήσεται ἑκάστῳ ἀπὸ τοῦ θεοῦ, ἔχειν τι ἀπό τινος (1 Cor. iv. 5 ;
vi. 19 ; 1 Tim. iii. 7), and after substantives, as δόξα ἀφ᾽ ἱμῶν 1 Thess.
ii. 6, διαθήκη ἀπὸ ὄρους Σινᾶ Gal. iv. 24, σημεῖον ἀπὸ σοῦ θέλομεν ἰδεῖν
Matt. xii. 38, and the like.

d) Where the Greeks preferred ὑπό.   Primarily with Active 6
verbs to designate the motive (Lat. *præ*, our *for, out of,
from*), as Matt. xiii. 44 ἀπὸ τῆς χαρᾶς αὐτοῦ ὑπάγει καὶ πωλεῖ
πάντα (on the addition, likewise unclassic, of the Pron. αὐτοῦ
see § 127, 26 p. 118 ; on the other hand, without a Pron. Acts
xii. 14), Matt. xiv. 26 ἀπὸ τοῦ φόβου ἔκραξαν, Luke xxii. 45
κοιμωμένους ἀπὸ τῆς λύπης ; similar to this use are such examples as ἀπὸ τοῦ ὄχλου οὐκ ἠδύνατο Luke (xix. 3), οὐκ ἴσχυον
. . . ἀπὸ τοῦ πλήθους τῶν ἰχθύων John (xxi. 6), οὐκ ἐνέβλεπον
ἀπὸ τῆς δόξης τοῦ φωτός Acts (xxii. 11).   In the second place,
with Neuter Verbs containing a Passive idea, and even with
actual Passives, to designate the personal author, hence
precisely for ὑπό and the Gen., or the Latin *a* with the Abl. ;
sometimes also to denote the cause, and so for the Dative
with the Passive otherwise usual.

This last-mentioned use has, indeed, been often disputed ; but incor- 280
rectly, if we compare the examples given below, in all of which the
Greeks would hardly have expressed themselves otherwise than by
ὑπό, or by means of very different constructions.   That the possibility
of this use has been doubted, is solely owing to the fact that earlier
expositors, ungrammatically enough to be sure, asserted that ἀπό was
used in the N. T. indiscriminately for ὑπό, and quite in the same sense.
The correct explanation, on the contrary, is this : that in cases where
the Greeks used ὑπό to designate an internal causal relation, the
N. T. writers contented themselves (more frequently than is the case
in the classics[1]) with a more external statement of relationship by
means of ἀπό, just as they (according to b) p. 324) so often used the
same preposition where the more exact view of the relation required
ἐκ.   The intrinsic force of ἀπό, accordingly, is on our supposition in
no wise altered, but only the construction with this prep. set as a loose
and inexact usage over against that which grammatically is preferable
and more correct.   Yet it is to be carefully noticed, that even in the
N. T. the lax usage is only exceptional and the construction with
ὑπό or the Dative to be assumed as a rule throughout, as well
as that many passages were referred to this usage by the (earlier)

---

[1] For that at least analogous modes of expression are to be found also in earlier
writers, and consequently that the above supposition is philologically well founded,
may be seen in Poppo on Thrc. 1. 17.

expositors where the interpretation of ἀπό in its original sense appears
to be thoroughly admissible; (cf. the note on p. 322 and Winer 371
(348) note).   Perhaps, too, it is not accidental that in several of the
following examples the governing verb itself is already compounded
with ἀπό; cf. the example from Acts xv. 38 in § 151, 2 p. 377.

Examples: 1) With Neuter verbs, Matt. xvi. 21 πολλὰ παθεῖν
ἀπὸ τῶν πρεσβυτέρων (var. ὑπό), cf. Mark viii. 31 etc.; 1 Thess. ii. 14
var., 2 Thess. i. 9 δίκην τίσουσιν ἀπὸ προσώπου τοῦ κυρίου καὶ ἀπὸ τῆς
δόξης τῆς ἰσχύος αὐτοῦ.   Similarly Rev. xviii. 15 οἱ πλουτήσαντες ἀπ᾽
αὐτῆς (deWette, *die von ihr d. h. durch sie reich geworden, that became
rich from her*, cf. ἐκ below).

2) With actual Passives, Mark viii. 31 [ὑπὸ]; Luke ix. 22; xvii.
25 πολλὰ παθεῖν καὶ ἀποδοκιμασθῆναι ἀπὸ τῶν πρεσβυτέρων etc. cf. 1 Pet.
ii. 4 var., Acts ii. 22 ἄνδρα ἀποδεδειγμένον ἀπὸ τοῦ θεοῦ,[1] 2 Cor. vii. 13
ἀναπέπαυται τὸ πνεῦμα αὐτοῦ ἀπὸ πάντων ὑμῶν, Jas. i. 13 ἀπὸ θεοῦ πειρά-
ζομαι, v. 4 (μισθὸς) ὁ ἀπεστερημένος ἀφ᾽ ὑμῶν (*kept back by you*), Rev.
xii. 6 τόπον ἡτοιμασμένον ἀπὸ τοῦ θεοῦ, Acts iv. 36 ἐπικληθεὶς Βαρνάβας
ἀπὸ τῶν ἀποστόλων where ἀπὸ has only by the recent editors been restored instead of the ὑπό of the Rec.; likewise x. 33 πάντα τὰ προστε-
ταγμένα σοι ἀπὸ [Lchm.] τοῦ κυρίου (var. παρά and ὑπό [the latter
given by cod. Sin. and adopted by Tdf. and Treg.]).[2]

To the above examples the following also may be added, 1 Cor. i. 30
ἐγενήθη σοφία ἡμῖν ἀπὸ θεοῦ (for θεός appears here as the efficient
cause, see the Comm.), Matt. xxviii. 4 ἀπὸ τοῦ φόβου αὐτοῦ ἐσείσθησαν,
Jude 23 χιτῶνα ἀπὸ τῆς σαρκὸς ἐσπιλωμένον, Rev. ix. 18 ἀπεκτάνθησαν
281 ἀπὸ τῶν τριῶν πληγῶν τούτων, a peculiarly turned expression for they
died *of* (*from*) the wounds (cf. 2 note p. 322).

REMARK.   On the local specification ἀπὸ σταδίων etc. see § 131, 11
p. 153.

7   ’ΕΚ.   Although this preposition often appears in peculiar
phrases, yet it departs in no point essentially from the ordinary
usage; hence for its use in the main the reader may be referred
to the exposition given in the dictionaries and the general
grammars.   Further, since the idea of the prep. is so forceful
and transparent that it could hardly be obscured by the modi-
fications of usage, a brief reference here to a few particular
cases will suffice.

Owing to the affinity in signification between ἐκ and ἀπό, it is

---

[1] In Luke i. 26 also the better attested reading (codd. Vat. Sin. [also Tdf. Treg.])
is ἀπεστάλη ἀπὸ τοῦ θεοῦ; and this is not to be translated, *away from God*.

[2] The existence of these variants in the best and oldest MSS. is a proof that that
loose use of ἀπό was known, and that an endeavor was made to get rid of it by
various corrections of a classic tone.

natural that both should often serve to denote one and the same
relation; hence both are united in John i. 45 (see 4 p. 324), 2 Cor.
iii. 5; Rev. ix. 18, and with a certain distinction in Luke ii. 4 (see 4
p. 324). Hence, further, (as follows from what is said in § 132) with
so many verbal ideas the Genitive was more closely defined now by ἐκ,
now by ἀπό. Thus μετανοεῖν in the Rev. is uniformly joined to
ἐκ (see Wahl) instead of to ἀπό (see 2 note p. 322), and τηρεῖν
(διατηρεῖν) is construed not like the other verbs signifying to be on
one's guard etc. (see 3 p. 323) with ἀπό but with ἐκ, John xvii. 15;
Acts xv. 29; Rev. iii. 10. It serves (far more frequently than ἀπό,
and rather in a classic acceptation) to designate the a u t h o r or the
c a u s e with Neuter and Passive verbs: so, for example, very commonly (like ex in Latin) after γεννηθῆναι, as well as the corresponding
predicates ἐν γαστρὶ ἔχειν Matt. i. 18, κοίτην ἔχειν Rom. ix. 10; further,
after the Neuter verbs ἀποθανεῖν, ἔπαινον ἔχειν, πλουτεῖν (cf. ἀπό), ζῆν,
ζωή ἐστιν ἔκ τινος, κεκοπιακὼς ἐξ ὁδοιπορίας and the like, after Passives
like ὠφελεῖσθαι, δεδομένον ἐστίν, λυπεῖσθαι, ζημιοῦσθαι, συνέχεσθαι, ἀδι-
κεῖσθαι, and in such phrases from the Rev. as πυροῦσθαι ἐκ πυρός,
σκοτοῦσθαι ἐκ καπνοῦ, φωτίζεσθαι ἐκ δόξης. Cf. also 2 Cor. i. 11; Eph.
iv. 16 and the Commentaries on these passages.

On the divers constructions of εἶναι and γίνεσθαι with ἐκ, both in a
proper and in a tropical sense, see § 132, 11 p. 162 sq. On the periphrasis with ἐκ for the Partitive Gen., and the construction (to be
referred to this Gen.) with διδόναι, λαμβάνειν, φαγεῖν, ἐσθίειν and the
like see ibid. 6, 7 p. 159, and with the idea of f u l n e s s ibid. 12 p. 163.
On the (substantival) phrases with ἐκ and the article see § 125, 9 p. 95.
Lastly, by means of ἐκ are formed many adverbial expressions, as ἐκ
ριζῶν radicitus, ἐξ αὐτῆς illico, ἐκ δεξιᾶς, ἐξ ἀριστερᾶς, ἐκ δευτέρου, ἐξ
ἱκανοῦ, ἐκ περισσοῦ, ἐκ συμφώνου, ἐξ ἀνάγκης, ἐξ ἰσχύος, the Hebraistic
ἐκ κοιλίας μητρός (cf. Isa. xlix. 1; Judges xvi. 17, etc.), and many others.

Owing to the obviousness of the relations they express, the 8
two opposite prepositions ἐκ and εἰς were employed in all sorts 282
of b r a c h y l o g i c a l and p r e g n a n t phrases, the meaning
of which is easily suggested by the phrase itself or by the
context.

For example: παρεγένετο ἐξ ὁδοῦ, πότε ἀναλύσῃ ἐκ τῶν γάμων, πλέκειν
στέφανον ἐξ ἀκανθῶν, ποιεῖν φραγέλλιον ἐκ σχοινίων, ὁ ὢν ἐκ τῆς γῆς ἐκ
τῆς γῆς ἐστιν καὶ ἐκ τῆς γῆς λαλεῖ John iii. 31, λαλεῖν ἐκ τοῦ κόσμου
1 John iv. 5, ἐκ τῶν ἰδίων John viii. 44, ἐξ εἰλικρινείας, ἐκ θεοῦ 2 Cor.
ii. 17, ἀναμένειν τὸ ' υἱὸν ἐκ τῶν οὐρανῶν sc. ἐρχόμενον 1 Thess. i. 10.
Similar constructions with εἰς are the following: Matt. x. 27 ὃ εἰς τὸ
οὖς ἀκούετε sc. λαληθέν, Acts xi. 22 ἠκούσθη ὁ λόγος εἰς τὰ ὦτα τῆς

ἐκκλησίας, Luke vii. 1 ἐπλήρωσεν πάντα τὰ ῥήματα αὐτοῦ εἰς τὰς ἀκοὰς τοῦ λαοῦ (i.e. which he spoke to or in their ears), Matt. x. 9 μὴ κτή- σησθε χρυσὸν εἰς τὰς ζώνας (in order to put it into etc.), Acts xvi. 24 τοὺς πόδας ἠσφαλίσατο εἰς τὸ ξύλον sc. δήσας. See besides, Mark x. 10 ; John xvi. 21 ; 2 Cor. v. 5 ; viii. 24 ; 1 Pet. iii. 20 ; — on εἶναι εἰς οἶκον, εἰς τὴν κοίτην, 15 below, p. 332 ; — on ἔνοχος εἰς τὴν γέενναν and the like, § 132, 23 note² p. 170.

That general predicates, like *to be, to go, to come*, are often omitted with both prepositions may be seen in its place, § 151, 24, b) p. 394.

ΠΡΟ. On the Hebraistic circumlocution πρὸ προσώπου see § 146, 1 p. 319 ; on πρὸ with the Infin. for πρίν, § 140, 11 p. 265 ; and respecting πρὸ ἐξ ἡμερῶν etc. § 131, 11 p. 153.

PREPOSITIONS WITH THE DATIVE.

9 **'ΕΝ** is by far the most common of these prepositions, and used in the most diversified references, both proper and tropical, external and internal. See the classification in Wahl's smaller clavis ; and on the numerous constructions of ἐν with verbs instead of the simple cases §§ 131–133. For our purpose (cf. 1 above, p. 321) we select the following :

a) There are a number of passages in which ἐν is joined to verbs which contain the idea of mo ti on, so that ἐν stands to a certain extent for εἰς ; and, on the other hand, εἰς is often found connected with the idea of r e st (see εἰς p. 332).

Although in presence of the countless examples of the correct grammatical use of these two prepositions in the N. T. there cannot be any talk of a complete obliteration of the distinction between them, it would nevertheless be idle, — in fact, contrary to the simple and natural interpretation of many passages, and prejudicial, — if we should attempt to deny that, as compared with the literary usage of classic prose, there is a certain carelessness and license in the employ- ment of both ; and this is in perfect harmony with the popular style of expression, (cf. the numerous passages in Homer where ἐν is used in the same way). In reference to ἐν there is the less reason for the denial, as according to p. 71 the local adverbs ἐκεῖ, ἐνθάδε, ποῦ, ὅπου, etc., are so often construed with verbs of motion ; and similar observa- 283 tions may be connected with other prepositions, see under ἐπί, παρά, πρός. The idea of the preposition itself, however, remains in all such cases u n a l t e r e d. When, therefore, ἐν stands with a verb of motion, it does not thereby receive the signification of εἰς ; on the contrary, grammatically this is always to be explained by the circumstance that the writer has in view the r e s u l t of the motion, or the sphere i n which the motion occurs, rather than the motion itself. Compare with this the Latin construction of *in* and the Ablat. with verba *ponendi*, etc. So we find, in analogy with that Latin usage, the following verbs joined to ἐν: τιθέναι (also τίθεσθαι in a tropical sense) and ἱστάναι (στῆσαι) together with their compounds; as, Matt. xviii. 2; xiv. 3; xxvii. 29, 60; Mark vi. 29; ix. 36; xv. 46; Luke i. 66; xxi. 14; xxiii. 53; John xix. 41; Acts iv. 7; v. 4 (ἔθου ἐν τῇ καρδίᾳ σου), 18, 25, 27; vii. 16; ix. 37; xix. 21 (θέσθαι ἐν τῷ πνεύματι), 2 Cor. v. 19. But the construction with εἰς continues at the same time in use; cf. Acts v. 18 with iv. 3; v. 25 with xii. 4; Mark vi. 29 with Acts xiii. 29. In other passages, with these verbs all reference to the whither is excluded, as Acts v. 27 (differently xxii. 30), Rom. ix. 33; 1 Cor. xii. 18, 28, etc. While with these verbs the construction with ἐν became, perhaps in consequence of Roman influence, a species of usage, isolated instances of something wholly analogous are found with other verbs of motion: thus in particular with the closely related verb διδόναι, as John iii. 35 (cf. xiii. 3), 2 Cor. i. 22; viii. 16; further, with ἐλθεῖν and its compounds, Luke ix. 46; xxiii. 42; 1 Thess. i. 8; Rev. xi. 11, ὑποχωρεῖν Luke v. 16 (καταβαίνειν John v. 4), ἀποστέλλειν Matt. x. 16; Luke x. 3, πέμπειν Phil. iv. 16, πίπτειν (cf. Pape sub voce) Heb. iv. 11. And then belong here, ἐμβάπτειν τὴν χεῖρα ἐν τῷ τρυβλίῳ Matt. xxvi. 23, ἔστρωσαν τὰ ἱμάτια ἐν τῇ ὁδῷ Matt. xxi. 8; Luke xix. 36, ἐπιστρέψαι ἀπειθεῖς ἐν φρονήσει δικαίων Luke i. 17, cf. Mark v. 30, τὸ ἐσπαρμένον ἐν τῇ καρδίᾳ Matt. xiii. 19, ἡ ἀγάπη ἐκκέχυται ἐν ταῖς καρδίαις Rom. v. 5. On the other hand, the following admit of a different explanation: 1 Cor. vii. 15 ἐν εἰρήνῃ κέκληκεν ἡμᾶς ὁ θεός, and Eph. iv. 4 ἐκλήθητε ἐν μιᾷ ἐλπίδι, see the Comm.; and if ἀγάπη is joined as well to εἴς τινα (2 Cor. ii. 4, 8 etc.) as to ἔν τινι (2 Cor. viii. 7; cf. 1 John iv. 9, 16), the reason is contained in the nature of ἀγάπη, — an idea which now may be conceived of as active, and now at rest.

b) Although the numerous shades of signification of ἐν are **10** all to be traced back more or less closely to the original idea of the preposition, yet in one respect in consequence of Oriental influence (cf. § 133, 17 p. 181) an element originally alien to the idea of the prep., and at variance with the ordinary Greek usage, has become blended with it. That is to say, ἐν in the Old and New Testaments is very commonly used, like the prep. בְּ in Hebrew, to designate the means: and that not only with things (equiv. to the instrumental Dative), but also with persons (equiv. to διά with the Gen., Latin *adjutus, opera*).

We will select only a few of the examples, since they are to be found

on almost every page: Luke xi. 19, 20 ἐν Βεελζεβοὺλ, ἐν δακτύλῳ θεοῦ
ἐκβάλλειν τὰ δαιμόνια, Matt. xxii. 43 ἐν πνεύματι καλεῖ αὐτὸν κύριον *in*
284 *the Spirit* i.e. impelled by the Spirit; and so frequently ἐν θεῷ, ἐν
Χριστῷ Ἰησοῦ, ἐν τῷ ὀνόματι κυρίου, Χριστοῦ, ἐν πνεύματι ἁγίῳ, ἐν τῷ
Ἀδάμ, ἐν σαρκί, etc., Acts iv. 7 ἐν ποίᾳ δυνάμει ἢ ἐν ποίῳ ὀνόματι ἐποιήσατε τοῦτο; 9 ἐν τίνι οὗτος σέσωσται; 10 ἐν τῷ ὀνόματι Ἰ. Χρ., ἐν τούτῳ
οὗτος παρέστηκεν ὑγιής, 1 Cor. v. 8 ἑορτάζωμεν μὴ ἐν ζύμῃ παλαιᾷ …
ἀλλ᾿ ἐν ἀζύμοις etc.   See also on the addition and the omission of ἐν with
the instrumental Dative, § 133, 19 p. 182 ; and on the diversified constructions (arising from this) of ἐν with verbal and adjectival ideas,
particularly with verbs expressing emotion, §§ 131–133 pp. 146 sqq.
On the Infin. with ἐν see § 140, 9 p. 263 sq.   When, on the contrary,
ἐν seems to stand for σύν (i.e. *with* the accompaniment of) it is always
to be referred to the idea *among, in the midst of,* — as Matt. xvi. 28
ἐρχόμενος ἐν τῇ βασιλείᾳ αὐτοῦ (not *to* his royalty, but *in the midst of,*
or in the splendor of, his royalty; see Fritzsche in loc. and cf. § 133,
22, b) p. 184), Luke xiv. 31 ἐν δέκα χιλιάσιν ὑπαντῆσαι τῷ μετὰ εἴκοσι
χιλιάδων ἐρχομένῳ, — or is to be explained as an instrumental ἐν by
supplying a verbal idea, as ἄνθρωπος ἐν πνεύματι ἀκαθάρτῳ (Mark i. 23,
§ 125, 11 p. 96), εἰσέρχεται ἐν αἵματι Heb. ix. 25, ἐν ῥάβδῳ ἔλθω ἢ ἐν
ἀγάπῃ πνεύματί τε πραΰτητος ; 1 Cor. iv. 21.

11   c) Among the various combinations of εἶναι (γίνεσθαι,
ἔχειν) with ἐν, we give prominence (as a peculiarity) to the
mode of periphrasing the predicate belonging to εἶναι etc. by
means of ἐν and an abstract term in the Dative.

Thus often in Luke, as ἐν ἐξουσίᾳ ἦν ὁ λόγος αὐτοῦ *his discourse was
powerful* (iv. 32), οἱ ἐν τρυφῇ ὑπάρχοντες *the luxurious* (vii. 25), γυνὴ
οὖσα ἐν ῥύσει αἵματος *a flowing woman* (viii. 43), ὑπάρχων ἐν βασάνοις
suffering pain (xvi. 23), ἐν ἔχθρᾳ εἶναι, ἐν κρίματι εἶναι, etc.   John vii. 4
ἐν παρρησίᾳ εἶναι *to be manifest,* 1 Thess. ii. 6 ἐν βάρει εἶναι *to be esteemed*
(or *severe*) ; further ἐν δόξῃ, ἐν ὑπεροχῇ, ἐν ἀκροβυστίᾳ, ἐν περιτομῇ εἶναι,
ἔχειν ἐν τῇ ἀσθενείᾳ, ἐν ἐπιγνώσει, ἐν ἑτοίμῳ, ἐν παραβάσει γίνεσθαι, etc.

12   d) Not less peculiar are many a d v e r b i a l e x p r e s s i o n s
formed with ἐν and the Dative, particularly if they stand in a
measure where the classic language would sooner have employed a participial clause or an adjective with ὤν.

Such (eagerly and often used) adverbial phrases in the N. T. are
the following : ἐν ἀληθείᾳ, ἐν ἐκτενείᾳ, ἐν δικαιοσύνῃ, ἐν σοφίᾳ, ἐν πραΰτητι
(equiv. to ἀληθῶς, ἐκτενῶς, δίκαιοι, σοφοὶ ὄντες, etc.), Acts ii. 46 μετε-
λάμβανον τροφῆς ἐν ἀγαλλιάσει καὶ ἀφελότητι καρδίας (equiv. to ἀγαλ-
λιώμενοι καὶ ἀφελεῖς ὄντες), 1 Cor. xv. 42, 43 σπείρεται ἐν φθορᾷ, ἐν
ἀτιμίᾳ, ἐν ἀσθενείᾳ · ἐγείρεται ἐν ἀφθαρσίᾳ, ἐν δόξῃ, ἐν δυνάμει, cf. vs. 44.

Thus such a phrase joined to a substantive, without the addition of ὤν or any other participle, often takes the place of an A d j e c t i v e belonging to the same (cf. § 125, 2 p. 91, 11 p. 95 sq., and the examples quoted there) ; as, Tit. iii. 5 ἔργα τὰ ἐν δικαιοσύνῃ, 2 Pet. ii. 7 ἡ ἐν ἀσελγείᾳ ἀναστροφή, 13 ἡ ἐν ἡμέρᾳ τρυφή.   The combination of ἐν with the Neuter of the Relative, ἐν ᾧ, is used as a Conjunction (in classic authors also, see Pape's Lex. I. 720, and cf. ἐξ οὗ, ἀνθ᾽ ὧν, etc.), sometimes in a temporal sense (Mark ii. 19 ; John v. 7, etc.), some- times in a tropical, *quatenus, quapropter, on the ground of this, that,* 285 see Fritzsche on Rom. viii. 3 ; Lünem. on Heb. ii. 18 ; vi. 17.   As a b r a c h y l o g i c a l peculiarity we may notice, further, Rom. xi. 2 ἐν Ἡλίᾳ i.e. *in the history of Elijah ;* cf. ἐπὶ τοῦ βάτου in 23 p. 336 and other parallel modes of expression in deWette's Introd. to the O. T. § 78.

REMARK. The extremely surprising combination ([given by codd. אAB and] adopted by Lchm. [Tdf. Treg.]) in Acts xxvi. 20 τοῖς ἐν Δαμασκῷ καὶ ἐν Ἱεροσολύμοις π ᾶ σ ά ν τ ε τ ὴ ν χ ώ ρ α ν τῆς Ἰουδαίας could only be explained by the ellipsis of some such Participle as ἐνοικοῦσιν ; but for this quite unusual ellipsis no analogous example is found, since no such Part. can be supplied here, as in Rev. xii. 12 Lchm. (see § 131, 14 p. 154), from what precedes.   Hence Tdf. [eds. 2, 7] has retained the reading εἰς πᾶσάν τε, (which, indeed, is also not congruous, and looks like an emendation made in the interests of grammar).

ΣΥΝ, like *cum* in Latin (or *sammt* in Germ. [Eng. *together* 13 *with*]), is often used instead of καί ; as, Mark iv. 10 ἠρώτων αὐτὸν οἱ περὶ αὐτὸν σὺν τοῖς δώδεκα τὰς παραβολάς, ix. 4 ; viii. 34 ; Luke xxiii. 11 ; Acts iii. 4 ; x. 2 ; xxiii. 15 ; 1 Cor. xvi. 19 ; Eph. iii. 18, etc.

Yet this phrase is no Latinism, at least the constructio ad synesin customary in Latin authors (i.e. the use of the Plural with a preceding or following Singular) is not found in connection with it.

Peculiar is the meaning b e s i d e s, *ad* (i.e. *super*), in Luke xxiv. 21 σὺν πᾶσιν τούτοις τρίτην ταύτην ἡμέραν ἄγει ; Vulg. *super hæc omnia,* deWette *bei alle dem.*

PREPOSITIONS WITH THE ACCUSATIVE.

ANA, a preposition used but rarely in the N.T., is employed 14 most commonly

1) In d i s t r i b u t i v e adjuncts ; in which connection we may notice, that according to p. 30 it is treated as an adverbial addition, for example before the subject, ἀνὰ εἷς ἕκαστος Rev. xxi. 21, or before

the object, Matt. xx. 9 ἔλαβον ἀνὰ δηνάριον, John ii. 6 ὑδρίαι χωροῦσαι.
ἀνὰ μετρητὰς δύο ἢ τρεῖς, Rev. iv. 8 ἔχον ἀνὰ πτέρυγας ἕξ, cf. Protev.
Jac. 7. 2 ; 8. 3 ;   and 2) in the phrase ἀνὰ μέσον *throughout*, as Matt.
xiii. 25 ; Mark vii. 31, *in the midst of* Rev. vii. 17, and simply *inter,
between*, 1 Cor. vi. 5 διακρῖναι ἀνὰ μέσον τοῦ ἀδελφοῦ αὐτοῦ where the
abridged form of expression (the use of the Singular with the omission
of the second party to the controversy) is noticeable.

15   *ΕΙΣ*.   The custom of connecting εἰς immediately with
verbs of rest has already been spoken of under ἐν (9 p. 328).
The rudiments of this brachylogical form of expression are
to be found in the popular language of all ages, and this idiom
has its analogies in all languages; cf. the examples in B.
286 under εἰς p. 414 (480).   Yet since the N. T. writers have
made a far more extended use of this liberty than is made
in the ordinary literary language, it is necessary to specify
here in detail the various species of construction, so far as the
examples given in the N. T. extend.

a) The expression with εἰς arose from its being **attracted**
by a verb of motion, present in the sentence, to which it in
part also **belongs**.

We are the more justified in explaining the extant instances in this
way (by the σχῆμα ἀπὸ κοινοῦ), agreeing as it does perfectly with the
classic literary usage, as they are almost all from the writings of Luke :
xxi. 37 ἐξερχόμενος ηὐλίζετο εἰς τὸ ὄρος, Acts ii. 39 ὑμῖν γάρ ἐστιν
ἡ ἐπαγγελία ... καὶ πᾶσιν τοῖς εἰς μακράν, ὅσους ἂν etc., vii. 12
ἀκούσας ὄντα σιτία εἰς Αἴγυπτον ἐξαπέστειλεν τοὺς πατέρας ἡμῶν,
Matt. iv. 13 ; ii. 23 ἐλθὼν κατῴκησεν εἰς πόλιν Ναζ., similarly Acts
vii. 4.   Hence the same mode of explanation is with reason to be
applied also to Luke ix. 61 ἐπίτρεψόν μοι ἀποτάξασθαι τοῖς εἰς τὸν οἶκόν
μου (see Meyer), and in Acts xii. 19 εἰς τὴν Καισάρειαν is to be referred
not merely to κατελθών but also to διέτριβεν.

16   b) Or it follows a verb of rest in which the (previous) **idea
of motion is still contained**, as the idea to place one's
self is in στῆναι, and in καθίζειν καθῆσθαι that of seating
one's self, etc.   (This case likewise is not uncommon in
Greek authors).

For example, Mark xiv. 60 ἀναστὰς ὁ ἀρχιερεὺς εἰς μέσον ἐπηρώτησεν,
Luke vi. 8 στῆθι εἰς τὸ μέσον, John xx. 19, 26 ; xxi. 4 ἔστη εἰς τὸ
αἰγιαλόν, 1 Pet. v. 12 ; Mark xiii. 3 καθημένου εἰς τὸ ὄρος τῶν ἐλαιῶν,
2 Thess. ii. 4.   Analogous are Acts xx. 14 συνέβαλεν ἡμῖν εἰς τὴν
Ἄσσον, Heb. xi. 9 Ἀβραὰμ παρῴκησεν εἰς γῆν τῆς ἐπαγγελίας ; cf. Acts
vii. 4.

c) Or it is used with the verbs εἶναι and γίνεσθαι. 17
The ideas of these verbs, being wholly general, and therefore
easily definable, acquire by being connected with εἰς the force
of equally general verbs of motion (*to come, go*) ; (cf. from
earlier authors Herod. 1. 21 ; 5. 38 ; Thuc. 6. 62, etc.).

Examples of γίνεσθαι are Luke i. 44 ὡς ἐγένετο ἡ φωνὴ εἰς τὰ ὦτά
μου, Acts xx. 16 ; xxv. 15 ; Gal. iii. 14, — which require no further
explanation.   More characteristic, on the other hand, are the examples with εἶναι, Luke xi. 7 εἰς τὴν κοίτην εἰσίν (popularly, *are to —*
Germ. *zu — bed* i.e. gone), Mark ii. 1 Tdf. [eds. 2, 7] ἠκούσθη ὅτι εἰς
οἶκόν ἐστιν (Lchm. [Treg. Tdf. cod. Sin.] ἐν οἴκῳ), John i. 18 ὁ ὢν εἰς
τὸν κόλπον τοῦ πατρός, 1 John v. 8 οἱ τρεῖς εἰς τὸ ἕν εἰσιν, cf. John xvii.
23 ; Acts viii. 23 εἰς γὰρ χολὴν πικρίας ... ὁρῶ σε ὄντα, Col. i. 6 τοῦ
εὐαγγελίου τοῦ παρόντος εἰς ὑμᾶς.   Whether Luke iv. 23 ὅσα ἠκούσαμεν
γενόμενα εἰς τὴν Καφαρναοὺμ, ποίησον καὶ ὧδε ἐν τῇ πατρίδι also belongs
here may be doubtful, since if we translate it *in Capernaum,* the idea
of motion (even antecedent) is excluded.   Hence Meyer thinks that
εἰς here has the tropical sense of *on* (*unto*).   Yet the other interpretation is more natural, and corresponds better with the second
clause.   Cf. the examples in the following paragraph.

d) But there still remains a number of instances which can 18
not without violence be adjusted to any of the above rules. 287
Hence we are compelled here either to s u p p l y a missing
idea of motion, or (as in the majority of cases is doubtless
more probable) to recognize (as above in the case of ἐν) a
m o r e n e g l i g e n t use of εἰς, and consequently the beginnings
of the subsequent obliteration of the distinction between the
two prepositions.   (Hence we find countless passages with εἰς
where complete rest is expressed in the Apocrypha of the N. T.)

For examples of this from later writers, see Jacobs ad Anth. Pal.
p. 49 (10), 712 ; Stephanus sub εἰς (p. 292 sq.) ; Protev. Jac. 4. 4 ;
5. 1 ; Thom. 11. 1 ; Nicod. 15. 1, 4 ; Herm. Vis. 4. 3 ; and the literature on the whole subject as referred to in Winer p. 418 (389).
Further, notice from the N. T., Acts viii. 40 εὑρέθη εἰς Ἄζωτον sc. ἐλθών
or γενόμενος, Mark i. 39 ἦν κηρύσσων εἰς τὰς συναγωγὰς αὐτῶν εἰς ὅλην
τὴν Γαλ. where an unforced interpretation, particularly of the second
εἰς, hardly permits us to take it otherwise than as equivalent to ἐν ὅλῃ
τῇ Γαλ., xiii. 9 παραδώσουσιν ὑμᾶς εἰς συνέδρια καὶ εἰς συναγωγὰς δαρήσεσθε
where in view of the parallel passage and to avoid asyndeton we
should not with Lchm. [Treg.] and Meyer put a comma after συναγωγάς,
Acts ii. 27, 31 ἐγκατελείφθη εἰς ᾅδου (ᾅδην Tdf. [*bis,* so ℵ ; but Lchm.

Treg. only in 27] see § 132, 27 p. 171), xix. 22 ἐπέσχεν χρόνον εἰς Ἀσίαν, xxi. 13 δεθῆναι καὶ ἀποθανεῖν εἰς Ἱερουσαλὴμ ἑτοίμως ἔχω, xxiii. 11 διαμαρτύρασθαι εἰς Ἱερουσαλήμ, εἰς Ῥώμην, xxv. 4 τηρεῖσθαι τὸν Παῦλον εἰς Καισάρειαν, Mark i. 9 ἐβαπτίσθη εἰς τὸν Ἰορδάνην (in the Jordan) : and its use in connection with the simple article, Mark xiii. 16 ὁ εἰς τὸν ἀγρόν hardly different from Matt. xxiv. 18 ὁ ἐν τῷ ἀγρῷ; also in Mark x. 10 the reading εἰς τὴν οἰκίαν is now restored as the only correct one in place of ἐν τῇ οἰκίᾳ. Cf. also the examples given above in 8 p. 327 sq.

In the passages where εἰς has a tropical, metaphysical, sense, since in them the idea of rest or of motion is at the most only secondary, it must be left to the interpreter to decide which meaning is best suited to the context in every particular case. But in general the notion of aim (corresponding to that of motion) is in such instances by far the prevalent one; cf. Winer 416 (388).

REMARK. On the circumlocution for the predicate Accusative with verbs signifying *to make to be, to elect*, by means of εἰς and the Acc., and on the corresponding (Old Testament) use of εἰς with εἶναι and γίνεσθαι, see § 131, 7 p. 150; on the circumlocution for the Dative by means of εἰς, see § 133, (3 p. 172). Adverbial expressions, as εἰς τὰ ἄμετρα, εἰς τὸ κενόν, εἰς περισσείαν, ὑπερβολήν, etc., are formed like those given in B. p. 414 (480) and to be explained in the same way.

PREPOSITIONS WITH THE GENITIVE AND ACCUSATIVE.

19   *ΔΙΑ.* The N. T. use of this preposition, both when it is connected with the Gen. and with the Acc., presents no anomalies. Even when according to our ideas it seems to express other relations, the interpreter will invariably bring to light a sense suited to the context if he endeavors to trace back its signification to the two fundamental ideas (*through* and *on account of*).

288   To the adverbial phrases given in the Gramm. (B. p. 414; H. § 629 fin.; D. § 478 fin.; J. § 627, 3 f.) may be added from the N. T. δι᾽ ὑπομονῆς, διὸ λόγου, διὰ προσκόμματος, διὰ βραχέων, δι᾽ ὀλίγων, διὰ πολλῶν, δι᾽ ὅλου, etc.

20   *ΚΑΤΑ.* In respect to this preposition also, only a few trivial peculiarities deserve to be noticed.

Peculiar to Luke is the local signification of κατά with the Gen. *throughout;* but always in connection with the Adject. ὅλος, so that in this way the relation is designated which the Greeks render by ἀνά and the Acc., as καθ᾽ ὅλης τῆς περιχώρου Luke iv. 14, καθ᾽ ὅλης τῆς

Ἰουδαίας xxiii. 5; Acts ix. 31, καθ' ὅλης τῆς Ἰόππης 42; x. 37.   In a
tropical sense h o s t i l e direction is by far its most common force;
hence in Gal. v. 17 ἐπιθυμεῖν κατά τινος is not a mere periphrasis for
the Gen.   On ὀμνύειν, ἐξορκίζειν, κατά τινος see § 131, 1 p. 147.   An
isolated use of κατά and the Gen. is its use as a periphrasis for an
a d j e c t i v a l notion, as 2 Cor. viii. 2 ἡ κατὰ βάθους πτωχεία deep poverty, with which has been compared Strabo 9. 5 ἐστὶ τὸ μαντεῖον ἄντρον
κοῖλον κατὰ βάθους.   On the periphrases for the Genitive, the
Possess. Pron., and also an attributive Adject. with a substantive, by
means of κ α τ ά and the A c c u s a t i v e (ἡ κατὰ θεὸν λύπη, οἱ κατὰ φύσιν
κλάδοι), see § 132, 2 p. 156 and 10 Rem. p. 162.   On κατά with
d i s t r i b u t i v e adjuncts see p. 30; and here again, as above with
ἀνά, it is to be noticed that the expression formed in this way with
κατά is joined to the verb as object, Acts xxi. 19 ἐξηγεῖτο καθ' ἓν
ἕκαστον.

ὙΠΕΡ and the Genitive is often used by Paul (after the 21
fashion of later writers, see B. p. 415; H. § 633 b.; D. § 480;
J. § 630, 2) for περί and the Genitive.

Thus with verba sentiendi etc., as 2 Thess. i. 4; Rom. ix. 27, etc.,
also in the sense of as respects, 2 Cor. viii. 23 εἴτε ὑπὲρ Τίτου, κοινωνὸς
ἐμός, etc.   In the MSS. it is often interchanged with περί, as in 2 Cor.
i. 8, etc.

ὑπέρ with the Acc. is used in later writers, (as παρά is in
the earlier classics), after Comparatives and similar verbal
ideas to designate the object surpassed.

Just so in the N. T.; as, Luke xvi. 8 φρονιμώτεροι ὑπὲρ τοὺς υἱοὺς
τοῦ φωτός, Heb. iv. 12 τομώτερος ὑπὲρ πᾶσαν μάχαιραν, Gal. i. 14 προέ-
κοπτον ὑπὲρ πολλούς, 2 Cor. xii. 13 ἡσσώθητε ὑπὲρ τὰς λοιπὰς ἐκκλησίας.
Hence it imparts, just as παρά does, to the preceding predicate a
comparative force by simple juxtaposition: Matt. x. 24 οὐκ ἔστιν μαθητὴς ὑπὲρ τὸν διδάσκαλον m o r e than his master, x. 37; Acts xxvi.
13; Phil. ii. 9 ὄνομα τὸ ὑπὲρ πᾶν ὄνομα.   On the adverbial ὑπέρ in
ὑπὲρ ἐγώ and other combinations see § 146, 4 p. 321.

PREPOSITIONS WITH ALL THREE CASES.

ἈΜΦΙ and ΠΕΡΙ.   Of these two prepositions the first is 22
not found in the N. T.   There is no example also of περί with
the Dative, the l o c a l reference of this combination being
transferred completely to the construction with περί and the
A c c u s a t i v e.

On the periphrasis οἱ περί τινα see § 125, 8 p. 95.   Περί and the 289
Gen. is employed, as in ordinary Greek usage, only in a t r o p i c a l

reference (*de*), and hence in Acts xxv. 18 περὶ οὗ does not belong to σταθέντες but to ἔφερον. Sometimes it stands in the sense of ὑπέρ *for* (as, on the other hand, ὑπέρ is used for περί, see ὑπέρ p. 335) : Matt. xxvi. 28; Gal. i. 4; Heb. v. 3.

23   ᾽ΕΠΙ is in use in the N. T. in almost all the manifold shades of signification which it has in Greek authors. We select the following as peculiarities :

ἐπί with the Genitive. The signification *in presence of, coram* (B. p. 416), springs from the original notion of approximation, of being in immediate proximity (*on, upon, near by*) ; and in a temporal reference the signification *immediately in, at* or *during*, corresponds precisely to this local signification.

Both meanings may often be pointed out in the N. T. :   a) of place, Mark xiii. 9 ἐπὶ ἡγεμόνων καὶ βασιλέων σταθήσεσθε, Matt. xxviii. 14 Tdf. [cod. Sin.] ἐὰν ἀκουσθῇ τοῦτο ἐπὶ τοῦ ἡγεμόνος *coram procuratore*, like Acts xxiii. 30 λέγειν ἐπὶ σοῦ, cf. 1 Cor. vi. 1, 6 ; 1 Tim. v. 19; vi. 13, etc., hence ἡ καύχησις ὑμῶν ἡ ἐπὶ Τίτου (2 Cor. vii. 14) *my encomiums of you uttered before Titus ;*   b) of time, Matt. i. 11 ἐπὶ τῆς μετοικεσίας Βαβυλῶνος, Rom. i. 10 ἐπὶ τῶν προσευχῶν μου δεόμενος, Eph. i. 16 ; Philem. 4, and in this way is explained most simply the brachylogical expression οὐκ ἀνέγνωτε ... ἐπὶ τοῦ βάτου (Mark xii. 26) or Μωυσῆς ἐμήνυσεν ἐπὶ τῆς βάτου (Luke xx. 37), very much as we say *at* i.e. in the occurrence at the bush; cf. ἐν Ἡλίᾳ in 12 above, p. 331.

Moreover, under the tropical meanings it is to be noticed also that λέγειν etc. ἐπί τινος is not synonymous with περί τινος, but in accordance with the primary sense of ἐπί can only mean, what is said concerns, is aimed at, has reference to, etc., as Gal. iii. 16 οὐ λέγει· Καὶ τοῖς σπέρμασιν, ὡς ἐπὶ πολλῶν, ἀλλ᾽ ὡς ἐφ᾽ ἑνός· Καὶ τῷ σπέρματι etc. In Acts xxi. 23 εὐχὴν ἔχοντες ἐφ᾽ ἑαυτῶν means literally *having a vow upon themselves.* Among the adverbial expressions we may notice the pretty common ἐπ᾽ ἀληθείας *in truth, actually, truly*, as Mark xii. 14, 32 ; Luke iv. 25 ; Acts iv. 27, etc., for which in Matt. xxii. 16 ἐν ἀληθείᾳ is used (differently in John iv. 23 sq., xvii. 19 ; 3 John 3, etc.).

24   ἐπί with the Dative. The signification *on, upon*, unusual in good prose (for which ἐπί with the Gen. is used), is found in the N. T. pretty frequently ; and that

a) With ideas of rest, as Matt. xiv. 8 δός μοι ἐπὶ πίνακι τὴν κεφαλὴν Ἰωάννου, Mark ii. 4 Tdf. [ed. 7], vi. 39, 55 ; John xi. 38; with both cases at the same time, Acts xxvii. 44 οὓς μὲν ἐπὶ σανίσιν, οὓς δὲ ἐπί

τινων etc.[1] To this is to be referred in a tropical sense the meaning 290
on the ground of; for similar to the sentences ἐπὶ ταύτῃ τῇ πέτρᾳ οἰκο-
δομήσω τὴν ἐκκλησίαν (Matt. xvi. 18), ἐποικοδομηθέντες ἐπὶ τῷ θεμελίῳ
(Eph. ii. 20), are Heb. viii. 6 ἐπὶ κρείττοσιν ἐπαγγελίαις νενομοθέτηται
(cf. vii. 11), Eph. ii. 10 κτισθέντες ἐπὶ ἔργοις ἀγαθοῖς, Phil. ii. 17 εἰ καὶ
σπένδομαι ἐπὶ τῇ θυσίᾳ καὶ λειτουργίᾳ etc., further, the common phrases
ἐπ᾽ ἐλπίδι, λαλεῖν, διδάσκειν, δέχεσθαί τινα ἐπί τῷ ὀνόματί τινος (Acts iv.
17; v. 28; Matt. xviii. 5, etc.) *on the ground of* hope, the name, etc.,
ζῆν ἐπ᾽ ἄρτῳ and many other verbal combinations, see § 133 pp. 174 sqq.

b) With ideas of m o t i o n, as Acts viii. 16 (τὸ πνεῦμα) ἦν ἐπ᾽ οὐδενὶ
αὐτῶν ἐπιπεπτωκός, particularly again in the tropical sense, so that then
it is often to be rendered by *towards* (*adversus* and *erga*), *for,* or
generally *with regard to,* as Luke xii. 52 διαμεμερισμένοι τρεῖς ἐπὶ δυσὶν
καὶ δύο ἐπὶ τρισίν; so in the following verse, and in fact alternating
with ἐπί and the Acc., John xii. 16 ταῦτα ἦν ἐπ᾽ αὐτῷ γεγραμμένα, Acts
xxi. 24 δαπάνησον ἐπ᾽ αὐτοῖς, Rom. x. 19 (quotn.), 2 Cor. ix. 14 χάριν
τοῦ θεοῦ ἐφ᾽ ὑμῖν, Gal. v. 13 ἐπ᾽ ἐλευθερίᾳ ἐκλήθητε, Rev. x. 11.

With ἐπί and the Dat. also many b r a c h y l o g i c a l phrases are
found, as Acts v. 35 προσέχετε ἑαυτοῖς ἐπὶ τοῖς ἀνθρώποις τούτοις τί
μέλλετε πράσσειν not *beware of these men* (see ἀπό and ἐκ), but *take
heed to yourselves in your treatment of these men,* so that thus it belongs
just as well to the main predicate προσέχετε as to the predicate of the
subordinate clause πράσσειν, see § 151, 16 p. 388; Mark vi. 52 οὐ
συνῆκαν ἐπὶ τοῖς ἄρτοις as if, *they remained hardened at the loaves* i.e.
they did not understand the occurrence with the loaves.

ἐπί with the Acc. designates as usual a movement *upon* or   25
tendency *towards* something, in a local and a figurative reference. But as ἐπί with the Dat. is used with verbs of motion,
so, on the other hand, ἐπί with the Acc. often stands in a
relation of r e s t, and that too as well in a local as in a tropical
view. Hence the frequent fluctuation in the text of the MSS.
between the two cases — more frequent than with almost any
other preposition; hence the double construction of many
verbs, e.g. those expressing an emotion, further of πιστεύειν,
πεποιθέναι, ἐλπίζειν, etc., with ἐπί τινι and ἐπί τινα §§ 131–133;
hence, finally, one and the same writer often employs in the
same circumstances both constructions without a perceptible

---

[1] Here too the style of Luke approximates to classic usage, in that he is decidedly averse to the construction with the Dative in this (outward) signification.
Hence in Acts ix. 33 ἐπὶ κραβάττου is now read again [so cod. Sin.], in Luke v.
25 Tdf. [Treg. cod. Sin.] ἐφ᾽ ὃ κατέκειτο (see No. 25), and also in Acts vii. 33
authorities differ [Lchm. Tdf. Treg. cod. Sin. ἐφ᾽ ᾧ]. On the other hand, Luke
xix. 44; xxi. 6; xxiii. 38; Acts iii. 10, 11 fall under a different head.

difference, even close together (see Luke xii. 53 in 24 p. 337).
Compare with this the similar observations in reference to the
loose employment of both cases under παρά and πρός p. 339 sq.,
as well as the free use of the two prep. ἐν and εἰς p. 328 sqq.

Examples of ἐπί with the Acc. in a relation of rest are found
everywhere Under the signification (moving) *over* may be brought
also, Matt. xiv. 29 περιπατῆσαι ἐπὶ τὰ ὕδατα, Mark xv. 33 σκότος ἐγένετο
ἐφ᾽ ὅλην τὴν γῆν, Rev. xiv. 6 εὐαγγελίσαι ἐπὶ πᾶν ἔθνος etc.; in other
instances, as in the case of εἰς, the idea of antecedent motion is included
291 in the verb, as ἔστησαν ἐπὶ τοὺς πόδας αὐτῶν, ἐπὶ τὴν θύραν Rev. iii. 20;
xi. 11; Acts x. 17, καθίζειν and καθῆσθαι ἐπὶ τὸ τελώνιον, τὸν πυλῶνα, etc.
Matt. ix. 9; Mark ii. 14; xi. 2; Luke v. 27; John xii. 15; Rev. iv.
4, etc. (hence ἀνέπεσεν ἐπὶ τὸ στῆθος John xxi. 20 *lay on the breast*);
but there still remain many passages where the idea of motion must
be supplied outright, or that of rest predominates (cf. εἰς p. 333), as
Matt. xviii. 12 ἀφήσει (τὰ πρόβατα) ἐπὶ τὰ ὄρη (not, *up on the mountains* — implying motion, but *leaveth them upon* or *at the mountains*),
Mark iv. 38 ἦν καθεύδων ἐπὶ τὸ προσκεφάλαιον, John i. 32, 33; iii. 36
μένει ἐπ᾽ αὐτόν, Acts iv. 22; 1 Pet. iv. 14 τὸ πνεῦμα ἐφ᾽ ὑμᾶς ἀναπαύεται,
Rev. iv. 4 στεφάνους ἐπὶ τὰς κεφαλάς, v. 1; vii. 15; xx. 1, etc. To
these may be added also the Accus. in the a d d i t i v e relation, as
λίθος ἐπὶ λίθον Matt. xxiv. 2, λύπην ἐπὶ λύπην Phil. ii. 27, also Luke
xi. 17 οἶκος ἐπὶ οἶκον πίπτει i.e. *house after house falls*, in this case
elsewhere the Dative is used, as Mark xiii. 2 (many MSS. [so Sin.,
followed by Treg. Tdf.] read here also ἐπὶ λίθον); and the formula
ἐπὶ τὸ αὐτὸ *together*, as well with words implying motion as with those
of rest, Luke xvii. 35; Acts ii. 1, etc. This last term, however, has
become completely an indeclinable adverb, like many other adverbial
expressions with ἐπί, as ἐπὶ τρίς, ἐφ᾽ ἱκανόν, ἐπὶ χρόνον, ἐφ᾽ ὅσον, ἐπὶ
πλεῖον and the like.

Further, we may notice as a peculiarity the construction of the
Gen. and the Acc. after ἐπί connected together in a single sentence,
Rev. xiii. 16; xiv. 9 ἐπὶ τοῦ μετώπου αὐτοῦ ἢ ἐπὶ τὴν χεῖρα αὐτοῦ.

REMARK. The quotation in Acts xv. 17 ἐφ᾽ οὓς ἐπικέκληται τὸ ὄνομά
μου ἐπ᾽ αὐτούς arose from a verbatim translation of the Hebrew
(כָּל שְׁמִי וְקָרָא), literally *my name is called upon them*, i.e. they are
called after my name.

26   *META.* The signification and use of this preposition agree
in all points with ordinary Greek usage; except that the N. T.
writers like to periphrase, in a brachylogical way by means of
μετά and the Gen., attributive limitations which otherwise
were commonly expressed by means of adjectives or participles.

For example: ἦλθεν μετὰ δυνάμεως *clothed with might*, περιβλέπω μετ᾽ ὀργῆς *angry*, μετὰ αἰσχύνης ἄρξῃ etc. (equiv. to αἰσχυνόμενος). In a similar way μετά with the Acc. is used brachylogically : John xiii. 27 μετὰ τὸ ψωμίον, τότε εἰσῆλθεν etc. *after* the morsel.   On the periphrasis with μετά for the Dative with verbs of *association* etc., see p. 177.

ΠΑΡΑ. Since the Dative designates in general a p p r o x - imation, when παρά and the Dat. are construed with verbs of motion the construction is not so much perfectly grammatical in itself considered, as in harmony particularly with what was said above under ἐν and ἐπί. It is wrong, therefore, to remove by emendation (whether with or without MS. authority) such instances even from classic writers (especially the later), see e.g. Xen. An. 2, 5, 27 ; Plut. Them. 5 ; Dio C. p. 15, 97 R. The general usus loquendi, that is to say of the literary language, was established, to be sure, upon the idea that rest is associated with παρά and the Dative ; but relics of the less exact mode of expression continue to come to light here and there.

In the N. T., the Dative with παρά in Luke xix. 7 παρὰ ἁμαρτωλῷ ἀνδρὶ εἰσῆλθεν καταλῦσαι may perhaps be connected (by the σχῆμα ἀπὸ κοινοῦ) as well with εἰσῆλθεν as with καταλῦσαι (its position draws it to εἰσῆλθεν), and in ix. 47 ἔστησεν αὐτὸ παρ᾽ ἑαυτῷ may be explained after the analogy of στῆσαι ἐν (see 9 p. 329).   But we should compare and connect with these instances the example under πρός below, and what was said above, p. 284, on Acts xxi. 16.   That παρά with the Acc., however, is used to denote rest, is quite common in all writers, see B. p. 418.   The three tropical senses of παρά with the Acc. there given are all to be found in the N. T. — the second (*on account of*) but once it is true, viz. 1 Cor. xii. 15, 16, but so much the more frequent are the other two : *beyond (praeter)* and *more than*.   In this last sense the construction with παρά takes the place of the Gen. of comparison or ἤ with the requisite case, not only after comparatives themselves (particularly in the Ep. to the Heb. for example i. 4 ; iii. 3 ; ix. 23 ; xi. 4 ; xii. 24 cf. Luke iii. 13), or comparative ideas, as ἄλλος (1 Cor. iii. 11), ἐλαττοῦν (Heb. ii. 7, 9), ὑπερφρονεῖν (Rom. xii. 3), but even when associated with the P o s i t i v e it imparts to it the force of a comparative, as Luke xiii. 2, 4 ἁμαρτωλοὶ παρὰ πάντας, ὀφειλέται ἐγένοντο παρὰ πάντας τοὺς ἀνθρώπους.   Cf. also the reading of cod. Vat. [and Sin. also] in Luke xviii. 14 Lchm. [Treg.], and the similar phenomena above in connection with ὑπέρ p. 335, and with ἤ § 149, 7 p. 360.

28   *ΠΡΟΣ* with the Genitive is only once extant, and then used quite in classic style: Acts xxvii. 34 τοῦτο πρὸς τῆς ὑμετέρας σωτηρίας ὑπάρχει.

Also πρός with the Dative is rare. But in Luke xix. 37 ἐγγίζοντος ἤδη πρὸς τῇ καταβάσει τοῦ ὄρους, ἐγγίζοντος does not mean *when he was near*, but *as he came near* (*to*) the mountain. Cf. παρά.

πρός with the Acc. corresponds to all the manifold shades of signification given in the grammars; only, after the analogy of παρά with the Acc. (which see, p. 339), it is more frequently used than by classic writers to denote r e s t also, and w i t h o u t the accessory notion of aim.

For example: Matt. xiii. 56 αἱ ἀδελφαὶ αὐτοῦ πρὸς ἡμᾶς εἰσίν, xxvi. 18 πρὸς σὲ ποιῶ τὸ πάσχα, Mark vi. 3; xiv. 49; John i. 1 ἦν πρὸς τὸν θεὸν, 1 John i. 2; Acts v. 10; xii. 20 ὁμοθυμαδὸν παρῆσαν πρὸς αὐτόν, 1 Cor. ii. 3; xvi. 7 ἐλπίζω ἐπιμεῖναι πρὸς ὑμᾶς (cf. ἐπί with the Acc. p. 338), 2 Cor. v. 8 (εὐδοκοῦμεν) ἐνδημῆσαι πρὸς τὸν κύριον etc. (see Wahl p. 279). In view of such unquestionable passages, it is un-necessary to search in others after an idea of motion or of aim (whether expressed, or first to be supplied) if the simple notion of rest suffices, and the immediate connection of the preposition with that appears to be the most natural; see e.g. Rom. iv. 2; 2 Cor. 1. 12.

An example of πρός in a C o m p a r a t i v e clause (see παρά above, p. 339) is Rom. viii. 18 τὰ παθήματα οὐκ ἄξια πρὸς τὴν μέλλουσαν δόξαν, cf. Ignat. ad Magn. 12 πρὸς ἕνα ὑμῶν οὐκ εἰμι. B r a c h y l o g i c a l and e l l i p t i c a l phrases, such as τί πρὸς σέ, ἁμαρτάνειν πρὸς θάνατον and the like, are easily explained by the vigorous force of the prep. A d v e r b i a l expressions, as in the Greek writers, are πρὸς φθόνον, 293 πρὸς καιρόν, πρὸς ὥραν (*for the moment, for a short time*) and others. On the periphrasis with πρός τι for the Dative, see pp. 172, 177.

29   *ΥΠΟ* is no longer construed with the D a t i v e. In con-nection with the G e n i t i v e and A c c u s a t i v e, the following particulars may be selected as peculiar in its use:

ὑπό with the Gen. is used with Passives not infrequently when a t h i n g or an a b s t r a c t notion is the efficient cause. In such cases, because the cause appears thus personified as it were, the expression is more forceful than the simple Dative, as Luke vii. 24 κάλαμον ὑπὸ ἀνέμου σαλευόμενον, viii. 14 ὑπὸ μεριμνῶν ... συμπνίγονται, Rom. xii. 21 μὴ νικῶ ὑπὸ τοῦ κακοῦ, Matt. viii. 24 etc. (see Wahl). On Heb. vii. 7 see § 128, 1 p. 122. Neuter verbs which contain a Passive sense prefer the connection with ἐκ and ἀπό, see these prep. pp. 325 sq. Instances of ὑπό are found only with γίνεσθαι (which thus becomes a

complete Passive) — as Luke xiii. 17 ἔχαιρεν ἐπὶ πᾶσιν τοῖς ὑπ᾽ αὐτοῦ
γινομένοις, Acts xx. 3, etc. — and, agreeably to their significations, with
πάσχειν (Matt. xvii. 12, etc.) and ὑπομένειν (Heb. xii. 3), once
also with πληγὰς λαμβάνειν i.e. *vapulare* 2 Cor. xi. 24.   As
peculiar, we may notice the elliptical and brachylogical mode of expression in 2 Cor. ii. 6 ἡ ἐπιτιμία ἡ ὑπὸ τῶν πλειόνων where the missing
Passive notion is to be derived from ἐπιτιμία, and in Rev. vi. 8 ἀποκτεῖναι ὑπὸ τῶν θηρίων τῆς γῆς i.e. *jubere (aliquem) interfici a bestiis*
(with which has been compared προαγορεύειν ὑπὸ κήρυκος in Herod. 9.
98, see Wesseling).   The second class of cases, also, described in
the Gram., viz. where ὑπό is used with Actives, an abstract idea being
subjoined as the moving cause of the action (e.g. *from* fear, *for* shame),
are rendered in the N. T. not by ὑπό, but by ἀπό again and ἐκ; see pp.
325 sq.   Whether in Rom. xiii. 1 οὐκ ἔστιν ἐξουσία εἰ μὴ ὑπὸ θεοῦ sc.
δεδομένη (Lchm. [Treg. Tdf.]) or ἀπὸ θεοῦ (Tdf. [eds. 2, 7]) is the
original reading is hard to decide, as they are equally attested by MSS.
[Sin. ὑπό], and both may be defended philologically.   With the
Accusative, ὑπό responds to the question *where* (taking the place
of the missing construction with the Dative) more frequently almost
than to the question *whither* (cf. the classic usage), particularly with
εἶναι and γίνεσθαι, in a local and a tropical reference: *under* ; as, John
i. 49 ὄντα ὑπὸ τὴν συκῆν, Matt. viii. 9 ἔχων ὑπ᾽ ἐμαυτὸν στρατιώτας,
1 Cor. x. 1 ; Gal. iii. 25 ; Rom. iii. 9 ; vi. 14, etc.

B. § 147, N. 2; J. § 650; W. p. 419 sq. (391 sq.); S. p. lxxxiv sq.

When two or more substantives connected together 30
by conjunctions depend on the same preposition, the
preposition is sometimes repeated, sometimes written but once.
As a ruling principle in such cases, the following may be laid
down : by omitting to repeat the preposition, the writer gives
an intimation that he regards the members rather as homogeneous, belonging together, or united into one whole ; by
repeating it, that he wants to have them taken as independent, 294
of a dissimilar or even contrary nature.

From this principle it follows,   1) that the prep. must always
be repeated in the adversative relation (ἀλλά, δέ, οὐ), and likewise
in the disjunctive (ἤ, οὐ μόνον ... ἀλλὰ καί, οὔτε ... οὔτε, etc.) if
the members are antithetic and after comparatives ; as, John vii. 22
οὐκ ἐκ τοῦ Μωυσέως ἐστὶν, ἀλλ᾽ ἐκ τῶν πατέρων, Acts viii. 34 (λέγει) περὶ
ἑαυτοῦ ἢ περὶ ἑτέρου τινός ; Col. iii. 17 ἐν λόγῳ ἢ ἐν ἔργῳ, Eph. i. 21 οὐ

μόνον ἐν τῷ αἰῶνι τούτῳ ἀλλὰ καὶ ἐν τῷ μέλλοντι, cf. Luke xx. 4;
1 Thess. i. 8; ii. 6; Rom. iv. 10; v. 1ℓ; 1 Cor. iv. 3, 21; Gal. iii. 2,
5; Acts xxv. 8, etc.   On the other hand, 2) if the members in
the disjunctive relation are similar, or if they stand in the copulative relation and so are united by καί (τε, τε καί, καί ... καί),
the preposition is either repeated or not, according as the members
either are to be regarded rather as independent and separate, or are
united into one whole, into a single composite expression.   For example: with ἤ, the preposition repeated, Acts iv. 7 ἐν ποίᾳ δυνάμει ἤ,
ἐν ποίῳ ὀνόματι ἐποιήσατε τοῦτο, 1 Cor. xiv. 6 λαλήσω ἢ ἐν ἀποκαλύψει
ἢ ἐν γνώσει ἢ ἐν προφητείᾳ ἢ ἐν διδαχῇ, John vii. 48; 2 Cor. ix. 7, etc.;
with ἤ, the preposition not repeated, Heb. x. 28 ἐπὶ δυσὶν ἢ τρισὶν
μάρτυσιν, Mark xiii. 32 περὶ τῆς ἡμέρας ἐκείνης ἢ τῆς ὥρας οὐδεὶς οἶδεν,
1 Tim. v. 19; ii. 9; 1 Pet. i. 11, etc.;   with καί etc. the preposition
repeated, Mark vi. 4 (ἄτιμος) ἐν τῇ πατρίδι αὐτοῦ καὶ ἐν τοῖς συγγενέσιν
αὐτοῦ καὶ ἐν τῇ οἰκίᾳ αὐτοῦ, Luke xxii. 33 καὶ εἰς φυλακὴν καὶ εἰς θάνατον
πορεύεσθαι, Mark ix. 22 καὶ εἰς πῦρ ἔβαλεν καὶ εἰς ὕδατα, 1 Cor. ii. 3 ἐν
ἀσθενείᾳ καὶ ἐν φόβῳ καὶ ἐν τρόμῳ, Acts xxvi. 4 ἐν τῷ ἔθνει μου ἔν τε
Ἱεροσολύμοις, 1 Thess. i. 5, etc.;   with καί etc. the preposition not
repeated, very common, Mark xiv. 43 παραγίνεται ὄχλος μετὰ μαχαιρῶν
καὶ ξύλων παρὰ τῶν ἀρχιερέων καὶ τῶν γραμματέων καὶ τῶν πρεσβυτέρων,
Acts i. 8 ἔν τε Ἱερουσαλὴμ καὶ πάσῃ τῇ Ἰουδαίᾳ, x. 39; vi. 9; xiv. 21,
etc.; Phil. iv. 3 μετὰ καὶ Κλήμεντος καὶ τῶν λοιπῶν συνεργῶν μου. Both
constructions are united in Phil. i. 7 ἐν τοῖς δεσμοῖς μου καὶ ἐν τῇ
ἀπολογίᾳ καὶ βεβαιώσει τοῦ εὐαγγελίου, where, therefore, the last two
members constitute one whole, etc.   In general, in this second class
of cases (i.e. where the members are homogeneous and the relation
copulative) no absolutely fixed rule can be laid down, since
the repetition or non-repetition of the prep. rested solely in the
writer's choice and way of looking at the subject, — is often more a
matter of feeling and rhetorical accent than of logical discrimination ;
and hence often in precisely the same cases the preposition is found
repeated and not repeated; cf. e.g. Luke xxiv. 27 with Acts xxviii. 23 ;
Matt. iv. 25 with Mark iii. 8, etc.   This holds trᵫe particularly, also,
when the Relative depends on the same prep. as the corresponding
Demonstrative, since even in Greek authors both constructions
(with and without the repetition of the prep.) occur equally. For
example: without repetition, Matt. xxiv. 50 ἐν ἡμέρᾳ ᾗ οὐ προσδοκᾷ,
Luke i. 25; Acts xiii. 39 (see above 2 note p. 322), Acts xiii. 2 εἰς
τὸ ἔργον ὃ προσκέκλημαι αὐτούς (where the construction spoken of
§ 131, 10 p. 152 may also have had influence) ; with repetition,
John iv. 53 ἐν ἐκείνῃ τῇ ὥρᾳ ἐν ᾗ εἶπεν [Tdf. om. first ἐν], Acts vii. 4 ;
xx. 18 ἀπὸ πρώτης ἡμέρας ἀφ' ἧς ἐπέβην etc.

B. § 147, N. 3 (Germ. ed.); H. § 616; J. § 651; S. p. lxxxiii.

When upon a substantive governed by a prepos.tiou a **31** limiting Genitive also depends, there are two general classes of cases as respects the preposition's position :

a) In case the nouns have no article, it is a fixed rule **295** that the preposition can never be separated by the limiting Genitive from its substantive, when this substantive (governed by the prep.) itself stands in the Genitive, even though the meaning excludes all possible ambiguity.

Hence we always find, ἐξ ἔργων νόμου, ἀπ᾽ ἄκρου γῆς, πρὸ καταβολῆς κόσμου, ἐξ ἀρχῆς κτίσεως, ἀπ᾽ ἀνατολῆς ἡλίου, διὰ τρυπήματος ῥαφίδος, διὰ λουτροῦ παλιγγενεσίας etc., and the pronouns σου, μου, αὐτοῦ, etc., which so often stand before their substantives, then follow them without exception ; thus, ἀπ᾽ ὀφθαλμῶν σου, ἐκ νεότητός μου, ἐκ δεξιῶν αὐτοῦ, διὰ and ἐκ μέσου αὐτῶν, etc. From this unquestionable observation it follows, that, wherever the sense might be ambiguous, the grammatical rule alone must decide. Accordingly, 2 Cor. iii. 18 ἀπὸ κυρίου πνεύματος can only mean *from the Lord of the Spirit*, and Matt. xxiv. 31 μετὰ σάλπιγγος φωνῆς μεγάλης only, *with a trumpet of loud sound* (see § 132, 10 p. 161). In phrases where the prep. governs a different case from the Genitive, the limiting Gen. can indeed be inserted immediately after the prep., as Matt. xiii. 33 εἰς ἀλεύρου σάτα τρία, Rev. vii. 17 ἐπὶ ζωῆς πηγὰς ὑδάτων where, however, it was necessary on other grounds also that ζωῆς should precede (see § 132, 1, b) p. 155). Yet this arrangement is extremely rare (compare the — critically uncertain, too — elliptical combinations ἐν Αἰγύπτου, εἰς ᾅδου, in § 132, 27 p. 171), and writers had become already so wonted to the natural arrangement that even here they uniformly said, εἰς ἄφεσιν ἁμαρτιῶν, εἰς ἀνάστασιν νεκρῶν, εἰς κῆπον ἑαυτοῦ, ἐπ᾽ ἐλπίδι ζωῆς αἰωνίου, etc. On the hyperbaton πρὸ ἓξ ἡμερῶν τοῦ πάσχα and the like, see § 131, 11 p. 153.

b) But if the noun governed by the preposition has the article, when there are two Genitives, at least the article of this governed noun must stand directly after the prep., and the second Gen., dependent on this substantive, may be inserted according to the general rule ; as, ἐκ τῆς Καίσαρος οἰκίας, ἐκ τῆς τοῦ διαβόλου παγίδος, διὰ τῆς ὑμῶν δεήσεως, διὰ τῆς ἑτέρων σπουδῆς, etc.

Commonly, however, even this does not take place, but the nouns follow in succession, as ἀπὸ τοῦ νόμου τῆς ἁμαρτίας, ἐκ τῶν ἡδονῶν ὑμῶν, μετὰ τῶν λαμπάδων ἑαυτῶν, ἐκ τῶν χειρῶν ἡμῶν, σὺν τῇ δυνάμει τοῦ κυρίου, etc.   The pronouns μου and σου, which, as is well known, cannot be inserted between the article and substantive, stand accordingly, as a rule, likewise afterwards (ὑπὸ τοῦ πατρός μου, etc.); but they can sometimes, owing to their propensity to precede their substantive (§ 127, 19 p. 115), be placed quite at the beginning, i.e. even before the preposition, as Matt. viii. 8 ἵνα μου ὑπὸ τὴν στέγην εἰσέλθῃς, John ix. 15 πηλὸν ἐπέθηκέν μου ἐπὶ τοὺς ὀφθαλμούς (cf. vss. 6, 11, and § 151, 14 p. 387); and so with αὐτοῦ, John xv. 10 αὐτοῦ ἐν τῇ ἀγάπῃ.

B. § 147, N. 5; H. § 615; C. §§ 703 b. 706; J. §§ 640. 644.

32   Strictly speaking, no examples are found in the N. T. in which prepositions continue to be used adverbially; and all the instances which might be reckoned under this head reduce themselves to (in part newly formed) compounds; see § 146, 4 p. 320.

296   B. § 147, N. 9; H. §§ 583, 605; C. § 699; J. § 641; W. p. 425 sq. (369 sq.).

33   That prepositions which by themselves govern the Genitive or the Dative, govern (especially ἐν, σύν, πρό) the same cases also when compounded with verbs, is a well-known fact; see the lexicons under συνζῆν, συνελθεῖν, συνέπεσθαι, συνανακεῖσθαι, συνσταυροῦν, ἐντυγχάνειν, ἐμβλέπειν, ἐμβριμᾶσθαι, ἐμμένειν, ἐνέχειν, ἐμπαίζειν, ἐμπλέκειν, ἐκπίπτειν, ἐκτινάσσειν, προστῆναι, προπορεύεσθαι, etc.   With other verbs the repetition of the preposition (or of a synonymous one) prevails, especially with verbs compounded with ἀπό and ἐκ, see under ἐμβάλλειν, ἐκβάλλειν, ἀπέχειν, ἀποστῆναι, ἀπαίρειν, ἐκπορεύεσθαι, ἀπαλλάσσειν, ἀπελαύνειν, ἀποκρύπτειν, ἀποπλανᾶν, προκηρύσσειν, ἐνευλογεῖσθαι, etc.

NEGATIVES.

B. § 148; H. § 832; C. § 686; D. § 528; J. § 739.

1   In no respect, perhaps, has the language of the N. T. adhered more closely to the usage established by the literary language, than in the employment of the two negatives οὐ and μή with their compounds; so that it proves to be easy to point out analogies in classic usage for the deviations even that occur.   Hence, for the general principles in all their extent, we refer the reader to the specifications given in the Grammars, and here need make mention only of particular instances of somewhat rare and peculiar use.

B. § 148, 2 b) and note; H. § 835; C. § 686 i. sq.; D. § 531; J. § 744, 1; W. p. 477 sq. (445 sq.)

2   The use of οὐ in the protasis of a conditional sentence occurs in the N. T. relatively very often; so that we are justified in inferring a difference in usage, since in classic

writers this use is only exceptional. It is true, the attempt has been made to explain the individual instances all according to the analogy of those which occur in classic authors, and consequently to consent to recognize merely an extension in the N. T. of a usage elsewhere rare. This method of treatment may be applied, indeed, to a portion of the extant passages, but is decidedly inapplicable to many, and is especially opposed by the circumstance that whereas after εἰ the predicate is so often negatived by οὐ, this n e v e r occurs under the same conditions in clauses with ἐάν; (cf. e.g. Matt. vi. 15 with Mark xi. 26). The usage of the N. T., on the contrary, may be referred to the following simple and almost invariable principles:

1) The first form of hypothesis (§ 139 A. pp. 220 sq.), i.e. εἰ with the Indicative as expressive of objective certainty, 297 takes the d i r e c t n e g a t i v e οὐ. Exceptions are extremely rare: 1 Tim. vi. 3 εἴ τις ἑτεροδιδασκαλεῖ καὶ μὴ προσέρχεται λόγοις etc.

2) The second form of hypothesis (ἐάν with the Subjunctive), and the fourth (εἰ with a Preterite Indicative), require i n-v a r i a b l y t h e d e p e n d e n t n e g a t i v e μή. (The third species of hypothesis, εἰ with the Optative, occurs in the N. T. only in a positive form.) On Matt. xxvi. 24 and Mark xiv. 21 see 3) d. p. 347.

3) The combination ἐκτὸς εἰ μή (see 13 p. 355) even when followed by the Indicative, the compound εἰ μή (used for the most part elliptically, i.e. without a predicate) in the signification except, nisi (see § 149, 4 p. 359), after a preceding negative or interrogative clause, as well as the elliptical for-mulæ εἰ δὲ μή, εἰ δὲ μή γε (§ 151, 23, e) p. 393) are, like established conjunctions or adverbs, no longer capable of changing their outward form.

Now since 2) and 3) admit of no exceptions and are perfectly gram-matical, it is only necessary here to establish the f i r s t class. We will so arrange the examples as first of all to exhibit those which stand in obvious analogy with those from classic authors treated of in B. l.c., and then proceed to those which ̲epart more or less from the ordinary usage.

a) The predicate of the conditional clause negatived by οὐ 3 is found in evident a n t i t h e s i s to a p o s i t i v e notion (com-

4₄

monly the same, but sometimes synonymous), either in what precedes or in what follows (see B. § 148, 2. g).

For example: in what precedes, Mark xi. 26 Lchm. ἀφίετε ἵνα etc. ... εἰ δὲ ὑμεῖς οὐκ ἀφίετε, οὐδὲ ὁ πατὴρ ἀφήσει,[1] John v. 47 εἰ γὰρ ἐπιστεύετε etc. ... εἰ δὲ τοῖς ἐκείνου γράμμασιν οὐ πιστεύετε, πῶς etc., Acts xxv. 11 εἰ μὲν οὖν ἀδικῶ ... · εἰ δὲ οὐδέν ἐστιν ὧν οὗτοι κατηγοροῦσίν μου. So in Rom. viii. 9; 1 Cor. vii. 9; Jas. iii. 2; in what follows, 1 Cor. ix. 2 εἰ ἄλλοις οὐκ εἰμὶ ἀπόστολος, ἀλλά γε ὑμῖν εἰμι, John x. 37 εἰ οὐ ποιῶ τὰ ἔργα ... , εἰ δὲ ποιῶ etc., Luke xi. 8 εἰ καὶ οὐ δώσει αὐτῷ ... , διά γε τὴν ἀναίδειαν αὐτοῦ δώσει αὐτῷ (cf. the similarly formed sentence in xviii. 4), 1 Cor. xi. 6 εἰ γὰρ οὐ κατακαλύπτεται γυνή with reference to the following κατακαλυπτέσθω.

In all the above passages the dependent negative would be in nowise erroneous, and by the Greeks would perhaps have been preferred. More necessary, on the other hand, is the use of the negative οὐ even according to classic usage, when to the negatived predicate another, still in the protasis, is immediately so appended or contrasted with an adversative particle that the entire emphasis falls upon this second part (cf. 8 p. 352); as, Jas. ii. 11 εἰ δὲ οὐ μοιχεύεις, φονεύεις δέ, 2 Pet. ii. 4, 5 εἰ γὰρ ὁ θεὸς ἀγγέλων ἁμαρτησάντων οὐκ ἐφείσατο, ἀλλὰ ... παρέδωκεν εἰς κρίσιν etc. (cf. with this the example Il. xv. 162, B. p. 493 Germ. ed.).

b) For the same reason as in a) the negative οὐ may be grammatically defended also in the following pretty common class of sentences (though the Greeks, however, here also would have perhaps preferred for the most part the dependent negative): where a negative protasis is associated with emphasis, or rather contrasted, with an apodosis likewise negatived (or negatively conceived).

The plainest example of this is 1 Cor. xv. 13–17 εἰ ἀνάστασις νεκρῶν οὐκ ἔστιν, οὐδὲ Χριστὸς ἐγήγερται· εἰ δὲ Χριστὸς οὐκ ἐγήγερται, κενὸν ἄρα τὸ κήρυγμα ἡμῶν· ... Χριστὸν οὐκ ἤγειρεν, εἴπερ ἄρα νεκροὶ οὐκ ἐγείρονται· εἰ γὰρ νεκροὶ οὐκ ἐγείρονται, οὐδὲ etc., Rom. xi. 21 εἰ ... οὐκ ἐφείσατο, οὐδὲ σοῦ φείσεται, Luke xvi. 31 εἰ Μωυσέως ... οὐκ ἀκούουσιν, οὐδ᾽ ἐάν τις ἐκ νεκρῶν ἀναστῇ πεισθήσονται, 2 Thess. iii. 10 εἴ τις οὐ θέλει ἐργάζεσθαι, μηδὲ ἐσθιέτω. See besides Heb. xii. 25, and, with the substitution of a question instead of a negation in the apodosis, Luke xvi. 11 sq. εἰ ... οὐκ ἐγένεσθε, τὸ ἀληθινὸν τίς ὑμῖν πιστεύσει; καὶ εἰ etc., John iii. 12 εἰ οὐ πιστεύετε, πῶς ... πιστεύσετε; 1 Tim. iii. 5 εἴ τις ...

298

---

[1] If vs. 26, which is wanting in several ancient mss. [Sin. also], was really first transferred (as is said) from Matt. vi. 15, then at least the alteration made in the words of Matthew turns out to correspond perfectly with N. T. usage.

οὐκ οἶδεν, πῶς ἐκκλησίας ἐπιμελήσεται; cf. 1 Cor. xv. 29; xv. 32 (substantially); and several of the passages quoted under a) may be brought under this head also, as Mark xi. 26; John v. 47; Acts xxv. 11; Rom. viii. 9.

c) Further, an endeavor has been made to bring a number of passages under the rule proposed by Hermann (ad Vig. p. 831), according to which οὐ is said to stand in conditional clauses when it blends as it were with the negatived word into a single (positive) notion.   Since, however, this view affords no satisfactory objective test, but, on the contrary, all conditional clauses in which the p r e d i c a t e is negatived may be brought with more or less ease under this category (e.g. οὐ φείδομαι equiv. to φθείρω, οὐκ ἀκούω equiv. to ἀνήκοός εἰμι, οὐκ οἶδεν equiv. to ἀγνοεῖ, οὐ δύναται equiv. to ἀδύνατόν ἐστιν, etc.), we can with tolerable confidence bring under this head only those passages in which a different part of the clause from the predicate is negatived, and consequently the predicate is evidently positive.

For example, 2 Cor. xii. 11 οὐδὲν ὑστέρησα . . . , εἰ καὶ οὐδέν εἰμι, Jas. i. 23 εἴ τις ἀκροατὴς λόγου ἐστὶν καὶ οὐ ποιητής where only the notion ποιητής i n a n t i t h e s i s to ἀκροατής is negatived (yet without constituting a single idea), and the predicate remains positive.   But Luke xii. 26 εἰ οὖν οὐδὲ ἐλάχιστον δύνασθε, τί περὶ τῶν λοιπῶν μεριμνᾶτε does not belong under this head, since by οὐδέ the predicate is also negatived, so that the sentence belongs with the passages under b). The other passages, also, with a negatived predicate adduced under 298 this head, we have already distributed under the first two more obvious rules; as, 1 Tim. iii. 5; Luke xvi. 31; Heb. xii. 25; 2 Pet. ii. 4; Jas. ii. 11.

d) In justification of the direct negative, reference has also been made to the special e m p h a s i s with which the predicate alone is rendered prominent as n e g a t i v e d.   This may be affirmed with reason of the two parallel passages Matt. xxvi. 24 and Mark xiv. 21 καλὸν ἦν αὐτῷ, εἰ οὐκ ἐγεννήθη ὁ ἄνθρωπος ἐκεῖνος (where, moreover, the direct negation appears to find an adequate occasion in the evident approximation of the sentence to the first form of hypothesis, cf. § 139, 27 c) p. 225), and also of John i. 25 τί βαπτίζεις, εἰ σὺ οὐκ εἶ ὁ Χριστός (if i.e. since thou certainly art not etc.).

Yet since the majority of such passages coincide with one of the objective characteristics propounded under a) and b), and accordingly have already been quoted there; further, since without such objective indications the interpreter is left to decide solely according to his feelings whether he will recognize a special emphasis or not; and especially, since in the N. T. the direct negative makes its appearance in clauses with the Indicative a l m o s t w i t h o u t an e x c e p t i o n (cf. 4 below), the circumstance above mentioned is not of itself suited to constitute a separate class or rule, at least for the New Testament.

e) Finally, the following additional examples are to be noticed as those which do not admit of being classed under any one of the above rules, and consequently belong to the characteristically free usage of the N. T., according to which conditional clauses of the first kind are uniformly negatived by οὐ:

Luke xiv. 26 εἴ τις ἔρχεται πρός με καὶ οὐ μισεῖ τὸν πατέρα ... οὐ δύναται etc., 2 John 10 (cf. 1 Tim. vi. 3), 1 Cor. xvi. 22 εἴ τις οὐ φιλεῖ τὸν κύριον, ἤτω ἀνάθεμα, 2 Thess. iii. 14 εἴ τις οὐχ ὑπακούει τῷ λόγῳ . . τοῦτον σημειοῦσθε, 1 Tim. v. 8 εἴ τις τῶν ἰδίων οὐ προνοεῖ, τὴν πίστιν ἤρνηται, Rev. xx. 15 εἴ τις οὐχ εὑρέθη ἐν τῇ βίβλῳ ... ἐβλήθη etc. Hardly would any classic writer have employed the direct negation in any of these passages, even on the assumption of a special emphasis in the negative. On the other hand, in Matt. xxvi. 42 οὐ is used more with reference to ἐὰν μή immediately following (with which the clauses with εἰ μή nisi after an antecedent οὐ are to be compared, see § 149, 4 p. 359); and in John x. 35 the clause καὶ οὐ δύναται λυθῆναι ἡ γραφή is to be taken as independent and parenthetic.

4   The use of the negative in R e l a t i v e S e n t e n c e s is quite like that in conditional sentences, as in general the former share in all essential particulars the nature and construction of the latter, (see B. § 139 B.). Accordingly, relative sentences in the Indicative, whether of a general nature or not, are almost exclusively n e g a t i v e d by οὐ, so that sentences with μή are extremely rare; on the other hand, relative sentences in the Subjunctive with ἄν (ἐάν) are without any exception negatived by μή.

300   Examples w i t h οὐ: Matt. xii. 2; Mark ii. 24; Luke vi. 2 ποιοῦσιν ὃ οὐκ ἔξεστιν ποιεῖν ἐν σαββάτῳ, Matt. x. 38 ὃς οὐ λαμβάνει τὸν σταυρὸν ... οὐκ ἔστιν μου ἄξιος, Gal. iii. 10 (quotn.) πᾶς ὃς οὐκ ἐμμένει etc., and after ὅστις with the Indic. Luke xiv. 27; xv. 7, etc.; further, in antithesis (similar to the instances unfolded above in 3 a) and b)), as Matt. xiii. 12; Mark iv. 25 ὃς ἔχει ... καὶ ὃς οὐχ ἔχει, Rom. vii. 15.

19 ὃ θέλω ... ὃ οὐ θέλω, xv. 21 (quotn.) οἷς οὐκ ἀνηγγέλη, ὄψονται, οἳ
οὐκ ἀκηκόασιν, συνήσουσιν, iv. 15 οὗ γὰρ οὐκ ἔστιν νόμος, οὐδὲ παράβασις.
Cf. besides, in 12 below, p. 354, the sentences with two (mutually
annulling) negatives in two clauses dependent on one another.
Examples w i t h μή and the Indicative (n e v e r in the historical
writings), 2 Pet i. 9 ᾧ γὰρ μὴ πάρεστιν ταῦτα, τυφλός ἐστιν, Tit. i. 11
διδάσκοντες ἃ μὴ δεῖ.   On the μή in Col. ii. 18, critically very doubtful
[wanting in ℵ* and omitted by Treg. Tdf.] (and in no wise necessary
to the sense), see Meyer.   Examples with μή and the Subjunctive
are very common in all parts of the N. T. e.g. Matt. x. 14, etc.; also
in antithesis, Luke viii. 18 cf. Matt. xiii. 12, etc.

On the other hand, in all illative, causal, and declarative   5
sentences, the language of the N. T. follows closely the ordinary
Greek usage.

Accordingly, after ὥστε with the Indicative οὐ is regularly used,
Matt. xix. 6; Gal. iv. 7, etc., after ὥστε with the Infin. invariably μή
(see 6) ; further, after ὅτι (because and that), καθότι, ἐπεί, ἐπειδή, etc.,
uniformly οὐ, Luke i. 34; 1 Cor. i. 21, etc.   John iii. 18 ὅτι (because)
μὴ πεπίστευκεν is to be regarded solely as a deviation from ordinary
usage (hence instances of the sort are often to be found also in later
writers, especially Lucian, see Herm. ad Vig. p. 806; Cobet, var. Lect.
315 sq., and on the usage of Arrian and Lucian, Ellendt præf. ad Arr.
p. 24; Du Mesnil, Stolp. Progr. 1867 p. 43) ; and on Heb. ix. 17
(ἐπεὶ μή ποτε ἰσχύει) see 10 p. 353.   Also after ὅτι in the signification
that, μή is sometimes used in later writers, e.g. App. B.C. 3, 96.

B. § 148, 2 d.; H. § 837; C. § 686 c.; D. § 594 Obs.; J. § 745; W. p. 481 sq. (449).

With the I n f i n i t i v e, the N. T. writers are so in the habit   6
of using the dependent negation, that they negative a statement by μ ή where the direct negation was not only admissible,
but in Greek authors even more usual ; so that, in point of
fact, examples of οὐ with the Infinitive are hardly to be met
with longer.

Hence, in particular, μή stands (as in Greek authors) without exception with an Infinitive introduced by the A r t i c l e, Matt. xiii. 5;
Rom. xiv. 13, 21, etc.; further, after ὥστε, Mark ii. 2; 1 Cor. i. 7, etc.,
no exception to which is established by Rom. vii. 6, since here only
παλαιότητι in c o n t r a s t with καινότητι is denied, and not the Infin.
Μή stands also after v e r b a d i c e n d i, etc., so far forth as a preference,
counsel, wish, command is contained in them, and after predicates
like δεῖ, δοκεῖ μοι, καλόν ἐστιν, ἄλογόν ἐστιν, etc., as Matt. v. 34, 39;
xxiii. 23; Luke xxi. 14; xxii. 40; Acts i. 4; xv. 28; 2 Pet. ii. 21;

301 Eph. iv. 17 ; Rom. ii. 21 ; xv. 1, etc.[1]   But also where the Infin. clause
(after the verba dicendi, etc.) contains only a declaration, and the
Greeks use, at least in part, the negative οὐ, we always find μή; as,
Luke xx. 7 ἀπεκρίθησαν μὴ εἰδέναι etc., Matt. xxii. 23 ; Mark xii. 18 ;
Luke ii. 26 ; Acts xxiii. 8 ; 2 Cor. xi. 5.

REMARK. In cases of accumulated (intensified) negation, the main
rule (B. § 148, 6, cf. 11 below p. 354) requires the same kind of
negative to be used with the Infin. as with the predicate, — consequently
οὐ; as, Luke xx. 40 οὐκέτι ἐτόλμων ἐπερωτᾶν οὐδέν, John iii. 27 οὐ
δύναται ἄνθρωπος λαμβάνειν οὐδέν, v. 19, 30 ; Rev. v. 4, etc.

B. § 148 e (f); H. § 839 · C. § 686 (d); D. p. 554; J. § 746; W. p. 482 sqq. (450 sqq.).

7   With Participles (as in Greek authors and under the
same conditions as there) both kinds of negation occur; only
in circumstances where either is admissible (see b below), the
disposition to employ μή etc. is incomparably stronger.

a) If the Participle has the Article (cf. the Infin.), it is
regularly negatived by μή ; thus, ὁ μὴ ὢν μετ᾽ ἐμοῦ, τοῖς μὴ
πεπλανημένοις, οἱ μὴ ἰδόντες καὶ πιστεύσαντες, etc.

Only those cases are exceptions where antithesis occurs, as Rom.
ix. 25 (quotn.) τὴν οὐκ ἠγαπημένην ἠγαπημένην, 1 Pet. ii. 10 οἱ οὐκ
ἠλεημένοι, νῦν δὲ ἐλεηθέντες, Gal. iv. 27 (quotn.) στεῖρα ἡ οὐ τίκτουσα
(Heb. אּל), Rom. iv. 12.   In Eph. v. 4 Tdf. [eds. 2, 7] the reading
τὰ οὐκ ἀνήκοντα would be an exception also,[2] but the reading is by no
means established [Tdf. now with Treg. Lchm. cod. Sin. ἃ οὐκ ἀνῆκεν] ;
cf. Rom. i. 28.

b) Should the Participle have no Article, μή is used
unqualifiedly when the participial clause is equivalent to a
hypothetical sentence, and so is to be resolved by *if;* as, εἰδότι
καὶ μὴ ποιοῦντι, ἁμαρτία αὐτῷ ἐστιν (Jas. iv. 17 ; Matt. xiii. 19,
etc.).   On the other hand, if the participial clause contains
an actual matter of fact, and so is to be resolved by means of
a Relative, or by *since, whilst, during, without,* etc., it is negatived (often when the circumstances are altogether the
same) sometimes by οὐ, sometimes, and indeed more commonly, by μή.

[1] In Acts xix. 27 [Treg.] Tdf. (κινδυνεύει . . . εἰς οὐδὲν [οὐθὲν ed. 8] λογισθῆναι)
rather the single fragment of the sentence (οὐδέν) is negatived, although usage
elsewhere would nevertheless have led us to expect μηδέν, and hence the other
strongly [yet not by cod. Sin.] supported reading (λογισθήσεται Lchm.) perhaps
is to be preferred. On 2 Tim. ii. 14 see 8 p. 352.

[2] In Greek authors also such cases, when no antithesis occurs (as in Ar. Eccl.
187), are extremely rare, e.g. Luc. adv. Ind. 5 ὁ κυβερνᾶν οὐκ εἰδὼς καὶ ἱππεύειν μὴ
μεμελετηκώς.

The original difference between the two negatives (although in point of fact no longer adhered to in employing them) is still evident in such sentences as Matt. xxii. 11, 12 εἶδεν ἄνθρωπον οὐκ ἐνδεδυμένον (who had not on), but subsequently εἰσῆλθες μὴ ἔχων ἔνδυμα (although thou hadst not etc.), 1 Pet. i. 8 ὃν οὐκ ἰδόντες (having in point of fact not seen him) ἀγαπᾶτε, εἰς ὃν ἄρτι μὴ ὁρῶντες (although ye do not see) πιστεύοντες δέ etc. Examples of the less common negative οὐ (οὐδέν) in a Participial clause which is temporal or causal, or to be resolved by means of a Relative, are Luke vi. 42 (οὐ βλέπων), John x. 12 οὐκ ὢν ποιμήν explained by οὐ οὐκ ἔστιν τὰ πρόβατα ἴδια, Acts xxvi. 22 οὐδὲν 302 ἐκτὸς λέγων, xxviii. 17 οὐδὲν ποιήσας (although in point of fact), vii. 5 (Gen. absol.), 1 Cor. ix. 26 πυκτεύω ὡς οὐκ ἀέρα δέρων, Gal. iv. 8 οὐκ εἰδότες, Col. ii. 19; Heb. xi. 1, 35. Examples of οὐ in consequence of the emphasis of antithesis, are 2 Cor. iv. 8, 9 ἐν παντὶ θλιβόμενοι ἀλλ' οὐ στενοχωρούμενοι, ἀπορούμενοι ἀλλ' οὐκ ἐξαπορούμενοι etc., Phil. iii. 3 οἱ πνεύματι θεοῦ λατρεύοντες ... καὶ οὐκ ἐν σαρκὶ πεποιθότες, 1 Cor. iv. 14 οὐκ ἐντρέπων ὑμᾶς γράφω ταῦτα, ἀλλ' ὡς etc.; and because a particular part of the sentence (rather than the whole) is denied, are Luke vii. 6 ἤδη αὐτοῦ οὐ μακρὰν ἀπέχοντος, Acts xvii. 27; xxvii. 20 χειμῶνος οὐκ ὀλίγου ἐπικειμένου.

Everywhere else the dependent negative μή is used, even with the most definite matters of fact, and in cases thoroughly concrete. Examples are so abundant in all parts of the N. T., that it is enough to give a few corresponding to those above with οὐ, or passages quite parallel: Matt. xviii. 25 μὴ ἔχοντος αὐτοῦ ἀποδοῦναι, ἐκέλευσεν etc., xxii. 25 μὴ ἔχων σπέρμα ἀφῆκεν τὴν γυναῖκα, 29 πλανᾶσθε, μὴ εἰδότες (because) τὰς γραφὰς μηδὲ etc., Acts v. 7; ix. 26; xii. 19 Ἡρώδης ἐπιζητήσας καὶ μὴ εὑρὼν ἐκέλευσεν etc., xvii. 6; Luke xviii. 2, etc.; even in antithesis, Mark v. 26 μηδὲν ὠφεληθεῖσα, ἀλλὰ μᾶλλον εἰς τὸ χεῖρον ἐλθοῦσα, Acts ix. 7 εἱστήκεισαν ἐνεοί, ἀκούοντες μὲν τῆς φωνῆς, μηδένα δὲ θεωροῦντες, 2 Cor. vi. 9.

c) When the Participle with εἶναι is used as a periphrasis for a finite verb (§ 144, 24 sq. p. 308 sq.), the dependent negative μή must be used, even in the most concrete cases, if it is not the copula (and thus the entire sentence), but the Participle alone, that is to be negatived.

Accordingly we must distinguish Luke vi. 43 οὐκ ἔστιν δένδρον καλὸν ποιοῦν καρπὸν σαπρόν, xxiii. 53 ἐν μνήματι, οὗ οὐκ ἦν οὐδεὶς οὔπω κείμενος, xii. 6; John iii. 24; Rom. iii. 12; 2 Cor. ii. 17; Jas. iii. 15, etc., from Luke xiii. 11 ἦν συγκύπτουσα καὶ μὴ δυναμένη ἀνακύψαι, i. 20 ἔσῃ σιωπῶν καὶ μὴ δυνάμενος λαλῆσαι, Acts ix. 9 ἦν ἡμέρας τρεῖς μὴ βλέπων.

d) Lastly, the Participle is negatived by μή (sometimes even in case of antithesis, cf. 8 below), whenever the entire sentence to which the Participle belongs requires the dependent negation.

Of this case also there are many examples : 1 Cor. vii. 29 (τοῦτο δέ φημι) ἵνα οἱ ἔχοντες γυναῖκας ὡς μὴ ἔχοντες ὦσιν, καὶ οἱ κλαίοντες ὡς μὴ etc., Eph. v. 27 ἵνα παραστήσῃ ἔνδοξον τὴν ἐκκλησίαν μὴ ἔχουσαν etc., Phil. iii. 9 εὑρεθῶ μὴ ἔχων etc., Rom. xii. 16, 17, 19, etc.

B. § 148, 2 g. (Germ. ed.); J. § 744, 1 Obs.; W. p. 479 (446 sq.).

8 Several examples of the use of the direct negative, in sentences which otherwise prefer μή, as soon as the negatived word stands in sharp antithesis (marked by ἀλλά, δέ, εἰ μή) to some other and following part of the sentence, have already been given above, see 3 a) p. 345, 7 a) and b) p. 350. According to this principle the direct negative makes its appearance in such cases (although by no means necessarily) even in sentences which positively require μή, as final and imperative sentences; see 7 d) above. The difference between these two modes of expression is this : when the direct negative is used, the negatived part of the sentence is, as it were, brought out **303** conspicuously from the rest (by supplying some such word as λέγω), and the emphasis falls on what follows introduced by ἀλλά, etc. (cf. 3 a) p. 345) ; on the other hand, where μή is used, both parts of the sentence remain equally related to the whole.

Examples: 1 Pet. iii. 3 ὧν ἔστω οὐχ ὁ ἔξωθεν ... κόσμος, ἀλλ᾽ ὁ κρυπτός etc. *whose adorning ought to be not* (or, *I do not say*) *the outward ... but* etc., Rev. ix. 4 ἵνα μὴ ἀδικήσουσιν τὸν χόρτον τῆς γῆς, οὐδὲ πᾶν χλωρὸν οὐδὲ πᾶν δένδρον, εἰ μὴ τοὺς ἀνθρώπους etc. Cf. 1 Cor. v. 10 ἔγραψα μὴ συναναμίγνυσθαι τοῖς πόρνοις, οὐ πάντως etc., on this see § 151, 19 p. 389. On the other hand, 1 Pet. v. 2, 3 ποιμάνατε ... μὴ ἀναγκαστῶς ἀλλ᾽ ἑκουσίως, μὴ αἰσχροκερδῶς ἀλλὰ προθύμως μηδὲ etc., Phil. ii. 2–4 πληρώσατέ μου τὴν χαρὰν ἵνα τὸ αὐτὸ φρονῆτε, ... μὴ τὰ ἑαυ·ῶν σκοποῦντες, ἀλλά etc., John xviii. 40, etc. 2 Tim. ii. 14 μή λογομάχει (Tdf. [Treg. cod. Sin.] λογομαχεῖν) ἐπ᾽ οὐδὲν χρήσιμον, without an adversative clause following, is more surprising, and only to be explained by the emphatic prominence given to an individual word.

On οὐ, as a second and independent negation of a particular part of a sentence, in sentences with μή, see 11 p. 354.

B. § 148, N. 3; H. § 840; C. §§ 685 a.; 686 e.; D. § 534; J. § 745, Obs. 5.

Examples of negatived **substantives**, i.e. of substantives trans- **9**
formed by the negative into their opposites and blending with it, as it
were, into a single word, occur only in O. T. quotations.   The negative
then is always οὐ, because compounds of the sort are formed in Hebrew
with לֹא, Rom. ix. 25 ; 1 Pet. ii. 10 οἵ ποτε οὐ λαός, νῦν δὲ λαός, Rom.
x. 19 ἐπ’ οὐκ ἔθνει.   In Greek elsewhere both species of negative are
met with, see particularly B. and J. as above.

On the negative with the Imperative, and the Subjunctive as its
substitute, see § 139, 6 p. 211.

B. § 148, 4 and N. 5; H. §§ 720 d.; 846; C. § 626; D. § 538 sq.; J. § 814; G. § 46 N. 4.

On μή as the conjunction after verbs and notions of fear and   **0**
anxiety, see § 139, 48 p. 241 sq.   Of the usage according to
which sentences with μή (μήπως, μήποτε), when **no verbum**
timendi is expressed, contain the idea of fear or anxiety,
the N. T. also affords a few evident examples.   Thus, with a
Subjunctive following, Matt. xxv. 9 λέγουσαι· μήποτε οὐ μὴ
ἀρκέσῃ ἡμῖν καὶ ὑμῖν ; and with a Future following, Rom. xi. 21
Tdf. [eds. 2, 7 ; ed. 8 omits μήπως with Lchm. Treg. cod. Sin.]
μήπως οὐδὲ σοῦ φείσεται.   See on the second negative in both
sentences No. 11 following.

As, according to B. § 139, m. 50 ; G. § 46, N. 5, etc. (cf. Gal. iv. 11
above in § 139, 48 p. 242), in sentences where a verb of fearing is
expressed, a preterite **Indicative** may be used after μή in order to
represent the object of fear as in a degree an actually existing fact,
so here too ; as, Gal. ii. 2 ἀνέβην δὲ καὶ ἀνεθέμην αὐτοῖς τὸ εὐαγγέλιον ...
κατ’ ἰδίαν δὲ τοῖς δοκοῦσιν, μή πως εἰς κενὸν τρέχω ἢ ἔδραμον i.e. *in the*
anxiety lest (or, *in order to see whether*, cf. Luke xi. 35 in § 139, 49
p. 243) *perchance my efforts are, or have already been, in vain.*   So
recent interpreters, — with this difference only, that they unnecessarily
still want to retain τρέχω as a Subjunctive.   On the contrary, it is in
the Indicative as really as the following ἔδραμον, and glancing at the
latter presents in advance the notion of the present as a like object of **304**
anxiety.   1 Thess. iii. 5 ἔπεμψα εἰς τὸ γνῶναι τὴν πίστιν ὑμῶν, μήπως
ἐπείρασεν ὑμᾶς ὁ πειράζων καὶ εἰς κενὸν γένηται ὁ κόπος ἡμῶν, *fearing*
(or, *in order to see whether*) *perchance the tempter has tempted you,*
and my labor thus might become in vain.   Heb. ix. 17 διαθήκη
βεβαία, ἐπεὶ μή ποτε ἰσχύει ὅτε ζῇ ὁ διαθέμενος affords an example of
the use (which increased more and more in later Greek) of μήποτε
with the Indicative, the notion of **anxiety** or of doubting inter-

45

rogation residing in the negative having gradually receded, and so μήποτε being used almost like οὔποτε in the sense of *probably never*.[1]

On μή as an **interrogative particle**, see § 139, 55 p. 248; and on οὐ μή as a strengthened negation with the Fut. and the Subjunct., ibid. 7 p. 211 sq. Of μὴ οὐ as a mere **intensification** there is no instance.

B. § 148, N. 7 a.; H. § 846; C. § 713 sub fin.; D. § 537; J. § 750.

11　Similar negatives as a **rule** strengthen each other, or the second is only the **continuation** of the first. Hence in sentences already, for any reason, negatived by (the conjunction) μή, as soon as a **particular part** of the sentence is to be negatived again, and independently of the first negation, this must be done in every instance by the other form of negation, **that is to say by** *οὐ*.

Examples from classic authors after the μή implying **anxiety** (Lat. *ne non*) may be seen in the Grammars. From the N. T. we have 2 Cor. xii. 20 φοβοῦμαι μήπως ἐλθὼν οὐχ οἵους θέλω εὕρω ὑμᾶς; see further Matt. xxv. 9 and Rom. xi. 21 in the preceding paragraph. For the same reason, in an interrogative sentence with the μή of **doubt**, as soon as an affirmative answer is expected (*nonne*), not μή again but οὐ must be introduced as the second negative; for examples of this, see § 139, 55 p. 248.

B. § 148, N. 7 b. and N. 8; J. § 747; W. p. 498 (464).

12　Cases may occur, however, in which two similar negatives **destroy each other**, inasmuch as both the sense and the natural position of the words exclude all ambiguity. In the N. T. there is only one passage where similar negatives destroy each other **in one and the same sentence**: 1 Cor. xii. 15 ἐὰν εἴπῃ ὁ πούς, ... οὐ παρὰ τοῦτο οὐκ ἔστιν ἐκ τοῦ σώματος. Here it was necessary to use the same negative twice, because the nature of the sentence did not 305 permit any other than the objective form of negation either at the beginning or in the middle; and that they mutually destroy each other follows from the sense inevitably.

---

[1] Still more frequently, in the writings e.g. of Aristotle, and especially in the literary language of the Alexandrians (the Grammarians, and the Scholiasts), it may be rendered simply by *perhaps* (i.e. ἴσως), which sprung by abbreviation from the complete sentence ὅρα μήποτε followed by the Subjunctive: *see to it lest perchance* etc.; as, Arist. Eth. Nic. 10 init. (μή ποτε οὐ καλῶς τοῦτ᾽ λέγεται), iii. 2 (μήποτ᾽ οὐ λέγουσι τὸ αἴτιον). Μή with the Indic. also is so used; as, Apoll. Adverb. 567. On this subject see further, Steph. Thes. sub voce; Bhdy. p. 397; Devar. ed. Klotz I. p. 137.

On the other hand, a double self-destroying negation for the purpose of an emphatic affirmation is more common in t w o sentences immediately dependent one on the other, viz. a l e a d i n g clause and a R e l a t i v e clause dependent upon it, after the analogy of the classic usage discussed in B. § 148, N. 8; C. § 559 c.; J. § 824, 2 (yet without such attraction as in οὐδεὶς ὅστις οὐ, οὐδενὶ ὅτῳ οὐ etc.); as, Matt. x. 26 οὐδέν ἐστιν κεκαλυμμένον ὃ οὐκ ἀποκαλυφθήσεται, καὶ κρυπτὸν ὃ οὐ γνωσθήσεται, xxiv. 2 οὐ μὴ ἀφεθῇ ὧδε λίθος ἐπὶ λίθον, ὃς οὐ καταλυθήσεται, Mark xiii. 2; Luke viii. 17; xii. 2; xxi. 6. Here belong those sentences, also, in which, instead of the negatived leading clause, the form of a question is chosen; as, Acts xix. 35 τίς ἐστιν ἀνθρώπων ὃς οὐ γινώσκει etc., Heb. xii. 7 τίς γὰρ υἱὸς ὃν οὐ παιδεύει πατήρ.

B. § 148, N. 9; H. § 838; C. § 713 d.; D. § 595; J. 749; G. pp. 198 sq.

The pleonastic use, too, of μή in dependent Infinitive **3** clauses after predicates which include within themselves a negative force, has been preserved, at least in certain parts of the N. T. (e.g. Luke's writings), especially with the Infinitive introduced by τοῦ.

See examples of this last kind in § 140, 16 p. 269. We have, besides, without τοῦ, Luke xx. 27 οἱ ἀντιλέγοντες ἀνάστασιν μὴ εἶναι, xxii. 34 Tdf. ἕως τρὶς ἀπαρνήσῃ μὴ εἰδέναι με, Heb. xii. 19 παρῃτήσαντο μὴ προστεθῆναι αὐτοῖς λόγον, Gal. v. 7 τίς ὑμᾶς ἐνέκοψεν τῇ ἀληθείᾳ μὴ πείθεσθαι. Analogous is the pleonastic οὐ when an Infin. is resolved into a clause with ὅτι, 1 John ii. 22 ὁ ἀρνούμενος ὅτι Ἰησοῦς οὐκ ἔστιν ὁ Χριστός, cf. Mark ix. 38 Lchm. [Tdf. cod. Sin.], and from classic authors, Demosth. Phil. p. 124 extr.; Xen. Anab. 2, 3, 25; Ath. 2. 17, etc. Pleonastic also is the negative in the common phrase ἐκτὸς εἰ μή i.e. *except if, except it be*, as 1 Cor. xiv. 5 μείζων ὁ προφητεύων, ... ἐκτὸς εἰ μὴ διερμηνεύῃ, xv. 2; 1 Tim. v. 19; see Lob. ad Phryn. p. 459, and on the Subjunct. § 139, 22 p. 221.

REMARK. In Rom. iv. 19 Lchm. [so Treg. Tdf.] in his text has **14** omitted the οὐ before κατενόησεν, with the oldest authorities [cod. Sin. also]. But since the context seems to require a negation, other editors have adopted οὐ, which likewise is sufficiently attested; or it is thought necessary, at least to supply the direct negative οὐ with κατενόησεν from the μή with ἀσθενήσας. That a single negative can belong ἀπὸ κοινοῦ to t w o notions is certain (see, among others, Poppo on Thuc. 1, 12; O. Schneider on Isocr. 4, 3; Grot. on Eur. Tro. 638; Mehlhorn on the Schema ἀπὸ κοινοῦ p. 14 sq.; Krüger, Gram. § 67, **8**

Anm. 4) ; e.g. Luke viii. 12 ἵνα μὴ πιστεύσαντες σωθῶσιν, and cf. the command ὀργίζεσθε καὶ μὴ ἁμαρτάνετε in § 144, 2 p. 290. But whether Greek usage permits the direct negative to be supplied from the dependent negative is more than doubtful. Further, against either supplying or adopting οὐ makes the manifest reference of the words to Gen. xvii. 17 ; for only to this passage, not to Gen. xv. 5 sq., does 306 the express mention of the νέκρωσις τῆς μήτρας Σάρρας in the n i n e -
t e e n t h vs. point us. But then the words μὴ ἀσθενήσας τῇ πίστει seem to be at variance with the narrative in Gen. xvii., and still more with the positive κατενόησεν immediately following, as well as with the drift of Paul's entire argument. In order to solve this difficulty the assumption is perhaps justifiable, that the words μὴ ἀσθενήσας τῇ πίστει are to be taken p r o l e p t i c a l l y, and that the true consequent clause does not begin till the twentieth vs. (εἰς δὲ τὴν ἐπαγγελίαν etc.). The words κατενόησεν etc. form, then, not so much a parenthetic insertion to designate more precisely the passage of the O. T. which the apostle had in mind, as an antithesis to the following οὐ διεκρίθη, such as is otherwise wont to be indicated by the particles μὲν ... δέ; hence the thought is as follows : *not wavering in faith, he considered, indeed, his senility and the deadness of Sarah's womb, but in reference to the promise of God* etc. The want of μέν would indeed be an offence in a classic writer ; but how often in all parts of the N. T. the sharpest antitheses are given merely by a simple δέ (see examples in § 149, 11 p. 364 and the note on p. 121), or even by καί (see the examples under § 149 8, b) p. 361 sq.), is well known; how much more occasion for this liberty was there here, where the writer might have contented himself with the simple participle (κατανοήσας), but, as he wrote, was precluded from that by the ἀσθενήσας which he had just used. This construction of the passage, moreover, is by no means destitute of parallels in the composition of the apostle. On the contrary, a number of passages stand in the plainest analogy to it : where two members of a sentence are connected with each other by οὐκ ... ἀλλά (δέ), and yet the thought in the first member is not to be denied absolutely, but only r e l a t i v e l y i n r e f e r e n c e t o t h e l e a d i n g t h o u g h t, in order, as Winer 497 (462) aptly says, " to direct undivided attention to the second and principal thought, the first comparatively disappearing from view," accordingly for r h e t o r i c a l reasons; cf. Fritzsche on Mark, Exc. II. Such passages are — from the historical writings Matt. x. 20 ; Mark ix. 37 ; Luke x. 20 ; John xii. 44 ; Acts v. 4 ; — from the Epistles, 1 Cor. xv. 10 ; 1 Thess. iv. 8, cf. also 1 Cor. i. 17 and de Wette's Comment. As in all these passages the writer hurries over the negative and parenthetic thought to the second and positive member, so Paul above hurries over the first and positive member to the second and negative (οὐ διεκρίθη).

OTHER PARTICLES.

B. § 149, m. 1; H. §§ 875; 795 a.; C. § 711 a.; J. §§ 626, Obs. 1; 696, Obs. 5.

Ὡς, οὕτως. The combination of ὡς with a preposition of direction **1** (*versus*) seems to have been unknown to the N. T. writers; for in the only passage where it occurs (Acts xvii. 14 ὡς ἐπί Grsb. Tdf. [eds. 2, 7]), the most important authorities [cod. Sin. also] read ἕως ἐπί, which Lchm. [so Tdf. Treg.] has adopted. The accented ὥς for οὕτως also is not found.

It is an extension of the familiar idiom by virtue of which οὕτως stands after participial clauses in order to resume them again in the conclusion (§ 144, 21 p. 306), when, the participial clause being wanting, this adverb by a somewhat **307** easy and popular mode of expression completely takes the place of the participle; as, Acts vii. 8 ἔδωκεν αὐτῷ δια-θήκην περιτομῆς· καὶ οὕτως (i.e. after this happened) ἐγέννησεν τὸν Ἰσαάκ, xxviii. 14; 1 Cor. ix. 24 οὐκ οἴδατε etc.; οὕτως (i.e. τοῦτο εἰδότες) τρέχετε, xiv. 25; Gal. vi. 2; 1 Thess. iv. 17; 2 Pet. i. 11.

In this way it passes over insensibly, like the Latin *sic*, into the meaning of the connective *then*, *so then*, as Acts xvii. 33; Rev. iii. 16. Quite analogous to this is its use after a protasis with εἰ (almost pleonastically like the German *so*, but more emphatic and resuming the protasis) to mark the beginning of the apodosis; as, 1 Thess. iv. 14 εἰ γὰρ πιστεύομεν ὅτι Ἰησοῦς ἀπέθανεν καὶ ἀνέστη, οὕτως καὶ ὁ θεὸς ἄξει etc., Rev. xi. 5 εἴ τις αὐτοὺς θέλει ἀδικῆσαι, οὕτως δεῖ αὐτὸν ἀποκτανθῆναι.

B. § 149, m. 2; H. § 508 b.; C. § 566 a.; J. § 882, 1.

Ἵνα. Of the elliptical use of ἵνα τί (equiv. to διὰ τί; *wherefore?*) **2** with an Indicative following (which occurs even in the earlier writers: Aristoph., Plato), there are many examples in the Old Test. as well as the New, and in later writers generally; as, Matt. ix. 4 ἵνα τί ἐνθυμεῖσθε πονηρὰ ἐν ταῖς καρδίαις ὑμῶν; xxvii. 46; Luke xiii. 7; Acts iv. 25 (quotn.), vii. 26; 1 Cor. x. 29; cf. Herm. ad Vig. p. 847.

B. § 149, m. 3; H. §§ 868; 869; C. § 701, N.; D. p. 571; J. §§ 800 sq.; 802 Obs. 8.

Ὅτι. Like the English *that* (cf. Germ. *dass*, Ital. *che*, French **3** *que*), ὅτι is the most frequent (subordinating) conjunction, and employed in manifold phrases; for, besides its common and most general sense (*that*), like the corresponding particles just mentioned in other languages, it is used sometimes pleo-nastically, sometimes elliptically, and sometimes passes over into the signification of other and more pointed particles (especially *because*).

On the pleonastic use of ὅτι after verba dicendi see § 139, 51 p. 245.

To the elliptical, belongs the expression τί ὅτι (which may be compared with the Lat. *quid quod;* but it is uttered without any rhetorical emphasis) in such sentences as Luke ii. 49 τί ὅτι ἐζητεῖτε με; (*why is it that* etc.), Acts v. 4, 9 ; Mark ii. 16 Lchm., — where, however, Tdf. [so Treg.] after cod B has given the preference to the interrogative ὅτι (§ 139, 59 p. 252), — and often in the Sept., as Gen. xviii. 13 ; xliv. 4 ; Judg. ix. 28, etc.; with the ellipsis supplied, John xiv. 22 τί γέγονεν ὅτι ἡμῖν μέλλεις ἐμφανίζειν σεαυτόν; John vii. 35 ποῦ οὗτος μέλλει πορεύεσθαι, ὅτι ἡμεῖς οὐχ εὑρήσομεν αὐτόν; is to be explained by a different kind of ellipsis; it arises from the two thoughts *Whither will he go?* and *How is it to be that we are not to find him?* united into a single sentence by abbreviation, in popular fashion. Similar is Matt. xvi. 7 οἱ δὲ διελογίζοντο λέγοντες· ὅτι ἄρτους οὐκ ἐλάβομεν, where *he says this because,* or *he has reference to the fact that* etc, is to be supplied. Of an elliptical nature, further, is the combination (peculiar to Paul) ὡς ὅτι in the sense of *quasi ;* 2 Thess. ii. 2 ὡς ὅτι ἐνέστηκεν ἡ ἡμέρα τοῦ κυρίου abbreviated from, *as* (happens when it is the case) *that the day of the Lord is at hand.* Similar, but with more of the common meaning of ὅτι, accordingly *as if that, because,* is the 308 use of ὡς ὅτι in 2 Cor. v. 19 ; xi. 21 (see Meyer on the passages, and the instances of ὡς ὅτι which he quotes from Greek writers; and on the not infrequent use of ὡς ὅτι in later writers, especially in the Alexandrian literary language, see Bast on Greg. Cor. p. 52). ὅτι equivalent to δῆλον ὅτι in 1 Tim. vi. 7 Lchm. [T. Tr. א*] (Tdf. [eds. 2, 7] δῆλον ὅτι) is exceptional. On the elliptical οὐχ ὅτι see § 150, 1 p. 372.

B. § 149, m. 4; H. § 872; C. § 701 f. sq.; J. §§ 850 sq.; 860, 5.

4　　*Εἰ.* The elliptical use of εἰ in oaths is a Hebraism current in the Sept. and transferred thence into the N. T. This εἰ arose from the literal translation of the Hebrew אִם, which imparts a negative force to the contents of the oath, and hence אִם לֹא a positive force *indeed! of a truth!,* see Gesen. Lehrg. p. 844 ; Gr. § 152, 2 f.

Examples of εἰ from the Sept. are, 1 Sam. iii. 14; 2 Sam. xx. 20 ; xi. 11 ; Ps. xcv. 11, etc., less frequently ἐάν Cant. ii. 7 ; Judg. v. 8, also the Infin. with μή Gen. xxi. 23, (the affirmative intensification אִם לֹא is either not translated at all, as Josh. xiv. 9 ; Isa. xiv. 24 ; Job xxx. 25 ; xxxi. 36, or by ἦ μήν Job i. 11 or εἰ μή xxii. 20, etc.). This mode of expression is evidently founded in an ellipsis (Aposiopesis), a thought being reserved in the mind which in other passages of the O. T. is expressed, and is commonly translated by the Sept. as follows :

τάδε ποιήσαι σοι ὁ θεὸς καὶ τάδε προσθείη, e.g. 1 Sam. iii. 17; 2 Sam.
iii. 35, etc. In the N. T. this εἰ is found in Mark viii. 12 (where it is
interpreted in the various readings by οὐ), and several times as a
quotation from Ps. xcv. 11 in the Ep. to the Heb., viz. iii. 11 cf. 18;
iv. 3, 5. On the other hand, εἰ μήν in Heb. vi. 14 is positive, like
the ἦ μήν in use elsewhere, and (according to Etym. mag. 416, 50)
only a different (itacistic) way of writing it; and in fact, in Gen. xxii.
17 (whence the above passage is taken) the MSS. offer both readings.
But it is construed with the Indic., except in Judith i. 12 where the
Infin. (current in Greek writers) is given: ὤμοσε εἰ μὴν ἐκδικήσειν.

The elliptical use of the combined particles εἰ μή (which have
become almost a single conjunction) in the sense of *except, nisi,*
after a preceding negation, is so general that passages in which the
predicate is added, as Mark vi. 5, are very rare; and the phrase
became so established in this sense, that, like εἴτε ... εἴτε in § 139, 22
p. 220 sq., it was retained even where the construction would sooner
lead us to expect ἐὰν μή (Matt. xxvi. 42; Gal. ii. 16, etc., cf. 6 p. 360),
as Mark vi. 8 ἵνα μηδὲν αἴρωσιν εἰ μὴ ῥάβδον etc., ix. 9, etc., and the
clause dependent on it was insensibly changed even as respects its
form into a leading clause, as 1 Cor. vii. 17 εἰ μὴ, ἑκάστῳ ὡς ἐμέρισεν ὁ
κύριος, οὕτως περιπατείτω,— with which may be compared the
similar grammatical phenomena in connection with ἵνα (§ 139, 37
p. 233), ὅτι (§ 139, 53 p. 246), ὥστε (§ 139, 50 p. 243). All that has
been said holds also with more or less force as respects the extended
combinations of particles εἰ μή τι (on which see § 139, 20, 22
pp. 219 sq.) and ἐκτὸς εἰ μή (see ibid 22 p. 221, and § 148, 13
p. 355).

B. § 149, m. 5; H. § 877, 5; D. p. 569; § 617 Obs.; J. §§ 839, Obs.; 860, 2.

'Επεί. In consequence of a brachylogical mode of expression,   5
this conjunction plainly has in several passages the signification
since or *for otherwise,* — it being necessary to supply or repeat
from the immediately preceding context the supposition suggested by our particle *otherwise, else.*

For example: Rom. iii. 6 μὴ ἄδικος ὁ θεός ..., ἐπεὶ πῶς κρινεῖ ὁ θεὸς
τὸν κόσμον; *for otherwise how* etc. (sc. εἰ ἄδικος ὁ θεός), xi. 6 ἐπεὶ ἡ
χάρις οὐκέτι γίνεται χάρις (sc. εἰ ἐξ ἔργων λεῖμμα γέγονεν or simply εἰ ἐξ 309
ἔργων γίνεταί τι); ... ἐπεὶ τὸ ἔργον οὐκέτι ἔστιν ἔργον (sc. εἰ χάριτι or
χάρις sc. ἔστιν), xi. 22 ἐπεὶ καὶ σὺ ἐκκοπήσῃ, sc. ἐὰν μὴ ἐπιμείνῃς etc.,
Heb. ix. 26; x. 2 in both which instances a hypothetical protasis of
the fourth kind is to be supplied for the apodosis, which is evidently
constructed on this model (cf. § 139, 14 and 15 p. 216). So, too,
1 Cor. v. 10, on which see § 151, 19 p. 390. See besides the very
similar idiom with ἀλλά in 14 p. 369.

B. § 149, m. 6.

6 ἐάν. By a certain inaccuracy of expression ἐάν stands once apparently for ὃς ἄν in Mark x. 30, 31 οὐδείς ἐστιν ὃς ἀφῆκεν οἰκίαν ... , ἐὰν μὴ λάβῃ etc. (D ὃς ἄν). This construction arose and is to be explained in the same way as εἰ μή (ἐὰν μή) *nisi*, by which the preceding negative is destroyed (see above, 4 p. 359), so that the meaning here is nearly as follows: *no one leaves* etc. *unless he receives*, i.e. e v e r y o n e who leaves etc. will receive.

The contracted κἄν (from καὶ ἐάν) stands several times, by an ellipsis, without a finite verb (cf. Demosth. p. 415, 24; Soph. El. 1483) almost adverbially in the sense of *if only, at least* (in which sense it occurs times without number in later writers and the Apocrypha); as, Acts v. 15 ἵνα ἐρχομένου Πέτρου κἂν ἡ σκιὰ ἐπισκιάσῃ i.e. *if* (it were) *only his shadow*, Mark vi. 56; 2 Cor. xi. 16 εἰ δὲ μή γε, κἂν ὡς ἄφρονα δέξασθέ με.

B. § 149, m. 7; H. § 860; C. §§ 713 h.; 511, 513; D. p. 569; J. §§ 875 Obs. 3; 779 Obs. 3.

7 ἤ. To the examples cited here of ἢ οὐ after a negative (or interrogative) clause instead of the simple ἤ, a parallel is apparently given in 1 Thess. ii. 19 τίς γὰρ ἡμῶν ἐλπὶς ἢ χαρὰ ... ἢ οὐχὶ καὶ ὑμεῖς; Yet since the antecedent question is not to be taken in an exclusive (negative) sense, as the καὶ before ὑμεῖς proves, the clause ἢ οὐχὶ etc. is to be joined to the first question as a second, which, because it assumes an affirmative answer, is negatived by οὐ.

On the other hand, indubitable instances are found of the other power of ἤ mentioned here, viz. to impart to a Positive notion the force of a Comparative; as, Matt. xviii. 8; Mark ix. 43, 45 καλόν ἐστίν σε κυλλὸν, χωλὸν εἰσελθεῖν ἤ etc., Luke xv. 7 χαρὰ ἔσται (sc. μείζων) ἐπὶ ἑνὶ ἁμαρτωλῷ μετανοοῦντι ἢ etc. Accordingly it imparts to the signification of θέλω the force of *malle* in 1 Cor. xiv. 19, and to λυσιτελεῖν the force of *satius esse* in Luke xvii. 2; cf. the parallel passages above from Matt. and Mark. See the similar phenomena under ὑπέρ (p. 335) and παρά with the Acc. (p. 339).

B. § 149, m. 8; H. §§ 855-57; C. § 701; D. §§ 549 sqq.; J. §§ 758 sq.

8 τέ, καί. The particle τε, which is but rarely employed in the Gospels, is used by Luke in the Acts with fondness, sometimes simply for the ordinary καί (ii. 37; iv. 33, etc.), sometimes in the combination τε καί. But where these two particles do not connect immediately with one another two similar or parallel terms, they can only signify *and also*, the τὲ in such case belonging to the sentence and καί to the single word, as Acts xxi. 28 οὗτός ἐστιν ὁ ἄνθρωπος ὁ ... πάντας πανταχῇ

διδάσκων, ἔτι τε καὶ ῞Ελληνας εἰσήγαγεν, Rom. i. 27 Tdf.[1] [cod. Sin.].
In the reverse order, καί connects the sentence, τὲ the particular term, **310**
as Acts xxvi. 10 καὶ πολλούς τε τῶν ἁγίων κατέκλεισα etc. A double
τὲ rarely appears except in composition or with corresponding particles
(εἴτε, μήτε, ἐάν τε), as Acts xxvi. 16; xvii. 4; Heb. vi. 2.

Καί is by far the most frequent of all the Greek particles in
the N. T.; and as it is used not only beyond comparison more
frequently than in the Greek literary language, but also in
another sense often, or rather under other circumstances, it
contributes much to the peculiar complexion of the N. T. style.
This extended use of καί (particularly in the Gospels, see § 144,
1 p. 288 sq.) proceeds from the practice, characteristic of all
popular languages, of placing in juxtaposition, with the simplest
connection and as independent little sentences, the several parts
especially of an historic narrative, which in a more choice style
are wont to be wrought together into a single whole. In the
Homeric language, and in part also in Herodotus, this takes
place commonly, indeed, by means of several of the many little
copulative conjunctions (τέ, δέ, ῥά, etc.); but in the N. T.,
predominantly by καί. Hence connection by means of καί
appears, times without number, in part for participial constructions (§ 144, 1 and 2 pp. 288 sq.), in part where the
Greeks would have employed divers other particles. But we
are not on this account warranted in supposing that it anywhere includes any other than its characteristic and proper
signification (*and, also, even*). The leading cases in which
its use deviates more or less from the ordinary usage are the
following:

a) With the use of καί in place of a Participle agrees its employment, where, as a rule, the first of two independent sentences
connected by καί expresses the relation of time for the second (the
leading) sentence; as, Matt. xxvi. 45 ἤγγικεν ἡ ὥρα καὶ ὁ υἱὸς τοῦ
ἀνθρώπου παραδίδοται, Mark xv. 25 ἦν δὲ ὥρα τρίτη καὶ ἐσταύρωσαν
αὐτόν, Luke xix. 43; xxiii. 44; John x. 22 Lchm., Acts v. 7; Heb.
viii. 8. Cf. the various constructions with καὶ ἐγένετο § 141, 6 p.
276.

b) Very commonly the N. T. language, particularly in the Gospels,

---

[1] Here, however, the other reading (δὲ Lchm. [Treg. *marg.*]) seems to be preferable; the apostle, instead of connecting the second member by τὲ (οἵ τε ἄρσενες
etc.), having given his discourse a different and more emphatic turn by means of
the words ὁμοίως δὲ καί. Cf. Wine ι 571 (531).

46

contents itself with this most simple method of connecting sentences
where other Greek writers are wont to employ either a simple
adversative particle (δέ, ἀλλά, μέντοι), or the corresponsive μὲν ...
δέ; as, Luke xx. 19; Mark xii. 12 ἐζήτουν αὐτὸν κρατῆσαι, καὶ ἐφοβήθησαν τὸν ὄχλον, Matt. xi. 25 ἔκρυψας ... καὶ ἀπεκάλυψας, Mark vii. 24;
John viii. 49 τιμῶ ... καὶ ὑμεῖς ἀτιμάζετε, vi. 36 (καὶ ... καί), xvii. 11
οὐκέτι εἰμὶ ... καὶ οὗτοι εἰσίν, vii. 30 (compared with 44), Luke xviii.
311 13 [Tdf. with ℵ and] (B ὁ δέ), 34 (D ἀλλ'), 1 Thess. ii. 18 (even
after a preceding μέν, cf. § 126, 3 p. 102, and Hartung, Part. II. p. 410),
Jas. iv. 2, etc.   On καὶ οὐ after positive clauses see also particularly
below, 13 e) p. 368.

c) In comparative sentences after ὡς, καθώς, the leading clause or
the member corresponding to ὡς etc. is often introduced merely by
καί, so that it then seems to stand for οὕτως.   More correct, however,
is the assumption that οὕτως drops out before καί, and καί while retaining its own proper meaning (i.e. *also*) takes upon itself besides
the relation to be expressed by οὕτως; as, Matt. vi. 10 γενηθήτω τὸ
θέλημά σου ὡς ἐν οὐρανῷ καὶ ἐπὶ γῆς *as in heaven, so* (*also*) *on earth*,
Acts vii. 51 καθὼς οἱ πατέρες ὑμῶν καὶ ὑμεῖς, John vi. 57 καθὼς ἐγὼ ζῶ ...,
καὶ ὁ τρώγων με ζήσει etc., xiii. 15, 33; Gal. i. 9; Phil. i. 20; 1 John
ii. 18, etc.   That a similar use occurs also in Greek authors, see
(among others) Kühner on Xen. Mem. 2, 2, 2.

d) There are several passages also, where, after an antecedent
dependent clause (protasis), the leading or consequent clause
begins with καί, very much as in Greek authors so often with (the
copulative and adversative) δέ (see B. § 149 m. 9; J. § 759, Obs. 3);
as, Luke ii. 21 ὅτε ἐπλήσθησαν αἱ ἡμέραι ..., καὶ ἐκλήθη τὸ ὄνομα
αὐτοῦ Ἰησοῦς, cf. 22; Acts xiii. 19 ὡς ἐτροφοφόρησεν αὐτοὺς ..., καὶ
καθελὼν etc., Phil. i. 22 (where after ἔργου no great punctuation mark
is to be placed, cf. § 144, 21 p. 306), 2 Cor. ii. 2 εἰ γὰρ ἐγὼ λυπῶ ὑμᾶς,
καὶ τίς ὁ εὐφραίνων με etc., Jas. iv. 15; Rev. iii. 20 Tdf. [cod. Sin.],
x. 7 (see deWette).[1]   Sentences in which the consequent clause is
preceded by καὶ ἰδού, as Luke vii. 12; Acts i. 10; x. 17 Tdf. [ed. 8
drops καί], have a predominantly Oriental (or O. T.) complexion.

On the other hand, the N. T. accords with ordinary usage
as respects,

e) The union by means of καί of two adjectival notions which are
not co-ordinate, as in the case of πολύς: Luke iii. 18; John xx.

---

[1] With these sentences belongs also Jas. iv. 15 ἐὰν ὁ κύριος θελήσῃ καὶ ζήσομεν
καὶ ποιήσομεν etc., where, however, it is doubtful whether the consequent clause
begins with the first καί or the second; but grammatically it is preferable to begin
it with the first καί, especially as the text now stands with a Future in both instances [so Lchm. Tdf. Treg., after ℵ etc.].

30 πολλὰ μὲν οὖν καὶ ἄλλα σημεῖα ἐποίησεν Ἰησοῦς, Acts xxv. 7 πολλα καὶ βαρέα αἰτιώματα, Tit. i. 10.

f) καί in the sense of *as* (*ac*) after ὁ αὐτός is not met with in the N. T. (the Dative is always used instead, B. § 133, 2 f.). Only in a single passage has καί the meaning *as*, viz. Eph. iv. 10 ὁ καταβὰς αὐτός ἐστιν καὶ ὁ ἀναβάς, where probably the ὁ before αὐτός has been omitted owing to the ὁ before καταβάς, (yet cf. Meyer [or Ellic.] in loc.). The common phrases ὁμοίως καί, ὡσαύτως καί, and ὁ αὐτὸς καί, on the other hand, are of an entirely different nature, and in them καί has only the meaning *also* (Matt. xxii. 26; xxvii. 44; Mark xiv. 31; 1 Cor. vii. 7; xv. 48; 1 Thess. ii. 14, etc.); so too after a Relative, ὡς καί, ὁποῖος καί, ὅσῳ καί, on which the general use of καί after Relatives (§ 143, 5 p. 282 sq.) may be compared; as, Luke xi. 1; Acts xv. 8; xxvi. 29; Heb. viii. 6.

g) καί as strengthening the Comparative, like the Latin *etiam*: Matt. xi. 9 ναὶ λέγω ὑμῖν, καὶ περισσότερον προφήτου, John xiv. 12 (*and even*), 2 Cor. xii. 15 Tdf. [eds. 2, 7; 8, Treg. א* om.], Heb. viii. 6.

h) Although sentences with καί according to their grammatical form can contain nothing else than specifications additional to what precedes, yet these specifications may at the same time serve also as explanatory supplements to the antecedent sentence or notion, so that they then sustain the relation of an epexegetical adjunct 312 to the latter. In such cases we are wont to render the καί by *namely, and indeed*; as, John i. 16 ἐκ τοῦ πληρώματος αὐτοῦ πάντες ἐλάβομεν, καὶ χάριν ἀντὶ χάριτος, 1 Cor. iii. 5; xv. 38; Acts xxiii. 6 περὶ ἐλπίδος καὶ ἀναστάσεως νεκρῶν ἐγὼ κρίνομαι.

i) On καὶ ... δέ see 10 p. 364; on καὶ in continuation of a negative (equiv. to οὐδέ etc.) 13 d) p. 368; and on the (apparent) omission of καί 14 p. 369.

B. § 149, m. 9; H. § 862; C. §§ 701 c.q.; 705 a.; D. §§ 559 sq.; J. §§ 764 sq.; 768 sq.

Δέ. Owing to the prevalent employment of καί as a particle **9** of transition and continuation, the number of passages where the particle δέ is used, as in the classics, rather copulatively, i.e. to subjoin a subordinate circumstance in a supplementary way or to form a connection with what follows, is comparatively small; as, Matt. xxi. 3; John vi. 10; Acts vi. 2; xxiv. 17; Rom. viii. 8, etc.

In other passages δέ has probably found its way by means of the copyists into the text instead of the more common particles of transition in the N. T. (γάρ, καί), which particles have sometimes been restored (e.g. Col. iii. 25; 1 Cor. vii. 38; Mark xvi. 8 Lchm. [Treg. Tdf. cod. Sin.], xiv. 2; xv. 33; Luke xii. 42, etc.); or δέ was first added by the copyists (as οὖν, καί often were also) to avoid the asyndeton displeasing to a Greek ear; this has been done times without number in John, as i. 26 Tdf. [Treg. cod. Sin.], 40, 43; ii. 4, 17; iv. 31, 50, 54; v. 29; vi. 43, 45, etc. Cf. § 151, 33 p. 402.

Of δέ in the Apodosis we find but one example, Acts xi. 17 εἰ οὖν τὴν ἴσην δωρεὰν ἔδωκεν ..., ἐγὼ δὲ τίς ἤμην etc. This δὲ Tdf. [eds. 2, 7; not 8] adopted, in opposition indeed to the oldest MSS. [Sin. also]; but this (genuine classic) use is so rare in the N.T. that we can understand the omission of the δέ by the copyists (cf. Acts xx. 4, 5). Tdf. has now adopted ὁ δὲ [ed. 7; in ed. 8 dropped δέ again] in the apodosis in 1 Pet. iv. 18 also, after cod. Vat. On the other hand, ἀλλά is often found in the apodosis in Paul's writings, e.g. Rom. vi. 5; 1 Cor. iv. 15; ix. 2.

B. § 149, m. 10; H. § 856 b.; J. § 769.

10 Καὶ ... δέ. Of the combination καὶ ... δέ in the sense of *and also*, (when the antithesis is stronger *but also*), there are a great many indubitable instances: Matt. x. 18 καὶ ἐπὶ ἡγεμόνας δὲ ἀχθήσεσθε, John viii. 16 (οὐ κρίνω) · καὶ ἐὰν κρίνω δὲ ἐγώ etc., Matt. xvi. 18; Mark iv. 36 Tdf., Luke ii. 35; John vi. 51; viii. 17; xv. 27; Acts iii. 24; xxii. 29; 2 Tim. iii. 12; Heb. ix. 21, etc.

B. § 149, m. 11; H. § 862 a.; C. § 701 sq.; D. § 559 sq.; J. § 764.

11 Μὲν ... δέ. In the use of these two particles the N. T. writers, especially Luke, the author of the Ep. to the Hebrews, and Paul, are by no means unpractised. Yet it is not to be overlooked, that, in general, antithetic relationship is far from always being indicated by these particles where native Greeks would hardly have omitted them. In their stead, N.T. writers contented themselves often with the simple δέ, and even merely with καί (see 8 b) p. 361 sq.).

Compare, for instance, the antithetic setting of the language in the maledictions (ταλανισμοί) in the twenty-third chap. of Matt., particularly vss. 3, 4, 8, 11, 23, 24, 25, and often besides in the same chapter. Here, indeed, there is no sharp antithesis; yet the Greeks would have employed the form of antithesis: μὲν ... δέ. Only in vss. 27, 28 is μὲν ... δέ actually used. Further, see John v. 29; viii. 15; Jas. ii. 2, 10, 14; iv. 6, the examples in § 127, 32 note p. 121, § 148, 14 p. 356, and many others especially from the Gospels and the Apocalypse (in which μέν is not used throughout). Hence it is probable that, as we saw above (9 p. 363 sq.) in the case of δέ so here, μέν first found its way into the text by the aid of (Grecizing) copyists; see particularly

in the recent editions, Mark i. 8; ix. 12 Tdf. (cf. Matt. xvii. 11), Acts
v. 23; 2 Cor. iv. 12; 1 Cor. xii. 20 var.; Matt. xxv. 33 var. Whether
in Rom. vi. 21 also (τὸ μὲν γὰρ τέλος etc.) μέν is to be expunged [so
Tdf. Treg. in text, with א*], because the following νυνὶ δέ does not
correspond with it, is much to be doubted. Cf. 1 Cor. iii. 4 in b)
below.

B. § 149, m. 13; H. § 862, 1 a.; D. §§ 562; 567; J. § 765, 7 sq.

Μέν. Every clause with μέν to which no following clause **12**
with δέ corresponds, is properly to be regarded as an anacoluthon.   Nevertheless, most of the instances of this sort which
occur in the N. T. admit (as in the classics) of being referred
to certain classes, of which the most evident, perhaps, are the
following:

a) Instead of δέ a different adversative particle is substituted; thus
ἀλλά in Acts iv. 16; Rom. xiv. 20; 1 Cor. xiv. 17; πλήν in Luke
xxii. 22, — even καί, see 8 b) p. 361 sq., and on ὃ μὲν ... καὶ ἄλλο and
the like § 126, 3 p. 102.

b) In enumerations the particle is often dropped in the second
member when it is sufficiently marked as such by some other word,
particularly by ἔπειτα, as John xi. 6; Jas. iii. 17; similarly 1 Cor.
xii. 28, — yet here the anacoluthon is stronger, the writer continuing
his enumeration (instead of with the pronominal οὓς δέ) by means of
the adverbial expressions πρῶτον, ἔπειτα, etc. In like manner δὲ is
wanting with ἄλλοι after οἱ μέν in many MSS. [Sin. also] in John vii.
12 Tdf. (cf. 9 p. 263). In 1 Cor. iii. 4 ἐγὼ μέν is immediately followed
indeed by ἕτερος δέ, but the two corresponding terms are strictly τὶς
and ἕτερος; yet this slight inaccuracy does not mar the perspicuity of
the whole.

c) Sometimes the first member of the antithesis is marked by μέν,
but the subsequent δέ was of necessity dropped because the writer
suddenly chose a n o t h e r c o n s t r u c t i o n which did not permit the
addition of δέ: thus Acts iii. 13 where the antithesis is contained in
the participial clause (ἐκείνου κρίναντος), xxvii. 21 where the antithesis
is indicated by the more forceful καὶ τὰ νῦν in the 22d verse; so it is
in Heb. xii. 9 by οὐ πολὺ μᾶλλον.

d) Sometimes the first member, marked by πρῶτον μέν, has no corresponding ἔπειτα, or other construction in its stead, the writer having
lingered so long over the first member that he loses the grammatical
sequence of thought, as Acts i. 1; Rom. i. 8; iii. 2; 1 Cor. xi. 18;
but the same thing happens also without any such reason, the writer
leaving it to the reader alone to complete the antithesis begun (the
completion being sometimes plainly s u g g e s t e d b y t h e c o n t e x t)
and beginning a new thought which has a greater claim upon him:

see e.g. Acts iii. 21; xix. 4 Tdf. [ed. 8 om. μέν; so cod. Sin.]; xxviii. 22; Rom. vii. 12; x. 1; xi. 13 Tdf. [ed. 8 adds οὖν; so Lchm. Treg.], 2 Cor. xii. 12; Col. ii. 23; Heb. vi. 16 Tdf. [ed. 8 om. μέν; so cod. Sin.]. Now since the copyists in such passages easily took offence at **314** μέν owing to the missing δέ, we find occurring here just the opposite of what was described in 11 p. 364, viz. the omission of μέν in the mss.; see Acts iii. 13; xix. 4; Rom. xi. 13; Heb. vi. 16. On μὲν οὖν see 16 p. 370.

B. § 149, m. 15; H. §§ 858. 859; C. §§ 701 a. e.; 713 b. c.; J. §§ 775; 776.

13   Οὐδέ, μηδέ· οὔτε, μήτε. a) The rule, that the double conjunction οὐδέ (μηδέ) ... οὐδέ (μηδέ) can only appear in continuation of an antecedent simple negative and to connect a new (negative) clause, is found confirmed in the N. T. almost throughout; see Matt. vi. 26; xii. 19; x. 9, 10; Mark xiii. 32; Luke xiv. 12; John i. 13, 25; Rom. xiv. 21; Col. ii. 21; 1 Thess. ii. 3 Lchm. [Treg. Tdf. cod. Sin.], Rev. v. 3; vii. 16; ix. 4.

Hence, examples to the contrary must either be so explained that the first negative is copulative and connects the entire sentence with what precedes, making reference to some negatived portion of the same (and so does not mean *neither*, but *also not*), as Gal. i. 12 Lchm. [Treg. cod. Sin.] (cf. p. 367 note), — or the negative stands for *ne ... quidem*, as Mark viii. 26 (μηδὲ εἰσέλθῃς ... μηδὲ εἴπῃς) is interpreted, see Meyer; yet the received reading here seems critically to be still quite unsettled, see Fritzsche in loc. and Lchm. praef. p. 44. In Vat. Sin. and a few other mss. the second clause is wholly wanting, and Sin. has simply μή instead of the first μηδέ; Tdf. has now [ed. 8] adopted this reading. In this way certainly we get rid of all difficulties.

What holds true of the double conjunction, holds also for the simple οὐδέ (μηδέ), inasmuch as in the signification *and not* (not *ne ... quidem*) it invariably forms the continuation of an antecedent negative, as well in sentences and larger portions of sentences, as with single words. Examples abound: Matt. vi. 25, 28; Luke x. 4; xii. 24, 33; Acts iv. 18; ix. 9; Rom. ix. 16; 2 Tim. i. 8; Gal. i. 1; 2 Pet. i. 8; Heb. ix. 12; xiii. 5, etc.

b) On the other hand, the double conjunction οὔτε (μήτε) ... οὔτε (μήτε), as a negatived καί ... καί, stands as well with entire sentences as particular parts of sentences, sometimes without a previous negative, sometimes with a preceding negative; in this latter case, the members negatived by οὔτε (μήτε) constitute as a rule a composite whole within the

limits of a sentence already negatived, — not a continuation of that sentence, (just as we say, *not ... neither ...
nor*).

Examples: without an antecedent negative, Matt. vi. 20; xi.
18; Mark xiv. 68 Lchm. [Treg. Tdf. cod. Sin.], John v. 37; Acts xv.
10; Rom. viii. 38; 1 Cor. iii. 7; viii. 8; Rev. iii. 15, etc.;   with
an antecedent negative, 2 Thess. ii. 2 εἰς τὸ μὴ ταχέως σαλευθῆναι ὑμᾶς
μηδὲ θροεῖσθαι, μήτε διὰ πνεύματος μήτε διὰ λόγου μήτε δι᾽ ἐπιστολῆς,
Matt. v. 34 sq., xii. 32; Luke ix. 3; Jas. v. 12, and according to
preponderant ms. authority [Sin. also] Acts xxiii. 8 Lchm. [Treg. Tdf.],
ἄγγελον and πνεῦμα then constituting the two members (τὰ ἀμφότερα)
of the negative partition. With the (more difficult and probable)
reading μηδὲ etc., the two members of the partition are to be taken
differently, see the note below. But in John i. 25 the reading now
is οὐκ ... οὐδέ ... οὐδέ, according to rule.

Consequently a single οὔτε (μήτε) after a preceding simple negative
(οὐ, οὐδείς) is, strictly taken, incorrect; since οὔτε contains no continued negation. And, in point of fact, recent criticism has enabled 315
us to set aside on ms. authority several such instances, see e.g. Mark
iii. 20; v. 3; xiv. 68 Lchm. [Treg. Tdf. cod. Sin.], Acts iv. 12; 1 Cor.
iii. 2; Eph. iv. 27; Rev. xii. 8; xx. 4, etc. Where it occurs, we
must of necessity supply an additional οὔτε after the first negative, as
in Rev. v. 4 οὐδεὶς ἄξιος εὑρέθη ἀνοῖξαι τὸ βιβλίον οὔτε βλέπειν αὐτό
where the parallel denial of both clauses (ἀνοῖξαι ... βλέπειν) is evident,
and so an οὔτε is to be supplied before ἀνοῖξαι. Hence in vs. 3 also
οὔτε is to be read with Lchm.[T.Tr. Sin.]before βλέπειν, inasmuch as
it is only in this way that the two members ἀνοῖξαι ... βλέπειν separate
themselves perspicuously and plainly from the preceding οὐδέ ... οὐδέ.[1]

---

[1] Where it is not possible to supply an οὔτε, the first (simple) negative must
directly take the place of οὔτε or μήτε (cf. Klotz ad Devar. II p. 709). This
case, however, occurs only extremely seldom, and is in every instance accompanied
by considerable variation in the mss., and consequently in the editions also. Thus,
in the above passage from Mark (xiv. 68), Tdf. in his 7th ed. reads οὐκ οἶδα οὔτε
ἐπίσταμαι, but in his 8th ed. οὔτε ... οὔτε again after codd. Vat. and Sin.; the
reading of cod. B in Luke vii. 33 (μὴ ... μήτε) is not adopted; and in Rev. ix. 20
(where Lchm. [so Treg.] reads οὔτε μετενόησαν), Tdf. [eds. 2, 7] has restored the
correct reading οὐ μετεν. (for which it would be still better to read [so T.] with cod.
Sin. οὐδέ) Jas. iii. 12 has been corrupted (see Lchm. I. præf. p. xliv). But when
οὐδέ (μηδέ) is followed by an οὔτε (μήτε), the οὐδέ negatives (and connects)
the entire sentence, and before the first predicate or member an οὔτε is to be
supplied, as in the above passages (cf. Hartung I. p. 201). Thus Gal. i. 12 Tdf.
οὐδὲ γὰρ ἐγὼ παρὰ ἀνθρώπου (sc. οὔτε) παρέλαβον αὐτὸ οὔτε ἐδιδάχθην. In Acts
xxiii. 8, with the reading μηδὲ ἄγγελον μήτε πνεύμα (so Tdf. eds. 2, 7, yet see
above) the two notions ἄγγελον and πνεῦμα are combined into a single main
idea (in connection with which the omission of μήτε before ἄγγελον was very

c) If the second or any following member is p o s i t i v e, οὔτε (μήτε) ... τε is used (as in Latin *neque ... et*) according to the grammatical rule ; as,

Acts xxvii. 20 μήτε ἡλίου μήτε ἄστρων ... χειμῶνός τε etc. Sometimes we find the less classic combination (see Klotz ad Devar. II. p. 714; App. B. C. 1, 29; Jos. B. J. 1, 13, 6; 2, 18, 5) οὔτε ... καί, 3 John 10 οὔτε αὐτὸς ἐπιδέχεται τοὺς ἀδελφοὺς καὶ ... κωλύει καὶ ... ἐκβάλλει, John iv. 11 οὔτε ἄντλημα ἔχεις καὶ τὸ φρέαρ ἐστὶν βαθύ.

d) From this last-named construction we must carefully distinguish the usage according to which καί stands after a simple negative (οὐ, μή, — but also after οὐδείς, μήποτε, μήπως, etc.) and connects the following clause so closely with the preceding clause (already negatived) that it is brought with the latter under the influence of the same negative, so that 316 καί then takes completely the place of the οὐδέ (μηδέ) used by the Greeks under such circumstances.

See Matt. x. 38; vii. 6; xiii. 15; x. 26; Luke xii. 2, 58; John xii. 40; 1 Thess. iii. 5; Heb. xii. 15; Rev. vi. 6, etc.

When the second clause with καί is a f f i r m a t i v e, the clauses do not belong directly together, and accordingly it is better to separate them by one of the larger punctuation marks; as, Heb. xii. 5; Rev. xii. 8, 9. Cf. e).

e) On the other hand, if after a preceding a f f i r m a t i v e clause the following clause uniting with it to form a single thought is to be n e g a t i v e d, only καὶ οὐ, καὶ μή can be employed, since οὐδέ (meaning *and not*) and οὔτε uniformly assume an antecedent negation. And here it is to be noticed, that this combination is introduced when the antithesis is the strongest (just because the antithesis is contained in the negative) ; the weaker contrast, on the contrary, is given by ἀλλ᾿ οὐ, ἀλλὰ μή, because ἀλλά, on the other hand, is the particle which acquires the sharpest adversative force (*but*, Germ.

natural) and constitute by virtue of the negative μηδὲ the continuation of the first (μὴ εἶναι ἀνάστασιν) ; so that then the τὰ ἀμφότερα following can congruously refer back to the two main ideas (resurrection and belief in spirits) thus separated. But in 1 Thess. ii. 3 the double οὐδέ is decidedly to be preferred, with Lchm. [Treg. Tdf. cod. Sin.]. The combination οὔτε ... οὐδέ (see Klotz l.c. p. 714) is anacoluthic, like μέν ... καί and the like, and does not occur in the N. T. except once in Acts ii. 31 cod. Vat. (not Sin.). But after a double οὔτε ... οὔτε the negative οὐδέ (i.e. *and not* or *not even*) can very well make its appearance again in continuation of the sentence thus negatived ; as, Luke xx. 35 Lchm. [Treg.], Acts xxiv. 13 Lchm. [Tdf. cod. Sin.]. On this cf. f) below.

sondern) after a preceding n e g a t i v e clause, inasmuch as it introduces the following affirmative and sets it over against the negative.

Examples are very frequent: John i. 20 ὡμολόγησεν καὶ οὐκ ἠρνήσατο, Luke i. 20 ἔσῃ σιωπῶν καὶ μὴ δυνάμενος λαλῆσαι, Rom. xii. 14 εὐλογεῖτε καὶ μὴ καταρᾶσθε, Matt. xxv. 42–44; xi. 17; xiii. 17; xxii. 3; xxiii. 3; John i. 5, 10, 11; iii. 10, 11, 12, 20; Luke iii. 8; vi. 37 etc., Rom. iii. 8; iv. 19 etc., Jas. i. 22, etc. — examples of ἀλλ' οὐ, John iii. 8 τὸ πνεῦμα πνεῖ ... ἀλλ' οὐκ οἶδας πόθεν ἔρχεται etc., xiii. 10 ὑμεῖς καθαροί ἐστε, ἀλλ' οὐχὶ πάντες etc.

But when καὶ οὐ or καὶ μή is introduced after a negatived sentence, the two sentences do not stand in a corresponsive relation, but are to be regarded more as independent sentences or clauses; as, Matt. xv. 32; Luke xii. 29; xviii. 2, etc.   Cf. d).

f) When a s i n g l e οὐδέ (as a rule in the midst of a sentence and without a preceding negative) contains an e m p h a t i c d e n i a l of the notion with which it is connected, it means *not even (ne ... quidem)*; as, Matt. vi. 29; Luke vii. 9; Acts xix. 2; 1 Cor. iii. 2; v. 1, etc.

Even after an antecedent negative it is possible to use this οὐδέ if no ambiguity arises, since similar negatives when multiplied do not destroy each other; as, Luke xviii. 13 οὐκ ἤθελεν οὐδὲ τοὺς ὀφθαλμοὺς ἐπᾶραι.   But whether in deteriorating Greek οὔτε is used, through negligence, instead of this οὐδέ, is a question that needs further investigation; the MSS. of the N. T. often exhibit it instead of οὐδέ, and Tdf. has now adopted it several times into the text (see Luke xii. 26 [ed. 7; ed. 8 οὐδέ, with Lchm. Treg. cod. Sin.], xx. 36 [so cod. Sin.], Mark iii. 20 [so cod. Sin.], and cf. v. 3 var., Theophilus ad Autol. 3. 29; Achil. Tat. 10. 20).

B. § 149, m. 16; H. § 863; C. § 701 b. N.; D. § 648 (1); J. § 773.

Ἀ λ λ ά. As ἐπεί, according to no. 5 above p. 359, sometimes has the 14 signification *for otherwise*, so ἀλλά in John xiii. 10 οὐκ ἔχει χρείαν ἢ τοὺς πόδας νίψασθαι, ἀλλ' ἔστιν καθαρὸς ὅλος means *but otherwise*.   The 317 special sense of οὐ (μὴ) ... ἀλλά has already been discussed § 148, 14 p. 355.   The combination οὐ γὰρ ἀλλά (*no; but* etc.) occurs in Acts xvi. 37.   On the elliptical ἀλλά after negative sentences see § 151, 23 c) p. 392.

In the combination of particles οὐ μόνον ... ἀλλὰ καί, the καί (as is the case with *etiam* in Latin) is sometimes omitted, and in this way the equipoise of the members is destroyed and the emphasis falls on the second part; (see Klotz ad Devar.. II. p. 10).

This relation of the two parts of the sentence is plainly indicated by the adjunct πολὺ μᾶλλον in Phil. ii. 12; but it is evident also without any adjunct, as Acts xix. 26 Tdf. [Treg. cod. Sin.] οὐ μόνον Ἐφέσου ἀλλὰ σχεδὸν πάσης Ἀσίας (where the addition of καί is very probably chargeable to the emendation of copyists), 1 John v. 6 οὐκ ἐν τῷ ὕδατι μόνον, ἀλλ᾽ ἐν τῷ ὕδατι καὶ ἐν τῷ αἵματι. On the elliptical οὐ μόνον δέ see § 151, 23 f) p. 293.

B. § 149, m. 17; H. § 870; C. §§ 701 j.; 708 c. e.; D. § 618; J. §§ 786; 872 i.

15   Γάρ. An example from the N. T. of γάρ in direct question (then) is John vii. 41 μὴ γὰρ ἐκ τῆς Γαλιλαίας ὁ Χριστὸς ἔρχεται; so often after strict interrogatives, as τί γὰρ Matt. xxvii. 23; πῶς γὰρ Acts viii. 31, etc. To the elliptical use of γάρ (as it occurs so often in Greek authors, see the Grammars) many passages belong, (see the same in Wahl sub voce); as, Acts xxii. 26; 2 Cor. ii. 17 ; Jas. iv. 14 Tdf. [Treg.].

B. § 149, m. 18; H. § 866; C. § 685 c.; D. p. 571; J. § 737.

16   Οὖν. The particle οὖν, which in general likes to append itself to other words, appears very often so closely connected with μέν as to blend with it, as it were, into a single particle. If now (as happens most frequently by far), no δέ answers to this μὲν οὖν, the μέν is not the corresponsive particle but a shorter form of μήν (as in μέντοι); hence in Greek authors the confirmatory combinations πάνυ μὲν οὖν, κομιδῇ μὲν οὖν (see Hartung II. p. 393). This μὲν οὖν is a favorite particle in transitions; and even when subsequently a clause with δέ follows, this clause by no means always stands in a corresponsive relation to the preceding, but simply continues the narration.

Luke often uses μὲν οὖν in this genuine classic way, particularly in the Acts (see Wahl). In the Gospel, on the other hand, it appears very rarely; so too in the other Gospels, (in Matt. not at all, in Mark doubtful). In the Epistles, too, it is often employed in the conclusion as a strengthened οὖν and without a following δέ.[1] Among the examples see especially Acts i. 18; xvii. 30; xxiii. 22; xxvi. 4, 9 ; Rom. xi. 13 Lchm. [Tdf. cod. Sin.], 1 Cor. vi. 4, 7 ; Phil. iii. 8 (ἀλλὰ μὲν οὖν), Heb. vii. 11 ; ix. 1.

318   To μὲν οὖν, become thus a single particle, the particle γε is some-

[1] On the other hand, the μὲν δή so often used in argument by Greek authors in the same sense, and without δέ, nowhere appears.

times appended for still greater unity: μ ε ν ο ῦ ν γ ε. This contains a correction of the preceding thought, and, at the same time, a confirmation of the following, but with a certain ironical tone: *immo vero, yea verily.* But the placing of this compound particle at the beginning of the sentence is quite unclassical (hence censured severely by Phrynichus p. 342 [ed. Lob.], and perhaps peculiar to the Alex. dialect only, cf. Sturz, Dial. Alex. p. 203): Luke xi. 28; Rom. ix. 20; x. 18.

ἄρα, οὐκοῦν. On the interrogative ἄρα, and the other N. T. interrogatives, see § 139, 55 p. 247; and on οὐκοῦν (*then, therefore, ergo*) ibid. p. 249.

B. § 149, m. 23; H. § 852, 14; C. § 476 d. sq.; D. p. 570; J. § 733.

The particle of swearing νή occurs but once, and then in Greek 17 fashion with the Acc.: 1 Cor. xv. 31. In another passage (ix. 15) it is a conjecture of Lachmann's (II. præf. p. xii.).

B. § 149, m. 26; H. § 865; C. § 685 c.; D. §§ 548 (4); 604; J. § 789; W. p. 444 sq. (414); S. p. xcvi. 18

῎Αρα. The question whether the conclusive particle ἄρα can begin a sentence, whether it then should be written ἄρα or ἆρα (cf. § 139, 55 p. 247), does not affect — at least as a question — the N. T. For although ἄρα is often placed after some other word or words, yet its standing first in this form (cf. the Lat. *igitur*) is no longer a subject of doubt, indeed, is already in such general use that even Luke and the author of the Ep. to the Heb. no longer take offence at it.

Examples of this use, especially at the beginning of an apodosis, are, Matt. xii. 28; Luke xi. 20, 48; 1 Cor. xv. 18; 2 Cor. v. 15; Heb. iv. 9; xii. 8, etc. Peculiar to P a u l is ἄρα strengthened by οὖν: ἄρα οὖν (never with the accent thrown back), in which strengthened form it is found standing only in the first place; as, Rom. v. 18; vii. 3, 25 etc., Gal. vi. 10; Eph. ii. 19; 1 Thess. v. 6; 2 Thess. ii. 15.[1] Another extension of the particle takes place by means of γε, rather in a restrictive sense, — standing first: Matt. vii. 20; xvii. 26; Acts xi. 18 Tdf. [ed. 8 drops γε, with Lchm. Treg. cod. Sin.]; following: Acts xvii. 27 (see § 139, 62 p. 256). It is the uniform and settled practice

---

[1] The same combination of particles occurs likewise at the beginning of sentences (but written ἄρ' οὖν) often in the best prose writers, and in sentences which contain no question; as, Plato, Gorg. p. 450 c. 477 a.; Charm. 159 b.; Euthyph. p. 5 a.; Prot. p. 313 c.; Xen. Cyr. 4, 3, 8, etc. Although the form of an interrogation may underlie such sentences, yet perhaps, considering the original identity of the two particles (cf. Klotz ad Devar. II. p. 167), it is preferable even here to write ἄρ' οὖν in order to distinguish them from actual questions with ἆρ' οὖν (Theaet. p. 188 a. c.; Gorg. 449 e., etc.).

in the N. T. to write ἄρα in the conclusive sense, and ἆρα in the interrogative.

B. § 149, m. 27; H. § 867, 4; C. § 720; D. p. 572; J. § 790.

19   Τοι. The particle τοίνυν stands second, as in Greek authors, in 1 Cor. ix. 26; first, in Heb. xiii. 13, and doubtfully [yet Tdf. Treg. cod. Sin. first] in Luke xx. 25. Lob. ad Phryn. p. 342 adduces several examples of this later usage.

B. § 150, m. 4; H. § 848 c.; C. § 717 g.; D. pp. 571, 578; J. §§ 762, 2; 891, 5 b.

1   Οὐχ ὅτι. In the N.T. also there is an elliptical combination
319 οὐχ ὅτι, but it differs wholly both as respects origin and signification from the combination in use by classic writers
(especially Plato).   For whereas the classic phrase assumes
in every case a negative notion, like *it makes no difficulty that*
etc. (hence its predicate is to be taken again in a positive
sense, and οὐχ ὅτι to be translated *although, quamquam*, e.g.
Plat. Prot. p. 336 Σωκράτη ἐγγυῶμαι μὴ ἐπιλήσεσθαι, οὐχ ὅτι
παίζει καί φησιν ἐπιλήσμων εἶναι), with οὐχ ὅτι in the N. T.
a positive notion, like *I do not mean to say that* etc., must be
supplied; so that the predicate belonging to οὐχ ὅτι is sharply
n e g a t i v e d, and receives in the clause following with ἀλλά,
δέ, εἰ μή its positive antithesis.

For example, John vi. 46 οὐχ ὅτι τὸν πατέρα ἑώρακέν τις εἰ μὴ ὁ ὢν
παρὰ τοῦ θεοῦ, ο ὗ τ ο ς ἑ ώ ρ α κ ε ν τὸν πατέρα, vii. 22; 2 Cor. i. 24; iii.
5; Phil. iii. 12; iv. 17 οὐχ ὅτι ἐπιζητῶ τὸ δόμα, ἀλλὰ ἐπιζητῶ etc.,
2 Thess. iii. 9.   The same ellipsis underlies all passages, and hence
must be applied also to Phil. iv. 11 : οὐχ ὅτι καθ᾽ ὑστέρησιν λέγω, literally
*I do not mean to say that I make this declaration in consideration of
my straitened condition* i.e. briefly *I do not say this* etc.

REMARK. The ellipsis in ο ὐ χ ο ἷ ο ν ὅ τ ι, in Rom. ix. 6 οὐχ οἷον δὲ
ὅτι ἐκπέπτωκεν ὁ λόγος τοῦ θεοῦ, is more difficult.   In default of parallel
instances in the N. T. (the numerous passages, too, quoted by Wetstein
from classic writers are essentially different), the force of this combination of particles must be derived solely from the context.   As
commonly in such cases, many different interpretations have been
brought forward; see the commentaries.   Among them all, the most
probable assumption seems to be this: that the phrase arose from
blending two formulas (see Meyer and Fritzsche in loc.), viz. οὐχ οἷον
followed by a finite verb, and the above οὐχ ὅτι.   But this οὐχ οἷον,
again, is not to be identified with the οὐχ οἷον used in the classics
instead of οὐχ ὅπως in the sense of *not only not* (see B. m. 2), but is

without doubt the one sharply censured by Phrynichus p. 372 as a
solecism (ἐν τῇ ἡμεδαπῇ; Phrynichus was an Asiatic) and explained
by οὐ δήπου, μὴ δήπου (*by no means*). This signification, united to
that of οὐχ ὅτι given above, gives as the meaning of the passage from
Paul, *by no means do I intend* (vss. 1–4) *to say, that God's
word has come to naught* etc.

B. § 150, m. 8; C. § 556 d.; J. § 816, 3 e.

ὅσος. Perhaps in imitation of the expression chosen by the LXX **2**
in Isa. xxvi. 20 (ἀποκρύβηθι μικρὸν ὅσον ὅσον), we find the same turn
in Heb. x. 37 ἔτι γὰρ μικρὸν ὅσον ὅσον ὁ ἐρχόμενος ἥξει καὶ οὐ χρονιεῖ
(the second part, too, an imitation of Hab. ii. 3). This idiom is also
not without parallels in Greek authors (Ar. Vesp. 213 τί οὐκ ἀπεκοιμή-
θημεν ὅσον ὅσον στίλην, Arrian. Ind. 29. 15 ὀλίγοι δὲ αὐτῶν σπείρουσιν
ὅσον [ὅσον] τῆς χώρης). In the passage before us an ellipsis of the
predicate εἶναι is commonly assumed, so that with ὁ ἐρχόμενος the
conclusion may be said to begin. Yet in view of the above parallels,
and of the single μικρὸν or ὀλίγον ὅσον used in the same way (see
Wetstein in loc.), it is probably better to put no stop after ὅσον, but **320**
to connect the expression immediately with ἥξει as an adverbial
adjunct. Compare here the observation made in connection with the
constructions of ἐγένετο (§ 141, 6, b) p. 277), that when such a consequent clause begins w i t h o u t καί, the predicate is wont to stand
b e f o r e the subject. Accordingly, since the subject stands first here,
in case the second clause were to be taken as a conclusion an additional
καί would probably have stood before it; just as is the fact in John
xiv. 19 ἔτι μικρὸν, κ α ὶ ὁ κ ό σ μ ο ς με οὐκέτι θεωρεῖ, xvi. 16 μικρὸν καὶ
οὐ θεωρεῖτέ με, where the second clause is necessarily taken as a
conclusion.

B. § 150, m. 12; H. 538 e.; C. § 567 e.; J. § 714 Obs. 2.

ἄλλος. To the familiar use of ἄλλος with objects of a different **3**
kind (ἄνδρες καὶ αἱ ἄλλαι γυναῖκες), Luke xxiii. 32 ἤγοντο καὶ ἕτεροι
δύο κακοῦργοι σὺν αὐτῷ ἀναιρεθῆναι has been compared. But the
passage does not present a g r a m m a t i c a l parallel, since a reporter
in the strict spirit of the l a w could hardly express himself otherwise
under the circumstances. Moreover, the hearer's feelings, injured
possibly by the expression, are straightway appeased by the words in
the following verse (ἐσταύρωσαν αὐτὸν καὶ τοὺς κακούργους). On the
recourse that has been had to the same idiom to explain ἕτερον in Gal.
i. 19 (ἕτερον δὲ τῶν ἀποστόλων οὐκ εἶδον εἰ μὴ Ἰάκωβον τὸν ἀδελφὸν τοῦ
Κυρίου), out of immoderate solicitude respecting the facts of history,
see the recent commentaries, and cf. Luke x. 1.

B. § 150, m. 13; H. § 863 c.; C. § 701 m. and N.; J. § 773, 5.

4   ἀλλ' ἤ. Not only is there an example in the N. T. — Luke xii. 51 οὐχὶ λέγω ὑμῖν, ἀλλ' ἤ (sc. παρεγενόμην δοῦναι) διαμερισμόν — of the ordinary use of ἀλλ' ἤ (nisi, unless, except), but also of the less usual (cf. B. p. 441 note) where in the preceding clause another and additional ἄλλος is expressed; as, 2 Cor. i. 13 οὐ γὰρ ἄλλα γράφομεν ὑμῖν, ἀλλ' ἤ ἃ ἀναγινώσκετε etc. But in 1 Cor. iii. 5 diplomatic authority [cod. Sin. also] is opposed to the adoption of ἀλλ' ἤ.

B. § 150, m. 20; H. § 721 b.; C. § 638 g.; D. § 517; J. § 856 Obs. 2.

5   ὤφελον. This word, in the form ὄφελον, has become in later writers and the N. T. completely an unchangeable conjunction. On its construction see § 139, 9 and 10 p. 214 sq.

B. § 150, m. 24; H. § 627; C. § 512 b.; D. p. 396; J. § 444 Obs. 5.

6   ἐν τοῖς. Just as this phrase, as a general neuter expression, is connected immediately with Feminines, so the same thing is done with the (partitive) Genitive πάντων; as in Thuc. 4. 52 τάς τε ἄλλας πόλεις καὶ πάντων μάλιστα τὴν Ἄντανδρον. Other instances of the sort in classic writers may be seen in Dorville ad Charit. p. 549 (571). Here belongs from the N. T. Mark xii. 28 ποία ἐστὶν πρώτη πάντων ἐντολή (Rec. πασῶν) ; but in Luke xix. 37 the reading of cod. Vat., adopted by Lchm. [Treg.], περὶ πάντων ὧν εἶδον δυνάμεων, is not confirmed by cod. Sin.

On the periphrasis οἱ περί τινα see § 125, 8 p. 95.

B. § 150, m. 31; J. § 696 Obs. 1; W. p. 621 (577); p. 633 (588).

7   ἀρξάμενος. By a very natural and easily intelligible brevity of expression, this Participle is often joined not only to the adverbial adjunct belonging to the idea of commencement (ἀπό), but at the same time also to that of the goal (ἕως) ; as, Matt. xx. 8 (ἀπόδος) ἀρξάμενος ἀπὸ τῶν ἐσχάτων ἕως τῶν πρώτων, Luke xxiii. 5 ; (John viii. 9) ; Acts i. 22. So, too, with the finite verb ἤρξατο, Acts i. 1. Another and similar 321 kind of logically inaccurate expression is Luke xxiv. 27 ἀρξάμενος ἀπὸ Μωυσέως καὶ ἀπὸ πάντων τῶν προφητῶν.

On the other hand, Luke xxiv. 47 Lchm. (γέγραπται) κηρυχθῆναι ... μετάνοιαν καὶ ἄφεσιν ἁμαρτιῶν εἰς πάντα τὰ ἔθνη, ἀρξάμενον ἀπὸ Ἰερουσαλήμ. If this reading is genuine, and we should apply to it for substance the idiom treated of in B. l.c., we should get the following sense, which suits the passage perfectly: that repentance and forgiveness be preached among all nations, before all, or first of all, in Jerusalem. But the rule that ἀρξάμενος must always agree in form

with the subject of the sentence would in that case be disregarded
here, where μετάνοιαν and ἄφεσιν are subject.   Yet it is not improbable
that this participle — which in this signification is added as a kind of
adverbial adjunct to the main predicate, so that even the grammatically
correct case in passages from classic authors is somewhat surprising
(see the examples in the Gramm.) — was, by frequent use, at length
changed into an adverb, and hence assumed the form which in such
cases first offered itself, viz. the Neuter (cf. τυχόν § 145, 8 p. 318).
This assumption has so much the more in its favor here, as by
substituting any other termination of the word we should encounter
still greater grammatical incongruities.   The rarity of the expression,
which occurs only here in this sense, produced many variants. Among
them that of cod. Vat. ἀρξάμενοι, adopted by Tdf. [Treg.], deserves
most consideration — (instead of it Tdf. in his ed. 7 read -νον again,
but in ed. 8 he has with cod. Sin. restored -νοι again) — and is to
be explained as an absol. Partic. referring to ἔθνη, according to § 123,
5 p. 78 and § 129, 8 b) p. 130.

B. § 150, m. 36; C. § 598.

'Εθέλειν. Since the trisyllabic form of this verb — which
in Greek authors when joined with an Infin. often serves as a
periphrasis for the adverb (*willingly, voluntarily*) with a finite
verb — does not occur in the N. T. (p. 57), the attempt has
sometimes been made there to extend the same mode of interpretation to θέλειν.

The chief demand for this extension is presented by John vi. 21
(ἤθελον οὖν λαβεῖν etc.), partly in view of the representation made by
Matt. and Mark, partly because if the matter stopped with mere
w i l l i n g, the narrative seems defective and incomplete.   But, on the
other hand, the interpretation *they did it willingly* does not correspond with the preceding ἐφοβήθησαν; for this leads us to expect
the idea of *emboldened, joyful*, which does not lie in ἤθελον. Correctly,
therefore, has Lücke acknowledged a diversity in the narrative of
John (a diversity which may be detected here in other particulars
also), and taken θέλειν in its proper signification; which it has, moreover, in all the other passages that have been brought under this
head.   For everywhere the rendering 'to like, be inclined, to do,' is
perfectly sufficient, as in John viii. 44; Mark xii. 38 where περιπατεῖν
is the simple object of θέλειν like the following ἀσπασμούς etc., Luke
xx. 46 where θελόντων corresponds to the synonymous φιλούντων that
follows.

REMARK. The case is different with the P a r t i c i p l e θέλων when
it is used absolutely (i.e. without an Infin. following) referring to a

noun, and the Infin. of the verb which is the predicate in the sentence
322 must be supplied (cf. § 151, 23 b) p. 392). In this way arises a signification of θέλων which we, if we choose to express ourselves in the
same brief manner, best reproduce by the adverb *purposely ;* as,
2 Pet. iii. 5 λανθάνει αὐτοὺς τοῦτο θέλοντας (sc. τοῦτο αὐτοὺς λανθάνειν)
they purposely know not i.e. *they choose not to know*, Col. ii. 18 μηδεὶς
ὑμᾶς καταβραβευέτω θέλων (sc. καταβραβεύειν ὑμᾶς) ἐν ταπεινοφροσύνῃ
etc. Yet in both passages various other interpretations have been
attempted (see the Commentaries); and in the latter passage, especially,
reference has been made to the usage of the LXX. who are accustomed to render the Hebrew בְּ חָפֵץ by θέλειν ἔν τινι (e.g. 1 Sam.
xviii. 22; 2 Sam. xv. 26; 1 Kings x. 9; 2 Chron. ix. 8). But the
absence of other precedents for this use of θέλειν in the N. T., as well
as the circumstance that the Dative with ἐν in the O. T. is always
personal (ἐν σοί), restricts us to the first interpretation.

CERTAIN PECULIAR KINDS OF CONSTRUCTION.
I. ATTRACTION.
B. § 151, I. 6; J. § 898, 2; W. pp. 626 sq. (581 sq.).

1 To facilitate a survey of the subject, we discuss fully in this
place a syntactic phenomenon which reappears in many kinds
of sentences, viz. the practice, very common in Greek, of subjoining the s u b j e c t of a dependent declarative sentence to
the main predicate to be governed as an o b j e c t. By this
means the great advantage accrues, that the two sentences can
be melted in this way in substance and in form completely
into one sentence.[1] As the subject is rendered sufficiently
familiar by the general grammars, we will content ourselves
here with a classification of the numerous examples in the
N. T. The construction occurs

a) In sentences w i t h ὅτι, after verba dicendi, sentiendi, etc., very
often in all parts of the N. T.; as, Matt. xxv. 24 ἔγνων σε ὅτι σκληρὸς
εἶ ἄνθρωπος, 1 Cor. xvi. 15 οἴδατε τὴν οἰκίαν Στεφανᾶ, ὅτι ἐστὶν ἀπαρχή
etc., John viii. 54 ὃν ὑμεῖς λέγετε ὅτι θεὸς ἡμῶν ἐστίν, iv. 35; ix. 19;
v. 42; Mark xii. 34; Acts iii. 10; iv. 13; xiii. 32; 1 Cor. iii. 20;
Rev. xvii. 8, etc.; also after ἔ χ ε ι ν in the sense of *to hold for, regard as*,
Mark xi. 32 εἶχον τὸν Ἰωάννην ὄντως ὅτι προφήτης ἦν. For emphasis'
sake the subject may be r e p e a t e d ꞏn the subordinate clause by
means of the Demonst. Pron. οὗτος (not αὐτός, cf. § 144, 21 p. 306),
Acts ix. 20 ἐκήρυσσεν τὸν Ἰησοῦν ὅτι οὗτός ἐστιν ὁ υἱὸς τοῦ θεοῦ. If

---

[1] Hence it is an erroneous practice to separate by punctuation marks, out of
regard for our style of expression, what the language so evidently combines into
one whole.

the predicate is a Passive, the Nominative is used with it, i.e. the **323** personal construction is introduced, though instances of this are very rare in the N. T.: 1 Cor. xv. 12 εἰ Χριστὸς κηρύσσεται ἐκ νεκρῶν ὅτι ἐγήγερται.

b) In indirect questions after the same verbs; as, Mark i. 24; Luke iv. 34 οἶδά σε τίς εἶ, Acts xv. 36 ἐπισκεψώμεθα τοὺς ἀδελφοὺς πῶς ἔχουσιν, John vii. 27; xiii. 28; Luke xix. 3; cf. the examples in § 139, 57 B. p. 250. That in 2 Cor. xiii. 5 (ἑαυτοὺς πειράζετε, εἰ ἐστὲ ἐν τῇ πίστει) the clauses are rather to be construed separately, is shown by the antecedent position of ἑαυτούς, so that ἑαυτούς is simply the object of πειράζετε, just as ἑαυτοὺς δοκιμάζετε.

c) Rarely in sentences with ἵνα, when according to N. T. usage after certain predicates (§ 139, 43 p. 238) it takes the place of the Infinitive elsewhere in use, as Rev. iii. 9 ποιήσω αὐτοὺς ἵνα ἥξουσιν καὶ προσκυνήσουσιν ... καὶ γνῶσιν etc.; and with μή in sentences expressing anxiety, as Acts v. 26; Gal. iv. 11, on both which passages see § 139, 48 p. 242. That Gal. vi. 1 (σκοπῶν σεαυτόν, μὴ καὶ σὺ πειρασθῇς) cannot be brought under this head, follows from the repetition of the subject (σύ), and from the signification of the verb σκοπεῖν; on it see § 139, 49 p. 243.

d) In the spirit of this construction, John, in chap. i. 15, instead of using a dependent clause (with ὅτι or in the Infin.), follows at once with the direct discourse (on this cf. especially John x. 36 and the other similar instances in § 141, 1 p. 272): οὗτος ἦν ὃν εἶπον· ὁ ὀπίσω μου ἐρχόμενος ἔμπροσθέν μου γέγονεν, for which subsequently (vs. 30) the other and ordinary construction appears: ὑπὲρ οὗ εἶπον· ὀπίσω μου ἔρχεται etc.

B. § 151, I. 8; H. § cf. 811 a.; C. cf. §§ 554 d.; 704 b.; J. § 647 Obs. 1; W. p. 629 (584).

Of that species of attraction, so common in the classics, **2** according to which adverbial adjuncts when they belong to a noun in the sentence, and especially to the article taking the place of a substantive, are attracted by the verb of the sentence (e.g. ὁ ἐκεῖθεν πόλεμος δεῦρο ἥξει *the war thence* (there) *will come hither*), there are several plain instances in the N. T. Those which there is adequate reason for bringing under this head (for too many have been brought under it, cf. p. 70 sq.) are reducible to the two leading classes following:

a) a reference to the question where is changed into one to the question whence; as,

Luke xi. 13 ὁ πατὴρ ὁ ἐξ οὐρανοῦ δώσει πνεῦμα ἅγιον τοῖς αἰτοῦσιν αὐτόν, Acts xv. 38 ἠξίου, τὸν ἀποστάντα ἀπ' αὐτῶν ἀπὸ Παμφυλίας καὶ

μὴ συνελθόντα ... μὴ συμπαραλαμβάνειν τοῦτον (where the interpretation *away from* Pamphylia appears forced), Matt. xxiv. 17 μὴ καταβάτω
ἆραι τὰ ἐκ τῆς οἰκίας αὐτοῦ (on the other hand, Mark, avoiding the
attraction, ἆραί τι ἐκ τῆς οἰκίας αὐτοῦ). Col. iv. 16 is to be regarded
rather as a species of brachylogy: τὴν ἐκ Λαοδικείας (sc. ἐπιστολὴν) ἵνα
καὶ ὑμεῖς ἀναγνῶτε i.e. (according to the understanding of almost all
recent expositors) my letter which is *now* in Laodicea and is to
reach you *from thence*. But the following cases positively do not
belong here: Luke xvi. 26 Tdf. ὅπως οἱ θέλοντες διαβῆναι ἔνθεν πρὸς
ὑμᾶς μὴ δύνωνται, μηδὲ οἱ ἐκεῖθεν (sc. θέλοντες διαβῆναι) πρὸς ἡμᾶς
διαπερῶσιν, Heb. xiii. 24 ἀσπάζονται ὑμᾶς οἱ ἀπὸ τῆς Ἰταλίας with which
324 may be compared Phil. iv. 22 ἀσπ. οἱ ἐκ τῆς Καίσαρος οἰκίας (§ 125, 9
p. 95). In Acts xiv. 26 also ὅθεν has its proper force, and the kind
of attraction occurring in Matt. xxv. 24, 26 has already been treated
of § 143, 12 p. 287 sq.

b) a reference to the question w h e r e is changed into one
to the question w h i t h e r.

The instances belonging here (πᾶσιν τοῖς εἰς μακράν Acts ii. 39, τοῖς
εἰς τὸν οἶκόν μου Luke ix. 61, ὁ εἰς τὸν ἀγρόν Mark xiii. 16) have
already found their place and explanation § 147, 15 p. 332, and 18
p. 333. Acts xxii. 5 (ἄξων καὶ τοὺς ἐκεῖσε ὄντας) perhaps may also be
brought under this head. Yet it is far more probable that ἐκεῖσε here
stands directly for ἐκεῖ, agreeably to the interchange so often occurring
with local adverbs (cf. p. 70 sq.); it is used in this way not only
often in the Apocrypha, but also in Greek writers e.g. Polybius, Dio
Cassius, Themistius, see Lob. ad Phryn. p. 44; Steph. Thes. sub voce.
The same thing early took place with the local adv. εἴσω (ἔσω), see
Pape, Steph., and Lob. p. 127; just as, on the other hand, ἐκεῖ and
ἔνδον answer to the question whither. Examples of ἔσω in the
relation of r e s t are Rom. vii. 22; 1 Cor. v. 12; 2 Cor. iv. 16 Lchm.
[Treg. Tdf. cod. Sin.], Eph. iii. 16, with which are to be compared
John xx. 26 (with εἶναι), Acts v. 23 (with εὕρομεν sc. ὄντα).

II. Anacoluthon.

B. p. 448 (524); H. § 886; C. (cf. Ind. sub verb.); D. § 625; J. § 900.

3 No figure of speech or species of construction (so far as the
absence of construction admits of being so called) is more
current in popular language than Anacoluthon, — sometimes
in the narrower sense, as an incomplete sentence: p r o p e r
a n a c o l u t h o n; sometimes in the broader, as an altered
structure: v a r i a t i o s t r u c t u r æ. Indeed, we may say that
the language of the people, or of an ordinary man, always

abounds more or less in anacoluthon (unconscious and un-
designed, to be sure).   Hence the great number of anacoluthic
thoughts, sentences, periods, in all the writers of the N. T.
(even those that write the most correctly), since many constructions of the sort had passed over into the Greek literary usage.
But we ought to consider only those instances as belonging to
a grammatical figure of speech which have actually acquired a
certain currency in the language, so that they are repeated, either generally or by particular writers; at least it
is only these that are fit to be discussed in a grammar.   But
all such anacolutha as cannot be regularly classified, — since
they are the result of the writer's mood at the moment, and
are therefore to be explained exclusively or predominantly by
the context in every case,— can be considered only incidentally,
and belong strictly, all of them, to exegesis.   Many of the 325
more common anacolutha, or changes of construction (for we
neglect for practical reasons to separate the two kinds of
sentences), have already been treated of in this Grammar in
other places; so that, to avoid repetition, only those instances
will receive special consideration which could not easily be
disposed of elsewhere.   We arrange, then, instances of anacoluthon under the following heads:

a. The simplest and most natural anacoluthon is that which   4
is known in grammar as the Nominative Absolute in the
strict sense (to be distinguished from the participial construction of the same name, § 144, 13 p. 298).   It arises from the
circumstance, that the speaker or writer begins the sentence
with a subject immediately before his mind — whether it be
the Nominative of a substantive, or of an adj. or partic. with
the article used in its stead, or of a pronoun, — and subsequently allows the sentence to take such a turn, that the
idea at the beginning no longer remains the subject, but ought
to stand in some one of the oblique cases.   It is then a very
common practice to leave the Nominative standing at the head
of the sentence (which consequently remains unfinished, strictly
speaking), and in the sequel to refer back to it by a Pronoun
in the requisite case.

For example, Acts vii. 40 ὁ Μωυσῆς οὗτος, ὃς ἐξήγαγεν ἡμᾶς ἐκ
γῆς Αἰγύπτου, οὐκ οἴδαμεν τί ἐγένετο αὐτῷ, Matt. x. 32 πᾶς οὖν ὅστις
ὁμολογήσει ἐν ἐμοὶ . . . , ὁμολογήσω κἀγὼ ἐι αὐτῷ, xii. 36 πᾶν ῥῆμα ἀργὸν

ὃ ..., ἀποδώσουσιν περὶ αὐτοῦ λόγον, John vi. 39 ἵνα πᾶν, ὃ δέδωκέν μοι, μὴ ἀπολέσω ἐξ αὐτοῦ (cf. § 127, 32 p. 121 sq.), xvii. 2 ἵνα π ᾶ ν ὃ (i.e. πάντες οὓς, see § 128, 1 p. 122) δέδωκας αὐτῷ, δώσῃ α ὐ τ ο ῖ ς etc.; hence in xv. 2 also (πᾶν κλῆμα ἐν ἐμοὶ μὴ φέρον καρπὸν, αἴρει αὐτό) we are to take the words πᾶν κλῆμα not as Accusative but as Nominative, — as their repetition by αὐτό shows. On Rom. ix. 10 (Ῥεβέκκα etc) see below, 23 f) p. 393. So the Participle with the article, as John vii. 38 ὁ π ι σ τ ε ύ ω ν εἰς ἐμὲ ..., ποταμοὶ ἐκ τῆς κοιλίας α ὐ τ ο ῦ ῥεύσουσιν etc., Rev. ii. 26 (ὁ νικῶν ... δώσω αὐτῷ), iii. 12, 21; cf. 5 following.

This usage so agrees with the character of the N. T. style, that even when in an inserted s u b o r d i n a t e clause the same subject accidentally recurs, we can explain the antecedent Nominative unhesitatingly by this construction, and are under no necessity of construing it into the dependent sentence, and so disturbing the natural sequence of the words.

326 1 John ii. 27 ὑ μ ε ῖ ς τὸ χρῖσμα, ὃ ἐ λ ά β ε τ ε ἀπ᾽ αὐτοῦ, μένει ἐν ὑ μ ῖ ν. The rhetorical figure is called forth here by the antithesis in which the idea placed first stands to another (viz. τὶς or οἱ πλανῶντες ὑμᾶς) ; and this is elsewhere rendered evident by the addition of μέν and δέ, as 1 Cor. xi. 14 ἀνὴρ μὲν, ἐὰν κομᾷ, ἀτιμία αὐτῷ ἐστιν, γυνὴ δὲ, ἐὰν κομᾷ, δόξα αὐτῇ ἐστιν, — yet the position of the words in this passage may also be explained according to 18 below, p. 389.

Similar is Luke xxi. 6 ταῦτα ἃ θεωρεῖτε, ἐλεύσονται ἡμέραι ἐν αἷς οὐκ ἀφεθήσεται λίθος etc., where a general pronoun precedes, and the more definite idea is not stated till afterwards.

5 REMARK. 1. Numerous instances analogous to the above-given examples may be adduced from other Greek writers, from Homer down (see among others Bhdy. Syntax p. 68). But it seems to be an e x c e p t i o n, and in conflict with the genius of the Greek language, when the notion that precedes in the Nominative remains the actual subject in the construction following, and yet an additional b a c k w a r d r e f e r e n c e is made by means of the pronoun αὐτός (not οὗτος, on which see § 144, 21 p. 306) ; — all the more because this pronoun in the Nom. in n a t i v e G r e e k writers has only the more pointed signification self. The example under this head is Luke xiii. 4 ἐκεῖνοι οἱ δέκα καὶ ὀκτώ, ἐφ᾽ οὓς ..., δοκεῖτε ὅτι α ὐ τ ο ὶ ὀφειλέται ἐγένοντο etc., cf. with this the same writer's usage treated of § 127, 9 p. 107. It seems to be exceptional likewise, when the term that precedes stands in the o b l i q u e case suited to the construction that follows, and yet the same case of the pronoun αὐτός recurs as though the Nominative had preceded, — an idiom which occurs repeatedly in the Rev., e.g. ii. 7, 17 τῷ νικοῦντι ... δώσω αὐτῷ (cf. the examples of a different kind

in 4 p. 380), vi. 4 τῷ καθημένῳ ... ἐδόθη αὐτῷ, but is found elsewhere also, as Matt. iv. 16; v. 40, and has its foundation in the copiousness of the N. T. language as respects the employment of pronouns, which has been often touched upon (see especially § 130, 2 p. 142); cf. besides § 145, 2 p. 315.

REMARK 2. Under the head of Nominative Absolute the two **6** passages quoted § 131, 13 b) p. 154 (viz. Rom. viii. 3; Heb. viii. 1) may also be brought. It is true that here, as was before remarked, the Neuter form in both instances makes it impossible to determine the case positively. Yet, since they likewise stand at the beginning of the sentence, they are rather to be regarded as Nominatives, after the analogy of the examples given above in 4 (especially Luke xxi. 6).

REMARK 3. Quite unparalleled is the placing of an Accusative **7** at the beginning (in a similar manner to the Nom. just described) in 2 Cor. xii. 17 μή τινα, ὧν ἀπέσταλκα πρὸς ὑμᾶς, δι᾽ αὐτοῦ ἐπλεονέκτησα ὑμᾶς; where the Accusative (τινα) is subsequently taken up again, or rather almost corrected, by the demons. pron. (δι᾽ αὐτοῦ). This irregularity is only explicable by assuming that the apostle, in beginning the sentence, had another construction in mind, but subsequently abandoned it. Such liberties in construction and loose connection of sentences, however, are quite natural in epistolary style (as in conversation); see below, especially 10 p. 383 and 12 p. 386.

b. The structure of periods in Greek depends in great part **8** on the artistic management of the various Participial construc- **327** tions (§ 144 p. 288 sqq.); yet grammatical precision of expression was forced sometimes to give way before the demands particularly of force and vivacity, or of symmetry. Probably most of the instances of (anarthrous) participles used anacoluthically in the Greek writers of the classic period are to be explained solely by the endeavor to meet these demands; (see B. II. 1.). But, speaking generally, the case is different in this respect with the language of the N.T. For, the more its diction approximates to the language of the people, which had no need of artistically constructed periods, or the less the writers were acquainted with the strictly Hellenic culture, the more do instances of anacoluthically used Participles multiply, without there being any rhetorical purpose involved in them. Hence many cases of such anacoluthon are found even in the Gospels; but especially in the lawless language of the Apocalypse, and in the long periods of Paul's Epistles, which often exceed all bounds, and consequently are deficient not infrequently in perspicuity.

In so far as the Participle stands for any reason in a C a s e
out of harmony with the leading clause to which it belongs, it
has already been subjected to a thorough and connected examination in § 144, 13 p. 298.   In so far, again, as under
different relations (whether it be that a finite verb is to be
supplied from the context, or that the construction is subsequently broken off and takes a different turn) it stands
a b s o l u t e l y, i.e. without any grammatical connection with
its leading clause, it has been treated of in the same section, 6
and 7, p. 292 sq.   It remains for us to speak here of yet a
third peculiarity in the employment of Participles — one which
is pre-eminently peculiar to the biblical language, and consists
in this : that a participial clause almost imperceptibly p a s s e s
o v e r i n t o a f i n i t e v e r b, consequently is completed after
the manner of a leading clause, yet without losing its force as a
participial clause in its r e l a t i o n to the w h o l e s e n t e n c e.
Here manifestly the Hebrew idiom (see Gesen. Lehrgeb. p. 802;
Gr. § 131, Rem. 2) has had great influence, since such constructions are foreign to Greek.[1]

No writer in the N. T. is more addicted to this mode of expression
than John; yet with Paul also the same is not uncommon.   For
example, John i. 32 τεθέαμαι τὸ πνεῦμα κ α τ α β α ῖ ν ο ν ... καὶ ἔ μ ε ι ν ε ν
ἐπ᾽ αὐτόν (yet regularly vs. 33), v. 44 ; 2 John 2 διὰ τὴν ἀλήθειαν τὴν
328 μένουσαν ἐν ἡμῖν, καὶ μεθ᾽ ἡμῶν ἔσται εἰς τὸν αἰῶνα.   In similar anacoluthic style we read, John xv. 5 ὁ μένων ἐν ἐμοὶ κ ἀ γ ὼ ἐν αὐτῷ, οὗτος
φέρει etc., 1 John iii, 24.   From Paul's Epistles : Col. i. 6 Tdf. [eds.
2, 7] τοῦ εὐαγγελίου τοῦ παρόντος εἰς ὑμᾶς ..., καὶ ἔστιν καρποφορούμενον
etc., 26 τὸ μυστήριον τὸ ἀποκεκρυμμένον ... νῦν δὲ ἐφανερώθη etc., 1 Cor.
vii. 37 μὴ ἔχων ἀνάγκην, ἐξουσίαν δὲ ἔχει, 2 Cor. vi. 9 ὡς ἀποθνῄσκοντες
καὶ ἰ δ ο ὺ ζ ῶ μ ε ν etc., Eph. i. 20 Tdf. [eds. 2, 7] (for the other
reading καθίσας [Tdf. ed. 8, Treg. cod. Sin.] is probably only a correction).   On Heb. viii. 10 ; x. 16 see § 144, 4 a) p. 291 ; besides cf.
Luke xix. 2 ; Rev. ii. 2, 9, 18 ; iii. 9 ; ix. 1, 17 ; x. 1, etc.

9   REMARK. A similar usage to this occurs, when R e l a t i v e a n d
o t h e r S u b o r d i n a t e c l a u s e s pass over in the same almost
unnoticed manner into leading clauses, and yet the continuation of
the sentence so formed (indicated generally by καὶ or δέ) does not
constitute the real leading clause for the antecedent subordinate clause.

[1] Foreign, inasmuch as we are not in the remotest degree warranted in inferring
an actual usage from isolated instances of a similar nature arising from negligence
or other causes; (cf. Thuc. 8, 45, 4 ; 7, 13, 2 ; Plat. Phaedr. p 230 d. ; Fritzsche,
Quaest. Luc. p. 112 ; Lehrs, Arist. p. 75).

For example: 1 Cor. vii. 13 γυνὴ ἥτις ἔχει ἄνδρα ἄπιστον καὶ οὗτος συνευδοκεῖ οἰκεῖν μετ' αὐτῆς, μὴ ἀφιέτω τὸν ἄνδρα, Tit. i. 2, 3 ζωῆς αἰωνίου, ἣν ἐπηγγείλατο ὁ θεὸς πρὸ χρόνων ..., ἐφανέρωσεν δὲ καιροῖς ἰδίοις τὸν λόγον αὐτοῦ etc., Rev. xvii. 2. It does not conflict with the character of the N. T. diction to suppose this construction to be present in many other passages ; but the less constrained arrangement of words in the ancient languages often prevents the nature of the clauses (whether leading or subordinate) from being any longer discovered positively. Compare, for example, Mark iv. 16 sq., the frequent connection of the Subjunctive with the Future (see the examples § 139, 7 note p. 211), and the similar use in § 143, 6 p. 283. Of a different sort, yet springing from the same principle, is Luke x. 8 εἰς ἣν δ' ἂν πόλιν εἰσέρχησθε καὶ δέχωνται ὑμᾶς etc., where the second clause passes over, not indeed into a leading clause, but into a different kind of s u b o r d i n a t e c l a u s e, as though ἐάν preceded.

c. This transition from one construction to another, or **10** m i n g l i n g o f t w o d i f f e r e n t c o n s t r u c t i o n s, is often to be found in the N. T. writings. Yet most of the instances are of so special a nature that it is difficult to distribute them under general heads. We confine ourselves, therefore, here, to illustrating the method of such mixed constructions by a number of the most evident examples.

Acts xxiv. 18 τινὲς δὲ ἀπὸ τῆς Ἀσίας Ἰουδαῖοι, οὓς ἔδει ἐπὶ σοῦ παρεῖναι καὶ κατηγορεῖν, εἴ τι ἔχοιεν. The clause τινὲς δὲ etc. is anacoluthic, whether connected with what precedes or not. The anacoluthon is occasioned by the R e l a t i v e c l a u s e f o l l o w i n g, which combines logically with the preceding clause into a single thought: but certain Asiatic Jews (who saw me there and maltreated me, see xxi. 27 sqq.), *these* ought to have appeared etc. In quite the same way an anacoluthon is produced by a Relative clause in xxiv. 5 sq. and Rom. xvi. 27, on which see § 144, 7 p. 293 sq.

Acts xxvii. 10 θεωρῶ, ὅτι μετὰ ὕβρεως καὶ πολλῆς ζημίας ... μέλλειν ἔσεσθαι τὸν πλοῦν. The sentence begins with ὅτι and passes over into the equivalent construction of the Acc. with the Infin. Something similar occurs often enough in classic writers, see B. § 139 m. 61 ; and compare the twice used ὅτι in Eph. ii. 11 sq. (after several parenthetic clauses).

1 Cor. xii. 2 according to the present reading: οἴδατε ὅτι ὅτε ἔθνη ἦτε πρὸς τὰ εἴδωλα τὰ ἄφωνα ὡς ἂν ἤγεσθε ἀπαγόμενοι. Here, after ex- **329** punging the inconvenient ὅτε (as many MSS. and editors do), we should encounter no further grammatical difficulty. But just this very circumstance confirms the clause ὅτε ἔθνη ἦτε, and the sense is not

opposed to it.   The sentence begins with ὅτι and after the parenthetic
clause ὅτε ἔθνη ἦτε passes over into an indirect question, very much as
we too might say *Ye know that, when ye were heathen, how ye then
were always led* etc.   Further, cf. on ἂν ἤγεσθε § 139, 13 p. 216.   The
combination ἤγεσθε ἀπαγόμενοι calls to mind the idiom in § 144, 30
p. 313.   For the other modes of explaining the passage see the Comm.

Mark vi. 8 sq. according to the present reading: παρήγγειλεν αὐτοῖς
ἵνα μηδὲν αἴρωσιν εἰς ὁδὸν εἰ μὴ ῥάβδον ... , ἀλλὰ ὑποδεδεμένους σανδάλια,
καὶ μὴ ἐνδύσησθε δύο χιτῶνας.   Here a threefold construction occurs :
after παρήγγειλεν at first ἵνα follows (according to § 139, 42 p. 237),
then the Accus. of the Participle ὑποδεδεμένους as if the construction
(equivalent to ἵνα) with the Infin. had preceded, and finally a transition
to direct discourse (see 11 below, p. 385).   The parallel passage
(Luke ix. 3) might be explained similarly ; yet it is more probable
that L u k e has so turned the common source whence both writers
drew, that another mode of explanation may be admitted ; see on this
point § 140, 18 p. 271.

Luke xi. 11 τίνα δὲ ἐξ ὑμῶν τὸν πατέρα αἰτήσει ὁ υἱὸς ἄρτον, μὴ λίθον
ἐπιδώσει αὐτῷ; arose from the blending into one sentence of the two
thoughts τίνα ἐξ ὑμῶν αἰτήσει ὁ υἱὸς ἄρτον; and μὴ λίθον ἐπιδώσει αὐτῷ
ὁ πατήρ; Matthew (vii. 9) has united these two thoughts into one
sentence differently, but likewise anacoluthically ; see on the passage
§ 143, 6 Remark p. 284.

Matt x. 25 ἀρκετὸν τῷ μαθητῇ ἵνα γένηται ὡς ὁ διδάσκαλος αὐτοῦ, καὶ ὁ
δοῦλος ὡς ὁ κύριος αὐτοῦ instead of καὶ τῷ δούλῳ ἀρκετὸν ἵνα γένηται ὡς etc.

Rom. ii. 7 sq. ἀποδώσει τοῖς μὲν δόξαν καὶ τιμὴν ... · τοῖς δὲ ... ὀργὴ
καὶ θυμός, where at the last words the apostle had in mind, instead of
the Active predicate (ἀποδοῦναι) used in the first member (but some
distance before), the Passive ; hence the transition from the Accus.
to the Nominative.   Such blending of an Active and a Passive construction is not altogether uncommon ; see e.g. Mark ix. 20 (in § 144,
13, c) p. 299), Acts v. 26 (in § 139, 48 p. 242), Rev. xi. 1 ἐδόθη μοι
κάλαμος ὅμοιος ῥάβδῳ, λ έ γ ω ν equiv. to ἔδωκέν μοι κάλαμον, λέγων ;
with this may be compared the frequent combination in the Sept.
ἀνηγγέλη αὐτῷ, λέγοντες (Gen. xxii. 20 ; xxxviii. 24 ; 2 Sam. xv. 31 ;
xix. 1, etc.).

Rom. xi. 22 ἴδε οὖν χρηστότητα καὶ ἀποτομίαν θεοῦ · ἐπὶ μὲν τοὺς
πεσόντας ἀποτομία etc., where the antecedent Accusatives, in continuing
the discourse, are taken up again by the Nom. without the introduction
of a new predicate.   This is less an anacoluthon than an almost parenthetic expansion (customary in Greek authors also) of the leading
thought ; see among other examples Il. ζ. 395 ; κ. 437 ; Plat. Soph
p. 266 d. (τίθημι δύο εἴδη etc.), p. 218 e. (τί δῆτα etc.) ; Bhdy. p. 68.

In Gal. ii. 6 the clause ἀπὸ δὲ τῶν δοκούντων εἶναί τι is left incomplete, but after the parenthesis (ὁποῖοί ποτε etc.) it is resumed in a changed construction by ἐμοὶ γὰρ οἱ δοκοῦντες etc.

Gal. ii. 4 : here likewise the clause διὰ δὲ τοὺς παρεισάκτους ψευδα- δέλφους etc. is left unfinished, so that after the parenthesis we must either supply, from what precedes, the thought *I did not have him* 350 *circumcised*, or we can avail ourselves of the Relative clause that follows (οἷς οὐδὲ πρὸς ὥραν etc.) in supplying the ellipsis, and arrange and complete the sentence grammatically thus : τοῖς δὲ παρεισάκτοις ... οὐδὲ πρὸς ὥραν εἴξαμεν. Cf. Acts xxiv. 18 above, p. 383.

Rev. xxi. 8 τοῖς δὲ δειλοῖς καὶ ἀπίστοις ... τὸ μέρος αὐτῶν ἐν τῇ λίμνῃ etc., where the Dative at the beginning presupposes a verbal predicate (*to fall to the lot of*), but in consequence of the substantive chosen (τὸ μέρος) is taken up again by the Gen. αὐτῶν.

Other examples of the blending of two constructions have been treated of in § 145, 9 p. 318 ; § 129, 14 p. 133 ; § 139, 58 p. 251.

d. A change of structure very current in Greek authors 1 consists in the mingling of the direct and the indirect forms of statement. Of course the transition from the cumbrous and rather disliked indirect form of discourse, to the lively and popular direct form, is more frequent in Greek and N. T. authors, than the reverse. It is not to be overlooked, that Luke, beyond all other writers, has mastered most this genuine Greek mode of expression ; whereas the examples from other N. T. authors result, perhaps, rather from inaccuracy or want of practice in composition.

Transitions from indirect to direct discourse : Luke v. 14 παρήγγειλεν αὐτῷ μηδενὶ εἰπεῖν, ἀλλὰ δεῖξον etc., Acts i. 4 παρήγγειλεν περιμένειν τὴν ἐπαγγελίαν ἣν ἠκούσατε, xiv. 22 ; xvii. 3 ; xxiii. 22. On Mark vi. 8 see 10 above p. 384.[1] Transitions from direct to indirect discourse : the three parallel passages Matt. ix. 6 ; Mark ii. 20 ; Luke v. 24 ἵνα δὲ εἰδῆτε ὅτι ... , εἶπεν τῷ παραλελυμένῳ, where after εἰδῆτε we expect a λέγω or λέξω, but instead the historian straightway comes in (λέγει) ; Acts xxiii. 23 εἶπεν· ἑτοιμάσατε στρατιώτας ... , κτήνη τε παραστῆσαι, Mark xi. 32 where in the words of the historian ἐφοβοῦντο τὸν λαόν we have the conclusion to the scribes' own words ἀλλὰ εἴπωμεν· ἐξ ἀνθρώπων; On John x. 36 see § 141, 1 p. 272, and on Luke ix. 3 no. 10 above, p. 384.

[1] When the indirect sentence is expressed by ὅτι with a finite verb instead of the Acc. with the Infin., the want of a prescribed sequence of words prevents us (as in 9 above in Relative clauses) from telling any longer with certainty whether following claıses are to be regarded as still dependent on ὅτι, or stand independently again John vi. 22 sq. may serve as an example.

49

12   e. A considerable portion of the larger instances of anacoluthon consist in this : that a given antecedent clause either
wants altogether its proper consequent clause, or
receives it only in substance, not in grammatical form, in one
of the following clauses.   Now in so far as the suppression of
so essential a portion of the sentence takes place designedly
and unmistakably for any ethical reason, it can be reckoned
among the rhetorical figures ; hence cases of the sort are wont
to be treated of in grammar under the special designation of
331 Aposiopesis (see 26 p. 396).   But in so far as the consequent clause fails to be given for formal reasons, to avoid
some sort of repetition, the instance falls under the head of
Ellipsis (see 23 g) p. 393).

Often, however, the reason for the suppression is an involuntary
one, and the anacoluthon solely a result of negligent and loose
connection, or called out by the troop of inrushing thoughts, by
parentheses of various sorts, by the remote position of the antecedent
clause, and other temporary causes.   Instances of the sort are found
with especial frequency in the writings of Paul, whose sentences, in
consequence of his wealth of thought and fulness of heart, often extended to entire pages, so that he not infrequently lost their grammatical connection.   For example, see Rom. v. 12 sq.; ii. 17–21 ; xii.
6–8, 15, 16 ; xvi. 25 sq.; Col. i ; Eph. i. and ii. ; Gal. iv. 19 sq. ; 2 Thess.
ii. 3, 4 ; 1 Tim. i. 3 sq.   In the Apocalypse such loose constructions
are the order of the day, see e.g. i. 12–16 ; iii. 12, 21 ; vii. 4, 9 ; xi. 8 ;
xiv. 12, and cf. § 123, 5 p. 78.[1]   Examples from other writers are
Mark iii. 14 sqq.; Heb. iii. 15 sq. ; 2 Pet. ii. 4–10.

13   REMARK. Sometimes the apodosis or conclusion does not correspond
to what precedes, because, instead of the consequent clause grammatically required, words from the O. T. follow unaltered ; as, Rom.
xv. 3, 21 ; 1 Cor. i. 31 (see on this las' passage also § 139, 37 p. 234) ;
cf. also 1, d) above, p. 377.

[1] The passage ii. 13 in the form given by the MSS. and adopted by Lchm.[Treg.]
does not offer a distant possibility of a grammatical construction, still less is anything analogous to it found elsewhere. In order, therefore, to restore the possibility
of a meaning, we must either (with the more modern MSS.) interpolate αἷς [א* ἐν
αἷς] after ἡμέραις or read ἐν αἷς ἡμέραις instead of ἐν ταῖς ἡμέραις. Perhaps the
corruption arose from the circumstance that some copyist, instead of the original
Genitive 'Αντίπα (see Tdf's note in ed. 7), substituted, on account of the apposition
following in the Nominative (§ 123, 5 p. 78), the Nominative form ('Αντίπας, which
then entailed necessarily the further changes (αἷς, ἐν αἷς, etc.).   [Tdf. now reads
τὴν πίστιν μου ἐν ταῖς ἡμέραις 'Αντείπας etc.]

III. Inversion (Hyperbaton).

B. p. 449 (526); H. § 885; C. 719; D. § 630; J. § 904; especially S. passim.

Although the arrangement of words in the ancient languages, taken as a whole, is freer than in the modern, yet it is not so capricious, at least in prose, that words necessarily belonging together could be dissociated without any reason. On the contrary, even in this respect language is confined always within certain limits. The reasons for the separation, which { 32 it must be confessed might often be very recondite according to our judgment, are predominantly rhetorical in nature, and consist in the requirements of euphony, of emphasis, of the antithetic or corresponsive location of particular members: — or, to express it generally, in the desire, constantly operative both in speaking and writing, to direct the hearer's or the reader's attention, at one time sooner, at another later, to single parts of the sentence, according to the nature of the thought. Here, however, as in the case of anacoluthon, we will pass in review only such instances of hyperbaton as are often repeated or possess a certain resemblance.

a. The Genitive is separated from its governing substan- 14 tive by other parts of the sentence, particularly by the predicate of the sentence. That perspicuity is not impaired, on the contrary often gains, by such an arrangement, appears from a nearer consideration of individual passages.

Among others look at Mark ii. 28 κύριός ἐστιν ὁ υἱὸς τοῦ ἀνθρώπου καὶ τοῦ σαββάτου, Rom. ix. 21 ἢ οὐκ ἔχει ἐξουσίαν ὁ κεραμεὺς τοῦ πηλοῦ (cf. § 140, 3 Remark p. 260), Eph. ii. 3 ἦμεν τέκνα φύσει ὀργῆς, 1 Thess. ii. 13 παραλαβόντες λόγον ἀκοῆς παρ' ἡμῶν τοῦ θεοῦ, where θεοῦ depends on λόγον as is evident from what follows (deWette, *das von uns verkündigte Wort Gottes*), 2 Cor. iii. 6 διακόνους καινῆς διαθήκης, οὐ γράμματος ἀλλὰ πνεύματος etc., where the two Genitives γράμματος and πνεύματος depend according to vss. 7 and 8 on διακόνους. In both these last passages a different arrangement was hardly possible, owing to the double Genitives. 1 Pet. iii. 21 οὐ σαρκὸς ἀπόθεσις ῥύπου, where emphasis occasioned the precedence of σαρκός. See also Acts iv. 33; xxii. 9; Gal. ii. 6; ii. 9; Jas. iii. 3; Heb. xii. 11 etc.; and on 2 Pet. iii. 2 see § 132, 1 b) p. 155. In Greek as in Latin there is a predilection for separating the Partitive Genitive in this way from its governing word, sometimes to such an extent that the two words belonging together occupy the first place in the clause and the last

(cf. Cic. de Or. 1, 1, 3, and Krüger, Lat. Gram. § 684, [S. p. xxxiii sq.]),
e.g. John iv. 39; xii. 11; 1 Cor. x. 27, etc.; and the Genitive of the
Personal Pronouns also, in so far as it serves as a periphrasis for the
Possessives, but (according to B. § 133 N. 10) in consequence of the
stronger attractive power of the verb is placed nearer it, so that it
then takes the place as it were of the Dative required by the verb.
See (besides the example from John ix. 6 given § 133, 16 p. 180)
John xiii. 6 σύ μου νίπτεις τοὺς πόδας; 14 ὀφείλετε ἀλλήλων νίπτειν
τοὺς πόδας.

15   b. A P a r t i c i p l e in apposition to a substantive, and having
an Infinitive clause also dependent upon it, stands by itself
between the subst. and its article and allows the Infinitive
adjunct to follow the substantive.

1 Cor. xii. 22 τὰ δοκοῦντα μέλη τοῦ σώματος ἀσθενέστερα ὑπάρχειν
instead of τὰ μέλη τοῦ σώματος τὰ δοκοῦντα ἀσθενέστερα ὑπάρχειν, Rom.
333 viii. 18 τὴν μέλλουσαν δόξαν ἀποκαλυφθῆναι, Gal. iii. 23. In a similar
manner A d v e r b i a l A d j u n c t s belonging immediately to a Participle having the article stand (not between the Art. and Part. but)
outside, as 2 Pet. iii. 2 μνησθῆναι τῶν προειρημένων ῥημάτων ὑπὸ τῶν
προφητῶν; (on this idiom, by no means rare in the classics, see B. 22d
Germ. ed. § 151, iii, 7, [for examples cf. S. p. lxxx col. 2]). Hence
grammatically it is quite admissible in 2 Thess. ii. 6 νῦν τὸ κατέχον
(particularly on comparing other passages where νῦν precedes in a
similar way, John iv. 18; Acts xv. 10; xxii. 16) to refer the νῦν to
κατέχον; yet see Meyer [i.e. Lünemann] in loc. On the other hand,
in Rom. vii. 21 recent interpreters have with reason contested the
opinion of those who draw τὸν νόμον into the Participial clause as
object; cf. Winer p. 557 (518).

16   c. I n t e r r o g a t i v e C l a u s e s often take the subject of the
clause or other words, on which in the course of the question
the main emphasis falls, before the interrogative word.

Thus often σὺ τίς εἶ John i. 19; viii. 25; xxi. 12; Rom. ix. 20;
xiv. 4; Jas. iv. 12, σὺ τί λέγεις John ix. 17, ... κρίνεις Rom. xiv. 10.
See besides Luke ix. 20; xvi. 11, 12 (in both instances the object,
owing to antithesis), xxiii. 31; John xxi. 21; Acts xv. 10; v. 35 (see
§ 147, 24 p. 337, [S. p. xxiv]).

17   d. In R e l a t i v e C l a u s e s this occurs less frequently, and
probably only when they precede, owing to the external similarity they then bear to interrogative clauses, — (hence in
Acts i. 2 the adjunct διὰ πνεύματος ἁγίου is with reason not
connected with the following Relative clause by the majority
of recent expositors).

John iv. 18 νῦν ὃν ἔχεις, 1 Cor. xv. 36 σὺ ὃ σπείρεις, and probably also John viii. 25 τὴν ἀρχὴν ὅ, τι καὶ λαλῶ ὑμῖν see Lücke in loc., and x. 29 if, with Tdf. [Treg. cod. Sin.] and cod. Vat. first hand, we read ὁ πατήρ ὃ δέδωκέν μοι, πάντων μεῖζόν ἐστι instead of ὁ πατήρ, ὃς δέδωκέν μοι, πάντων μείζων ἐστί. Cf. besides the paragraph on inverted attraction with Relative clauses § 143, 13 p. 288, [S. p. xxix].

e. This transposition takes place, further, in clauses with **18** subordinating conjunctions; so that, in consequence, the emphasized word precedes the conjunction, — as is so often the case in Latin also.

For example: before ἵνα, 2 Cor. ii. 4 τὴν ἀγάπην ἵνα γνῶτε, ἣν ἔχω εἰς ὑμᾶς, Acts xix. 4; Col. iv. 16; Gal. ii. 10; Eph. iii. 18 Lchm. (see § 144, 13, b) p. 299), 1 Cor. ix. 15 Tdf.; before ἐάν, 1 Cor. vi. 4. On 1 Cor. xi. 14 cf. 4 above, p. 380; before ὡς, Rom. xii. 3; 1 Cor. iii. 5; vii. 17; before ἕως, 2 Thess. ii. 7.

f. Smaller words, Particles, Negatives, because in **19** their ordinary place they might easily remain unnoticed, stand not infrequently, in case of emphasis, in a position where, taken with rigorous logic, they do not belong; but this certainly occurs also often without any other design than regard for euphony and rhythmical flow, — a consideration which in Greek writers (in the N. T. especially with Luke and the author of the Ep. to the Heb.) readily occasions the displacement of unemphatic words.

Acts xxvi. 24 τὰ πολλά σε γράμματα εἰς μανίαν περιτρέπει, Heb. iv. 11 ἵνα μὴ ἐν τῷ αὐτῷ τις ὑποδείγματι πέσῃ, Rom. v. 6 ἔτι γὰρ Χριστὸς ὄντων ἡμῶν ἀσθενῶν κατὰ καιρὸν ... ἀπέθανεν, where the ἔτι is repeated again by several ancient MSS. [cod. Sin. also] (and Lchm. [Treg. Tdf.]) in the place where it properly belongs (after ἀσθενῶν). On **334** the trajection of ὅμως see § 144, 23 p. 308. • Negatives transposed : Acts vii. 48 ἀλλ' οὐχ ὁ ὕψιστος ἐν χειροποιήτοις κατοικεῖ. In Rom. iii. 9 τί οὖν ; προεχόμεθα; οὐ πάντως, several interpreters have taken οὐ πάντως as an inversion for πάντως οὐ (1 Cor. xvi. 12). It is evident, however, that nothing but deference to our usage (because we invert in translation our corresponding words *altogether not, ganz und gar nicht*) produced the assumption. Both adverbial expressions πάντως οὐ and οὐ πάντως correspond precisely to the N. T. periphrases for the negative adjectives by means of πᾶς οὐ and οὐ πᾶς (see § 127, 32 p. 121); and as in that case both combinations are rendered by *no one*, so here the two adverbial expressions may in a similar manner be reproduced by *in no wise* (i.e. not at all). The separation of the two words (as in the case of the adjective) was impossible in the passage before us, owing to the ellipsis; but there is nothing to prevent our filling out the expression (in accordance with p. 122) thus: οὐ προεχόμεθα πάντως. On the other hand, in 1 Cor. v. 10 ἔγραψα ὑμῖν μὴ συναναμίγνυσθαι πόρνοις, οὐ πάντως τοῖς πόρνοις etc. the first (dependent) negative, precisely according to the rule in § 148, 8 p. 352, is not continued in the following clause (in this case μὴ πάντως would have been absolutely required) but revoked, or rather in a certain sense restricted, by the second (direct) negative :- *I wrote to you to hold no intercourse with fornicators;* (by that *I mean*) *not completely, not altogether* etc., *for otherwise* (ἐπεὶ ὠφείλετε, see § 149, 5 p. 359) *ye must* etc. Mark iv. 16 καὶ οὗτοί εἰσιν ὁμοίως οἱ ἐπὶ τὰ πετρώδη σπειρόμενοι οἳ for καὶ ὁμοίως οἱ ἐπὶ τὰ π. σπειρόμενοι οὗτοί εἰσιν οἵ etc. In 2 Tim. ii. 6 the assumption of an hyperbaton (πρῶτον belonging to κοπιῶντα) has been discarded by recent expositors, and in Acts i. 21 ἐφ' ἡμᾶς belongs to the entire predicate εἰσῆλθεν καὶ ἐξῆλθεν taken as one idea: *to go out and in.*

20 g. Lastly, entire clauses also are sometimes moved forward, sometimes displaced. This occurs, however, more or less in all languages, and the reason for the change of location is, as a rule, plainly to be perceived.

Somewhat abnormal and unusual, according to N. T. usage, is the placing of the final clause first in John xix. 28 μετὰ τοῦτο εἰδὼς ... ἵνα τελειωθῇ ἡ γραφὴ, λέγει · διψῶ (see Lücke), xix. 31; Rom. ix. 11 (see Fritzsche, Com. II. p. 297); also the arrangement in John xi. 15 χαίρω δι' ὑμᾶς, ἵνα πιστεύσητε, ὅτι etc. where ὅτι depends on χαίρω; and further, the position of the Relative clause in John x. 36 (see on this § 141, 1 p. 272), and of the indirect interrogative clause in 1 Cor. xv. 2 δι' οὗ καὶ σώζεσθε, τίνι λόγῳ εὐηγγελισάμην ὑμῖν εἰ κατέχετε.

REMARK. On the phrases πρὸ ἓξ ἡμερῶν τοῦ πάσχα, ὡς ἀπὸ σταδίων etc. see § 131, 11 p. 153; and on ἐπὶ σταδίους δώδεκα χιλιάδων (Rev. xxi. 16) see § 132, 11 Rem. p. 163.

IV. ELLIPSIS (BRACHYLOGY, PREGNANT CONSTRUCTION).

B. § 151, 1 sqq.; H. §§ 880 sq.; C. cf. Index s. v.; D. §§ 627, 628; J. §§ 891 sq.

22 A large part of those instances to which with more or less reason the grammatical notion of Ellipsis, or the omission of a 335 part of a sentence, can be applied, have already been assigned to other places in this Grammar. We will give as complete a reference to them as possible, before we proceed to treat of those cases of ellipsis which ought to be grouped together here.

On the ellipsis of the subject, in so far as it is to be supplied

from the context or some other source, see § 129, 14 sqq. p. 132 sqq.;
of the substantive with an adjective § 123, 8 p. 81; § 134, 6
p. 189; of a substantive with the article followed by a Genitive or
some sort of an adverbial adjunct (ὁ τοῦ, οἱ περὶ, ἡ σήμερον, etc.) § 125,
7–10 pp. 94 sq.;   of the object or of ἑαυτόν § 130, 4 p. 144; of the
Genitive κυρίου with ὄνομα and of τῆς ὁδοῦ see p. 163;   of the pronominal words in two connected clauses § 130, 2 p. 142;   of an
indefinite pronominal term (τινές) with a partitive Gen., or its
periphrasis by means of ἐκ, § 132, 6 p. 158;   of the copula § 129,
20 sq. pp. 136 sq.;   of other general verbal notions akin to the
copula (as παρεῖναι, γίνεσθαι, ἐλθεῖν, our as respects, concerns, etc.) in
such sentences as τί ἐμοὶ καὶ σοί etc. § 129, 23 p. 137;   of ἤ after
πλεῖον etc. § 132, 21 p. 168;   of ἄν with ἔδει, ἀνῆκεν, etc., § 139, 15
p. 216 sq.;   of ἄν with conditional sentences of the fourth kind § 139,
27 p. 225;   of a Passive idea in the participle with the Dative
(consilii) § 133, 24 p. 185;   of a finite verb with the participle
§ 144, 6 and 7 pp. 292 sq.;   of a verb or term of fearing, anxiety,
before μή, μήποτε, etc. § 148, 10 p. 353;   of λέγω (in explanation)
with the Infin. absol. § 140, 18 p. 271, and with the negative οὐ § 148
8 p. 352;   on the elliptical mode of expression in proverbs and
proverbial phrases § 144, 5 p. 291 sq., cf. below no. 24, a) p. 394;
on the elliptical use of εἰ μή § 149, 4 p. 359;   of κἄν ibid. 6 p. 360;
on the ellipsis of an entire clause or thought before ὅτι § 149,
3 p. 358;   before γάρ ibid. 15 p. 370;   before ἵνα, and on the
elliptical ἵνα (ἀλλ᾽ ἵνα) in general, § 139, 47 p. 241;   on the ellipsis
of the consequent clause in so far as the sentence becomes in
this way anacoluthic, see the chapters on Anacoluthon and Aposiopesis.

Under the head of ellipsis in the broader (improper) sense 23
belong all those cases where certain parts of the sentence are
simply not repeated, because they are already contained in
what precedes.   Since this occurs in all languages, in the
following exposition (for simplicity's sake and in order not to
heap up a mass of perfectly plain and intelligible examples)
regard will be paid to those instances only in which an actual
deviation from our usage occurs.

a) The member dropped is of such a nature that, were the
sentence complete, it would have been repeated without
further change of form.

Passing over such passages as Luke xx. 24; Rom. iii. 27; viii. 4;
1 Cor. vii. 3; John iv. 26; Rom. xiii. 1, etc., where our language is
wont for the most part to express itself in the same way, we encounter
the greatest peculiarity in the following passages: 2 Cor. i. 6; v. 13;

vii. 12, in which passages the predicate, or its equivalent, must be re-
336 peated in the consequent clause from the antecedent clause; Rom.
xi. 6 where in the antecedent clause as well as in the consequent the
predicate must be supplied from what precedes; John iv. 53; Acts
xxiii. 34; 1 Cor. xv. 27 where in the clauses beginning with ὅτι the
predicate is wanting; Rom. ii. 28 where the words Ἰουδαῖος and
περιτομή strictly ought to have been expressed twice; Rom. iv. 16 διὰ
τοῦτο ἐκ πίστεως, ἵνα κατὰ χάριν (to be completed from vss. 13 and 14),
etc. The article is used alone with the omission of a participle
(contained in what precedes) in Matt. xxv. 17, 22 ὁ τὰ δύο sc. λαβών,
cf. Gal. iv. 29 and 24 b) below, p. 394.

b) A portion of the sentence must be repeated from the
preceding context, but with a change of form. Here, too,
it is superfluous to adduce all the examples, since we often
express ourselves in quite the same way.

For example: Mark xiv. 29 εἰ πάντες σκανδαλισθήσονται, ἀλλ' οὐκ
ἐγώ sc. σκανδαλισθήσομαι (as Matt. actually has it), xv. 8 ἤρξατο αἰτεῖσθαι, καθὼς ἀεὶ ἐποίει αὐτοῖς sc. ποιεῖν or ἵνα ποιήσῃ, 1 Cor. ix. 25 (sc.
ἵνα λάβωσιν), Heb. v. 5 (sc. ἐδόξασεν αὐτὸν γενηθῆναι ἀρχιερέα), Gal.
iii. 5 where also, according to 24 b) p. 394, a simple τοῦτο ποιεῖ may
be supplied. Further, see Matt. xxvi. 5; Luke xxiii. 41; John xiii.
9; xviii. 40; Rom. xi. 16; xii. 6 sqq., 1 Cor. xi. 1; xiv. 27; vii. 21;
ix. 12; Gal. ii. 16; Phil. iii. 4; Eph. v. 24; 2 Tim. i. 5; Heb. xii. 25.
Of course ellipses of this sort, especially the more surprising, were
apt to be filled out by the copyists, and hence many other passages
where the ellipsis is found in the minority of MSS. may originally have
belonged under this head; as Eph. v. 22 Tdf. Respecting the
instances where the subject is supplied in this way from the context,
see § 129, 14, 15 pp. 132 sq.

c) When in a following clause, instead of the negatived
member that precedes, the affirmative is to be supplied,
an intimation of this is given by the conjunction ἀλλά (as in
the opposite case by ἀλλ' οὐ Mark xiv. 29 etc.). (Cf. the
elliptical wohl aber in Germ.)

For example: 1 Cor. vii. 19; iii. 1, 7; x. 24 μηδεὶς τὸ ἑαυτοῦ ζητείτω,
ἀλλὰ (but every man) τὸ τοῦ ἑτέρου, Gal. vi. 15; Eph. iv. 29. In
2 Cor. viii. 5 καὶ οὐ καθὼς ἠλπίσαμεν, ἀλλ' ἑαυτοὺς ἔδωκαν etc. the predicate is expressed, indeed, in the clause that follows, but instead not
in the preceding clause: and (they gave) not barely as we hoped, but
even themselves did they give etc.

d) From a preceding specific erm a more general one,

or at least a kindr?d idea merely, is to be educed for what follows.

Rom. xiv. 21 καλὸν τὸ μὴ φαγεῖν κρέα μηδὲ πιεῖν οἶνον μηδὲ ἐν ᾧ ... προσκόπτει nor in general to do anything etc., 23; Heb. x. 6, 8 ὁλοκαυτώματα καὶ περὶ ἁμαρτίας sc. προσφοράν, 38 (on which see § 129, 15 p. 133), John xii. 5 where, strictly speaking, we must supply with ἐδόθη *the proceeds* gained from the sale of the ointment, 2 Cor. v. 12 where from συνιστάνομεν a γράφομεν or λέγομεν τοῦτο is to be derived. On Rev. xii. 12 Lchm. [Treg.] see § 131, 14 p. 154.

e) After εἰ δὲ μή or εἰ δὲ μή γε (see B. l.c. 7) the ellipsis became, as is well known, so general, that this formula acquired almost the force of an unchangeable particle, serving 337 to negative the preceding clause regardless of its form and to introduce what follows; much as we use the word *otherwise*.

Hence it stands not only (as in Greek authors) after antecedent negations, Luke v. 36 sq. and its parallels, 2 Cor. xi. 16, but also as a continuation of a condition expressed by ἐάν, Luke x. 6; xiii. 9, indeed is even so used that a second clause with ἐάν, taking up as it were in what follows the εἰ δὲ μή and paraphrasing it, is added, Rev. ii. 5 (cf. Clement's 2d Ep. ad Cor. c. 6). In general it stands readily after Imperatives, so that the predicate in an altered form strictly ought to be repeated according to b) above; as, Matt. vi. 1; John xiv. 11; 2 Cor. xi. 16; Rev. ii. 5, 16.

f) Particularly characteristic of Paul is the elliptical construction after the formula οὐ μόνον δὲ ... followed by ἀλλὰ καί; what is omitted may in every instance easily be supplied from the context.

For example: Rom. v. 3, 11; viii. 23; ix. 10 (where the second clause also is elliptical, or rather anacoluthic, the antecedent Nom. Ῥεβέκκα being taken up again, according to 4 above, p. 380, by the Dative αὐτῇ in vs. 12), 2 Cor. viii. 19; On the other hand, more complete is 1 Tim. v. 13 (2 Tim. iv. 8 etc.). In Greek authors also, particularly the later (Diog. Laert., Lucian), a similar usage is found.

g) Lastly, to avoid repetitions sometimes the entire consequent clause is omitted, or is wrought immediately into the antecedent clause.

So particularly in comparative sentences (as the same thing often occurs in Latin authors also, e.g. Cic. sen. 2. 5; 11. 36); as, 2 Cor. iii. 13 καὶ οὐ καθάπερ Μωυσῆς ἐτίθει κάλυμμα etc., Matt. xxv.

14 sq.; 1 John iii. 12. On this cf. besides 12 above, p. 386, and especially 26 below (Aposiopesis) p. 396.

24 The actual ellipses, i.e. those which are not resorted to in order to avoid a repetition, but where the missing member is to be supplied from the words immediately given, are for the most part contained in the list given above (22 p. 390 sq.). Here are still to be mentioned

a) The omission of the predicate in standing formulas and proverbial phrases, such as are found in all languages (cf. § 144, 5 p. 291).

For example: τί ἐμοὶ καὶ σοί (Matt. viii. 29; Mark i. 24; Luke viii. 28; John ii. 4), τὸ αἷμα ἐφ᾽ ἡμᾶς (Matt. xxvii. 25), ὀφθαλμὸν ἀντὶ ὀφθαλμοῦ (Matt. v. 38), etc., see the remaining examples in § 129, 23 p. 138; further, the familiar epistolary salutation χαίρειν, in which the accompanying Dative easily suggests the missing term λέγω (2 John 10, 11); as, Acts xv. 23; xxiii. 26; Jas. i. 1.

b) And in other sentences also, when the words actually expressed are sufficiently definite to cause the missing 338 predicate to suggest itself.

Thus the term εἶπεν is omitted when the direct discourse itself immediately follows (as in Lat.), e.g. Acts ii. 38 Πέτρος δὲ πρὸς αὐτούς · μετανοήσατε etc., xxv. 22, probably also 2 Cor. ix. 6 τοῦτο δὲ (sc. λέγω [Eng. *but this I say*]; deWette, *wisset*). On this cf. § 140, 18 p. 271. Further, other general terms are omitted whose more precise nature is indicated by a case or an adverb or a preposition (especially ἐκ and εἰς), as Luke xxii. 26 ὑμεῖς δὲ οὐχ οὕτως (sc. ποιήσετε), Phil. iii. 14 ἐν δὲ (sc. ποιῶ) cf. Gal. iii. 5, etc.; John xxi. 21 οὗτος δὲ τί; (say γίνεται), Rom. iv. 9 ὁ μακαρισμὸς οὗτος ἐπὶ τὴν περιτομὴν etc. (sc. γίνεται or λέγεται)[1], v. 18 εἰς πάντας ἀνθρώπους (sc. ἀπέβη, ἐγένετο), Gal. ii. 9 ἵνα ἡμεῖς εἰς τὰ ἔθνη, αὐτοὶ δὲ εἰς etc. (sc. ἐρχώμεθα), iii. 18 εἰ γὰρ ἐκ νόμων ἡ κληρονομία, v. 8 ἡ πεισμονὴ οὐκ ἐκ τοῦ καλοῦντος ἡμᾶς, 13 μόνον μὴ τὴν ἐλευθερίαν εἰς ἀφορμὴν τῇ σαρκί (where the idea omitted is something like *possess, make use of*, and is intimated by the μή of the Imperative). The more specific predicates, if they have not already been expressly mentioned in the preceding context, are less frequently omitted, because their omission easily causes obscurity. Yet we easily supply in Gal. i. 20 (ἰδοὺ ἐνώπιον τοῦ θεοῦ ὅτι) the idea *I swear*, in Rev. vi. 6 (τρεῖς χοίνικες δηναρίου) from the accompanying Gen. of price the notion of a verb of buying or appraising, in 2 Cor. ix. 7 the term δότω from the drift of the entire section (chaps. viii. and ix.). 1 Cor. iv. 6 is more difficult; here we must supply with ἵνα μάθητε τὸ
[[1]cf. p. 138.]

μὴ ὑπὲρ ἃ γέγραπται an Infin., say φρονεῖν (which as an explanatory addition is found even in the mss.). In some passages the elliptically used article necessarily points to a Participle (cf. 23, a) p. 392): Acts xiii. 9 Σαῦλος, ὁ καὶ Παῦλος sc. καλούμενος, Rom. xiii. 7 ἀπόδοτε ... τῷ τὸν φόρον (sc. αἰτοῦντι) τὸν φόρον, τῷ τὸ τέλος etc. 2 Cor. viii. 15 (quotn.) ὁ τὸ πολὺ (sc. συλλέγων) οὐκ ἐπλεόνασεν, καὶ ὁ τὸ ὀλίγον etc. Several examples quite similar are adduced from Lucian by Du Mesnil, Stolper Progr. (1867) p. 9.

REMARK. Here belongs also the phrase ὅρα μή, uttered after the manner of an aposiopesis (no. 26 p. 396) and left incomplete: Rev xix. 10; xxii. 9.

c) To the instances where an entire thought or a complete clause must be supplied (see 22 p. 390) belongs the construction, when, between premise and conclusion, the middle member or logical link is wanting, — the writer in his haste to reach the main thought giving it at once in the form of the conclusion.

Rom. xi. 18 μὴ κατακαυχῶ τῶν κλάδων · εἰ δὲ κατακαυχᾶσαι, οὐ σὺ τὴν ῥίζαν βαστάζεις etc. supply, *remember that* etc. Likewise, 1 Cor. xi. 16; John ix. 36 τίς ἐστιν, κύριε, ἵνα πιστεύσω εἰς αὐτόν, 1 John v. 9. Also in 1 Cor. xv. 32 εἰ νεκροὶ οὐκ ἐγείρονται, φάγωμεν καὶ πίωμεν, αὔριον γὰρ ἀποθνήσκομεν, strictly taken, such a middle member is omitted, and yet the conclusion (φάγ. καὶ πίω.) in the spirited style connects finely with the premise. To the same desire to omit superfluous and unessential words and give the main thought itself as soon as possible, is to be traced the omission before a Relative clause of the Demonstrative, grammatically required, together with the copula belonging to it; as, 2 Cor. iv. 6 ὁ θεὸς ὁ εἰπὼν ἐκ σκότους φῶς λάμψαι, ὃς ἔλαμψεν i.e. *he* it is who etc. (cf. v. 5); Luke viii. 13 οἱ δὲ ἐπὶ τῆς 339 πέτρας (sc. οὗτοί εἰσιν) οἵ, ὅταν ἀκούσωσιν etc.

It is obvious that the majority of ellipses have arisen from 25 an endeavor after brevity of expression; hence many of them have been treated by grammarians and interpreters under the designation of Brachylogy (Breviloquence) or Pregnant Construction. Since, however, it is difficult — so elastic is the idea of Brachylogy — to draw a boundary even approximately precise between it and Ellipsis, it seemed to be more convenient and more promotive of perspicuity to unite all the instances of the sort under the one general head of Ellipsis.

It may be particularly mentioned here, also, that many of the syntactic combinations already treated of in other parts of this Grammar may be viewed as brachylogic, inasmuch as the term or member omitted, or rather not specially expressed, does not admit of being represented so definitely as in the foregoing paragraphs by one or more words fitting into the context. Thus the usage is decidedly brachylogical, of substituting in comparisons at once the whole instead of the part to which, strictly speaking, the comparison extends; on this see § 132, 20 p. 167 in connection with § 133, 10 p. 177.

Brachylogic, further, are many of the adjuncts in the Acc. with Passive and Middle notions (see among other examples 2 Cor. vi. 13 and iii. 18 in § 134, 7 p. 190) ; the omission of a verbum *dicendi, sentiendi, quærendi* before a direct discourse, sentences with ὅτι, questions etc., see § 139, 57, 58 pp. 250 sq., § 141, 1 and Note p. 272 sq.; clauses with ἐπεί and ἀλλά in the pregnant signification *since then, since otherwise, otherwise however*, see § 149, 5 p. 359 and 14 p. 369; the adverbial specifications of the departure and the goal at the same time with ἄρχεσθαι, see § 150, 7 p. 374; as well as all the numerous instances of the so-called pregnant construction with prepositions, see § 147 under the several prepositions, especially under ἀπό p. 322 sq., ἐκ p. 327, εἰς p. 332 sq.

V. Aposiopesis.

B. p. 452 (529); H. § 883; D. § 627; J. § 860, 3; 897.

36   In perfect agreement with the classic examples of Aposiopesis after an antecedent conditional clause is Luke xiii. 9 κἂν μὲν ποιήσῃ καρπόν · εἰ δὲ μή γε, εἰς τὸ μέλλον ἐκκόψεις αὐτήν.

Analogous in form to this are the following: Luke xix. 42 εἰ ἔγνως καὶ σὺ καί γε ἐν τῇ ἡμέρᾳ σου ταύτῃ τὰ πρὸς εἰρήνην σου · νῦν δὲ etc., where the form of the suppressed apodosis is sufficiently indicated by the formula νῦν δέ, which is so often introduced after conditional sentences of the fourth kind (John viii. 40; ix. 41; xv. 22, 24 etc.; 1 Cor. xii. 20; Heb. ix. 26; xi. 16), Luke xxii. 42 Tdf. [eds. 2, 7; ed. 8 παρενέγκαι, so cod. Sin.] (where the reading παρένεγκε [Lchm. Treg.] probably came from the copyists, who either were not acquainted with the idiom or wanted to make the words conform to those in the parallel passages). Similar also are John vi. 62; Acts 340 xxiii. 9; Rom. ix. 22; in these passages the editors indicate the presence of this kind of ellipsis by an interrogation mark (as denoting a thought remaining as it were without answer, or the answer to which is left to the hearer).

On the origin of the formula of swearing with εἰ without an apodosis following, see § 149, 4 p. 358.

VI. PLEONASM.

B. p. 452 (530); H. § 884; C. cf. Index; D. § 629; J. § 899.

The majority of pleonastic modes of expression, like the elliptical, so far forth as they are of a grammatical nature have been considered and discussed at other points in this Grammar, to which the following summary reference may be of service:

On the superfluous use of Pronouns, particularly of the Pron. αὐτός, the Possessives, and their periphrases by means of the Personals, see § 127, 9 sq. p. 107 sq., 26 p. 118; § 130, 2 p. 142; of the oblique cases of αὐτός in Hebrew fashion in Relative sentences, § 143, 1 p. 280; on οὗτος and οὕτως after Participles (and substantives) with and without the article, § 144, 21 p. 306; on οὗτος before clauses with ὅτι and ἵνα, § 127, 6 p. 105; on οὕτως at the beginning of the conclusion, § 149, 1 p. 357; on τις in the combination εἷς τις, § 124, 1 p. 85; on μᾶλλον with the Comparative, § 123, 11 p. 83; on καί after ὡς, ὡσαύτως, at the beginning of the conclusion, etc., § 149, 8 c) and f) p. 362 sq.; on ὅτι before the Infin., and before other declarative clauses (ὅτι, ὡς), see 10 above, p. 383; on the Negatives οὐ and μή after predicates in which a negative idea is contained, as well as μή in the formula ἐκτὸς εἰ μή, § 148, 13 p. 355; on οὐ in ἤ οὐ see § 149, 7 p. 360; on the Hebraistic circumlocution for prepositions by means of the phrases διὰ χειρός, διὰ στόματος, πρὸ προσώπου, and the like, § 133, 20 p. 182; § 146, 1 p. 319, and § 147 under the several Prep.; on Participles in such combinations as εἶπεν, ἐλάλησεν λέγων, the Hebraistic combinations ἰδὼν εἶδον etc., § 144, 30 p. 313; on the Dative in similar combinations, § 133, 22 p. 183 sq.; on the Imperatives ὅρα, βλέπετε before other Imperatives, § 139, 49 p. 242 sq.

The pleonastic fashion of subjoining to local adverbs answering to the question *whence* the Prep. ἀπό, ἐκ, has been already mentioned on p. 70. A similar redundance (of which numerous examples can be adduced from Greek authors also, see the grammars) occurs, too, with other adverbial expressions, e.g. John xi. 7 ἔπειτα μετὰ τοῦτο, xiii. 27 μετὰ τὸ ψωμίον τότε (see § 147, 26 p. 339), particularly in the repetition in an adverbial form of the idea of the Prep. with which the verb is compounded, as ἐκβάλλειν and ἐξάγειν ἔξω (Luke iv. 29; xxiv. 50, etc.), προδραμὼν ἔμπροσθεν (xix. 4), πάλιν ἀνακάμπτειν (Acts xviii. 21), with which agree the pleonasms with substantives, ὁ οἰκοδεσπότης τῆς οἰκίας Luke xxii. 11, τὰ βαΐα τῶν φοινίκων John xii. 13.

A great portion of the pleonasms of the N. T. are of a rhetorical nature or belong to the peculiar style of the several

writers, who vary in their fondness for expressing themselves
in the verbose Oriental fashion.　To these Oriental pleonasms
341 belong such phrases as ὁρᾶν ὀφθαλμοῖς (1 John i. 1); μέλλουσιν
ἔρχεσθαι καὶ ἁρπάζειν αὐτόν (John vi. 15) ; ἀνοίξας τὸ στόμα
αὐτοῦ καὶ ἀρξάμενος ἀπὸ τῆς γραφῆς ταύτης εὐηγγελίσατο etc.
(Acts viii. 35, cf. x. 34 ; Matt. v. 2) ; ἐπάρας τοὺς ὀφθαλμοὺς
καὶ θεασάμενος (John vi. 5) ; the frequently repeated ἰδού
(often twice and more in the same sentence), particularly in
the historic style ; the periphrastic way of expressing a simple
event by means of ἐγένετο δὲ, or καὶ ἐγένετο, with a finite verb
following, or an Infinitive (§ 141, 6 p. 276) ; the tropes χεὶρ
κυρίου, οἱ ὀφθαλμοὶ κυρίου ; the many phrases and periphrases
formed with the word ὄνομα ; and many others.　The subject,
consequently, is less of a grammatical nature, than of a stylistic
nature in the main.　Of the copious details, those which admit
of being brought under somewhat definite linguistic heads are
the following :

a) The (frequent) literal and commonly asyndetic
repetition of a member of a sentence, particularly in successive
parallel sentences, is designed for oratorical effect.

Thus the forceful threefold ἐβλήθη in Rev. xii. 9, the double ἰδοὺ
νῦν in 2 Cor. vi. 2, the thrice used πάντα ἄνθρωπον in Col. i. 28, the
threefold ἀλλά in 1 Cor. vi. 11, the fivefold πάντες (connected by καὶ)
in x. 1 sq.　Further, see Rom. viii. 15 (πνεῦμα twice), John i. 10 (καὶ
ὁ κόσμος twice), xiv. 27 (εἰρήνην twice, asyndetically), xix. 10 (ἐξουσίαν
ἔχω twice), Matt. xii. 37 (ἐκ τῶν λόγων σου twice), 1 Cor. xiii. 11 (ὡς
νήπιος thrice, asyndetically), xiv. 24 (ὑπὸ πάντων twice, asyndetically),
i. 20 (ποῦ three times, asyndetically), iv. 8 (ἤδη twice), 2 Cor. xi. 26
(κινδύνοις eight times, asyndetically), vii. 2 (οὐδένα three times, asyndetically), xi. 20 (εἴ τις five times, asyndetically), Phil. iii. 2 (βλέπετε
three times, asyndetically), iv. 8 (ὅσα six times, asyndetically), Eph.
vi. 12 (πρός four times, asyndetically), 1 Tim. v. 10 (εἰ five times,
asyndetically), 1 John i. 1 sq. (ὃ four times, asyndetically), an entire
telic clause twice in 2 Cor. xii. 7.　The repetition of the same word
in immediate succession in ἔπεσεν, ἔπεσεν Βαβυλὼν ἡ μεγάλη, Rev.
xiv. 8 ; xviii. 2, is emphatic ; the doubling of the Imperative attests
the clamorousness of the demand, as in σταύρωσον, σταύρωσον John
xix. 6 ; the repetition of the person addressed, anxious solicitude of
the speaker in respect to himself,— as Matt. xxv. 11 κύριε, κύριε, ἄνοιξον
ἡμῖν, Luke viii. 24 ἐπιστάτα, ἐπιστάτα, ἀπολλύμεθα, — or earnest and
reproachful admonition in respect to the person addressed, as Luke x.

41 Μάρθα, Μάρθα, μεριμνᾷς etc., xxii. 31 Σίμων, Σίμων, ᾿δοὺ ὁ σατανᾶς etc., Acts ix. 4 etc. Σαούλ, Σαούλ, τί με διώκεις ;

b) The altered repetition of a particular member aims to give it prominence in order to turn attention to it, sometimes also merely to take it up again in a more suitable position.

This repetition occurs most commonly by means of the Demonstrative οὗτος and adverb οὕτως, sometimes in the following clause (see the examples in § 144, 21 p. 306), sometimes in the very same clause, as John iv. 6 Ἰησοῦς κεκοπιακὼς ... ἐκαθέζετο οὕτως, Matt. xiii. 20 sqq. 342 ὁ δὲ ἐπὶ τὰ πετρώδη σπαρεὶς οὗτός ἐστιν etc., Acts ii. 23 Ἰησοῦν τὸν Ναζωραῖον ... τοῦτον ἀνείλατε, xv. 38 ; Rom. vii. 10 εὑρέθη μοι ἡ ἐντολὴ ἡ εἰς ζωὴν, αὕτη εἰς θάνατον, ix. 6, etc. The periphrastic repetition aims at perspicuity, see the following section.

c) A peculiar kind of altered repetition, which in the N. T. is especially characteristic of John, but is often found also in all Greek literature from Homer on (see the examples in B. VI. 2 ; J. § 899, 6), consists in the repetition of the negatived contrary, and that too always immediately afterwards and connected by καί.

John i. 20 ὡμολόγησεν καὶ οὐκ ἠρνήσατο, 1 John i. 6 ψευδόμεθα καὶ οὐ ποιοῦμεν τὴν ἀλήθειαν (yet here with a certain difference), ii. 4, 27 ἀληθές ἐστιν καὶ οὐκ ἔστιν ψεῦδος, Luke i. 20 σιωπῶν καὶ μὴ δυνάμενος λαλῆσαι, Acts xviii. 9 λάλει καὶ μὴ σιωπήσῃς, Heb. xii. 8 νόθοι ἐστὲ καὶ οὐχ υἱοί; cf. John i. 3, etc. Both emphasis and perspicuity are the aim of this mode of expression.

d) Those instances in which an entire clause (antecedent or parenthetic) is repeated for the sake of perspicuity belong rather to Exegesis or Stylistics. See e.g. Rom. vi. 16 ᾧ παριστάνετε ἑαυτούς ... ᾧ ὑπακούετε, — at which Lchm. (II. praef. x) takes offence without reason ; see Meyer in loc.

VII. Epexegesis.

B. p. 453 (530); C. § 668; J. § 667; 835, 2.

Epexegetical additions in the books of the N. T., especially 29 in the MSS., are innumerable. Many of these, however, long ago came into suspicion with N. T. critics as probably being glosses and interpretations added by some later hand, admitted into the text of the MSS. by the carelessness of the copyists, and thence into the printed editions; and they have now, through the laborious, acute and comparative criticism of recent editors, been removed from the text.

A large part of the genuine epexegetical additions are announced by the adverbial τουτέστιν (see p. 11), particularly in the Epp. to the Rom. and the Heb.; see the lexicons. But there are many also without that adjunct: thus the Infinitive, with and without τοῦ, after abstracts, in explanation or extension of their meaning, as Rev. xiii. 6 βλασφημίας πρὸς τὸν θεόν, βλασφημῆσαι τὸ ὄνομα αὐτοῦ καὶ τὴν σκηνὴν αὐτοῦ καὶ τοὺς ἐν τῷ οὐρανῷ σκηνοῦντας; see the exx. with τοῦ in § 140, 14 p. 268; after Pronouns and Adverbs to designate them more closely, as 1 Cor. xvi. 21 τῇ ἐμῇ χειρὶ Παύλου, John ix. 13 ἄγουσιν αὐτὸν πρὸς τοὺς Φαρισαίους, τόν ποτε τυφλόν, Acts viii. 38; 1 Thess. iv. 3 τοῦτό ἐστιν τὸ θέλημα τοῦ θεοῦ, ὁ ἁγιασμὸς ὑμῶν, Jas. iv. 1 οὐκ ἐντεῦθεν, ἐκ τῶν ἡδονῶν ὑμῶν; (cf. with this the preparatory οὗτος, etc., § 127, 6 p. 105), Mark ii. 20; Luke v. 35 τότε ... ἐν ἐκείνῃ τῇ ἡμέρᾳ or ἐκείναις ταῖς ἡμέραις (cf. the opposite case John xiii. 27);[1] and also after words of other kinds that need explanation, e.g. John 343 vi. 1 πέραν τῆς θαλάσσης τῆς Γαλιλαίας, τῆς Τιβεριάδος, Eph. i. 7 ἐν ᾧ ἔχομεν τὴν ἀπολύτρωσιν, τὴν ἄφεσιν τῶν παραπτωμάτων, 13 ὁ λόγος τῆς ἀληθείας, τὸ εὐαγγέλιον τῆς σωτηρίας ὑμῶν, Rom. viii. 23 υἱοθεσίαν ἀπεκδεχόμενοι, τὴν ἀπολύτρωσιν τοῦ σώματος ἡμῶν, Phil. iv. 18; Eph. ii. 15, etc. To determine how far additions connected by καί also are of an epexegetical nature as respects sense, is a matter for the interpreter; as respects grammatical form, they cannot be denominated epexegetical, owing to the connection by καί; see § 149, 8 h) p. 363.

REMARK. On Rev. ii. 5 (εἰ δὲ μή ... ἐὰν μὴ μετανοήσῃς) see 23, e) p. 393.

VIII. ZEUGMA.

B. p. 453 (530 sq.); H. § 882; C. § 497; D. § 628; J. § 895, 5.

30 That in the N. T. there are indubitable instances of this grammatical figure of speech may be seen from the following examples:

1 Cor. xiv. 34 Tdf. [eds. 2, 7] οὐ γὰρ ἐπιτρέπεται αὐταῖς λαλεῖν, ἀλλὰ ὑποτάσσεσθαι etc., where ἐπιτρ. strictly suits λαλεῖν only, and from it is to be derived the requisite notion of necessity for ὑποτάσσεσθαι (hence the early alteration into the Imperative: ὑποτασσέσθωσαν Lchm. [Treg. Tdf. cod. Sin.]), Luke i. 64 ἀνεῴχθη τὸ στόμα αὐτοῦ παραχρῆμα

---

[1] Here belongs also Acts xix. 40 μηδενὸς αἰτίου ὑπάρχοντος, περὶ οὗ δυνησόμεθα δοῦναι λόγον τῆς συστροφῆς ταύτης, which arose from μηδ. αἰτ. ὑπάρχ., ὅτι or ἵνα περὶ τούτου (sc. περὶ τῆς συστροφῆς ταύτης) δυνησόμεθα etc. On this cf. § 139, 32 p. 229 sq.

καὶ ἡ γλῶσσα αὐτοῦ (cf., on the other hand, Mark vii. 35 ἠνοίγησαν αὐτοῦ αἱ ἀκοαί, καὶ ἐλύθη ὁ δεσμὸς τῆς γλώσσης αὐτοῦ), 1 Cor. iii. 2 γάλα ὑμᾶς ἐπότισα, οὐ βρῶμα. An analogous instance also to those given in the grammars, where the o p p o s i t e idea must be educed, is found in 1 Tim. iv. 3 κωλυόντων γαμεῖν, ἀπέχεσθαι βρωμάτων, where from the negative κωλυόντων the positive notion κελειόντων or the general λεγόντων (cf. § 139, 42 note p. 237 ; § 141, 2 p. 273) must be educed.

REMARK. Acts xx. 34 probably is hardly to be called a zeugma. And that in Jas. i. 9, 10 by assuming this figure to occur, the peculiar force and beauty of the thought is positively impaired, is universally acknowledged now by the interpreters.

IX. ASYNDETON (POLYSYNDETA).

B. p. 453 (531); H. § 854; C. § 707 g.-j.; D. § 626; J. § 792.

The inquiry how far the several clauses, both within the 31 confines of a larger period and also the larger clauses among themselves, are joined together by conjunctions, or stand side by side asyndetically, or are connected differently and by means of different conjunctions than is wont to be the case in Greek authors, opens a wide field ; and to treat it exhaustively would require a special and detailed examination in which the style of the individual writers should be carefully discriminated. Much that belongs to such a discussion, however, has already been treated of in other parts of this Grammar, 344 particularly in §§ 139, 149, 150 ; e.g. the frequent connection of sentences and members of sentences by means of καί (John x. 3, 12 ; Acts xiii. 36 ; xvii. 28 ; 1 Cor. xii. 4 sq. ; Jas. v. 17, 18 ; see the other examples of polysyndetic connection in § 144, 1 p. 288 sq.), the use of the simple δέ or even καί instead of μὲν ... δέ elsewhere more usual (§ 149, 11 p. 364 ; 8 b) p. 361 sq.), of οὕτως at the beginning of the conclusion (§ 149, 1 p. 357), etc.

Here may be mentioned also, the connection (certainly unclassic) of historical events, in pursuing a narrative, by means of the adverb τότε, which thus (like the Latin *tum*) acquires almost the character of a c o n j u n c t i o n. This use is particularly current in Matthew, e.g. iii. 15 εἶπεν πρὸς αὐτόν· ἄφες ἄρτι ... τότε ἀφίησιν αὐτόν, iv. 9 sq. λέγει αὐτῷ· ταῦτά σοι πάντα δώσω ...· τότε λέγει αὐτῷ ὁ Ἰησοῦς etc., 11 τότε ἀφίησιν αὐτὸν ὁ διάβολος, ix. 6, etc.

A great number of examples of a s y n d e t o n, i.e. of asyn- 32 detically repeated single parts of a sentence, are already contained in 28 a) p. 398. It remains for us to consider here the most common instances of asyndetic juxtaposition of a different nature: and 1) those in which single parts of a sentence, 2) those in which entire independent sentences, succeed one another without a connective.

1) In the case of single parts of a sentence, asyndetic sequence occurs

a) With two Imperatives of which the first contains merely the formal introduction to the second and main command, as in Matt. v. 24 ὕπαγε διαλλάγηθι, xviii. 15 ὕπαγε ἔλεγξον, Mark i. 44; ii. 9 Tdf. [eds. 2, 7 ; ed. 8 adds καὶ, so cod. Sin.], 11 ἔγειρε ἆρον τὸν κράββατόν σου. Cf. with this the combinations ὁρᾶτε βλέπετε ἀπὸ . . . , ὁρᾶτε μηδεὶς γινωσκέτω, in § 139, 49 p. 243.

b) In enumerations, — whether consisting of substantives, as Rom. i. 29 sq. ψιθυριστάς, καταλάλους, ὑβριστάς etc., 2 Cor. xii. 20 ἔρις, ζῆλος, θυμοί etc., Gal. v. 20 ; 1 Tim. vi. 4 (see, on the other hand, the polysyndeton in Rev. v. 12, etc.), or epithets, as 1 Tim. iii. 2 sq. δεῖ τὸν ἐπίσκοπον ἀνεπίλημπτον εἶναι, μιᾶς γυναικὸς ἄνδρα, νηφάλιον, σώφρονα etc., Tit. i. 6 ; ii. 4; Jas. i. 8, etc.

c) for rhetorical reasons (cf. 28 a) p. 398), e.g. Mark iv. 39 σιώπα, πεφίμωσο, 1 Cor. iv. 8 ἤδη κεκορεσμένοι ἐστέ, ἤδη ἐπλουτήσατε, χωρὶς ἡμῶν ἐβασιλεύσατε, Jas. v. 5, 6 (ἐτρυφήσατε καὶ ἐσπαταλήσατε, ἐθρέψατε, κατεδικάσατε, ἐφονεύσατε), 1 Tim. iii. 16 etc., particularly in contrasting antithetic ideas and clauses, since the antithesis (as in Latin) comes out more emphatically by means of rhetorical asyndeton, than where the contrast is made by the help of adversative conjunctions, as 1 Cor. xv. 42 sq. σπείρεται ἐν φθορᾷ, ἐγείρεται ἐν ἀφθαρσίᾳ · σπείρεται ἐν ἀτιμίᾳ, ἐγείρεται ἐν δόξῃ etc., John iv. 22 ὑμεῖς προσκυνεῖτε ὃ οὐκ οἴδατε, ἡμεῖς προσκυνοῦμεν ὃ οἴδαμεν, vi. 63, etc. Compare with this the mode of contrasting two sentences in § 139, 28 p. 226.

33 2) Entire independent sentences, on the other hand, are subjoined asyndetically to what precedes, especially in the three following cases:

345 a) Pre-eminently characteristic of John is asyndeton in the narration of historic facts following each other, — their intimate connection being indicated, as a rule, by letting the predicate precede at the very head of the sentence; as, John i. 40 λέγει αὐτοῖς etc., 42 εὑρίσκει οὗτος πρῶτος etc., 46 εὑρίσκει Φίλιππος τὸν Ναθαναὴλ, 47 λέγει αὐτῷ, 48 εἶδεν Ἰησοῦς, 49 λέγει αὐτῷ . . . ἀπεκρίθη Ἰησοῦς, 50, 51 ἀπεκρίθη etc., Matt. xx. 7 λέγουσιν αὐτῷ · . . . λέγει αὐτοῖς · xxv 21 ἔφη αὐτῷ ὁ κύριος, xxvii. 65 ἔφη αὐτοῖς etc. That this species of

asyndeton has been marred by the copyists times without number, by
the insertion of such particles as δέ, γάρ, οὖν, etc., see e.g. in § 149, 9
p. 363, and cf. the critical commentaries on the N. T.

b) Further, entire passages of considerable length often stand
asyndetically, especially in the didactic style, in order to indicate the
commencement of a n e w s u b j e c t: see e.g. from the Ep. to the Rom.
viii. 16; ix. 1; x. 1; xiii. 1; from the 1st Ep. to the Cor. iv. 14; v. 9;
vi. 1; vi. 12; ix. 1; x. 23; xiv. 1, etc.

c) Lastly, s m a l l e r, p r o v e r b - l i k e, didactic utterances and
sayings are put together asyndetically.　Of these the Sermon on the
Mount and the discourses of Jesus in the Gospel of John afford
numerous examples, as well as the many separate commands and
exhortations in the hortatory portions of the Epistles and the Apocalypse.　See Matt. chaps. v. to vii.; John iii. 5–8; xii. 19; v. 23, 28,
30–33, 35 sqq.; vii. 16 sqq.; 1 Thess. v. 14; James chaps. iv. and v;
Rev. ii 10, 11; iii. 2, 6, etc.

I. INDEX OF SUBJECTS.

The Figures refer to Pages.

Absolute cases, see Accusative, Genitive, Participle, etc.

Abstracts in the Plur. 77; without an Art. 89; in the Acc. with cognate verb 148, and in the Dat. 183.

Accusative, the Alexandrian in ν 13. Syntax of 146 sqq.; with intransitives 147; of an abstract akin to the verb 148, 189; double 149, 152; Greek 152, cf. 183, 189; pronominal neuter instead of a different case 152; of time and distance 152 sq., cf. 170; as an adverb 153; as a parenthetic adjunct 153; of exclamation 154; of the object with the Passive 148, 188; with the Middle 191 sq.; absolute of participles 317, cf. 374 sq.; absolute at the beginning 381. With Infin. 272 sqq., interchanged with ὅτι 383.

Acts The, see Luke.

Adjectives, lingering in Nom. 78; diverging in Gend. or Num. 80; for adverbs 82 sq.; predicative without Art. 94, and with Art. 124; use of neuter 122; Gen. of a subst. for 161; κατά and Acc. for 156, 162; κ. with Gen. for 335; ἐν with Dat. for 331; verbal 41, 190.

Adverbs: 69, 319; adjectives for 82 sq.; neuters as 96, 123; as predicates 131; in elliptical construction 138; participles for 299; in cases of attraction 377; of place, loose use and attraction of 70, 105, cf. 221 note. Cf. Particles.

Adverbial adjuncts in the Nom. 139; separated from the Part. 388; subjoined to a subst. with the Art. 91; without the Art. 95 sq.

Aeolisms 61, 69.

Alexandrian dialect 1. Forms: Acc. in ν 13; names of Mts. 22; τέσσερα, κεκαθερισμένος, etc. 29; Aorist 39; 3d Plur. in -σαν 43; ἐραυνάω 58; ἧκα 59; λήμψομαι 62; καμμύω 62; κατενύγην 63; χεῶ 68; ἐδίδετο, etc. 47. Phrases and constructions, see Septuagint. Cf. Language.

Anacoluthon 378 sqq.; with μέν 365.

Analytical tendency in later (and especially N.T.) Greek: see Resolution, Periphrasis, Possessive adjuncts, Subject, Object, Pleonasm, αὐτός, ἐγώ, etc.

Anastrophe 72.

Antithesis: antithetic arrangement of words etc. with negatives 346, 349, 350, 352; indicated by δέ, καί, etc. 364 sq.; without a connective 402

Aorist, the Alexandrian 39; Passive with Mid. or Intrans. force 51 sq., 191; in sense of Perf. 197 sq.; prophetic 198; proleptic 198; for the Pluperf. 199; gnomic (of habitude) 201; and Imperfect cf. 200.

Apodosis wanting 386, 393. Cf. Aposiopesis, δέ, καί, οὕτως.

Aposiopesis: 396; cf. 358, 386.

Apposition 77 sq.; attracted by the Rel. 77; in the Nom. for some other case 78; in the Gen. 78, cf. 79 note; to the omitted subject 132; to the Voc. 141.

Article the, εἷς for the indefinite 85; the definite 85 sq.; with proper names 86; with pronouns 87, 119; not used for the indefinite 87 sq., 93; the rhetorical 88, 124; omitted 87 sqq., 91 sq.; with more closely defined substantives 90 sq.; used twice or thrice 90, 98; expressed but once 92 sq., 97 sqq.; after τινές and other indefinite expressions 93, 295; used absolutely, or in lieu of a subst. 94; with a Gen. following 95; with an adverbial limitation 95, 96; before entire clauses 96 sq.; with several connected substs. 97 sq.; as a Demonstrative (postpositive, ὅς μέν etc.) 101 sq. Wanting with Poss. adjuncts 119; with Demonstratives when predicative 120; with predicates 124; inserted with predicates 124 With the Voc. 140; with participles 124, 141, 309; with the Infin, 266 sqq.

405

Asking, verbs of, see ἐρωτᾶν, δεῖσθαι, etc.

Aspiration, before a smooth breathing etc. 7.

Asyndeton 226, 398, 401 sq.

Attic declension 13, 21; Attic Gen.14.

Attraction 376 sq.; of an appositive 77 sq.; with the Infin. 278; in relative sentences 285 sq.; faulty 287; with adverbs 287, 377; inverse 288; of the participle 305.

Attributives, agreement of with substantives 80 sq.; with the Art. 87, 89 sq.; belonging to several substantives 129. See Adjectives, Pronouns, Participles, etc.

Augment: neglected 32, 33, 34; double 35; superfluous 53, 63.

Blending of two constructions 318; of the Active and the Passive 384; of the direct and the indirect statement 385. Cf. variatio structurae.

Brachylogy 395 sq.; in comparisons 167, 177; with direct discourse, questions, etc. 250 sq.; 272 sq.; with ἐπεί, ἀλλά 359, 369; with ἄρχεσθαι 374; with ἀπό 322 sq.; ἐκ 327; εἰς 332 sq. For other reffs. see 396.

Breathings 7; over ρ 33.

Capernaum, ἡ ἰδία πόλις 118.

Cardinals, see Numerals

Cases, the oblique 141 sqq.; of participles 305, 308. See Acc. Dat. Gen. etc.

Causal sentences 232 sq.; particles 233.

Cities names of, how declined 18; Gend. of 21; use of Art. with 86.

Clauses, leading instead of subordinate 289; dependent passing over into leading 282 sq., 357, 383.

Command, construction with words of 275 sq.

Comparative degree, forms of 27 sq.; for the Pos. 83; for the Superl. 83; strengthening of 83; with ὑπέρ 335; παρά 339; πρός 340; expressed by ἤ 360.

Comparison 27; double 28; breviloquence in 167 sq., 177, 393; gnomic Aor. in 202.

Complutensian text 3.

Compound verbs, construction of 344.

Conditional Sentences 220 sqq.; rhetorical forms of 226; asyndetic juxtaposition in 226; Imperative in 227; use of οὐ in 344 sqq.

Conjunctions, displaced 389. See Particles.

Consonants, mutations of 7; doubling of 8; changes in ν 8; final 9.

Constructio ad synesin 80, 105 sq., 129 sq., 281 sq.; personal construction 377.

Contraction, in substantives 12 sqq.; neglected in ὀστέον 13, in ὀρέων etc. 14, in βόας etc. 14, in χρυσέων 26; in verbs 44 sqq.; in ἐκχέετε 44. Takes place contrary to rule (ἡμίσους etc.) 14.

Copula, omission of 136 sq.

Countries, the Art. with names of 86.

Crasis 10.

Dative, with substs. 92, 179 sq.; in elliptical phrases 138; of closer limitation instead of the Acc. 152, cf. 183; of punishment 165; of the Person, or object affected 171 sqq.; periphrasis for (with Prep. εἰς, πρός, ἐνώπιον, etc)172,188; with πιστεύειν 173; ἐλπίζειν 175; ὁμολογεῖν 176; with verbs of approach, contention, etc. 177; of exhorting, censuring, etc. 177; with ὁ αὐτός 177; commodi, etc. 178; ethicus 179; of subjective judgment 179; with compounds 180, 344; of the Thing 181 sqq.; instrumental 181, with ἐν 182; of mode, closer limitation, etc. 183; of cognate abstract (χαρᾷ χαίρειν, etc.) 183; with verbs of going 184; of emotion 185; consilii 185; of time 186; two Datives 186 sq.; with the Passive 187; with verbal Adjs. 190; with adverbs 320; Datives absolute 143 N.[2]; 316; Pauline Dat. after ζῆν, στήκειν, etc. 178.

Dawes's Canon 213; see Goodwin in Trans. of Amer. Philolog. Assoc. for 1869–70, pp. 46–55.

Declension of nouns, unusual forms in first 11; second 12; third 13 sq.; of foreign proper names 15 sqq.; anomalous 22 sq.; of adjectives 25 sq.

Demonstratives 103 sqq.; omitted before Rel. 104 sq., 286, cf. 395; preparatory (before ἵνα, ὅτι, and the Infin.) 105, 240, 262, 263, cf. 400; constr. ad syn. with 105 sq. See Pronouns.

II. INDEX OF GREEK WORDS AND FORMS.

The Figures refer to Pages.

changed into ε in γήρει 15 ; in τέσσερα 29 ; κεκαθερισμένος 29; in verbs in -άω 44.

a Gen. -ης after a vowel or ρ 11 ; with proper names 17.

-τ. Gen. -ας with proper names 17.

-ι Gen. -ων in names of cities 18.

'Αβαρίμ, τό 22.

Ἄβυσσος, ἡ 12.

ἀγαθός comparison 27.

ἀγαθωσύνη 73.

ἀγαλλιάομαι 51 ; constr. of 185 ; with Participle 300.

ἄγαλμα omission of 82.

ἀγαπᾶν ἀγάπην 148 sq.

ἀγάπη with ἐν and εἰς 329.

ἀγαπητός constr. of 190.

ἄγε Interjection 70.

ἄγειν 53 ; used impersonally 134 ; and its compounds used intransitively 144.

ἄγια, τά, ἄγια ἁγίων 24, 83.

ἁγιωσύνη 73.

ἄγνυμι 53.

ἀγοράζειν τιμῆς 164.

'Αγρίππας 20.

ἀγωνίζεσθαι ἀγῶνα 148.

ἀδελφός omission of 94.

ᾄδης meaning and construction of 171.

ἀδύνατόν ἐστι with Infin. 260.

'Αερμών, τό and ἡ 22.

ἄζυμα, τά 23.

ἀθῷος ἀπό 158.

αι and ε interchanged 5, 40 note.

-αι in 1st Aor. Opt. Act. 42.

αἰχμαλωτεύειν αἰχμαλωσίαν 148.

Αἴγυπτος without Art. 87 ; ἐν Αἰγύπτου 171.

αἰνεῖν constr. of 176 note.

-αινω Aor. of verbs in 41.

αἱρέω 53.

-αιρω Aor. of verbs in 41.

αἴρω : Aor. Pass. in reflex. sense 52 ; sc. ἄγκυραν 146 ; constr. of 157 sq.

αἰσχύνεσθαι ἀπό 192, 323.

αἰτεῖν and compounds constr. of 149, 189; Aor. Mid. 191 ; Act. and Mid. 193 ; αἰτεῖσθαι ἵνα 237.

αἰτιώματα, αἰτιάματα 73.

αἰῶνες, οἱ 24.

αἰώνιος 26.

ἀκατάπαστος, ἀκατάπαυστος 65.

ἀκμήν adhuc 153.

ἀκούειν Fut. of 53 ; constr. of 165 sq 301 sq.; ἀκοῇ 184 ; Perf. force of Pres. 203.

ἄκρος in Neut. with Gen. following 94.

'Ακύλας 20.

ἅλας, [ἅλα], ἅλς 24.

ἀλείφεσθαι with Acc. 192.

ἀλλά elided 10 ; οὐκ ... ἀλλά 356 ; for δέ 365; ἀλλ' οὐ 368 ; ἀλλά but otherwise 369 ; οὐ γὰρ ἀλλά 369 ; ἀλλ' ἤ 374 ; ἀλλά in ellipsis 392.

ἀλλήλων 31.

ἄλλομαι 54.

ἄλλος and ἕτερος 32, 102, 122 ; followed by Part. with Art. 93, 295; redundant 373.

ἅλς, ὁ, ἅλας and ἅλα, τό, 24.

ἁμαρτάνειν 54 ; ἁμαρτίαν 148 ; signif. and constr. of 173.

ἀμύνειν in Middle 194 note.

ἀμφιάζω 49.

ἀμφιέννυμι, ἀμφιέζω 49 ; in Mid. 191.

ἄν rare 72 ; for ἐάν ? 72, 220 ; use of 216 ; with Ind. Pret. 216, 224 ; supposed omission of with ἔδει etc. 216 ; with Subjunc. 217, 231 ; with Optat. 217 ; in interrog. clauses 254 ; Subjunc. with οὐ μή for οὐκ ἄν with Opt. 218 ; with Aor. Subjunc. 219 ; ὡς ἄν without a verb 219 ; omission of 225 sq. ; in relative sentences 227 sq.; with the Fut. 228, 231 cf. 222 ; ὅπου ἄν 228 ; with particles of time 231 ; with ὅπως 234.

-αν in 2d Aor. 3d Plur. 43 ; for -ασι in Perf. 43.

ἀνά 331 ; used adverbially in distributive sense 30, 331 sq.; ἀνὰ μέσον 332.

ἀναβαίνειν Fut. force of 204.

ἀνάγαιον, ἀνώγαιον, ἀνώγεων 13.

ἀνάγομαι, ἀνήχθην 51.

ἀναθεματίζειν ἀναθέματι 184.

ἀναλύειν used intransitively 145.

'Ανανίας 20.

ἀναπαύεσθαι constr. of 158 ; ἀναπαήσονται, ἀναπαύσονται 65.

414

ἀνάστα -στηθι 47.
ἀνάστασις νεκρῶν 89.
ἀναστρέφειν 145.
ἀναφανέντες Κύπρον 190.
'Ἀνδρέας 18.
ἀνέβη ἐπὶ καρδίαν 135.
ἀνέχομαι augment 35 ; ἀνέχεσθαι with Gen. 161.
ἀνῆκεν 216.
ἀνήρ, ἄνδρες omission and insertion of 82 ; when anarthrous 89.
ἀνθυπατεύειν 169.
῎Αννα, -ας 17.
῎Αννας 20.
ἀνοίγω forms of 63 ; without object 145.
ἄνομος with Gen. 169.
ἀνορθώθη 34.
ἀντί 321; ἀνθ' ὧν 105 ; ἀντί with verbs of buying etc. 164 ; with Infin. 263.
ἀντιλαμβάνεσθαι always with Gen. 160; Mid. 194.
'Ἀντίπας 20.
ἀντιπέρα -ν accent etc. 321.
ἀντίχριστος anarthrous use of 89.
ἀνώτερος etc. 28.
ἄξιος constr. of 240 cf. 229.
ἀπαγγέλλειν ἵνα 237.
ἀπαντήσω 53.
ἀπαρνήσεται 53.
ἀπάρτι 321.
ἀπειλέω 54.
ἀπείραστος with Gen. 170.
ἀπεκρίθη, ἀπεκρίνατο 51.
ἀπεκατεστάθην augment 35.
ἀπεκτάνθην 41.
ἀπέναντι 319
ἀπέχει impersonal use of 135; ἀπέχειν intrans. 144 ; ἀπέχειν Perf. force of Pres. 203.
ἀπό elided 10 ; ἀπὸ ἄνωθεν, μακρόθεν, etc. 70 ; uses of 321 sq. ; in specifns. of space and time 153 ; before Gen. of separation 157 sq. ; with words of plenty 163 ; of hearing etc. 166 ; after Passives 187; and Middles 192; before adverbs 320; for Gen. alone or instead of an Acc. 323; for ἐκ 324; with ἐκ in specifications of origin 324 ; for παρά 324 ; after μανθάνειν 324 ; for ὑπό 325; for Dat. after Pass. 325 ; ἀπὸ προσώπου 323, 324 ; ἀφ' ἧς and ἀφ' οὗ of time 82, 105.
ἀπογενέσθαι with Dat. 178.
ἀπόδεκτός with Dat. 190.
ἀποθνήσκειν with Acc. 149; with Dat. 178; οἱ ἀποθνήσκοντες 206.
ἀποκαλύπτειν 146.
ἀποκρύπτειν constr. of 149 ; in Pass. 189.
ἀποκτεῖναι ἐν θανάτῳ 184.
ἀποκτέννω, ἀποκταίνω 61.
ἀποκύω, ἀποκυέω 62.
ἀπόλλυμι 64 ; οἱ ἀπολλύμενοι 206.

'Ἀπολλώς inflection 21
ἀπολογεῖσθαί τινι 172.
ἀπορρίπτειν 145.
ἀποστέλλειν 146 ; ἐν 329.
ἀποστρέφεσθαι 192.
ἀποτάξασθαί τινι 179.
ἀποφεύγειν constr. of 158.
ἄπταιστος 42
ἅπτεσθαι constr. of 167.
'Ἀπφία 8.
ἆρα in questions 247 ; interchanged with ἄρα 247, 371; ἄρα οὖν 371; ἆραγε 371.
ἄραφος, ἄρραφος 32.
ἀργός Fem. ἀργή 25.
ἀργύρια, τά 24.
ἀρεσκεία 12.
ἀρεστός with Dat. 190.
'Ἀρέτας 20.
ἀριθμόν used adv. 153.
ἀρκεῖν ἵνα 240.
ἀρκετὸν εἶναι ἵνα 240 ; with Infin. 263.
ἁρμόσασθαι 193.
ἀρνέομαι as Dep. Mid. 51.
ἀρξάμενος ἀπό as a fixed formula 79; ἀρξάμενος 374.
ἁρπάζειν 54.
ἄρρην and ἄρσην 7 ; Acc. -αν 13.
'Ἀρτεμᾶς 20.
ἀρτέμων 24.
ἄρχειν constr. of 169.
ἀρχήν used adv. 153.
-άρχης, -αρχός 73.
-ας Prop. names in 17, 19.
-ᾶς Gen. ᾶ 20.
ἀσαίνομαι? 263.
ἄσπιλος 158.
ἀσφαλῆν -ήν -ῇ 14.
ἀσφαλισθῆναι 52.
ἄτερ 320.
αὐθεντεῖν 169.
αὐλίζομαι with Aor. Pass. 51.
αὐξάνω, αὔξω 54, 145 ; αὔξησιν 148; in Pass. 189.
αὔρα omission of 82.
αὐτός constr. ad syn. with 105 sq.; loose reference 106 ; for unemphatic he 107 sq ; in the Sept. 108 sq. ; for Christ 108; αὐτή or αὕτη? 109 ; αὐτό and τοῦτο 109; αὐτοί 109; αὐτὸ τοῦτο, τοῦτο αὐτὸ 109 sq., 280 ; αὐτοὶ οὗτοι 110; use of Art. with 119 ; Gen. of no longer used with Adj. Prons. 117; excessive use of 107, 118, 142 sq., 306, 315, 380; ὁ αὐτός with Dat. 177 ; supposed resumptive use of with Infin. 279; in relative sentences 280, 283; after a Part. 143, 306 ; ἐπὶ τὸ αὐτό 338.
αὐτοῦ, αὑτοῦ, ἑαυτοῦ 111 sq.; used for the reflex. of the 1st or 2d Pers. 113 ; position of in reference to the Art. 116.

ἀφαιρεῖν, -σθαι, constr. of **149, 158**; in Pass. 189.
ἀφανίζειν sc. χρήματα 146.
ἀφεῖς 49.
ἀφέωνται, ἀφίενται 49.
ἄφες with Subjunctive 210.
ἀφελπίζω 7.
ἀφίδω 7.
ἀφιέναι ἵνα 238; ἀφιέι χι with Infin. 258; with Part. 304; in the sense of *permit* 210, 258; *leave* 304.
ἀφίονται 49.
ἀφορίζω Fut. of 37.
ἄχρις and ἄχρι 10; moods with **231**.
-άω changed into -έω 44.

Βάαλ, ὁ, ἡ 21.
βαθέως 26.
βαίνειν 54.
βάλλειν Aor. Pass. in reflex. sense 52; intrans. 145; εἰς τ. καρδ. ἵνα 238.
βάπτειν with Gen. 170.
βαπτίζειν ἐν ὕδατι and ὕδατι, etc. 182.
βαπτισθῆναι βάπτισμα 148.
Βαραχίας 17.
Βαρνάβας 20.
Βαρραβᾶς 20.
Βαρσαβᾶς 20.
βαρέω, βαρύνω 54.
βασκαίνειν 41.
βασιλεύειν constr. of **169.**
βασίλισσα 73.
βάτος, ἡ 12.
βέβαιος 25.
Βεελζεβούλ spelling **6.**
Βελίαρ 6.
Βηθανία 17.
Βηθλεέμ, ἡ 21.
Βηθσαϊδά 17.
Βηθφαγῆ -γῆ 15.
βιάζεσθαι 53.
βιόω 54.
βλαστᾷ 55.
βλαστάνειν 55.
βλασφημεῖν 146.
βλέπειν i.q. φυλάσσεσθαι constr. of 242 sq., 323; with Part. 301.
βότρυς Acc. Plur. -ας 14.
βούλομαι augment 33; βούλει 42; with the Subj. 208; ἐβουλόμην without ἄν 217.
βοῦς, βόας 14.
βραδύς foll. by Infin. etc. 265, 269.

Γάζα 17.
γάμοι, οἱ 23.
γαμέω 55, 145, 177.
γάρ interrog. and ellipt **180 of 370.**
γεγονώς i.q. *natus* 55.
Γεδεών inflection 15.
γέεννα 17.
Γεθσημανῆ -νεῖ -νεί **15.**
γελάσω 53.

γέμειν constr. of **163, 164.**
γεμίζειν constr. of 163.
γεύεσθαι constr. of 167.
γῆ omission of 82; anarthrous use of **89**
γῆρας Dat. -ει 15.
γίνομαι 55; Aor. Pass. and Mid. 52; καὶ ἐγένετο and ἐγένετο δέ 135, 276, cf. 312; ellipsis of 138; εἴς τι 150, 333; with Gen. 162 sq.; Fut. force of Pres. 204; μὴ γένοιτο 248; ἐγέν. foll. by Infin. and τοῦ 270, foll. by an Infin. and finite verb 276 sq., or by Acc. and Infin. 277; with Part. in periphrasis 308 sq.; followed by ἐι 330; ὑπό 340 sq.
γινώσκω 55; Pass. with Dat. 187; with Part. 301.
γλῶσσα spelling 7.
γνοῖ Aor. Subjunctive 46.
γνώμη omission of 82.
γνωρίζω Fut. of 37.
γνωστός with Dat. 190.
Γόμορρα inflection 18.
γονυπετεῖν constr. of 148.
γράφω, ἔγραψα in letters 198; γραφ. ἵνα or ὅτι 237.
γυνή without the Art. 89; omission of 94.

Δαμασκός 18.
Δανείδ spelling 6.
δέ 363; in the apodosis 364; often added by the copyists 363 sq., 403; καὶ ... δέ 364; μὲν ... δέ 364 sq.; omitted 365.
δεῖ 135, 147, 164, 259; to be supplied 272; not to be supplied 273; ἔδει without ἄν 216, 225 sq.
δέομαι 55; constr. of 164; ἵνα 237; with εἰ 256; with Infin. 258, and εἰς 265, 273.
δείκνυμι forms of 45.
δέρειν πολλάς sc. πληγάς 148; in Pass. 189.
δέσμιος Ἰησοῦ 169.
δεσμός forms of Plur. 23.
δεῦρο, δεῦτε 70.
Δημᾶς 20.
δηναρίου Gen. of price 164.
διά elided 10; with Gen. of Pers. 182; in modal periphrasis 183; after Passives 187; with Infin. 263; general use of 334; in adverbial phrases **334.**
διάβολος anarthrous 89.
διάγειν intrans. 144.
διακατελέγχεσθαι 177.
διακονέω augment 35; Pass. 188.
διάκονοι omission of 82.
διακρίνεσθαι constr. of 177; διακριθῆναι intrans. 52.
διαλέγεσθαι constr. of 177.
διαλείπω (οὐ) followed by a Part. **300.**
διαμαρτυρεῖσθαι ἵνα 237.

διαστέλλεσθαι ἵνα 237.
διατάσσειν and -εσθαι 193.
διατελεῖν with complement. clause 104.
διατίθεσθαι διαθήκην 148.
διατρίβειν 145.
διδάσκειν constr. of 149; διδασκαλίας 148; in Pass. 188.
διδοῖ 46.
δίδωμι forms of 45 sq., 47; in sense of acquire? 133; δ. δόματα 148; constr. with Gen. 159; Aor. and Perf. interchanged 199; ἵνα 238; followed by interrog. clause 251; followed by Infin. 258, 260, 261, with εἰς 265; ἐν 329.
διερμήνευεν 34.
δικαιοῦσθαι ἀπό 322.
διό, διόπερ 233.
διορύσσειν sc. τεῖχος 146.
διότι 233.
διπλοῦς, -πλός, -πλότερος 27.
διψάω contraction 44; with Acc. 147.
διώκειν ἵνα 237; διώξω 53.
δοῖ 46.
δοκῶ μοι, ἐμαυτῷ 111.
δόξα θεοῦ anarthrous 89.
δύναμαι augment 33; forms, etc. 55; ἐδυνάμην without ἄν 216.
δύνασαι, δύνῃ 55.
δυνατός with Dat. 190; δυνατός εἰμι with Infin. 260.
δύο inflection 28; δύο δύο 30.
δύω 56.
δῷ 46.
δώῃ (δῴη, δῴῃ) 46, 233.
δῴην 46.
δώσῃ 36.

ε initial in compos. changed into η 74.
ε interchanged with αι 5, 40 note.
-ε Voc. in 12.
ἔα 72.
ἐάν, ἤν, ἄν 72; ἐάν for ἄν 72; with Subjunc. 220; with Indic. 221, 222; negatives after 345; in asseveration 358; i.q. ὃς ἄν 360; transposition in clauses with 389.
ἐάντε ... ἐάντε 221 note.
ἑαυτόν ellipsis of 144; with Acc. and Inf. contrary to rule 274.
ἑαυτοῦ, etc., not αὑτοῦ, etc., 111; position of 116; ἑαυτοῖς, etc., for reflex. of 1st and 2d. Pers. 113.
ἐβάσκανεν 41.
ἐγάμησα, ἔγημα 55.
ἐγγίζω Fut. of 37.
ἐγγύς, ἐγγύτερον as Pred. 131; with Gen. or Dat. 170.
ἐγείρω, Aor. Pass. in reflex. sense 52; intrans. ἔγειραι, ἔγειρε 56; ἐγείρεται (Fut.) 204.
ἐγκαίνια, τά 23.
ἐγκαλεῖν constr. of 177; in Pass. 188.

ἐγκανᾶ 9.
ἐγκαλεῖσθαι στάσεως 177.
ἐγχρίειν constr. of 149 sq.
ἐγώ, etc., N. T. use of with verbs 131 sq
ἐδαφίζω Fut. of 37.
ἐδολιοῦσαν 43.
ἐδέετο, ἐδεεῖτο 55.
ἐδίδοτο -ετο 47.
ἔδομαι, φάγομαι 58.
ἔδοτο -ετο 47.
ἔδυν 56.
Ἐζεκίας 17.
ἐθέλω, θέλω 57.
ἔθνη as Masc. 130.
ἐθύθη, ἐτύθη 7.
ει for ι 5.
ει augment 34.
εἰ without an apodosis 215; with Indic. 220; with Subj. 221; with Optat. 223 sq.; with the Pret. 224; with Pres. for Pret. 224; for ὅτι after θαυμάζω etc. 246, cf. 215; redundant 248, 249; in questions 250; negatives after 345 sq.; in oaths 358; εἰ καί, εἴ πως, εἰ ἄρα followed by Subj. and Opt. (if perchance) 256; εἰ οὐ 345; εἰ μή nisi 345, 348, 359; εἰ δὲ μή, εἰ δὲ μή γε 345, 393; εἰ μήν 359; εἰ μήτι 219, 221, 359; ἐκτὸς εἰ μή 359.
-εια, abstracts in 12.
εἶδαν, εἶδον, ἴδον, ἴδα 39.
εἰδέα 5.
εἰδέναι never with Part. 301.
εἶδον καὶ ἰδού 139.
εἰκῆ, εἰκῇ 69.
εἰκόναν 13.
εἴκοσι and εἴκοσιν 9.
εἰλάμην 40.
εἰλισσόμενος 34.
εἰμί only in composition 50.
εἰμί forms 49 sq.; ὁ ὢν καὶ ὁ ἦν 50; ellipsis of in 3d Sing. 136; in 3d Plur. 137; in 1st and 2d Pers. 137; in Subjunc. Optat. Imperat. 137; of Indic. in doxologies 137; εἴς τι 150; with Gen. 159, 162 sq.; καὶ ἔσται followed by Fut. 278; Part. omitted 304, 308; with Part. in periphrasis 308 sq.; ἔσομαι with Perf. Part. 311; ἦν, ἦσαν with Part. like ἐγένετο δέ, etc. 312; ἦν, ἦσαν with Pres. Part. in Mark and Luke 312; with ἐν 330.
εἵνεκεν 10; with Inf. 266.
εἰπεῖν 57; εἰπόν accent 57; ἵνα 237 note; with Infin. 275; εἶπεν omitted 394.
εἴρηκεν used absolutely 134.
-εῖς Acc. Plur. from -εύς 14.
εἰς with Infin. 264 cf. 244, 259; in brachylog. and pregn. constr.327sq.; with verbs of rest 328, 329 sq.; interchanged with ἐν 333; with εἶναι.

53

γίνεσθαι, 150, 333 ; and Acc. after verbs signifying *to appoint* etc. 150 ; in circumlocution for Dative 172 ; in adverbial phrases 334.

εἰς τριάκοντα etc. 30.

εἷς for πρῶτος 29 ; for τὶς 85 ; εἷς τις 85 ; in the sense of *alter*, ὁ ἕτερος, 30, 102 ; for the reciprocal Pron. 31 ; Hebraistic? use of 102 ; εἷς . . . οὐ (μή) 121 ; ἕως ἑνός 121.

εἷς καθ' εἷς 28, 30.

-εισαν in 3d Plur. Pluperf. 43.

εἴτε . . . εἴτε with Subjunc. 221, in questions 250.

εἶχαν 40.

ἐκ use of 326 ; in periphrasis 156 ; instead of simple Gen. 157 ; with Gen. of separation 157 ; with part. Gen. 156, 158 ; with words of plenty etc. 163 ; of buying etc. 164 ; of hearing 166 ; after Passives 187, 327 ; and ἀπό 326 sq. ; after Neuter verbs 327 ; in adverbial expressions 327 ; in brachylogical phrases 327 ; in phrases with the Art. 95 ; denoting origin etc. 324.

ἐκαθεζόμην, ἐκαθήμην 56.

ἕκαστος use of Art. with 120 ; εἷς ἕκαστος 120 ; ἀνὰ εἷς ἕκαστος 30 ; with Plur. verb 131.

ἑκατονταετής accent 29.

ἑκατοντάρχης, ἑκατόνταρχος 73.

ἐκδικεῖν τι ἔκ τινος 182.

ἐκδόσεται 47.

ἐκεῖ 71, 378.

ἐκεῖνος and οὗτος 104 ; use of Art. with 119 sq. ; resumptive of Part. 306.

ἐκεῖσε 71, 378.

ἐκκαθάρῃ 41.

ἐκκλίνειν 145.

ἔκπαλαι 321.

ἐκτὸς εἰ μή *except* 221, 345, 355, 359.

ἐκτρέπεσθαι 192.

ἐκφεύγειν constr. of 146 sq.

ἐκφυῇ, ἐκφύη 68.

ἐκχέετε 44.

ἐκχεῶ, ἐκχέω 68.

Ἐλαιών, τὸ ὄρος τῶν ἐλαιῶν, etc., 22, cf. 151.

ἐλάσσων and ἐλάττων 7 ; neut. indeclinable 127 sq.

ἐλαττόω spelling 7.

ἐλαχιστότερος 28.

ἐλεέω, ἐλεάω 57.

ἔλεος, τό 22.

ἐλευθεροῦν constr. of 158.

ἐλθεῖν to be supplied 138.

ἐλκόω augment 34.

ἐλλόγα, -ᾶτο etc. 58.

ἐλπίζω Fut. of 37 ; constructions of 175, 337 ; with Infin. especially Aor. 259 ; with ὅτι and Fut. Ind. 259 ; ἐπ' ἐλπίδι 337.

ἐλπίς 7.

Ἐλύμας 20.

ἐλῶ 53.

ἐμαυτοῦ etc. use of 110 sq.

ἐμβριμάομαι Aor. of 52.

ἐμμέσῳ 8 sq. ; ἐν μέσῳ anarthrous 89 ; with Gen. following 94.

ἐμός : τῇ ἐμῇ χειρὶ Παύλου 117.

ἐμοῦ for μου 117.

ἐμπαίξουσιν 64.

ἐμπιπλῶν 66.

ἐμπνέων with Gen. 167.

ἐμπορεύεσθαι with Acc. 147.

ἔμπροσθεν 172, 176, 319.

ἐμφανίζω Fut. of 37.

ἐν unassimilated in comp. 8.

ἐν in periphrasis of Gen. 156, 158 ; with Dat. inst. 181, 182, 329, cf. 264 ; not a mere sign of Dat. 181 ; in modal periphrasis 183 ; with Infin. 263 sq. ; with verbs of motion 328 ; for διά with persons 329 ; with εἶναι, γίνεσθαι 330 ; with ἔχειν 330 ; in adverbial phrases 330 ; ἐν τοῖς 374 ; ἐν ᾧ 105, 331 ; ἐν κυρίῳ Χριστῷ etc. 174, 175, 185, 330 ; ἐν Ἠλίᾳ 331 ; ἐν and εἰς interchanged 333.

ἔναντι, ἐναντίον 173, 180, 319.

ἐνδείκνυσθαι 192.

ἐνδιδύσκω 56 ; ἐνδιδύσκεσθαι constr. of 191.

ἐνδύεσθαι constr. of 191 ; ἐνδύεσθαι ἔνδυμα 148, 191.

ἕνεκα, ἕνεκεν, εἵνεκεν 10 ; followed by Infin. 266.

ἐνεργεῖν and -εῖσθαι 193.

ἐνέχειν 144 ; -εσθαι 161.

ἐνθάδε 71.

ἔνι for ἔνεστι 72.

ἐνισχύειν 145.

ἔννομος with Gen. 169.

ἐνορκίζειν constr. of 147.

ἔνοχος constr. of 170.

ἐντέλλεσθαι, ἐντολὰς διδόναι, ἵνα 237 ; Infin. after 273, 275.

ἐντραπήσονται *verebuntur* 52.

ἐντρέπεσθαι τινα 192.

ἐνώπιον and κατενώπιον 172, 176, 180, 188, 319.

ἑόρακα 64.

ἐξαγοράζεσθαι 192.

ἐξαυτῆς 82.

ἐξεκρέμετο 61.

ἔξεστιν constr. with 278 ; ἐξόν use of 318.

ἐξήραμμαι 41.

ἐξομολογεῖσθαι 176.

ἐξορκίζειν constr. of 147 ; ἵνα 237.

ἐξ οὗ *since* 105.

ἐξουδενέω -όω 28.

ἐξουθενέω -όω 28.

ἐξ ... οὐία with Infin. 260 ; ἔχειν with Infin. 260.

ἐπαινέσω 53.
ἐπαισχύνθη 34 ; ἐπαισχύνεσθαι constr. of 192.
ἐπανάγειν intrans. 144.
ἐπάναγκες 27.
ἐπάνω in the sense of πλέον 168, 319.
Ἐπαφρᾶς 20.
ἐπεί 233 ; i.q. for otherwise 359.
ἐπειδή 233.
ἔπειτα after a Part. 306 ; without δέ 365.
ἔπεσα, ἔπεσαν, ἔπεσον 39.
ἐπέχειν 144.
ἐπί with verbs of accusing 165 ; ἐφ' ᾧ i.q. ἐπὶ τί 253 ; before adverbs 321; with Gen. of place 336 ; of time 336 ; in adverb. phrases 336 ; with Dative 336 sq. ; with words of rest and of motion 337; in brachylogical phrases 337; with Accusative 337; with idea of rest 338 ; additive 338 ; ἐπὶ τὸ αὐτό and other adverbial phrases 338.
ἐπιβάλλειν 145 ; ἐπιβαλών 145.
ἐπιβλέπω : its use in Mid. and Imperat. 273.
ἐπιθυμεῖν κατά τινος 235 ; ἐπιθυμίᾳ 184.
ἐπικαλεῖν with Dat. 151 note.
ἐπιλαμβάνεσθαι constr. of 160, 192.
ἐπιλελησμένον ἐστίν in Pass. sense 52.
ἐπιμένω (with Participle) expressing continuance 300.
ἐπιορκήσω 53.
ἐπιούσιος 73 sq.
ἐπίστασθαι with Part. 301.
ἐπίστασις meaning of 180.
ἐπίστηθι 47.
ἐπιστρέφειν 145.
ἐπιφᾶναι 41.
ἐπιφώσκω 68.
ἐπουράνιος 25.
ἐραυνάω, ἐρευνάω 58.
ἐργάζομαι augment 33.
ἔρημος Fem. 25.
ἐρημοῦται Fut. ? 38.
ἐρίζω Fut. of 37.
ἐρ θεία 12 ; ἐριθεῖαι Plur. 77.
ἔρις, ἔριδες, ἔρεις 24.
Ἑρμᾶς 20.
ἐρρέθην, ἐρρήθην 57.
ἔρχομαι 58 ; Fut. force of 204, 255 ; used for εἶμι 50 ; ὁ ἐρχόμενος of the Messiah 204, 206 ; τὰ ἐρχόμενα etc. 204 ; ἐλθεῖν ἐν 329.
ἐρωτάω contraction 44 ; ἵνα 237 ; with Infin. 258 ; and εἰς 265 ; followed by direct discourse 272, cf. δεῖσθαι
-ες for -ας in Perf. 2d Sing. 43.
ἐσθίω, ἔσθω 58 ; with Gen. 159.
ἐστάθην, ἔστην 47, 52.
ἔστακα 48.
ἑστάναι 48.
ἔστησα intransitively ? 47.
ἑστώς, ἑστός, ἑστηκός 48.

ἔσχατος in Neut. with Gen. following 94 ; use of with ἡμέρα 94.
ἔσω not εἴσω 72 ; in the relation of res: 378 ; ἐσώτερος 28.
ἕτερος followed by Part. with Art. 93 ; superfluous 373, cf. ἄλλος.
ἑτοιμάζειν sc. κατάλυμα 146 ; ἵνα 237.
ἑτεροζυγεῖν τινί 177.
ἕτοιμος 25 ; foll. by Infin. etc. 260, 269.
ἔτος Gen. Plur. -ῶν 14 ; accent of compounds of 29.
εὐ augment of verbs beginning with 34.
Εὔα 17.
εὐαγγελίζω augment 35 ; use of Act. 148; constr. of 148, 150; Pass. 188.
εὐαρεστέω augment 35; constr. of 185 ; Pass. 188.
εὐδοκέω augment of 34; constr. of 185; εὐδόκησα in quotns. 203 ; εὐδόκησεν sc. ὁ θεός 134.
εὐθυδρομέω augment 34.
εὐκαιρίαν ζητεῖν ἵνα 237.
εὐνουχίζω augment 34.
εὐλαβεῖσθαι constr. of 241 sq.
εὐλογητὸς ὁ θεός etc. 137.
εὐπορέω augment 34.
εὐρακύλων 16.
εὑρήσῃς etc. 36.
εὑρίσκω 58 ; augment of 34 ; Act. and Mid. 193 ; with Part. i.q. εἶναι 301 ; with Part. omitted 304; εὑρεθῆναί τινι 187.
εὗρον, εὗραν 40.
-εύς contracts in 14.
εὐχαριστεῖν constr. of 300.
εὔχομαι augment 34 ; constr. of 177, 237 ; ηὐχόμην without ἄν 217.
ἔφανα 41.
ἐφάπαξ 321.
ἔφιδε, ἔπιδε 7.
ἔχειν intrans. 144 ; καλῶς, ἐσχάτως, 144; κατά τινος 144 ; ἐν γαστρί 144 ; κατὰ κεφαλῆς 146 ; -εσθαι with Gen. 161 ; Aor. Mid. 191 ; signif. of Mid. 192 ; οὐκ ἐχ. foll. by Rel. clause 229 ; οὐκ ἐχ. τί for ὅ 251, 229 sq.; followed by Infin. 251 ; with ἐν 330; signifying to hold for etc. 376.
ἐχέθην, ἐχύθην 69.
ἐχθές not χθές 72.
-έω giving place to -άω 57, 63 cf. 44.
-έως Gen. in 14, 26.
ἕως, ἕως οὗ, etc., constr. of 230 sq. 319 ; ἄν with Fut. 231 ; with Infin. 266 ; as Prep. 319 ; before adverbs 320 ; transposition in clauses with 389.

ζ used for σ before μ 5.
Ζακχαῖος 18.
Ζαχαρίας 19.
ζάω forms and signif. 58 sq. ; constr. of 149, 178 ; Infin. as a subst. 262.
ζῆλος gender of 23.

ζηλοῦν ἵνα 237.
Ζηνᾶς 20.
ζητεῖν ἵνα 237, 240; with Infin. 258 cf.
　279 sq.
ζωὴ αἰώνιος use of Art. with 90.
ζῶον construed as Masc. 130.

η used for ι 5.
-η proper names in 17.
ἤ omitted after πλέον etc. 168; in ques-
　tions 249; ἤ οὐ 360; giving com-
　parative force 360.
ἡγεμονεύειν constr. of 169.
ἡγέομαι 59; constr. of 169.
ᾔδεισαν 51.
ἥκω 59; Perf. force of Pres. 203.
ἦλθα, ἦλθαν, ἦλθον 39.
Ἠλίας 18.
ἡλίκος in exclamation 253.
ἥλιος anarthrous 89.
ἡμέρα omission of 81; in adverbial speci-
　fications 139.
ἥμισυς forms of 14.
ἡμῶν for possessive 116; position of 116.
ἠνεῴχθησαν 35.
ἥξη 36.
ἤρεμος 28.
ἠρώτουν 44.
-ης proper names in 17,　, 19; -ῆς Gen.
　-ῆ 20.
Ἡσαΐας 17.
ἡττάομαι 59; constr. of 168.
ἥττημα 7.
ἤφιεν 49.
ἦχος gender of 23.

θάλασσα spelling 7; anarthrous use of 89.
θάλλω 59.
θάνατος anarthrous use of 89; θανάτῳ
　τελευτᾶν 184.
θαρρέω and θαρσέω 7.
θαυμάζω 59; θαῦμα 148; constr. of 185,
　264.
θεαθῆναι 52.
θέλω 57; with Subjunc. 208 cf. 240; with
　εἰ 215, 246; ἵνα 237, 240; in the
　sense of malle 360; never equiv. to
　adverb 375; θέλων used absolutely
　i.q. purposely 376; θέλειν ἔν τινι 376.
-θεν, -θε particles of place in 70.
θεός Voc. 12, 140; anarthrous use of 89;
　ellipsis of as Subj. 134; as a limiting
　Dat. 179 sq.
θερίζω Fut. of 37.
θεωρεῖτε Fut.? 38; with Part. 301.
Θευδᾶς 20.
θηρίον construed as Masc. 80.
θθ for τθ 8.
θνήσκω 60.
θριαμβεύειν constr. of 147.
Θυάτειρα inflection of 18.
θυμοί Plur. 77.
θύραι, αἱ 24.

θύω, ἐθύθη 7.

ι represented in MSS. by ει or by η 5;
　subscr. omitted in Infin. 44, in ad-
　verbs 69; -ί as an adverbial ending
　73.
Ἰάειρος 18.
Ἰακώβ and Ἰάκωβος 6, 18.
Ἰαμβρῆς 20.
Ἰαννῆς 20.
ἴαται, ἰαθήσεται 52.
ἴδα, ἴδον 39.
ἴδε and ἰδού ecce 62, 70; with a Nom.
　139; in place of ἦν 312; repeated
　398; εἶδον καὶ ἰδού 139; καὶ ἰδού
　before the apodosis 362.
ἰδέα spelling 5.
ἴδιος use of for ἑαυτοῦ etc. 117; οἱ ἴδ.,
　τὰ ἴδ. used substantively 118; in
　strict sense 118; a favorite word in
　2 Pet. 118; omission of Art. with
　119.
ἰδού see ἴδε.
Ἱερᾷ πόλει not Ἱεραπόλει 74.
Ἱερεμίας 17.
Ἱεριχώ 15.
Ἱερουσαλήμ, ἡ, Ἱεροσόλυμα, τὰ 6,16,18,21.
Ἰεχονίας 18.
-ίζω Fut. of verbs in 36.
ἵημι Aor. of 46; forms of 48.
Ἰησοῦς 21.
ἱκανὸν εἶναι ἵνα 240; foll. by Infin. 260.
ἱκνέομαι 60.
ἱμάτια, τά 24; ellipsis of 82.
ἵνα in final sentences 229, 233, 377; force
　of in N.T. 235 sq.; with Indic. Fut.
　and Pres. 234; with Imperat. 234;
　classes of preds. which it follows
　237 sq.; nearly equiv. to ὥστε 238 cf.
　264; omission of (?) 238, 243; in-
　terchanged with the Infin. (with ana
　without τοῦ) 238, 240, 264, 267 sq.;
　may be translated that, even so that
　239; in elliptical constructions 241;
　for Fut. Part. of purpose 241; for
　the Imperat. 241; ἵνα μή ne dicam
　241; ἵνα τί 357; attraction with 377;
　transposition in clauses with 389.
Ἰορδάνης 17, 21.
Ἰούδας 18.
Ἰουνίας 18.
ἴουσιν Gen. 48.
-ις Gen. -εως, contracts in 14.
ἴσα as predicate 131.
ἵστημι, ἱστάνω etc. forms of 44 sq., 47;
　and στῆσαι with ἐν 329; στῆναι with
　εἰς 332; with ἐπί 336.
ἰχθύς uncontracted 14.
Ἰωάννα 17.
Ἰωάννης, Ἰωάνης 17.
Ἰωνᾶς 20.
Ἰωσῆς 19, 20.
Ἰωσίας 18.

κυριεύε.ν constr. of 169.
κύριος anarthrous 89.
κωλύειν constr. of 158.
Κῶς inflection 21.

λάβε or λαβέ 62.
λαγχάνειν constr. of 160, 269.
λάθρα, λάθρᾳ 69.
λαλεῖν τινι and μετά τινος 172.
λαμβάνω Alex. spelling 62 ; τὶ εἴς τι 151 ;
　with Gen. 159 ; with gerundial In-
　fin. 261 ; with ἀπό and παρά 324
　and note.
λανθάνειν with a Participle 299.
λαός 13 ; with Plural verb 130.
λάσκω 62.
λέγειν : λέγει sc. ὁ θεός or ἡ γραφή 134 ;
　λέγειν καλῶς, κακῶς with Acc. 146;
　τινί and πρός τινα 172; ellipsis of
　271 sq., 352, 394 ; for κελεύειν (Infin.
　after) 273, 276 ; ἐπί τινος and περί
　τινος 336.
λεγιών -εών 16.
λείπω Aor. of 62.
Λευΐς (-είς) inflection 21.
λήμψομαι 62.
ληνός, ὁ, ἡ 12, 81.
Λίβανος, ὁ 22.
λιμός, ἡ 12, 81.
λιμπάνω 62.
λογισθῆναι 52.
λογίζομαι εἴς τι 151 ; ὡς 151.
λοιπόν adverbially 96,123; τοῦ λοιποῦ 170.
Λουκᾶς 20.
Λύδδα inflection 18.
λυσιτελεῖν satius esse 360.
Λύστρα inflection 19.

-μα nouns in 73.
μαθητεύειν constr. of 147.
Μαθθαῖος 18.
μακαρίζω Fut. of 37.
μακράν sc. ὁδόν 153.
μᾶλλον pleonastic (with the Compar.) 83.
μαμωνᾶς 20.
Μανασσῆς 19.
μανθάνειν constr. of 167; with Participle
　303 ; with ἀπό and παρά 324.
μαρανθήσεται wither away 52.
Μάρθα -ας 17.
Μαριάμ and Μαρία 6, 17.
μαρτυρεῖν μαρτυρίαν 148 ; with Dat. 178 ;
　Pass. 188 ; with εἰς and Infin. 265.
Ματθίας 18.
Ματταθίας 18.
μάχαιρα -ης 11.
μάχεσθαι with periphrasis for Dat. 177 ;
　μάχην 148.
μεγαλωσύνη 73.
μεγιστᾶνες 24.
μεθύω, μεθύσκομαι 62.
Μελεᾶς 20.
μειζότερος 28.
μέλλω augm. 33; with Infin. esp. Pres. 259.

μέλομαι 62 ; μέλει μοι constr. of 164.
μεμβράνα 17.
μεμίαμμαι 41.
μεμίανται 3d Plur. 41.
μεμνηστευμένη 32.
μέμφεσθαι constr. of 177.
μέν introduced by the copyists 364 sq.
　variations in 365 ; without a fol-
　lowing δέ 365 ; omitted 366 ; μέν ...
　δέ 364 ; μὲν οὖν 370; μενοῦνγε 370sq.;
　μὲν δή not found 370 note.
μένειν with Acc. 147.
μεριμνᾶν with three cases 186.
μέσος in Neut. with Gen. following 94 ;
　μέσον as Prep. 123, 319 ; ἀνὰ μέσον
　332.
Μεσσίας 18.
μετά with Infin. Acc. 265 ; constructions
　with 338 sq. ; used brachylogically
　339.
μεταδίδωμι constr. of 160.
μετανοεῖν ἀπό 322 note ; ἐκ 327.
μεταστραφήτω reflexive 52.
μετασχηματίζω Fut. of 37.
μετέχειν constr. of 160.
μετοικίζω Fut. of 37.
μέχρις and μέχρι 10 ; Moods with 231.
μή (μήπως etc.) final 233 ; after verbs of
　fearing 241 sq., 377 ; without a verb
　of fearing expressed 353 ; with the
　Indic. 243, 353 ; with a following οὐ
　248, 354.
μή interrogative (μήποτε, μήτι) 248 ;
　whether not, whether not perchance 250,
　255 sq. ; μὴ οὐ 248, 354.
μή negative with the Infin. 269, 349, 355;
　in conditional sentences 345 ; in
　relative sentences 348; with parti-
　ciples 350 sq. ; pleonastic with the
　Infin. 355 ; cf. οὐ.
μηδέ 366 sq. ; cf. οὐδέ.
μηδείς emphatic substitutes for 121 ;
　μηδέν with Mass. or Fem. substs.
　127, 152 ; μηδὲν σοί elliptically 138.
μηθείς 28.
μῆναν 13.
μήποτε, οὔποτε 354; i.q. ἴσως 354 note.
μήτε 366.
μήτηρ omission of 94.
μήτις 31.
-μι verbs in 44 sq.
μιγνύειν constr. of 177.
μιαρός, μιαρός 29.
μίλιον 18.
μνημονεύειν constr. of 164.
μνησθῆναι 52.
μοιχεῖαι Plur. 77.
μόνος and μόνον 83.
μου etc. used for reflexives 110, 115; for
　possessives 115; position of 343, 344.
μύω, καμμύω 62.
Μωυσῆς, Μωϋσῆς, Μωσῆς 19.

πίνω forms of 66 ; with Gen. 159.
πίπτω 67 ; ἐν 329.
πιστεύω signification and constructions of 173 sq., 337 ; τῇ καρδίᾳ and ἐν τ. κ. 182 ; Infin. after 273.
πιστὸς ἐν etc. 174.
-πλασίων 30.
πλεῖον indecl. 127.
πλεονεκτεῖν constr. of 168 ; in Pass. 188.
πλεονεξίαι 77.
πληγή omitted 82.
πλῆθος with Plur. pred. 130.
πλημμύρης 11.
πλήν in N. T. 320 ; for δέ 365.
πλησίον as Pred. 131.
πλοῦς Gen. of 13.
πλοῦτος, τό and ὁ 22.
πνεῦμα ἅγιον anarthrous 89.
ποδήρην 13.
ποιεῖν εὖ, καλῶς 146 ; with Part. 300 ; with Acc. of time i.q. spend 146 ; constr. of 149, 150 ; Middle 193 ; τί ποιήσομεν and ποιήσωμεν 209 ; ἵνα 238, 240 ; Infin. with τοῦ 270 ; to be supplied 394.
πολλά adverb 123.
πολύς followed by Part. with Art. 93.
πονηρίαι Plur. 77.
πορεύεσθαι : εἰς and ἐν εἰρήν. 184 ; Fut. force of Pres. 204.
πόρρω as Pred. 131.
πότερον ... ἤ 32, 250.
ποτίζειν constr. of 149 ; in Pass. 188.
Ποτίολοι 18.
ποῦ, ποῖ 71.
Πούδης 17.
πραέως 26.
πρᾷος, πραΰς 26.
πραότης, πραΰτης 26.
πρασιαὶ πρασιαί 30, 139.
πράττειν εὖ, with Participle 300.
πρέπει 135 ; constrns. with 278.
πρὶν ἤ constr. with 231, 232, 279.
τοῦ in specifins. of space and time 153 ; foll. by τοῦ and Infin. 265 ; πρὸ προσώπου 319.
προάγειν intrans. and with new obj. 144 ; Fut. force of Pres. 204.
προβάλλειν 145.
προέρχεσθαι with Acc. of pers. 144.
προκόπτειν 145.
προορώμην 64.
πρός with Infin. Acc. 266 ; with Gen. and Dat. 340 ; with Acc. to denote rest 340 ; in comparison 340 ; in elliptical and adverbial phrases 340 ; as periphrasis for Dat. 172, 177 ; πρός με, πρός σε 31.
τροσαναλῶσαι 172.
προσέπαισαν 40 note.
προσευχῇ προσεύχεσθαι 184 ; ἵνα 237.
προσέχειν 144 ; ἀπό 323 ; ἐπί 337.
προσήλυτος 74.

προσκαλεῖσθαί τινα 192.
προσκυνεῖν constr. of 147.
προσλαμβάνεσθαι constr. of 60 sq., 192.
προσπαίω 40.
προστίθεσθαι with Part. i.q. again 299 sq.
προσωπολημψίαι Plur. 77.
πρόσωπον in circumlocution 90, 319.
πρότερος and πρῶτος 32.
προφητεύω augment 35.
πρῶρα accent and spelling 11 ; Gen. -ης 11.
πρωτοκλισίαι Plur. 77.
πρῶτος and πρῶτον 83 ; πρῶτος for πρότερος 32, 84.
πύλη omission of 82.
πυνθάνομαι constr. of 167.

ρ Gen. after in -ης 11.
ρ doubling of after augment 32.
ῥαββί spelling 6.
ῥαπίζω Fut. of 37.
ῥεραντισμένοι 33.
ῥεριμμένον 33.
ῥέω 67.
Ῥήγνυμι sc. φωνήν 146.
ῥῆμα κυρίου, λέγων 298.
ρρ and ρσ 7.

-σαι 2d Pers. Sing. in 42.
σσ and ττ 7.
σάββατον etc. 23.
-σαι in 2d Sing. Pass. 42.
σαλπίζω forms 37 ; σαλπίζει sc. σαλπιγκτής 134.
σαλπιστής 37.
Σαλωμών 16.
Σαμάρεια 17.
Σαούλ and Σαῦλος 6, 18.
Σάπφειρα, -ης 8, 11.
Σαρών Acc. -ῶνα, -άρωνα, -νᾶ 16.
σατανᾶς 20 ; without the Art. 89.
σεαυτοῦ etc. use of 110.
σημᾶναι 41.
σημεῖον περιτομῆς 78.
σημειοῦσθαι 192.
-σθωσαν 3d Plur. Imperative 42.
Σιδών -ῶνος 16.
σίκερα, τό 24.
Σίλας, Σιλουανός 20.
Σιλωάμ, ὁ and ἡ 21.
Σίμων -ωνος 16.
Σινᾶ, τό 21.
σινάπεως 14.
Σιών. τό 21 ; ἡ 22.
σκανδαλισθῆναι etc. sense 52.
σκάπτειν sc. γῆν 146.
σκέπτομαι 67.
Σκευᾶς 20.
σκοπεῖν μή 243
σκότος, τό 22.
Σόδομα, τά 21.
Σολομών declension and accent 16.
σός 115.

σου for reflexive 110, 115 ; for possessive 115 ; position of 344.

ϳουδάριον 18.

Σουσάννα 17.

σπάσασθαι μάχαιραν 192.

σπεῖρα accent 11 ; -ρης 11.

σπείρειν σπόρον 148.

σπλαγχνίζεσθαι sense 52 ; constr. 164.

σπουδάσω 53.

σσ and ττ 7.

σταθήσομαι sense 47.

στάχυς uncontracted 14.

Στεφανᾶς 20.

στήκω forms of 48 ; with Dat. 178 note[2].

στῆναι cf. ἵστημι.

στηρίζω characteristic 36.

στοιχεῖν with Dat. 184.

στόμα use of in circumln. 90, 183, 187, 320 and note.

στρατεύεσθαι στρατείαν 148.

στρατιά with Plur. pred. 130.

στρατοπεδάρχης 73.

στρέφειν intrans. 145.

στρώννυμι 67 ; sc. κλίνην 146.

στρωννύω 45.

συγγενῆν 13 ; συγγενεῦσι 25.

συγκαλεῖν and -εῖσθαι 193.

συλλαμβάνειν and συλ. ἐν γαστρί 146.

συμβάλλειν 145.

Συμεών indecl. 16.

συμπόσια συμπόσια 30, 139.

συμφέρειν ἵνα 240.

σύμφυτοι with Gen. 169.

συμφωνεῖν with Gen. and with ἐκ 164.

συν unassimilated in compos. 8 ; used for καί 331 ; besides 331.

συνειδυίης 12.

συνεργεῖν 193.

-συνη abstract nouns in 73.

συνήθειά ἐστιν ἵνα 240.

συνήχθησαν meaning and use of 52.

συνιέναι constr. of 167.

συνιοῦσιν, -ιουσιν 48.

συνιστάναι ἵνα 237.

συνίων, -ιῶν, (-ιών) 48 sq.

σχίζω Fut. of 37.

ταβέρναι 17.

ταπεινώθητε reflexive 52.

τὰ πολλά adverbially 96.

-τάτως adverbs in 69.

ταὐτά and τὰ αὐτά 10.

ταχύς comparison of 27.

τέ connecting Participles 297 ; τε καί 360 sq. ; καί τε 361 ; τέ . . . τέ 361.

τέκνον with Gen. of abstract 161 sq.

τελευτάω 145.

τελέω with Part. 300.

-τεος verbals in 190.

τέρας uncontracted 15.

-τέρως adverbs in 69.

τεσσαρεσκαιδέκατος 29.

τέσσερες, τεσσεράκοντα 29.

τέτευχα, τέτυχα 67.

τηρεῖν ἐκ 327.

τίθημι forms of 45, 46 ; constr. of 150 ; ἵνα 238 ; ἐν 329.

τιμῆς dearly 164.

τίς, τὶς 31.

τὶς, τὶ for Indef. Art. 85 ; followed by Part. with Art. 93, 295 ; in pregnant or emphatic sense 114 cf. p. 127 ; omitted 158, 159.

τίς, τί, for simple Rel. and vice versa 115 ; for πότερος 115 ; τί ἐμοὶ καὶ σοί 138 ; τί πρὸς σέ etc. 138 ; τί quam 253 ; τί ὅτι 358.

τοίνυν 372.

τοιοῦτος, τοσοῦτος with Art. 87.

-τος verbals in 41 sq., 190.

τότε as a connective 401.

τοὐναντίον 10.

τοὔνομα 10 ; used adverbially 139.

τοῦτ' ἔστι, τουτέστι 11, 400.

τοῦτο as a preparatory Demons. before ἵνα, ὅτι, or the Infin., 105, 240, 262, 263 cf. 400.

ττ and σσ 7.

τυγχάνω 67 ; τυχόν used absolutely 318.

υ and οι interchanged 5.

ὑγιαίνειν ἐν τῇ πίστει and τῇ πίστει 182.

ὑγιής Acc. -ῆ 15.

ὕδωρ or ὑετός to be supplied 82.

υἱός Voc. 12 ; with Gen. of abstract 161 sq.

ὑμέτερος use of 116.

-υμι and -ύω 45.

ὑμῶν for possessive 116 ; between Subst. and Art 116.

ὑπάγειν intrans. for ἰέναι 144, 204, cf. 255 ; Fut. force of Pres. 204.

ὑπάρχειν with Part. 300 ; without ὤν 304.

ὑπέρ for περί 335 ; with Acc. in comparison 335 ; adverbially and in composition 321 ; ὑπὲρ ἐγώ 321.

ὑπεράνω 321.

ὑπερεκπερισσοῦ with Gen. compar. 168, 321.

ὑπερέχειν intrans. and with new obj. 144 ; with Gen. or Acc. 169.

ὑπερλίαν 321.

ὑπό after Passives 187, 340 ; with Gen. and Acc. 340 sq. ; with Acc. particularly after εἶναι, γίνεσθαι 341.

ὑποδεῖσθαι constr. of 191.

ὑποκάτω 321.

ὑποκρίσεις Plur. 77.

ὑποτάγητε reflexive 52.

ὑστερεῖν constr. of 158, 169.

ὕψιστος without the Art. (ἐν ὑψίστοις) 89 and note.

φαγεῖν with Gen. 159.

φάγεσαι 42, 58.

φάγος, φαγός 73.

φαιλόνης 17.

III. INDEX OF PASSAGES CITED FROM THE SEPTUAGINT.

The Figures refer to Pages.

IV. INDEX OF PASSAGES IN THE NEW TEST EXPLAINED OR CITED.

The Figures refer to Pages; those followed by an Asterisk indicate passages not merely referred to or quoted, but commented upon.

Acts viii. 21	180	Acts x. 40	9
Acts viii. 22	256, 322*	Acts x. 41	93, 122
Acts viii. 23	301, 333	Acts x. 43	174
Acts viii. 24	287	Acts x. 45	233
Acts viii. 26	104*, 314	Acts x. 47	269
Acts viii. 27	296		
Acts viii. 28	312	Acts xi. 7	301
Acts viii. 30	247, 301	Acts xi. 11	82
Acts viii. 31	222, 223, 224, 254, 370	Acts xi. 12	306
Acts viii. 34	341	Acts xi. 14	126
Acts viii. 35	150, 398	Acts xi. 15	264
Acts viii. 38	400	Acts xi. 17	174, 226*, 364*
Acts viii. 39	54	Acts xi. 18	371
Acts viii. 40	266, 333	Acts xi. 21	183
		Acts xi. 22	327
Acts ix. 1	167*	Acts xi. 26	278
Acts ix. 2	163, 224, 233	Acts xi. 28	12, 41, 81, 259, 283
Acts ix. 3	34*, 277	Acts xi. 29	34, 131
Acts ix. 4	6, 112, 166, 302*, 399*	Acts xi. 30	182
Acts ix. 6	47, 50		
Acts ix. 7	166, 351	Acts xii. 1	324
Acts ix. 8	63 (bis)	Acts xii. 2	11
Acts ix. 9	351, 366	Acts xii. 3	300
Acts ix. 12	214	Acts xii. 4	283, 329
Acts ix. 13	149, 167	Acts xii. 6	9, 259
Acts ix. 15	268	Acts xii. 7	40, 47
Acts ix. 20	376	Acts xii. 10	39, 63
Acts ix. 21	124, 309	Acts xii. 11	40, 182
Acts ix. 22	9, 69, 124	Acts xii. 14	48, 63, 325
Acts ix. 24	233	Acts xii. 16	39, 300
Acts ix. 26	351	Acts xii. 18	7, 250
Acts ix. 27	160	Acts xii. 19	275, 332, 351
Acts ix. 31	184, 335	Acts xii. 20	107, 340
Acts ix. 32	18, 277	Acts xii. 21	106*
Acts ix. 33	337*	Acts xii. 24	48
Acts ix. 34	47, 146		
Acts ix. 35	16, 18, 283	Acts xiii. 2	152, 342
Acts ix. 36	286	Acts xiii. 3	142
Acts ix. 37	277, 329	Acts xiii. 9	395
Acts ix. 38	18	Acts xiii. 10	89, 140, 258*
Acts ix. 39	45, 193, 283	Acts xiii. 11	144
Acts ix. 40	63	Acts xiii. 13	95*
Acts ix. 42	174, 335	Acts xiii. 16	141
Acts ix. 43	277	Acts xiii. 18	29
		Acts xiii. 19	362
Acts x. 1	93, 139	Acts xiii. 21	6, 86
Acts x. 2	331	Acts xiii. 22	150, 283
Acts x. 10	106*	Acts xiii. 24	319
Acts x. 11	29, 63, 196	Acts xiii. 25	240, 252*
Acts x. 13	138	Acts xiii. 26	141, 162
Acts x. 14	121	Acts xiii. 27	297*
Acts x. 15	29, 138	Acts xiii. 29	158, 329
Acts x. 17	254, 338, 362	Acts xiii. 32	150, 376
Acts x. 18	254	Acts xiii. 36	401
Acts x. 22	166, 188	Acts xiii. 39	287, 322*, 342
Acts x. 24	193	Acts xiii. 40	243
Acts x. 25	270	Acts xiii. 41	140, 175, 214 (bis)
Acts x. 31	52	Acts xiii. 43	98, 100
Acts x. 33	82, 300, 326*	Acts xiii. 45	314
Acts x. 34	398	Acts xiii. 46	113
Acts x. 36	153*, 288	Acts xiii. 47	150, 194, 268
Acts x. 37	79*, 153, 335	Acts xiii. 48	26
Acts x. 39	40, 53, 283, 286, 342		

1 Cor. i. 26	137, 138
1 Cor. i. 27	123
1 Cor. i. 28	100, 123
1 Cor. i. 29	121, 173, 214
1 Cor. i. 30	326*
1 Cor. i. 31	234, 386
1 Cor. ii. 1	206
1 Cor. ii. 3	340, 342
1 Cor. ii. 4	73*
1 Cor. ii. 9	135
1 Cor. ii. 10	58
1 Cor. ii. 13	170
1 Cor. iii. 1	33, 392
1 Cor. iii. 2	149, 367, 369, 401
1 Cor. iii. 4	365 (bis)*
1 Cor. iii. 5	363, 374, 389
1 Cor. iii. 6	54
1 Cor. iii. 7	367, 392
1 Cor. iii. 8	98, 117
1 Cor. iii. 10	255
1 Cor. iii. 11	339
1 Cor. iii. 14	34
1 Cor. iii. 15	60
1 Cor. iii. 17	128, 281
1 Cor. iii. 19	291*
1 Cor. iii. 20	376
1 Cor. iii. 21	163, 244
1 Cor. iv. 2	304
1 Cor. iv. 3	240, 342
1 Cor. iv. 5	88*, 244, 325
1 Cor. iv. 6	21, 31, 131, 235, 394*
1 Cor. iv. 7	42, 307
1 Cor. iv. 8	215*, 398, 402
1 Cor. iv. 9	101
1 Cor. iv. 12	117
1 Cor. iv. 14	119*, 192, 198, 206, 351, 403
1 Cor. iv. 15	364
1 Cor. iv. 16	273
1 Cor. iv. 18	318
1 Cor. iv. 19	204
1 Cor. iv. 20	138
1 Cor. iv. 21	208, 330, 342
1 Cor. v. 1	369
1 Cor. v. 3	307
1 Cor. v. 7	7
1 Cor. v. 8	243, 330
1 Cor. v. 9	403
1 Cor. v. 10	100*, 217, 352, 359, 390*
1 Cor. v. 12	138, 378
1 Cor. vi. 1	336, 403
1 Cor. vi. 4	370, 389
1 Cor. vi. 5	72, 332
1 Cor. vi. 6	177, 336
1 Cor. vi. 7	113, 370
1 Cor. vi. 11	398
1 Cor. vi. 12	403
1 Cor. vi. 13	138
1 Cor. vi. 15	208
1 Cor. vi. 16	134
1 Cor. vi. 19	77, 113, 163, 286, 325
1 Cor. vi. 20	164
1 Cor. vii. 1	287
1 Cor. vii. 2	117
1 Cor. vii. 3	391
1 Cor. vii. 5	219*
1 Cor. vii. 7	102, 119, 363
1 Cor. vii. 9	346
1 Cor. vii. 12	109
1 Cor. vii. 13	383
1 Cor. vii. 14	125
1 Cor. vii. 15	127, 329
1 Cor. vii. 16	255
1 Cor. vii. 17	133, 359, 389
1 Cor. vii. 18	226
1 Cor. vii. 19	127, 392
1 Cor. vii. 21	226, 392
1 Cor. vii. 23	164
1 Cor. vii. 25	307
1 Cor. vii. 27	226
1 Cor. vii. 28	55*, 178, 199
1 Cor. vii. 29	352
1 Cor. vii. 31	181*
1 Cor. vii. 32	152, 186
1 Cor. vii. 32 sq.	255
1 Cor. vii. 34	55*
1 Cor. vii. 35	113, 169
1 Cor. vii. 36	132
1 Cor. vii. 37	263, 270, 382
1 Cor. vii. 38	363
1 Cor. vii. 39	55*, 177, 260
1 Cor. viii. 3	55*
1 Cor. viii. 6	283
1 Cor. viii. 7	186
1 Cor. viii. 8	367
1 Cor. viii. 10	265, 295
1 Cor. viii. 11	45
1 Cor. viii. 13	37*
1 Cor. ix. 1	403
1 Cor. ix. 1 sqq.	247
1 Cor. ix. 2	346, 364
1 Cor. ix. 4	66, 248, 260
1 Cor. ix. 5	248, 260
1 Cor. ix. 6	126, 248, 260, 268
1 Cor. ix. 7	159
1 Cor. ix. 8	249
1 Cor. ix. 9	164, 249
1 Cor. ix. 10	268
1 Cor. ix. 11	37, 221*, 247
1 Cor. ix. 12	117, 392
1 Cor. ix. 15	98, 217, 234, 240 (bis), 371, 389
1 Cor. ix. 17	190
1 Cor. ix. 18	88, 240, 265
1 Cor. ix. 21	60, 169
1 Cor. ix. 24	357
1 Cor. ix. 25	392
1 Cor. ix. 26	351, 372

A GLOSSARY OF TECHNICAL TERMS

(GRAMMATICAL AND RHETORICAL).

The more familiar terms, and those which (like Anacoluthon, Aposiopesis, Asyndeton, Brachylogy, Ellipsis, Epexegesis, Hyperbaton, Pleonasm, Polysyndeton, etc.,) find special elucidation in the body of the foregoing work, and a place in its Index, are not included in the following List. In preparing it free use has been made of the various books on Rhetoric, Hermeneutics, Grammar, etc., together with the N. T. Commentaries.

Aetiologic, giving the cause; aetiological particles i.e. causal conjunctions.

Adversative: cf. Metabasis.

Amphiboly: ambiguity arising from the possibility of two constructions; as in ὁ δίκαιος ἐκ πίστεως ζήσεται (Rom. i. 17).

Anacoenosis: see Communicatio.

Anadiplosis or epanastrophe: the repetition of the end of one clause at the beginning of the next with an extension of the thought; as, ἔθνη ... κατέλαβε δικαιοσύνην, δικαιοσύνην δὲ τὴν ἐκ πίστεως (Rom. ix. 30).

Anantapodoton: a conditional (or similar) proposition which wants its apodosis (or consequent clause); as, 2 Pet. ii. 4 εἰ γὰρ etc. (Rom. v. 12 ὥσπερ δι' ἑνὸς ἀνθρώπου etc.).

Anaphora or epanaphora: the repetition of one or more words at the beginning of successive clauses; as, οὐκ εἰμὶ in 1 Cor. ix. 1, or τίς in vs. 7.

Anarthrous: without the Article.

Anastrophized: having its accent thrown back; as, ἔνι when i.q. ἔνεστι, cf. p. 72.

Annominatio: a paronomasia (which see) in which regard is had not merely to a resemblance in sound, but in sense as well; as, Rom. i. 28 οὐκ ἐδοκί-μασαν τὸν θεὸν ... παρέδωκεν αὐτοὺς ὁ θεὸς εἰς ἀδόκιμον νοῦν, Win. 638 (592).

Antanaclasis: the repetition of one and the same word in an opposite (or different) sense; as, νεκρούς in Matt. viii. 22.

Antiphrasis: the use of a word (generally one having a good sense) instead of its opposite; as, οἰκοδομηθήσεται (edified) in 1 Cor. viii. 10.

Antiptosis: the putting of one Case for another; cf. Win. 636 (590).

Ascensive: augmentative or climactic, as καί in κἀγώ Rom. iii. 7 even I (forming an 'ascent' to the ἐγώ by a tacit comparison, as it were).

Attributive: a word etc. used adjectively.

Catachresis: the abuse of a word, or its bold use in an extraordinary application; as, διὰ νόμου πίστεως Rom. iii. 27.

470

Categoric Plural: the use of the Plural denoting a class when but one individual is referred to, — (in order to give vagueness or a certain fulness to the expression); as, Matt. ii. 20 τεθνήκασι οἱ ζητοῦντες (referring to Herod).

Chiasmus or chiasma: a rhetorical arrangement of words or clauses so that they correspond to one another crosswise, like the letter X; as, Matt. xii. 22 ὥστε τὸν τύφλον κ. κωφὸν

κ. λαλεῖν κ. βλέπειν

Communicatio, or anacoenosis, occurs when a writer associates his readers with himself, either adopting their opinions or assuming that they share his; cf. e.g. in Rom. iii. 9 the *we* of προεχόμεθα; with that of προητιασάμεθα.

Comparatio compendiaria: an abbreviated comparison; as, Matt. v. 20, cf p. 168.

Constructio ad synesin (or sensum): a regard, in construction, for sense to the neglect of the grammatical form. See the Index.

Constructio praegnans occurs when one clause virtually contains within itself another; as, Mark ii. 1 εἰς οἶκόν ἐστι i.e. he has gone *into* and now *is in the house,* cf. p. 395. Cf. Pregnant.

Co-ordinate (cf. subordinate): descriptive of a proposition or clause which, while sustaining a logical relation to another, is so connected with it as to be its equal in grammatical rank.

Correlation, law of (or of sympathy): that usage respecting the Article according to which, if one substantive has another depending upon it in the Gen., they either both take the Art. or are both without it.

Corresponsive καί the, introduces a consequence answering to what precedes; as, διὸ καὶ παρέδωκεν αὐτοὺς ὁ θεὸς Rom. i. 24.

Dawes's Canon: see Index.

Descensive: indicating progress downwards; as, καί in εἴγε καὶ εἰκῇ Gal. iii. 4: *if indeed it be even* (i.e. only) *in vain.*

Dilogy: sometimes, a (designedly) ambiguous expression; sometimes, a repetition for the sake of emphasis.

Diplasiasmus: a doubling — whether of words, syllables, or consonants; as, Matt. xxiii. 37 Ἱερουσαλήμ, Ἱερουσαλήμ.

Dynamic: an epithet applied to the Dative Case viewed as denoting efficiency; more commonly known as the instrumental Dative, (corresponding to the Latin Ablative). It is also used as descriptive of the Middle Voice, when that voice expresses not merely the action of the verb, but implies also a certain intensity or earnestness as respects the agent.

Ecbatic: denoting a mere event or issue as distinguished from the fulfilment of a purpose (cf. telic); as e g. ἵνα in the (alleged) sense of *so that,* see p. 239.

Enallage: an exchange of one gender, number, person, voice, mood, tense, etc. of a word for another. Cf. Index.

Epanadiplosis: the use of the same word both at the beginning and at the end of a sentence; as, χαίρετε in Phil. iv. 4.

Epanalepsis: the resumption of a word or a thought after intervening matter; as, 1 Cor. viii. 4 cf 1; xi. 20 cf. 18.

Epanaphora: see Anaphora.

Epanastrophe: see Anadiplosis.

Epanorthosis: the rectification of an expression by qualifying it, or by substituting another in its stead; as, John xvi. 32 ἐμὲ μόνον ἀφῆτε· καὶ οὐκ εἰμὶ μόνον etc.

Epistrophe or Epiphora: the recurrence of the same word at the end of successive clauses; as, κἀγώ in 2 Cor. xi. 22.

Epizeuxis: the repetition of a word, — generally to express earnestness or emphasis; as, Matt. vii. 21 κύριε, κύριε.

Ethical i.e. indicating the state of mind. Prepositions are used ethically when used to denote mental relations. The Ethical Dative is a Dative (generally of a Pron. of the 1st or 2d Pers.) indicating interest or emotion; it is often untranslatable, cf. p. 179 The Ethical Future is a Future expressing not mere futurity, but what *may* or *ought* to take place; cf. Win. 279 (262).

Extensive (as contrasted with intensive) use, for example of πᾶς: viz. to denote frequency as distinguished from force; as, Eph. i. 8 πᾶσα σοφία all (i.e. 'every kind of' rather than 'the highest') *wisdom*. Cf. Win. 111 (105 sq.).

Figura Etymologica: a verb with an Accusative of kindred signification; as, John vii. 24 κρίσιν κρίνετε.

Gnomic or iterative Aorist, see pp. 201 sq.

Granville Sharp's rule (respecting the Article): 'when καὶ connects two personal nouns of the same case, if the Art. precedes the first noun and is not repeated before the second, the latter always relates to the same person that is expressed or described by the first.' It was applied by him (in "Remarks on the Uses of the Definitive Art. in the Gr. Text of the N. T." 3d ed. 1803) to proving the Deity of Christ from such expressions as βασιλεία τοῦ Χριστοῦ καὶ Θεοῦ Eph. v. 5.

Hendiadys (ἓν διὰ δυοῖν): one notion expressed as though it were two; cf. Win. 630 (585).

Hypallage: the transfer of an attribute of one substantive to another; cf. ποτήριον ... ἐκχυνόμενον Luke xxii. 20, and Win. 634 (589).

Hypotactic: see paratactic.

Hysteron Proteron: an inversion of the natural order of words, — what should come 'last' being put 'first'; cf. Win. 553 (514).

Idiosis: the transfer, by a writer, to himself in his private capacity of what holds true universally, or of an entire class; as in Rom. vii. 7 sqq.

Intensive: cf. extensive.

Litotes, substantially synonymous with Meiosis; which see.

Meiosis: the employment of a disparaging or over-weak expression in order to enforce a thought; particularly, the expression of a thought by denying its contrary; as, οὐκ ἐπαινῶ 1 Cor. xi. 22.

Metabasis, metabatic, etc., marking a transition; as δέ when its copulative force is predominant, — distinguished from the oppositive δέ (as it occurs, for example, after a negative), and from the adversative ἀλλά. Cf. Win. 441 sq. (411 sq.).

Metaplasm: a formation from a non-existent Nom. or theme; see Index.

Metaschematismus: the transfer to an individual of what holds true of the whole class to which he belongs; cf. 1 Cor. iv. 6.

Metonymy: the exchange of one term or name for another with which it has some relation; as, Rom. ii. 27 ἡ ἀκροβυστία i.q. ἔθνη vs. 14.

Mimesis : a lively imitation or reproduction of the words etc. of another; as, Col. ii. 21.

Nomen conjugatum : a noun akin in form or meaning to the word with which it is connected; as, Col. ii. 29 αὔξει αὔξησιν.

Oxymoron : a pointed expression produced by uniting words of opposite sig· nification; as, Rom. i. 20 τὰ ἀόρατα . . . καθορᾶται.

Paraleipsis : the mention of a thing by pretending to pass it by; as, Philem. 19 ἵνα μὴ λέγω etc.

Paratactic the (as distinguished from the hypotactic or syntactic) arrangement of clauses, is the ranging of them one after another in simple succession, instead of indicating their logical relations to one another; as, Matt. xviii. 21 ποσάκις ἁμαρτήσει εἰς ἐμὲ ὁ ἀδελφός μου καὶ ἀφήσω etc.

Parathetic (or loose) compounds (as distinguished from synthetic, which see) are those formed by the mere juxtaposition of separate words, as, ἀνα-λαμβάνω. On parathetic Apposition see Win. 528 (492).

Paronomasia : a combination of words similar in sound; as, Rom. i. 29 sq. πορνείᾳ, πονηρίᾳ, φθόνου, φόνου . . . ἀσυνέτους, ἀσυνθέτους, — cf. Win. 636 sq. (591 sq.).

Polyptoton : the recurrence of different cases etc. of the same word; as, 2 Cor. ix. 8 ἐν παντὶ πάντοτε πᾶσαν αὐτάρκειαν ἔχοντες. Cf. the Latin epigram "Mors mortis morti mortem nisi morte tulisset, Aeternæ vitæ janua clausa foret" (quoted by Alf. on Heb. ii. 14).

Predicate, a tertiary, is the predicate of a predicate (which latter is connected with its subject by some other verb than a copula or a verb signifying to name etc.); in other words, it is the anticipation of a distinct additional proposition (cf. Donaldson, Gr. Gram. §§ 417, 489). It is most conveniently translated by ' taking the tertiary predicate as the primary one, and making the verb which contains the primary predicate dependent on a relative.' For example, in John v. 36 ἐγὼ ἔχω τὴν μαρτυρίαν μείζω τοῦ Ἰωάννου the Adj. μείζω, being without the Art., implies an additional (tertiary) predication respecting the (secondary) predicate μαρτυρίαν, which may be brought out by the translation " The testimony which I have is greater than John."

Pregnant use of a word : when it is used to imply a second relation, the antecedent or consequent of that which it strictly expresses; as, John viii. 47 ὁ ὢν ἐκ τοῦ θεοῦ . . . ἀκούει i.e. 'heareth [and obeyeth].' On pregnant construction cf. Constructio Praegnans.

Prolepsis : anticipation. It may be either of a rhetorical nature, as when an objection is anticipated and answered (e.g. Rom. vⁱ '5), or of a grammatical i.e. in the reference of a word (cf. pp. 198 sq. 356).

Prosopopoeia : personification, or the ascribing of personal properties to inanimate objects or abstract ideas; as, Matt. vi. 3 μὴ γνώτω ἡ ἀριστερά σου etc.

Prosphonesis or apostrophe : the rhetorical use of direct address; as, Rom. ii. 1.

Rational concord : construction according to the sense rather than the form, see Constructio ad synesin.

Recitative ὅτι : a redundant ὅτι which the Greek allows to remain even when a quotation is introduced in direct form; as, Matt vii. 23 τότε ὁμολογήσω αὐτοῖς· ὅτι οὐδέποτε ἔγνων ὑμᾶς.

Sense-construction : see Constructio ad synesin.

Sharp, see Granville Sharp's Rule.

Schema (i.e. figure or construction): σχῆμα ἀπὸ κοινοῦ occurs when a word (or its influence) is common to two clauses, so that its case etc. is determined by the second rather than by that to which it primarily belongs; as, Acts ix. 27 Βαρνάβας ἐπιλαβόμενος αὐτὸν ἤγαγε where αὐτόν although primarily belonging to ἐπιλ. is governed by ἤγαγε. See Index p. 412 and under "Luke."

σχῆμα Ἀττικόν: the use of a Neuter Plural with a verb in the Singular, as, John x. 25 τὰ ἔργα . . . μαρτυρεῖ περὶ ἐμοῦ.

σχῆμα Βοιώτιον or Πινδαρικόν: the use of a Masc. or Fem. Plural with a verb in the Singular; to this Luke ix. 28 ἐγένετο . . . ὡσεὶ ἡμέραι ὀκτώ has been incorrectly referred, cf. Win. 516 (481), 563 (523 sq.).

σχῆμα κατ᾽ ἐξοχήν occurs when an individual of a genus (connected by καί) is distinguished by a separate mention; as, Acts v. 29 ὁ Πέτρος καὶ οἱ ἀπόστολοι.

σχῆμα καθ᾽ ὅλον καὶ μέρος: when to a totality (often a Plural) the specification of a particular part is afterwards subjoined; cf. 2 Cor. xii. 7 ἐδόθη μοι σκόλοψ τῇ σαρκί, see p. 186.

σχῆμα Κολοφώνιον: the use of a Dative (often instead of a Gen.) in immediate dependence on a substantive; as, 2 Cor. ix. 11 εὐχαριστίαν τῷ θεῷ, cf. p. 180.

σχῆμα παρονομασία, cf. Figura etymologica.

σχῆμα πρὸς τὸ σημαινόμενον or νοούμενον, cf. Constructio ad synesin.

Subordinate: a word or clause so related to another as to be complementary to it and grammatically dependent upon it.

Synchoresis: a concession made for the purpose of pointing a retort; as, James ii. 19 σὺ πιστεύεις . . . καλῶς ποιεῖς· καὶ τὰ δαιμόνια πιστεύουσι etc.

Synecdoche: the designation of a whole by a part, a genus by a species etc., or vice versa; as, Rom. xiii. 1 πᾶσα ψυχὴ ὑποτασσέσθω let every *soul* (i.e. every person). Hence the Accusative specifying the part etc. is called the Acc. of synecdoche.

Synizesis: in grammar, the union of two vowels in pronunciation; in rhetoric, equivalent to zeugma; which see.

Syntactic structure: see paratactic.

Synthetic (or close) compounds (as distinguished from parathetic, which see) are those in which the component elements have been moulded together into one inseparable whole; as, κακοῦργος. On synthetic Apposition see Win. 528 (492).

Tapeinosis: essentially synonymous with Meiosis, which see.

Tautology: needless or pleonastic repetition; cf. Luke i. 35 πνεῦμα ἅγιον ἐπελεύσεται . . . δύναμις ὑψίστου ἐπισκιάσει etc.

Telic: denoting end or purpose; cf. Ecbatic.

Tertiary predicate: see Predicate.

Whole and Part Figure: see σχῆμα καθ᾽ ὅλον καὶ μέρος.

Zeugma: the connection of a verb, adjective, etc., with a number of words, when it really suits but one of them; as, Luke i. 64 ἀνεῴχθη τὸ στόμα αὐτοῦ καὶ ἡ γλῶσσα. Cf. pp. 400 sq.

HELPS TO BIBLICAL STUDY.

Gardiner. *Biblical Works by Frederic Gardiner, D.D., Professor in the Berkeley Divinity School:*

A Harmony of the Four Gospels in Greek, according to the Text of Tischendorf, with a Collation of the Textus Receptus, and of the Texts of Griesbach, Lachmann, and Tregelles. Revised Edition. With an Appendix on the Principles of Textual Criticism, and the Canons of Eusebius. [See full title below.] 8vo. $2.50

The Principles of Textual Criticism, with a List of all the known Greek Uncials, and a Table representing graphically the parts of the Text of the New Testament contained in each, also the Canons of Eusebius. 8vo. pp. 64. Paper Covers, 50 cts. Cloth, flexible, 75 cts.

A Harmony of the Four Gospels in English, according to the Authorized Version; corrected by the best Critical Editions of the Original. [Arranged in paragraphs.] 8vo. pp. 324. $1.75

Diatessaron. The Life of Our Lord in the Words of the Gospels. [Arranged in one continuous narrative.] 16mo. .80

Cary. *An Introduction to the Greek of the New Testament.* By George L. Cary, of the Meadville Theological Seminary. 12mo. pp. 72. 75 cents.
" This is substantially a primary Greek Grammar of the New Testament, intended for those who have had no previous knowledge of the language."—*Central Baptist.*
" The simplicity of its method, its conciseness and perspicuity admirably adapt it to the use of such persons." — *Theological and Homiletic Monthly.*

Buttmann. *A Grammar of the New Testament Greek.* By Alexander Buttmann. Authorized Translation [by Prof. J. Henry Thayer, D.D.]; with numerous additions and corrections by the Author. 8vo. pp. xx and 474. $2.75
Buttmann's Grammar is more exclusively philological than that of Winer, it has less the character of a concise commentary. It is thoroughly scholarly, lucid, and compact. For comparing New Testament and Classic usage running references are made throughout the book to the Grammars of Hadley, Crosby, Donaldson, Jelf, and others. Winer and Buttmann supplement each other admirably.
From the American Presbyterian Review. — " By far the most important work on the Grammar of the New Testament Greek which has been produced of late years."

Winer. *A Grammar of the Idiom of the New Testament:* prepared as a Solid Basis for the Interpretation of the New Testament. By Dr. George Benedict Winer. Seventh Edition, enlarged and improved. By Dr. Gottlieb Lünemann, Professor of Theology at the University of Göttingen. Revised and Authorized Translation. [By Prof. J. Henry Thayer, D.D.]. 8vo. pp. 744. $4.00
Winer is the most valuable of all aids for a thorough and fundamental theological scholarship. Nothing has been left undone by Professor Thayer to make this the most complete and correct edition of the most celebrated of all New Testament Grammars. Three full Indexes have been added. One of them, that of passages in the New Testament explained or cited, occupies sixty pages. The texts that are merely cited are distinguished from these which are commented upon. In an important sense the book gives a grammatical commentary on the more difficult texts of the New Testament. **K-6**